microbiology fundamentals

a clinical approach

Selected Material for University of Missouri – Columbia

Marjorie Kelly Cowan
Miami University

with

Jennifer Bunn, RN
Clinical Advisor

and

Jennifer Herzog
Herkimer County Community College
Digital Author

Learning Solutions

Boston Burr Ridge, IL Dubuque, IA New York San Francisco St. Louis
Bangkok Bogotá Caracas Lisbon London Madrid
Mexico City Milan New Delhi Seoul Singapore Sydney Taipei Toronto

Microbiology Fundamentals: A Clinical Approach
Selected Material for University of Missouri – Columbia

This book is a McGraw-Hill Learning Solutions textbook and contains select material from *Microbiology Fundamentals: A Clinical Approach* by Marjorie Kelly Cowan, Jennifer Bunn and Jennifer Herzog. Copyright © 2013 by The McGraw-Hill Companies, Inc. Reprinted with permission of the publisher. Many custom published texts are modified versions or adaptations of our best-selling textbooks. Some adaptations are printed in black and white to keep prices at a minimum, while others are in color.

6 7 8 9 0 DRY DRY 14

ISBN-13: 978-0-07-768885-1
ISBN-10: 0-07-768885-6
Part of:
ISBN-13: 978-0-07-768886-8
ISBN-10: 0-07-768886-4

Learning Solutions Consultant: Elizabeth Wildes
Production Editor: Jennifer Bartell
Printer/Binder: RR Donnelley

Brief Table of Contents

About the Authors

Kelly Cowan, PhD, has been a microbiologist at Miami University since 1993, where she teaches microbiology for pre-nursing/allied health students at the university's Middletown campus, a regional commuter campus that accepts first-time college students with a high school diploma or GED, at any age. She started life as a dental hygienist. She then went on to attain her PhD at the University of Louisville, and later worked at the University of Maryland's Center of Marine Biotechnology and the University of Groningen in The Netherlands. Kelly has published (with her students) twenty-four research articles stemming from her work on bacterial adhesion mechanisms and plant-derived antimicrobial compounds. But her first love is teaching—both doing it and studying how to do it better. She is chair of the Undergraduate Education Committee of the American Society for Microbiology (ASM). When she is not teaching or writing, Kelly hikes, reads, takes scuba lessons, and still tries to (s)mother her three grown kids.

Jennifer Bunn, RN, is a registered nurse, having spent most of her career in rural medicine, where she has had the opportunity to interact with patients of all ages. Her experience includes emergency medicine, pediatrics, acute care, continuing care, and labor and delivery. Currently, Jennifer works in home care. Over the span of her career she has enjoyed mentoring and precepting LPN and RN students. She is also a CPR instructor. She has written medical content for websites, as well as articles and blogs in the health care niche. She is a perfect fit for this project, helping pre-nursing and other medical professional students see how microbiology is relevant to their lives and to their future careers.

Jennifer Herzog, MS, MPhil, is an assistant professor of biology at Herkimer County Community College, where she regularly teaches biology and microbiology to nonmajors and allied health students. She has been an active member of the American Society for Microbiology for nearly 20 years, most recently serving as Chair of the ASM Conference for Undergraduate Education. In addition, she currently authors the "Journal Watch" section of the ASM's *Journal of Microbiology & Biology Education* and serves on the ASM's Microbe Library Editorial Review Board.

Preface

Students:

Thanks for picking up this book! I designed and wrote this book after years of frustration, teaching from books that didn't focus on the right things for students—who need a solid (but concise) introduction to microbiology. Most of the other books are way too big, way too detailed, and way too dull! The worst part is, they don't accomplish the main goal, which is to clearly communicate to students the important features of microbes and infectious disease. They all get bogged down in an overwhelming amount of detail.

While I was writing this book, I kept in mind the principles I wanted my students to grab on to and to retain for years to come. While there is enough detail to give you the context around the principles, there is not so much that you will be overwhelmed. Biological processes are described right next to the illustrations that show them. The format is easier to read than most books, as there is only one column of text on a page, and wider margins. The margins allow room for interesting illustrations and clinical content. My co-author, Jen Bunn, is a registered nurse, who brings her years of experience to life on the page and shows you how this information will matter to you when you are working as a health care provider. And the digital materials, authored by Jen Herzog, are the icing on the cake—you can do as much as you want in terms of study and practice anywhere you have access to a computer or a tablet.

The "two Jens" and I are really hopeful that this is a different kind of book, and one that you will truly enjoy working with. I know I can't wait to use it in my own classes!

—Kelly Cowan

I dedicate this book, and all my books, to public health workers who devote their lives to bringing the advances and medicines enjoyed by the industrialized world to *all* humans.

Connecting Instructors to Students

McGraw-Hill Higher Education and Blackboard® have teamed up! What does this mean for you?

The **Best** of **Both Worlds**

Mc Graw Hill

Bb Blackboard

Do More

Your life, simplified. Now you and your students can access McGraw-Hill Connect® and Create™ right from within your Blackboard course—all with one single sign-on! Say goodbye to the days of logging in to multiple applications.

Deep integration of content and tools. Not only do you get single sign-on with Connect and Create, you also get deep integration of McGraw-Hill content and content engines right in Blackboard. Whether you're choosing a book for your course or building Connect assignments, all the tools you need are right where you want them—inside of Blackboard.

Seamless gradebooks. Are you tired of keeping multiple gradebooks and manually synchronizing grades into Blackboard? We thought so. When a student completes an integrated Connect assignment, the grade for that assignment automatically (and instantly) feeds your Blackboard grade center.

A solution for everyone. Whether your institution is already using Blackboard or you just want to try Blackboard on your own, we have a solution for you. McGraw-Hill and Blackboard can now offer you easy access to industry leading technology and content, whether your campus hosts it or we do. Be sure to ask your local McGraw-Hill representative for details.

Introducing McGraw-Hill ConnectPlus® Microbiology

McGraw-Hill ConnectPlus® Microbiology integrated learning platform provides auto-graded assessments, a customizable, assignable eBook, an adaptive diagnostic tool, and powerful reporting against learning outcomes and level of difficulty—all in an easy-to-use interface. Connect Microbiology is specific to your book and can be completely customized to your course and specific learning outcomes, so you help your students connect to just the material they need to know.

Save time with auto-graded assessments and tutorials

Fully editable, customizable, auto-graded interactive assignments using high-quality art from the textbook, animations, and videos from a variety of sources take you way beyond multiple choice. Assignable content is available for every Learning Outcome in the book. Extremely high-quality content, created by digital author Jennifer Herzog, includes case study modules, What's the Diagnosis clinical activities, tutorial animations, NCLEX practice questions, and more!

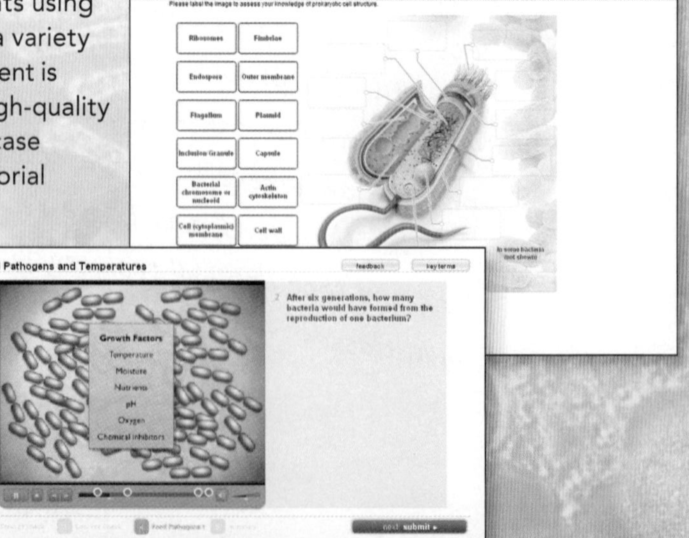

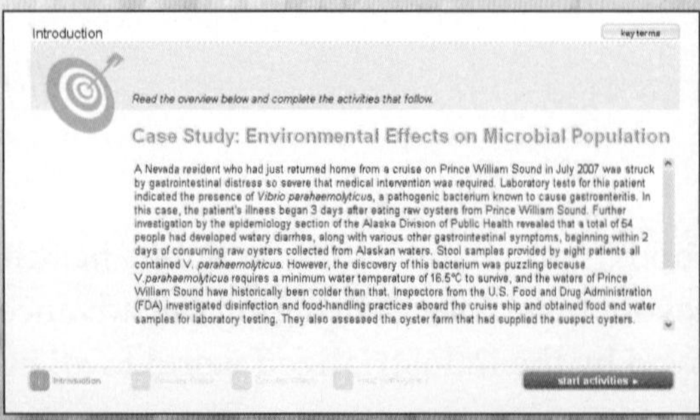

...Through Innovative Digital Solutions

New! Unique Interactive Question Types Pre-tagged to ASM's Curriculum Guidelines for Undergraduate Microbiology

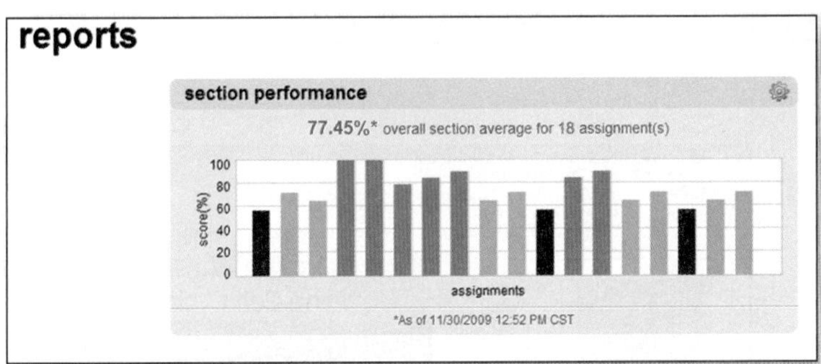

Gather assessment information

Generate powerful data related to student performance against learning outcomes, specific topics, level of difficulty, and more.

All ConnectPlus content is pre-tagged to Learning Outcomes for each chapter as well as topic, section, Bloom's Level, and ASM Curriculum Guidelines (once they're finalized) to assist you in both filtering out unneeded questions for ease of creating assignments and in reporting on your students' performance against these points. This will enhance your ability to effectively assess student learning in your courses by allowing you to align your learning activities to peer-reviewed standards from an international organization.

Mc Graw Hill create **Craft your teaching resources to match the way you teach!** With McGraw-Hill Create™ you can easily rearrange chapters, combine material from other content sources, and quickly upload your own content. Access thousands of leading McGraw-Hill textbooks for content that fits your objectives and arrange your book to fit your teaching style. Create even allows you to personalize your book's appearance by selecting the cover and adding your name, school, and course information. Order a Create book and you'll receive a complimentary print review copy in 3 to 5 business days or a complimentary electronic review copy (eComp) via email in minutes. Go to **www.mcgrawhillcreate.com** today and register to experience how McGraw-Hill Create empowers you to teach your students your way.

Microbiology Fundamentals Laboratory Manual

Steven Obenauf, Broward College
Susan Finazzo, Georgia Perimeter College

Written specifically for pre-nursing and allied health microbiology students, this manual features brief, visual exercises with a clinical emphasis.

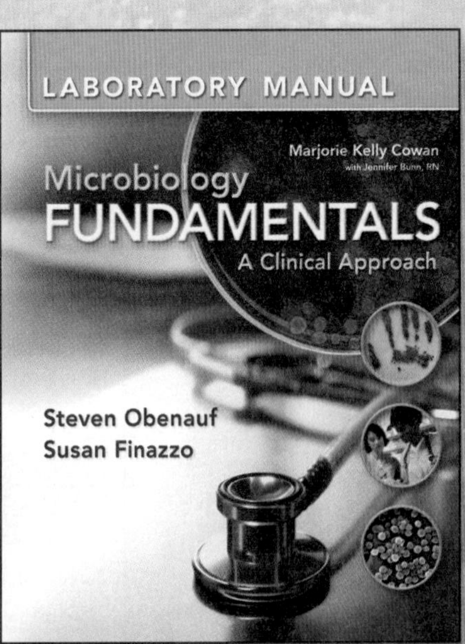

LABORATORY MANUAL
Marjorie Kelly Cowan
Microbiology
FUNDAMENTALS
A Clinical Approach
Steven Obenauf
Susan Finazzo

INSTRUCTORS

Connect via Customization

Presentation Tools allow you to customize your lectures.

Enhanced Lecture Presentations contain lecture outlines, Flex Art, art, photos, tables, and animations embedded where appropriate. Fully customizable, but complete and ready to use, these presentations will enable you to spend less time preparing for lecture!

Flex Art Fully editable (labels and leaders) line art from the text, with key figures that can be manipulated. Take the images apart and put them back together again during lectures so students can understand one step at a time.

Animations Over 100 animations bringing key concepts to life, available for instructors and students.

Animation PPTs Animations are truly embedded in PowerPoint® for ultimate ease of use! Just copy and paste into your custom slide show and you're done!

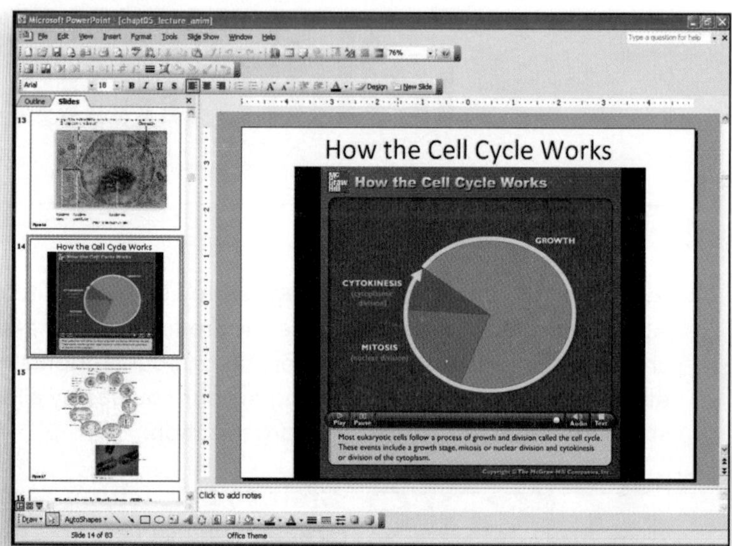

Take your course online—*easily*— with one-click Digital Lecture Capture.

McGraw-Hill Tegrity® records and distributes your lecture with just a click of a button. Students can view them anytime, anywhere via computer, iPod, or mobile device. Tegrity indexes as it records your slideshow presentations, and anything shown on your computer so students can use keywords to find exactly what they want to study.

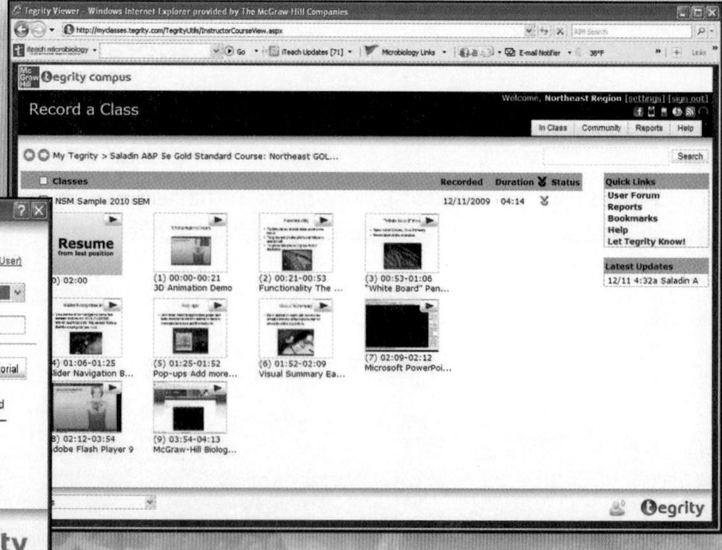

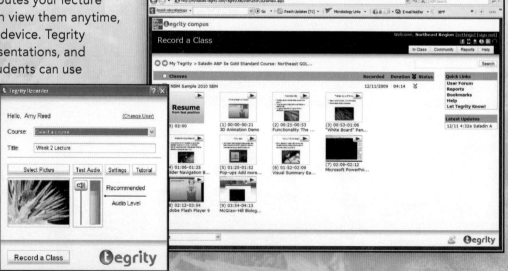

STUDENTS

Connect 24/7 with Personalized Learning Plans

Access content anywhere, any time, with a customizable, interactive eBook.

McGraw-Hill ConnectPlus® eBook takes digital texts beyond a simple PDF. With the same content as the printed book, but optimized for the screen, ConnectPlus has embedded media, including animations and videos, which bring concepts to life and provide "just in time" learning for students.

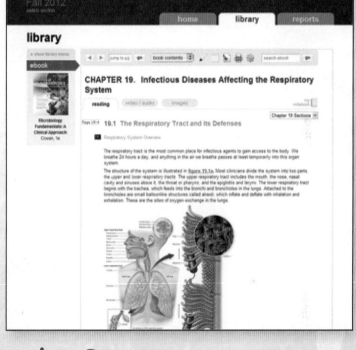

"Use of technology, especially LearnSmart, assisted greatly in keeping on track and keeping up with the material."
—student, Triton College

McGraw-Hill LearnSmart™ A Diagnostic, Adaptive Learning System

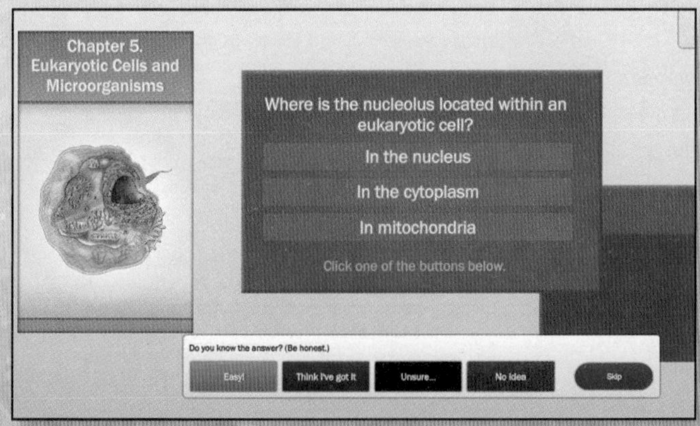

McGraw-Hill LearnSmart™ is an adaptive diagnostic tool, powered by Connect Microbiology, which is based on artificial intelligence and constantly assesses a student's knowledge of the course material.

Sophisticated diagnostics adapt to each student's individual knowledge base in order to match and improve what they know. Students actively learn the required concepts more easily and efficiently.

Self-study resources are also available at www.mhhe.com/cowan.

"I love LearnSmart. Without it, I would not be doing as well."
—student, Triton College

Clinical applications help students see the relevance of microbiology.

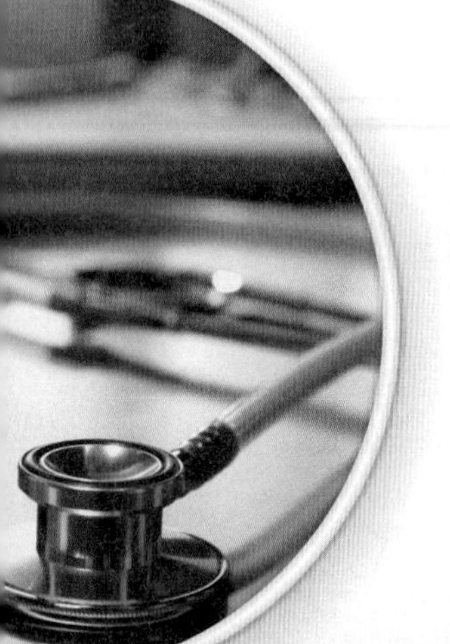

Case File Each chapter begins with a case written from the perspective of a former microbiology student.

These high-interest introductions provide a specific example of how the chapter content is relevant to real life and future health care careers.

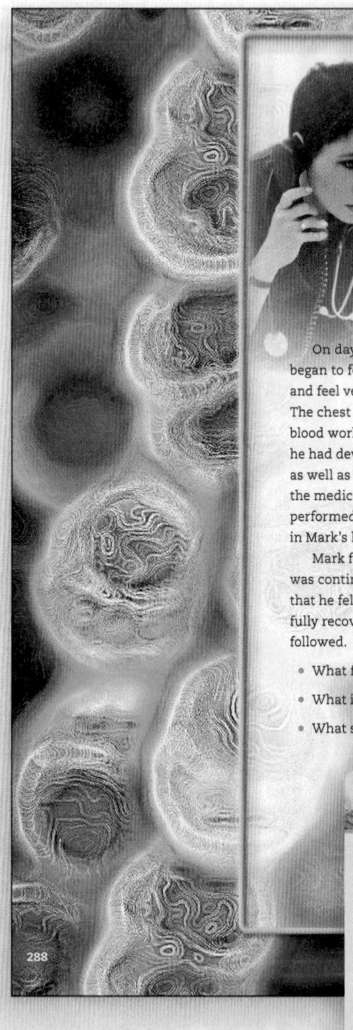

CASE FILE

An Unexpected Outcome

As a respiratory tech on a surgical ward, I helped to care for Mark, a 65-year-old man who was admitted to the hospital for a relatively routine surgery: a total hip replacement. He was told before his surgery that he would need to stay in the hospital for only 4 to 5 days, at which time he would be discharged home to continue recuperating and begin outpatient physical therapy.

On day 4 of recovery, the night before he was to be discharged, Mark began to feel unwell. He developed chills and a fever, and began to cough and feel very weak. A chest X ray was performed and blood work was drawn. The chest X ray revealed a consolidation in his left lower lobe, while his blood work revealed an elevated white blood cell count. Mark was told that he had developed pneumonia. He was started on an antibiotic intravenously, as well as oxygen and medications given via nebulizer, which aerosolized the medications so that they could be inhaled deeply into the lungs. I performed chest physiotherapy several times a day to help loosen secretions in Mark's lungs.

Mark felt well enough to go home after 4 days of IV antibiotic therapy. He was continued on oral antibiotics for the pneumonia he developed and found that he felt quite weak for several days after returning home. He eventually fully recovered from his surgery and the respiratory complication that followed.

- What factors may have led to Mark developing pneumonia?
- What is the special name for infections contracted in the hospital?
- What signs of pneumonia did Mark exhibit? What symptoms?

Case File Wrap-Up appears on page 316.

288

Clinical Advisor

This textbook features a clinical advisor, Jennifer Bunn, RN, who carefully reviewed the entire manuscript and authored the following features, described on these pages:

- Added clinical relevance throughout the chapter
- Relevant case studies
- Medical Moment boxes
- NCLEX® Prep questions

"Jen added things that were fascinating to ME! And will enrich my teaching. Pre-allied health students are so eager to start 'being' nurses, etc., they love these clinical details."

—Kelly Cowan

Medical Moment
These boxes give students a more detailed clinical application of a concept from the page spread where they are located.

Medical Moment

Athlete's Foot: A Fungal Scourge

Tinea pedis (commonly known as athlete's foot) is a fungal infection affecting the foot. You do not need to be an athlete to get athlete's foot—tinea pedis, like other fungal infections, thrives in warm, moist areas. It is highly contagious and can be spread easily from person to person. Locker rooms, pools, and showers are the perfect breeding grounds for this hardy fungus. People whose feet sweat excessively, or who wear closed tight shoes, are at higher risk for developing athlete's foot, as are people whose feet are wet for prolonged periods of time.

Athlete's foot causes itching, redness, and flaking of the skin between the toes. A burning or a stinging sensation may occur. Cracks and blisters that crust and ooze may develop, adding to the unpleasantness of the condition. When the fungus attacks the nails, they may discolor, flake, and crumble.

Diagnosis is readily made on the basis of the appearance of the skin. Sometimes a skin culture is needed to confirm the diagnosis. Antifungals, either topically or orally, will usually clear up the condition. Keeping the feet dry is the best means to prevent athlete's foot.

CLINICAL

NCLEX® PREP

4. Which of the following statements about mumps are true?
   a. The most common mode of transmission is airborne.
   b. The MMR vaccine is a live attenuated vaccine.
   c. Treatment for mumps is supportive.
   d. Mumps often results in sterility in males.
   e. both b and c

NCLEX® Prep Questions Found throughout the chapter, these multiple-choice questions are application-oriented and designed to help students learn the microbiology information they will eventually need to pass the NCLEX examination. Students will begin learning to think critically, apply information, and over time, prep themselves for the examination.

Additional questions are available in Connect for homework and assessment.

Inside the Clinic Each chapter ends with a reading that emphasizes the nursing aspect of microbiology.

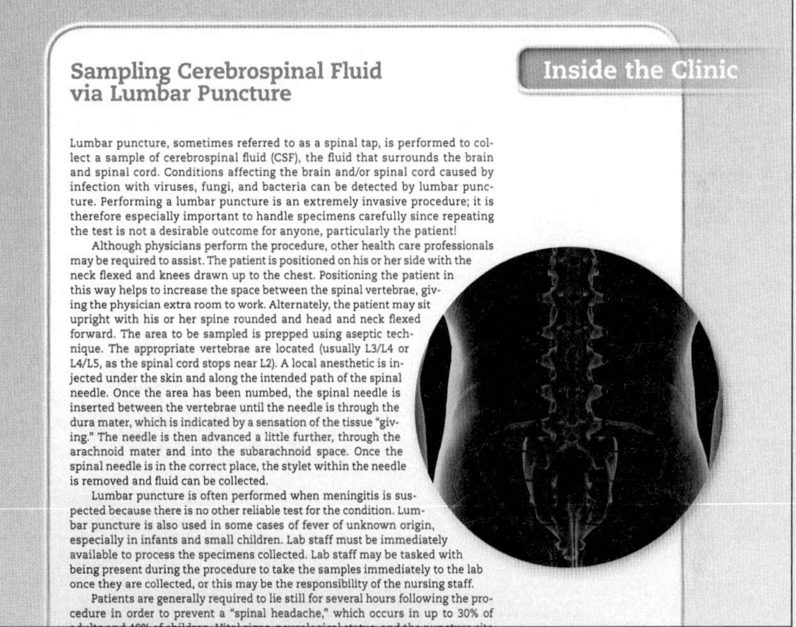

Sampling Cerebrospinal Fluid via Lumbar Puncture

Inside the Clinic

Lumbar puncture, sometimes referred to as a spinal tap, is performed to collect a sample of cerebrospinal fluid (CSF), the fluid that surrounds the brain and spinal cord. Conditions affecting the brain and/or spinal cord caused by infection with viruses, fungi, and bacteria can be detected by lumbar puncture. Performing a lumbar puncture is an extremely invasive procedure; it is therefore especially important to handle specimens carefully since repeating the test is not a desirable outcome for anyone, particularly the patient!

Although physicians perform the procedure, other health care professionals may be required to assist. The patient is positioned on his or her side with the neck flexed and knees drawn up to the chest. Positioning the patient in this way helps to increase the space between the spinal vertebrae, giving the physician extra room to work. Alternately, the patient may sit upright with his or her spine rounded and head and neck flexed forward. The area to be sampled is prepped using aseptic technique. The appropriate vertebrae are located (usually L3/L4 or L4/L5, as the spinal cord stops near L2). A local anesthetic is injected under the skin and along the intended path of the spinal needle. Once the area has been numbed, the spinal needle is inserted between the vertebrae until the needle is through the dura mater, which is indicated by a sensation of the tissue "giving." The needle is then advanced a little further, through the arachnoid mater and into the subarachnoid space. Once the spinal needle is in the correct place, the stylet within the needle is removed and fluid can be collected.

Lumbar puncture is often performed when meningitis is suspected because there is no other reliable test for the condition. Lumbar puncture is also used in some cases of fever of unknown origin, especially in infants and small children. Lab staff must be immediately available to process the specimens collected. Lab staff may be tasked with being present during the procedure to take the samples immediately to the lab once they are collected, or this may be the responsibility of the nursing staff.

Patients are generally required to lie still for several hours following the procedure in order to prevent a "spinal headache," which occurs in up to 30% of

Clinical Examples Throughout Clinical insights and examples are woven throughout the chapter—not just in boxed elements.

anaphylactic attacks are urged to carry at all times injectable ephrine (adrenaline) and an identification tag indicating their sensitivity. ephrine reverses constriction of the airways and slows the release of allergic mediators. Although epinephrine works quickly and well, it has a very short half-life. It is very common to require more than one dose in anaphylactic reactions. Injectable epinephrine buys the individual time to get to a hospital for continuing treatment.

Allergy "Vaccines"

70% of allergic patients benefit from controlled in

270 CHAPTER 10 Antimicrobial Treatment

Intravenous catheters must be kept clean to avoid infection.

Spectrum of Activity

Scores of antimicrobial drugs cal and pharmaceutical literat most of them are variants of a ways of categorizing antimicr vious section, is to designate Broad-spectrum drugs are effe narrow-spectrum drugs gener that tetracyclines are broad-s narrow-spectrum agents.

Since penicillin is such a molecule over the years illustr we provide an overview in tab narrow-spectrum, and suscept developed to overcome those

Referring back to table 10 drugs based on which of the f

Antibiotics and Biof

As you read in chapter 6, bi living counterparts. One of t perspective—is that they are against them when they are assumed that it was a proble bial drugs could not penetrate organisms. While that is a fac to biofilm resistance: the diffe to surfaces they express differ ceptibility profiles.

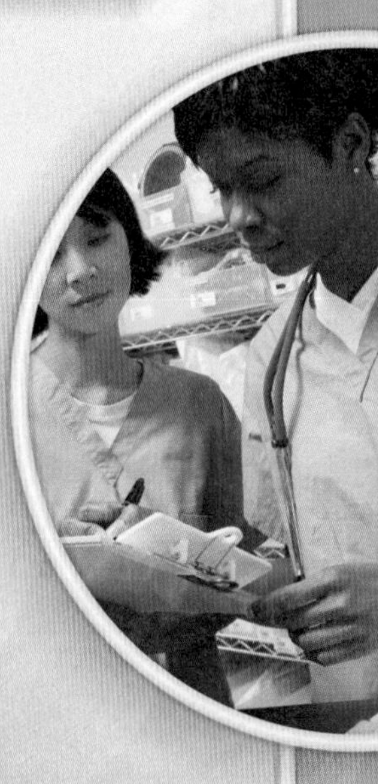

VISUAL

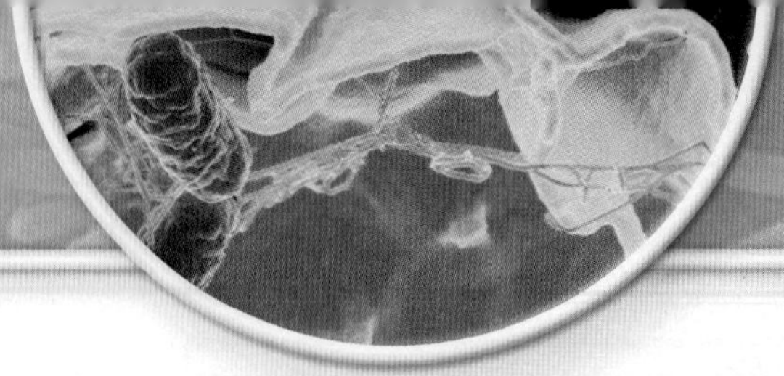

Visually appealing layouts and vivid art closely linked to narrative complement the way 21st-century students learn.

Engaging, Accurate, and Educational Art Visually appealing art and page layouts engage students in the content, while carefully constructed figures help them work through difficult concepts.

Whenever possible, figures are shown in context to help students relate the figure content to real-life situations.

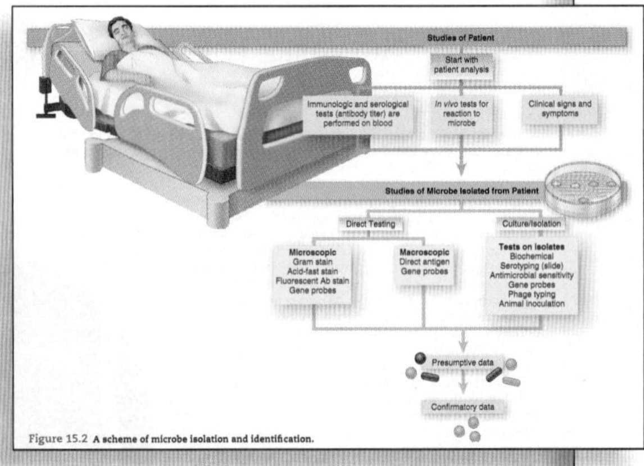

Figure 15.2 A scheme of microbe isolation and identification.

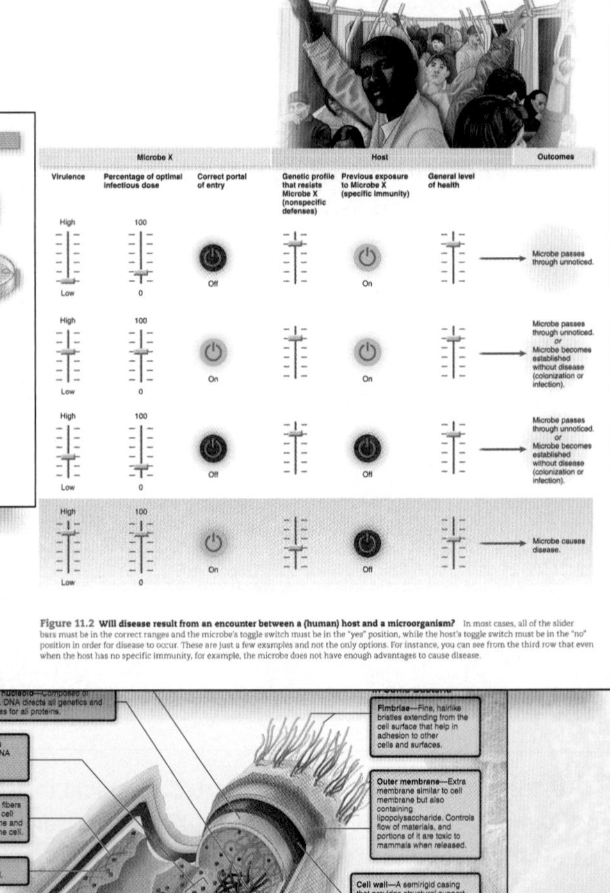

Figure 11.2 Will disease result from an encounter between a (human) host and a microorganism? In most cases, all of the slider bars must be in the correct ranges and the microbe's toggle switch must be in the "yes" position, while the host's toggle switch must be in the "no" position in order for disease to occur. These are just a few examples and not the only options. For instance, you can see from the third row that even when the host has no specific immunity, for example, the microbe does not have enough advantages to cause disease.

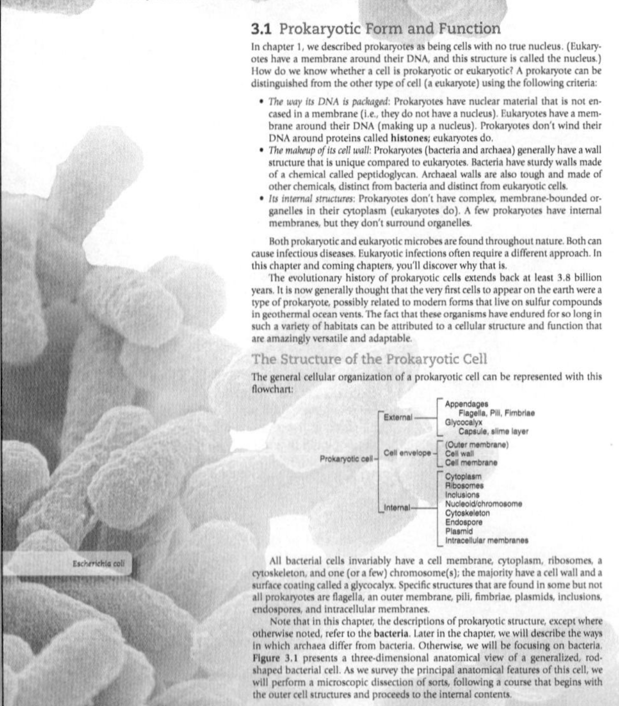

62 CHAPTER 3 Prokaryotic Profiles: The Bacteria and Archaea

3.1 Prokaryotic Form and Function

In chapter 1, we described prokaryotes as being cells with no true nucleus. (Eukaryotes have a membrane around their DNA, and this structure is called the nucleus.) How do we know whether a cell is prokaryotic or eukaryotic? A prokaryote can be distinguished from the other type of cell (a eukaryote) using the following criteria:

- *The way its DNA is packaged*: Prokaryotes have nuclear material that is not encased in a membrane (i.e., they do not have a nucleus). Eukaryotes have a membrane around their DNA (making up a nucleus). Prokaryotes don't wind their DNA around proteins called **histones**; eukaryotes do.
- *The makeup of its cell wall*: Prokaryotes (bacteria and archaea) generally have a wall structure that is unique compared to eukaryotes. Bacteria have sturdy walls made of a chemical called peptidoglycan. Archaeal walls are also tough and made of other chemicals, distinct from bacteria and distinct from eukaryotic cells.
- *Its internal structures*: Prokaryotes don't have complex, membrane-bounded organelles in their cytoplasm (eukaryotes do). A few prokaryotes have internal membranes, but they don't surround organelles.

Both prokaryotic and eukaryotic microbes are found throughout nature. Both can cause infectious diseases. Eukaryotic infections often require a different approach. In this chapter and coming chapters, you'll discover why that is.

The evolutionary history of prokaryotic cells extends back at least 3.8 billion years. It is now generally thought that the very first cells to appear on the earth were a type of prokaryote, possibly related to modern forms that live on sulfur compounds in geothermal ocean vents. The fact that these organisms have endured for so long in such a variety of habitats can be attributed to a cellular structure and function that are amazingly versatile and adaptable.

The Structure of the Prokaryotic Cell

The general cellular organization of a prokaryotic cell can be represented with this flowchart:

Prokaryotic cell
- External
  - Appendages
    - Flagella, Pili, Fimbriae
  - Glycocalyx
    - Capsule, slime layer
- Cell envelope
  - (Outer membrane)
  - Cell wall
  - Cell membrane
- Internal
  - Cytoplasm
  - Ribosomes
  - Inclusions
  - Nucleoid/chromosome
  - Cytoskeleton
  - Endospore
  - Plasmid
  - Intracellular membranes

All bacterial cells invariably have a cell membrane, cytoplasm, ribosomes, a cytoskeleton, and one (or a few) chromosome(s); the majority have a cell wall and a surface coating called a glycocalyx. Specific structures that are found in some but not all prokaryotes are flagella, an outer membrane, pili, fimbriae, plasmids, inclusions, endospores, and intracellular membranes.

Note that in this chapter, the descriptions of prokaryotic structure, except where otherwise noted, refer to the **bacteria**. Later in the chapter, we will describe the ways in which archaea differ from bacteria. Otherwise, we will be focusing on bacteria. **Figure 3.1** presents a three-dimensional anatomical view of a generalized, rod-shaped bacterial cell. As we survey the principal anatomical features of this cell, we will perform a microscopic dissection of sorts, following a course that begins with the outer cell structures and proceeds to the internal contents.

Escherichia coli

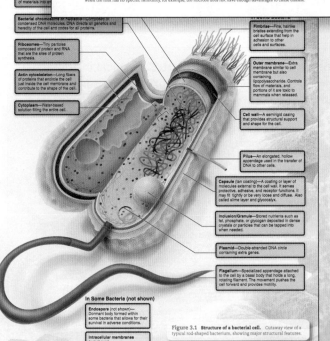

In All Bacteria

Bacterial chromosome or nucleoid—Composed of condensed DNA molecules. DNA directs all genetics and heredity of the cell and codes for all proteins.

Ribosomes—Tiny particles composed of protein and RNA that are the sites of protein synthesis.

Actin cytoskeleton—Long fibers of proteins that encircle the cell just inside the cell membrane and contribute to the shape of the cell.

Cytoplasm—Water-based solution filling the entire cell.

Fimbriae—Fine, hairlike bristles extending from the cell surface that help in adhesion to other cells and surfaces.

Outer membrane—Extra membrane similar to cell membrane but also containing lipopolysaccharide. Controls flow of materials, and portions of it are toxic to mammals when released.

Cell wall—A semirigid casing that provides structural support and shape for the cell.

Pilus—An elongated, hollow appendage used in the transfer of DNA to other cells.

Capsule (tan coating)—A coating or layer of molecules external to the cell wall. It serves protective, adhesive, and receptor functions. It may fit tightly or be very loose and diffuse. Also called slime layer and glycocalyx.

Inclusion/Granule—Stored nutrients such as fat, phosphate, or glycogen deposited in dense crystals or particles that can be tapped into when needed.

Plasmid—Double-stranded DNA circle containing extra genes.

Flagellum—Specialized appendage attached to the cell by a basal body that holds a long, rotating filament. The movement pushes the cell forward and provides motility.

In Some Bacteria (not shown)

Endospore (not shown)—Dormant body formed within some bacteria that allows for their survival in adverse conditions.

Intracellular membranes (not shown)

Figure 3.1 **Structure of a bacterial cell.** Cutaway view of a typical rod-shaped bacterium, showing major structural features.

VISUAL

Visual Tables The most important points explaining a concept are distilled into table format and paired with explanatory art.

496 CHAPTER 18 Infectious Diseases Affecting the Cardiovascular and Lymphatic Systems

HIGHLIGHT DISEASE

Causative Agent

Plasmodium species are protozoa in the sporozoan group. The genus *Plasmodium* contains four species: *P. malariae, P. vivax, P. falciparum*, and *P. ovale*. Humans are the primary vertebrate hosts for most of the species. The four species show variations in the pattern and severity of disease.

Table 18.1 Life Cycle of the Malarial Parasite

1 The *asexual phase* (and infection) begins when an infected female *Anopheles* mosquito injects saliva containing anticoagulant into a capillary in preparation for taking a blood meal. In the process, she inoculates the blood with motile, spindle-shaped asexual cells called **sporozoites** (Gr. *sporo*, seed, and *zoon*, animal).

2 The sporozoites circulate through the body and migrate to the liver in a short time. Within liver cells, the sporozoites undergo asexual division called *schizogony* (Gr. *schizo*, to divide, and *gone*, seed), which generates numerous daughter parasites, or *merozoites*. This phase of *pre-erythrocytic development* lasts from 5 to 16 days, depending upon the species of *Plasmodium*. Its end is marked by eruption of the liver cell, which releases from 2,000 to 40,000 mature merozoites into the circulation.

3 During the *erythrocytic phase*, merozoites attach to special receptors on RBCs and invade them, converting in a short time to ring-shaped trophozoites. This stage feeds upon hemoglobin, grows, and undergoes multiple divisions to produce a cell called a *schizont*, which is filled with more merozoites. Bursting RBCs liberate merozoites to infect more red cells. Eventually, certain merozoites differentiate into two types of specialized gametes called *macrogametocytes* (female) and *microgametoctyes* (male). Because the human does not provide a suitable environment for the next phase of development, this is the end of the cycle in humans.

4 The *sexual phase* (sporogony) occurs when a mosquito draws infected red blood cells into her stomach. In the stomach, the microgametocyte releases gametes that fertilize the larger macrogametocytes. The resultant diploid cell (ookinete) implants into the stomach wall of the mosquito, becoming an oocyst, which undergoes multiple mitotic divisions, ultimately releasing sporozoites that migrate to the salivary glands and lodge there. This event completes the sexual cycle and makes the sporozoites available for infecting the next victim.

78 CHAPTER 3 Prokaryotic Profiles: The Bacteria and Archaea

Figure 3.20 **A typical sporulation cycle in *Bacillus* species from the active vegetative cell to release and germination.** The process takes, on average, about 10 hours. Inset is a high magnification (10,000×) cross section of a single spore showing the dense protective layers that surround the core with its chromosome.

6 to 8 hours in most spore-forming species. **Figure 3.20** illustrates the major physical and chemical events in this process.

Return to the Vegetative State: Germination

After lying in a state of inactivity for an indefinite time, endospores can be revitalized when favorable conditions arise. The breaking of dormancy, or germination, happens in the presence of water and a specific chemical or environmental stimulus (germination agent). Once initiated, it proceeds to completion quite

Process Figures Complex processes are broken into easy-to-follow steps. Numbered steps in the art coordinate with numbered text boxes to walk students through the figure.

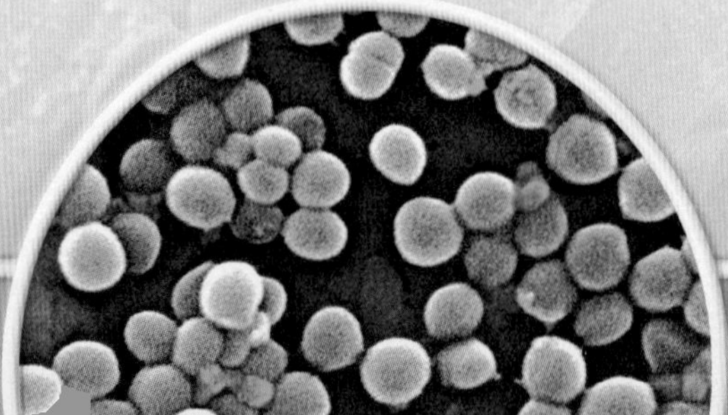

BRIEF

Streamlined coverage of core concepts help students retain the information they will need for advanced courses.

Chemistry topics required for understanding microbiology are combined with the foundation content found in chapter 1.

Genetics content is synthesized into one chapter covering the concepts that are key to microbiology students.

Core concepts in environmental and applied microbiology are combined into one chapter.

Brief Table of Contents

iii

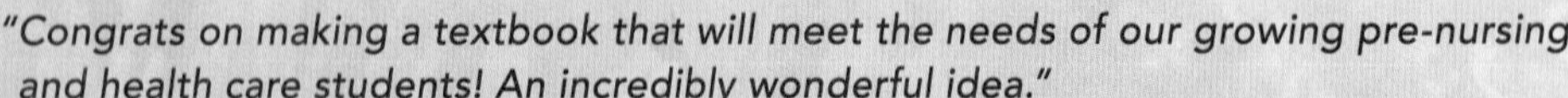

"Congrats on making a textbook that will meet the needs of our growing pre-nursing and health care students! An incredibly wonderful idea."
—Ingrid Hermann, Santa Fe College

"A streamlined microbiology book with a good balance between level of detail and readability. A must-have if the target audience is students in the health professions."
—Peter Kourtev, Central Michigan University

BRIEF

Eliminated Duplication Detail is incorporated into figures so students can learn in context with the art. This allows a more concise narrative flow while still retaining core information.

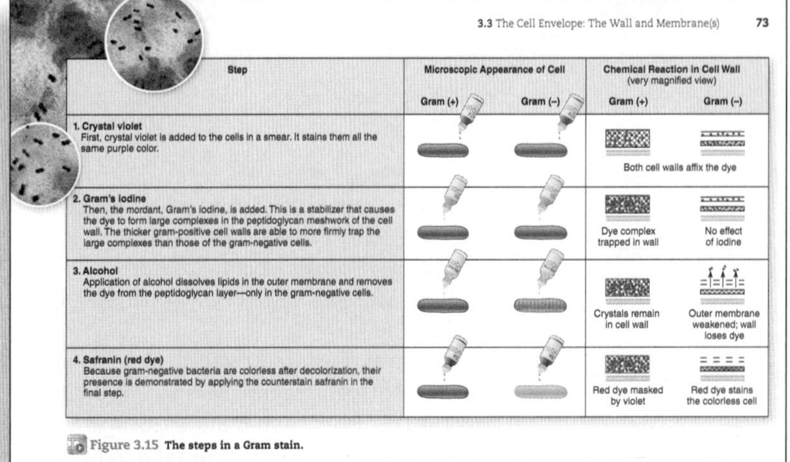
3.3 The Cell Envelope: The Wall and Membrane(s) 73

Step	Microscopic Appearance of Cell		Chemical Reaction in Cell Wall (very magnified view)	
	Gram (+)	Gram (–)	Gram (+)	Gram (–)
1. Crystal violet First, crystal violet is added to the cells in a smear. It stains them all the same purple color.			Both cell walls affix the dye	
2. Gram's iodine Then, the mordant, Gram's iodine, is added. This is a stabilizer that causes the dye to form large complexes in the peptidoglycan meshwork of the cell wall. The thicker gram-positive cell walls are able to more firmly trap the large complexes than those of the gram-negative cells.			Dye complex trapped in wall	No effect of iodine
3. Alcohol Application of alcohol dissolves lipids in the outer membrane and removes the dye from the peptidoglycan layer—only in the gram-negative cells.			Crystals remain in cell wall	Outer membrane weakened; wall loses dye
4. Safranin (red dye) Because gram-negative bacteria are colorless after decolorization, their presence is demonstrated by applying the counterstain safranin in the final step.			Red dye masked by violet	Red dye stains the colorless cell

Figure 3.15 **The steps in a Gram stain.**

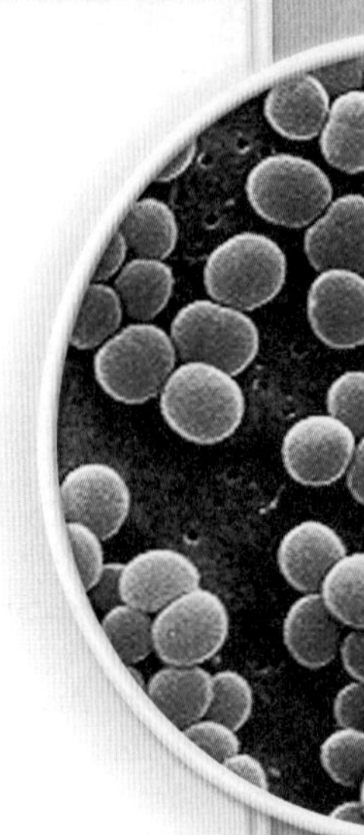

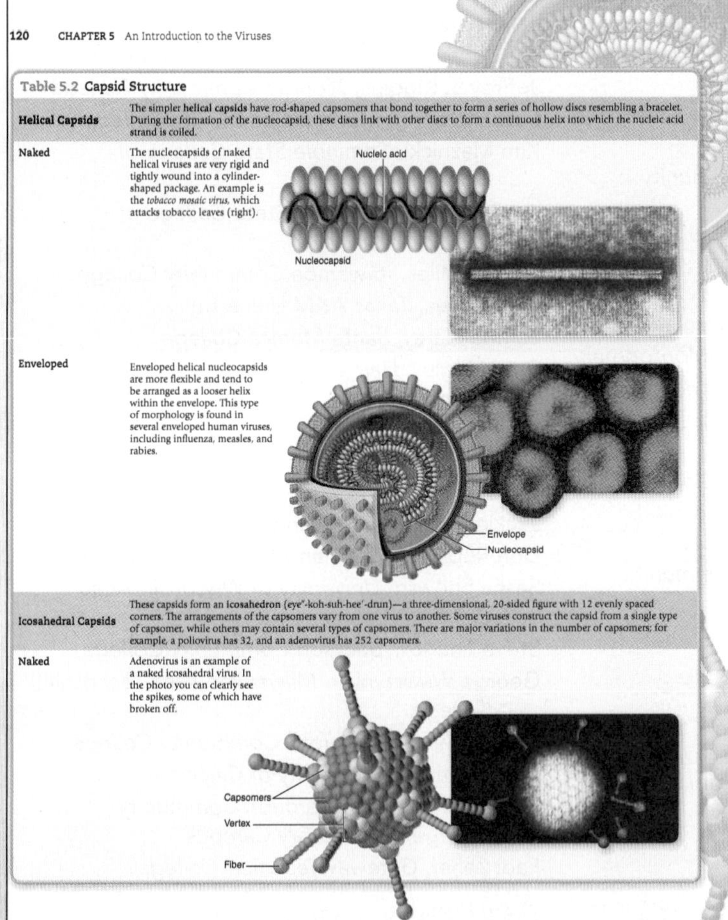
120 CHAPTER 5 An Introduction to the Viruses

Table 5.2 Capsid Structure

Helical Capsids	The simpler **helical capsids** have rod-shaped capsomers that bond together to form a series of hollow discs resembling a bracelet. During the formation of the nucleocapsid, these discs link with other discs to form a continuous helix into which the nucleic acid strand is coiled.
Naked	The nucleocapsids of naked helical viruses are very rigid and tightly wound into a cylinder-shaped package. An example is the *tobacco mosaic virus,* which attacks tobacco leaves (right).
Enveloped	Enveloped helical nucleocapsids are more flexible and tend to be arranged as a looser helix within the envelope. This type of morphology is found in several enveloped human viruses, including influenza, measles, and rabies.
Icosahedral Capsids	These capsids form an **icosahedron** (eye″-koh-suh-hee′-drun)—a three-dimensional, 20-sided figure with 12 evenly spaced corners. The arrangements of the capsomers vary from one virus to another. Some viruses construct the capsid from a single type of capsomer, while others may contain several types of capsomers. There are major variations in the number of capsomers; for example, a poliovirus has 32, and an adenovirus has 252 capsomers.
Naked	Adenovirus is an example of a naked icosahedral virus. In the photo you can clearly see the spikes, some of which have broken off.

Tables Tables are used to further streamline content and help students understand relationships between concepts.

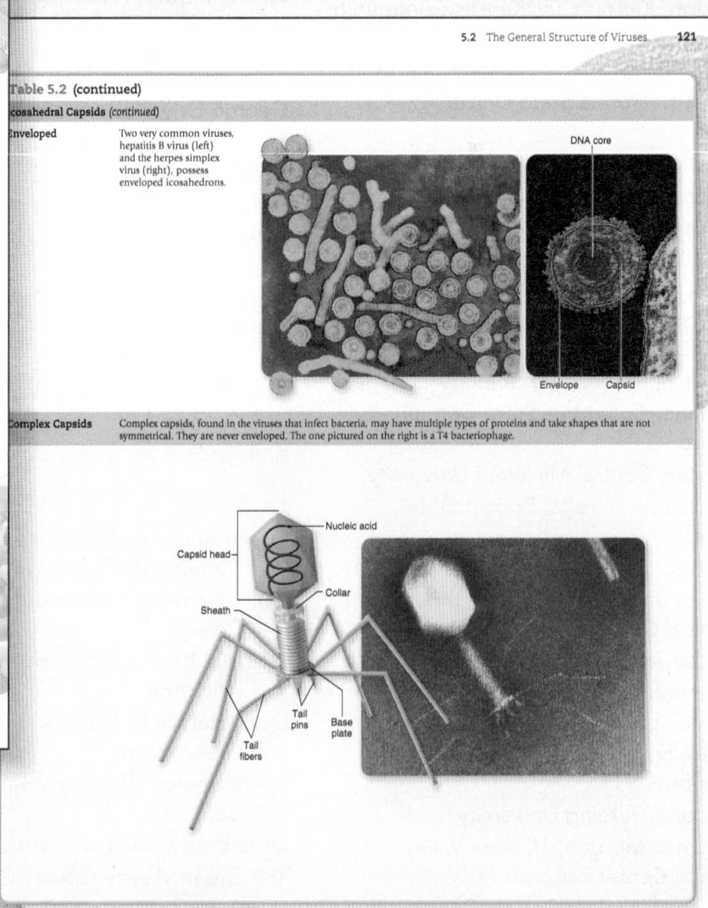
5.2 The General Structure of Viruses 121

Table 5.2 (continued)

Icosahedral Capsids *(continued)*	
Enveloped	Two very common viruses, hepatitis B virus (left) and the herpes simplex virus (right), possess enveloped icosahedrons.
Complex Capsids	Complex capsids, found in the viruses that infect bacteria, may have multiple types of proteins and take shapes that are not symmetrical. They are never enveloped. The one pictured on the right is a T4 bacteriophage.

Reviewers

Reviewers

Jennifer Bess, *Hillsborough Community College*
Evelyn J. Biluk, *Chippewa Valley Technical College—River Falls*
Charlotte Borgeson, *University of Nevada—Reno*
Chad Brooks, *Austin Peay State University*
Linda Bruslind, *Oregon State University*
Claire Carpenter, *Yakima Valley Community College*
James K. Collins, *University of Arizona*
George Ealy, *Keiser University*
Luti Erbeznik, *Oakland Community College*
Ted Fleming, *Bradley University*
Amy Goode, *Illinois Central College*
Todd Gordon, *Kansas City, Kansas Community College*
Ellen Gower, *Greenville Technical College*
Judy Haber, *California State University—Fresno*
Julie Harless, *Lone Star College–Montgomery*
Ingrid Hermann, *Santa Fe College*
Alison Hoversten-Davis, *East Los Angeles College*
Janice Ito, *Leeward Community College*
Debra Jackson, *University of Louisiana at Monroe*
Judy Kaufman, *Monroe Community College*
Amine Kidane, *Columbus State Community College*
Peter Kourtev, *Central Michigan University*
Ernesto Lasso de la Vega, *Edison State University*
Suzanne Long, *Monroe Community College*
Geralyne Lopez-de-Victoria, *Midlands Technical College*
Martha R. Lowe, *Bergen Community College*
Laurie Shannon Meadows, *Roane State Community College*
Tracey Mills, *Ivy Tech Community College–Columbus*
Steven Moore, *Harding University*
Marla Tanzman Morgen, *Hudson Valley Hospital Center Laboratory*
Ellyn Mulcahy, *Johnson County Community College*
Steven D. Obenauf, *Broward College*
Gregory Paquette, *University of Rhode Island*
Amanda Parker, *Pearl River Community College–Forrest County Center*
Jeanie G. Strobert Payne, *Bergen Community College*
Marcia Pierce, *Eastern Kentucky University*
Deborah Polayes, *George Mason University*
Michael J. Putnam, *Alfred State College*
Ben Rowley, *University of Central Arkansas*
Tina Salmassi, *California State University—Los Angeles*
John P. Seabolt, *University of Kentucky*
Tracey Steeno, *Northeast Wisconsin Technical College*
Delon Washo-Krupps, *Arizona State University*
Van Wheat, *South Texas College*
John Whitlock, *Hillsborough Community College*

Board of Advisors

George Ealy, *Keiser University*
Michael Griffin, *Angelo State University*
Julie Harless, *Lone Star College—Montgomery*
Jeffrey S. Kiggins, *Monroe Community College*
Amy Miller, *University of Cincinnati, Blue Ash College*
Tracey Mills, *Ivy Tech Community College*
Marla T. Morgen, *Hudson Valley Hospital Center Microbiology Laboratory*
Jerred Seveyka, *Yakima Valley Community College*
Kathryn Sutton, *Clarke University*

Focus Group Attendees

Corrie Andries, *Central New Mexico Community College*
John Bacheller, *Hillsborough Community College*
Michelle Badon, *University of Texas at Arlington*
David Battigelli, *University of North Carolina—Greensboro*
Lance Bowen, *Truckee Meadows Community College*
Dave Brady, *Southwestern Community College*
Toni Brem, *Wayne County Community College*
Lisa Burgess, *Broward College*
Liz Carrington, *Tarrant County College, Southeast*
Joe Caruso, *Florida Atlantic University*
Robin Cotter, *Phoenix College*
Elizabeth Emmert, *Salisbury University*
Jason Furrer, *University of Missouri*
Chris Gan, *Highline Community College*
Zaida M. Gomez-Kramer, *University of Central Arkansas*
Brinda Govindan, *San Francisco State University*
Julianne Grose, *Brigham Young University*
Zaf Hatahet, *Northwestern State University*
James Herrick, *James Madison University*
Jim Johnson, *Central Washington University*
Jeffrey S. Kiggins, *Monroe Community College*
Suzanne Long, *Monroe Community College*
Kim Maznicki, *Seminole State College of Florida*
Amee Mehta, *Seminole State College of Florida*
Sharon Miles, *Itawamba Community College*
Rita Moyes, *Texas A&M University*
Valerie Narey, *Santa Monica College*
Ruth Negley, *Harrisburg Area Community College*
Julie Oliver, *Cosumnes River College*
Jean Revie, *South Mountain Community College*
Jackie Reynolds, *Richland College*
Don Rubbelke, *Lakeland Community College*
Sasha Showsh, *University of Wisconsin—Eau Claire*
Steve Thurlow, *Jackson Community College*
George Wawrzyniak, *Milwaukee Area Technical College*
Janice Webster, *Ivy Tech Community College*
MJ Weintraub, *University of Cincinnati*
John Whitlock, *Hillsborough Community College, Dale Mabry Campus*
Fadi Zaher, *Gateway Technical College*

Accuracy Checkers

Kris Hueftle, *Florence-Darlington Technical College*
Martin Henry H. Stevens, *Miami University*

Contents

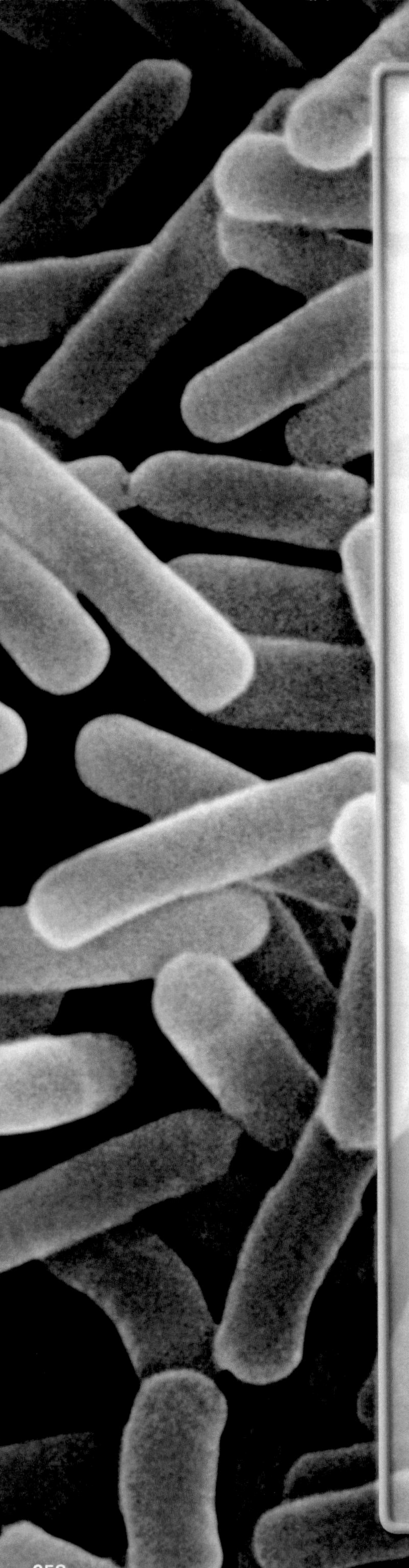

CASE FILE

An Unexpected Effect

Janet, a 25-year-old secretary, was admitted to my floor of the hospital with symptoms of kidney infection, including chills, fever, flank pain, nausea, and malaise. A preliminary urinalysis showed the presence of white blood cells, nitrates, protein, and blood in the urine. Blood drawn for a complete blood count showed an elevated white blood cell count, indicative of a bacterial infection. The urine was sent for culture and sensitivity testing. Meanwhile, the physician caring for Janet ordered intravenous fluids to rehydrate her. She also ordered the drug gentamicin, to be commenced immediately via the intravenous route while awaiting the culture and sensitivity (C&S) report, which would not be available for at least 18 hours.

The C&S report confirmed that Janet's kidney Infection was caused by a *Proteus* species and that it was sensitive to gentamicin. After a few days, Janet felt much better. Her fever was gone and the flank pain had subsided. However, Janet remarked to me that she was experiencing ringing in her ears. I reported it to the doctor, who immediately ordered the gentamicin to be discontinued and changed Janet's antibiotic therapy to another antibiotic shown to be effective against *Proteus*.

- What type of antibiotic is gentamicin? What is gentamicin's metabolic target?
- Why did Janet's doctor discontinue gentamicin therapy after she learned that Janet was experiencing tinnitus (ringing in the ears)? Is this considered a toxic or an allergic response?

Case File Wrap-Up appears on page 284.

CHAPTER 10

Antimicrobial Treatment

IN THIS CHAPTER...

10.1 Principles of Antimicrobial Therapy

1. State the main goal of antimicrobial treatment.
2. Identify the sources for most currently used antimicrobials.
3. Describe two methods for testing antimicrobial susceptibility.
4. Define therapeutic index, and identify whether a high or a low index is preferable.

10.2 Interactions Between Drug and Microbe

5. Explain the concept of selective toxicity.
6. List the five major targets of antimicrobial agents.
7. Identify which categories of drugs are most selectively toxic and why.
8. Distinguish between broad-spectrum and narrow-spectrum antimicrobials, and explain the significance of the distinction.
9. Identify the microbes against which the various penicillins are effective.
10. Explain the significance of penicillinases.
11. Identify two antimicrobials that act by inhibiting protein synthesis.
12. Explain how drugs targeting folic acid synthesis work.
13. Identify one example of a fluoroquinolone.
14. Name a drug that targets the cellular membrane.
15. Discuss how treatment of biofilm infections differs from that of nonbiofilm infections.
16. Name the four main categories of antifungal agents.
17. Explain why antiprotozoal and antihelminthic drugs are likely to be more toxic than antibacterial drugs.
18. List the three major targets of action of antiviral drugs.

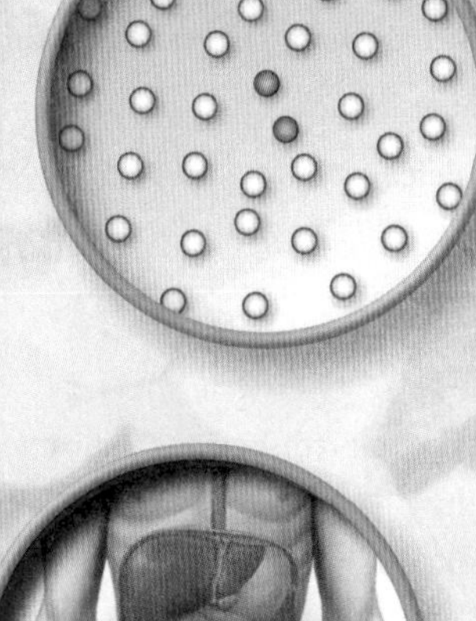

10.3 Antimicrobial Resistance

19. Discuss two possible ways that microbes acquire antimicrobial resistance.
20. List five cellular or structural mechanisms that microbes use to resist antimicrobials.
21. Discuss at least two novel antimicrobial strategies that are under investigation.

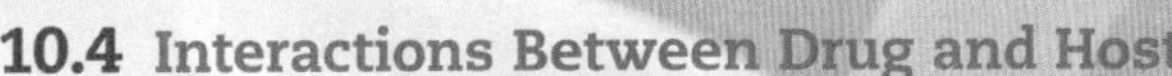

10.4 Interactions Between Drug and Host

22. Distinguish between drug toxicity and allergic reactions to drugs.
23. Explain what a superinfection is and how it occurs.

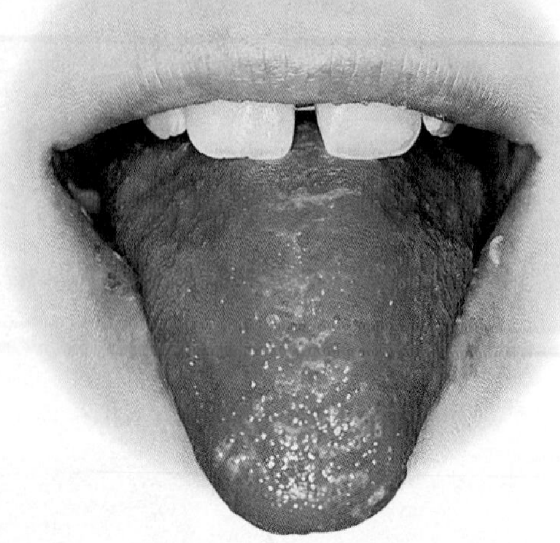

Scarlet fever, once common, is now treatable with antibiotics. Strawberry tongue is one of its symptoms.

10.1 Principles of Antimicrobial Therapy

A hundred years ago in the United States, one out of three children was expected to die of an infectious disease before the age of 5. Early death or severe lifelong debilitation from scarlet fever, diphtheria, tuberculosis, meningitis, and many other bacterial diseases was a fearsome yet undeniable fact of life to most of the world's population. The introduction of modern drugs to control infections in the 1930s was a medical revolution that has added significantly to the life span and health of humans. It is no wonder that, for many years, antibiotics in particular were regarded as miracle drugs. Although antimicrobial drugs have greatly reduced the incidence of certain infections, they have definitely not eradicated infectious disease and probably never will. In fact, many doctors are now warning that we are dangerously close to a postantibiotic era, where the drugs we have are no longer effective.

The goal of antimicrobial chemotherapy is deceptively simple: Administer a drug to an infected person, which destroys the infective agent without harming the host's cells. In actuality, this goal is rather difficult to achieve, because many (often contradictory) factors must be taken into account. The ideal drug should be easy to administer, yet be able to reach the infectious agent anywhere in the body; be absolutely toxic to the infectious agent, while being nontoxic to the host; and remain active in the body as long as needed, yet be safely and easily broken down and excreted. Additionally, microbes in biofilms often require different drugs than when they are not in biofilms. In short, the perfect drug does not exist—but by balancing drug characteristics against one another, a satisfactory compromise can usually be achieved **(table 10.1)**.

Chemotherapeutic agents are described with regard to their origin, range of effectiveness, and whether they are naturally produced or chemically synthesized. A few of the more important terms you will encounter are found in **table 10.2**.

NCLEX® PREP

1. Jim has been diagnosed with meningococcal disease. His family has been started on an antibiotic to prevent contracting the disease. This is an example of
   a. chemotherapy.
   b. prophylaxis.
   c. antimicrobial resistance.
   d. host defense.

Table 10.1 Characteristics of the Ideal Antimicrobial Drug

- Selectively toxic to the microbe but nontoxic to host cells
- Microbicidal rather than microbistatic
- Relatively soluble; functions even when highly diluted in body fluids
- Remains potent long enough to act and is not broken down or excreted prematurely
- Does not lead to the development of antimicrobial resistance
- Complements or assists the activities of the host's defenses
- Remains active in tissues and body fluids
- Readily delivered to the site of infection
- Reasonably priced
- Does not disrupt the host's health by causing allergies or predisposing the host to other infections

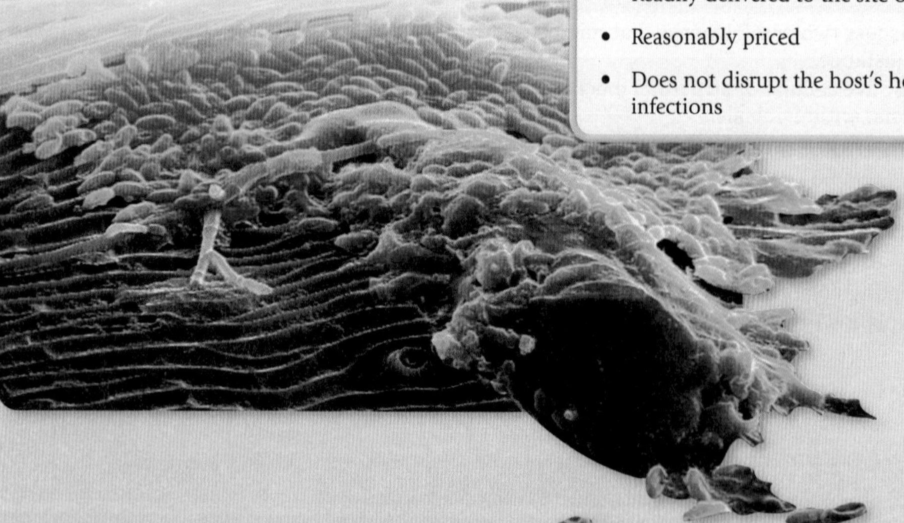

Bacterial biofilm formed on the surface of a spider.

Table 10.2 Terminology of Chemotherapy

Chemotherapeutic Drug	Any chemical used in the treatment, relief, or prophylaxis of a disease
Prophylaxis	Use of a drug to prevent imminent infection of a person at risk
Antimicrobial Chemotherapy	The use of chemotherapeutic drugs to control infection
Antimicrobials	All-inclusive term for any antimicrobial drug, regardless of its origin
Antibiotics	Substances produced by the natural metabolic processes of some microorganisms that can inhibit or destroy other microorganisms
Semisynthetic Drugs	Drugs that are chemically modified in the laboratory after being isolated from natural sources
Synthetic Drugs	Drugs produced entirely by chemical reactions
Narrow Spectrum (Limited Spectrum)	Antimicrobials effective against a limited array of microbial types—for example, a drug effective mainly on gram-positive bacteria
Broad Spectrum (Extended Spectrum)	Antimicrobials effective against a wide variety of microbial types—for example, a drug effective against both gram-positive and gram-negative bacteria

A Note About Chemotherapy

The word "chemotherapy" is commonly associated with the treatment of cancer. As you see in table 10.2, its official meaning is broader than that and can also be applied to antimicrobial treatment.

In this chapter, we describe different types of antibiotic drugs, their mechanism of action, and the types of microbes on which they are effective. The organ system chapters 16 through 21 list specific disease agents and the drugs used to treat them.

The Origins of Antimicrobial Drugs

Nature is a prolific producer of antimicrobial drugs. Antibiotics, after all, are natural metabolic products of aerobic bacteria and fungi. By inhibiting the growth of other microorganisms in the same habitat (antagonism), antibiotic producers presumably enjoy less competition for nutrients and space. The greatest numbers of current antibiotics are derived from bacteria in the genera *Streptomyces* and *Bacillus* and from molds in the genera *Penicillium* and *Cephalosporium.* Not only have chemists created new drugs by altering the structure of naturally occurring antibiotics, they are actively searching for metabolic compounds with antimicrobial effects in species other than bacteria and fungi.

Before actual antimicrobial therapy can begin, it is important that at least three factors be known:

1. the nature of the microorganism causing the infection,
2. the degree of the microorganism's susceptibility (also called sensitivity) to various drugs, and
3. the overall medical condition of the patient.

Identifying the Agent

Identification of infectious agents from body specimens should be attempted as soon as possible. It is especially important that such specimens be taken before any antimicrobial drug is given, before the drug reduces the numbers of the infectious agent. Direct examination of body fluids, sputum, or stool is a rapid initial method for detecting and perhaps even identifying bacteria or fungi. A doctor often begins the therapy on the basis of such immediate findings, or even on the basis of an informed best guess. For instance, if a sore throat appears to be caused by *Streptococcus pyogenes,* the physician might prescribe penicillin, because this species seems to

First mass-produced in 1944, penicillin saved many lives in WWII.

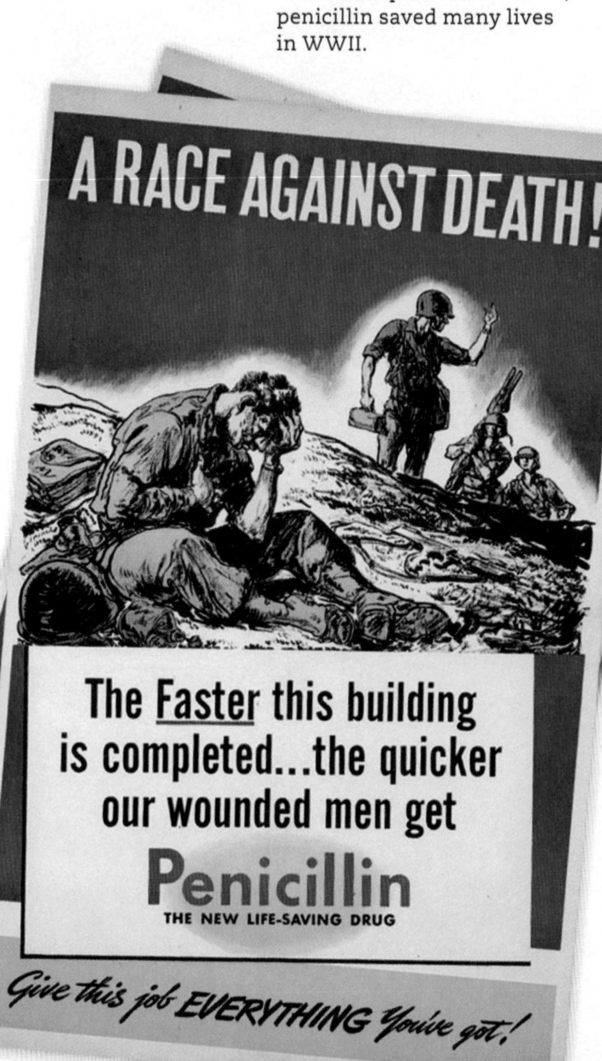

be almost universally sensitive to it so far. If the infectious agent is not or cannot be isolated, epidemiological statistics may be required to predict the most likely agent in a given infection. For example, *Streptococcus pneumoniae* accounts for the majority of cases of meningitis in children, followed by *Neisseria meningitidis* (discussed in detail in chapter 17).

Testing for the Drug Susceptibility of Microorganisms

Testing is essential in those groups of bacteria commonly showing resistance, such as *Staphylococcus* species, *Neisseria gonorrhoeae, Streptococcus pneumoniae, Enterococcus faecalis,* and the aerobic gram-negative intestinal bacilli. However, not all infectious agents require antimicrobial sensitivity testing. Drug testing in fungal or protozoan infections is difficult and is often unnecessary. When certain groups, such as group A streptococci and all anaerobes (except *Bacteroides*), are known to be uniformly susceptible to penicillin G, testing may not be necessary unless the patient is allergic to penicillin.

Selection of a proper antimicrobial agent begins by demonstrating the *in vitro* activity of several drugs against the infectious agent by means of standardized methods. In general, these tests involve exposing a pure culture of the bacterium to several different drugs and observing the effects of the drugs on growth.

The *Kirby-Bauer* technique is an agar diffusion test that provides useful data on antimicrobial susceptibility. In this test, the surface of a plate of special medium is spread with the test bacterium, and small discs containing a premeasured amount of antimicrobial are dispensed onto the bacterial lawn. After incubation, the zone of inhibition surrounding the discs is measured and compared with a standard for each drug **(table 10.3** and **figure 10.1).** The profile of antimicrobial sensitivity, or *antibiogram,* provides data for drug selection. The Kirby-Bauer procedure is less effective for bacteria

Penicillins attack bacterial cell walls.

Table 10.3 Results of a Sample Kirby-Bauer Test

Drug	Zone Sizes (mm) Required for: Susceptibility (S)	Resistance (R)	Example Results (mm) for *Staphylococcus aureus*	Evaluation
Bacitracin	>13	<8	15	S
Chloramphenicol	>18	<12	20	S
Erythromycin	>18	<13	15	I
Gentamicin	>13	<12	16	S
Kanamycin	>18	<13	20	S
Neomycin	>17	<12	12	R
Penicillin G	>29	<20	10	R
Polymyxin B	>12	<8	10	R
Streptomycin	>15	<11	11	R
Vancomycin	>12	<9	15	S
Tetracycline	>19	<14	25	S

R = resistant, I = intermediate, S = sensitive

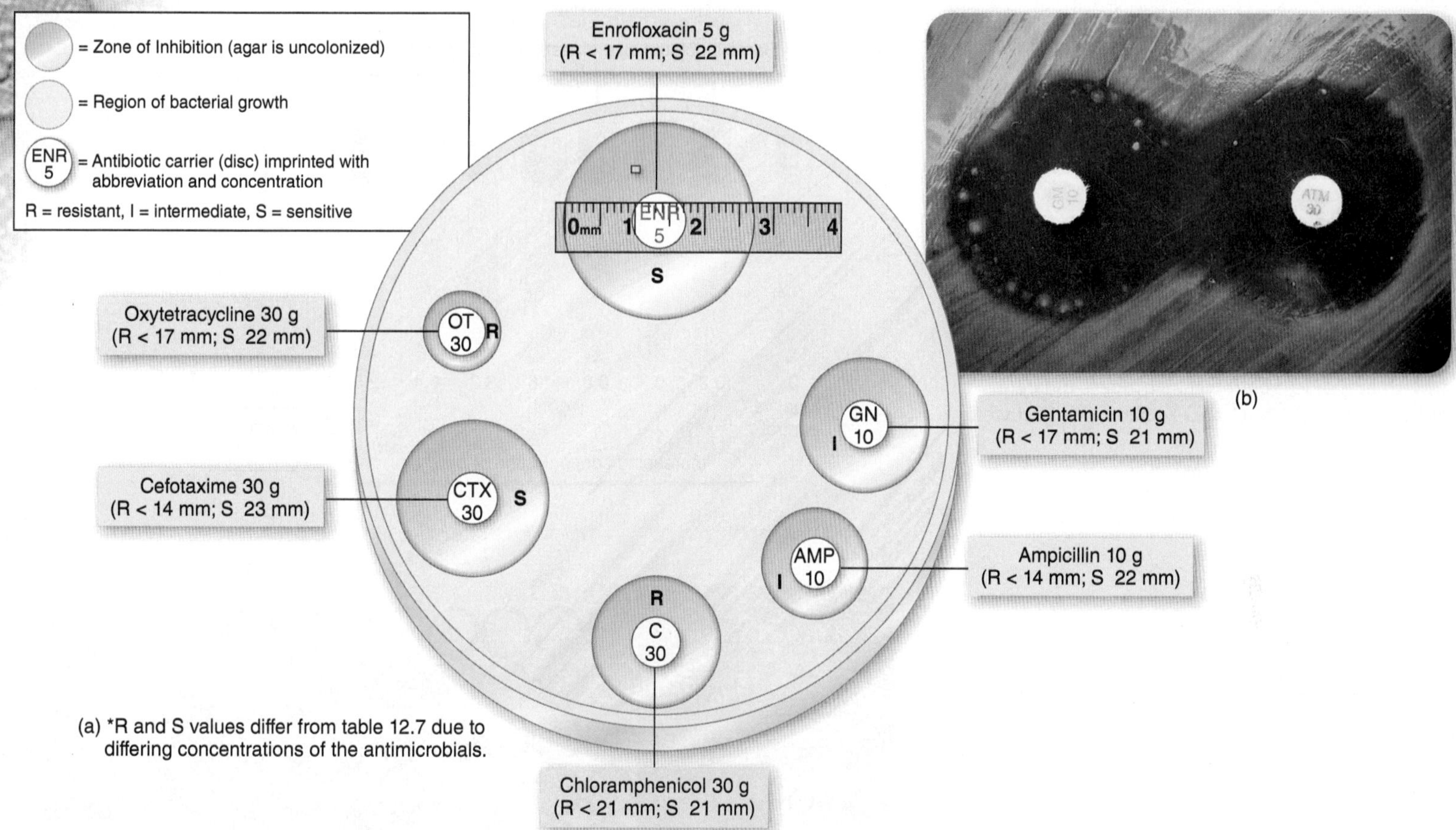

Figure 10.1 Technique for preparation and interpretation of disc diffusion tests. **(a)** Standardized methods are used to spread a lawn of bacteria over the medium. A dispenser delivers several drugs onto a plate, followed by incubation. Interpretation of results: During incubation, antimicrobials become increasingly diluted as they diffuse out of the disc into the medium. If the test bacterium is sensitive to a drug, a zone of inhibition develops around its disc. Roughly speaking, the larger the size of this zone, the greater is the bacterium's sensitivity to the drug. The diameter of each zone is measured in millimeters and evaluated for susceptibility or resistance by means of a comparative standard (see table 10.3). **(b)** Results of test with *Escherichia hermannii* indicate a synergistic effect between two different antibiotics (note the expanded zone between these two drugs).

that are anaerobic, highly fastidious, or slow-growing (*Mycobacterium*). An alternative diffusion system that provides additional information on drug effectiveness is the E-test **(figure 10.2)**.

More sensitive and quantitative results can be obtained with tube dilution tests. First the antimicrobial is diluted serially in tubes of broth, and then each tube is inoculated with a small uniform sample of pure culture, incubated, and examined for growth (turbidity). The smallest concentration (highest dilution) of drug that visibly inhibits growth is called the **minimum inhibitory concentration**, or **MIC**. The MIC is useful in determining the smallest

Figure 10.2 Alternative to the Kirby-Bauer procedure. Another diffusion test is the E-test, which uses a strip to produce the zone of inhibition. The advantage of the E-test is that the strip contains a gradient of drug calibrated in micrograms. This way, the MIC can be measured by observing the mark on the strip that corresponds to the edge of the zone of inhibition. (IP = imipenem and TZ = tazobactam)

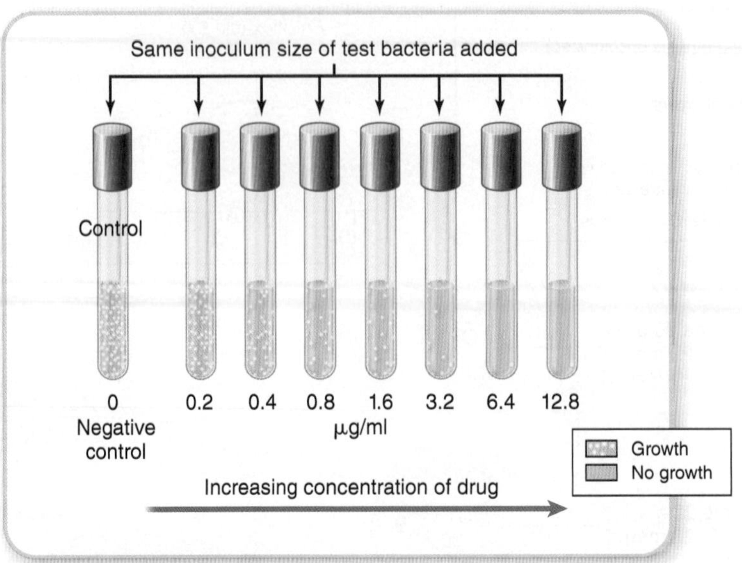

(a)

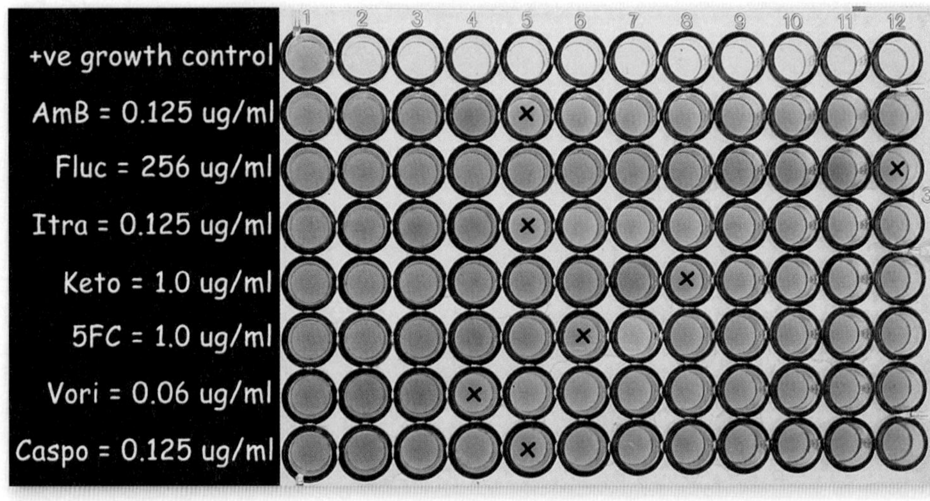

(b)

Figure 10.3 Tube dilution test for determining the minimum inhibitory concentration (MIC). (a) The antibiotic is diluted serially through tubes of liquid nutrient from right to left. All tubes are inoculated with an identical amount of a test bacterium and then incubated. The first tube on the left is a control that lacks the drug and shows maximum growth. The dilution of the first tube in the series that shows no growth (no turbidity) is the MIC. (b) Microbroth dilution in a multiwell plate adapted for eukaryotic pathogens. Here, amphotericin B, flucytosine, and several azole drugs are tested on a pathogenic yeast. Pink indicates growth and blue, no growth. Numbers indicate the dilution of the MIC, and Xs show the first well without growth.

effective dosage of a drug and in providing a comparative index against other antimicrobials **(figure 10.3)**. In many clinical laboratories, these antimicrobial testing procedures are performed in automated machines that can test dozens of drugs simultaneously.

The MIC and Therapeutic Index

The results of antimicrobial sensitivity tests guide the physician's choice of a suitable drug. If therapy has already commenced, it is imperative to determine if the tests bear out the use of that particular drug. Once therapy has begun, it is important to observe the patient's clinical response, because the *in vitro* activity of the drug is not always correlated with its *in vivo* effect. When antimicrobial treatment fails, the failure is due to one or more the following:

- the inability of the drug to diffuse into that body compartment (the brain, joints, skin);
- resistant microbes in the infection that didn't make it into the sample collected for testing; or
- an infection caused by more than one pathogen (mixed), some of which are resistant to the drug.

If therapy does fail, a different drug, combined therapy, or a different method of administration must be considered.

Because drug toxicity to the host is of concern, it is best to choose the one with high selective toxicity for the infectious agent and low human toxicity. The **therapeutic index (TI)** is defined as the ratio of the dose of the drug that is toxic to humans as compared to its minimum effective (therapeutic) dose. The closer these two figures are (the smaller the ratio), the greater is the potential for toxic drug reactions. For example, a drug that has a therapeutic index of:

$$\frac{10\ \mu g/ml\ (\text{toxic dose})}{9\ \mu g/ml\ (\text{MIC})} \quad TI = 1.1$$

is a riskier choice than one with a therapeutic index of:

$$\frac{10\ \mu g/ml}{1\ \mu g/ml} \quad TI = 10$$

When a series of drugs being considered for therapy have similar MICs, the drug with the highest therapeutic index usually has the widest margin of safety.

The physician must also take a careful history of the patient to discover any preexisting medical conditions that will influence the activity of the drug or the response of the patient. A history of allergy to a certain class of drugs precludes the use of that drug and any drugs related to it. Underlying liver or kidney disease will ordinarily necessitate the modification of drug therapy, because these organs play such an important part in metabolizing or excreting the drug. Infants, the elderly, and pregnant women require special precautions. For example, age can diminish gastrointestinal absorption and organ function, and most antimicrobial drugs cross the placenta and could affect fetal development.

The intake of other drugs must be carefully scrutinized, because incompatibilities can result in increased toxicity or failure of one or more of the drugs. For example, the combination of aminoglycosides and cephalosporins can be toxic to kidneys; antacids reduce the absorption of isoniazid; and the interaction of tetracycline or rifampin with oral contraceptives can abolish the contraceptive's effect. Some drugs (penicillin with certain aminoglycosides, or amphotericin B with flucytosine) act synergistically, so that reduced doses of each can be used in combined therapy. Other concerns in choosing drugs include any genetic or metabolic abnormalities in the patient, the site of infection, the route of administration, and the cost of the drug.

The Art and Science of Choosing an Antimicrobial Drug

Even when all the information is in, the final choice of a drug is not always easy or straightforward. Consider the hypothetical case of an elderly alcoholic patient with pneumonia caused by *Klebsiella* and complicated by diminished liver and kidney function. All drugs must be given parenterally because of prior damage to the gastrointestinal lining and poor absorption. Drug tests show that the infectious agent is sensitive to third-generation cephalosporins, gentamicin, imipenem, and azlocillin. The patient's history shows previous allergy to the penicillins, so these would be ruled out. Drug interactions occur between alcohol and the cephalosporins, which are also associated with serious bleeding in elderly patients, so this may not be a good choice. Aminoglycosides such as gentamicin are nephrotoxic and poorly cleared by damaged kidneys. Imipenem causes intestinal discomfort, but it has less toxicity and would be a viable choice.

In the case of a cancer patient with severe systemic *Candida* infection, there will be fewer criteria to weigh. Intravenous amphotericin B or fluconazole are the only possible choices, despite drug toxicity and other possible adverse side effects. In a life-threatening situation in which a dangerous chemotherapy is perhaps the only chance for survival, the choices are reduced and the priorities are different.

Antibiotics have become commonly prescribed medicine.

ASSESS YOUR PROGRESS

1. State the main goal of antimicrobial treatment.
2. Identify the sources for most currently used antimicrobials.
3. Describe two methods for testing antimicrobial susceptibility.
4. Define therapeutic index, and identify whether a high or a low index is preferable.

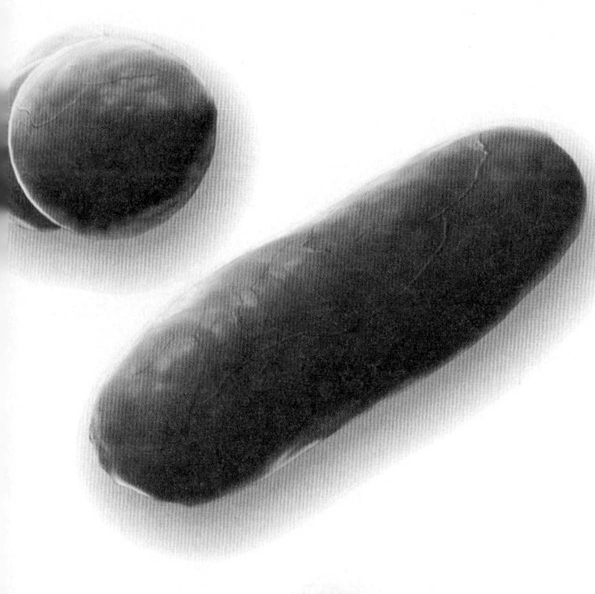

10.2 Interactions Between Drug and Microbe

The goal of antimicrobial drugs is either to disrupt the cell processes or structures of bacteria, fungi, and protozoa or to inhibit virus replication. Most of the drugs used in chemotherapy interfere with the function of enzymes required to synthesize or assemble macromolecules, or they destroy structures already formed in the cell. Above all, drugs should be **selectively toxic,** which means they should kill or inhibit microbial cells without simultaneously damaging host tissues. This concept of selective toxicity is central to antibiotic treatment, and the best drugs are those that block the actions or synthesis of molecules in microorganisms but not in vertebrate cells. Examples of drugs with excellent selective toxicity are those that block the synthesis of the cell wall in bacteria (penicillins). They have low toxicity and few direct effects on human cells because human cells lack the chemical peptidoglycan, and are thus unaffected by this action of the antibiotic. Among the most toxic to human cells are drugs that act upon a structure common to both the infective agent and the host cell, such as the cell membrane (e.g., amphotericin B, used to treat fungal infections). As the characteristics of the infectious agent become more and more similar to those of the host cell, selective toxicity becomes more difficult to achieve, and undesirable side effects are more likely to occur.

Mechanisms of Drug Action

If the goal of chemotherapy is to disrupt the structure or function of an organism to the point where it can no longer survive, then the first step toward this goal is to identify the structural and metabolic needs of a living cell. Once the requirements of a living cell have been determined, methods of removing,

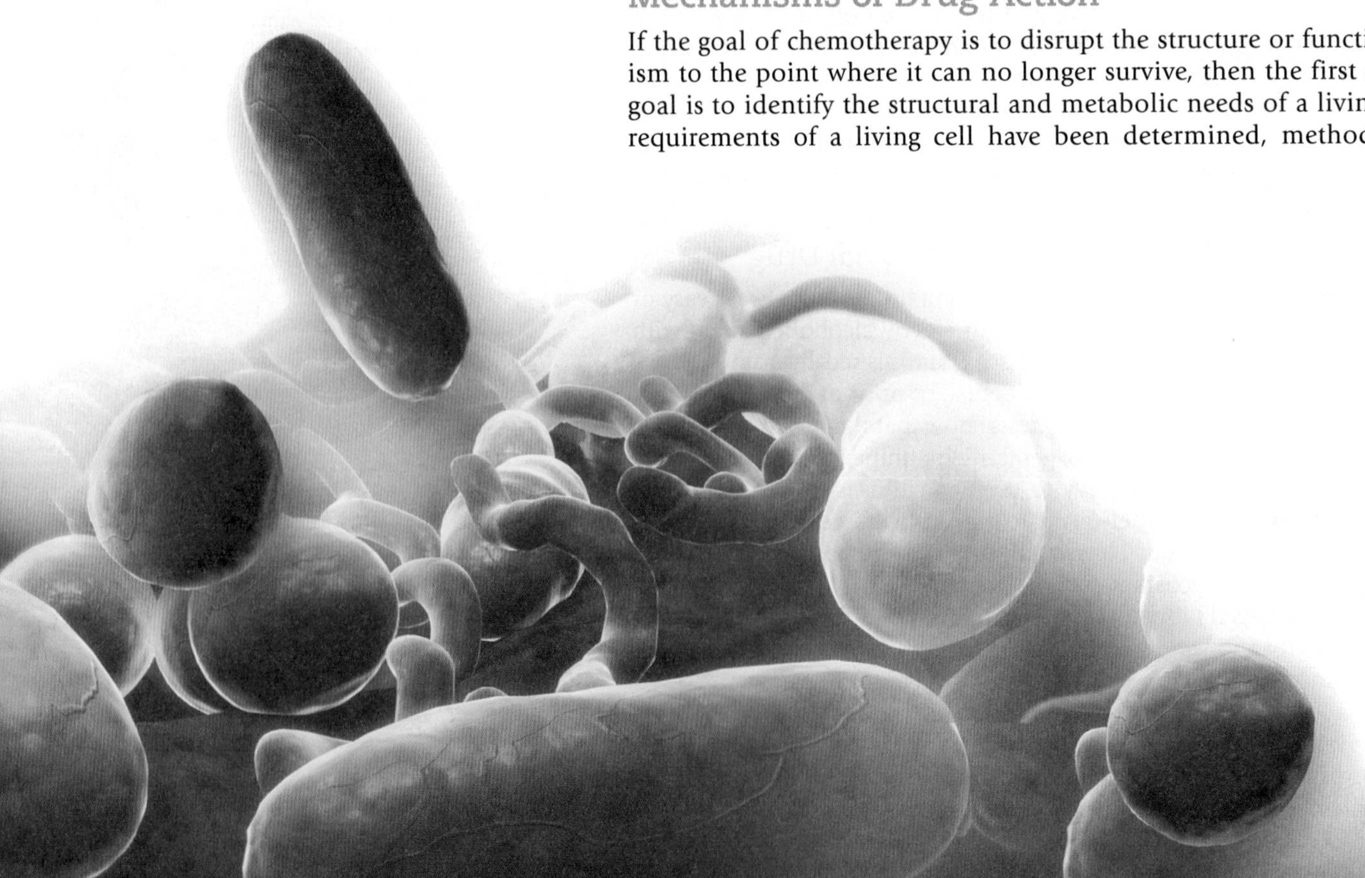

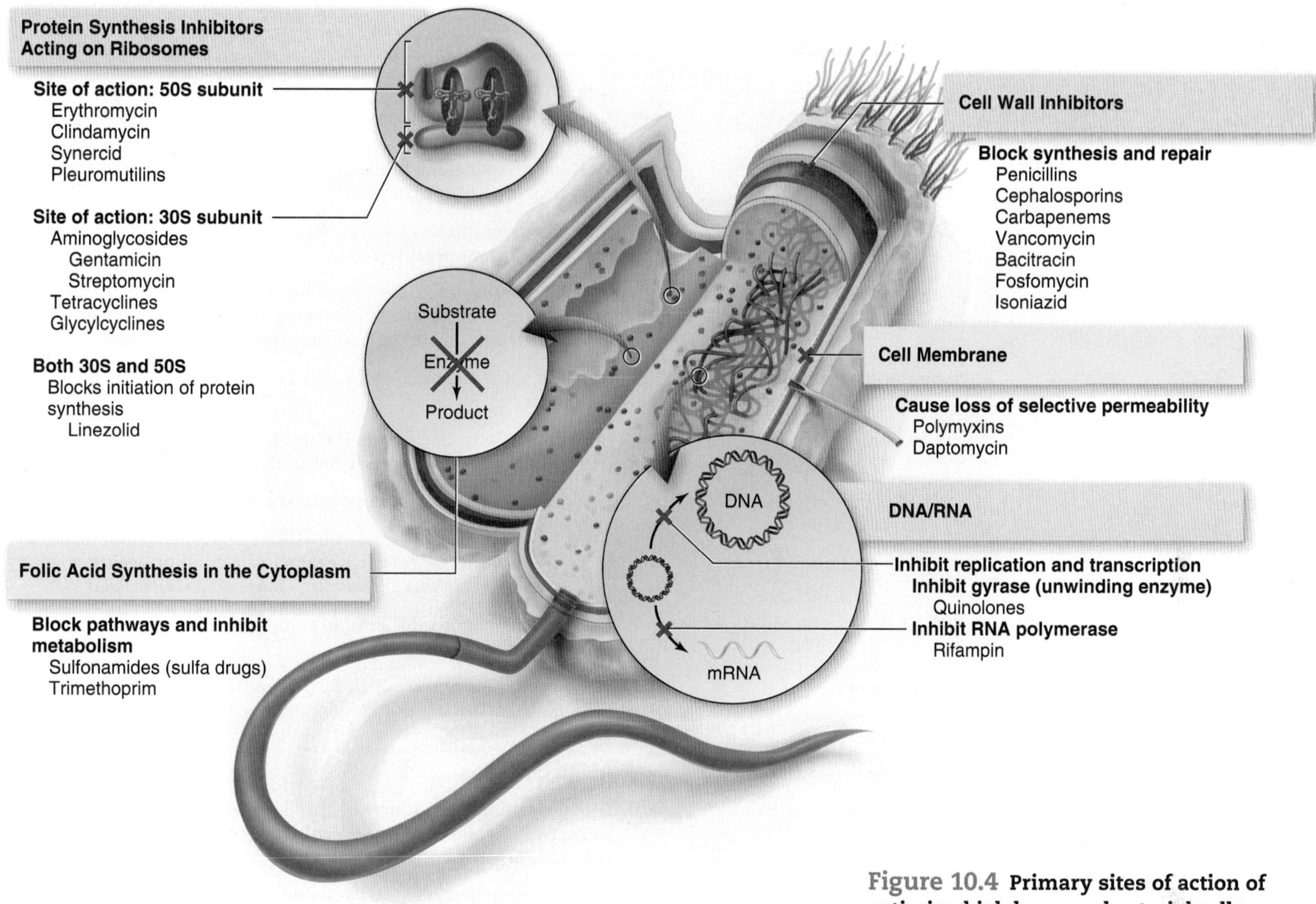

Figure 10.4 Primary sites of action of antimicrobial drugs on bacterial cells.

disrupting, or interfering with these requirements can be employed as potential chemotherapeutic strategies. The metabolism of an actively dividing cell is marked by the production of new cell wall components (in most cells), DNA, RNA, proteins, and cell membrane. Consequently, antimicrobial drugs are divided into categories based on which of these metabolic targets they affect. These categories are outlined in **figure 10.4** and include the following:

1. inhibition of cell wall synthesis,
2. inhibition of nucleic acid (RNA and DNA) structure and function,
3. inhibition of protein synthesis,
4. interference with cell membrane structure or function, and
5. inhibition of folic acid synthesis.

As you will see, these categories are not completely discrete, and some effects can overlap. **Table 10.4** describes these categories, as well as common drugs comprising each of these categories.

Table 10.4 Specific Drugs and Their Metabolic Targets

Drug Class/Mechanism of Action	Subgroups	Uses/Characteristics
Drugs That Target the Cell Wall		
Penicillins	Penicillins G and V	Most important natural forms used to treat gram-positive cocci, some gram-negative bacteria (meningococci, syphilis, spirochetes)
	Ampicillin, carbenicillin, amoxicillin	Have a broader spectra of action, are semisynthetic; used against gram-negative enteric rods
	Methicillin, nafcillin, cloxacillin	Useful in treating infections caused by some penicillinase-producing bacteria (enzymes capable of destroying the beta-lactam ring of penicillin, which makes some bacteria resistant to penicillin)
	Mezlocillin, azlocillin	Extended spectrum; can be substituted for combinations of antibiotics
	Clavulanic acid	Inhibits beta-lactamase enzymes; added to penicillins to increase their effectiveness in the presence of penicillinase-producing bacteria
Cephalosporins	Cephalothin, cefazolin	First generation*; most effective against gram-positive cocci, few gram-negative bacteria
	Cefaclor, cefonicid	Second generation; more effective than first generation against gram-negative bacteria such as *Enterobacter*, *Proteus*, and *Haemophilus*
	Cephalexin, cefotaxime	Third generation; broad-spectrum, particularly against enteric bacteria that produce beta-lactamases
	Ceftriaxone	Third generation; semisynthetic broad-spectrum drug that treats wide variety of urinary, skin, respiratory, and nervous system infections
	Cefpirome, cefepime	Fourth generation
	Ceftobiprole	Fifth generation; used against methicillin-resistant *Staphylococcus aureus* (MRSA) and also against penicillin-resistant gram-positive and gram-negative bacteria
Carbapenems	Doripenem, imipenem	Powerful but potentially toxic; reserved for use when other drugs are not effective
	Aztreonam	Narrow-spectrum; used to treat gram-negative aerobic bacilli causing pneumonia, septicemia, and urinary tract infections; effective for those who are allergic to penicillin
Miscellaneous Drugs That Target the Cell Wall	Bacitracin	Narrow-spectrum; used to combat superficial skin infections caused by streptococci and staphylococci; main ingredient in Neosporin
	Isoniazid	Used to treat *Mycobacterium tuberculosis*, but only against growing cells; used in combination with other drugs in active tuberculosis
	Vancomycin	Narrow spectrum of action; used to treat staphylococcal infections in cases of penicillin and methicillin resistance or in patients with an allergy to penicillin
	Fosfomycin tromethamine	Phosphoric acid agent; effective as an alternative treatment for urinary tract infection caused by enteric bacteria
Drugs That Target Protein Synthesis		
Aminoglycosides Insert on sites on the 30S subunit and cause the misreading of the mRNA, leading to abnormal proteins	Streptomycin	Broad-spectrum; used to treat infections caused by gram-negative rods, certain gram-positive bacteria; used to treat bubonic plague, tularemia, and tuberculosis; vancomycin also targets protein synthesis as well as cell walls

*New improved versions of drugs are referred to as new "generations."

Table 10.4 (continued)

Drug Class/Mechanism of Action	Subgroups	Uses/Characteristics
Drugs That Target Protein Synthesis *(continued)*		
Tetracyclines Block the attachment of tRNA on the A acceptor site and stop further protein synthesis	Tetracycline, terramycin	Effective against gram-positive and gram-negative rods and cocci, aerobic and anaerobic bacteria, mycoplasmas, rickettsias, and spirochetes
Glycylcyclines	Tigecycline	Newer derivative of tetracycline; effective against bacteria that have become resistant to tetracyclines
Macrolides Inhibit translocation of the subunit during translation (erythromycin)	Erythromycin, clarithromycin, azithromycin	Relatively broad-spectrum, semisynthetic; used in treating ear, respiratory, and skin infections, as well as *Mycobacterium* infections in AIDS patients
Miscellaneous Drugs That Target Protein Synthesis	Clindamycin	Broad-spectrum antibiotic used to treat penicillin-resistant staphylococci, serious anaerobic infections of the stomach and intestines unresponsive to other antibiotics
	Quinupristin and dalfopristin (Synercid)	A combined antibiotic from the streptogramin group of drugs; effective against *Staphylococcus* and *Enterococcus* species causing endocarditis and surgical infections, including resistant strains
	Linezolid	Synthetic drug from the oxazolidinones; a novel drug that inhibits the initiation of protein synthesis; used to treat antibiotic-resistant organisms such as MRSA and VRE
Drugs That Target Folic Acid Synthesis		
Sulfonamides Interfere with folate metabolism by blocking enzymes required for the synthesis of tetrahydrofolate, which is needed by the cells for folic acid synthesis and eventual production of DNA, RNA, and amino acids	sulfasoxazole	Used to treat shigellosis, acute urinary tract infections, certain protozoan infections
	Silver sulfadiazine	Used to treat burns, eye infections (in ointment and solution forms)
	Trimethoprim	Inhibits the enzymatic step immediately preceding the step inhibited by sulfonamides; trimethoprim often given in conjunction with sulfamethoxazole because of this synergistic effect; used to treat *Pneumocystis jiroveci* in AIDS patients
Drugs That Target DNA or RNA		
Fluoroquinolones Inhibit DNA unwinding enzymes or helicases, thereby stopping DNA transcription	Nalidixic acid	First generation; rarely used anymore
	Ciprofloxacin, ofloxacin	Second generation
	levofloxacin	Third generation; used against gram-positive organisms, including some that are resistant to other drugs
	Trovafloxacin	Fourth generation; effective against anaerobic organisms
Miscellaneous Drugs That Target DNA or RNA	Rifamycin (altered chemically into rifampin)	Limited in spectrum because it cannot pass through the cell envelope of many gram-negative bacilli; mainly used to treat infections caused by gram-positive rods and cocci and a few gram-negative bacteria; used to treat leprosy and tuberculosis
Drugs That Target Cell Membranes		
Polymyxins Interact with membrane phospholipids; distort the cell surface and cause leakage of protein and nitrogen bases, particularly in gram-negative bacteria	Polymyxin B and E	Used to treat drug-resistant *Pseudomonas aeruginosa* and severe urinary tract infections caused by gram-negative rods
	Daptomycin	Most active against gram-positive bacteria

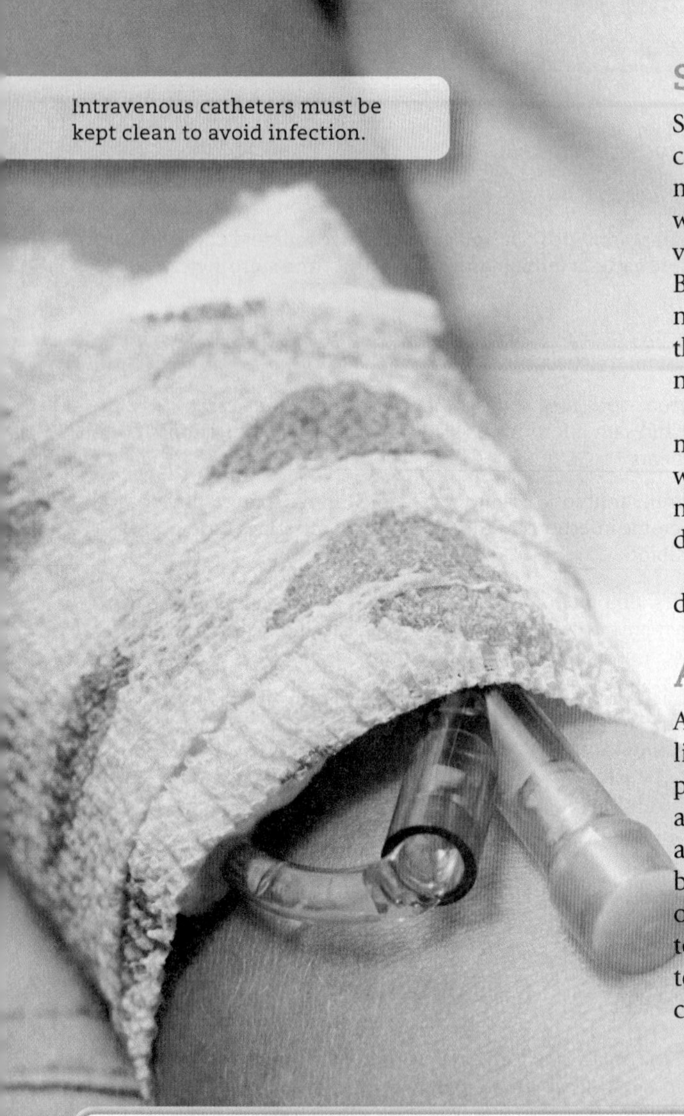

Intravenous catheters must be kept clean to avoid infection.

Spectrum of Activity

Scores of antimicrobial drugs are marketed in the United States. Although the medical and pharmaceutical literature contains a wide array of names for antimicrobials, most of them are variants of a small number of drug families. One of the most useful ways of categorizing antimicrobials, which you have already encountered in the previous section, is to designate them as either **broad-spectrum** or **narrow-spectrum.** Broad-spectrum drugs are effective against more than one group of bacteria, whereas narrow-spectrum drugs generally target a specific group. **Table 10.5** demonstrates that tetracyclines are broad-spectrum, whereas polymyxin and even penicillins are narrow-spectrum agents.

Since penicillin is such a familiar antibiotic, and since the alterations in the molecule over the years illustrate how antibiotics are developed and improved upon, we provide an overview in **table 10.6**. Here you will see that original penicillin was narrow-spectrum, and susceptible to microbial counterattacks. Later penicillins were developed to overcome those two limitations.

Referring back to table 10.4, you can view details about various antimicrobial drugs based on which of the five major mechanisms they target.

Antibiotics and Biofilms

As you read in chapter 6, biofilm inhabitants behave differently than their free-living counterparts. One of the major ways they differ—at least from a medical perspective—is that they are often unaffected by the same antimicrobials that work against them when they are free-living. When this was first recognized, it was assumed that it was a problem of penetration, that the (often charged) antimicrobial drugs could not penetrate the sticky extracellular material surrounding biofilm organisms. While that is a factor, there is something more important contributing to biofilm resistance: the different phenotype expressed by biofilm bacteria. Secured to surfaces they express different genes and therefore have different antibiotic susceptibility profiles.

Table 10.5 Spectrum of Activity for Antibiotics

Bacteria	Mycobacteria	Gram-negative Bacteria	Gram-positive Bacteria	Chlamydias	Rickettsias
Examples of diseases	Tuberculosis	Salmonellosis, plague, gonorrhea	Strep throat, staph infections*	Chlamydia, trachoma	Rocky Mountain spotted fever
Spectrum of activity of various antibiotics	Isoniazid Streptomycin Tobramycin Polymyxin Carbapenems Tetracyclines Sulfonamides Cephalosporins Penicillins				
Are there normal biota in this group?	Yes	Yes	Yes	Probably	None known

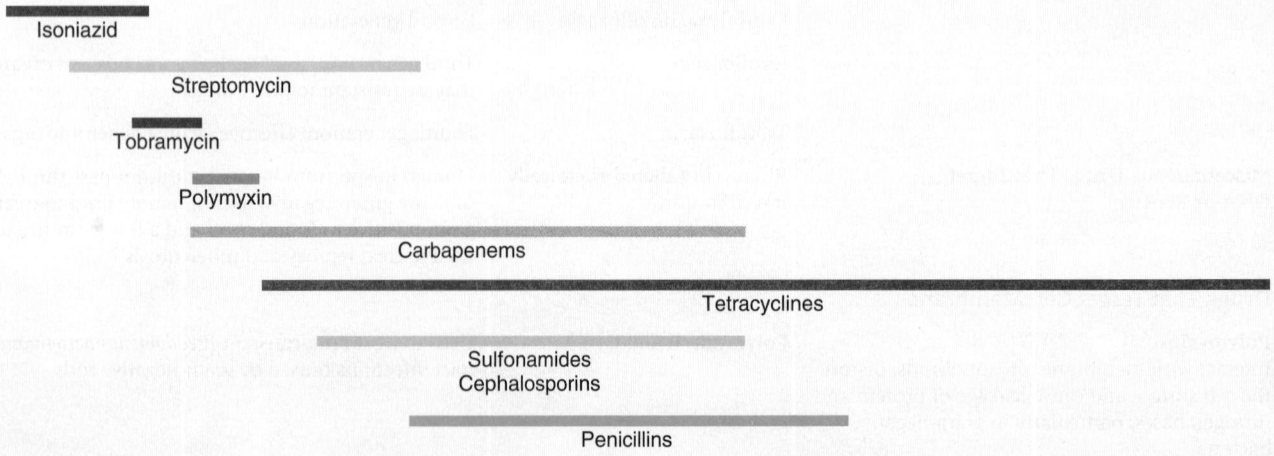

*Note that some members of a bacterial group may not be affected by the antibiotics indicated, due to acquired or natural resistance. In other words, exceptions do exist.

Table 10.6 Characteristics of Selected Penicillin Drugs

Name	Spectrum of Action	Uses, Advantages	Disadvantages
Penicillin G 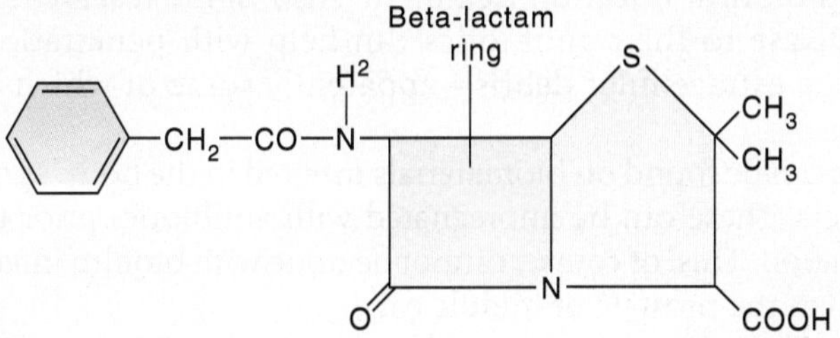	Narrow	Best drug of choice when bacteria are sensitive; low cost; low toxicity	Can be hydrolyzed by penicillinase; allergies occur; requires injection
Penicillin V	Narrow	Good absorption from intestine; otherwise, similar to penicillin G	Hydrolysis by penicillinase; allergies
Oxacillin, cloxacillin 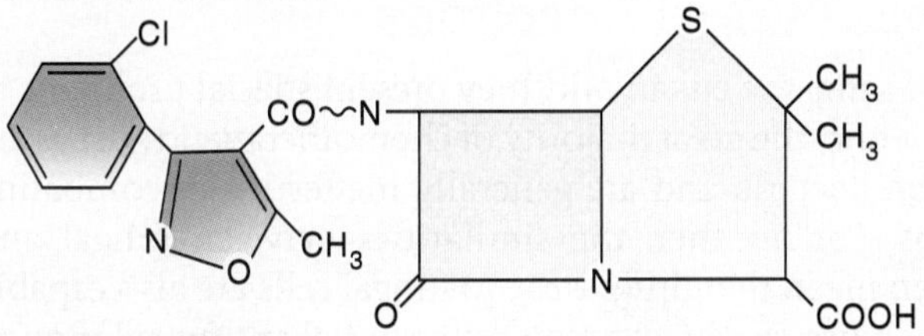	Narrow	Not susceptible to penicillinase; good absorption	Allergies; expensive
Methicillin, nafcillin 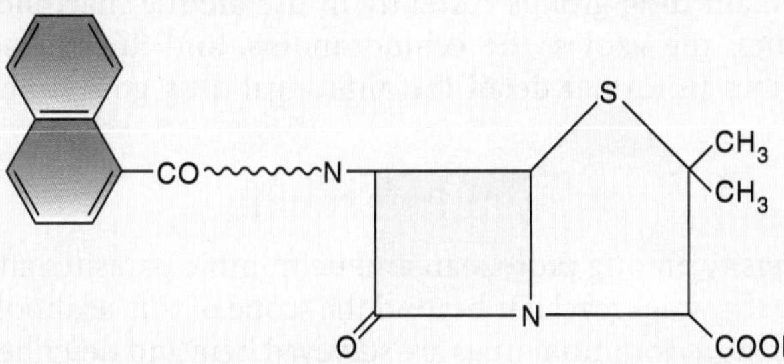	Narrow	Not usually susceptible to penicillinase	Poor absorption; allergies; growing resistance
Ampicillin	Broad	Works on some gram-negative bacilli	Can be hydrolyzed by penicillinase; allergies; only fair absorption
Amoxicillin	Broad	Gram-negative infections; good absorption	Hydrolysis by penicillinase; allergies
Carbenicillin 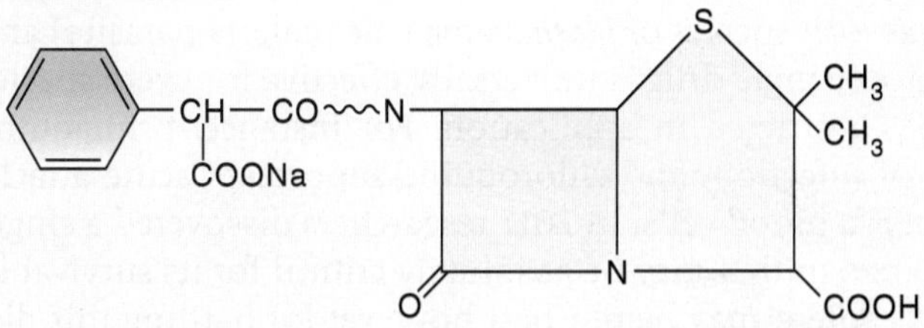	Broad	Works on more gram-negative bacilli than ampicillin	Poor absorption; used only parenterally
Azlocillin, mezlocillin, ticarcillin 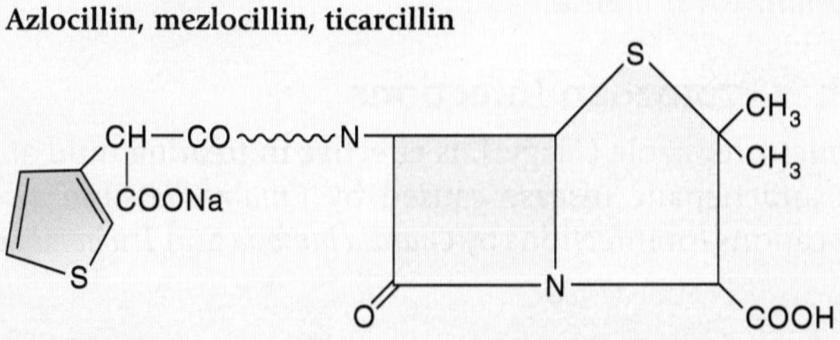	Very broad	Effective against *Pseudomonas* species; low toxicity compared with aminoglycosides	Allergies; susceptible to many beta-lactamases

Years of research have so far not yielded an obvious solution to this problem, though there are several partially successful strategies. One of these involves interrupting the quorum sensing pathways that mediate communication between cells and may change phenotypic expression. Daptomycin, a lipopeptide that is effective in deep tissue infections with resistant bacteria, has also shown some success in biofilm infection treatment. Also, some researchers have found that adding DNase to their antibiotics can help with penetration of the antibiotic through the extracellular debris—apparently some of which is DNA from lysed cells.

Many biofilm infections can be found on biomaterials inserted in the body, such as cardiac or urinary catheters. These can be impregnated with antibiotics prior to insertion to prevent colonization. This, of course, cannot be done with biofilm infections of natural tissues, such as the prostate or middle ear.

Interestingly, it appears that chemotherapy with some antibiotics—notably aminoglycosides—can cause bacteria to form biofilms at a higher rate than they otherwise would. Obviously there is much more to come in understanding biofilms and their control.

Agents to Treat Fungal Infections

Because the cells of fungi are eukaryotic, they present special problems in chemotherapy. For one, the great majority of chemotherapeutic drugs are designed to act on bacteria and are generally ineffective in combating fungal infections. For another, the similarities between fungal and human cells often mean that drugs toxic to fungal cells are also capable of harming human tissues. A few agents with special antifungal properties have been developed for treating systemic and superficial fungal infections. Four main drug groups currently in use are the macrolide polyene antibiotics, the azoles, the echinocandins, and flucytosine. **Table 10.7** describes in further detail the antifungal drug groups and their actions.

Agents to Treat Protozoal Infections

The enormous diversity among protozoan and helminthic parasites and their corresponding therapies reach far beyond the scope of this textbook; however, a few of the more common drugs are surveyed here and described again for particular diseases in the organ systems chapters.

Antimalarial Drugs: Quinine and Its Relatives

Quinine, extracted from the bark of the cinchona tree, was the principal treatment for malaria for hundreds of years, but it has been replaced by the synthesized quinolones, mainly chloroquine and primaquine, which have less toxicity to humans. Because there are several species of *Plasmodium* (the malaria parasite) and many stages in its life cycle, no single drug is universally effective for every species and stage, and each drug is restricted in application. For instance, primaquine eliminates the liver phase of infection, and chloroquine suppresses acute attacks associated with infection of red blood cells. In 2011 researchers discovered a single protein in the malarial protozoan that may be absolutely critical for its survival in all its stages. Targeting that protein may be our best hope yet for battling this disease that has devastated humans for millenia.

Antimalarial quinine is extracted from the bark of the cinchona tree.

Chemotherapy for Other Protozoan Infections

A widely used amoebicide, metronidazole (Flagyl), is effective in treating mild and severe intestinal infections and hepatic disease caused by *Entamoeba histolytica*. Given orally, it also has applications for infections by *Giardia lamblia* and *Trichomonas*

Table 10.7 Agents Used to Treat Fungal Infections

Drug Group	Drug	Action
Macrolide polyenes	Amphotericin B 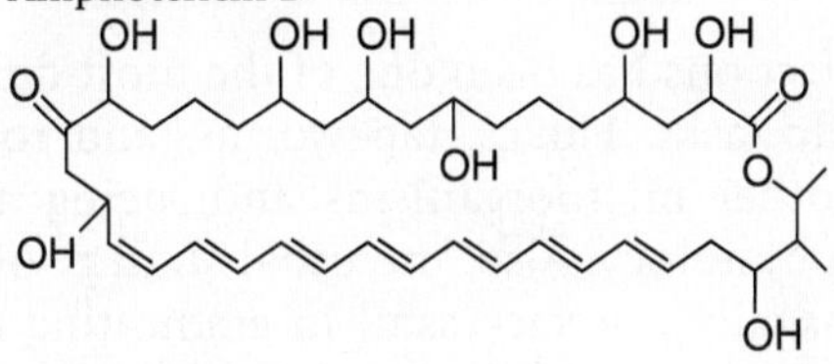	• Bind to fungal membranes, causing loss of selective permeability; extremely versatile • Can be used to treat skin, mucous membrane lesions caused by *Candida albicans* • Injectable form of the drug can be used to treat histoplasmosis and *Cryptococcus* meningitis
Azoles	Ketoconazole, fluconazole, miconazole, and clotrimazole (shown) 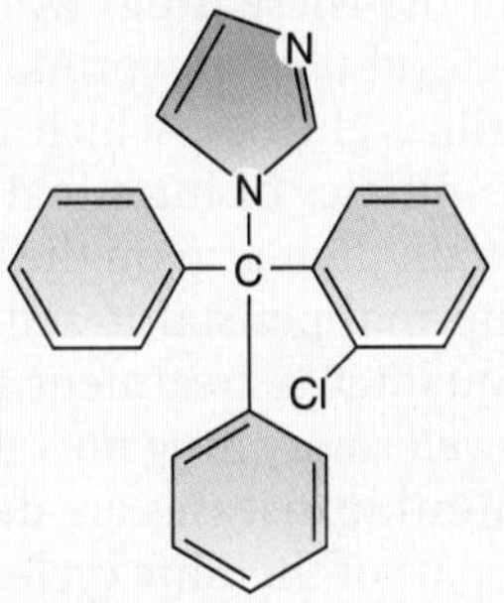	• Interfere with sterol synthesis in fungi • Ketoconazole—cutaneous mycoses, vaginal and oral candidiasis, systemic mycoses • Fluconazole—AIDS-related mycoses (aspergillosis, *Cryptococcus* meningitis) • Clotrimazole and miconazole—used to treat infections in the skin, mouth, and vagina
Echinocandins	Micafungin, caspofungin (shown) 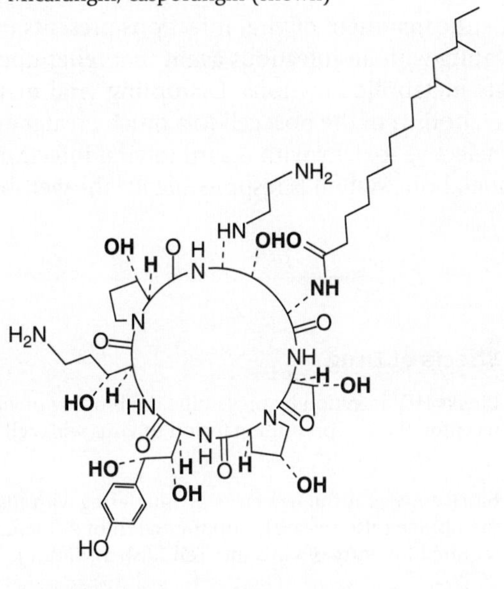	• Inhibit fungal cell wall synthesis • Used against *Candida* strains and aspergillosis
Nucleotide cytosine analog	Flucytosine 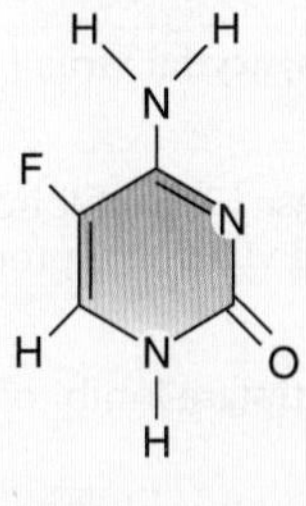	• Rapidly absorbed orally, readily dissolves in the blood and CSF (cerebrospinal fluid) • Used to treat cutaneous mycoses • Usually combined with amphotericin B to treat systemic mycoses because many fungi are resistant to this drug

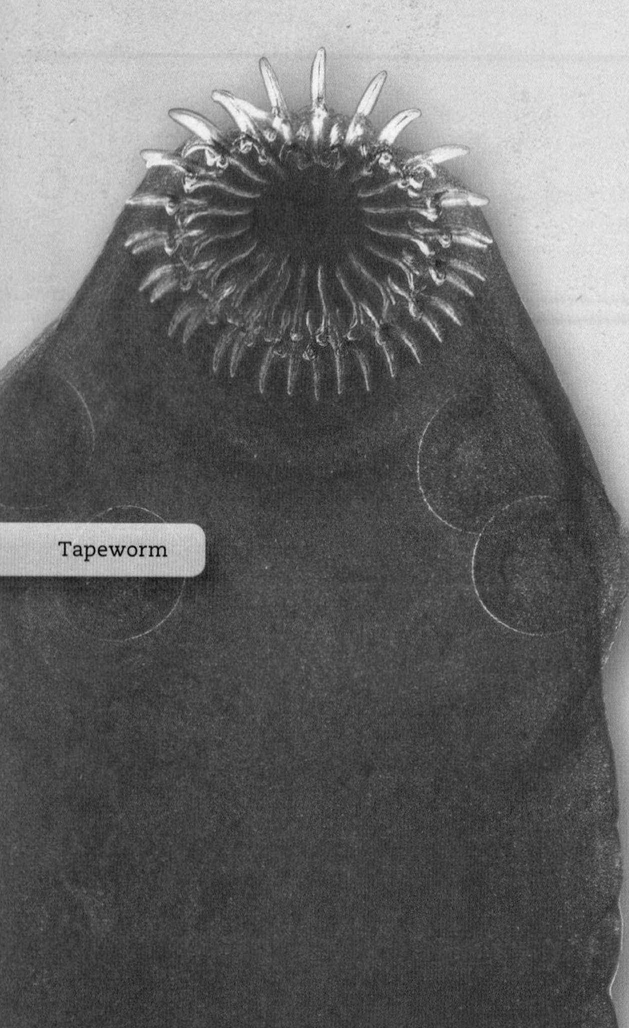

vaginalis (described in chapters 20 and 21, respectively). Other drugs with antiprotozoan activities are quinacrine (a quinine-based drug), sulfonamides, and tetracyclines.

Agents to Treat Helminthic Infections

Treating helminthic infections has been one of the most difficult and challenging of all chemotherapeutic tasks. Flukes, tapeworms, and roundworms are much larger parasites than other microorganisms and, being animals, have greater similarities to human physiology. Also, the usual strategy of using drugs to block their reproduction is usually not successful in eradicating the adult worms. The most effective drugs immobilize, disintegrate, or inhibit the metabolism of all stages of the life cycle.

Mebendazole and albendazole are broad-spectrum antiparasitic drugs used in several roundworm intestinal infestations. These drugs work locally in the intestine to inhibit the function of the microtubules of worms, eggs, and larvae. This means the parasites can no longer utilize glucose, which leads to their demise. The compound pyrantel paralyzes the muscles of intestinal roundworms. Consequently, the worms are unable to maintain their grip on the intestinal wall and are expelled along with the feces by the normal peristaltic action of the bowel. Two newer anthelminthic drugs are praziquantel, a treatment for various tapeworm and fluke infections, and ivermectin, a veterinary drug now used for strongyloidiasis and oncocercosis in humans. Helminthic diseases are described in chapter 20 because these organisms spend a large part of their life cycles in the digestive tract.

Agents to Treat Viral Infections

The chemotherapeutic treatment of viral infections presents unique problems. With viruses, we are dealing with an infectious agent that relies upon the host cell for the vast majority of its metabolic functions. Disrupting viral metabolism requires that we disrupt the metabolism of the host cell to a much greater extent than is desirable. Put another way, selective toxicity with regard to viral infection is difficult to achieve because a single metabolic system is responsible for the well-being of both virus and

Table 10.8 Actions of Antiviral Drugs

Mode of Action	Examples	Effects of Drug
Inhibition of Virus Entry Receptor/fusion/uncoating inhibitors	Enfuvirtide (Fuzeon®)	Blocks **HIV** infection by preventing the binding of viral proteins to cell receptor, thereby preventing fusion of virus with cell
	Amantadine and its relatives, zanamivir (Relenza®), oseltamivir (Tamiflu©)	Block entry of **influenza virus** by interfering with fusion of virus with cell membrane (also release); stop the action of influenza neuraminidase, required for entry of virus into cell (also assembly)
Inhibition of Nucleic Acid Synthesis	Acyclovir (Zovirax®), other "cyclovirs," vidarabine	Purine analogs that terminate DNA replication in **herpesviruses**
	Ribavirin	Purine analog, used for **respiratory syncytial virus (RSV)** and some **hemorrhagic fever viruses**
	Zidovudine (AZT), lamivudine (3TC), didanosine (ddI), zalcitabine (ddC), and stavudine (d4T)	Nucleotide analog reverse transcriptase (RT) inhibitors; stop the action of reverse transcriptase in **HIV**, blocking viral DNA production
	Nevirapine, efavirenz, delavirdine	Nonnucleotide analog reverse transcriptase inhibitors; attach to **HIV** RT binding site, stopping its action
Inhibition of Viral Assembly/Release	Indinavir, saquinavir	Protease inhibitors; insert into **HIV** protease, stopping its action and resulting in inactive noninfectious viruses

host. Although viral diseases such as measles, mumps, and hepatitis are routinely prevented by the use of effective vaccinations, epidemics of AIDS, influenza, and even the "commonness" of the common cold attest to the need for more effective medications for the treatment of viral pathogens.

The first successful antiviral drugs were developed to target specific points in the infectious cycle of viruses. Three major modes of action are as follows:

1. barring penetration of the virus into the host cell,
2. blocking the transcription and translation of viral molecules, and
3. preventing the maturation of viral particles.

Table 10.8 presents a comprehensive overview of the most widely used antiviral drugs. Hundreds of new drugs are in development.

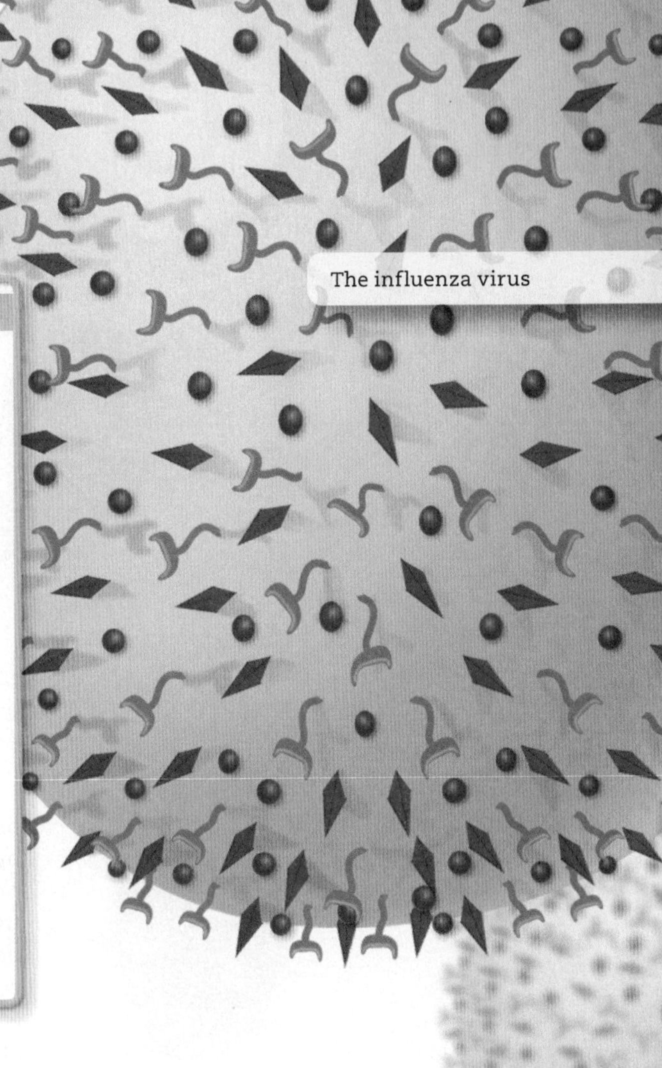
The influenza virus

ASSESS YOUR PROGRESS

5. Explain the concept of selective toxicity.
6. List the five major targets of antimicrobial agents.
7. Identify which categories of drugs are most selectively toxic and why.
8. Distinguish between broad-spectrum and narrow-spectrum antimicrobials, and explain the significance of the distinction.
9. Identify the microbes against which the various penicillins are effective.
10. Explain the significance of beta-lactamases.
11. Identify two antimicrobials that act by inhibiting protein synthesis.
12. Explain how drugs targeting folic acid synthesis work.
13. Identify one example of a fluoroquinolone.
14. Name a drug that targets the cellular membrane.
15. Discuss how treatment of biofilm infections differs from that of nonbiofilm infections.
16. Name the four main categories of antifungal agents.
17. Explain why antiprotozoal and antihelminthic drugs are likely to be more toxic than antibacterial drugs.
18. List the three major targets of action of antiviral drugs.

10.3 Antimicrobial Resistance

One unfortunate outcome of the use of antimicrobials is the development of microbial **drug resistance,** an adaptive response in which microorganisms begin to tolerate an amount of drug that would ordinarily be inhibitory. The ability to circumvent or inactivate antimicrobial drugs is due largely to the genetic versatility and adaptability of microbial populations. The property of drug resistance can be intrinsic as well as acquired. Intrinsic drug resistance can best be exemplified by the fact that bacteria must, of course, be resistant to any antibiotic that they themselves produce. Of much greater importance is the acquisition of resistance to a drug by a microbe that was previously sensitive to the drug. In our context, the term *drug resistance* will refer to this last type of acquired resistance.

How Does Drug Resistance Develop?

Contrary to popular belief, antibiotic resistance is not a recent phenomenon. Resistance to penicillin developed in some bacteria as early as 1940, three years before the drug was even approved for public use. The scope of the problem only became apparent in the 1980s and 1990s, when scientists and physicians observed treatment failures on a large scale.

Microbes become newly resistant to a drug after one of the following two events occurs:

1. spontaneous mutations in critical chromosomal genes, or
2. acquisition of entire new genes or sets of genes via horizontal transfer from another species.

Drug resistance that is found on chromosomes usually results from spontaneous random mutations in bacterial populations. The chance that such a mutation will be advantageous is minimal, and the chance that it will confer resistance to a specific drug is lower still. Nevertheless, given the huge numbers of microorganisms in any population and the constant rate of mutation, such mutations do occur. The end result varies from slight changes in microbial sensitivity, which can be overcome by larger doses of the drug, to complete loss of sensitivity. There may be a third mechanism of acquiring resistance to a drug, which is a phenotypic, not a genotypic, adaptation. Recent studies suggest that bacteria can "go to sleep" when exposed to antibiotics, meaning they will slow or stop their metabolism so that they cannot be harmed by the antibiotic. They can then rev back up after the antibiotic concentration decreases. In the next sections, we will focus on the two genetic changes that can result in acquired resistance.

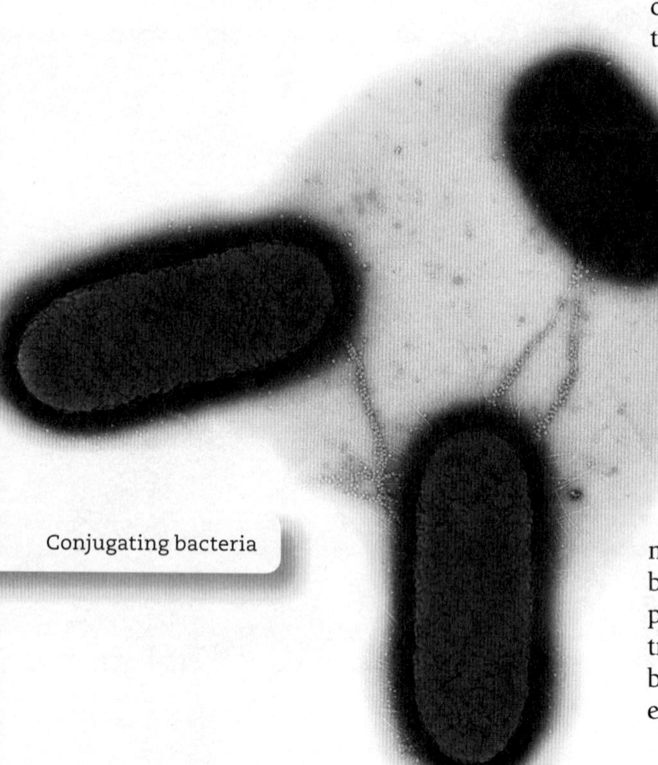
Conjugating bacteria

Resistance occurring through horizontal transfer originates from plasmids called **resistance (R) factors** that are transferred through conjugation, transformation, or transduction. Studies have shown that plasmids encoded with drug resistance are naturally present in microorganisms before they have been exposed to the drug. Such traits are "lying in wait" for an opportunity to be expressed and to confer adaptability on the species. Many bacteria also maintain transposable drug resistance sequences (transposons) that are duplicated and inserted from one plasmid to another or from a plasmid to the chromosome. Chromosomal genes and plasmids containing codes for drug resistance are faithfully replicated and inherited by all subsequent progeny. This sharing of resistance genes accounts for the rapid proliferation of drug-resistant species. As you have read in earlier chapters, gene transfers are extremely frequent in nature, with genes coming from totally unrelated bacteria, viruses, and other organisms living in the body's normal biota and the environment.

We also have a new appreciation for where the reservoirs of antibiotic-resistance genes might be. Recently it was discovered that a wide variety of soil bacteria can not only survive in the presence of many antibiotics, but can also use the antibiotics as fuel. This indicates that there is a large population of natural environmental bacteria with capabilities that might be transferred to disease-causing bacteria. It is also clear that non-disease-causing inhabitants of our bodies and the bodies of our pets harbor many antibiotic-resistance genes that can and do easily jump to pathogenic bacteria with which they share space.

Specific Mechanisms of Drug Resistance

Mutations and horizontal transfer, described above, result in mutants acquiring one of several mechanisms of drug resistance. **Table 10.9** lists the most common mechanisms of drug resistance and provides specific examples of each.

Table 10.9 Mechanisms of Drug Resistance

Mechanism	Example	
New enzymes are synthesized, inactivating the drug (occurs when new genes are acquired).	Bacterial exoenzymes called beta-lactamases hydrolyze the beta-lactam ring structure of some penicillins and cephalosporins, rendering the drugs inactive.	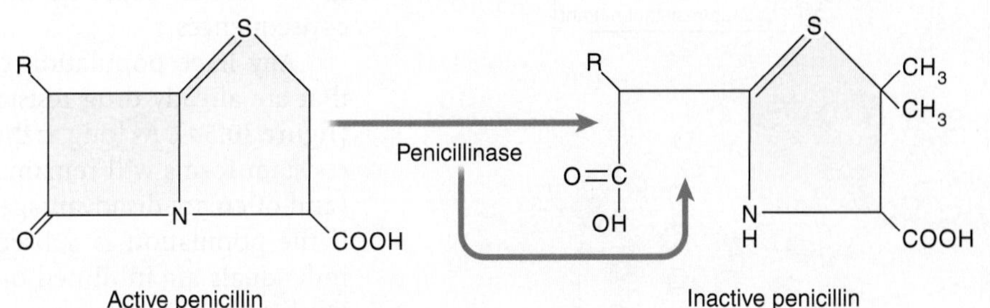
Permeability or uptake of the drug into the bacterium is decreased (occurs via mutation).		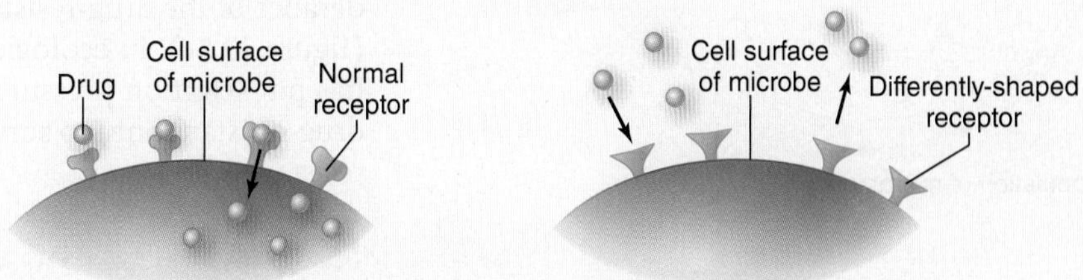
Drug is immediately eliminated (occurs through the acquisition of new genes).	Many bacteria possess multidrug-resistant (MDR) pumps that actively transport drugs out of cells, conferring drug resistance on many gram-positive and gram-negative pathogens.	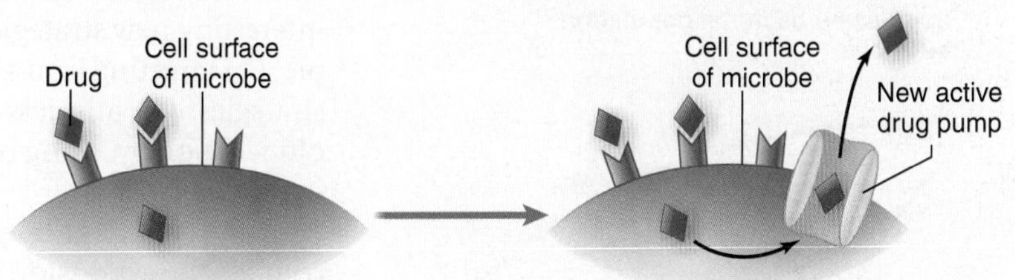
Binding sites for drugs are decreased in number and/or affinity (occurs via mutation or through the acquisition of new genes).	Erythromycin and clindamycin resistance is associated with an alteration on the 50S ribosomal binding site.	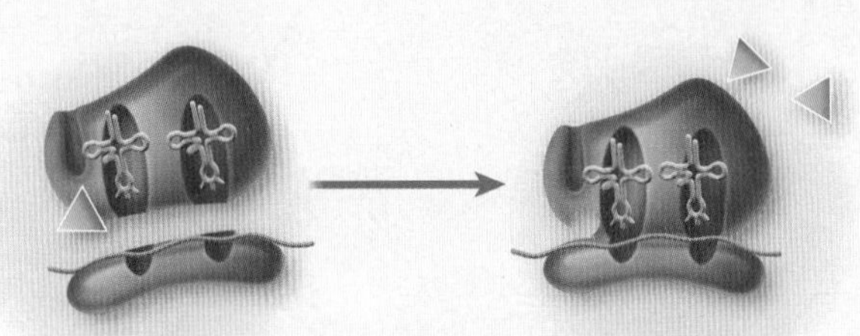
An affected metabolic pathway is shut down, or an alternative pathway is used (occurs via mutation of original enzymes).	Sulfonamide and trimethoprim resistance develop when microbes deviate from the usual patterns of folic acid synthesis.	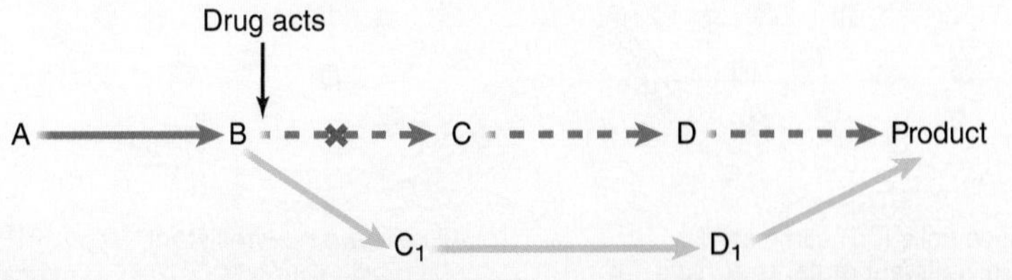

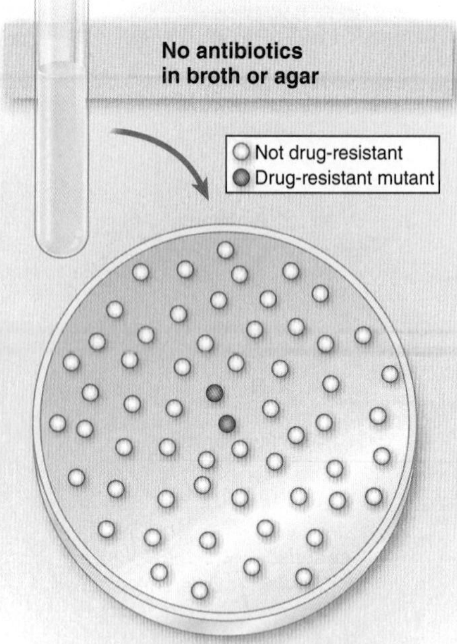

(a) Population of microbial cells

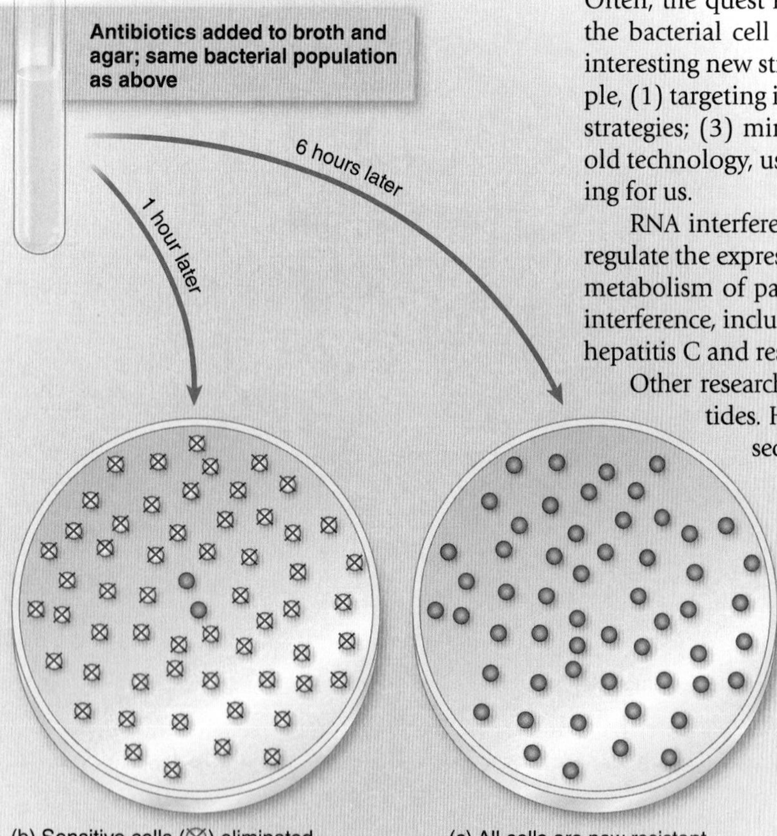

(b) Sensitive cells (⊠) eliminated by drug; resistant mutants survive

(c) All cells are now resistant

Figure 10.5 The events in natural selection for drug resistance. **(a)** Populations of microbes can harbor some members with a prior mutation that confers drug resistance. **(b)** Environmental pressure (here, the presence of the drug) selects for survival of these mutants. **(c)** They eventually become the dominant members of the population.

Natural Selection and Drug Resistance

So far, we have been considering drug resistance at the cellular and molecular levels, but its full impact is felt only if this resistance occurs throughout the cell population. Let us examine how this might happen and its long-term therapeutic consequences.

Any large population of microbes is likely to contain a few individual cells that are already drug resistant because of prior mutations or transfer of plasmids **(figure 10.5*a*)**. As long as the drug is not present in the habitat, the numbers of these resistant forms will remain low because they have no particular growth advantage (and often are disadvantaged relative to their nonmutated counterparts). However, if the population is subsequently exposed to this drug **(figure 10.5*b*)**, sensitive individuals are inhibited or destroyed, and resistant forms survive and proliferate. During subsequent population growth, offspring of these resistant microbes will inherit this drug resistance. In time, the replacement population will have a preponderance of the drug-resistant forms and can eventually become completely resistant **(figure 10.5*c*)**. In ecological terms, the environmental factor (in this case, the drug) has put selection pressure on the population, allowing the more "fit" microbe (the drug-resistant one) to survive, and the population has evolved to a condition of drug resistance.

New Approaches to Antimicrobial Therapy

Often, the quest for new antimicrobial strategies focuses on finding new targets in the bacterial cell and custom-designing drugs that aim for them. There are many interesting new strategies that have not yet resulted in a marketable drug—for example, (1) targeting iron-scavenging capabilities of bacteria; (2) using RNA interference strategies; (3) mimicking molecules called defense peptides; and (4) exploiting an old technology, using bacteriophages, the natural enemies of bacteria, to do the killing for us.

RNA interference, you recall from chapter 8, refers to small pieces of RNA that regulate the expression of genes. This is being exploited in attempts to shut down the metabolism of pathogenic microbes. There have been several human trials of RNA interference, including trials to evaluate the effectiveness of synthetic RNAs in treating hepatitis C and respiratory syncytial virus.

Other researchers are looking into proteins called host or bacterial defense peptides. Host defense peptides are peptides of 20 to 50 amino acids that are secreted as part of the mammalian innate immune system. They have names such as defensin, magainins, and protegrins. Some bacteria produce similar peptides. These are called bacteriocins and lantibiotics. Both host and bacterial defense peptides have multiple activities against bacteria—inserting in their membranes and also targeting other structures in the cells. For this reason, researchers believe they may be more effective than narrowly targeted drugs in current use, and will be much less likely to foster resistance.

Sometimes the low-tech solution can be the best one. Eastern European countries have gained a reputation for using mixtures of bacteriophages as medicines for bacterial infections. There is little argument about the effectiveness of these treatments, though they have never been approved for use in the West. One recent human trial used a mixture of bacteriophages specific for *Pseudomonas aeruginosa* to treat ear infections caused by the bacterium. These infections are found in the form of biofilms and have been extremely difficult to treat. The phage preparation called Biophage-PA successfully treated patients who had experienced long-term antibiotic-resistant infections. Other researchers are incorporating phages into wound dressings. One clear advantage to bacteriophage treatments is the extreme specificity of the phages—only one species of bacterium is affected, leaving the normal inhabitants of the body, and the body itself, alone.

There are new approaches being considered for antiviral treatment as well. Viruses mutate to become resistant to the drugs used to treat them even more quickly than do bacteria. As we learned earlier, current antivirals target parts of the virus that make it able to attach, multiply, or package itself. They are usually specific for one type of molecule, such as an enzyme. This makes it extremely likely that the molecule will incorporate a mutation quickly and then become resistant to the drug. The new investigative strategy is to exploit the one thing all viruses have in common: their complete dependence on the host cell. What if a drug targets a host protein, which would mutate much, much more slowly? For this strategy to work, a protein that was essential for viral reproduction, but not necessary to the host cell function, must be found. It turns out there are a lot of these. One promising host cell target is a protein called TSG101. It is a protein that the cell uses to transport materials internally, and that is hijacked by viruses to help them exit the cell. Crippling this protein has little effect on the human cell, and is devastating to the virus. The startling fact about this line of research is that it could yield a class of drugs that are active against viruses that have not even been discovered yet—as it is not dependent on particular attributes of a particular virus.

Ebola virus

Helping Nature Along

Other novel approaches to controlling infections include the use of **probiotics** and **prebiotics.** Probiotics are preparations of live microorganisms that are fed to animals and humans to improve the intestinal biota. This can serve to replace microbes lost during antimicrobial therapy or simply to augment the biota that is already there. This is a slightly more sophisticated application of methods that have long been used in an empiric fashion, for instance, by people who consume yogurt because of the beneficial microbes it contains. Recent years have seen a huge increase in the numbers of probiotic products sold in ordinary grocery stores **(figure 10.6).** Experts generally find these products safe, and in some cases they can be effective. Probiotics are thought to be useful for the management of food allergies; their role in the stimulation of mucosal immunity is also being investigated.

Prebiotics are nutrients that encourage the growth of beneficial microbes in the intestine. For instance, certain sugars such as fructans are thought to encourage the growth of *Bifidobacterium* in the large intestine and to discourage the growth of potential

Figure 10.6 **Examples of probiotic grocery items.**

NCLEX® PREP

2. Yogurt is an example of a ______, containing live microorganisms that can improve intestinal biota.

a. prebiotic
b. antibiotic
c. superbiotic
d. probiotic

Medical Moment

Herbal Remedies and Antibiotics

These days, many people are choosing to take their health into their own hands. This fact is illustrated by the explosive growth in the use of herbal supplements and remedies.

One problem with the use of herbal supplements and remedies is that people often take them together with medications prescribed by their physicians for other conditions without being aware of possible interactions. In addition, they fail to disclose the use of herbal supplements to their physicians. This practice can lead to unexpected and adverse reactions.

Antibiotics are one of the most frequently prescribed medications. An example of a reaction that can occur when herbal supplements are taken in conjunction with an antibiotic occurs with the use of St. John's wort, a popular supplement used to treat depression. St. John's wort can increase the speed at which medications are broken down by the liver, including some antibiotics and antifungal drugs (i.e., itraconazole), rendering these medications less effective. St. John's wort may also cause photosensitivity, as can some antibiotics, such as sulfamethoxazole and trimethoprim (Septra®). Patients and health care professionals need to be aware of the possible interactions between antibiotics and herbal supplements.

pathogens. You can be sure that you will hear more about prebiotics and probiotics as the concepts become increasingly well studied by scientists. Clearly, the use of these agents is a different type of antimicrobial strategy than we are used to, but it may have its place in a future in which traditional antibiotics are more problematic.

ASSESS YOUR PROGRESS

19. Discuss two possible ways that microbes acquire antimicrobial resistance.
20. List five cellular or structural mechanisms that microbes use to resist antimicrobials.
21. Discuss at least two novel antimicrobial strategies that are under investigation.

10.4 Interactions Between Drug and Host

Until now, this chapter has focused on the interaction between antimicrobials and the microorganisms they target. During an infection, the microbe is living in or on a host; therefore, the drug is administered to the host though its target is the microbe. Therefore, the effect of the drug on the host must always be considered.

Although selective antimicrobial toxicity is the ideal constantly being sought, chemotherapy by its very nature involves contact with foreign chemicals that can harm human tissues. In fact, estimates indicate that at least 5% of all persons taking an antimicrobial drug experience some type of serious adverse reaction to it. The major side effects of drugs fall into one of three categories: direct damage to tissues through toxicity, allergic reactions, and disruption in the balance of normal microbial biota. The damage incurred by antimicrobial drugs can be short term and reversible or permanent, and it ranges in severity from cosmetic to lethal.

Toxicity to Organs

Drugs can adversely affect the following organs: the liver (hepatotoxic), kidneys (nephrotoxic), gastrointestinal tract, cardiovascular system and blood-forming tissue (hemotoxic), nervous system (neurotoxic), respiratory tract, skin, bones, and teeth. The potential toxic effects of drugs on the body, along with the responsible drugs, are detailed in **table 10.10.**

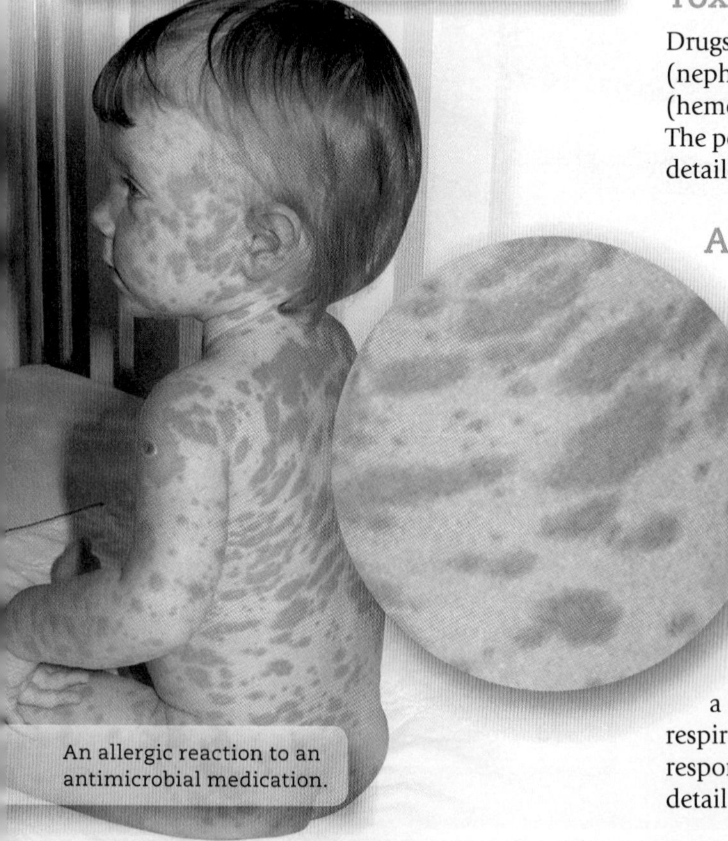

An allergic reaction to an antimicrobial medication.

Allergic Responses to Drugs

One of the most frequent drug reactions is heightened immunosensitivity, or **allergy.** This reaction occurs because the drug acts as an antigen (a foreign material capable of stimulating the immune system) and stimulates an allergic response. This response can be provoked by the intact drug molecule or by substances that develop from the body's metabolic alteration of the drug. In the case of penicillin, for instance, it is not the penicillin molecule itself that causes the allergic response but a product, *benzylpenicilloyl*. Allergic reactions have been reported for every major type of antimicrobial drug, but the penicillins account for the greatest number of antimicrobial allergies, followed by the sulfonamides.

People who are allergic to a drug become sensitized to it during the first contact, usually without symptoms. Once the immune system is sensitized, a second exposure to the drug can lead to a reaction such as a skin rash (hives), respiratory inflammation, and, rarely, anaphylaxis, an acute, overwhelming allergic response that develops rapidly and can be fatal. (This topic is discussed in greater detail in chapter 14.)

Table 10.10 Major Adverse Toxic Reactions to Common Drug Groups

Antimicrobial Drug	Primary Damage or Abnormality Produced
Antibacterials	
Penicillin G	Skin
Carbenicillin	Abnormal bleeding
Ampicillin	Diarrhea and enterocolitis
Cephalosporins	Inhibition of platelet function
	Decreased circulation of white blood cells; nephritis
Tetracyclines	Diarrhea and enterocolitis
	Discoloration of tooth enamel
	Reactions to sunlight (photosensitivity)
Chloramphenicol	Injury to red and white blood cell precursors
Aminoglycosides (streptomycin, gentamicin, amikacin)	Diarrhea and enterocolitis
	Malabsorption
	Loss of hearing, dizziness, kidney damage
Isoniazid	Hepatitis (liver inflammation)
	Seizures
	Dermatitis
Sulfonamides	Formation of crystals in kidney; blockage of urine flow
	Hemolysis
	Reduction in number of red blood cells
Polymyxin	Kidney damage
	Weakened muscular responses
Quinolones (ciprofloxacin, norfloxacin)	Headache, dizziness, tremors, GI distress
Rifampin	Damage to hepatic cells
	Dermatitis
Antifungals	
Amphotericin B	Disruption of kidney function
Flucytosine	Decreased number of white blood cells
Antiprotozoan Drugs	
Metronidazole	Nausea, vomiting
Chloroquine	Vomiting
	Headache
	Itching
Antihelminthics	
Niclosamide	Nausea, abdominal pain
Pyrantel	Intestinal irritation
	Headache, dizziness
Antivirals	
Acyclovir	Seizures, confusion
	Rash
Amantadine	Nervousness, light-headedness
	Nausea
AZT	Immunosuppression, anemia

NCLEX® PREP

3. Drugs that adversely affect the liver are said to be ______. Examples of drugs that may damage the liver are drugs that are used to treat tuberculosis: ______ and ______.
   - a. neurotoxic; acyclovir; ciprofloxacin
   - b. cardiotoxic; chloroquine; sulfamethoxazole
   - c. hepatotoxic; rifampin; isoniazid
   - d. nephrotoxic; amphotericin B; cephalexin

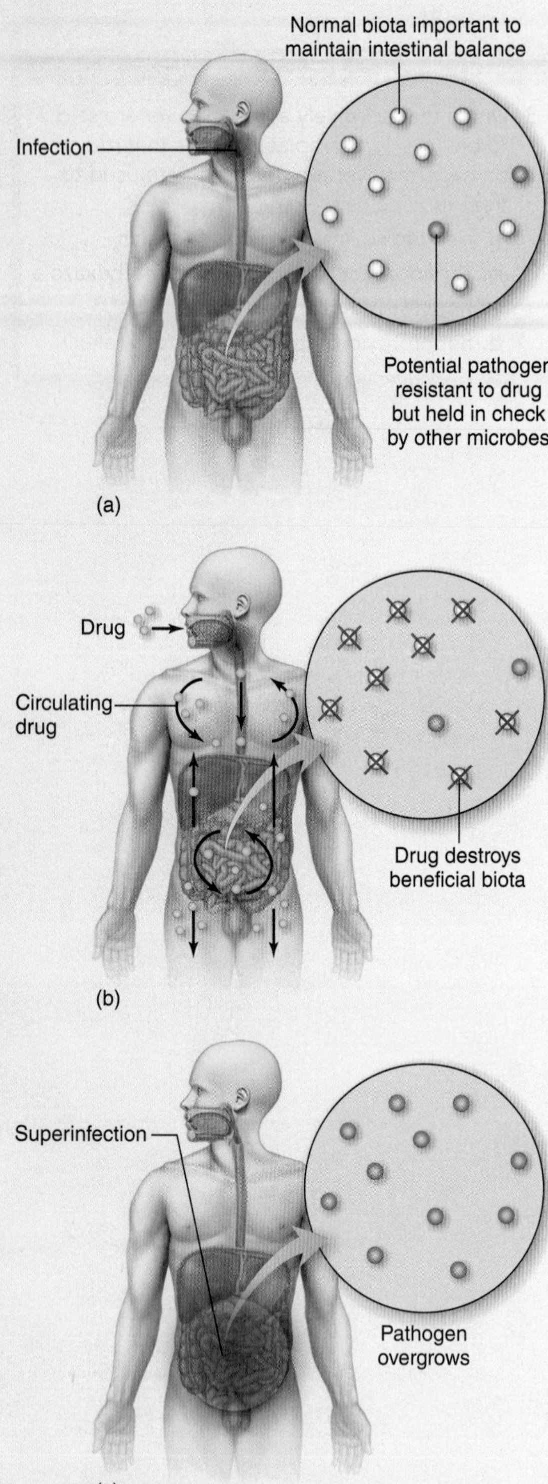

Figure 10.7 The role of antimicrobials in disrupting microbial biota and causing superinfections. **(a)** A primary infection in the throat is treated with an oral antibiotic. **(b)** The drug is carried to the intestine and is absorbed into the circulation. **(c)** The primary infection is cured, but drug-resistant pathogens have survived and create an intestinal superinfection.

Suppression and Alteration of the Microbiota by Antimicrobials

Most normal, healthy body surfaces, such as the skin, large intestine, outer openings of the urogenital tract, and oral cavity, provide numerous habitats for a virtual "garden" of microorganisms. These normal colonists, or residents, called the **biota,** or microbiota, consist mostly of harmless or beneficial bacteria, but a small number can potentially be pathogens. Although we defer a more detailed discussion of this topic to chapter 11 and later chapters, here we focus on the general effects of drugs on this population.

If a broad-spectrum antimicrobial is introduced into a host to treat infection, it will destroy microbes regardless of their roles as normal biota, affecting not only the targeted infectious agent but also many others in sites far removed from the original infection **(figure 10.7)**. When this therapy destroys beneficial resident species, other microbes that were once in small numbers begin to overgrow and cause disease. This complication is called a **superinfection.**

Some common examples demonstrate how a disturbance in microbial biota leads to replacement biota and superinfection. A broad-spectrum cephalosporin used to treat a urinary tract infection by *Escherichia coli* will cure the infection, but it will also destroy the lactobacilli in the vagina that normally maintain a protective acidic environment there. The drug has no effect, however, on *Candida albicans,* a yeast that also resides in normal vaginas. Released from the inhibitory environment provided by lactobacilli, the yeasts proliferate and cause symptoms. *Candida* can cause similar superinfections of the oropharynx (thrush) and the large intestine.

Oral therapy with tetracyclines, clindamycin, and broad-spectrum penicillins and cephalosporins is associated with a serious and potentially fatal condition known as *antibiotic-associated colitis* (pseudomembranous colitis). This condition is due to the overgrowth in the bowel of *Clostridium difficile,* an endospore-forming bacterium that is resistant to the antibiotic. It invades the intestinal lining and releases toxins that induce diarrhea, fever, and abdominal pain. (You'll learn more about infectious diseases of the gastrointestinal tract, including *C. difficile,* in chapter 20.)

An Antimicrobial Drug Dilemma

We began this chapter with a view of the exciting strides made in chemotherapy during the past few years, but we must end it on a note of qualification and caution. There is now a worldwide problem in the management of antimicrobial drugs. The remarkable progress in treating many infectious diseases has spawned a view of antimicrobials as a "cure-all" for infections as diverse as the common cold and acne. And, although it is true that few things are as dramatic as curing an infectious disease with the correct antimicrobial drug, in many instances, drugs have no effect or can be harmful. For example, roughly 200 million prescriptions for antimicrobials are written in the United States every year. A recent study disclosed that 75% of antimicrobial prescriptions are for pharyngeal, sinus, lung, and upper respiratory infections. A fairly high percentage of these are viral in origin and will have little or no benefit from antibacterial drugs.

In the past, many physicians tended to use a "shotgun" antimicrobial therapy for minor infections, which involves administering a broad-spectrum drug instead of a more specific narrow-spectrum one. This practice led to superinfections and other adverse reactions. Importantly, it also caused the development of resistance in "bystander" microbes (normal biota) that were exposed to the drug as well. This helped to spread antibiotic resistance to pathogens. With growing awareness of the problems of antibiotic resistance, this practice is much less frequent.

Tons of excess antimicrobial drugs produced in this country are exported to other countries, where controls are not as strict. Nearly 200 different antibiotics are sold over the counter in Latin America and Asian countries. It is common for people in these countries to self-medicate without understanding the correct medical indication. Drugs used in this way are largely ineffectual but, worse yet, they are known to be responsible for emergence of drug-resistant bacteria that subsequently cause epidemics.

In the final analysis, every allied health professional should be critically aware not only of the admirable and utilitarian nature of antimicrobials, but also of their limitations.

ASSESS YOUR PROGRESS

22. Distinguish between drug toxicity and allergic reactions to drugs.
23. Explain what a superinfection is and how it occurs.

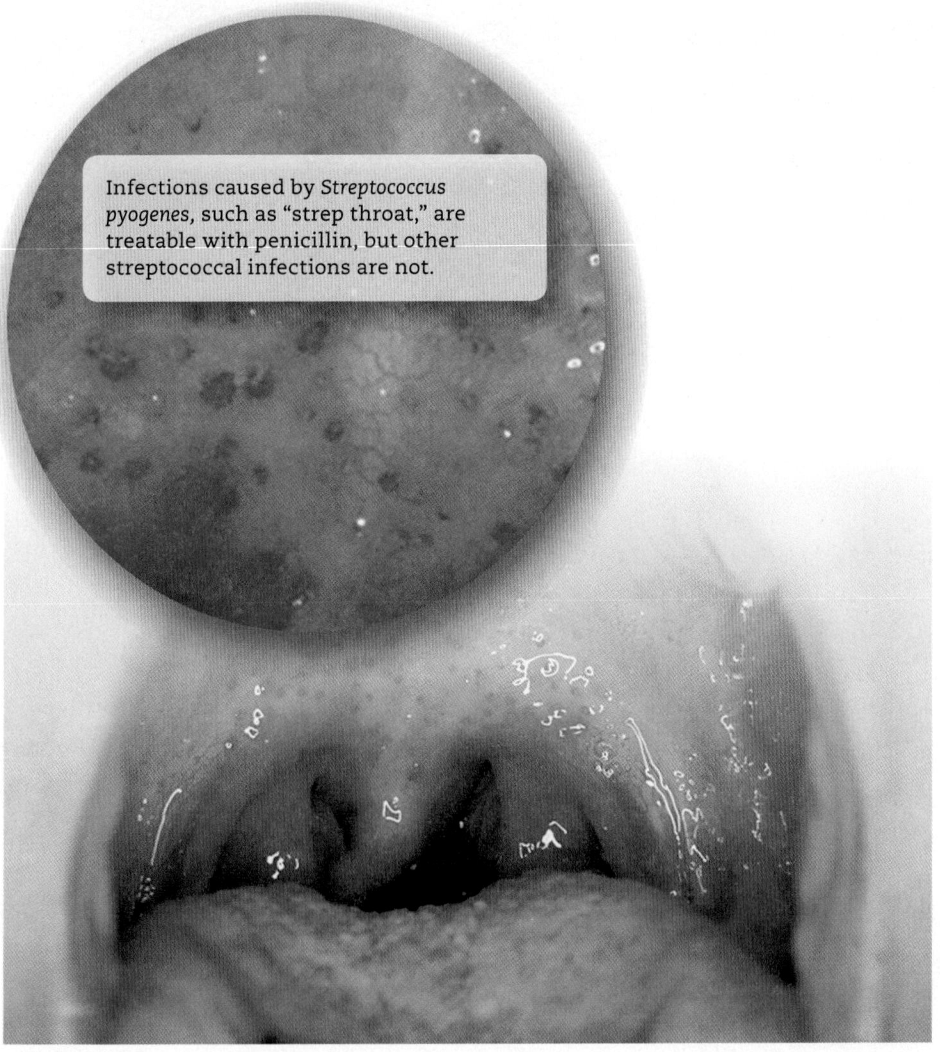

Infections caused by *Streptococcus pyogenes*, such as "strep throat," are treatable with penicillin, but other streptococcal infections are not.

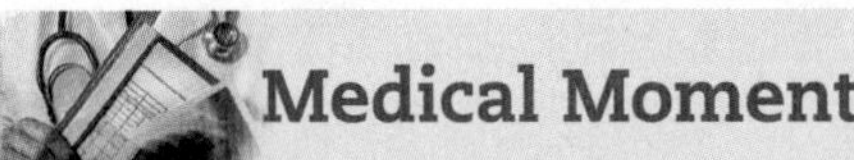

Medical Moment

Asking About Antibiotic Allergies

It is estimated that 1 person in 10 is allergic to penicillin. Approximately 300 deaths per year in the United States can be attributed to penicillin allergy. This illustrates the importance of knowing a patient's allergy status. When a patient has a medication allergy, they will have a brightly colored wristband applied upon admission to the hospital. It lists any allergies the patient has. This allows anyone caring for the patient to be able to identify quickly and easily what the patient is allergic to. Before electronic medical records came into being, allergy bracelets were one of the most important defenses against medication errors.

The computer age has added another layer of safety in medication administration. A patient's allergies can now be recorded electronically, alerting physicians and pharmacists if a medication is inadvertently prescribed to which a patient is allergic. However, health care personnel cannot become too complacent and depend solely upon computers to do their job—a medication should never be administered to a patient without health care staff first asking about allergies.

NCLEX® PREP

4. Mary has a urinary tract infection and is prescribed cephalexin for 10 days. Toward the end of her course of treatment, Mary develops a vaginal yeast infection. The yeast infection is an example of a/an
   a. superinfection.
   b. expected complication.
   c. allergic reaction.
   d. toxic reaction.

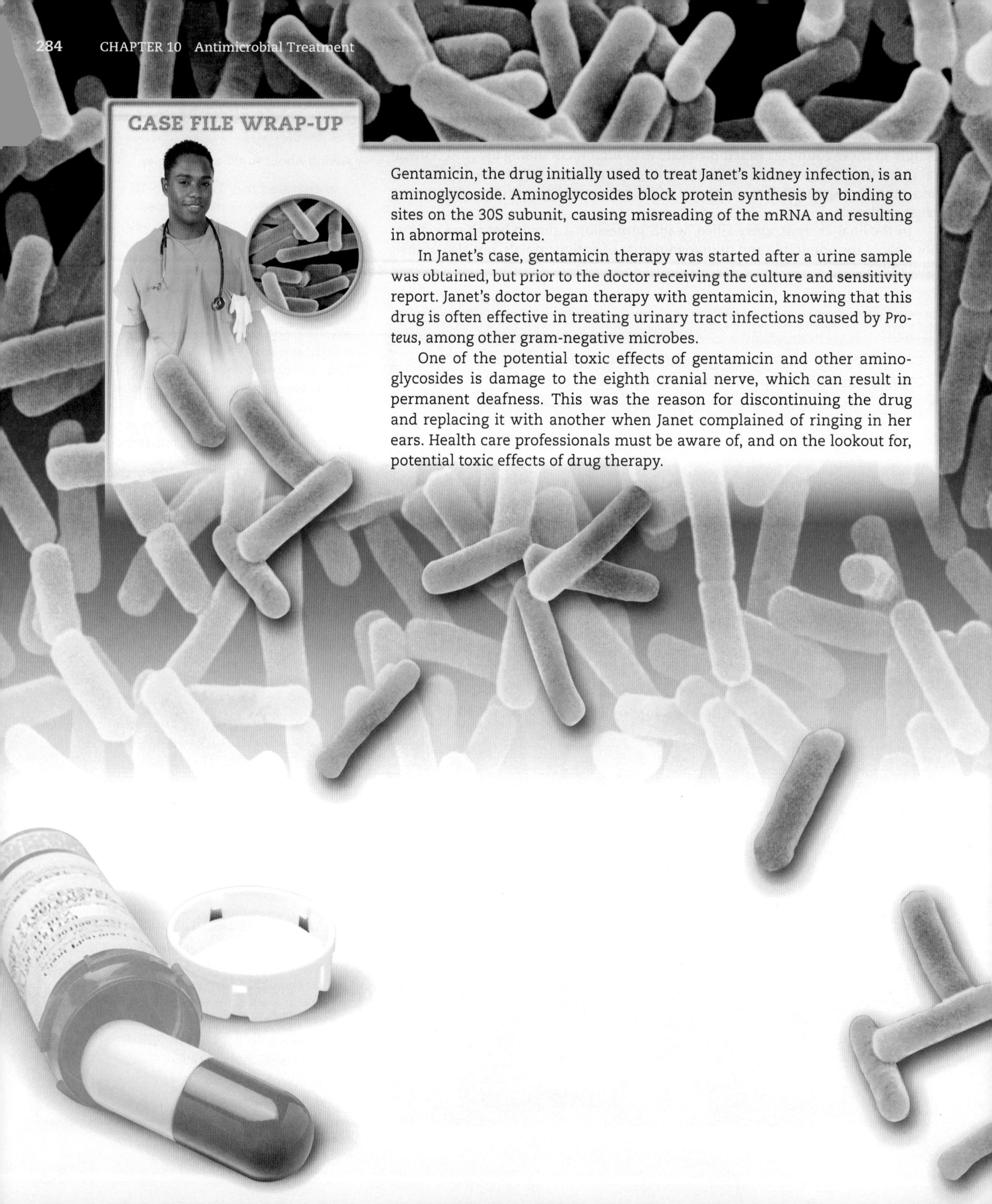

CASE FILE WRAP-UP

Gentamicin, the drug initially used to treat Janet's kidney infection, is an aminoglycoside. Aminoglycosides block protein synthesis by binding to sites on the 30S subunit, causing misreading of the mRNA and resulting in abnormal proteins.

In Janet's case, gentamicin therapy was started after a urine sample was obtained, but prior to the doctor receiving the culture and sensitivity report. Janet's doctor began therapy with gentamicin, knowing that this drug is often effective in treating urinary tract infections caused by *Proteus*, among other gram-negative microbes.

One of the potential toxic effects of gentamicin and other aminoglycosides is damage to the eighth cranial nerve, which can result in permanent deafness. This was the reason for discontinuing the drug and replacing it with another when Janet complained of ringing in her ears. Health care professionals must be aware of, and on the lookout for, potential toxic effects of drug therapy.

Demanding Antibiotics: The Consumer's Role in Drug Resistance

Inside the Clinic

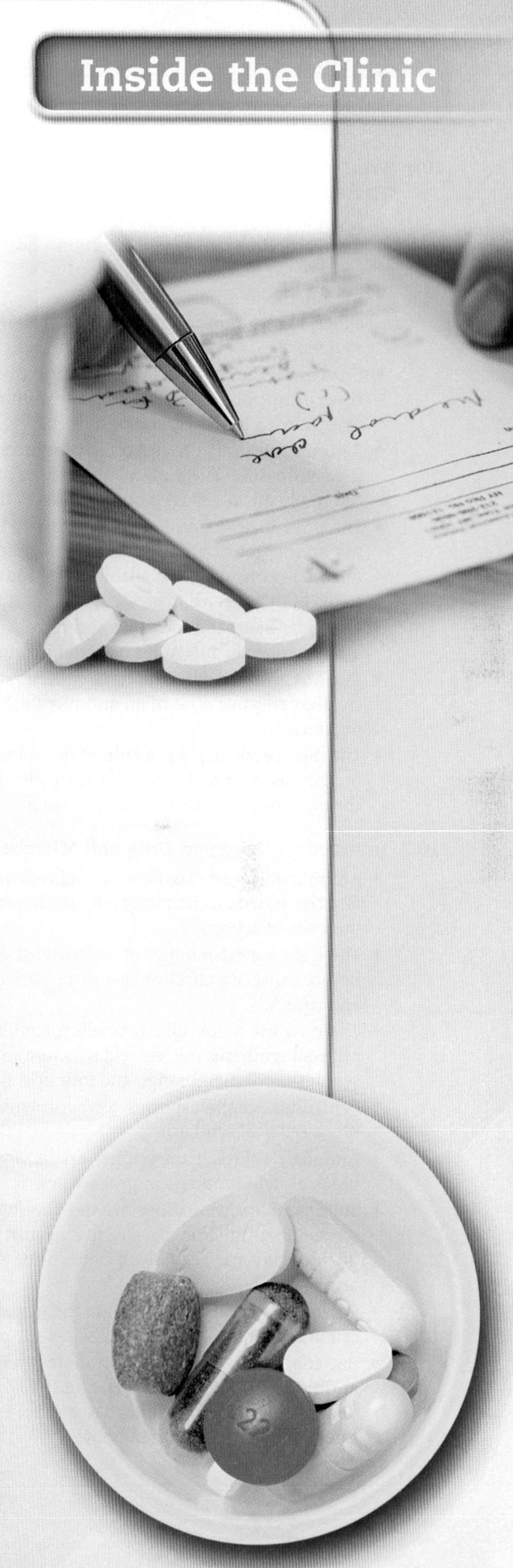

There have been many reasons cited for the rise of antibiotic resistance, including the use of antibiotics in livestock to improve health and size of livestock, the indiscriminate use of antibiotics in developing countries (particularly the sale of antibiotics without a prescription), and inappropriate prescribing of antibiotics by physicians (e.g., antibiotics prescribed to treat viral infections).

Most physicians have become more aware that prescribing practices for antibiotics must be tightened. However, many of their patients have yet to learn this important lesson. Many people continue to visit their physician with a viral Infection, such as the common cold, and demand a prescription for an antibiotic. Society has become accustomed to being provided with an antibiotic prescription for whatever ails them, and health care consumers often demand antibiotics even when their condition does not warrant one. Putting pressure on their physicians sometimes yields the coveted prescription, a dangerous practice for the individual patient and society as a whole.

Health care education is the responsibility not only of physicians, but also of nurses, pharmacists, and other professionals who deal directly with patients. Patients demanding antibiotics for viral infections often require an explanation as to why antibiotics are not appropriate for use against viruses. They also require an explanation as to why using antibiotics in such a manner is actually irresponsible practice. Hearing this information from trusted health care professionals may have a bigger impact on the public than hearing the same information via government education ads.

The following are some suggestions on instructions that can be given to patients to decrease the spread of antibiotic-resistant organisms:

- Finish all antibiotics as prescribed—do not stop taking antibiotics partway through their course, even if you feel better. Antibiotics should be stopped only if your doctor instructs you to quit taking them (i.e., in the event of an allergic reaction).
- Don't ask your physician to prescribe antibiotics for viral infections. Your doctor will know whether you require an antibiotic, and it can be dangerous to take antibiotics when they are not necessary. Antibiotics are not effective against viruses.
- Never share antibiotics with others.
- Do not flush unused antibiotics down the toilet or dispose of them in your garbage disposal system. Do not throw out unused antibiotics in the garbage. Antibiotics can end up in the water supply, increasing the problem of antibiotic resistance. Instead, take them to your pharmacy and ask them to dispose of the medication for you.
- If you are a parent, ensure that your children are given or take antibiotics as prescribed by a physician, and be sure they finish the entire course.
- Avoid illness in the first place—be sure you are fully immunized against preventable diseases. Wash your hands frequently to prevent the spread of disease. Hand washing is the most effective means of preventing illness from occurring.

Chapter Summary

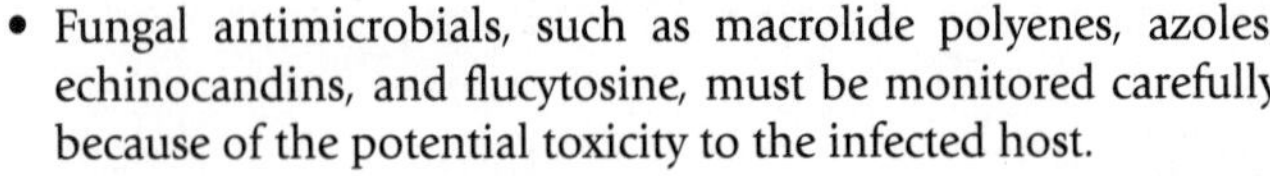

10.1 Principles of Antimicrobial Therapy

- Antimicrobial chemotherapy involves the use of drugs to control infection on or in the body.
- Antimicrobial drugs are produced either synthetically or from natural sources.
- Broad-spectrum antimicrobials are effective against many types of microbes. Narrow-spectrum antimicrobials are effective against a limited group of microbes.
- Bacteria and fungi are the primary sources of most currently used antibiotics. The molecular structures of these compounds can be chemically altered or mimicked in the laboratory.
- The three major considerations necessary to choose an effective antimicrobial are the nature of the infecting microbe, the microbe's sensitivity to available drugs, and the overall medical status of the infected host.
- The Kirby-Bauer test identifies antimicrobials that are effective against a specific infectious bacterial isolate.
- The MIC (minimum inhibitory concentration) identifies the smallest effective dose of an antimicrobial toxic to the infecting microbe.
- The therapeutic index is a ratio of the amount of drug toxic to the infected host and the MIC. The smaller the ratio, the greater the potential for toxic host-drug reactions.

10.2 Interactions Between Drug and Microbe

- Antimicrobials are classified into approximately 20 major drug families, based on chemical composition, source or origin, and their site of action.
- There are a great number of antibacterial drugs, but a limited number that are effective against protozoa, helminths, fungi, and viruses.
- There are five main cellular targets for antibiotics in microbes: cell wall synthesis, nucleic acid structure and function, protein synthesis, cell membranes, and folic acid synthesis.
- Penicillins, cephalosporins, carbapenems, and vancomycin block cell wall synthesis.
- Aminoglycosides, tetracyclines, erythromycin, and ketolides block protein synthesis in prokaryotes.
- Sulfonamides, trimethoprim, and the fluoroquinolones are synthetic antimicrobials effective against a broad range of microorganisms. They block steps in the synthesis of nucleic acids.
- Polymyxins and daptomycin are the major drugs that disrupt cell membranes.
- Bacteria in biofilms respond differently to antibiotics than when they are free-floating. It is therefore difficult to eradicate biofilms in the human body.
- Fungal antimicrobials, such as macrolide polyenes, azoles, echinocandins, and flucytosine, must be monitored carefully because of the potential toxicity to the infected host.
- There are fewer antiprotozoal drugs than antibacterial drugs because protozoa are eukaryotes like their human hosts, and they have several life stages, some of which can be resistant to the drug.
- Antihelminthic drugs immobilize or disintegrate infesting helminths or inhibit their metabolism in some manner.
- Antiviral drugs interfere with viral replication by blocking viral entry into cells, blocking the replication process, or preventing the assembly of viral subunits into complete virions.
- Many antiviral agents are analogs of nucleotides. They inactivate the replication process when incorporated into viral nucleic acids. HIV antivirals interfere with reverse transcriptase or proteases to prevent the maturation of viral particles.

10.3 Antimicrobial Resistance

- Microorganisms are termed drug resistant when they are no longer inhibited by an antimicrobial to which they were previously sensitive.
- Microbes acquire genes that code for methods of inactivating or escaping the antimicrobial, or acquire mutations that affect the drug's impact.
- Mechanisms of microbial drug resistance include drug inactivation, decreased drug uptake, decreased drug receptor sites, and modification of metabolic pathways formerly attacked by the drug.
- Widespread indiscriminate use of antimicrobials has resulted in an explosion of microorganisms resistant to all common drugs.

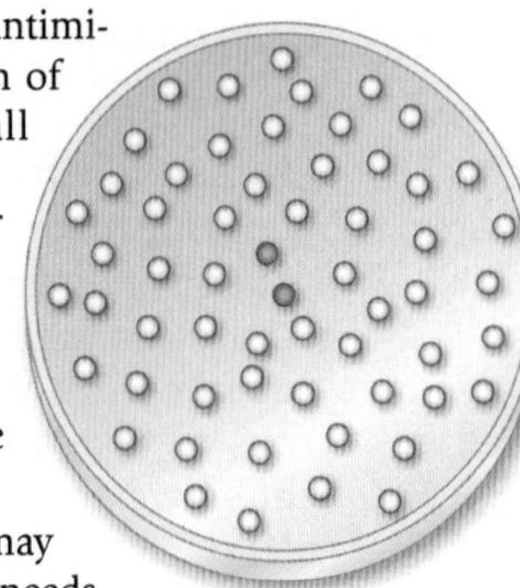

- Research strategies for new types of antibiotics include targeting iron-scavenging pathways of microbes, the use of RNA interference, mimicking natural defense peptides, and the use of bacteriophages.
- New targets for antiviral therapy may focus on host factors that the virus needs for its reproduction.
- Probiotics and prebiotics are methods of crowding out pathogenic bacteria and providing a favorable environment for the growth of beneficial bacteria.

10.4 Interactions Between Drug and Host

- The three major side effects of antimicrobials are toxicity to organs, allergic reactions, and problems resulting from alteration of normal biota.
- Antimicrobials that destroy most but not all normal biota can allow the unaffected normal biota to overgrow, causing a superinfection.

Multiple-Choice Questions Knowledge and Comprehension

Select the correct answer from the answers provided.

1. A compound synthesized by bacteria or fungi that destroys or inhibits the growth of other microbes is a/an
   a. synthetic drug.
   b. antibiotic.
   c. antimicrobial drug.
   d. competitive inhibitor.
2. Which statement is *not* an aim in the use of drugs in antimicrobial chemotherapy? The drug should
   a. have selective toxicity.
   b. be active even in high dilutions.
   c. be broken down and excreted rapidly.
   d. be microbicidal.
3. Drugs that prevent the formation of the bacterial cell wall are
   a. quinolones.
   b. beta-lactams.
   c. tetracyclines.
   d. aminoglycosides.
4. Microbial resistance to drugs is acquired through
   a. conjugation.
   b. transformation.
   c. transduction.
   d. all of these.
5. Phage therapy is a technique that uses
   a. chemicals to destroy phages infecting human cells.
   b. chemicals to foster the growth of beneficial phages in the body.
   c. phages to foster the growth of normal biota.
   d. phages to target pathogenic bacteria in the body.
6. Most antihelminthic drugs function by
   a. weakening the worms so they can be flushed out by the intestine.
   b. inhibiting worm metabolism.
   c. blocking the absorption of nutrients.
   d. inhibiting egg production.
7. The MIC is the ________ of a drug that is required to inhibit growth of a microbe.
   a. largest concentration
   b. standard dose
   c. smallest concentration
   d. lowest dilution
8. An antimicrobial drug with a ________ therapeutic index is a better choice than one with a ________ therapeutic index.
   a. low; high
   b. high; low

Critical Thinking Application and Analysis

Critical thinking **is the ability to reason and solve problems using facts and concepts. These questions can be approached from a number of angles and, in most cases, they do not have a single correct answer.**

1. Can you think of a situation in which it would be better for a drug to be microbistatic rather than microbicidal? Discuss thoroughly.
2. Why does the penicillin group of drugs have milder toxicity than other antibiotics?
3. Explain the phenomenon of drug resistance from the standpoint of microbial genetics (include a description of R factors).
4. You have been directed to take a sample from a growth-free portion of the zone of inhibition in the Kirby-Bauer test and inoculate it onto a plate of nonselective medium.
   a. What does it mean if growth occurs on the new plate?
   b. What if there is no growth?
5. a. Explain the basis for combined therapy.
   b. Give reasons why it could be helpful to use combined therapy in treating HIV infection.

Visual Connections Synthesis

This question connects previous images to a new concept.

1. **From chapter 8, table 8.5.** Place Xs over this figure in places where bacterial protein synthesis might be inhibited by drugs.

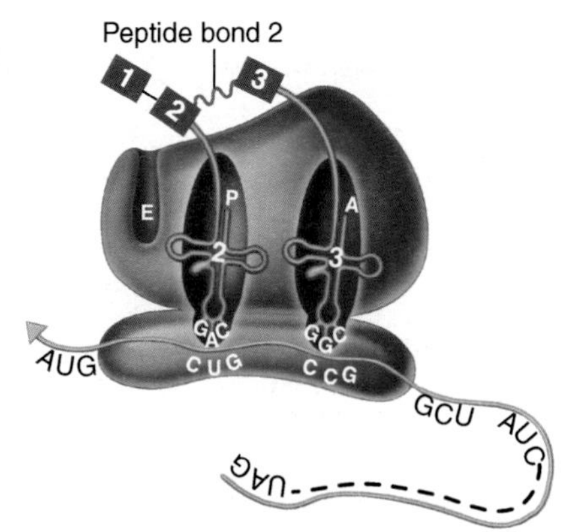

A Rash of Symptoms

During my pediatric rotation, I met Robby, a 7-year-old boy brought to the emergency room by his very worried mother. Immediately I noticed a rash on Robby's cheeks, which were also bright red. Robby's mother lifted his shirt, and I noticed a blotchy, lacey-appearing rash over most of his chest and abdomen. The rash was also evident on Robby's arms and legs.

I learned in school to always ask about associated symptoms and signs when confronted with a rash of unknown etiology, so I asked Robby's mother about other symptoms he was experiencing. Robby's mother stated that Robby had also had a slight fever (up to 38.3°C [101°F]). He had eaten very little in the past 2 days and had also complained of a headache. He was sleeping more than usual. Robby's mother did notice that the rash worsened when Robby's temperature was higher and following his bath.

Robby's mother was concerned about whether the rash was contagious—and, if so, whether the rest of the family was at risk.

- What disease was Robby likely experiencing?
- What is the treatment? What complications could occur, if any?

Case File Wrap-Up appears on page 454.

CHAPTER 16

Infectious Diseases Affecting the Skin and Eyes

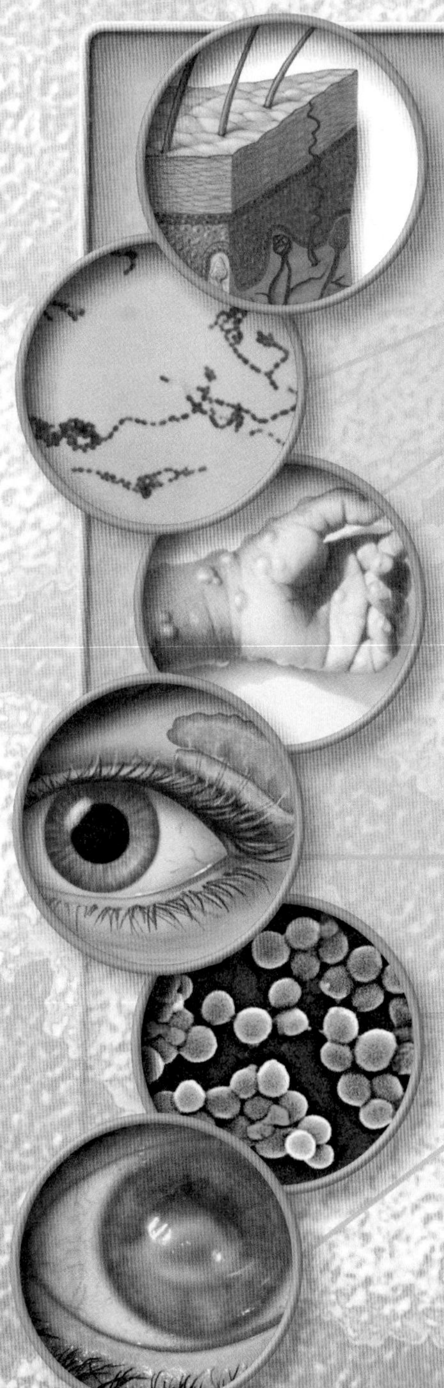

IN THIS CHAPTER...

16.1 The Skin and Its Defenses

1. Describe the important anatomical features of the skin.
2. List the natural defenses present in the skin.

16.2 Normal Biota of the Skin

3. List the types of normal biota presently known to occupy the skin.

16.3 Skin Diseases Caused by Microorganisms

4. List the possible causative agents, modes of transmission, virulence factors, diagnostic techniques, and prevention/treatment for the highlighted condition, maculopapular rash diseases.
5. Discuss important features of the other infectious skin diseases. These are impetigo, cellulitis, staphylococcal scalded skin syndrome, vesicular/pustular rash diseases, wartlike eruptions, large pustular skin lesions, and cutaneous mycoses.
6. Provide an update of the status of MRSA infections in the United States.
7. Discuss the relative dangers of rubella and rubeola viruses in different populations.

16.4 The Surface of the Eye and Its Defenses

8. Describe the important anatomical features of the eye.
9. List the natural defenses present in the eye.

16.5 Normal Biota of the Eye

10. List the types of normal biota presently known to occupy the eye.

16.6 Eye Diseases Caused by Microorganisms

11. List the possible causative agents, modes of transmission, virulence factors, diagnostic techniques, and prevention/treatment for the highlighted condition, conjunctivitis.
12. Discuss important features of keratitis caused by either HSV or by *Acanthamoeba*.

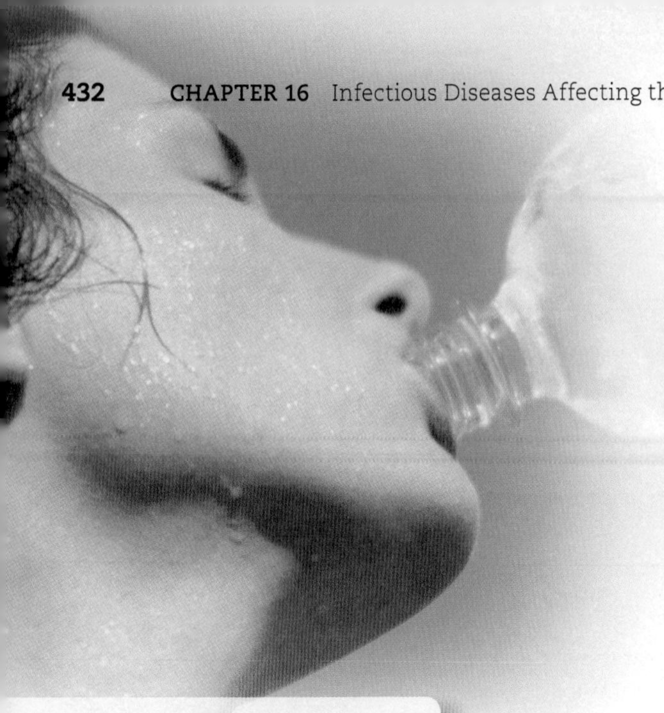

Sweat is cooling and it has several antimicrobial properties.

16.1 The Skin and Its Defenses

The organs under consideration in this chapter—the skin and eyes—form the boundary between the human and the environment. The skin, together with the hair, nails, and sweat and oil glands, forms the **integument.** The skin has a total surface area of 1.5 to 2 square meters. Its thickness varies from 1.5 millimeters at places such as the eyelids to 4 millimeters on the soles of the feet. Several distinct layers can be found in this thickness, and we summarize them here. Follow **figure 16.1** as you read.

The outermost portion of the skin is the epidermis, which is further subdivided into four or five distinct layers. On top is a thick layer of epithelial cells called the stratum corneum, about 25 cells thick. The cells in this layer are dead and have migrated from the deeper layers during the normal course of cell division. They are packed with a protein called **keratin**, which the cells produce in very large quantities. Cells emerge from the deepest levels of the epidermis. Because this process is continuous, the entire epidermis is replaced every 25 to 45 days. Keratin gives the cells their ability to withstand damage, abrasion, and water penetration; the surface of the skin is termed keratinized for this reason. Below the stratum corneum are three or four more layers of epithelial cells. The lowest layer, the stratum basale, or basal layer, is attached to the underlying dermis and is the source for all of the cells that make up the epidermis.

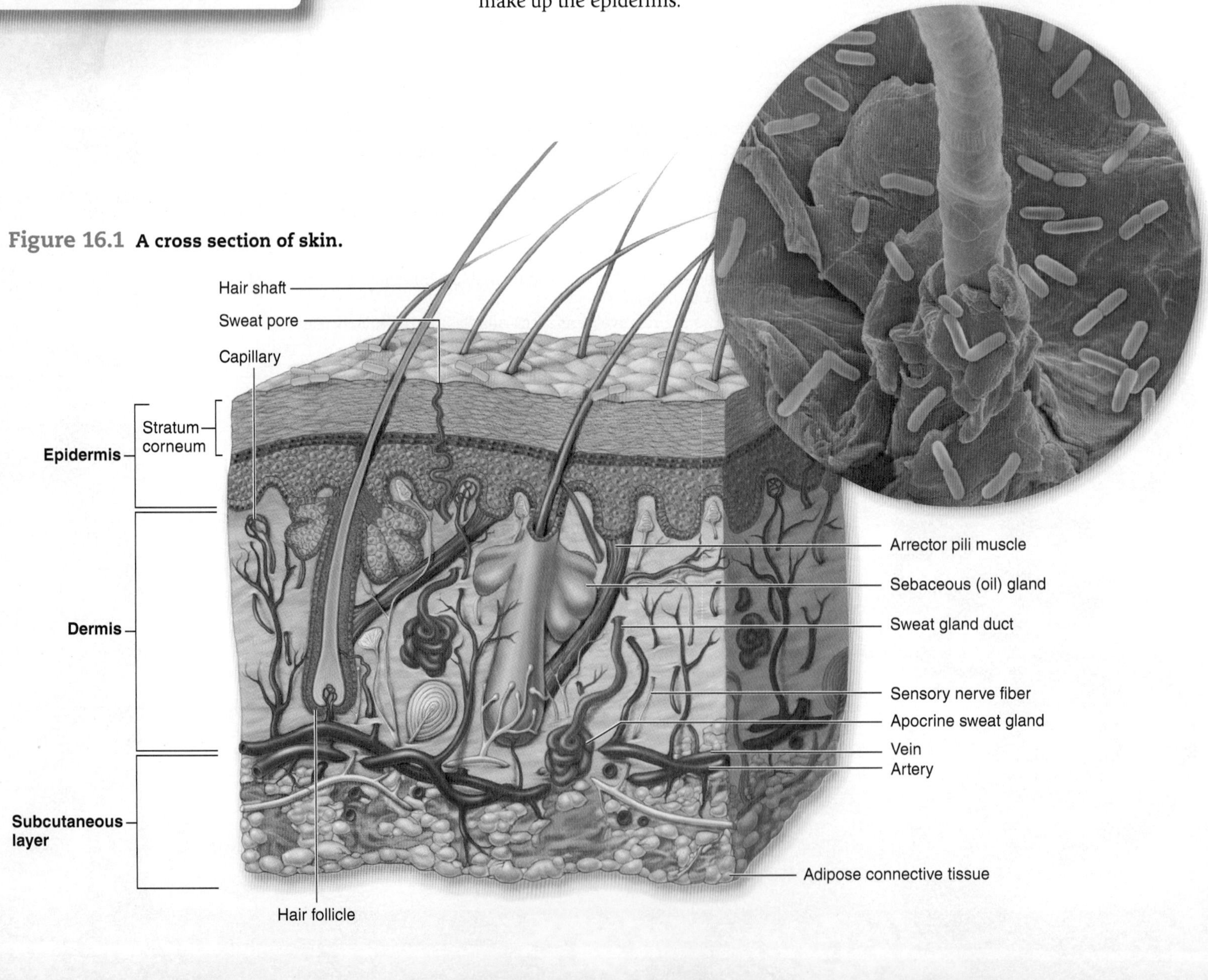

Figure 16.1 A cross section of skin.

The dermis, underneath the epidermis, is composed of connective tissue instead of epithelium. This means that it is a rich matrix of fibroblast cells and fibers such as collagen, and it contains macrophages and mast cells. The dermis also harbors a dense network of nerves, blood vessels, and lymphatic vessels. Damage to the epidermis generally does not result in bleeding, whereas damage deep enough to penetrate the dermis results in broken blood vessels. Blister formation, the result of friction trauma or burns, causes a separation between the dermis and epidermis.

The "roots" of hairs, called follicles, are in the dermis. **Sebaceous** (oil) **glands** and scent glands are associated with the hair follicle. Separate sweat glands are also found in this tissue. All of these glands have openings on the surface of the skin, so they pass through the epidermis as well.

Millions of cells from the stratum corneum slough off every day, and attached microorganisms slough off with them. The skin is also brimming with antimicrobial substances. Perhaps the most effective skin defense against infection is the one most recently discovered. In the past 20 years, small molecules called **antimicrobial peptides** have been identified in epithelial cells. These are positively charged chemicals that act by disrupting (negatively charged) membranes of bacteria. There are many different types of these peptides, and they seem to be chiefly responsible for keeping the microbial count on skin relatively low.

The sebaceous glands' secretion, called **sebum,** has a low pH, which makes the skin inhospitable to most microorganisms. Sebum is oily due to its high concentration of lipids. The lipids can serve as nutrients for normal microbiota, but breakdown of the fatty acids contained in lipids leads to toxic by-products that inhibit the growth of microorganisms not adapted to the skin environment. This mechanism helps control the growth of potentially pathogenic bacteria. Sweat is also inhibitory to microorganisms, because of both its low pH and its high salt concentration. **Lysozyme** is an enzyme found in sweat (and tears and saliva) that specifically breaks down peptidoglycan, which you learned in chapter 3 is a unique component of bacterial cell walls.

NCLEX® PREP

1. Skin is thickest on the __________ and thinnest on the ________.
   a. chest; cheeks
   b. buttocks; nose
   c. soles; eyelids
   d. abdomen; dorsum of the hands

ASSESS YOUR PROGRESS

1. Describe the important anatomical features of the skin.
2. List the natural defenses present in the skin.

16.2 Normal Biota of the Skin

Microbes that do live on the skin surface as normal biota must be capable of living in the dry, salty conditions they find there. Microbes are rather sparsely distributed over dry, flat areas of the body, such as on the back, but they can grow into dense populations in moist areas and skin folds, such as the underarm and groin areas. The normal microbiota also live in the protected environment of the hair follicles and glandular ducts.

As discussed in chapter 11, we don't know how many species call the skin "home" because the majority of them are probably not cultivable. Early data have begun to emerge from the Human Microbiome Project (HMP). Predominant bacterial genera are *Streptococcus, Staphylococcus, Propionibacterium,* and *Corynebacterium.* The fungus *Malassezia* is also present in high numbers. It came as a surprise that two dominant genera on human skin are *Pseudomonas* and *Janthinobacterium,* both gram-negative rods. Neither was thought to be numerous on skin before the genomic methodology was applied. Another important finding from the HMP is that there is a rich diversity of microbes—many of them well known to be pathogenic—living under the skin. Their role in dermatologic diseases of all kinds is now being investigated. The bottom line: The skin microbiota is more dynamic and more diverse than we ever imagined.

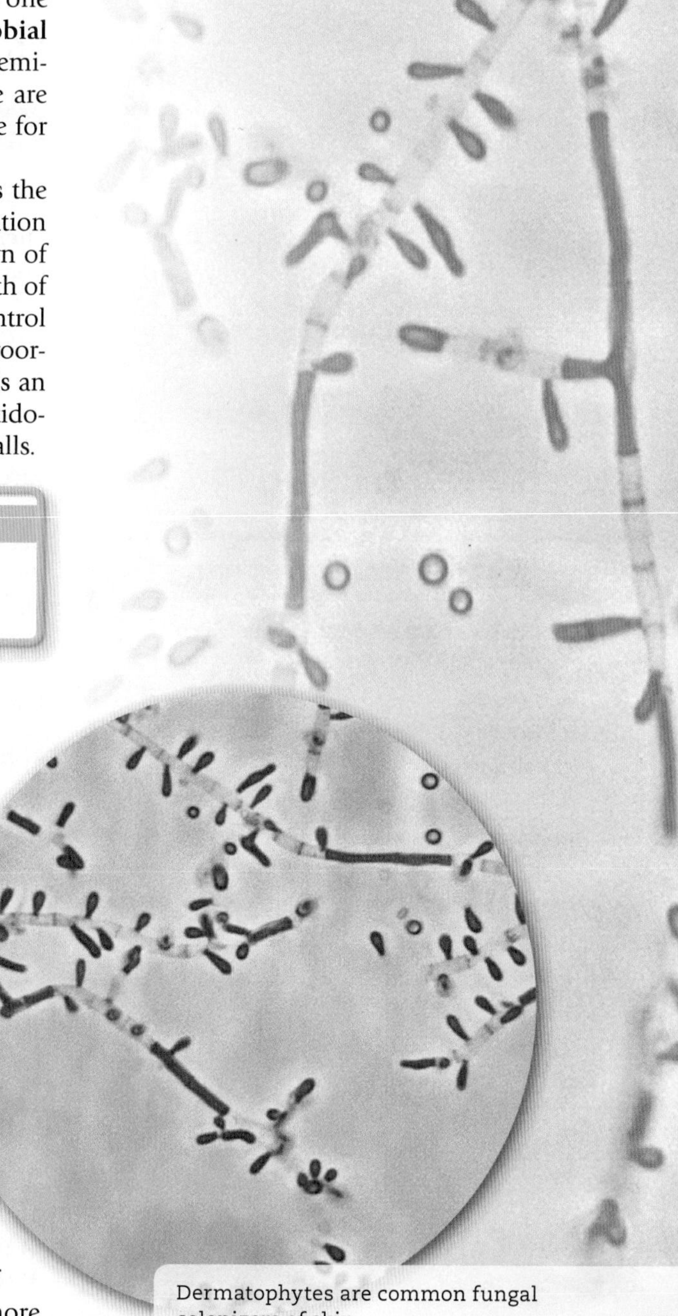

Dermatophytes are common fungal colonizers of skin.

Defenses and Normal Biota of the Skin

	Defenses	Normal Biota
Skin	Keratinized surface, sloughing, low pH, high salt, lysozyme	*Streptococcus, Staphylococcus, Corynebacterium, Propionibacterium, Pseudomonas, Janthinobacterium*

ASSESS YOUR PROGRESS

3. List the types of normal biota presently known to occupy the skin.

16.3 Skin Diseases Caused by Microorganisms

HIGHLIGHT DISEASE

Maculopapular Rash Diseases

There are a variety of microbes that can cause the type of skin eruptions classified as **maculopapular,** a term denoting flat to slightly raised colored bumps.

Measles

Every year hundreds of thousands of children in the developing world die from this disease (about 540 a day), even though an extremely effective vaccine has been available since 1964. Health campaigns all over the world seek to make measles vaccine available to all, and have been very effective. Since 2002, worldwide deaths from measles have dropped 74%. Ironically, it seems that more work and education need to be done in *developed* countries now. Many parents are opting not to have their children vaccinated, due to unfounded fears about the link between the vaccine and autism. We would do well to remember that before the vaccine was introduced, measles killed 6 million people each year.

Measles is also known as **rubeola.** Be very careful not to confuse it with the next maculopapular rash disease, rubella.

NCLEX® PREP

2. Koplik's spots are associated with which maculopapular rash disease?

- **a.** measles
- **b.** rubella
- **c.** cellulitis
- **d.** roseola

▸ Signs and Symptoms

The initial symptoms of measles are sore throat, dry cough, headache, conjunctivitis, lymphadenitis, and fever. In a short time, unusual oral lesions called *Koplik's spots* appear as a prelude to the characteristic red maculopapular **exanthem** (eg-zan′-thum) that erupts on the head and then progresses to the trunk and extremities until most of the body is covered **(figure 16.2).** The rash gradually coalesces into red patches that fade to brown.

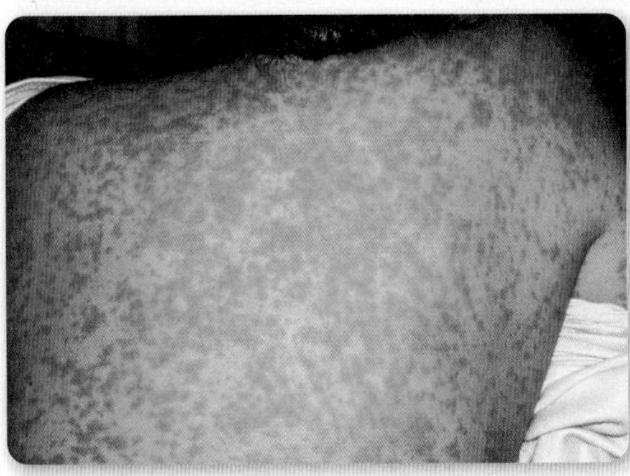

Figure 16.2 The rash of measles.

In a small number of cases, children develop laryngitis, bronchopneumonia, and bacterial secondary infections such as ear and sinus infections. Occasionally (1 in 100 cases), measles progresses to pneumonia or encephalitis, resulting in various central nervous system (CNS) changes ranging from disorientation to coma. Permanent brain damage or epilepsy can result.

A large number of measles patients experience secondary bacterial infections.

The most serious complication is **subacute sclerosing panencephalitis (SSPE),** a progressive neurological degeneration of the cerebral cortex, white matter, and brain stem. Its incidence is approximately one case in a million measles infections, and it afflicts primarily male children and adolescents. The pathogenesis of SSPE appears to involve a defective virus, one that has lost its ability to form a capsid and be released from an infected cell. Instead, it spreads unchecked through the brain by cell fusion, gradually destroying neurons and accessory cells and breaking down myelin. The disease causes profound intellectual and neurological impairment. The course of the disease invariably leads to coma and death in a matter of months or years.

The measles virus is a member of the *Morbillivirus* genus. It is a single-stranded enveloped RNA virus in the family *Paramyxoviridae*.

▶ Pathogenesis and Virulence Factors

The virus implants in the respiratory mucosa and infects the tracheal and bronchial cells. From there, it travels to the lymphatic system, where it multiplies and then enters the bloodstream. Viremia carries the virus to the skin and to various organs.

The measles virus induces the cell membranes of adjacent host cells to fuse into large **syncytia** (sin-sish′-uh), giant cells with many nuclei. These cells no longer perform their proper function. The virus seems proficient at disabling many aspects of the host immune response, especially cell-mediated immunity and delayed-type hypersensitivity.

▶ Transmission and Epidemiology

Measles is one of the most contagious infectious diseases, transmitted principally by respiratory droplets. There is no reservoir other than humans, and a person is infectious during the periods of incubation, prodrome phase, and the skin rash but usually not during convalescence. Only relatively large, dense populations of susceptible individuals can sustain the continuous chain necessary for transmission.

▶ Culture and Diagnosis

The disease can be diagnosed on clinical presentation alone; but if further identification is required, an ELISA test is available that tests for patient IgM to measles antigen, indicating a current infection.

▶ Prevention

The MMR vaccine (for measles, mumps, and rubella) contains live attenuated measles virus, which confers protection for up to 20 years. Measles immunization is recommended for all healthy children at the age of 12 to 15 months, with a booster before the child enters school.

▶ Treatment

Treatment relies on reducing fever, suppressing cough, and replacing lost fluid. Complications require additional remedies to relieve neurological and respiratory symptoms and to sustain nutrient, electrolyte, and fluid levels. Vitamin A supplements are recommended by some physicians; they have been found effective in reducing the symptoms and decreasing the rate of complications.

Rubella

This disease is also known as German measles. Rubella is derived from the Latin for "little red," and that is a good way to remember it because it causes a relatively minor rash disease with few complications. Sometimes it is called the 3-day measles. The only exception to this mild course of events is when a fetus is exposed to the virus while in its mother's womb (in utero). Serious damage can occur, and for that reason women of childbearing years must be sure to have been vaccinated well before they plan to conceive.

▶ Signs and Symptoms

The two clinical forms of rubella are referred to as postnatal infection, which develops in children or adults, and **congenital** (prenatal) infection of the fetus, expressed in the newborn as various types of birth defects.

A Note About the Chapter Organization

Beginning in this chapter, we discuss conditions caused by microbial infection. The chapter organization mirrors the clinical experience. In a clinical setting, patients present themselves to health care practitioners with a set of symptoms, and the health care team makes an "anatomical" diagnosis—such as a *generalized vesicular rash*. The anatomical diagnosis allows practitioners to narrow down the list of possible causes to microorganisms that are known to be capable of creating such a condition. Then the proper tests can be performed to arrive at an etiologic diagnosis (i.e., determining the exact microbial cause). So the order of events is as follows:

1. anatomical diagnosis,
2. differential diagnosis,
3. etiological diagnosis.

In practice, this process may be shortened. For instance, if a patient has a disease such as mumps, the distinctive signs and symptoms of that disease may allow the practitioner to make the anatomical and the etiological diagnosis at the same time, followed by confirmation of the etiology through laboratory methods, if necessary.

In this book, we organize diseases according to the anatomical diagnosis (which appears as a gold-colored heading). Then the agents in the differential diagnosis are each addressed, each of them appearing as turquoise headings. When we finish addressing each agent that could cause the condition we sum them up in a Disease Table, whether there is only one possible cause or whether there are nine or 10.

Some conditions are truly iconic examples of how infectious agents work in the human body. Meningitis in the nervous system is a good example. These "paradigm" diseases are highlighted at the beginning of the disease sections in these chapters. The other conditions are treated more briefly, since there is a wealth of good information available about these diseases; however, we do summarize every disease in a table containing all its important features, so that your textbook is a complete reference resource.

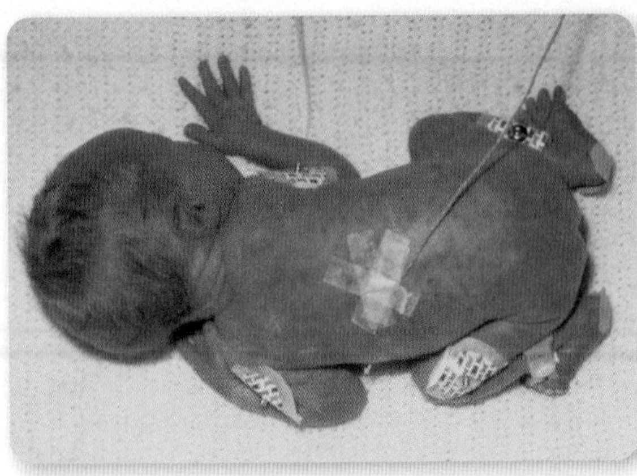

Figure 16.3 An infant born with congenital rubella can display a papular pink or purple rash.

Postnatal Rubella The rash of pink macules and papules first appears on the face and progresses down the trunk and toward the extremities, advancing and resolving in about 3 days. The rash is milder looking than the measles rash (see Disease Table 16.1). Adult rubella is often characterized by joint inflammation and pain rather than a rash.

Congenital Rubella Rubella is a strongly **teratogenic** virus. Transmission of the rubella virus to a fetus in utero can result in a serious complication called **congenital rubella (figure 16.3).** The mother is able to transmit the virus even if she is asymptomatic. Infection in the first trimester is most likely to induce miscarriage or multiple permanent defects in the newborn. The most common of these is deafness and may be the only defect seen in some babies. Other babies may experience cardiac abnormalities, ocular lesions, deafness, and mental and physical retardation in varying combinations. Less drastic sequelae that usually resolve in time are anemia, hepatitis, pneumonia, carditis, and bone infection.

▶ Causative Agent

The rubella virus is a *Rubivirus,* in the family Togaviridae. It is a nonsegmented single-stranded RNA virus with a loose lipid envelope. There is only one known serotype of the virus, and humans are the only natural host. The virus has the ability to stop mitosis, which is an important process in a rapidly developing embryo and fetus. It also induces apoptosis (programmed cell death) of normal tissue cells. This inappropriate cell death can do irreversible harm to organs it affects. And last, the virus damages vascular endothelium, leading to poor development of many organs.

▶ Transmission and Epidemiology

Rubella is a disease with worldwide distribution. Infection is initiated through contact with respiratory secretions and occasionally urine. The virus is shed during the prodromal phase and up to a week after the rash appears. Congenitally infected infants are contagious for a much longer period of time. Because the virus is only moderately communicable, close living conditions are required for its spread. This disease is well controlled in the United States, with fewer than 10 cases reported in each of the last several years. Most cases are reported among adolescents and young adults in military training camps, colleges, and summer camps.

▶ Culture and Diagnosis

Diagnosing rubella relies on the same twin techniques discussed earlier for measles. Because it mimics other diseases, rubella should not be diagnosed on clinical grounds alone. IgM antibody to rubella virus can be detected early using an ELISA technique or a latex-agglutination card. Other conditions and infections can lead to false-positives, however, and the IgM test should be augmented by an acute and convalescent measurement of IgG antibody. It is important to know whether the infection is indeed rubella, especially in women, because if so, they will be immune to reinfection. Women in developed countries routinely undergo antibody testing at the beginning of pregnancy to determine their immune status.

▶ Prevention and Treatment

The attenuated rubella virus vaccine is usually given to children in the combined form (MMR vaccination) at 12 to 15 months and a booster at 4 or 6 years of age. The vaccine for rubella can be administered on its own, without the measles and mumps components. Postnatal rubella is generally benign and requires only symptomatic treatment. No specific treatment is available for the congenital manifestations.

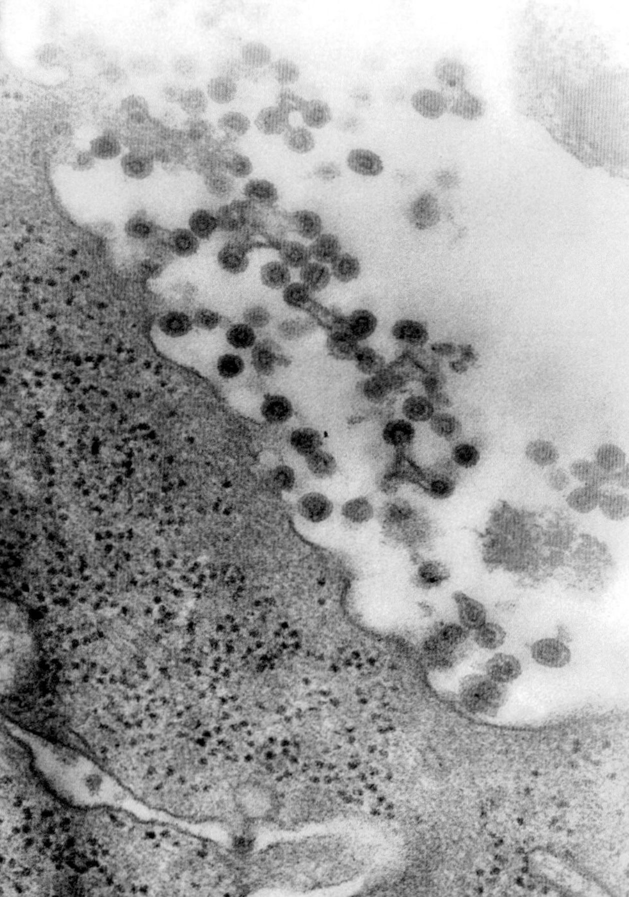

Fifth Disease

This disease, more precisely called *erythema infectiosum,* is so named because about 100 years ago it was the fifth of the diseases recognized by doctors to cause rashes in children. The first four were scarlet fever, measles, rubella, and another rash that was thought to be distinct but was probably not. Fifth disease is a very mild disease that often results in a characteristic "slapped-cheek" appearance because of a confluent reddish rash that begins on the face. Within 2 days, the rash spreads on the body but is most prominent on the arms, legs, and trunk. The rash of fifth disease may reoccur for several weeks and may be brought on by any activity that increases body heat (i.e., exercise, fever, sunlight, warm baths, and even high emotion).

The causative agent is parvovirus B19. You may have heard of "parvo" as a disease of dogs, but strains of this virus group infect humans. Fifth disease is usually diagnosed by the clinical presentation, but sometimes it is helpful to rule out rubella by testing for IgM against rubella.

This infection is very contagious. There is no vaccine and no treatment for this usually mild disease.

Roseola

This disease is common in young children and babies. It is sometimes known as "sixth disease." It can result in a maculopapular rash, but a high percentage (up to 70%) of cases proceed without the rash stage. Children sick with this disease exhibit

Disease Table 16.1 Maculopapular Rash Diseases

Disease	Measles (Rubeola)	Rubella	Fifth Disease	Roseola	Scarlet Fever
Causative Organism(s)	Measles virus	Rubella virus	Parvovirus B19	Human herpesvirus 6 or 7	*Streptococcus pyogenes* (lysogenized)
Most Common Modes of Transmission	Droplet contact	Droplet contact	Droplet contact, direct contact	?	Droplet or direct contact
Virulence Factors	Syncytium formation, ability to suppress cell-mediated immunity (CMI)	In fetuses: inhibition of mitosis, induction of apoptosis, and damage to vascular endothelium	–	Ability to remain latent	Erythrogenic toxin
Culture/Diagnosis	ELISA for IgM, acute/convalescent IgG	Acute IgM, acute/convalescent IgG	Usually diagnosed clinically	Usually diagnosed clinically	Examination of skin lesions, throat culture (beta-hemolytic on blood agar, sensitive to bacitracin, rapid antigen tests)
Prevention	Live attenuated vaccine (MMR)	Live attenuated vaccine (MMR)	–	–	–
Treatment	No antivirals; vitamin A, antibiotics for secondary bacterial infections	–	–	–	Penicillin, cephalexin in penicillin-allergic
Distinguishing Features of the Rashes	Starts on head, spreads to whole body, lasts over a week	Milder red rash, lasts approximately 3 days	"Slapped-cheek" rash first, spreads to limbs and trunk, tends to be confluent rather than distinct bumps	High fever precedes rash stage—rash not always present	Sandpaper feel to affected skin; severe sore throat
Appearance of Lesions					

HIGHLIGHT DISEASE

a high fever (up to 41°C, or 105°F) that comes on quickly and lasts for up to 3 days. Seizures may occur during this period, but other than that patients remain alert and do not act terribly ill. On the fourth day, the fever disappears, and it is at this point that a rash can appear, first on the chest and trunk and less prominently on the face and limbs. By the time the rash appears, the disease is almost over.

Roseola is caused by a human herpesvirus called HHV-6, and sometimes by HHV-7. Like all herpesviruses, it can remain latent in its host indefinitely after the disease has cleared. Very occasionally, the virus reactivates in childhood or adulthood, leading to mononucleosis-like or hepatitis-like symptoms. It is thought that 100% of the U.S. population is infected with this virus by adulthood. Some people experienced the disease roseola when they became infected, and some of them did not. The suggestion has been made that this virus causes other disease conditions later in life, such as multiple sclerosis. No vaccine and no treatment exist for roseola.

Scarlet Fever

To complete our survey of infections that can cause maculopapular rashes, we include a disease that has primary symptoms elsewhere but can produce a distinctive red rash on the skin as well. Scarlet fever is most often the result of a respiratory infection with *Streptococcus pyogenes* (most often, pharyngitis). Occasionally, scarlet fever will follow a streptococcal skin infection, such as impetigo or cellulitis. If the *S. pyogenes* strain contains a bacteriophage carrying a gene for an exotoxin called erythrogenic toxin, scarlet fever can result. More details on scarlet fever are given in chapter 19; it is included in Disease Table 16.1 mainly for purposes of differentiating the rash from the others in this group.

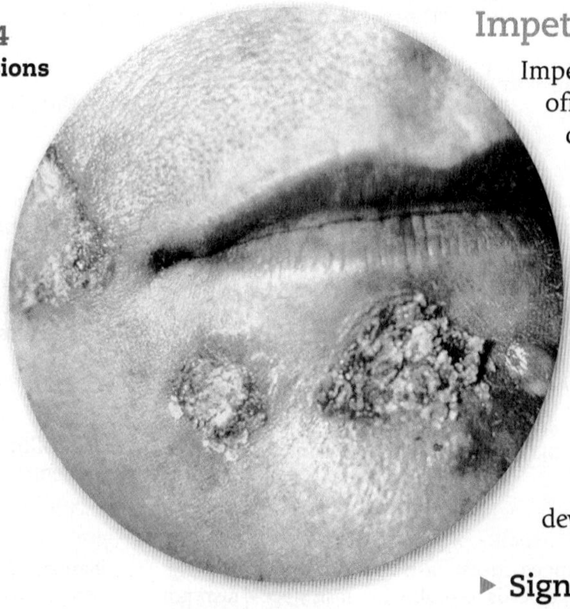

Figure 16.4
Impetigo lesions on the face.

Impetigo

Impetigo is a superficial bacterial infection that causes the skin to flake or peel off **(figure 16.4)**. It is not a serious disease but is highly contagious, and children are the primary victims. Impetigo can be caused by either *Staphylococcus aureus* or *Streptococcus pyogenes*, and some cases are probably caused by a mixture of the two. It has been suggested that *S. pyogenes* begins all cases of the disease, and in some cases *S. aureus* later takes over and becomes the predominant bacterium cultured from lesions. Because *S. aureus* produces a bacteriocin (toxin) that can destroy *S. pyogenes*, it is possible that *S. pyogenes* is often missed in culture-based diagnosis.

Impetigo, whether it is caused by *S. pyogenes*, *S. aureus*, or both, is highly contagious and transmitted through direct contact but also via fomites and mechanical vector transmission. The peak incidence is in the summer and fall.

The only current prevention for impetigo is good hygiene. Vaccines are in development for both of the etiologic agents, but none are currently available.

▸ Signs and Symptoms

The "lesion" of impetigo looks variously like peeling skin, crusty and flaky scabs, or honey-colored crusts. Lesions are most often found around the mouth, face, and extremities, though they can occur anywhere on the skin. It is very superficial and it itches. The symptomatology does not indicate whether the infection is caused by *Staphylococcus* or *Streptococcus*.

Impetigo Caused by *Staphylococcus aureus*

Staphylococcus aureus is a gram-positive coccus that grows in clusters, like a bunch of grapes. It is nonmotile. Much of its destructiveness is due to its array of **superantigens** (see chapter 12).

This species is considered the sturdiest of all non-spore-forming pathogens, with well-developed capacities to withstand high salt (7.5% to 10%), extremes in pH, and high temperatures (up to 60°C for 60 minutes). *S. aureus* also remains viable after months of air drying and resists the effect of many disinfectants and antibiotics. These properties contribute to the reputation of *S. aureus* as a troublesome hospital pathogen.

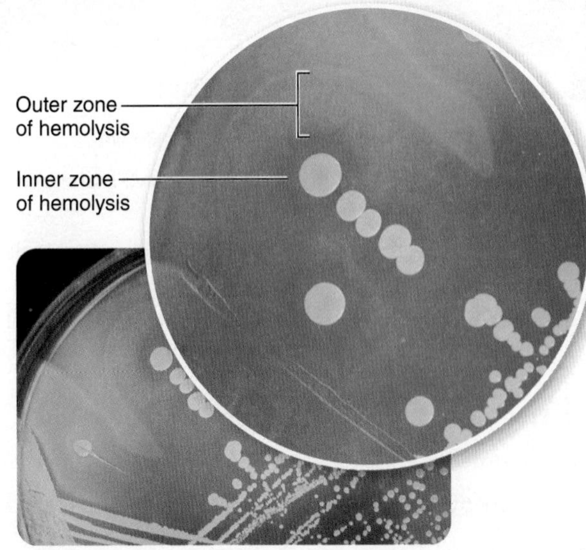

Figure 16.5 *Staphylococcus aureus.* Blood agar plate growing *S. aureus*. Some strains show two zones of hemolysis, caused by two different hemolysins. The inner zone is clear, whereas the outer zone is fuzzy and appears only if the plate has been refrigerated after growth.

Pathogenesis and Virulence Factors

The most important virulence factors relevant to *S. aureus* impetigo are exotoxins called exfoliative toxins A and B, which are coded for by a phage that infects some *S. aureus* strains. At least one of the toxins attacks a protein that is very important for epithelial cell-to-cell binding in the outermost layer of the skin. Breaking up this protein leads to the characteristic blistering seen in the condition. The breakdown of skin architecture also facilitates the spread of the bacterium. All pathogenic *S. aureus* strains typically produce **coagulase,** an enzyme that coagulates plasma. Because 97% of all human isolates of *S. aureus* produce this enzyme, its presence is considered the most diagnostic species characteristic.

Other enzymes expressed by *S. aureus* include hyaluronidase, which digests the intercellular "glue" (hyaluronic acid) that binds connective tissue in host tissues; staphylokinase, which digests blood clots; a nuclease that digests DNA (DNase); and lipases that help the bacteria colonize oily skin surfaces.

Culture and/or Diagnosis

Primary isolation of *S. aureus* is achieved by inoculation on blood agar **(figure 16.5).** For heavily contaminated specimens, selective media such as mannitol salt agar are used. The production of catalase, an enzyme that breaks down hydrogen peroxide accumulated during oxidative metabolism, can be used to differentiate the staphylococci, which produce it, from the streptococci, which do not.

One key technique for separating *S. aureus* from other species of *Staphylococcus* is the coagulase test **(figure 16.6).** By definition, any isolate that coagulates plasma is *S. aureus;* all others are coagulase negative.

Figure 16.6 The coagulase test. Staphylococcal coagulase is an enzyme that reacts with factors in plasma to initiate clot formation. In the coagulase test, a tube of plasma is inoculated with the bacterium. If it remains liquid, the test is negative. If the plasma develops a lump or becomes completely clotted, the test is positive.

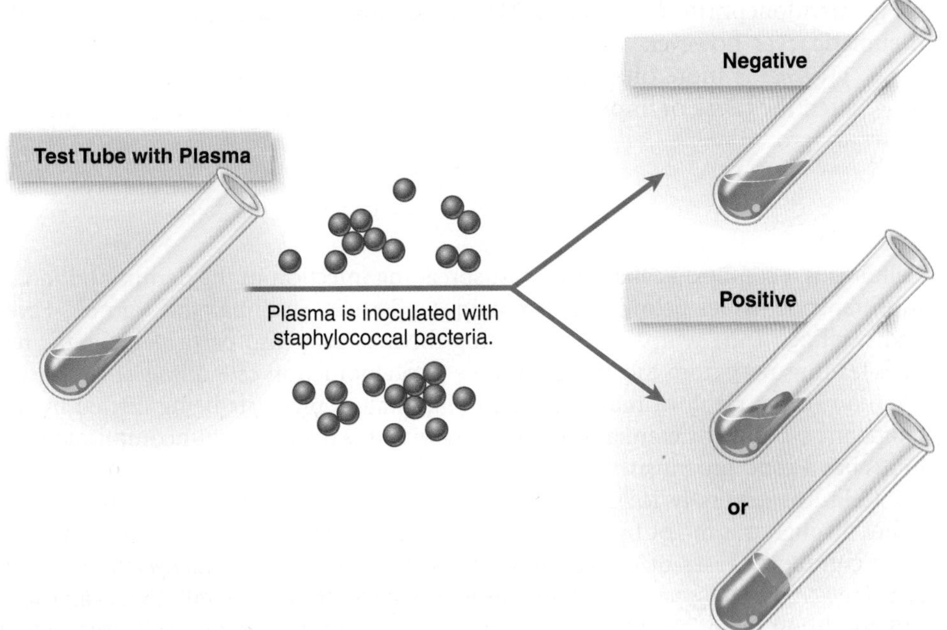

A Note About MRSA

Everyone who has any recent work experience in health care knows the term *MRSA*, which stands for methicillin-resistant *Staphylococcus aureus*. MRSAs are *S. aureus* strains that are resistant to penicillin derivatives. (Methicillin is a penicillin derivative that is used only in the laboratory for testing purposes.). Now it is very common for nosocomial infections to be caused by MRSA. These MRSA strains must be treated very aggressively with vancomycin or other new antibiotics (telavancin, tigecycline, or ceftobiprole) because they are resistant to multiple first-line and second-line antibiotics.

During the period between 2004 and 2006, a disturbing *S. aureus* trend that had been bubbling under the surface emerged into the public eye. While the health care establishment had grown accustomed to (though not complacent about) hospital-acquired MRSA (HA-MRSA), people who had no recent history in hospitals or health care facilities started turning up with MRSA infections. These infections are classified as *community-acquired* MRSA and given the acronym CA-MRSA. Between 1998 and 2008, there was a 10-fold increase in children admitted to hospitals with MRSA. In other words, they had MRSA before they got there. The rate of nonresistant *Staphylococcus aureus* admissions did not change.

Disease Table 16.2 Impetigo

Causative Organism(s)	*Staphylococcus aureus*	*Streptococcus pyogenes*
Most Common Modes of Transmission	Direct contact, indirect contact	Direct contact, indirect contact
Virulence Factors	Exfoliative toxin A, coagulase, other enzymes	Streptokinase, plasminogen-binding ability, hyaluronidase, M protein
Culture/Diagnosis	Routinely based on clinical signs; when necessary, culture and Gram stain, coagulase and catalase tests, multitest systems, PCR	Routinely based on clinical signs; when necessary, culture and Gram stain, coagulase and catalase tests, multitest systems, PCR
Prevention	Hygiene practices	Hygiene practices
Treatment	Topical mupirocin or pleuromutilin, oral cephalexin	Topical mupirocin or pleuromutilin, oral cephalexin
Distinctive Features	Seen more often in older children, adults	Seen more often in newborns; may have some involvement in all impetigo (preceding *S. aureus* in staphylococcal impetigo)

Medical Moment

Another Strep Infection

Erysipelas is often associated with infection of the skin caused by *S. pyogenes*, which can enter the skin through a small wound or incision on the face or extremities. The infection then spreads to the dermis and subcutaneous tissues. Close to the portal of entry, the skin becomes reddened and edematous and may resemble an orange peel in consistency. Fever, chills, headache, vomiting, and generalized malaise may accompany these symptoms. As the infection progresses, the lesion continues to spread outward. The edge of the lesion is slightly elevated and is red and hot to the touch. The lesion may remain superficial or may produce long-term systemic complications. Severe cases in which large portions of the skin are involved may even be fatal.

In the past, the face was most often affected. Today, however, the legs are the most common area to be affected. The disease often affects infants, children, and the elderly, as well as those with poorly functioning immune systems, alcoholism, diabetes, or other skin impairment (i.e., eczema). Treatment involves either oral or intravenous antibiotics, depending on the severity of the infection.

Impetigo Caused by *Streptococcus pyogenes*

Streptococcus pyogenes is thoroughly described in chapter 19. The important features are briefly summarized here, and the features pertinent to impetigo are listed in **Disease Table 16.2.**

S. pyogenes is a gram-positive coccus and is beta-hemolytic on blood agar. In addition to impetigo, it causes streptococcal pharyngitis (strep throat), scarlet fever, pneumonia, puerperal fever, necrotizing fasciitis, serious bloodstream infections, and poststreptococcal conditions such as rheumatic fever.

If the precise etiologic agent must be identified, there are well-established methods for identifying group A streptococci. Refer to chapter 19.

▸ Pathogenesis and Virulence Factors

Like *S. aureus*, this bacterium possesses a huge arsenal of enzymes and toxins. Some of these are listed in Disease Table 16.2.

Rarely, impetigo caused by *S. pyogenes* can be followed by acute poststreptococcal glomerulonephritis (see chapter 19). The strains that cause impetigo never cause rheumatic fever, however.

S. pyogenes is more often the cause of impetigo in newborns, and *S. aureus* is more often the cause of impetigo in older children, but both can cause infection in either age group.

Cellulitis

Cellulitis is a condition caused by a fast-spreading infection in the dermis and in the subcutaneous tissues below. It causes pain, tenderness, swelling, and warmth. Fever and swelling of the lymph nodes draining the area may also occur. Frequently, red lines leading away from the area are visible (a phenomenon called *lymphangitis*); this symptom is the result of microbes and inflammatory products being carried by the lymphatic system. Bacteremia could develop with this disease, but uncomplicated cellulitis has a good prognosis.

Cellulitis generally follows introduction of bacteria or fungi into the dermis, either through trauma or by subtle means (with no obvious break in the skin). The most common causes of the condition in healthy people are *Staphylococcus aureus* and *Streptococcus pyogenes*, although almost any bacterium and some fungi can cause this condition in an immunocompromised patient. In infants, group B streptococci are a frequent cause (see chapter 21).

Disease Table 16.3 Cellulitis

Causative Organism(s)	*Staphylococcus aureus*	*Streptococcus pyogenes*	Other bacteria or fungi
Most Common Modes of Transmission	Parenteral implantation	Parenteral implantation	Parenteral implantation
Virulence Factors	Exfoliative toxin A, coagulase, other enzymes	Streptokinase, plasminogen-binding ability, hyaluronidase, M protein	–
Culture/Diagnosis	Based on clinical signs	Based on clinical signs	Based on clinical signs
Prevention	–	–	–
Treatment	Oral or IV antibiotic (often cephalexin); surgery sometimes necessary	Oral or IV antibiotic penicillin; surgery sometimes necessary	Aggressive treatment with oral or IV antibiotic (cephalexin or penicillin); surgery sometimes necessary
Distinctive Features	–	–	More common in immunocompromised

Mild cellulitis responds well to oral antibiotics chosen to be effective against both *S. aureus* and *S. pyogenes*. More involved infections and infections in immunocompromised people require intravenous antibiotics. If there are extensive areas of tissue damage, surgical debridement (duh-breed'-munt) is warranted.

Staphylococcal Scalded Skin Syndrome (SSSS)

This syndrome is another **dermolytic** condition caused by *Staphylococcus aureus*. It affects mostly newborns and babies, although children and adults can experience the infection. Transmission may occur when caregivers carry the bacterium from one baby to another. Adults in the nursery can also directly transfer *S. aureus* because approximately 30% of adults are asymptomatic carriers. Carriers can harbor the bacteria in the nasopharynx, axilla, perineum, and even the vagina. (Fortunately, only about 5% of *S. aureus* strains are lysogenized by the type of phage that codes for the toxins responsible for this disease.)

Like impetigo, this is an exotoxin-mediated disease. The phage-encoded exfoliative toxins A and B are responsible for the damage. Unlike impetigo, the toxins enter the bloodstream from some focus of infection (the throat, the eye, or sometimes an impetigo infection) and then travel to the skin throughout the body. These toxins cause **bullous lesions,** which often appear first around the umbilical cord (in neonates) or in the diaper or axilla area. A split occurs in the epidermal tissue layers just above the stratum basale (see figure 16.1). Widespread **desquamation** of the skin follows, leading to the burned appearance referred to in the name **(figure 16.7).**

Once a tentative diagnosis of SSSS is made, immediate antibiotic therapy should be instituted.

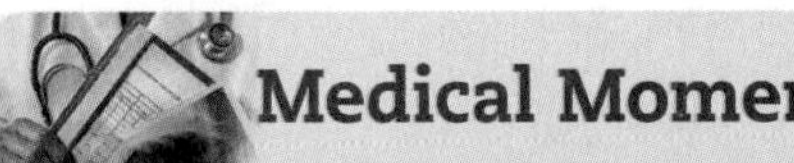

Medical Moment

Additional Staph Infections

S. aureus has been discussed in this chapter as an important human pathogen causing several skin conditions such as impetigo, cellulitis, and scalded skin syndrome. Other conditions may also be caused by *S. aureus*, such as folliculitis, furuncles, and carbuncles.

Folliculitis is a mild, superficial inflammation of the hair follicles or glands. The disease is often self-limiting but can lead to a more serious infection of the subcutaneous tissues, such as an **abscess**. An abscess is a localized staphylococcal skin infection resulting in an inflamed lesion surrounding a core of pus (purulent material).

Abscesses can be further subdivided into furuncles and carbuncles. A **furuncle** results when a single hair follicle or sebaceous gland becomes inflamed and progresses into a large, red, and exquisitely painful abscess. They often occur in clusters on parts of the body where skin comes in contact with other skin or clothing (i.e., back of the neck, buttocks, or axillae). A **carbuncle** is a cluster of furuncles that are interconnected to form larger and deeper lesions, which may grow as large as baseballs. They are extremely painful and may give rise to systemic disease.

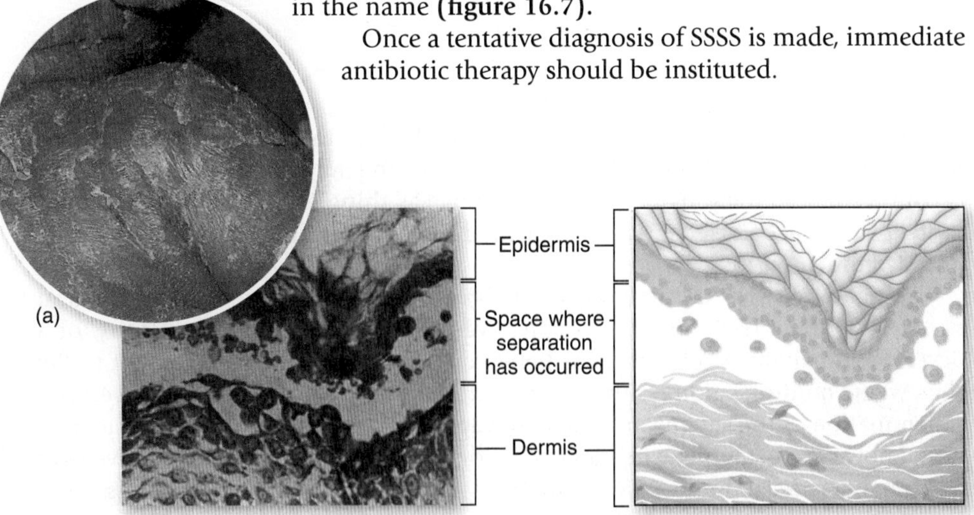

Figure 16.7 Staphylococcal scalded skin syndrome (SSSS) in a newborn child. **(a)** Exfoliative toxin produced in local infections causes blistering and peeling away of the outer layer of skin. **(b)** Photomicrograph of a segment of skin affected with SSSS. The point of epidermal shedding, or desquamation, is in the epidermis. The lesions will heal well because the level of separation is so superficial.

Disease Table 16.4 Scalded Skin Syndrome

Causative Organism(s)	*Staphylococcus aureus*
Most Common Modes of Transmission	Direct contact, droplet contact
Virulence Factors	Exfoliative toxins A and B
Culture/Diagnosis	Histological sections; culture performed but false-negatives common because toxins alone are sufficient for disease
Prevention	Eliminate carriers in contact with neonates
Treatment	Immediate systemic antibiotics (cloxacillin or cephalexin)
Distinctive Features	Split in skin occurs *within* epidermis

Vesicular or Pustular Rash Diseases

There are two diseases that present as generalized "rashes" over the body in which the individual lesions contain fluid. The lesions are often called *pox,* and the two diseases are chickenpox and smallpox. Chickenpox is very common and mostly benign, but even a single case of smallpox constitutes a public health emergency. Both are viral diseases.

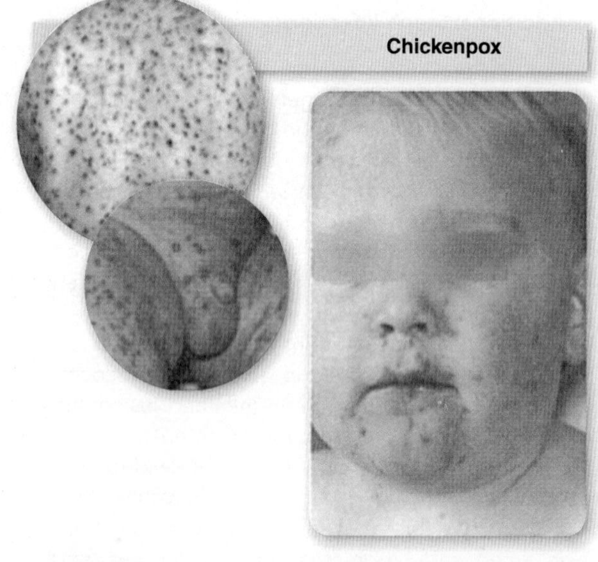

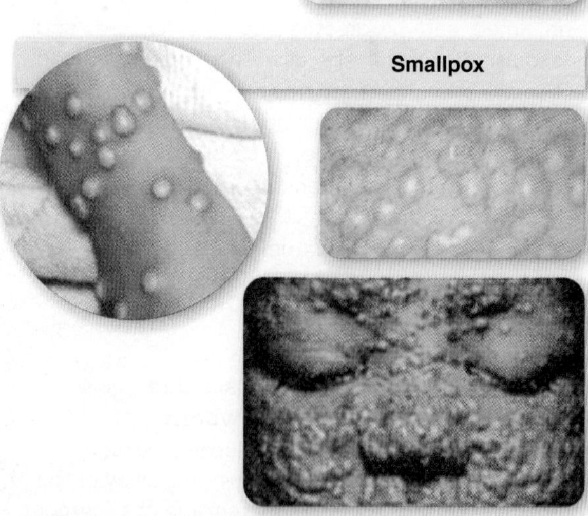

Figure 16.8 Images of chickenpox and smallpox.

Chickenpox

After an incubation period of 10 to 20 days, the first symptoms to appear are fever and an abundant rash that begins on the scalp, face, and trunk and radiates in sparse crops to the extremities. Skin lesions progress quickly from macules and papules to itchy vesicles filled with a clear fluid. In several days, they encrust and drop off, usually healing completely but sometimes leaving a tiny pit or scar. Lesions number from a few to hundreds and are more abundant in adolescents and adults than in young children. **Figure 16.8** contains images of the chickenpox lesions in a child and in an adult. The lesion distribution is *centripetal,* meaning that there are more in the center of the body and fewer on the extremities, in contrast to the distribution seen with smallpox. The illness usually lasts 4 to 7 days; new lesions stop appearing after about 5 days. Patients are considered contagious until all of the lesions have crusted over.

Approximately 0.1% of chickenpox cases are followed by encephalopathy, or inflammation of the brain caused by the virus. It can be fatal, but in most cases recovery is complete.

Shingles

After recuperation from chickenpox, the virus enters into the sensory endings that innervate dermatomes, regions of the skin supplied by the cutaneous branches of nerves, especially the thoracic (**figure 16.9*a***) and trigeminal nerves. From here, it becomes latent in the ganglia and may reemerge as **shingles** (also known as **herpes zoster**) with its characteristic asymmetrical distribution on the skin of the trunk or head (**figure 16.9*b***).

Shingles develops abruptly after reactivation by such stimuli as psychological stress, X-ray treatments, immunosuppressive and other drug therapy, surgery, or a developing malignancy. The virus is believed to migrate down the ganglion to the skin, where multiplication resumes and produces crops of tender, persistent vesicles. Inflammation of the ganglia and the pathways of nerves can cause pain and tenderness, known as postherpetic neuralgia, that can last for several months. Involvement of cranial nerves can lead to eye inflammation and ocular and facial paralysis.

▶ Causative Agent

Human herpesvirus 3 (HHV-3, also called **varicella** [var″-ih′sel′-ah]) causes chickenpox, as well as the condition called herpes zoster or shingles. The virus is sometimes referred to as the varicella-zoster virus (VZV). Like other herpesviruses, it is an enveloped DNA virus.

▶ Pathogenesis and Virulence Factors

HHV-3 enters the respiratory tract, attaches to respiratory mucosa, and then invades and enters the bloodstream. The viremia disseminates the virus to the skin, where the virus causes adjacent cells to fuse and eventually lyse, resulting in the characteristic lesions. The virus enters the sensory nerves at this site, traveling to the dorsal root ganglia.

The ability of HHV-3 to remain latent in ganglia is an important virulence factor, because resting in this site protects it from attack by the immune system and provides a reservoir of virus for the reactivation condition of shingles.

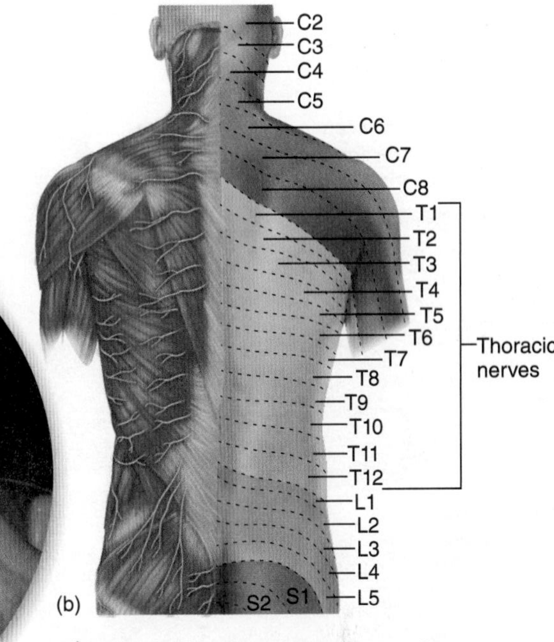

Figure 16.9 Varicella-zoster virus reemergence as shingles. (a) Clinical appearance of shingles lesions. (b) Dermatomes are areas of the skin served by a single ganglion. Shingles generally affects a single dermatome for this reason.

▶ Transmission and Epidemiology

Humans are the only natural hosts for HHV-3. The virus is harbored in the respiratory tract but is communicable from both respiratory droplets and the fluid of active skin lesions. People can acquire a chickenpox infection by being exposed to the fluid of shingles lesions.

Infected persons are most infectious a day or two prior to the development of the rash. Chickenpox is so contagious that if you are exposed to it you almost certainly will get it.

▶ Prevention

Live attenuated vaccine was licensed in 1995. In 2006, the FDA approved a unique vaccine called Zostavax. It is intended for adults age 60 and over and is for the prevention of shingles.

▶ Treatment

Uncomplicated varicella is self-limiting and requires no therapy aside from alleviation of discomfort. Secondary bacterial infection, as just noted, is treated with topical or systemic antibiotics. Oral acyclovir or related antivirals should be administered to people considered to be at risk for serious complications within 24 hours of onset of the rash.

Smallpox

Largely through the World Health Organization's comprehensive global efforts, naturally occurring smallpox is now a disease of the past. However, after the terrorist attacks on the United States on September 11, 2001, and the anthrax bioterrorism shortly thereafter, the U.S. government began taking the threat of smallpox bioterrorism very seriously. Vaccination, which had been discontinued, was once again offered to certain U.S. populations.

▶ Signs and Symptoms

Infection begins with fever and malaise, and later a rash begins in the pharynx, spreads to the face, and progresses to the extremities. Initially, the rash is **macular**, evolving in turn to **papular**, **vesicular**, and **pustular** before eventually crusting over,

NCLEX® PREP

3. The following statements are true regarding shingles, *except*
   a. the condition is caused by a reactivation of the varicella virus that may remain latent in the ganglia of nerve fibers for years.
   b. you can "come down" with shingles by being exposed to the fluid of shingles lesions.
   c. psychological stress can reactivate the virus, which causes shingles.
   d. shingles may cause eye inflammation and facial paralysis.

Vaccinia virus, the cause of cowpox, is used as a vaccine against smallpox, caused by the variola virus.

leaving nonpigmented sites pitted with scar tissue. There are two principal forms of smallpox, variola minor and variola major. Variola major is a highly virulent form that causes toxemia, shock, and intravascular coagulation. People who have survived any form of smallpox nearly always develop lifelong immunity.

It is vitally important for health care workers to be able to recognize the early signs of smallpox. The diagnosis of even a single suspected case must be treated as a health and law enforcement emergency. The symptoms of variola major progress as follows: After the prodrome period of high fever and malaise, a rash emerges, first in the mouth. Severe abdominal and back pain sometimes accompany this phase of the disease. A rash appears on the skin and spreads throughout the body within 24 hours. A distribution of the rash on the body is shown in figure 16.8.

By the third or fourth day of the rash, the bumps become larger and fill with a thick opaque fluid. A major distinguishing feature of this disease is that the pustules are indented in the middle. Also, patients report that the lesions feel as if they contain a BB pellet. Within a few days, these pustules begin to scab over. After 2 weeks, most of the lesions will have crusted over; the patient remains contagious until the last scabs fall off because the crusts contain the virus. During the entire rash phase, the patient is very ill. The lesions occur at the dermal level, which is the reason that scars remain after the lesions are healed.

A patient with variola minor has a rash that is less dense and is generally less ill than someone with variola major.

Causative Agent

The causative agent of smallpox, the variola virus, is orthopoxvirus, an enveloped DNA virus. Other members of this group are the monkeypox virus and the vaccinia virus from which smallpox vaccine is made. Variola is a hardy virus, surviving outside the host longer than most viruses.

Disease Table 16.5 Vesicular or Pustular Rash Diseases

Disease	Chickenpox	Smallpox
Causative Organism(s)	Human herpesvirus 3 (varicella-zoster virus)	Variola virus
Most Common Modes of Transmission	Droplet contact, inhalation of aerosolized lesion fluid	Droplet contact, indirect contact
Virulence Factors	Ability to fuse cells, ability to remain latent in ganglia	Ability to dampen, avoid immune response
Culture/Diagnosis	Based largely on clinical appearance	Based largely on clinical appearance
Prevention	Live attenuated vaccine; there is also vaccine to prevent reactivation of latent virus (shingles)	Live virus vaccine (vaccinia virus)
Treatment	None in uncomplicated cases; acyclovir for high risk	–
Distinctive Features	No fever prodrome; lesions are superficial; in centripetal distribution (more in center of body)	Fever precedes rash; lesions are deep and in centrifugal distribution (more on extremities)
Appearance of Lesions		

▶ Transmission and Epidemiology

Smallpox is spread primarily through droplets, although fomites such as contaminated bedding and clothing can also spread it.

In the early 1970s, smallpox was endemic in 31 countries. Every year, 10 to 15 million people contracted the disease, and approximately 2 million people died from it. By 1977, after 11 years of intensive effort by the world health community, the last natural case occurred in Somalia.

▶ Prevention

In chapter 13, you read about Edward Jenner and his development of vaccinia virus to inoculate against smallpox. To this day, the vaccination for smallpox is based on the vaccinia virus. Immunizations were stopped in the United States in 1972. Since the terrorist events of 2001, most military branches are requiring that their personnel take the vaccination before deploying to certain parts of the world. In 2007, a new vaccine was approved by the Food and Drug Administration; it is called ACAM 2000.

Vaccination is also useful for postexposure prophylaxis, meaning that it can prevent or lessen the effects of the disease after you have already been infected with it.

Close up of a profile view of a smallpox scab on skin.

▶ Treatment

There is no treatment for smallpox.

Wartlike Eruptions

All types of warts are caused by viruses. Most common warts are probably caused by one of more than 100 human papillomaviruses, or HPVs. HPVs are also the cause of genital warts, described in chapter 21. Another virus in the poxvirus family causes a condition called **molluscum contagiosum,** which causes bumps that may look like warts.

Warts

Warts, also known as **papillomas,** afflict nearly everyone. Children seem to get them more frequently than adults, and there is speculation that people gradually build up immunity to the various HPVs that they encounter over time, as is the case with the viruses that cause the common cold.

Some HPVs can infect mucous membranes; others invade skin. Painless, elevated, rough growths on the fingers and occasionally on other body parts are called common, or seed, warts. **Plantar warts** are deep, painful papillomas on the soles of the feet. Flat warts are smooth, skin-colored lesions that develop on the face, trunk, elbows, and knees.

Transmission occurs through direct contact, and often warts are transmitted from one part of the body to another by autoinoculation. Because the viruses are fairly stable in the environment, they can also be transmitted indirectly from towels or from a shower stall, where they persist inside the protective covering of sloughed-off keratinized skin cells. The incubation period can be from 1 to 8 months. Almost all nongenital warts are harmless, and they tend to resolve themselves over time.

Warts disappear on their own 60% to 70% of the time, usually over the course of 2 to 3 years. Physicians do approve of home remedies for resolving warts. These include nonprescription salicylic acid preparations, as well as the use of adhesive tape. Yes, you read that right: Well-controlled medical studies have shown that adhesive tape (even duct tape!) can cause warts to disappear, presumably because the tape creates an airtight atmosphere that stops virus reproduction. But a psychological component, similar to a placebo effect, cannot be ruled out. (Neither of these treatments should be used for genital warts; see chapter 21.) Physicians have

Disease Table 16.6 Warts and Wartlike Eruptions

Causative Organism(s)	Human papillomaviruses	Molluscum contagiosum viruses
Most Common Modes of Transmission	Direct contact, autoinoculation, indirect contact	Direct contact, including sexual contact, autoinoculation
Virulence Factors	–	–
Culture/Diagnosis	Clinical diagnosis, also histology, microscopy, PCR	Clinical diagnosis, also histology, microscopy, PCR
Prevention	Avoid contact	Avoid contact
Treatment	Home treatments, cryosurgery (virus not eliminated)	Usually none, although mechanical removal can be performed (virus not eliminated)
Appearance of Lesions		

other techniques for removing warts, including a number of drugs and/or cryosurgery. No treatment guarantees that the viruses are eliminated; therefore, warts can always grow back.

Molluscum Contagiosum

This disease is distributed throughout the world, with highest incidence occurring on certain Pacific islands, although its incidence in North America has been increasing since the 1980s. Skin lesions take the form of smooth, waxy nodules on the face, trunk, and limbs. The firm nodules may be indented in the middle **(Disease Table 16.6).** This condition is common in children, where it most often causes nodules on the face, arms, legs, and trunk. In adults, it appears mostly in the genital areas. In immunocompromised patients, the lesions can be more disfiguring and more widespread on the body. It is particularly common in AIDS patients and often presents as facial lesions.

The molluscum contagiosum virus is a poxvirus, containing double-stranded DNA and possessing an envelope. It is spread via direct contact and also through fomites. Adults who acquire this infection often acquire it through sexual contact.

In most cases, no treatment is indicated, although a physician may remove the lesions or treat them with a topical chemical. Treatment of lesions does not ensure elimination of the virus.

Large Pustular Skin Lesions

Leishmaniasis

Two infections that result in large lesions (greater than a few millimeters across) deserve mention in this chapter on skin infections. The first is leishmaniasis, a zoonosis transmitted among various mammalian hosts by female sand flies. This infection can express itself in several different forms, depending on which species of the protozoan *Leishmania* is involved. Cutaneous leishmaniasis is a localized infection of the capillaries of the skin caused by *L. tropica,* found in Mediterranean, African, and Indian regions. A form of mucocutaneous leishmaniasis called espundia is caused by *L. braziliensis,* endemic to parts of Central and South America. It affects both the skin and mucous membranes. Another form of this infection is systemic leishmaniasis.

Disease Table 16.7 Large Pustular Skin Lesions

Disease	Leishmaniasis	Cutaneous Anthrax
Causative Organism(s)	*Leishmania* spp.	*Bacillus anthracis*
Most Common Modes of Transmission	Biological vector	Direct contact with endospores
Virulence Factors	Multiplication within macrophages	Endospore formation; capsule, lethal factor, edema factor (see chapter 18)
Culture/Diagnosis	Culture of protozoa, microscopic visualization	Culture on blood agar; serology, PCR performed by CDC
Prevention	Avoiding sand fly	Avoid contact; vaccine available but not widely used
Treatment	Sodium stibogluconate	Ciprofloxacin, doxycycline, levofloxacin
Distinctive Features	Mucocutaneous and systemic forms	Can be fatal
Appearance of Lesions		

Leishmania is transmitted to the mammalian host by the sand fly when it ingests the host's blood. The disease is endemic to equatorial regions that provide favorable conditions for the sand fly. At particular risk are travelers or immigrants who have never had contact with the protozoan and lack specific immunity.

There is no vaccine; avoiding the sand fly is the only prevention.

Cutaneous Anthrax

This form of anthrax is the most common and least dangerous version of infection with *Bacillus anthracis*. (The spectrum of anthrax disease is discussed fully in chapter 18.) It is caused by endospores entering the skin through small cuts or abrasions. Germination and growth of the pathogen in the skin are marked by the production of a papule that becomes increasingly necrotic and later ruptures to form a painless, black **eschar** (ess′-kar) (see Disease Table 16.7). In the fall of 2001, 11 cases of cutaneous anthrax occurred in the United States as a result of bioterrorism (along with 11 cases of inhalational anthrax). Mail workers and others contracted the infection when endospores were sent through the mail. The infection can be naturally transmitted by contact with hides of infected animals (especially goats).

Left untreated, even the cutaneous form of anthrax is fatal approximately 20% of the time. A vaccine exists but is recommended only for high-risk persons and the military.

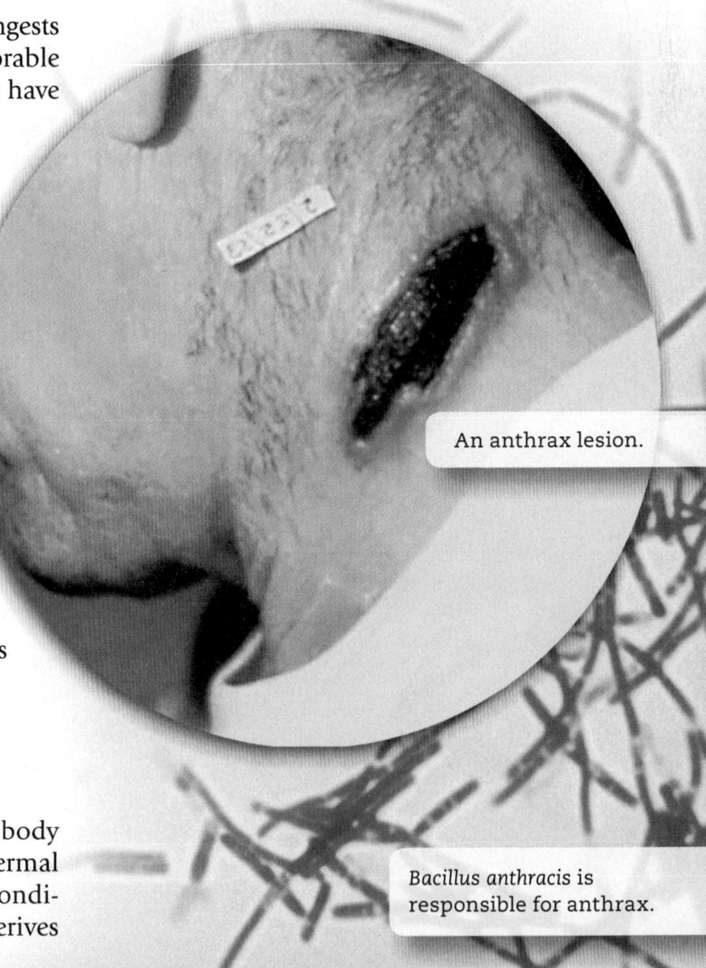

An anthrax lesion.

Cutaneous and Superficial Mycoses

Ringworm

A group of fungi that is collectively termed **dermatophytes** causes a variety of body surface conditions. These mycoses are strictly confined to the nonliving epidermal tissues (stratum corneum) and their derivatives (hair and nails). All these conditions have different names that begin with the word **tinea** (tin′-ee-ah), which derives

Bacillus anthracis is responsible for anthrax.

Table 16.1 Signs and Symptoms of Cutaneous Mycoses

Ringworm of the Scalp (Tinea Capitis)	This mycosis results from the fungal invasion of the scalp and the hair of the head, eyebrows, and eyelashes.
Ringworm of the Beard (Tinea Barbae)	This tinea, also called *barber's itch,* affects the chin and beard of adult males. Although once a common aftereffect of unhygienic barbering, it is now contracted mainly from animals.
Ringworm of the Body (Tinea Corporis)	This extremely prevalent infection of humans can appear nearly anywhere on the body's glabrous (smooth and bare) skin.
Ringworm of the Groin (Tinea Cruris)	Sometimes known as *jock itch,* crural ringworm occurs mainly in males on the groin, perianal skin, scrotum, and, occasionally, the penis. The fungus thrives under conditions of moisture and humidity created by sweating.
Ringworm of the Foot (Tinea Pedis)	Tinea pedis has more colorful names as well, including athlete's foot and jungle rot. Infections begin with blisters between the toes that burst, crust over, and can spread to the rest of the foot and nails.
Ringworm of the Nail (Tinea Unguium)	Fingernails and toenails, being masses of keratin, are often sites for persistent fungus colonization. The first symptoms are usually superficial white patches in the nail bed. A more invasive form causes thickening, distortion, and darkening of the nail.

from the erroneous belief that they were caused by worms. That misconception is also the reason these diseases are often called *ringworm*—ringworm of the scalp (tinea capitis), beard (tinea barbae), body (tinea corporis), groin (tinea cruris), foot (tinea pedis), and hand (tinea manuum). (Don't confuse these "tinea" terms with genus and species names. It is simply an old practice for naming the conditions.) Most of these conditions are caused by one of three different dermatophytes, which are discussed here.

The signs and symptoms of ringworm conditions are summarized in **table 16.1.**

▶ Causative Agents

There are about 39 species in the genera *Trichophyton*, *Microsporum*, and *Epidermophyton* that can cause the preceding conditions **(figure 16.10).** The causative agent of a given type of ringworm varies from one geographic location to another and is not restricted to a particular genus and species.

Diagnosis of tinea of the scalp caused by some species is aided by use of a long-wave ultraviolet lamp that causes infected hairs to fluoresce. Samples of hair, skin scrapings, and nail debris treated with heated potassium hydroxide (KOH) show a thin, branching fungal mycelium if infection is present.

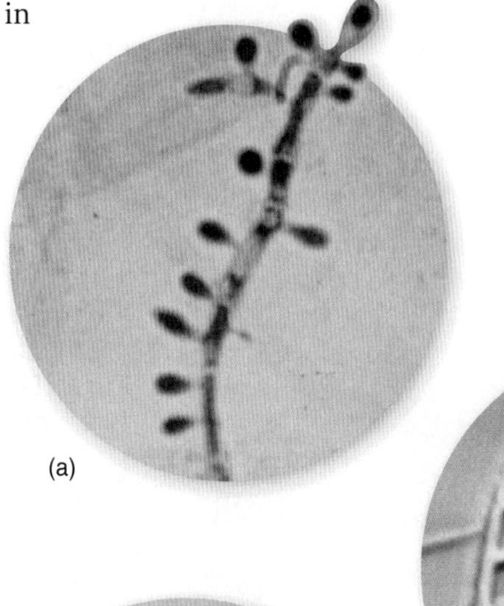

▶ Pathogenesis and Virulence Factors

The dermatophytes have the ability to invade and digest keratin, which is naturally abundant in the cells of the stratum corneum. The fungi do not invade deeper epidermal layers.

▶ Transmission and Epidemiology

Transmission of the fungi that cause these diseases is via direct and indirect contact with other humans or with infected animals. Some of these fungi can be acquired from the soil.

Therapy is usually a topical antifungal agent. Ointments containing tolnaftate, miconazole, itraconazole, terbinafine, or thiabendazole are applied regularly for several weeks. Some drugs work by speeding up loss of the outer skin layer.

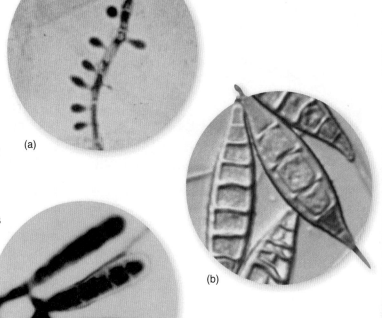

(a) (b) (c)

Figure 16.10 Examples of dermatophyte spores. **(a)** Regular, numerous microconidia of *Trichophyton*. **(b)** Macroconidia of *Microsporum canis*, a cause of ringworm in cats, dogs, and humans. **(c)** Smooth-surfaced macroconidia in clusters characteristic of *Epidermophyton*.

Superficial Mycoses

Agents of **superficial mycoses** involve the outer epidermal surface and are ordinarily innocuous infections with cosmetic rather than inflammatory effects. Tinea versicolor is caused by the yeast genus *Malassezia*, a genus that has at least 10 species living on human skin. The yeast feeds on the high oil content of the skin glands. Even though these yeasts are very common (carried by nearly 100% of humans tested), in some people its growth elicits mild, chronic scaling and interferes with production of pigment by melanocytes.

Disease Table 16.8 Cutaneous and Superficial Mycoses

Disease	Cutaneous Infections	Superficial Infections (Tinea Versicolor)
Causative Organism(s)	*Trichophyton, Microsporum, Epidermophyton*	*Malassezia* spp.
Most Common Modes of Transmission	Direct and indirect contact, vehicle (soil)	Endogenous "normal biota"
Virulence Factors	Ability to degrade keratin, invoke hypersensitivity	–
Culture/Diagnosis	Microscopic examination, KOH staining, culture	Usually clinical, KOH can be used
Prevention	Avoid contact	None
Treatment	Topical tolnaftate, itraconazole, terbinafine, miconazole, thiabendazole	Topical antifungals

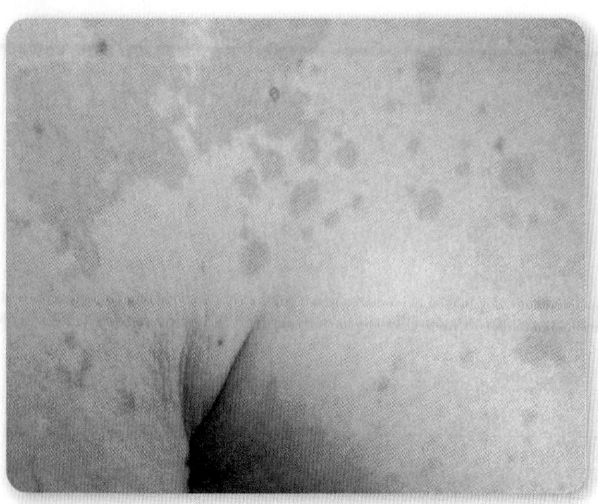

Figure 16.11 Tinea versicolor. Mottled, discolored skin pigmentation is characteristic of superficial skin infection by *Malassezia furfur.*

The trunk, face, and limbs may take on a mottled appearance **(figure 16.11).** Other superficial skin conditions in which *Malassezia* is implicated are folliculitis, psoriasis, and seborrheic dermatitis (dandruff).

ASSESS YOUR PROGRESS

4. List the possible causative agents, modes of transmission, virulence factors, diagnostic techniques, and prevention/treatment for the highlighted condition, maculopapular rash diseases.
5. Discuss important features of the other infectious skin diseases. These are impetigo, cellulitis, staphylococcal scalded skin syndrome, vesicular/pustular rash diseases, wartlike eruptions, large pustular skin lesions, and cutaneous mycoses.
6. Provide an update of the status of MRSA infections in the United States.
7. Discuss the relative dangers of rubella and rubeola viruses in different populations.

16.4 The Surface of the Eye and Its Defenses

The eye is a complex organ with many different tissue types, but for the purposes of this chapter we consider only its exposed surfaces, the *conjunctiva* and the *cornea* **(figure 16.12).** The **conjunctiva** is a very thin membranelike tissue that covers the eye (except for the cornea) and lines the eyelids. It secretes an oil- and mucus-containing fluid that lubricates and protects the eye surface. The **cornea** is the dome-shaped central portion of the eye lying over the iris (the colored part of the eye). It has five to six layers of epithelial cells that can regenerate quickly if they are superficially damaged. It has been called "the windshield of the eye."

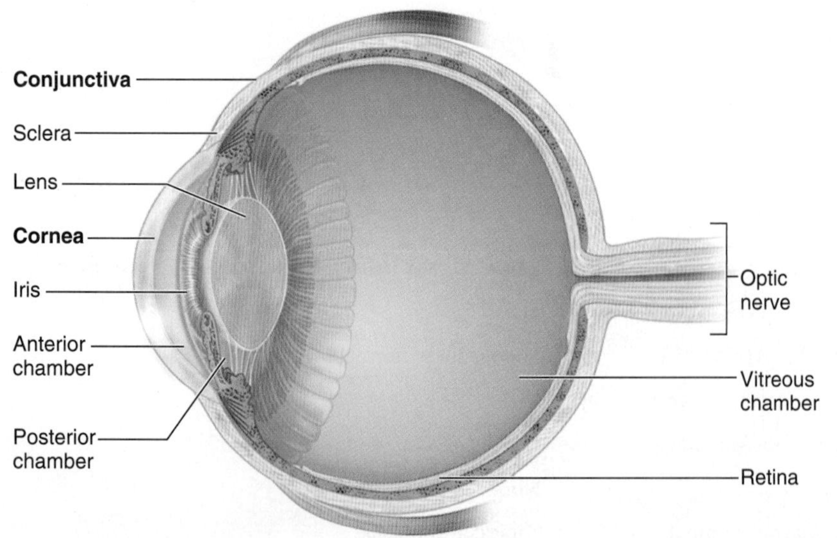

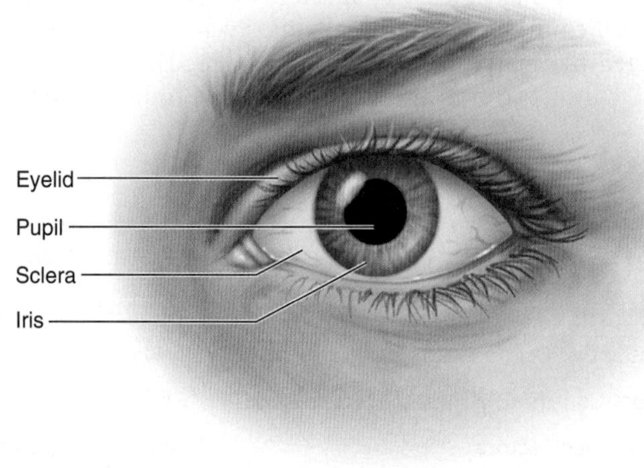

Figure 16.12 The anatomy of the eye.

The eye's best defense is the film of tears, which consists of an aqueous fluid, oil, and mucus. The tears are formed in the lacrimal gland at the outer and upper corner of each eye **(figure 16.13)**, and they drain into the lacrimal duct at the inner corner. Tears contain sugars, lysozyme, and lactoferrin. These last two substances have antimicrobial properties. The mucus layer contains proteins and sugars and plays a protective role. And, of course, the flow of the tear film prevents the attachment of microorganisms to the eye surface.

Because the eye's primary function is vision, anything that hinders vision would be counterproductive. For that reason, inflammation does not occur in the eye as readily as it does elsewhere in the body. Flooding the eye with fluid containing a large number of light-diffracting objects, such as lymphocytes and phagocytes, in response to every irritant would mean almost constantly blurred vision. So even though the eyes are relatively vulnerable to infection (not being covered by keratinized epithelium), the evolution of the vertebrate eye has of necessity favored reduced innate immunity. This characteristic is sometimes known as **immune privilege.**

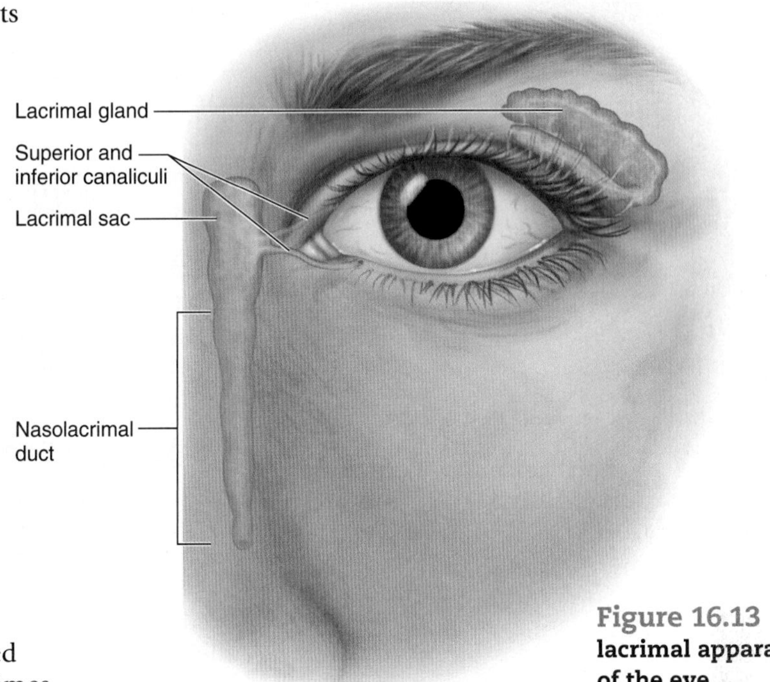

Figure 16.13 The lacrimal apparatus of the eye.

ASSESS YOUR PROGRESS

8. Describe the important anatomical features of the eye.
9. List the natural defenses present in the eye.

16.5 Normal Biota of the Eye

The normal biota of the eye—so far as is currently known—is generally sparse. When people are tested, up to 20% have no recoverable (i.e., culturable) bacteria in their eyes. The few bacteria that are found resemble the normal biota of the skin—namely, staphylococci, streptococci, *Corynebacterium*, and some yeast. *Neisseria* species can also live on the surface of the eye.

Defenses and Normal Biota of the Eyes

	Defenses	Normal Biota
Eyes	Mucus in conjunctiva and in tears, lysozyme and lactoferrin in tears	Sparsely populated with *Staphylococcus aureus, Staphylococcus epidermidis,* and *Corynebacterium* species

ASSESS YOUR PROGRESS

10. List the types of normal biota presently known to occupy the eye.

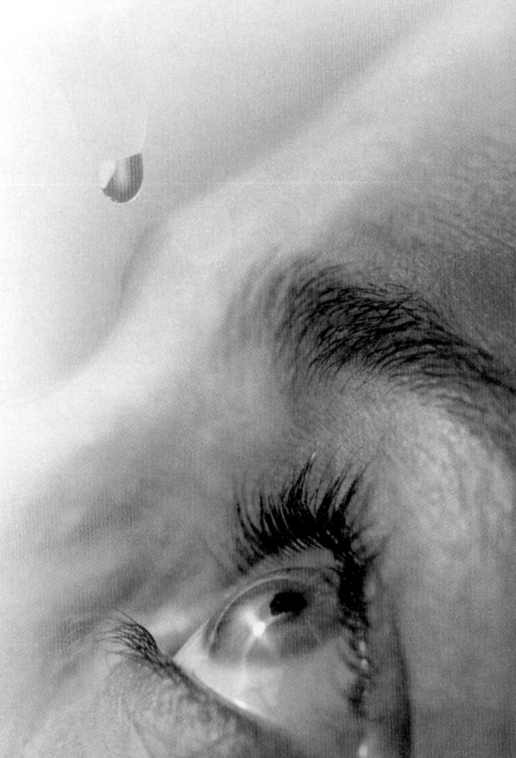

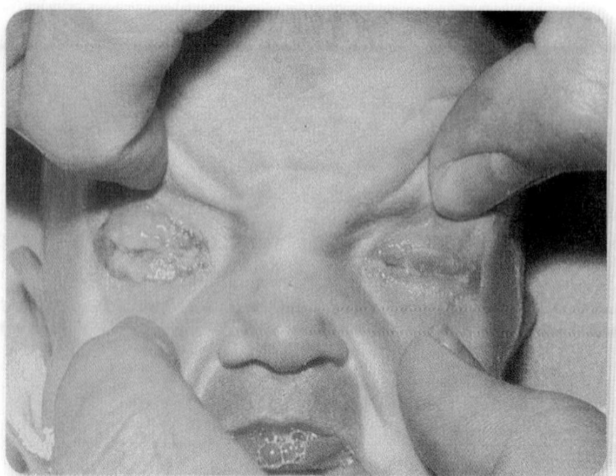

Figure 16.14 Neonatal conjunctivitis.

16.6 Eye Diseases Caused by Microorganisms

In this section, we cover the infectious agents that cause diseases of the surface structures of the eye—namely, the cornea and conjunctiva.

HIGHLIGHT DISEASE

Conjunctivitis

Infection of the conjunctiva is relatively common. It can be caused by specific microorganisms that have a predilection for eye tissues, by contaminants that proliferate due to the presence of a contact lens or an eye injury, or by accidental inoculation of the eye by a traumatic event.

Signs and Symptoms

Just as there are many different causes of conjunctivitis, there are many different clinical presentations. Most bacterial infections produce a milky discharge, whereas viral infections tend to produce a clear watery exudate. It is typical for a patient to wake up in the morning with an eye "glued" shut by secretions that have accumulated and solidified through the night. Some conjunctivitis cases are caused by an allergic response, and these often produce copious amounts of clear fluid as well. The informal name for common conjunctivitis is pinkeye.

Causative Agents and Their Transmission

Cases of neonatal eye infection with *Neisseria gonorrhoeae* or *Chlamydia trachomatis* are usually transmitted vertically from a genital tract infection in the mother (discussed in chapter 21). Either one of these eye infections can lead to serious eye damage if not treated promptly **(figure 16.14).** Note that herpes simplex can also cause neonatal conjunctivitis, but it is often accompanied by generalized herpes infection (covered in chapter 21).

Bacterial conjunctivitis in other age groups is most commonly caused by *Staphylococcus epidermidis, Streptococcus pyogenes,* or *Streptococcus pneumoniae,* although *Haemophilus influenzae* and *Moraxella* species are also frequent causes. *N. gonorrhoeae* and *C. trachomatis* can also cause conjunctivitis in adults. These infections may result from autoinoculation from a genital infection or from sexual activity, although *N. gonorrhoeae* can be part of the normal biota in the respiratory tract. A wide variety of bacteria, fungi, and protozoa can contaminate contact lenses and lens cases and then be transferred to the eye, resulting in disease that may be very serious. Viral conjunctivitis is commonly caused by adenoviruses, although other viruses may be responsible. Both bacterial and viral conjunctivitis are transmissible by direct and even indirect contact and are usually highly contagious.

Prevention and Treatment

Newborn children in the United States are administered antimicrobials in their eyes after delivery to prevent neonatal conjunctivitis from either *N. gonorrhoeae* or *C. trachomatis.* Treatment of those infections, if they are suspected, is started before lab results are available and usually is accomplished with erythromycin, both topical and oral. If *N. gonorrhoeae* is confirmed, oral therapy is usually switched to ceftriaxone. If antibacterial therapy is prescribed for other conjunctivitis cases, it should cover all possible bacterial pathogens. Ciprofloxacin eyedrops are a common choice. Erythromycin or gentamicin are also often used. Because conjunctivitis is usually diagnosed based on clinical signs, a physician may prescribe prophylactic antibiotics even if a viral cause is suspected. If symptoms don't begin improving within 48 hours, more extensive diagnosis may be performed. **Disease Table 16.9** lists the most common causes of conjunctivitis; keep in mind that other microorganisms can also cause conjunctival infections.

NCLEX® PREP

4. Conjunctivitis may cause
   a. reddened conjunctiva.
   b. watering of the eye.
   c. mild pain.
   d. photophobia.
   e. all of the above.

Disease Table 16.9 Conjunctivitis

Disease	Neonatal Conjunctivitis	Bacterial Conjunctivitis	Viral Conjunctivitis
Causative Organism(s)	*Chlamydia trachomatis* or *Neisseria gonorrhoeae*	*Streptococcus pyogenes, Streptococcus pneumoniae, Staphylococcus aureus, Haemophilus influenzae, Moraxella,* and also *Neisseria gonorrhoeae, Chlamydia trachomatis*	Adenoviruses and others
Most Common Modes of Transmission	Vertical	Direct, indirect contact	Direct, indirect contact
Virulence Factors	–	–	–
Culture/Diagnosis	Gram stain and culture	Clinical diagnosis	Clinical diagnosis
Prevention	Screen mothers; apply antibiotic or silver nitrate to newborn eyes	Hygiene	Hygiene
Treatment	Topical and oral antibiotics	Broad-spectrum topical antibiotic, often ciprofloxacin	None, although antibiotics often given because type of infection not distinguished
Distinctive Features	In babies <28 days old	Mucopurulent discharge	Serous (clear) discharge

Keratitis

Keratitis is a more serious eye infection than conjunctivitis. Invasion of deeper eye tissues occurs and can lead to complete corneal destruction. Any microorganism can cause this condition, especially after trauma to the eye, but this section focuses on one of the more common causes: herpes simplex virus. It can cause keratitis in the absence of predisposing trauma.

The usual cause of herpetic keratitis is a "misdirected" reactivation of (oral) herpes simplex virus type 1 (HSV-1). The virus, upon reactivation, travels into the ophthalmic rather than the mandibular branch of the trigeminal nerve. Infections with HSV-2 can also occur as a result of a sexual encounter with the virus or transfer of the virus from the genital to eye area. Blindness due to herpes is the leading infectious cause of blindness in the United States.

The viral condition is treated with trifluridine or acyclovir or both.

Disease Table 16.10 Keratitis

Causative Organism(s)	Herpes simplex virus	Miscellaneous microorganisms
Most Common Modes of Transmission	Reactivation of latent virus, although primary infections can occur in the eye	Often traumatic introduction (parenteral)
Virulence Factors	Latency	Various
Culture/Diagnosis	Usually clinical diagnosis; viral culture or PCR if needed	Various
Prevention	–	–
Treatment	Topical trifluridine and/or oral acyclovir	Specific antimicrobials

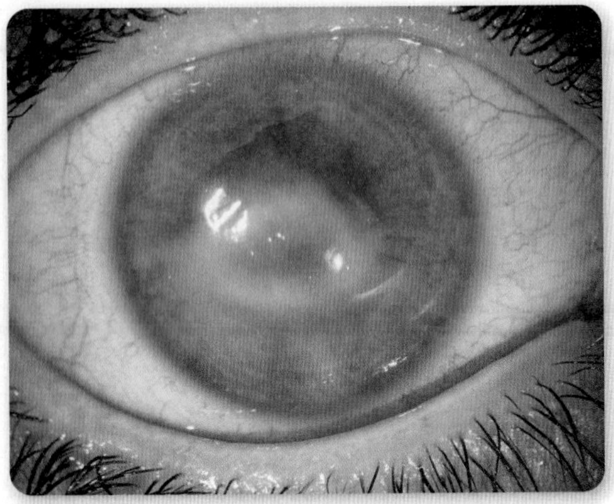

Figure 16.15 ***Acanthamoeba* infection of the eye.**

In the last few years, another form of keratitis has been increasing in incidence. An amoeba called *Acanthamoeba* has been causing serious keratitis cases, especially in people who wear contact lenses. This free-living amoeba is everywhere—it lives in tap water, freshwater lakes, and the like. The infections are usually associated with less-than-rigorous contact lens hygiene, or previous trauma to the eye **(figure 16.15)**.

ASSESS YOUR PROGRESS

11. List the possible causative agents, modes of transmission, virulence factors, diagnostic techniques, and prevention/treatment for the highlighted condition, conjunctivitis.

12. Discuss important features of keratitis caused by either HSV or by *Acanthamoeba*.

CASE FILE WRAP-UP

Parvovirus B19 is the cause of fifth disease.

The physician examined Robby and determined that he is suffering from fifth disease, a common childhood viral illness. It is also referred to as "slapped-cheek" disease because of the characteristic appearance of the cheeks of children with this illness. Robby's symptoms—mild fever, malaise, and a maculopapular rash prominent on the trunk and limbs—is typical of the illness. There is no specific treatment; the illness runs its course in 5 to 10 days, although the rash may reappear intermittently even after the illness has subsided. Fifth disease is very contagious. Most adults will have been exposed to the virus and will be immune as adults.

Summing Up

Taxonomic Organization Microorganisms Causing Diseases of the Skin and Eyes

Microorganism	Pronunciation	Location of Disease Table
Gram-positive bacteria		
Staphylococcus aureus	staf″-uh-lo-kok′-us are′-ee-us	Impetigo, p. 440 Cellulitis, p. 441 Scalded skin syndrome, p. 442
Streptococcus pyogenes	strep″-tuh-kok′-us pie′-ah″-gen-eez	Impetigo, p. 440 Cellulitis, p. 441 Scarlet fever, p. 437
Bacillus anthracis	buh-sill′-us an′-thray″-sus	Cutaneous anthrax, p. 447
Gram-negative bacteria		
Neisseria gonorrhoeae	nye-seer″-ee-uh′ gon′-uh-ree″-uh	Neonatal conjunctivitis, p. 453
Chlamydia trachomatis	kluh-mi″-dee-uh′ truh-koh′-muh-tis	Neonatal conjunctivitis, p. 453
DNA viruses		
Human herpesvirus 3	hew′-mun hur″-peez-vie′-russ	Chickenpox, shingles, p. 444
Variola virus	vayr′-ee-oh″-luh vie′-russ	Smallpox, p. 444
Parvovirus B19	par″-voh-vie′-russ	Fifth disease, p. 437
Human herpesvirus 6 and 7	hew′-mun hur″-peez-vie′-russ	Roseola, p. 437
Human papillomavirus	hew′-mun pap′-uh-loh″-muh-vie′-russ	Warts, p. 446
Molluscum contagiosum virus	muh-lus′-cum cun-tay′-gee-oh″-sum vie′-russ	Warts and wartlike eruptions, p. 446
Herpes simplex virus	hur″-peez sim′-plex vie′-russ	Keratitis, p. 454
RNA viruses		
Measles virus	mee′-zulls vie′-russ	Measles, p. 437
Rubella virus	roo′-bell″-uh vie′-russ	Rubella, p. 437
Fungi		
Trichophyton	try″-ko-fie′-tahn	Ringworm, p. 449
Microsporum	my″-krow′-spoor′-um	Ringworm, p. 449
Epidermophyton	ep′-uh-dur″-moh-fie′-tahn	Ringworm, p. 449
Malassezia spp.	mal′-uh-see″-zee-uh	Superficial mycoses, p. 449
Protozoa		
Leishmania spp.	leesh-mayn″-ee-uh	Leishmaniasis, p. 447
Acanthamoeba	ay-kanth″-uh-mee′-buh	Keratitis, p. 454

Inside the Clinic

Flesh-Eating Disease: Necrotizing Fasciitis

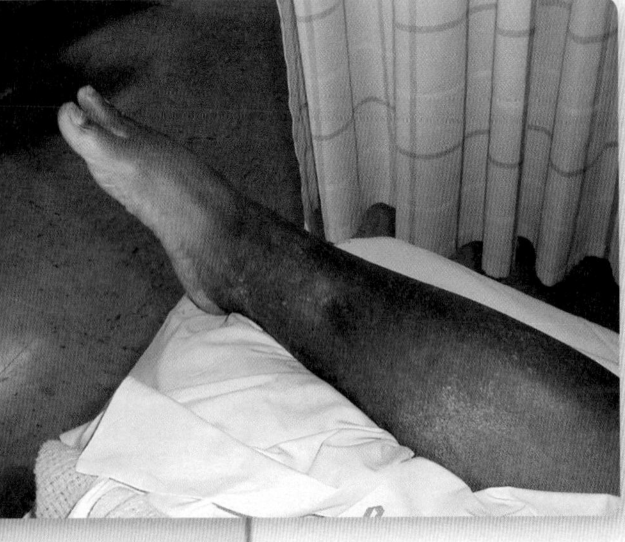

In 2008 in Winnipeg, Manitoba, 12 cases of necrotizing fasciitis were diagnosed among Winnipeg's homeless population. Nine of the twelve people infected had experienced a recent injury, including one person who had suffered burns. Manitoba health officials stated that the province had recorded 16 cases of necrotizing fasciitis in 2008, a fourfold increase in the number of cases typically reported each year. A total of five people died. Health officials pointed out that lack of hygiene, overcrowding in shelters, and the homeless population's tendency not to seek treatment for illness were likely all factors that may have caused the homeless population to be at higher risk for the deadly disease. Statistics for the province show that the numbers of cases of the disease have been increasing in recent years: 56 cases were reported in the 2-year period spanning 2006 to 2008. In contrast, there were only 12 cases between 2004 and 2005.

Numbers like these tend to attract scrutiny. Necrotizing fasciitis has received a lot of attention in recent years. The disease is sometimes referred to as flesh-eating disease, although this is a misnomer. The bacteria involved in necrotizing fasciitis do not actually "eat" flesh; rather, the bacteria digest connective tissue in the skin, and the toxins released by the bacteria poison the epidermal and dermal tissues. As the flesh dies, it separates from surrounding tissue and sloughs off, and the bacteria spread into the deeper tissues, such as the muscle.

Two pathogenic bacteria that cause necrotizing fasciitis are streptococci and staphylococci, commonly found on the skin. Either (or both) of these bacteria can be introduced into body tissues via small breaks in the skin, such as abrasions or cuts, where they begin to reproduce rapidly. Why are these bacteria so potentially deadly? Both of these bacteria possess an array of superantigens. Superantigens are capable of stimulating a huge array of T cells, even those with the incorrect specificity. As a result, cytokines such as tumor necrosis factor and interleukins are released in massive numbers. This cytokine "storm" can result in extensive damage and death. *S. pyogenes* and *S. aureus* both possess these dangerous properties and are often implicated in cases of flesh-eating disease.

Necrotizing fasciitis can progress rapidly. Initially, patients may complain of pain, which may be out of proportion to the outward appearance of the skin. If the infection affects superficial tissue, swelling and signs of inflammation may progress rapidly. Infections involving deeper tissues may not show outward signs of inflammation initially. Skin may eventually turn a blue or purplish color and blisters may form. Subcutaneous tissues eventually die. Fever is typical, and the affected person will appear to be very ill. Without rapid recognition and treatment, the disease is often fatal. Those who survive may lose affected limbs. People with compromised immune systems, chronic diseases such as diabetes, and those who abuse alcohol and drugs are at higher risk for the disease.

Infectious Diseases Affecting
The Skin and Eyes

Keratitis

Herpes simplex virus
Acanthamoeba

Large Pustular Skin Lesions

Leishmania species
Bacillus anthracis

Staphylococcal Scalded Skin Syndrome

Staphylococcus aureus

Maculopapular Rash Diseases

Measles virus
Rubella virus
Parvovirus B19
Human herpesvirus 6 or 7

Impetigo

Staphylococcus aureus
Streptococcus pyogenes

Wart and Wartlike Eruptions

Human papillomaviruses
Molluscum contagiosum viruses

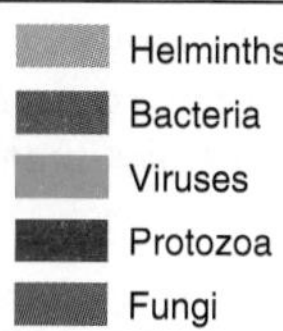

Conjunctivitis

Neisseria gonorrhoeae
Chlamydia trachomatis
Various bacteria
Various viruses

Vesicular or Pustular Rash Disease

Human herpesvirus 3 (varicella)
Variola virus

Cellulitis

Staphylococcus aureus
Streptococcus pyogenes

Cutaneous and Superficial Mycoses

Trichophyton
Microsporum
Epidermophyton
Malassezia

CONNECT®

System Summary Figure 16.16

Chapter Summary

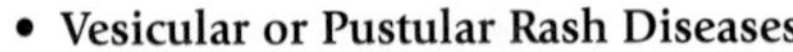

16.1 The Skin and Its Defenses

- The epidermal cells contain the protein keratin, which "waterproofs" the skin and protects it from microbial invasion.
- Other defenses include antimicrobial peptides, low pH sebum, high salt and lysozyme in sweat, and antimicrobial peptides.

16.2 Normal Biota of the Skin

- The skin has a diverse array of microbes as its normal biota, especially gram-positive cocci, corynebacteria, and *Janthinobacterium*.

16.3 Skin Diseases Caused by Microorganisms

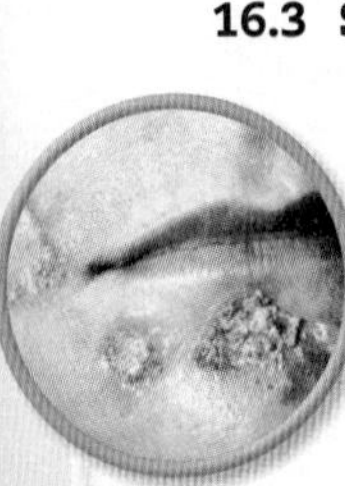

- Maculopapular Rash Diseases
  - **Measles:** Measles or *rubeola* results in characteristic red maculopapular exanthem that erupts on the head and then progresses to the trunk and extremities until most of the body is covered. The MMR vaccine (measles, mumps, and rubella) contains attenuated measles virus.
  - **Rubella:** Also known as German measles, can appear in two forms: postnatal and congenital (prenatal) infection of the fetus. The MMR vaccination contains protection from rubella.
  - **Fifth Disease:** Also called *erythema infectiosum*, fifth disease is a very mild but highly contagious disease that often results in characteristic "slapped-cheek" appearance. Causative agent is parvovirus B19.
  - **Roseola:** Can result in a maculopapular rash; is caused by a human herpesvirus called HHV-6 and sometimes by HHV-7.
  - **Scarlet Fever:** May accompany infection of throat or skin with *Streptococcus pyogenes*.
- **Impetigo:** A highly contagious superficial infection that can cause skin to peel or flake off. Causative organisms can be either *Staphylococcus aureus* or *Streptococcus pyogenes* or both.
- **Cellulitis:** Results from a fast-spreading infection of the dermis and subcutaneous tissue below. Most commonly caused by *S. aureus* or *S. pyogenes*.
- **Staphylococcal Scalded Skin Syndrome (SSSS):** Caused by *S. aureus*. Affects mostly newborns and babies and is similar to a systemic form of impetigo.
- Vesicular or Pustular Rash Diseases
  - **Chickenpox:** Skin lesions progress quickly from macules and papules to itchy vesicles filled with clear fluid.
  - **Shingles:** Chickenpox virus becomes latent in the ganglia and may reemerge to cause shingles. Human herpesvirus 3 causes chickenpox, as well as herpes zoster or shingles.
  - **Smallpox:** Naturally occurring smallpox has been eradicated from the world. Causative agent is the variola virus, an enveloped DNA virus.
- **Wartlike Eruptions:** Most common warts are caused by human papillomavirus or a poxvirus, molluscum contagiosum, which causes bumps that may look like warts. Rarely, a skin wart can become malignant when caused by a particular type of HPV.
- Large Pustular Skin Lesions
  - **Leishmaniasis:** A zoonosis transmitted by the female sand fly when it ingests the host's blood.
  - **Cutaneous Anthrax:** Most common and least dangerous version of infections with *Bacillus anthracis*.
- **Ringworm (Cutaneous Mycoses):** A group of fungi collectively termed dermatophytes cause mycoses in the nonliving epidermal tissues, hair, and nails. Often called "ringworm." Species in the genera *Trichophyton*, *Microsporum*, and *Epidermophyton* are the cause.
- **Superficial Mycoses:** Agents of superficial mycoses, such as *Malassezia* species, involve only the outer epidermis.

16.4 The Surface of the Eye and Its Defenses

- The flushing action of the tears, which contain lysozyme and lactoferrin, is the major protective feature of the eye.

16.5 Normal Biota of the Eye

- The eye has similar microbes as the skin but in lower numbers.

16.6 Eye Diseases Caused by Microorganisms

- **Conjunctivitis:** Infection of the conjunctiva (commonly called pinkeye) can be caused by either bacteria or viruses. Both bacterial and viral conjunctivitis are highly contagious.
- **Keratitis:** A more serious eye infection than conjunctivitis. Herpes simplex viruses (HSV-1 and HSV-2) and *Acanthamoeba* cause two different forms of the disease.

Multiple-Choice Questions Knowledge and Comprehension

Select the correct answer from the answers provided.

1. An effective treatment for a cutaneous mycosis like tinea pedis would be
   a. penicillin.
   b. miconazole.
   c. griseofulvin.
   d. doxycycline.

2. What is the antimicrobial enzyme found in sweat, tears, and saliva that can specifically break down peptidoglycan?
   a. lysozyme
   b. beta-lactamase
   c. catalase
   d. coagulase

3. Which of the following is probably the most important defense factor for skin?
   a. phagocytes
   b. sebum
   c. dryness
   d. antimicrobial peptides
4. Name the organism(s) most commonly associated with cellulitis.
   a. *Staphylococcus aureus*
   b. *Propionibacterium acnes*
   c. *Streptococcus pyogenes*
   d. both a and b
   e. both a and c
5. Herpesviruses can cause all of the following diseases, *except*
   a. chickenpox.
   b. shingles.
   c. keratitis.
   d. smallpox.
   e. roseola.
6. Which disease is incorrectly matched with the causative agent?
   a. viral conjunctivitis/adenovirus
   b. shingles/adenovirus
   c. smallpox/variola virus
   d. warts/*Staphylococcus aureus*
7. Dermatophytes are fungi that infect the epidermal tissue by invading and attacking
   a. collagen.
   b. keratin.
   c. fibroblasts.
   d. sebaceous glands.
8. Poor contact lens hygiene is likely to get you a case of
   a. herpetic keratitis.
   b. *Wolbachia* infection.
   c. *Acanthamoeba* keratitis.
   d. ophthalmic gonorrhea.

Critical Thinking Application and Analysis

***Critical thinking* is the ability to reason and solve problems using facts and concepts. These questions can be approached from a number of angles and, in most cases, they do not have a single correct answer.**

1. Discuss the reasons why the Human Microbiome Project is a step forward in characterizing normal and pathogenic biota in humans.
2. How is the occurrence of shingles related to chickenpox?
3. Why would antibiotics in the penicillin family be ineffective in treating fungal infections?
4. Smallpox has been widely reported as a possible bioterror weapon. Given what you know about the etiology of the disease and the current state of the world's immunity to smallpox, discuss how effective (or ineffective) a smallpox weapon might be. What kind of defense could be mounted against such an attack?
5. Despite the availability of the measles vaccine, outbreaks of measles still occur. Discuss some of the reasons for these occurrences.

Visual Connections Synthesis

This question connects previous images to a new concept.

1. **From chapter 11, figure 11.3.** How does this figure help explain impetigo caused by *Staphylococcus aureus* or *Streptococcus pyogenes?*

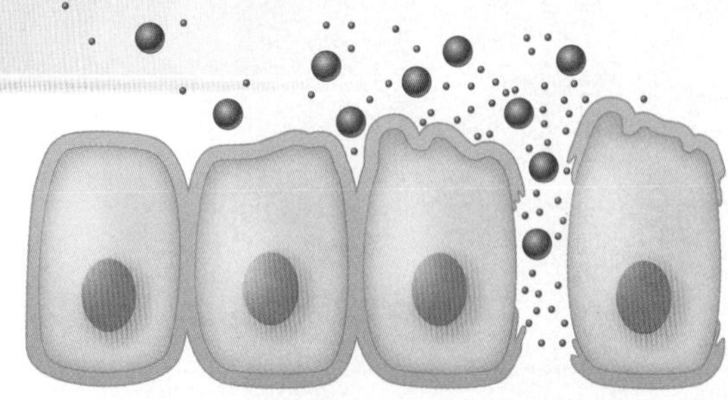

An Unanticipated Complication

While working on a pediatric unit, I was responsible for caring for Cody, a 7-year-old boy who had been admitted to the unit for treatment of a severe case of otitis media. Cody had been treated for an ear infection 2 weeks previously and had seemed to improve with oral antibiotic therapy. However, shortly after completing the antibiotic regimen, Cody became ill again, spiking a high fever and becoming dehydrated due to vomiting. He was admitted for rehydration and was started on antibiotics for a relapse of otitis media.

Although Cody seemed to improve initially, he did not improve as quickly as he should have. He continued to run a very high fever and was unable to eat. He was lethargic and slept much of the time. When awake, he complained of a headache.

The third day after admission, Cody suffered a seizure. His level of consciousness decreased. This change in condition made his physician suspect that Cody was suffering from more than an ear infection. The doctor ordered blood cultures, a complete blood count (CBC), and electrolytes. He also performed a lumbar puncture. I was surprised when Cody's physician explained to me that he believed Cody had developed bacterial meningitis. Soon after, he was transferred to the pediatric intensive care unit (PICU).

- What symptoms did Cody experience that are consistent with meningitis?
- Why would it be important to know which childhood vaccinations Cody had received?

Case File Wrap-Up appears on page 484.

CHAPTER 17

Infectious Diseases Affecting the Nervous System

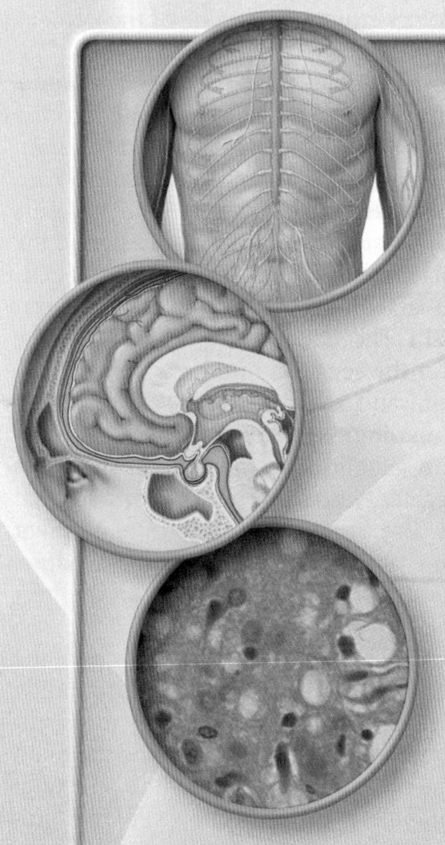

IN THIS CHAPTER...

17.1 The Nervous System and Its Defenses

1. Describe the important anatomical features of the nervous system.
2. List the natural defenses present in the nervous system.

17.2 Normal Biota of the Nervous System

3. Discuss the current state of knowledge of the normal flora of the nervous system.

17.3 Nervous System Diseases Caused by Microorganisms

4. List the possible causative agents, modes of transmission, virulence factors, diagnostic techniques, and prevention/treatment for the highlighted conditions meningitis and poliomyelitis.
5. Identify the most common and also the most deadly of the multiple possible causes of meningitis.
6. Explain the difference between the oral polio vaccine and the inactivated polio vaccine, and under which circumstances each is appropriate.
7. Discuss important features of the diseases most directly involving the brain. These are meningoencephalitis, encephalitis, and subacute encephalitis.
8. Identify which encephalitis-causing viruses you should be aware of in your geographic area.
9. Discuss important features of the other diseases in the nervous system. These are rabies, poliomyelitis, tetanus, and botulism.

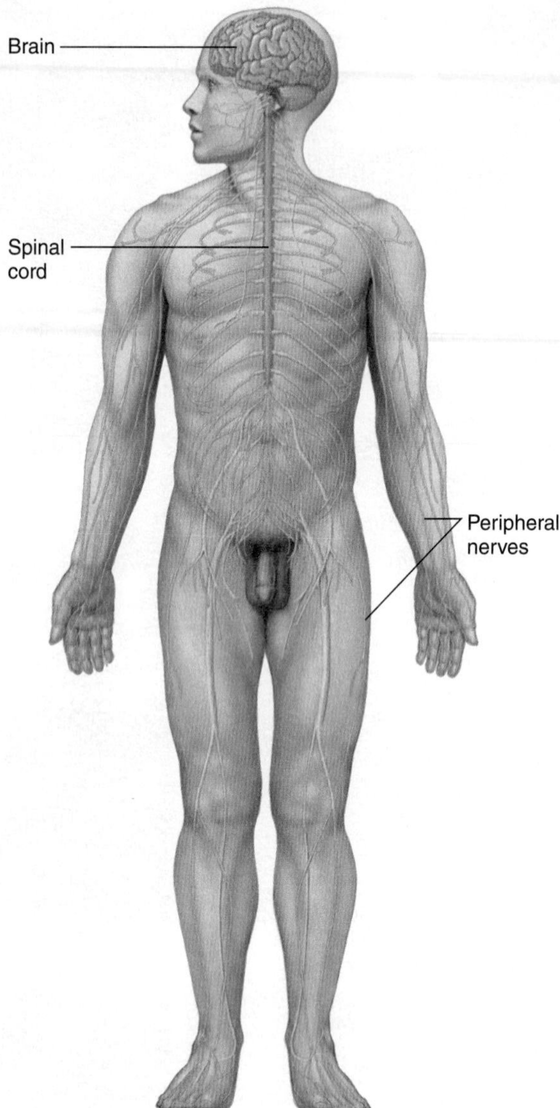

Figure 17.1 Nervous system. The central nervous system and the peripheral nerves.

17.1 The Nervous System and Its Defenses

The nervous system has two component parts: the central nervous system (CNS), consisting of the brain and spinal cord, and the peripheral nervous system (PNS), which contains the nerves that emanate from the brain and spinal cord to sense organs and to the periphery of the body **(figure 17.1)**. The nervous system performs three important functions—sensory, integrative, and motor. The sensory function is fulfilled by sensory receptors at the ends of peripheral nerves. They generate nerve impulses that are transmitted to the central nervous system. There, the impulses are translated, or integrated, into sensation or thought, which in turn drives the motor function. The motor function necessarily involves structures outside of the nervous system, such as muscles and glands.

The brain and the spinal cord are dense structures made up of cells called **neurons**. They are both surrounded by bone. The brain is situated inside the skull, and the spinal cord lies within the spinal column **(figure 17.2)**, which is composed of a stack of interconnected bones called vertebrae. The soft tissue of the brain and spinal cord is encased within a tough casing of three membranes called the **meninges**. The layers of membranes, from outer to inner, are the dura mater, the arachnoid mater, and the pia mater. Between the arachnoid mater and pia mater is the subarachnoid space (i.e., the space under the arachnoid mater). The subarachnoid space is filled with a clear serumlike fluid called cerebrospinal fluid (CSF). The CSF provides nutrition to the CNS, while also providing a liquid cushion for the sensitive brain and spinal cord. The meninges are a common site of infection, and microorganisms can often be found in the CSF when meningeal infection **(meningitis)** occurs.

The PNS consists of nerves and ganglia. A ganglion is a swelling in the nerve where the cell bodies of the neurons congregate. Nerves are bundles of neuronal axons that receive and transmit nerve signals. The axons and dendrites of adjacent neurons communicate with each other over a very small space, called a synapse. Chemicals called neurotransmitters are released from one cell and act on the next cell in the synapse.

The defenses of the nervous system are mainly structural. The bony casings of the brain and spinal cord protect them from traumatic injury. The cushion of surrounding CSF also serves a protective function. The entire nervous system is served by the vascular system, but the interface between the blood vessels serving the brain and the brain itself is different from that of other areas of the body and provides a third structural protection. The cells that make up the walls of the blood vessels allow very few molecules to pass through. In other parts of the body, there is freer passage of ions, sugars, and other metabolites through the walls of blood vessels. The restricted permeability of blood vessels in the brain is called the **blood-brain barrier**, and it prohibits most microorganisms from passing into the central nervous system. The drawback of this phenomenon is that drugs and antibiotics are difficult to introduce into the CNS also.

The CNS is considered an "immunologically privileged" site. These sites are able to mount only a partial, or at least a different, immune response when exposed to immunologic challenge. The functions of the CNS are so vital for the life of an organism that even temporary damage that could potentially result from "normal" immune responses would be very detrimental. The uterus and parts of the eye are other immunologically privileged sites. Specialized cells in the central nervous system perform defensive functions. Microglia are a type of cell having phagocytic capabilities, and brain macrophages also exist in the CNS, although the activity of both of these types of cells is thought to be less than that of phagocytic cells elsewhere in the body.

NCLEX® PREP

1. The term "immunologically privileged" means that
   - **a.** a site can mount only a partial immune response when faced with an immunologic challenge.
   - **b.** the CNS is impervious to microorganisms.
   - **c.** a barrier (such as the blood-brain barrier) protects the CNS against all microorganisms.
   - **d.** the immune response of the brain is superior to that of other body sites.

ASSESS YOUR PROGRESS

1. Describe the important anatomical features of the nervous system.
2. List the natural defenses present in the nervous system.

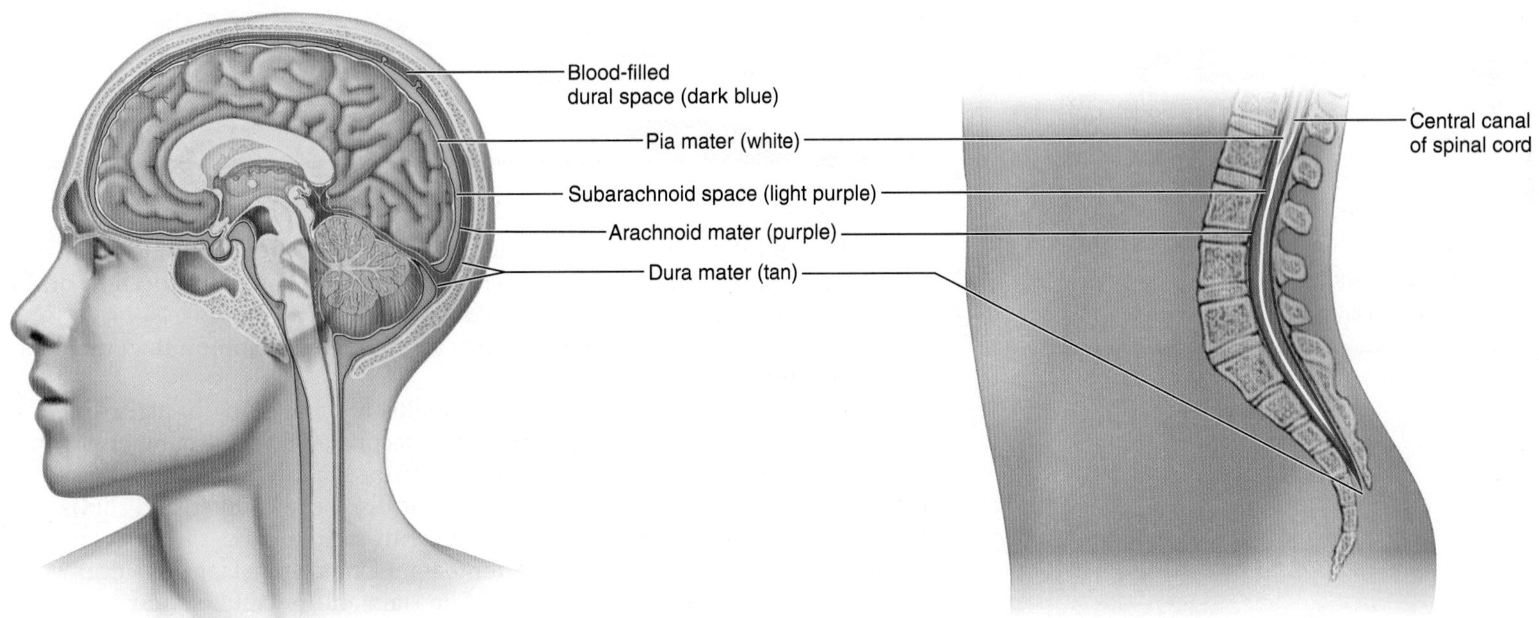

Figure 17.2 **Detailed anatomy of the brain and spinal cord.**

17.2 Normal Biota of the Nervous System

It is still believed that there is no normal biota in either the CNS or PNS, and that finding microorganisms of any type in these tissues represents a deviation from the healthy state. Viruses such as herpes simplex live in a dormant state in the nervous system between episodes of acute disease, but they are not considered normal biota. The Human Microbiome Project is not sampling this system at the present time.

Nervous System Defenses and Normal Biota

	Defenses	Normal Biota
Nervous System	Bony structures, blood-brain barrier, microglial cells, and macrophages	None

ASSESS YOUR PROGRESS

3. Discuss the current state of knowledge of the normal flora of the nervous system.

NCLEX® PREP

2. The central nervous system
   a. consists of the brain and spinal cord.
   b. receives signals (generated nerve impulses) and translates them, resulting in sensation or thought, which drives motor function.
   c. is protected by bone (skull and spinal column).
   d. has three membranes called meninges, which encase the soft tissues of the brain and spinal cord.
   e. all of the above

NCLEX® PREP

3. *N. meningitidis* counters the body's defenses with
   a. IgA protease.
   b. a capsule.
   c. spore formation.
   d. both a and b.
   e. both b and c.

17.3 Nervous System Diseases Caused by Microorganisms

HIGHLIGHT DISEASE

Meningitis

Meningitis, an inflammation of the meninges, is an excellent example of an anatomical syndrome. Many different microorganisms can cause an infection of the meninges, and they produce a similar constellation of symptoms. Noninfectious causes of meningitis exist as well, but they are much less common than the infections listed here.

The more serious forms of acute meningitis are caused by bacteria, but it is thought that their entrance to the CNS is often facilitated by coinfection or previous infection with respiratory viruses. Meningitis in neonates is most often caused by different microorganisms than those causing the disease in children and adults, and therefore it is described separately in the following section.

Whenever meningitis is suspected, lumbar puncture (spinal tap) is performed to obtain CSF, which is then examined by Gram stain and/or culture. Most physicians will begin treatment with a broad-spectrum antibiotic immediately and shift treatment if necessary after a diagnosis has been confirmed.

Signs and Symptoms

No matter the cause, meningitis results in these typical symptoms: headache, painful or stiff neck, fever, and nausea and vomiting. Early symptoms may be mistaken for flu symptoms. Photophobia (sensitivity to light) may also be noted. Skin rashes may be present in specific types of meningitis. There is usually an increased number of white blood cells in the CSF. Specific microorganisms may cause additional, and sometimes characteristic, symptoms, which are described in the individual sections that follow.

Like many other infectious diseases, meningitis can manifest as acute or chronic disease. Some microorganisms are more likely to cause acute meningitis, and others are more likely to cause chronic disease.

In a normal healthy patient, it is very difficult for microorganisms to gain access to the nervous system. Those that are successful usually have specific virulence factors.

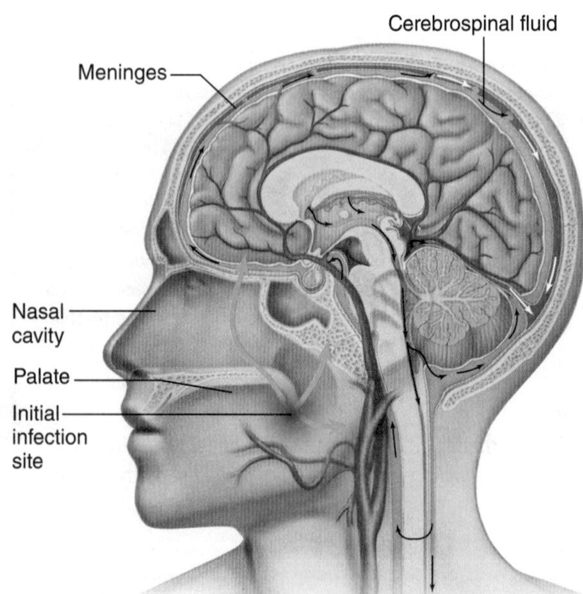

Figure 17.3 Dissemination of the meningococcus from a nasopharyngeal infection. Bacteria spread to the roof of the nasal cavity, which borders a highly vascular area at the base of the brain. From this location, they can enter the blood, causing meningococcemia, and escape into the cerebrospinal fluid, leading to infection of the meninges.

Neisseria meningitidis

Neisseria meningitidis appears as gram-negative diplococci lined up side by side and is commonly known as the meningococcus. It is often associated with epidemic forms of meningitis. This organism causes the most serious form of acute meningitis. Although 12 different strains with different capsular antigens exist, serotypes A, B, and C are responsible for most cases of infection.

Pathogenesis and Virulence Factors

Bacteria entering the blood vessels rapidly penetrate the meninges and produce symptoms of meningitis. The most serious complications of meningococcal infection are due to meningococcemia **(figure 17.3)**, which can accompany meningitis but can also occur on its own. The pathogen releases endotoxin into the generalized circulation, which is a potent stimulus for certain white blood cells. Damage to the blood vessels caused by cytokines released by the white blood cells leads to vascular collapse, hemorrhage, and crops of lesions called **petechiae** (pee-tee'-kee-eye) on the trunk and appendages. A petechia (singular) is a small, 1 to 2 mm red or purple spot that may occur anywhere on the body **(figure 17.4)**.

In a small number of cases, meningococcemia becomes an overwhelming disease with a high mortality rate.

The disease has a sudden onset, marked by fever higher than 40°C, or 104°F, sore throat, chills, delirium, severe widespread areas of bleeding under the skin, shock, and coma. Generalized intravascular clotting, cardiac failure, damage to the adrenal glands, and death can occur within a few hours. The bacterium has an IgA protease and a capsule, both of which counter the body's defenses.

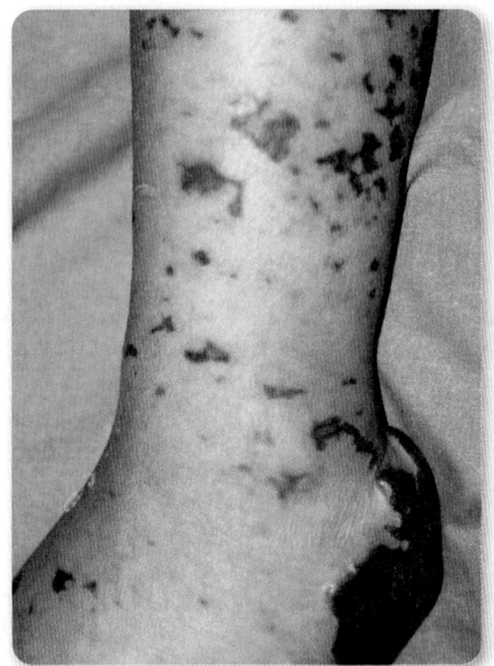

Figure 17.4 Petechiae associated with meningococcal meningitis.

Transmission and Epidemiology

Because meningococci do not survive long in the environment, these bacteria are usually acquired through close contact with secretions or droplets.

Meningococcal meningitis has a sporadic or epidemic incidence in late winter or early spring. The continuing reservoir of infection is humans who harbor the pathogen in the nasopharynx. The carriage state, which can last from a few days to several months, exists in 3% to 30% of the adult population and can exceed 50% in institutional settings. The scene is set for transmission when carriers live in close quarters with nonimmune individuals, as might be expected in families, day care facilities, college dormitories, and military barracks. The highest risk groups are young children (6 to 36 months old) and older children and young adults (10 to 20 years old).

Culture and Diagnosis

Suspicion of bacterial meningitis constitutes a medical emergency, and differential diagnosis must be done with great haste and accuracy. It is most important to confirm (or rule out) meningococcal meningitis, because it can be rapidly fatal. Treatment is usually begun with this bacterium in mind until it can be ruled out. Cerebrospinal fluid, blood, or nasopharyngeal samples are stained and observed directly for the typical gram-negative diplococci. Cultivation may be necessary to differentiate the bacterium from other species. Specific rapid tests are also available for detecting the capsular polysaccharide or the cells directly from specimens without culturing.

It is usually necessary to differentiate this species from normal *Neisseria* that also live in the human body and can be present in infectious fluids. Immediately after collection, specimens are streaked on Modified Thayer-Martin medium (MTM) or chocolate agar and incubated in a high CO_2 atmosphere. Presumptive identification of the genus is obtained by a Gram stain and oxidase testing on isolated colonies **(figure 17.5)**.

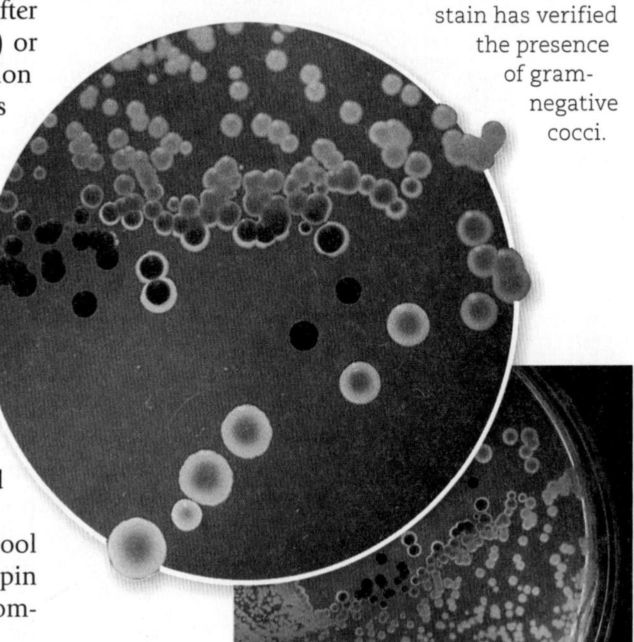

Figure 17.5 The oxidase test. A drop of oxidase reagent is placed on a suspected *Neisseria* or *Branhamella* colony. If the colony reacts with the chemical to produce a purple to black color, it is oxidase-positive; those that remain white to tan are oxidase-negative. Because several species of gram-negative rods are also oxidase-positive, this test is presumptive for these two genera only if a Gram stain has verified the presence of gram-negative cocci.

Prevention and Treatment

The infection rate in most populations is about 1%, so well-developed natural immunity to the meningococcus appears to be the rule. A sort of natural immunization occurs during the early years of life as one is exposed to the meningococcus and its close relatives. Because even treated meningococcemial disease has a mortality rate of up to 15%, it is vital that chemotherapy begin as soon as possible with one or more drugs. Penicillin G is the most potent of the drugs available for meningococcal infections; it is generally given in high doses intravenously. Patients may also require treatment for shock and intravascular clotting.

When family members, medical personnel, or children in day care or school have come in close contact with infected people, preventive therapy with rifampin or tetracycline may be warranted. A new vaccine was licensed in 2005 and is recommended for children at elevated risk during their preadolescent visit.

Disease Table 17.1 Meningitis

Causative Organism(s)	*Neisseria meningitidis*	*Streptococcus pneumoniae*	*Haemophilus influenzae*
Most Common Modes of Transmission	Droplet contact	Droplet contact	Droplet contact
Virulence Factors	Capsule, endotoxin, IgA protease	Capsule, induction of apoptosis, hemolysin and hydrogen peroxide production	Capsule
Culture/Diagnosis	Gram stain/culture of CSF, blood, rapid antigenic tests	Gram stain/culture of CSF	Culture on chocolate agar
Prevention	Conjugated vaccine; rifampin or tetracycline used to protect contacts	Two vaccines: Prevnar (children), and Pneumovax 23 (adults)	Hib vaccine
Treatment	Penicillin G or cefotaxime	Cefotaxime; check for resistance (add vancomycin in that case)	Cefotaxime
Distinctive Features	Petechiae, meningococcemia; most serious form of meningitis	Serious, acute, most common meningitis in adults	Serious, acute, less common since vaccine became available

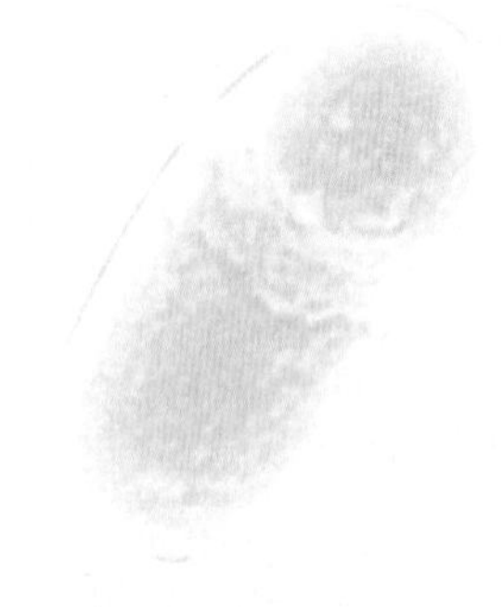

Streptococcus pneumoniae

You will see in chapter 19 that *Streptococcus pneumoniae* causes the majority of bacterial pneumonias. (It is also referred to as the **pneumococcus.**) Meningitis is also caused by this bacterium; indeed, it is the most frequent cause of community-acquired meningitis and is also very severe. It does not cause the petechiae associated with meningococcal meningitis, and that difference is useful diagnostically. As many as 25% of pneumococcal meningitis patients will also have pneumococcal pneumonia. Pneumococcal meningitis is most likely to occur in patients with underlying susceptibility, such as alcoholic patients and patients with sickle-cell disease or those with absent or defective spleen function.

This bacterium is covered thoroughly in chapter 19, because it is a common cause of ear infections and pneumonia. It obviously has the potential to be highly pathogenic, while appearing as normal biota in many people. It can penetrate the respiratory mucosa; gain access to the bloodstream; and then, under certain conditions, enter the meninges.

Like the meningococcus, this bacterium has a polysaccharide capsule that protects it against phagocytosis. It also produces an alpha-hemolysin and hydrogen peroxide, both of which have been shown to induce damage in the CNS. It also appears capable of inducing brain cell apoptosis.

The bacterium is a small gram-positive flattened coccus that appears in end-to-end pairs. It has a distinctive appearance in a Gram stain of cerebrospinal fluid. Staining or culturing the nasopharynx is not useful because it is often normal biota there. Treatment requires a drug to which the bacterium is not resistant; penicillin is therefore not a good choice. Cefotaxime is often used, but drug susceptibilities must always be tested. It is recommended that a steroid be administered 20 minutes prior to antibiotic administration. This will dampen the inflammatory response to cell wall components that are released by antibiotic treatment of the gram-positive bacterium.

As mentioned in chapter 19, two vaccines are available for *S. pneumoniae:* a seven-valent conjugated vaccine (Prevnar), which is now recommended as part of the childhood immunization schedule, and a 23-valent polysaccharide vaccine (Pneumovax 23), which is available for adults.

Listeria monocytogenes	*Cryptococcus neoformans*	*Coccidioides* species	Viruses
Vehicle (food)	Vehicle (air, dust)	Vehicle (air, dust, soil)	Droplet contact
Intracellular growth	Capsule, melanin production	Granuloma (spherule) formation	Lytic infection of host cells
Cold enrichment, rapid methods	Negative staining, biochemical tests, DNA probes	Identification of spherules, cultivation on Sabouraud's agar	Initially, absence of bacteria/fungi/protozoa, followed by viral culture or antigen tests
Cooking food, avoiding unpasteurized dairy products	–	Avoiding airborne spores	–
Ampicillin, trimethoprim-sulfamethoxazole	Amphotericin B and fluconazole	Amphotericin B or oral or IV itraconazole	Usually none (unless specific virus identified and specific antiviral exists)
Asymptomatic in healthy adults; meningitis in neonates, elderly, and immunocompromised	Acute or chronic, most common in AIDS patients	Almost exclusively in endemic regions	Generally milder than bacterial or fungal

Haemophilus influenzae

The meningitis caused by this bacterium is severe. Before the vaccine was introduced in 1988, it was a very common cause of severe meningitis and death. In the course of the last 13 years, meningitis caused by this bacterium is much less common in the United States, a situation that can always change if a lower percentage of people get the vaccine.

Listeria monocytogenes

Listeria monocytogenes is a gram-positive bacterium that ranges in morphology from coccobacilli to long filaments in palisades formation **(figure 17.6).** Cells do not produce capsules or spores and have from one to four flagella. *Listeria* is not fastidious and is resistant to cold, heat, salt, pH extremes, and bile. It grows inside host cells and can move directly from an infected host cell to an adjacent healthy cell.

Listeriosis in healthy adults is often a mild or subclinical infection with nonspecific symptoms of fever, diarrhea, and sore throat. However, listeriosis in elderly or immunocompromised patients, fetuses, and neonates (described later) usually affects the brain and meninges and results in septicemia. (Septicemia is a term that means the multiplication of bacteria in the bloodstream.) The death rate is around 20%. Pregnant women are especially susceptible to infection, which can be transmitted to the infant prenatally when the microbe crosses the placenta or postnatally through the birth canal. Intrauterine infections usually result in premature abortion and fetal death.

Apparently, the primary reservoir is soil and water, and animals, plants, and food are secondary sources of infection. Most cases of listeriosis are associated with ingesting contaminated dairy products, poultry, and meat. Recent epidemics have spurred an in-depth investigation into the prevalence of *L. monocytogenes* in these sources. A 2003 U.S. government report concluded that consumers are exposed to low to moderate levels of *L. monocytogenes* on a regular basis. The pathogen has been isolated in 10% to 15% of ground beef and in 25% to 30% of chicken and turkey carcasses and is also present in 5% to 10% of luncheon meats, hot dogs, and cheeses.

Diagnosing listeriosis is hampered by the difficulty in isolating it. The chances of isolation, however, can be improved by using a procedure called *cold enrichment,*

Figure 17.6 *Listeria monocytogenes.* The bacterium is generally rod shaped. In Gram stains, individual cells tend to stack up in structures called palisades. That arrangement, pointed out here, is more obvious on a gram stain where many more bacteria are seen.

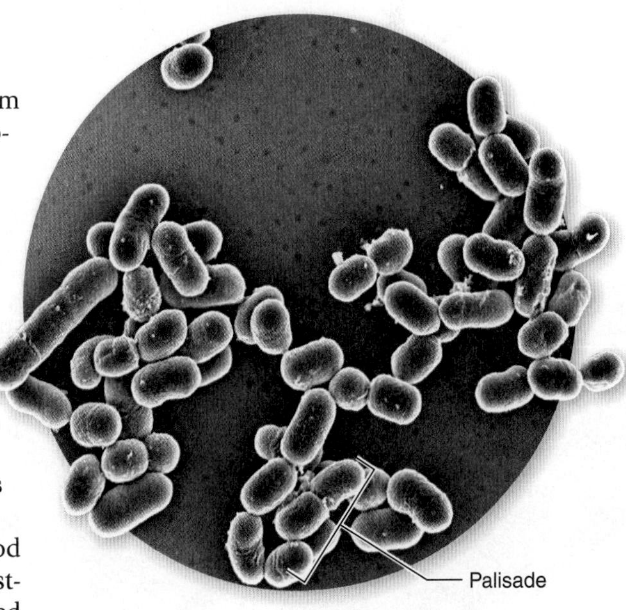

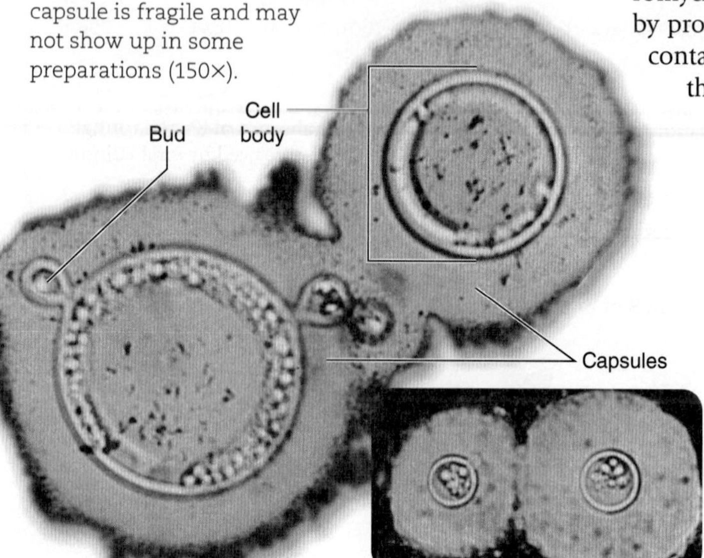

Figure 17.7 *Cryptococcus neoformans* from infected spinal fluid stained negatively with India ink. Halos around the large spherical yeast cells are thick capsules. Also note the buds forming on one cell. Encapsulation is a useful diagnostic sign for cryptococcosis, although the capsule is fragile and may not show up in some preparations (150×).

in which the specimen is held at 4°C and periodically plated onto media, but this procedure can take 4 weeks. Rapid diagnostic kits using ELISA, immunofluorescence, and gene probe technology are now available for direct testing of dairy products and cultures. Antibiotic therapy should be started as soon as listeriosis is suspected. Ampicillin and trimethoprim-sulfamethoxazole are the first choices, followed by erythromycin. Prevention can be improved by adequate pasteurization temperatures and by proper washing, refrigeration, and cooking of foods that are suspected of being contaminated with animal manure or sewage. Pregnant women are cautioned by the U.S. Food and Drug Administration not to eat soft, unpasteurized cheeses.

Cryptococcus neoformans

The fungus *Cryptococcus neoformans* causes a more chronic form of meningitis with a more gradual onset of symptoms, although in AIDS patients the onset may be fast and the course of the disease more acute. It is sometimes classified as a meningoencephalitis (inflammation of both brain and meninges). Headache is the most common symptom, but nausea and neck stiffness are very common. This fungus is a widespread resident of human habitats. It has a spherical to ovoid shape, with small, constricted buds and a large capsule that is important in its pathogenesis **(figure 17.7).**

The primary ecological niche of *C. neoformans* is the bird population. It is prevalent in urban areas where pigeons congregate, and it proliferates in the high-nitrogen environment of droppings that accumulate on pigeon roosts. Masses of dried yeast cells are readily scattered into the air and dust. Its role as an opportunist is supported by evidence that healthy humans have strong resistance to it and that frank (obvious) infection occurs primarily in debilitated patients.

By far the highest rates of cryptococcal meningitis occur among patients with AIDS. This meningitis is frequently fatal. Other conditions that predispose individuals to infection are steroid treatment, diabetes, and cancer. It is not considered communicable among humans.

▸ Prevention and Treatment

Systemic cryptococcosis requires immediate treatment with amphotericin B and fluconazole over a period of weeks or months. There is no prevention.

Coccidioides species

The morphology of the fungus *Coccidioides* species is very distinctive. At 25°C, it forms a moist white to brown colony with abundant, branching, septate hyphae. These hyphae fragment into thick-walled, blocklike **arthroconidia** (arthrospores) at maturity **(figure 17.8*a*).** On special media incubated at 37°C to 40°C, an arthrospore germinates into the parasitic phase, a small, spherical cell called a spherule **(figure 17.8*b*)** that can be found in infected tissues as well.

There are two species of *Coccidioides*: *C. immitis* is responsible for disease in California's San Joaquin valley and *C. posadasil* is more widely distributed in the United States southwest, Mexico, and South America.

▸ Pathogenesis and Virulence Factors

This is a true systemic fungal infection of high virulence, as opposed to an opportunistic infection. It usually begins with pulmonary infection but can disseminate quickly throughout the body. Coccidioidomycosis of the meninges is the most serious manifestation. All persons inhaling the arthrospores probably develop some degree of infection, but certain groups have a genetic susceptibility that gives rise to more serious disease. After the arthrospores are inhaled, they develop into spherules in the lungs. These spherules release scores of endospores into the lungs. (Unfortunately "endospores" is the term used for this phase of the infection even though we have learned that endospores are *bacterial* structures.) At this point, the patient either

Meningitis-causing agents have their own research branch at the CDC.

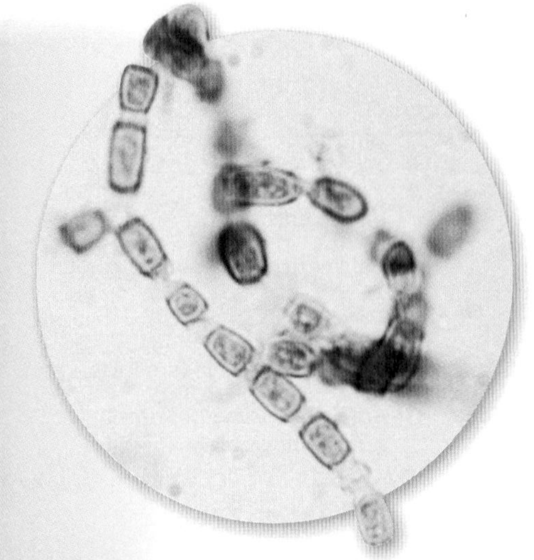

(a) Arthrospores

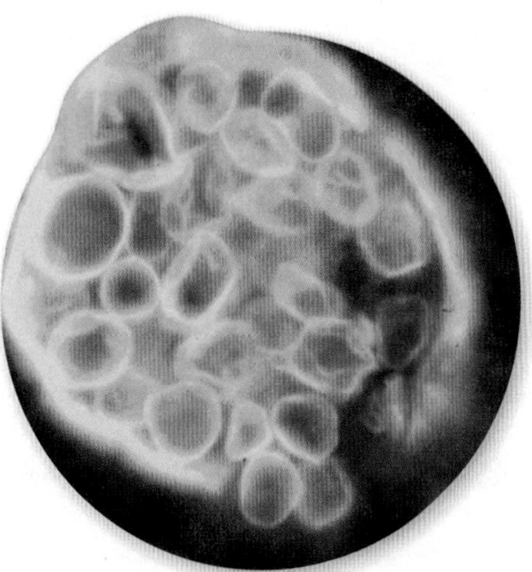
(b) Spherules containing endospores

Figure 17.8 Two phases of *Coccidioides* infection. **(a)** Arthrospores are present in the environment and are inhaled. **(b)** In the lungs, the brain, or other tissues, arthrospores develop into spherules that are filled with endospores. Endospores are released and induce damage.

experiences mild respiratory symptoms, which resolve themselves, or the endospores cause disseminated disease. Disseminated disease can include meningitis, osteomyelitis, and skin granulomas.

The highest incidence of coccidioidomycosis, estimated at 100,000 cases per year, occurs in the southwestern United States, although it also occurs in Mexico and parts of Central and South America. Especially concentrated reservoirs exist in the San Joaquin Valley of California and in southern Arizona. Outbreaks are usually associated with farming activity, archeological digs, construction, and mining. A highly unusual outbreak of coccidioidomycosis was traced to the Northridge, California, earthquake in 1994. Clouds of dust bearing loosened spores were given off by landslides, and local winds then carried the dust into the outlying residential areas.

Viruses

A wide variety of viruses can cause meningitis. Because no bacteria or fungi are found in the CSF in viral meningitis, the condition is often called *aseptic meningitis.* Aseptic meningitis may also have noninfectious causes.

The majority of cases of viral meningitis occur in children, and 90% are caused by enteroviruses. A common cause of viral meningitis is initial infection with HSV-2, concurrent with a genital infection. But many other viruses also gain access to the central nervous system on occasion.

Viral meningitis is generally milder than bacterial or fungal meningitis, and it is usually resolved within 2 weeks. The mortality rate is less than 1%. Diagnosis begins with the failure to find bacteria, fungi, or protozoa in CSF and can be confirmed, depending on the virus, by viral culture or specific antigen tests. In most cases, no treatment is indicated.

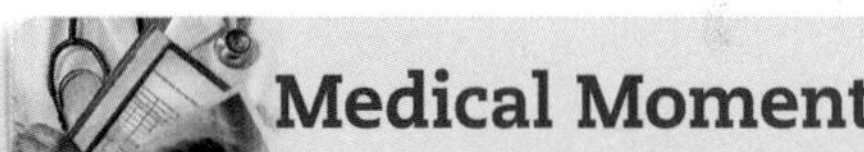

Medical Moment

Tuberculous Meningitis

We'll study tuberculosis in detail in chapter 19, focusing on how it affects the respiratory system. But it also can affect the nervous system severely. It has been estimated that approximately one-third of the world's population is infected with the agent of tuberculosis (TB). Of this number, approximately 10% will develop clinical disease. Tuberculous meningitis remains the most prevalent chronic CNS disease in developing countries.

Tuberculous meningitis (TBM) occurs in the following two steps:

1. The causative agent of TB, *Mycobacterium tuberculosis*, enters the host and multiplies in the lungs, spreading to regional lymph nodes; bacilli then seed to the brain or meninges, resulting in the formation of small foci of caseous lesions (Rich foci).
2. Rich foci increase in size until they rupture, entering the subarachnoid space and causing meningitis.

Tuberculous meningitis may present acutely, affecting the cranial nerves, or may present more subtly, with altered mental state, headache, and stiff neck. Patients may complain of fever, headache, vomiting, and photophobia prior to this stage. These early symptoms may last for as long as 9 months or as little as 1 day.

TBM can be difficult to diagnose. Patients with TBM must be diagnosed and treated quickly, as a delayed or missed diagnosis can become fatal rapidly. Isoniazid, rifampin, and pyrazinamide are the mainstays of treatment.

Neonatal Meningitis

Meningitis in newborns is almost always a result of infection transmitted by the mother, either in utero or (more frequently) during passage through the birth canal. As more premature babies survive, the rates of neonatal meningitis increase, because the condition is favored in patients with immature immune systems. In the United States, the two most common causes are *Streptococcus agalactiae* and *Escherichia coli. Listeria monocytogenes* is also found frequently in neonates. It has already been covered here but is included in **Disease Table 17.2** as a reminder that it can cause

Disease Table 17.2 Neonatal Meningitis

Causative Organism(s)	*Streptococcus agalactiae*	*Escherichia coli*, strain K1	*Listeria monocytogenes*
Most Common Modes of Transmission	Vertical (during birth)	Vertical (during birth)	Vertical
Virulence Factors	Capsule	–	Intracellular growth
Culture/Diagnosis	Culture mother's genital tract on blood agar; CSF culture of neonate	CSF Gram stain/culture	Cold enrichment, rapid methods
Prevention	Culture and treatment of mother	–	Cooking food, avoiding unpasteurized dairy products
Treatment	Penicillin G plus aminoglycosides	Cefotaxime plus aminoglycoside	Ampicillin, trimethoprim-sulfamethoxazole
Distinctive Features	Most common; positive culture of mother confirms diagnosis	Suspected if infant is premature	–

neonatal cases as well. In the developing world, neonatal meningitis is more commonly caused by other organisms.

Streptococcus agalactiae

This species of *Streptococcus* belongs to group B of the streptococci. It colonizes 10% to 30% of female genital tracts and is the most frequent cause of neonatal meningitis (for details about this condition in women, see chapter 21). The treatment for neonatal disease is penicillin G, sometimes supplemented with an aminoglycoside. Women who are considered high risk (previous baby with group B streptococcal disease, early rupture of membranes, premature labor) are typically screened for the presence of these bacteria by means of a cervical and rectal swab between 35 and 37 weeks of gestation. Women who are found to harbor the bacteria are offered intravenous antibiotics at the beginning of active labor and throughout labor until delivery is accomplished to avoid passing the bacteria to their infant during the birthing process. Penicillin is the drug of choice; if the mother is allergic to penicillin, IV erythromycin or cefuroxime may be administered instead.

Escherichia coli

The K1 strain of *Escherichia coli* is the second most common cause of neonatal meningitis. Most babies who suffer from this infection are premature, and their prognosis is poor. Twenty percent of them die, even with aggressive antibiotic treatment, and those who survive often have brain damage.

The bacterium is usually transmitted from the mother's birth canal. It causes no disease in the mothers but can infect the vulnerable tissues of a neonate. It seems to have a predilection for the tissues of the central nervous system. Cefotaxime is usually administered intravenously, in combination with aminoglycosides.

HIGHLIGHT DISEASE

Poliomyelitis

Poliomyelitis (poh″-lee-oh′my″-eh′ly′tis) (polio) is an acute enteroviral infection of the spinal cord that can cause neuromuscular paralysis. Because it often affects small children, in the past it was called infantile paralysis. No civilization or culture has escaped the devastation of polio. The efforts of a WHO campaign have significantly reduced the global incidence of polio. It was the campaign's goal to eradicate all of the remaining wild polioviruses by 2000, and then by 2005. It didn't happen. Eventually, billionaire Bill Gates got involved and contributed $700 million to help eradicate the disease. During the course of 2010 and 2011, it continued to ripple through many countries that had previously been declared polio-free.

Signs and Symptoms

Most infections are contained as short-term, mild viremia. Some persons develop mild nonspecific symptoms of fever, headache, nausea, sore throat, and myalgia. If the viremia persists, viruses can be carried to the central nervous system through its blood supply. The virus then spreads along specific pathways in the spinal cord and brain. Being **neurotropic,** the virus infiltrates the motor neurons of the anterior horn of the spinal cord, although it can also attack spinal ganglia, cranial nerves, and motor nuclei. Nonparalytic disease involves the invasion but not the destruction of nervous tissue. It gives rise to muscle pain and spasm, meningeal inflammation, and vague hypersensitivity.

In paralytic disease, invasion of motor neurons causes various degrees of flaccid paralysis over a period of a few hours to several days. Depending on the level of damage to motor neurons, paralysis of the muscles of the legs, abdomen, back, intercostals, diaphragm, pectoral girdle, and bladder can result. In rare cases of **bulbar poliomyelitis,** the brain stem, medulla, or even cranial nerves are affected. This situation leads to loss of control of cardiorespiratory regulatory centers, requiring mechanical respirators. In time, the unused muscles begin to atrophy, growth is slowed, and severe deformities of the trunk and limbs develop. Common sites of deformities are the spine, shoulder, hips, knees, and feet. Because motor function but not sensation is compromised, the crippled limbs are often very painful.

In recent times, a condition called post-polio syndrome (PPS) has been diagnosed in long-term survivors of childhood infection. PPS manifests as a progressive muscle deterioration that develops in about 25% to 50% of patients several decades after their original polio attack.

Disease Table 17.3	Poliomyelitis
Causative Organism(s)	Poliovirus
Most Common Modes of Transmission	Fecal-oral, vehicle
Virulence Factors	Attachment mechanisms
Culture/Diagnosis	Viral culture, serology
Prevention	Live attenuated (OPV) (developing world) or inactivated vaccine (IPV) (developed world)
Treatment	None, palliative, supportive

Causative Agent

The poliovirus is in the family *Picornaviridae,* genus *Enterovirus*—named for its small **(pico)** size and its RNA genome **(figure 17.9).** It is nonenveloped and nonsegmented. The naked capsid of the virus confers chemical stability and resistance to acid, bile, and detergents. By this means, the virus survives the gastric environment and other harsh conditions, which contributes to its ease of transmission.

Pathogenesis and Virulence Factors

After being ingested, polioviruses adsorb to receptors of mucosal cells in the oropharynx and intestine. Here, they multiply in the mucosal epithelia and lymphoid tissue. Multiplication results in large numbers of viruses being shed into the throat and feces, and some of them leak into the blood. Depending on the number of viruses in the blood and their duration of stay there, an individual may exhibit no symptoms, mild nonspecific symptoms such as fever or short-term muscle pain, or devastating paralysis.

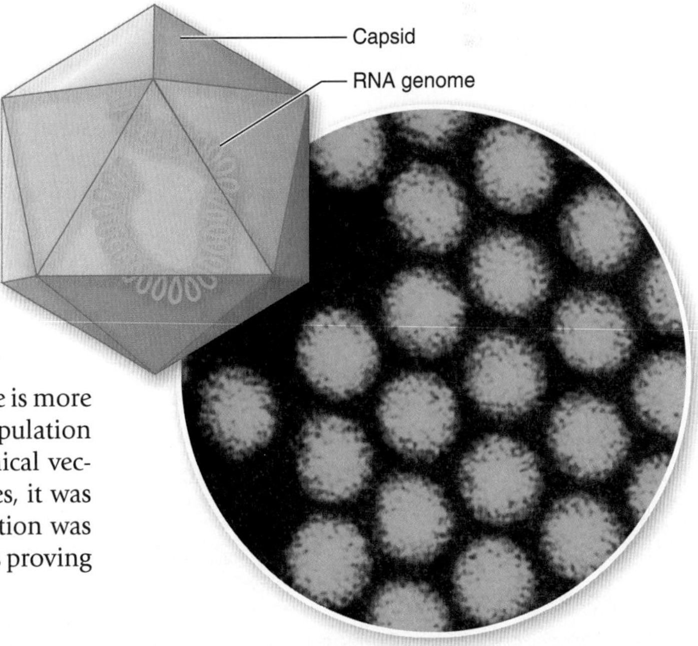

Figure 17.9 Typical structure of a picornavirus. **(a)** A poliovirus, a type of picornavirus that is one of the simplest and smallest viruses (30 nm). It consists of an icosahedral capsid shell around a molecule of RNA. **(b)** A mass of stacked poliovirus particles in an infected host cell (300,000×).

Transmission and Epidemiology

Sporadic cases of polio can break out at any time of the year, but its incidence is more pronounced during the summer and fall. The virus is passed within the population through food, water, hands, objects contaminated with feces, and mechanical vectors. Although the 20th century saw a very large rise in paralytic polio cases, it was also the century during which effective vaccines were developed. The infection was eliminated from the Western Hemisphere in the late 20th century. Sadly, it is proving extremely difficulty to eradicate from the developing world.

Prevention and Treatment

Treatment of polio rests largely on alleviating pain and suffering. During the acute phase, muscle spasm, headache, and associated discomfort can be alleviated by pain-relieving drugs. Respiratory failure may require artificial ventilation maintenance. Prompt physical therapy to diminish crippling deformities and to retrain muscles is recommended after the acute febrile phase subsides.

The mainstay of polio prevention is vaccination as early in life as possible, usually in four doses starting at about 2 months of age. Adult candidates for immunization are travelers and members of the armed forces. The two forms of vaccine currently in use are inactivated poliovirus vaccine (IPV), developed by Jonas Salk in 1954, and oral poliovirus vaccine (OPV), developed by Albert Sabin in the 1960s.

For many years, the oral vaccine was used in the United States because it is easily administered by mouth, but it is not free of medical complications. It contains an attenuated virus that can multiply in vaccinated people and be spread to others. In very rare instances, the attenuated virus reverts to a neurovirulent strain that causes disease rather than protects against it. For this reason, IPV, using killed virus, is the only vaccine used in the United States.

HIGHLIGHT DISEASE

Meningoencephalitis

Two microorganisms cause a distinct disease called *meningoencephalitis* (disease in both the meninges and brain), and they are both amoebas. *Naegleria fowleri* and *Acanthamoeba* are accidental parasites that invade the body only under unusual circumstances.

Naegleria fowleri

Most cases of *Naegleria* infection reported worldwide occur in people who have been swimming in warm, natural bodies of fresh water. Infection can begin when amoebas are forced into human nasal passages as a result of swimming, diving, or other aquatic activities. Once the amoeba is inoculated into the favorable habitat of the nasal mucosa, it burrows in, multiplies, and subsequently migrates into the brain and surrounding structures. The result is primary amoebic meningoencephalitis (PAM), a rapid, massive destruction of brain and spinal tissue that causes hemorrhage and coma and invariably ends in death within a week or so (**figure 17.10**). We should note that this organism is very common—children often carry the amoeba as harmless biota, especially during the summer months, and the series of events leading to disease is exceedingly rare.

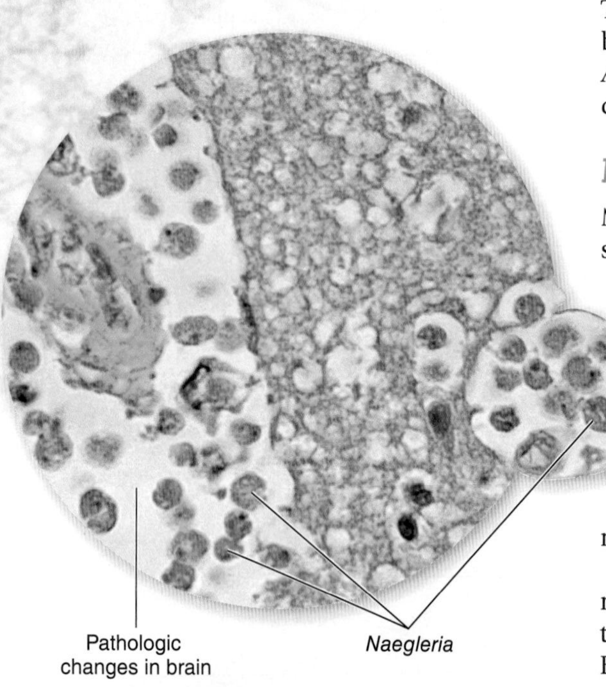

Figure 17.10 ***Naegleria fowleri* in the brain.** The trophozoite form invades brain tissue, destroying it.

Unfortunately, *Naegleria* meningoencephalitis advances so rapidly that treatment usually proves futile. Studies have indicated that early therapy with amphotericin B, sulfadiazine, or tetracycline in some combination can be of some benefit. Because of the wide distribution of the amoeba and its hardiness, no general means of control exists. Public swimming pools and baths must be adequately chlorinated and checked periodically for the amoeba.

Acanthamoeba

This protozoan differs from *Naegleria* in its portal of entry; it invades broken skin, the conjunctiva, and occasionally the lungs and urogenital epithelia. Although it causes a meningoencephalitis somewhat similar to that of *Naegleria*, the course of infection

Disease Table 17.4 Meningoencephalitis

	Primary Amoebic Meningoencephalitis	Granulomatous Amoebic Meningoencephalitis
Causative Organism(s)	*Naegleria fowleri*	*Acanthamoeba*
Most Common Modes of Transmission	Vehicle (exposure while swimming in water)	Direct contact
Virulence Factors	Invasiveness	Invasiveness
Culture/Diagnosis	Examination of CSF; brain imaging, biopsy	Examination of CSF; brain imaging, biopsy
Prevention	Avoid warm fresh water	–
Treatment	Amphotericin B; mostly ineffective	Surgical excision of granulomas; ketoconazole may help

is lengthier. The disease is called granulomatous amoebic meningoencephalitis (GAM). At special risk for infection are people with traumatic eye injuries, contact lens wearers, and AIDS patients exposed to contaminated water. We discussed ocular infections in chapter 16. Cutaneous and CNS infections with this organism are occasional complications in AIDS.

Pools are chlorinated to prevent *Naeglaria* and other outbreaks.

Acute Encephalitis

Encephalitis (inflammation of the brain) can present as acute or **subacute.** It is always a serious condition, as the tissues of the brain are extremely sensitive to damage by inflammatory processes. Acute encephalitis is almost always caused by viral infection. One category of viral encephalitis is caused by viruses borne by insects (called arboviruses, which is short for arthropod-borne viruses), including West Nile virus. Alternatively, other viruses, such as members of the herpes family, are causative agents. Bacteria such as those covered under meningitis can also cause encephalitis, but the symptoms are usually more pronounced in the meninges than in the brain.

The signs and symptoms of encephalitis vary, but they may include behavior changes or confusion because of inflammation. Decreased consciousness and seizures frequently occur. Symptoms of meningitis are often also present. Few of these agents have specific treatments, but because swift initiation of acyclovir therapy can save the life of a patient suffering from herpesvirus encephalitis, most physicians will begin empiric therapy with acyclovir in all seriously ill neonates and most other patients showing evidence of encephalitis. Treatment will, in any case, do no harm in patients who are infected with other agents.

Arthropod-Borne Viruses (Arboviruses)

Most arthropods that serve as infectious disease vectors feed on the blood of hosts. Infections show a peak incidence when the arthropod is actively feeding and reproducing, usually from late spring through early fall. Warm-blooded vertebrates also maintain the virus during the cold and dry seasons. Humans can serve as dead-end, accidental hosts, as in equine encephalitis, or they can be a maintenance reservoir, as in yellow fever (discussed in chapter 18).

Arboviral diseases have a great impact on humans **(figure 17.11).** Although exact statistics are unavailable, it is believed that millions of people acquire infections each year and thousands of them die. One common outcome of arboviral infection is an

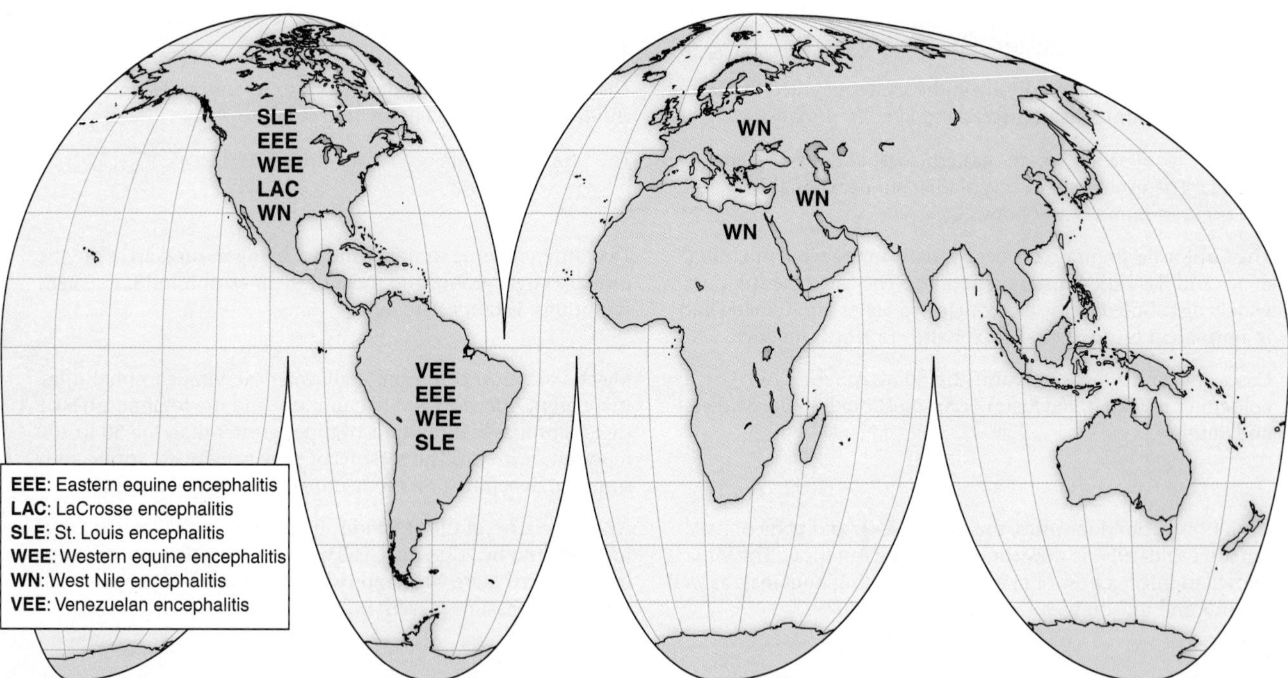

Figure 17.11 Worldwide distribution of major arboviral encephalitides.

Public health officials regularly take samples of standing water in rain gutters, swimming pools, and elsewhere, looking for larval mosquitoes like those seen here.

acute fever, often accompanied by rash. Viruses that primarily cause these symptoms are covered in chapter 18.

The arboviruses discussed in this chapter can cause encephalitis, and we consider them as a group because the symptoms and management are similar. The transmission and epidemiology of individual viruses are different, however, and are discussed for each virus in **table 17.1.** All of the infections here are transmitted by mosquitoes.

▶ Pathogenesis and Virulence Factors

Arboviral encephalitis begins with an arthropod bite, the release of the virus into tissues, and its replication in nearby lymphatic tissues. All the arboviruses we describe here are transmitted by mosquitoes. Prolonged viremia establishes the virus in the brain, where inflammation can cause swelling and damage to the brain, nerves, and meninges. Symptoms are extremely variable and can include coma, convulsions, paralysis, tremor, loss of coordination, memory deficits, changes in speech and personality, and heart disorders. In some cases, survivors experience some degree of permanent brain damage. Young children and the elderly are most sensitive to injury by arboviral encephalitis.

▶ Culture and Diagnosis

Except during epidemics, detecting arboviral infections can be difficult. The patient's history of travel to endemic areas or contact with vectors, along with serum analysis, is highly supportive of a diagnosis. Rapid serological tests are available for some of the viruses.

▶ Treatment

No satisfactory treatment exists for any of the arboviral encephalitides (plural of *encephalitis*). As mentioned earlier, empiric acyclovir treatment may be begun in case the infection is actually caused by either herpes simplex virus or varicella zoster. Treatment of the other infections relies entirely on support measures to control fever, convulsions, dehydration, shock, and edema.

Most of the control safeguards for arbovirus disease are aimed at the arthropod vectors. Mosquito abatement by eliminating breeding sites and by broadcast-spreading insecticides has been highly effective in restricted urban settings. Birds play a role as reservoirs of the virus, but direct transmission between birds and humans does not occur.

Table 17.1 Arboviral Encephalitis

	Geographic Distribution	Notes
Western Equine Encephalitis (WEE)	This disease occurs sporadically in the western United States and Canada, appearing first in horses and later in humans.	The disease is extremely dangerous to infants and small children, with a case fatality rate of 3% to 7%.
Eastern Equine Encephalitis (EEE)	Endemic to an area along the eastern coast of North America and Canada. The usual pattern is sporadic, but occasional epidemics can occur in humans and horses.	The case fatality rate can be very high (70%).
California Encephalitis	The California strain occurs occasionally in the western United States and has little impact on humans. The LaCrosse strain is widely distributed in the eastern United States and Canada and is a prevalent cause of viral encephalitis in North America.	Two different virus strains; children living in rural areas are the primary target group, and most of them exhibit mild, transient symptoms. Fatalities are rare.
St. Louis Encephalitis (SLE)	Cases appear throughout North and South America, but epidemics in the United States occur most often in the Midwest and South.	May be the most common of all American viral encephalitides. Inapparent infection is very common, and the total number of cases is probably thousands of times greater than the 50 to 100 reported each year. The seasons of peak activity are spring and summer, depending on the region and species of mosquito.
West Nile Encephalitis	Commonly found in Africa, the Middle East, and parts of Asia, but after mid-1999 is now common in the Americas. The virus is known to infect a host of mammals (including humans), as well as birds and mosquitoes.	A close relative of the SLE virus. It emerged in the United States in 1999, and by 2008 the CDC was reporting that 1% of people in the United States—or approximately 3 million people—had evidence of past or present infection.

Disease Table 17.5 Encephalitis

Causative Organism(s)	Arboviruses (viruses causing WEE, EEE, California encephalitis, SLE, West Nile encephalitis)	Herpes simplex virus type 1 or 2	JC virus	Immunologic reaction to other viral infections
Most Common Modes of Transmission	Vector (mosquito bites)	Vertical or reactivation of latent infection	? Ubiquitous	Sequelae of measles, other viral infections, and occasionally, vaccination
Virulence Factors	Attachment, fusion, invasion capabilities	–	–	–
Culture/ Diagnosis	History, rapid serological tests	Clinical presentation, PCR, Ab tests, growth of virus in cell culture	PCR of cerebrospinal fluid	History of viral infection or vaccination
Prevention	Insect control; vaccines for WEE and EEE available	Maternal screening for HSV	None	–
Treatment	None	Acyclovir	Zidovudine or other antivirals	Steroids, anti-inflammatory agents
Distinctive Features	History of exposure to insect important	In infants, disseminated disease present; rare between 30 and 50 years	In severely immunocompromised, especially AIDS	History of virus/vaccine exposure critical

Herpes Simplex Virus (HSV)

Herpes simplex type 1 and 2 viruses can cause encephalitis in newborns born to HSV-positive mothers. In this case, the virus is disseminated and the prognosis is poor. Older children and young adults (ages 5 to 30), as well as older adults (over 50 years old), are also susceptible to herpes simplex encephalitis caused most commonly by HSV-1. In these cases, the HSV encephalitis represents a reactivation of dormant HSV from the trigeminal ganglion.

It should be noted the varicella-zoster virus (see chapter 16) can also reactivate from the dormant state, and it is responsible for rare cases of encephalitis.

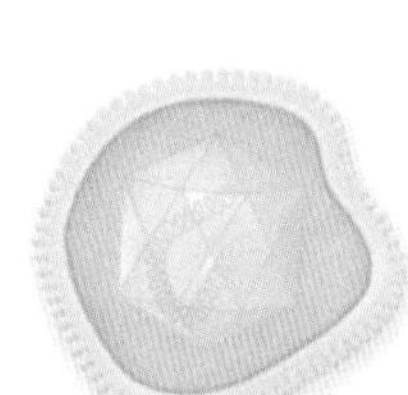

JC Virus

The **JC virus (JCV)** gets its name from the initials of the patient in whom it was first diagnosed as the cause of illness. Serological studies indicate that infection with this polyoma virus is commonplace. In patients with immune dysfunction, especially in those with AIDS, it can cause a condition called **progressive multifocal leukoencephalopathy** (loo″-koh-en-sef″uh-lop′-uh-thee) **(PML).** This uncommon but generally fatal infection is a result of JC virus attack of accessory brain cells. The infection demyelinizes certain parts of the cerebrum. This virus should be considered when encephalitis symptoms are observed in AIDS patients. Recently a few deaths from this condition have been prevented with high doses of zidovudine.

Subacute Encephalitis

When encephalitis symptoms take longer to show up, and when the symptoms are less striking, the condition is termed subacute encephalitis. The most common cause of subacute encephalitis is the protozoan *Toxoplasma.* Another form of subacute encephalitis can be caused by persistent measles virus as many as 7 to 15 years after the initial infection. Finally, a class of infectious agents known as prions can cause a condition called spongiform encephalopathy.

NCLEX® PREP

4. The following statements are true of arboviruses, *except*
   a. arboviruses show a peak incidence when the arthropod is actively feeding and reproducing.
   b. humans may be accidental reservoirs or maintenance reservoirs.
   c. fever and rash are common outcomes of arboviral infection.
   d. West Nile virus is not considered to be an arbovirus.

Toxoplasma gondii

Infection in the fetus and in immunodeficient people, especially those with AIDS, is severe and often fatal. Although infection in otherwise healthy people is generally unnoticed, recent data tell us it can have profound effects on their brain, and the responses it controls. People with a history of *Toxoplasma* infection are more likely to display thrill-seeking behaviors. Also, people with infection histories seem to have slower reaction times.

T. gondii is a very successful parasite with so little host specificity that it can attack at least 200 species of birds and mammals. However, its primary reservoir and hosts are members of the feline family, both domestic and wild.

▸ Signs and Symptoms

Most cases of toxoplasmosis are asymptomatic or marked by mild symptoms such as sore throat, lymph node enlargement, and low-grade fever. In patients whose immunity is suppressed by infection, cancer, or drugs, the outlook may be grim. The infection causes a more chronic or subacute form of encephalitis than do most viruses, often producing extensive brain lesions and fatal disruptions of the heart and lungs. A pregnant woman with toxoplasmosis has a 33% chance of transmitting the infection to her fetus. Congenital infection occurring in the first or second trimester is associated with stillbirth and severe abnormalities such as liver and spleen enlargement, liver failure, hydrocephalus, convulsions, and damage to the retina that can result in blindness.

▸ Pathogenesis and Virulence Factors

Toxoplasma is an obligate intracellular parasite, making its ability to invade host cells an important factor for virulence.

▸ Transmission and Epidemiology

The parasite undergoes a sexual phase in the intestine of cats and is then released in feces, where it becomes an infective *oocyst* that survives in moist soil for several months. These forms eventually enter an asexual cyst state in tissues, called a *pseudocyst.* Most of the time, the parasite does not cycle in cats alone and is spread by oocysts to intermediate hosts, including rodents and birds. The cycle returns to cats when they eat these infected prey animals. Cattle and sheep can also be infected.

In 2007, scientists at Stanford University found that the protozoan crowds into a part of the rat brain that usually directs the rat to avoid the smell of cat urine (a natural defense against a domestic rat's major predator). When *Toxoplasma* infects rat brains, the rats lose their fear of cats. Infected rats are then easily eaten by cats, ensuring the continuing *Toxoplasma* life cycle. All other neurological functions in the rat are left intact.

Humans appear to be constantly exposed to the pathogen. The rate of prior infections, as detected through serological tests, can be as high as 90% in some populations. Many cases are caused by ingesting pseudocysts in contaminated meats. A common source is raw or undercooked meat. The grooming habits of cats spread fecal oocysts on their body surfaces, and unhygienic handling of them presents an opportunity to ingest oocysts. Infection can also occur when oocysts are inhaled in air or dust contaminated with cat droppings and when tachyzoites cross the placenta to the fetus.

In view of the fact that the oocysts are so widespread and resistant, hygiene is of paramount importance in controlling toxoplasmosis. Adequate cooking or freezing below −20°C destroys both oocysts and tissue cysts. Oocysts can also be avoided by washing the hands after handling cats or soil possibly contaminated with cat feces,

NCLEX® PREP

5. *Toxoplasma gondii*
   a. may severely affect the developing fetus.
   b. may cause asymptomatic or mild disease (sore throat, low-grade fever).
   c. does not affect the eyes.
   d. is not associated with undercooked meat.
   d. both a and b
   e. both c and d

especially sandboxes and litter boxes. Pregnant women should be especially attentive to these rules and should never clean the cat's litter box.

Prions

As you read in chapter 5, prions are **proteinaceous infectious particles** containing, apparently, no genetic material. They are known to cause diseases called **transmissible spongiform encephalopathies (TSEs),** neurodegenerative diseases with long incubation periods but rapid progressions once they begin. The human TSEs are **Creutzfeldt-Jakob disease (CJD),** Gerstmann-Strussler-Scheinker disease, and fatal familial insomnia. TSEs are also found in animals and include a disease called scrapie in sheep and goats, transmissible mink encephalopathy, and bovine spongiform encephalopathy (BSE). This last disease is commonly known as mad cow disease and was in the headlines in the 1990s due to its apparent link to a variant form of Creutzfeldt-Jakob human disease in Great Britain. We consider CJD in this section.

Prions were found in the meat of cattle fed with animal scraps. The highest number of cases occurred in the 1990s in the United Kingdom but isolated cases have been found in the United States and Canada, as recently as 2011.

▶ Signs and Symptoms of CJD

Symptoms of CJD include altered behavior, dementia, memory loss, impaired senses, delirium, and premature senility. Uncontrollable muscle contractions continue until death, which usually occurs within 1 year of diagnosis.

▶ Causative Agent of CJD

The transmissible agent in CJD is a prion. In some forms of the disease, it involved the transformation of a normal host protein (called PrP), a protein that is supposed to function to help the brain develop normally, and that has recently been found to protect against Alzheimer's disease. Once this happens, the abnormal PrP itself becomes catalytic and able to spontaneously convert other normal human PrP proteins into the abnormal form. This becomes a self-propagating chain reaction that creates a massive accumulation of altered PrP, leading to plaques, spongiform damage (i.e., holes in the brain) **(figure 17.12),** and severe loss of brain function.

Using the term **transmissible agent** may be a bit misleading, however, as some cases of CJD arise through genetic mutation of the *PrP* gene, which can be a heritable trait. So it seems that although one can acquire a defective PrP protein via transmission, one can also have an altered *PrP* gene passed on through heredity.

Prions are incredibly hardy "pathogens." They are highly resistant to chemicals, radiation, and heat. They can withstand prolonged autoclaving.

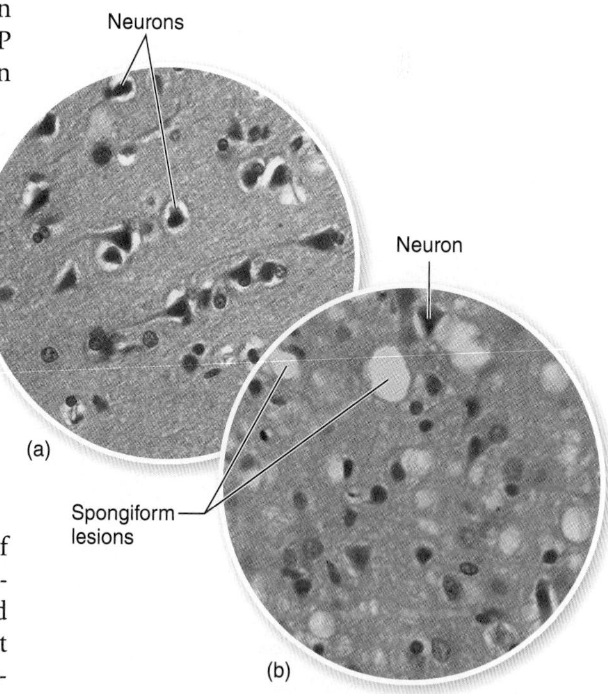

Figure 17.12 The microscopic effects of spongiform encephalopathy. (a) Normal cerebral cortex section, showing neurons and glial cells. (b) Sectioned cortex in CJD patient shows numerous round holes, producing a "spongy" appearance. This destroys brain architecture and causes massive loss of neurons and glial cells.

▶ Transmission and Epidemiology

In the late 1990s, it became apparent that humans were contracting a variant form of CJD (vCJD) after ingesting meat from cattle that had been afflicted by bovine spongiform encephalopathy. Presumably, meat products had been contaminated with fluid or tissues infected with the prion. Cases of this disease have centered around Great Britain, where many cows were found to have BSE. The median age at death of patients with vCJD is 28 years. In contrast, the median age at death of patients with other forms of CJD is 68 years.

Health care professionals should be aware of the possibility of CJD in patients, especially when surgical procedures are performed, as cases have been reported of transmission of CJD via contaminated surgical instruments. Due to the heat and chemical resistance of prions, normal disinfection and sterilization procedures are usually not sufficient to eliminate them from instruments and surfaces. The latest

Disease Table 17.6 Subacute Encephalitis

Causative Organism(s)	*Toxoplasma gondii*	Subacute sclerosing panencephalitis	Prions
Most Common Modes of Transmission	Vehicle (meat) or fecal-oral	Persistence of measles virus	CJD = direct/parenteral contact with infected tissue, or inherited vCJD = vehicle (meat, parenteral)
Virulence Factors	Intracellular growth	Cell fusion, evasion of immune system	Avoidance of host immune response
Culture/Diagnosis	Serological detection of IgM, culture, histology	EEGs, MRI, serology (Ab versus measles virus)	Biopsy, image of brain
Prevention	Personal hygiene, food hygiene	None	Avoiding tissue
Treatment	Pyrimethamine and/or leucovorin and/or sulfadiazine	None	None
Distinctive Features	Subacute, slower development of disease	History of measles	Long incubation period; fast progression once it begins

CDC guidelines for handling of CJD patients in a health care environment should be consulted.

Rabies

Rabies is a slow, progressive zoonotic disease characterized by a fatal encephalitis. It is so distinctive in its pathogenesis and its symptoms that we discuss it separately from the other encephalitides. It is distributed nearly worldwide, except for perhaps two dozen countries that have remained rabies-free by practicing rigorous animal control.

▶ Signs and Symptoms

The average incubation period of rabies is 1 to 2 months or more, depending on the wound site, its severity, and the inoculation dose. The incubation period is shorter in facial, scalp, or neck wounds because of closer proximity to the brain. The prodromal phase begins with fever, nausea, vomiting, headache, fatigue, and other nonspecific symptoms.

Until recently, humans were never known to survive rabies. But a handful of patients have recovered in recent years after receiving intensive, long-term treatment.

▶ Pathogenesis and Virulence Factors

Infection with rabies virus typically begins when an infected animal's saliva enters a puncture site. The virus occasionally is inhaled or inoculated through the membranes of the eye. The rabies virus remains up to a week at the trauma site, where it multiplies. The virus then gradually enters nerve endings and advances toward the ganglia, spinal cord, and brain. Viral multiplication throughout the brain is eventually followed by migration to such diverse sites as the eye, heart, skin, and oral cavity. The infection cycle is completed when the virus replicates in the salivary gland and is shed into the saliva. Clinical rabies proceeds through several distinct stages that almost inevitably end in death, unless post-exposure vaccination is performed before symptoms begin.

Scientists have discovered that virulence is associated with an envelope glycoprotein that seems to give the virus its ability to spread in the CNS and to invade certain types of neural cells.

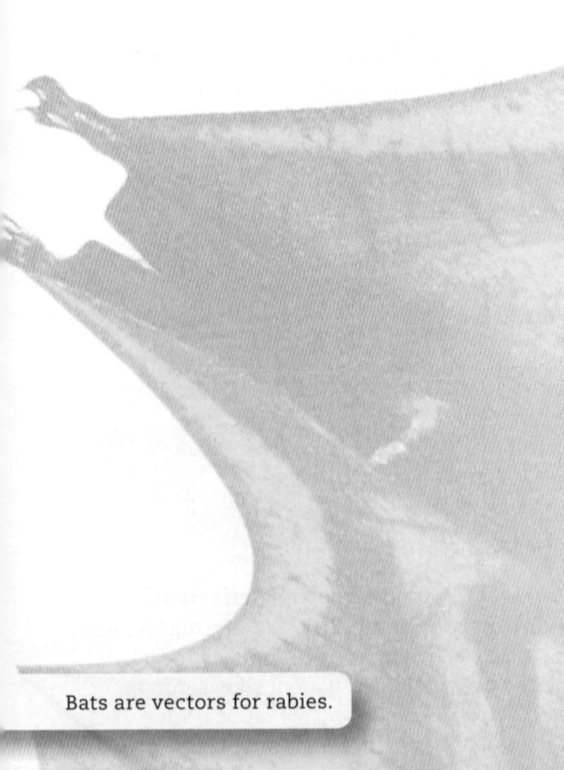

Bats are vectors for rabies.

▸ Transmission and Epidemiology

The primary reservoirs of the virus are wild mammals such as canines, skunks, raccoons, badgers, cats, and bats that can spread the infection to domestic dogs and cats. Both wild and domestic mammals can spread the disease to humans through bites, scratches, and inhalation of droplets. The annual worldwide total for human rabies is estimated at about 55,000 cases, but only a tiny number of these cases occur in the United States, the majority of these transmitted to humans from bats. Most U.S. cases of rabies occur in wild animals (about 6,000 to 7,000 cases per year), while dog rabies has declined **(figure 17.13)**.

The epidemiology of animal rabies in the United States varies. The most common wild animal reservoir host has changed from foxes to skunks to raccoons. Regional differences in the dominant reservoir also occur. Rats, skunks, and bobcats are the most common carriers of rabies in California, raccoons are the predominant carriers in the East, and coyotes dominate in Texas.

Diagnosis requires multiple tests. Reverse transcription PCR is used with saliva samples but must be accompanied by detection of antibodies to the virus in serum or spinal fluid. Skin biopsies are also used.

Disease Table 17.7 Rabies

Causative Organism(s)	Rabies virus
Most Common Modes of Transmission	Parenteral (bite trauma), droplet contact
Virulence Factors	Envelope glycoprotein
Culture/ Diagnosis	RT-PCR of saliva; Ab detection of serum or CSF; skin biopsy
Prevention	HDCV—inactivated vaccine
Treatment	Postexposure passive and active immunization

▸ Prevention and Treatment

A bite from a wild or stray animal demands assessment of the animal, meticulous care of the wound, and a specific treatment regimen. A wild mammal, especially a skunk, raccoon, fox, or coyote that bites without provocation, is presumed to be rabid, and therapy is immediately begun.

Rabies is one of the few infectious diseases for which a combination of passive and active postexposure immunization is indicated (and successful). Initially the wound is infused with human rabies immune globulin (HRIG) to impede the spread of the virus, and globulin is also injected intramuscularly to provide immediate systemic protection. A full course of vaccination is started simultaneously. The current vaccine of choice is the **human diploid cell vaccine (HDCV)**. The routine

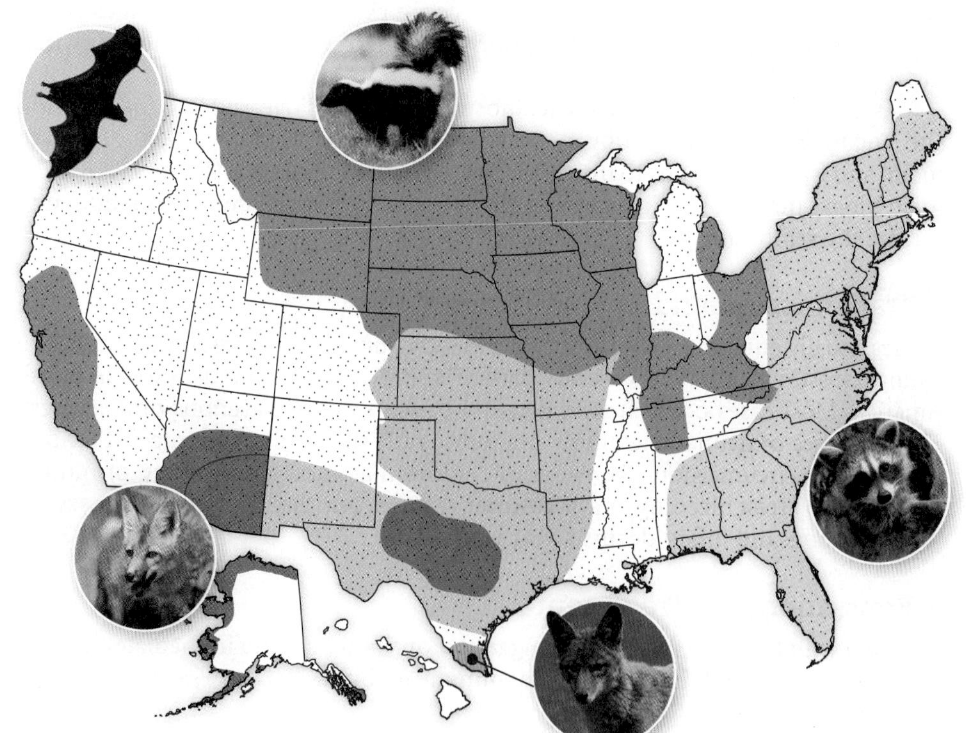

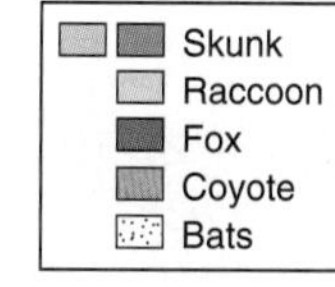

Figure 17.13 Distribution of rabies in the United States. Rabies is found in 10 distinct geographic areas. In each area, a particular animal is the reservoir as illustrated by four different colors. The prevalence in bats is shown by the black dots.

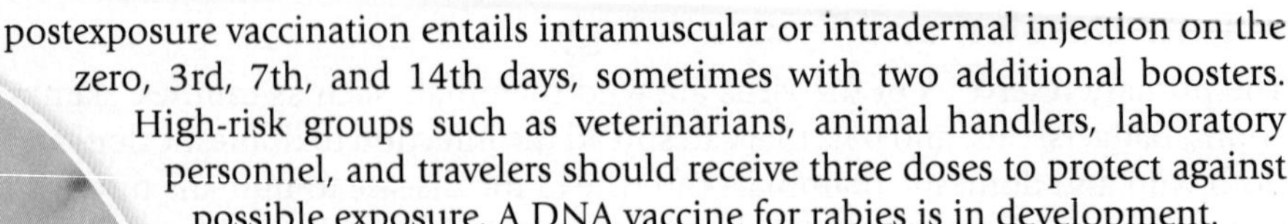

Figure 17.14 *Clostridium tetani*. Its typical tennis racket morphology is created by terminal endospores that swell the end of the cell (170×).

postexposure vaccination entails intramuscular or intradermal injection on the zero, 3rd, 7th, and 14th days, sometimes with two additional boosters. High-risk groups such as veterinarians, animal handlers, laboratory personnel, and travelers should receive three doses to protect against possible exposure. A DNA vaccine for rabies is in development.

Tetanus

Tetanus is a neuromuscular disease whose alternate name, lockjaw, refers to an early effect of the disease on the jaw muscle. The etiologic agent, *Clostridium tetani,* is a common resident of cultivated soil and the gastrointestinal tracts of animals. It is a gram-positive, spore-forming rod. The endospores it produces often swell the vegetative cell **(figure 17.14).** Spores are produced only under anaerobic conditions.

▸ Signs and Symptoms

C. tetani releases a powerful neurotoxin, **tetanospasmin,** that binds to target sites on peripheral motor neurons, spinal cord and brain, and in the sympathetic nervous system. The toxin acts by blocking the inhibition of muscle contraction. Without inhibition of contraction, the muscles contract uncontrollably, resulting in spastic paralysis. The first symptoms are clenching of the jaw, followed in succession by extreme arching of the back, flexion of the arms, and extension of the legs **(figure 17.15).** Lockjaw confers the bizarre appearance of *risus sardonicus* (sardonic grin), which looks eerily as though the person is smiling **(figure 17.16).** Death most often occurs due to paralysis of the respiratory muscles and respiratory arrest.

▸ Pathogenesis and Virulence Factors

The mere presence of spores in a wound is not sufficient to initiate infection because the bacterium is unable to invade damaged tissues readily. It is also a strict anaerobe, and the spores cannot become established unless tissues at the site of the wound are necrotic and poorly supplied with blood, conditions that favor germination.

As the vegetative cells grow, the tetanospasmin toxin is released into the infection site. The toxin spreads to nearby motor nerve endings in the injured tissue, binds to them, and travels via axons to the ventral horns of the spinal cord (figure 17.16). The toxin blocks the release of neurotransmitter, and only a small amount is required to initiate the symptoms.

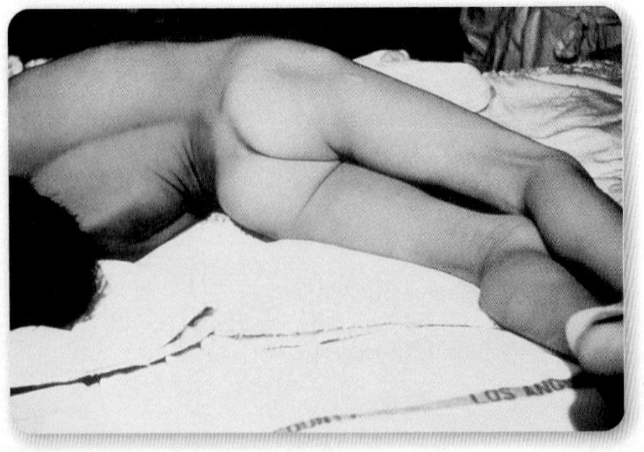

Figure 17.15 Late-stage tetanus.

▸ Transmission and Epidemiology

Spores usually enter the body through accidental puncture wounds, burns, umbilical stumps, frostbite, and crushed body parts. The incidence of tetanus is low in North America. Most cases occur among geriatric patients and intravenous drug abusers. The incidence of neonatal tetanus—predominantly the result of an infected umbilical stump or circumcision—is higher in cultures that apply dung, ashes, or mud to these sites to arrest bleeding or as a customary ritual. The disease accounts for several hundred thousand infant deaths a year worldwide.

▸ Prevention and Treatment

A patient with a clinical appearance suggestive of tetanus should immediately receive antitoxin therapy with human tetanus immune globulin (TIG).

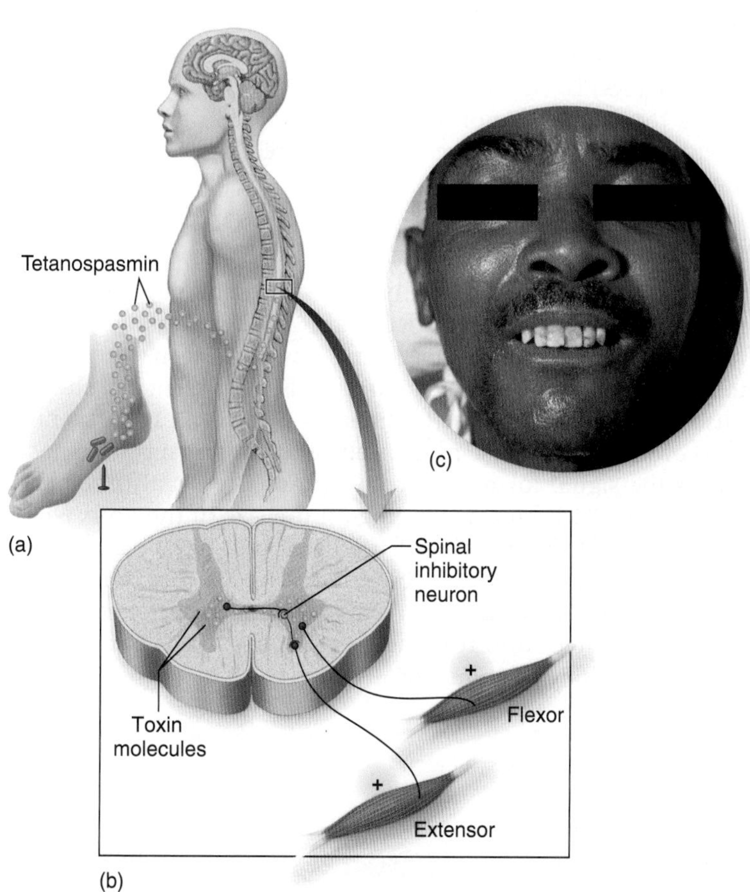

Figure 17.16 The events in tetanus. **(a)** After traumatic injury, bacteria infecting the local tissues secrete tetanospasmin, which is absorbed by the peripheral axons and is carried to the target neurons in the spinal column. **(b)** In the spinal cord, the toxin attaches to the junctions of regulatory neurons that inhibit inappropriate contraction. Released from inhibition, the muscles, even opposing members of a muscle group, receive constant stimuli and contract uncontrollably. **(c)** Muscles contract spasmodically, without regard to regulatory mechanisms or conscious control. Note the clenched jaw, called *risus sardonicus*.

Disease Table 17.8 Tetanus	
Causative Organism(s)	*Clostridium tetani*
Most Common Modes of Transmission	Parenteral, direct contact
Virulence Factors	Tetanospasmin exotoxin
Culture/ Diagnosis	Symptomatic
Prevention	Tetanus toxoid immunization
Treatment	Combination of passive antitoxin and tetanus toxoid active immunization, supportive

The recommended vaccination series for 1- to 3-month-old babies consists of three injections of DTaP (diphtheria, tetanus, and acellular pertussis) given 2 months apart, followed by booster doses about 1 and 4 years later. Children thus immunized probably have protection for 10 years. At that point, and every 10 years thereafter, they should receive a dose of TD, tetanus-diphtheria vaccine. Additional protection against neonatal tetanus may be achieved by vaccinating pregnant women, whose antibodies will be passed to the fetus. Toxoid should also be given to injured persons who have never been immunized, have not completed the series, or whose last booster was received more than 10 years previously. The vaccine can be given simultaneously with passive TIG immunization to achieve immediate as well as long-term protection.

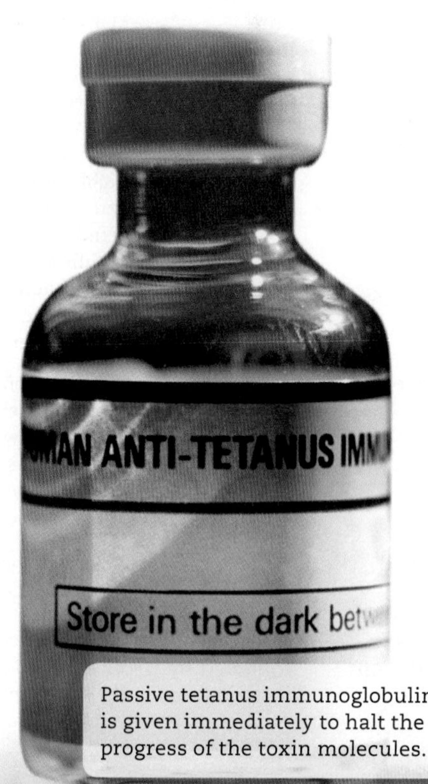

Passive tetanus immunoglobulin is given immediately to halt the progress of the toxin molecules.

Disease Table 17.9 Botulism

Causative Organism(s)	*Clostridium botulinum*
Most Common Modes of Transmission	Vehicle (food-borne toxin, airborne organism); direct contact (wound); parenteral (injection)
Virulence Factors	Botulinum exotoxin
Culture/Diagnosis	Culture of organism; demonstration of toxin
Prevention	Food hygiene; toxoid immunization available for laboratory professionals
Treatment	Antitoxin, supportive care

Botulism

Botulism is an **intoxication** (i.e., caused by an exotoxin) associated with eating poorly preserved foods, although it can also occur as a true infection. Until recent times, it was relatively common and frequently fatal, but modern techniques of food preservation and medical treatment have reduced both its incidence and its fatality rate.

▶ Signs and Symptoms

There are three major forms of botulism, distinguished by their means of transmission and the population they affect. **Table 17.2** summarizes these. The symptoms are largely the same in all three forms, however. From the circulatory system, an exotoxin called the **botulinum toxin** travels to its principal site of action, the neuromuscular junctions of skeletal muscles **(figure 17.17).** The effect of botulinum is to prevent the release of the neurotransmitter substance, acetylcholine, that initiates the signal for muscle contraction. The usual time before onset of symptoms is 12 to 72 hours, depending on the size of the dose. Neuromuscular symptoms first affect the muscles of the head and include double vision, difficulty in swallowing, and dizziness, but there is no sensory or mental lapse. Later symptoms are descending muscular paralysis and respiratory compromise. In the past, death resulted from respiratory arrest, but mechanical respirators have reduced the fatality rate to about 10%.

Table 17.2 Three Types of Botulism

		Transmission and Epidemiology	Culture and Diagnosis
Food-Borne Botulism	Pure intoxication	Many botulism outbreaks occur in home-processed foods, including canned vegetables, smoked meats, and cheese spreads. Several factors in food processing can lead to botulism. Endospores are present on the vegetables or meat at the time of gathering and are difficult to remove completely. When contaminated food is put in jars and steamed in a pressure cooker that does not reach reliable pressure and temperature, some spores survive (botulinum spores are highly heat resistant). At the same time, the pressure is sufficient to evacuate the air and create anaerobic conditions. Storage of the jars at room temperature favors spore germination and vegetative growth, and one of the products of the cell's metabolism is botulinum, the most potent microbial toxin known. Bacterial growth may not be evident in the appearance of the jar or can or in the food's taste or texture, and only minute amounts of toxin may be present. Botulism is never transmitted from person to person.	Some laboratories attempt to identify the toxin in the offending food. Alternatively, if multiple patients present with the same symptoms after ingesting the same food, a presumptive diagnosis can be made. The cultivation of *C. botulinum* in feces is considered confirmation of the diagnosis since the carrier rate is very low.
Infant Botulism	Infection followed by intoxication	This is currently the most common type of botulism in the United States, with approximately 75 cases reported annually. The exact food source is not always known, although raw honey has been implicated in some cases, and the endospores are common in dust and soil. Apparently, the immature state of the neonatal intestine and microbial biota allows the spores to gain a foothold, germinate, and give off neurotoxin. As in adults, babies exhibit flaccid paralysis, usually manifested as a weak sucking response, generalized loss of tone (the "floppy-baby syndrome"), and respiratory complications. Although adults can also ingest botulinum spores in contaminated vegetables and other foods, the adult intestinal tract normally inhibits this sort of infection.	Finding the toxin or the organism in the feces confirms the diagnosis.
Wound Botulism	Infection followed by intoxication	Perhaps three or four cases of wound botulism occur each year in the United States. In this form of the disease, endospores enter a wound or puncture, much as in tetanus, but the symptoms are similar to those of food-borne botulism. Increased cases of this form of botulism are being reported in intravenous drug users as a result of needle puncture.	The toxin should be demonstrated in the serum, or the organism should be grown from the wound.

▶ Causative Agent

Clostridium botulinum, like *Clostridium tetani,* is an endospore-forming anaerobe that does its damage through the release of an exotoxin. *C. botulinum* commonly inhabits soil and water and occasionally the intestinal tract of animals. It is distributed worldwide but occurs most often in the Northern Hemisphere. The species has seven distinctly different types (designated A, B, C, D, E, F, and G) that vary in distribution among animals, regions of the world, and types of exotoxin. Human disease is usually associated with types A, B, E, and F, and animal disease with types A, B, C, D, and E.

Both *C. tetani* and *C. botulinum* produce neurotoxins; but tetanospasmin, the toxin made by *C. tetani,* results in spastic paralysis (uncontrolled muscle contraction). In contrast, botulinum, the *C. botulinum* neurotoxin, results in flaccid paralysis, a loss of ability to contract the muscles.

▶ Pathogenesis and Virulence Factors

As just described, the symptoms are caused entirely by the exotoxin botulinum.

▶ Culture and Diagnosis

Diagnostic standards are slightly different for the three different presentations of botulism. Because minute amounts of the toxin are highly dangerous, laboratory testing should be performed only by experienced personnel. A suspected case of botulism should trigger a phone call to the state health department or the CDC before proceeding with diagnosis or treatment.

▶ Prevention and Treatment

The CDC maintains a supply of type A, B, and E trivalent horse antitoxin, which, when administered soon after diagnosis, can prevent the worst outcomes of the disease. Patients are also managed with respiratory and cardiac support systems. In all cases, hospitalization is required and recovery takes weeks. There is an overall 5% mortality rate.

ASSESS YOUR PROGRESS

4. List the possible causative agents, modes of transmission, virulence factors, diagnostic techniques, and prevention/treatment for the highlighted conditions meningitis and poliomyelitis.
5. Identify the most common and also the most deadly of the multiple possible causes of meningitis.
6. Explain the difference between the oral polio vaccine and the inactivated polio vaccine, and under which circumstances each is appropriate.
7. Discuss important features of the diseases most directly involving the brain. These are meningoencephalitis, encephalitis, and subacute encephalitis.
8. Identify which encephalitis-causing viruses you should be aware of in your geographic area.
9. Discuss important features of the other diseases in the nervous system. These are rabies, poliomyelitis, tetanus, and botulism.

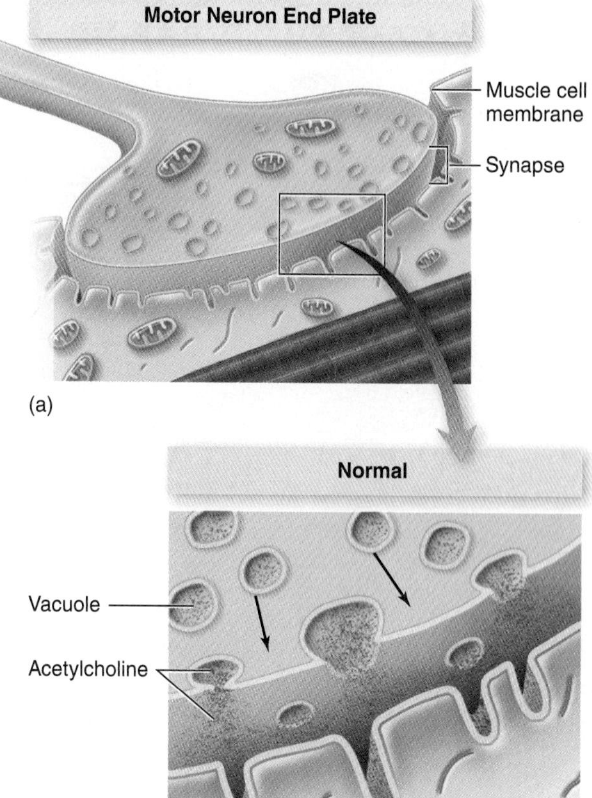

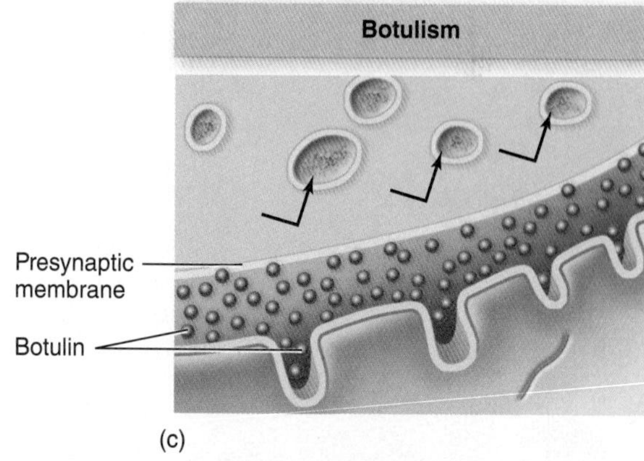

Figure 17.17 The physiological effects of botulism toxin (botulinum). **(a)** The relationship between the motor neuron and the muscle at the neuromuscular junction. **(b)** In the normal state, acetylcholine released at the synapse crosses to the muscle and creates an impulse that stimulates muscle contraction. **(c)** In botulism, the toxin enters the motor end plate and attaches to the presynaptic membrane, where it blocks release of the chemical. This prevents impulse transmission and keeps the muscle from contracting. This causes flaccid paralysis.

CASE FILE WRAP-UP

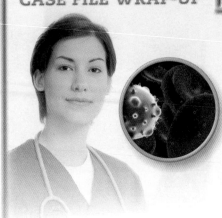

The results of Cody's lumbar puncture confirmed his physician's suspicion that he had developed meningitis. *H. influenzae* type B (Hib) was identified from the specimen of CSF obtained via the lumbar puncture. Cody's mother confirmed that he had not been given his childhood vaccinations. When questioned, the mother stated that she believed vaccinations could cause autism; therefore, Cody had not been immunized against Hib.

Meningitis caused by Hib can result from the spread of the bacteria from inadequately treated otitis media. This type of meningitis can be very severe. A vaccine has been available since 1988, but due to Cody not receiving his childhood vaccinations, he was susceptible to the disease. Although he eventually recovered, Cody suffered permanent hearing loss.

Summing Up

Taxonomic Organization Microorganisms Causing Disease in the Nervous System

Microorganism	Pronunciation	Location of Disease Table
Gram-positive endospore-forming bacteria		
Clostridium botulinum	klos-trid″-ee-um bot′-yew-lin″-um	Botulism, p. 482
Clostridium tetani	klos-trid″-ee-um tet′-a-nie	Tetanus, p. 481
Gram-positive bacteria		
Streptococcus agalactiae	strep″-tuh-kok′-us ay-ga-lact′-tee-ay	Neonatal meningitis, p. 470
Streptococcus pneumoniae	strep″-tuh-kok′-us nu-mo′-nee-ay	Meningitis, p. 466
Listeria monocytogenes	lis-teer′-ee-uh mon′-oh-sy-toj″-eh-nees	Meningitis, p. 466 Neonatal meningitis, p. 470
Gram-negative bacteria		
Escherichia coli	esh′-shur-eesh″-ee-uh col′-eye	Neonatal meningitis, p. 470
Haemophilus influenzae	huh-mah′-fuh-luss in′-floo-en″-zay	Meningitis, p. 466
Neisseria meningitidis	nye-seer″-ee-uh′ men′-in-jit″-ih-dus	Meningitis, p. 466
DNA viruses		
Herpes simplex virus type 1 and 2	hur′-peez sim′-plex vie′-russ	Encephalitis, p. 475
JC virus	jay′-cee″ vie′-russ	Progressive multifocal leukoencephalopathy, p. 475
RNA viruses		
Arboviruses	ar′-bow-vie′-russ-suz	Encephalitis, p. 475
Western equine encephalitis virus, Eastern equine encephalitis virus, California encephalitis virus (California and LaCrosse strains), St. Louis encephalitis virus, West Nile virus	wes′-turn ee′-cwine en-sef′-ah-ly′-tiss vie′-russ, ee′-stern ee′-cwine en-sef′-ah ly″-tuss vie′-russ, cal′-i-for′-nee-uh en-sef′-ah-ly″-tiss vie′-russ, saynt lew′-iss en-cef′-ah-ly″-tiss vie′- russ, west ny′-il vie′-russ	
Poliovirus	poh′-lee-oh vie′-russ	Poliomyelitis, p. 471
Rabies virus	ray′-bees vie′-russ	Rabies, p. 479
Fungi		
Cryptococcus neoformans	crip-tuh-kok′-us nee′-oh-for″-mans	Meningitis, p. 466
Coccidioides	cox-sid″-ee-oid′-ees	Meningitis, p. 466
Prions		
Creutzfeldt-Jakob prion	croytz′-felt yaw′-cob pree′-on	Creutzfeldt-Jakob disease, p. 478
Protozoa		
Acanthamoeba	ay-kanth″-uh-mee′-buh	Meningoencephalitis, p. 472
Naegleria fowleri	nay-glar′-ee-uh fow-lahr′-ee	Meningoencephalitis, p. 472
Toxoplasma gondii	tox′-oh-plas″-mah gon′-dee-eye	Subacute encephalitis, p. 478

Inside the Clinic

Winning the Battle: Bacterial Meningitis

A CDC study, reported in the *New England Journal of Medicine* in the May 26, 2011 issue, shows a substantial decrease in meningitis cases between the study years 1998 and 2007. This is good news, although the disease still claims approximately 500 lives and causes significant morbidity in 4,000 people every year. Even though fewer people are contracting the disease, those who do get the disease are just as sick. Meningitis is still a serious cause of morbidity and mortality, even in the United States.

Five types of bacteria were responsible for most cases of meningitis in the decades spanning the 1970s and 1980s. These included the following:

Haemophilus influenzae,
Neisseria meningitidis,
Streptococcus pneumoniae,
Group B streptococcus, and
Listeria monocytogenes.

Since the introduction of the vaccine for *H. influenzae* in 1990, vaccinations have also been developed for certain strains of *S. pneumoniae* and *N. meningitidis*. The incidence of *N. meningitidis* decreased by 58% during the study period, while the incidence of one strain of *S. pneumoniae* decreased by an incredible 92%! Overall, these vaccinations are responsible for decreasing the incidence of bacterial meningitis by 31% during the years studied. The vaccination against pneumococcal infection and the Hib vaccines are now included in the routine childhood immunization protocols. The meningococcal vaccine is available for high-risk groups, including children at risk between the ages of 2 and 10 years of age and people who are living in close quarters where *N. meningitidis* can be easily spread, such as college dorms and military barracks.

During the study period, those who were diagnosed with bacterial meningitis were more likely to be children under 2 months of age and people of African American heritage. It is easy to understand why children under 2 months of age would be at higher risk, as vaccinations would not yet have been given, but why are African Americans at higher risk? Researchers speculate that access to care may be an issue. It has also been speculated that African Americans may have a built-in genetic susceptibility to the bacteria that cause meningitis. In some cases, it could be a combination of these two factors.

Although great strides have been made in reducing the incidence of meningitis, *L. monocytogenes* remains a significant cause of the disease. To avoid meningitis caused by *L. monocytogenes*, people must avoid consuming undercooked meats and unpasteurized dairy products. Pregnant women, in particular, should mind their diet carefully to avoid contracting the bacterium.

Cross-sectional view of infected meningeal tissue.

Infectious Diseases Affecting
The Nervous System

Encephalitis
Arboviruses
Herpes simplex virus type 1 or 2
JC virus

Subacute Encephalitis
Toxoplasma gondii
Prions

Rabies
Rabies virus

Tetanus
Clostridium tetani

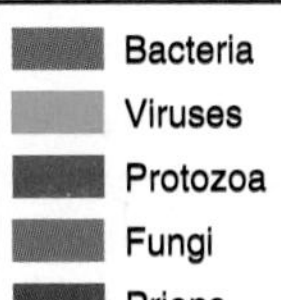

Creutzfeldt-Jakob Disease

Prion

Meningoencephalitis
Naegleria fowleri
Acanthamoeba

Meningitis
Neisseria meningitidis
Streptococcus pneumoniae
Haemophilus influenzae
Listeria monocytogenes
Cryptococcus neoformans
Coccidioides species
Various viruses

Neonatal Meningitis
Streptococcus agalactiae
Escherichia coli
Listeria monocytogenes

Polio
Poliovirus

Botulism
Clostridium botulinum

System Summary Figure 17.18

Chapter Summary

17.1 The Nervous System and Its Defenses

- The nervous system has two parts: the central nervous system (the brain and spinal cord), and the peripheral nervous system (nerves and ganglia).
- The soft tissue of the brain and spinal cord is encased within the tough casing of three membranes called the *meninges.* The subarachnoid space is filled with a clear serumlike fluid called cerebrospinal fluid (CSF).
- The nervous system is protected by the *blood-brain barrier,* which limits the passage of substances from the bloodstream to the brain and spinal cord.

17.2 Normal Biota of the Nervous System

- At the present time, we believe there is no normal biota in either the central nervous system (CNS) or the peripheral nervous system (PNS).

17.3 Nervous System Diseases Caused by Microorganisms

- **Meningitis:** Inflammation of the meninges. The more serious forms are caused by bacteria, often facilitated by coinfection or previous infection with respiratory viruses.
  - *Neisseria meningitidis:* Gram-negative diplococcus; causes most serious form of acute meningitis.
  - *Streptococcus pneumoniae:* Gram-positive coccus; most frequent cause of community-acquired pneumococcal meningitis.
  - *Haemophilus influenzae:* Declined sharply because of vaccination.
  - *Listeria monocytogenes:* Most cases are associated with ingesting contaminated dairy products, poultry, and meat.
  - *Cryptococcus neoformans:* Fungus; causes chronic form with more gradual onset of symptoms.
  - *Coccidioides* species: True systemic fungal infection; begins in lungs but can disseminate quickly throughout body; highest incidence in southwestern United States, Mexico, and parts of Central and South America.
  - Viruses: Very common, particularly in children; 90% are caused by enteroviruses.
- **Neonatal Meningitis:** Usually transmitted vertically. Primary causes are *Streptococcus agalactiae, Escherichia coli,* and *Listeria monocytogenes.*
- **Poliomyelitis:** Acute enterovirus infection of spinal cord; can cause neuromuscular paralysis. Two effective vaccines exist: Inactivated Salk poliovirus vaccine (IPV) is the only one used now in the United States; attenuated oral Sabin poliovirus vaccine (OPV) still being used in the developing world.
- **Meningoencephalitis:** Caused mainly by two amoebas, *Naegleria fowleri* and *Acanthamoeba.*
- **Acute Encephalitis:** Usually caused by viral infection. Arboviruses carried by arthropods often are responsible. Begins with arthropod bite, release of virus into tissues, and replication in nearby lymphatic tissues.
  - Western Equine Encephalitis (WEE): Occurs sporadically in western United States and Canada.
  - Eastern Equine Encephalitis (EEE): Endemic to eastern coast of North America and Canada.
  - California Encephalitis: Caused by two different viral strains, the California strain and the LaCrosse strain.
  - St. Louis Encephalitis (SLE): May be most common of American viral encephalitides. Appears throughout North, South America; epidemics occur most often in Midwest and South.
  - West Nile Encephalitis: West Nile virus is close relative of SLE virus. Emerged in United States in 1999.
  - Herpes simplex virus: Herpes simplex virus type 1 and 2 cause encephalitis in newborns born to HSV-positive mothers, older children and young adults (ages 5 to 30), older adults.
  - JC virus: Can cause progressive multifocal leukoencephalopathy (PML), particularly in immunocompromised individuals. Fatal infection.
- **Subacute Encephalitis:** Symptoms take longer to manifest.
  - *Toxoplasma gondii:* Protozoan, causes toxoplasmosis, most common form of subacute encephalitis. Relatively asymptomatic in the healthy; can be severe in immunodeficient people and fetuses.
  - Prions: Proteinaceous infectious particles containing no genetic material. Cause transmissible spongiform encephalopathies (TSEs), neurodegenerative diseases with long incubation periods but rapid progressions once they begin. Human TSEs are Creutzfeldt-Jakob disease (CJD), Gerstmann-Strussler-Scheinker disease, and fatal familial insomnia.
- **Rabies:** Slow, progressive zoonotic disease characterized by fatal encephalitis. Rabies virus is in the family *Rhabdoviridae.*
- **Tetanus:** Neuromuscular disease, also called lockjaw; caused by *Clostridium tetani* neurotoxin, *tetanospasmin,* which binds target sites on spinal neurons, blocks inhibition of muscle contraction.
- **Botulism:** Caused by exotoxin of *C. botulinum;* associated with eating poorly preserved foods; can also occur as true infection. Three major forms: food-borne, infant botulism, and wound botulism.

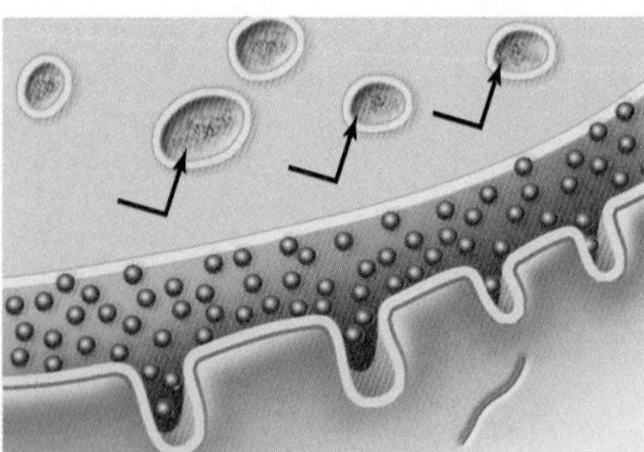

Multiple-Choice Questions Knowledge and Comprehension

Select the correct answer from the answers provided.

1. Which of the following organisms does *not* cause meningitis?
   a. *Haemophilus influenzae*
   b. *Streptococcus pneumoniae*
   c. *Neisseria meningitidis*
   d. *Clostridium tetani*
2. The first choice antibiotic for bacterial meningitis is the broad-spectrum
   a. cephalosporin.
   b. penicillin.
   c. ampicillin.
   d. vancomycin.
3. Meningococcal meningitis is caused by
   a. *Haemophilus influenzae.*
   b. *Streptococcus pneumoniae.*
   c. *Neisseria meningitidis.*
   d. *Listeria monocytogenes.*
4. Which of the following neurological diseases is *not* caused by a prion?
   a. Creutzfeldt-Jakob disease
   b. scrapie
   c. mad cow disease
   d. St. Louis encephalitis
5. *Cryptococcus neoformans* is primarily transmitted by
   a. direct contact.
   b. bird droppings.
   c. fomites.
   d. sexual activity.
6. CJD is caused by a/an
   a. arbovirus.
   b. prion.
   c. protozoan.
   d. bacterium.
7. What food should you avoid feeding a child under 1 year old because of potential botulism?
   a. honey
   b. milk
   c. apple juice
   d. applesauce
8. Which of the following is *not* caused by an arbovirus?
   a. St. Louis encephalitis
   b. Eastern equine encephalitis
   c. West Nile encephalitis
   d. mad cow disease

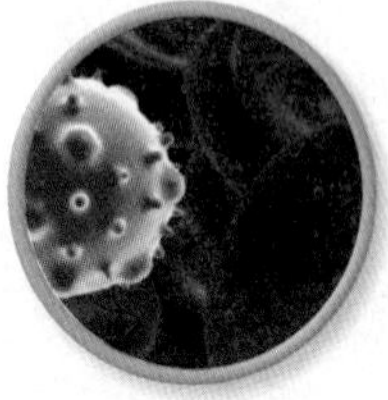

Critical Thinking Application and Analysis

***Critical thinking* is the ability to reason and solve problems using facts and concepts.These questions can be approached from a number of angles and, in most cases, they do not have a single correct answer.**

1. Why is encephalitis often difficult to diagnosis?
2. Discuss the transmission of CJD.
3. In the section on meningococcal meningitis, the following sentence appears: "If no samples were obtained prior to antibiotic treatment, a PCR test is the best bet for identifying the pathogen." Why?
4. Why is there no normal biota associated with the nervous system?
5. Even though the oral polio vaccine is not used in the developed world, it is still widely used in the developing world, in part because it confers what might be called "accidental" herd immunity. Can you speculate on what this is?

Visual Connections Synthesis

This question connects previous images to a new concept.

1. **From chapter 2, figure 2.19*a*.** Without looking back to the figure in chapter 2, speculate on which meningitis-causing organism you are seeing here. How could your presumptive diagnosis be confirmed?

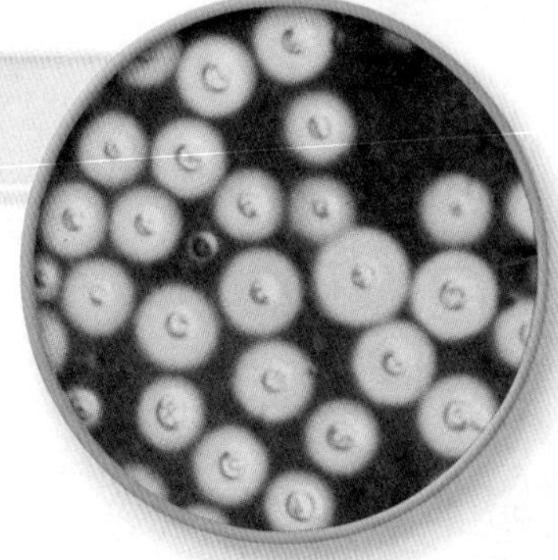

www.mcgrawhillconnect.com

Enhance your study of this chapter with study tools and practice tests. Also ask your instructor about the resources available through ConnectPlus, including the media-rich eBook, interactive learning tools, and animations.

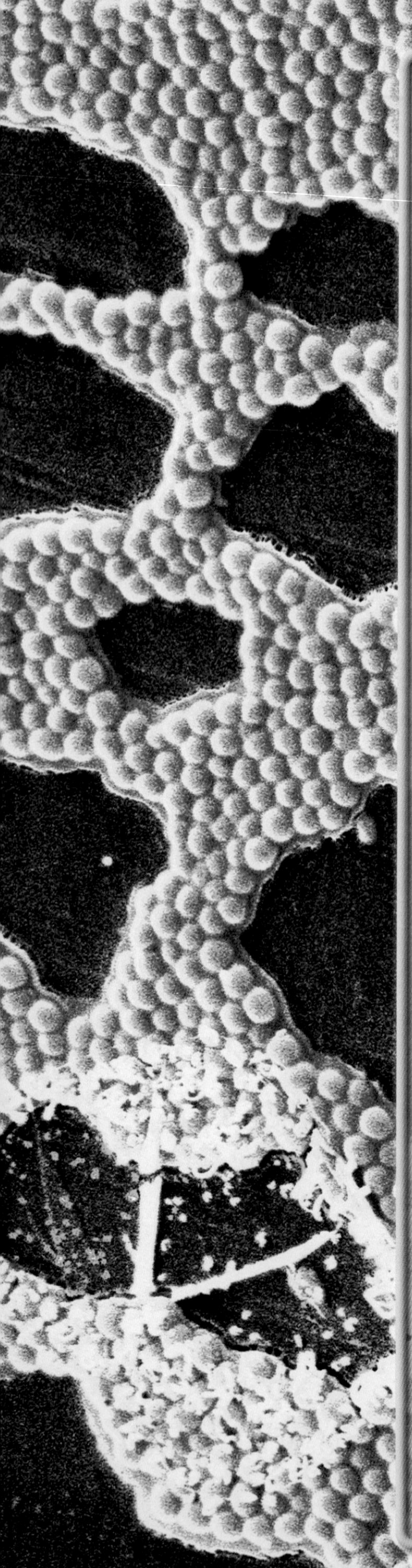

CASE FILE

A Shocking Situation

While working as a laboratory technician, I was called to the emergency room (ER) to draw blood from a young woman. The patient was being treated for cancer and had a central line in place for chemotherapy. The history provided to me by the nursing staff indicated that the patient had developed a sudden high fever. She was lethargic, had very low blood pressure, and appeared quite ill. She had been instructed to report any fever immediately due to her compromised immune state, and her family had brought her to the ER as soon as they realized how ill she was.

The nursing staff pointed out that the patient's catheter site was draining purulent material. A swab of the site had already been obtained. I drew blood for a complete blood count (CBC), electrolytes and creatinine, and obtained blood cultures from two different sites as instructed. The physician arrived and informed me that he would be removing the central line and inserting it in another site. Once the line was removed, the end would be cut off and brought to the lab for culture and sensitivity testing. Intravenous fluids were already being administered to combat the patient's hypotension, and broad-spectrum antibiotics were started immediately.

- What condition was the patient suffering from?
- What was the likely cause of her illness?
- What symptoms did the patient display that were consistent with the illness?

Case File Wrap-Up appears on page 518.

CHAPTER 18

Infectious Diseases Affecting the Cardiovascular and Lymphatic Systems

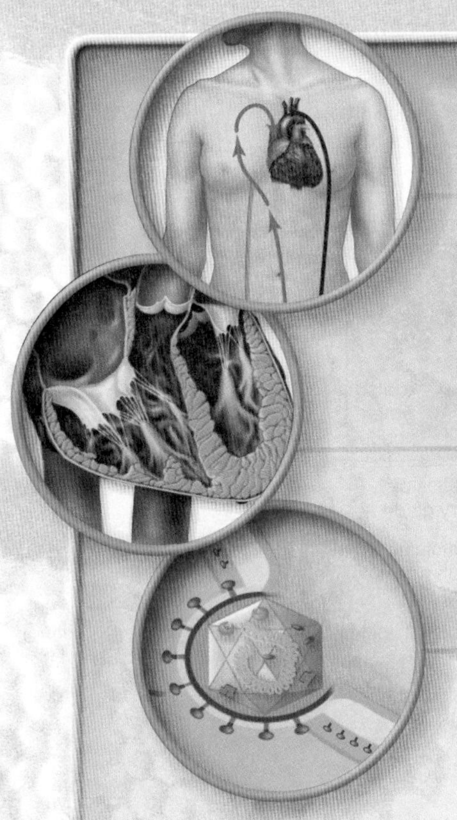

IN THIS CHAPTER...

18.1 The Cardiovascular and Lymphatic Systems and Their Defenses

1. Describe the important anatomical features of the cardiovascular and lymphatic systems.
2. List the natural defenses present in the cardiovascular and lymphatic systems.

18.2 Normal Biota of the Cardiovascular and Lymphatic Systems

3. Discuss the "what" and the "why" of the normal biota of the cardiovascular and lymphatic systems.

18.3 Cardiovascular and Lymphatic System Diseases Caused by Microorganisms

4. List the possible causative agents, modes of transmission, virulence factors, diagnostic techniques, and prevention/treatment for the highlighted conditions, malaria and HIV.
5. Discuss the epidemiology of malaria.
6. Discuss the epidemiology of HIV infection in the developing world.
7. Discuss the important features of infectious cardiovascular diseases that have more than one possible cause. These are the two forms of endocarditis, septicemia, hemorrhagic fever diseases, and nonhemorrhagic fever diseases.
8. Discuss factors that distinguish hemorrhagic and nonhemorrhagic fever diseases.
9. Discuss what series of events may lead to septicemia and how it should be prevented and treated.
10. Discuss the important features of infectious cardiovascular diseases that have only one possible cause. These are plague, tularemia, Lyme disease, infectious mononucleosis, and anthrax.
11. Describe what makes anthrax a good agent for bioterrorism, and list the important presenting signs to look for in patients.

18.1 The Cardiovascular and Lymphatic Systems and Their Defenses

The Cardiovascular System

The cardiovascular system is the pipeline of the body. It is composed of the blood vessels, which carry blood to and from all regions of the body, and the heart, which pumps the blood. This system moves the blood in a closed circuit, and it is therefore known as the *circulatory system*. The cardiovascular system provides tissues with oxygen and nutrients and carries away carbon dioxide and waste products, delivering them to the appropriate organs for removal. A closely related but largely separate system, the **lymphatic system,** is a major source of immune cells and fluids, and it serves as a one-way passage, returning fluid from the tissues to the cardiovascular system. **Figure 18.1** shows you how the two systems work together. You first saw this figure in chapter 12.

Figure 18.1 **The anatomy of the cardiovascular and lymphatic systems.**

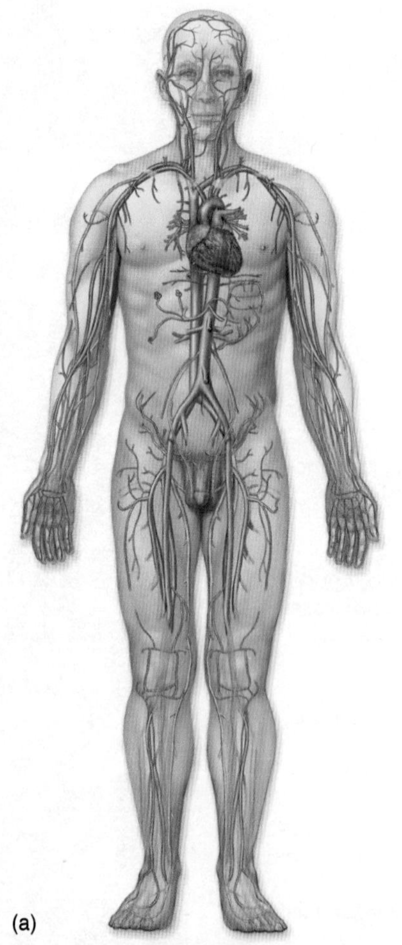

The Circulatory System: Surveillance

Body compartments are screened by circulating WBCs.

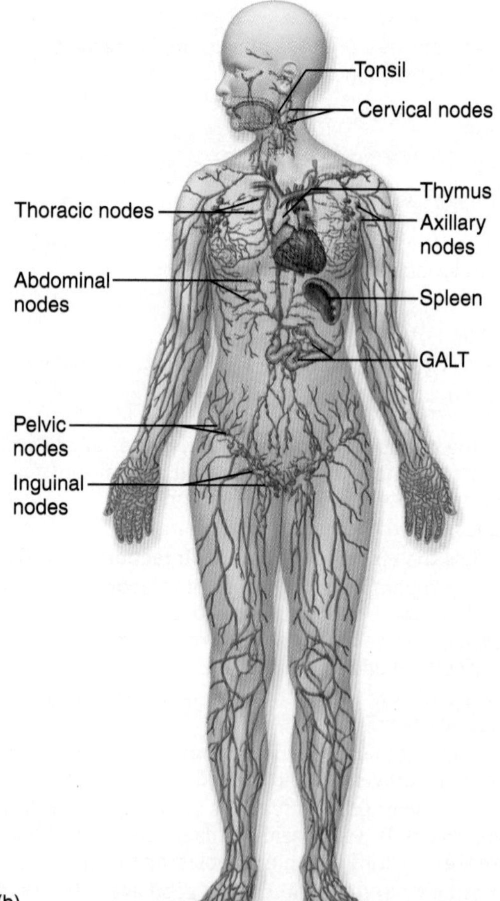

The Lymphatic System

The lymphatic system consists of a branching network of vessels that extend into most body areas. Note the higher density of lymphatic vessels in the "dead-end" areas of the hands, feet, and breast, which are frequent contact points for infections. Other lymphatic organs include the lymph nodes, spleen, gut-associated lymphoid tissue (GALT), the thymus gland, and the tonsils.

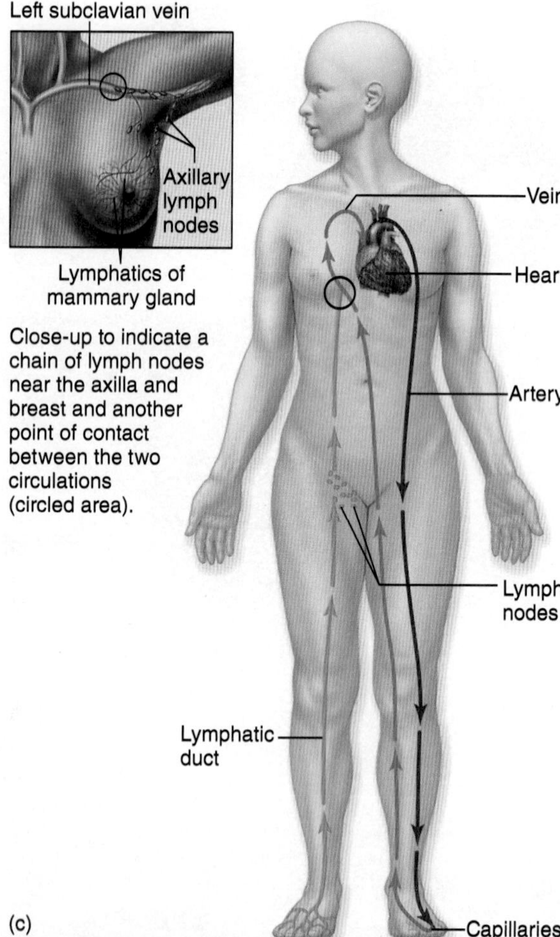

The Lymphatic and Circulatory Systems

Comparison of the generalized circulation of the lymphatic system and the blood. Although the lymphatic vessels parallel the regular circulation, they transport in only one direction unlike the cyclic pattern of blood. Direct connection between the two circulations occurs at points near the heart where large lymph ducts empty their fluid into veins (circled area).

The heart is a fist-size muscular organ that pumps blood through the body. It is divided into two halves, each of which is divided into an upper and lower chamber **(figure 18.2).** The upper chambers are called atria (singular, atrium), and the lower are ventricles. The entire organ is encased in a fibrous covering, the pericardium, which is an occasional site of infection. The actual wall of the heart has three layers: from outer to inner, they are the epicardium, the myocardium, and the endocardium. The endocardium also covers the valves of the heart, and it is a relatively common target of microbial infection.

The blood vessels consist of *arteries, veins,* and *capillaries.* Arteries carry oxygenated blood away from the heart under relatively high pressure. They branch into smaller vessels called arterioles. Veins actually begin as smaller venules in the periphery of the body and coalesce into veins. The smallest blood vessels, the capillaries, connect arterioles to venules. Both arteries and veins have walls made of three layers of tissue. The innermost layer is composed of a smooth epithelium called endothelium. Its smooth surface encourages the smooth flow of cells and platelets through the system. The next layer is composed of connective tissue and muscle fibers. The outside layer is a thin layer of connective tissue. Capillaries, the smallest vessels, have walls made of only one layer of endothelium.

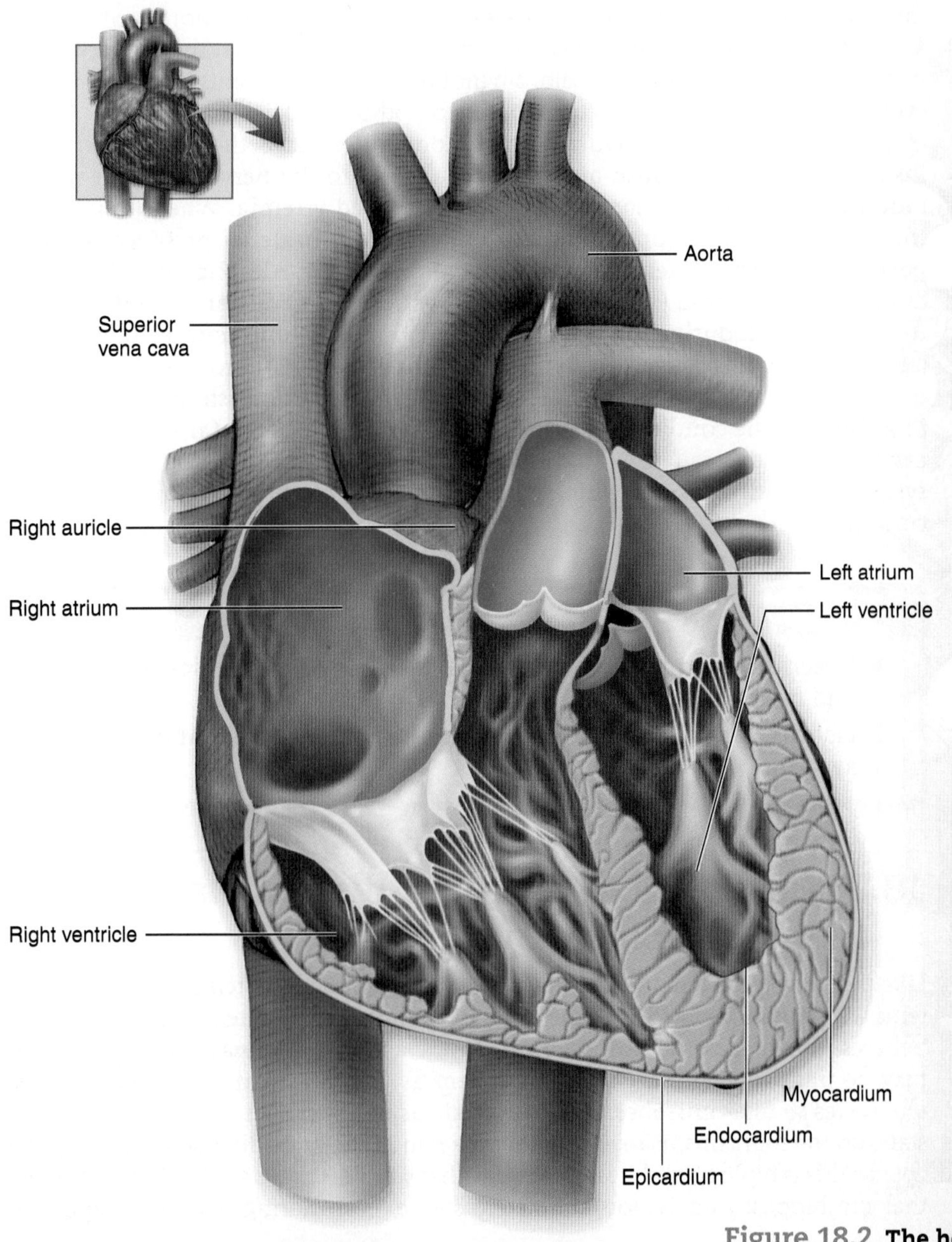

Figure 18.2 The heart.

Conceptual image of blood cells in an artery.

Medical Moment

Lymphangitis

Lymphangitis is an infection of the lymph vessels, which can occur as a result of bacterial infection. Staphylococcal and streptococcal skin infections are a common cause of lymphangitis. Lymphangitis can be a serious condition that may progress rapidly to sepsis if improperly treated.

Generally, an individual with a skin infection will notice a red streak spreading toward the armpit or groin area. Fever, pain, and flulike symptoms, as well as enlarged lymph nodes (lymphadenopathy) are all common symptoms of lymphangitis. Often the lymph nodes closest to the infected area are the ones affected.

Prompt recognition and treatment are essential. A swab of the affected area or blood cultures may yield the causative organism. Antibiotics should be started immediately. Anti-inflammatory drugs may help to reduce inflammation. In addition, warm compresses may help to decrease swelling and ease discomfort.

Lymphangitis may be confused with thrombophlebitis. However, lymphangitis can often be recognized by the presence of a skin infection and other signs of infection such as fever and chills. Most people recover from lymphangitis without any complications, but swelling of the affected area may continue for several weeks.

The Lymphatic System

The lymphatic system consists mainly of the lymph vessels, which roughly parallel the blood vessels; lymph nodes, which cluster at body sites such as the groin, neck, armpit, and intestines; and the spleen. It serves to collect fluid that has left the blood vessels and entered tissues, filter it of impurities and infectious agents, and return it to the blood.

Defenses of the Cardiovascular and Lymphatic Systems

The cardiovascular system is highly protected from microbial infection. Microbes that successfully invade the system, however, gain access to every part of the body, and every system may potentially be affected. For this reason, bloodstream infections are called **systemic** infections.

Multiple defenses against infection reside in the bloodstream. The blood is full of leukocytes, with approximately 5,000 to 10,000 white blood cells per milliliter of blood. The various types of white blood cells include the lymphocytes, responsible for specific immunity, and the phagocytes, which are so critical to nonspecific as well as specific immune responses. Very few microbes can survive in the blood with so many defensive elements. That said, a handful of infectious agents have nonetheless evolved exquisite mechanisms for avoiding blood-borne defenses.

Medical conditions involving the blood often have the suffix *-emia*. For instance, viruses that cause meningitis can travel to the nervous system via the bloodstream. Their presence in the blood is called **viremia.** When fungi are in the blood, the condition is termed **fungemia,** and bacterial presence is called **bacteremia,** a general term denoting only their *presence.* Although the blood contains no normal biota (see next section), bacteria frequently are introduced into the bloodstream during the course of daily living. Brushing your teeth or tearing a hangnail can introduce bacteria from the mouth or skin into the bloodstream; this situation is usually temporary. But when bacteria flourish and grow in the bloodstream, the condition is termed **septicemia.** Septicemia (also called sepsis) can very quickly lead to cascading immune responses, resulting in decreased systemic blood pressure, which can lead to **septic shock,** a life-threatening condition.

ASSESS YOUR PROGRESS

1. Describe the important anatomical features of the cardiovascular and lymphatic systems.
2. List the natural defenses present in the cardiovascular and lymphatic systems.

NCLEX® PREP

1. Endocarditis is an inflammation of which portion of the heart?
   - a. pericardium
   - b. endocardium
   - c. epicardium
   - d. myocardium

18.2 Normal Biota of the Cardiovascular and Lymphatic Systems

Like the nervous system, the cardiovascular and lymphatic systems are "closed" systems with no normal access to the external environment. Therefore, current science believes they possess no normal biota. In the absence of disease, microorganisms may be transiently present in either system as just described. The lymphatic system serves to filter microbes and their products out of tissues. Thus, in the healthy state, no microorganisms *colonize* either the lymphatic or cardiovascular systems. Of course, this is biology, and it is never quite that simple. Recent studies have suggested that the bloodstream is not completely sterile, even during periods of apparent health. It is tempting to speculate that these low-level microbial "infections" may contribute to diseases for which no etiology has previously been found or for conditions currently thought to be noninfectious.

Cardiovascular and Lymphatic Systems Defenses and Normal Biota

	Defenses	Normal Biota
Cardiovascular System	Blood-borne components of nonspecific and specific immunity—including phagocytosis, specific immunity	None
Lymphatic System	Numerous immune defenses reside here.	None

ASSESS YOUR PROGRESS

3. Discuss the "what" and the "why" of the normal biota of the cardiovascular and lymphatic systems.

18.3 Cardiovascular and Lymphatic System Diseases Caused by Microorganisms

Categorizing cardiovascular and lymphatic infections according to clinical presentation is somewhat difficult because most of these conditions are systemic, with effects on multiple organ systems. We start with two extremely important conditions, malaria and HIV.

HIGHLIGHT DISEASE

Malaria

Throughout human history, including prehistoric times, malaria has been one of the greatest afflictions, in the same rank as bubonic plague, influenza, and tuberculosis. Even now, as the dominant protozoan disease, it threatens 40% of the world's population every year. The origin of the name is from the Italian words *mal,* bad, and *aria,* air.

▸ Signs and Symptoms

After a 10- to 16-day incubation period, the first symptoms are malaise, fatigue, vague aches, and nausea with or without diarrhea, followed by bouts of chills, fever, and sweating. These symptoms occur at 48- or 72-hour intervals, as a result of the synchronous rupturing of red blood cells. The interval, length, and regularity of symptoms reflect the type of malaria. Patients with falciparum malaria, the most virulent type, often display persistent fever, cough, and weakness for weeks without relief. Complications of malaria are hemolytic anemia from lysed blood cells and organ enlargement and rupture due to cellular debris that accumulates in the spleen, liver, and kidneys. One of the most serious complications of falciparum malaria is termed *cerebral malaria.* In this condition, small blood vessels in the brain become obstructed due to the increased ability of red blood cells (RBCs) to adhere to vessel walls (a condition called *cytoadherence* induced by the infecting protozoan). The resulting decrease in oxygen in brain tissue can result in coma and death. In general, malaria has the highest death rate in the acute phase, especially in children. Certain kinds of malaria (those caused by *Plasmodium vivax* and *P. ovale*) are subject to relapses because some infected liver cells harbor dormant protozoans for up to 5 years.

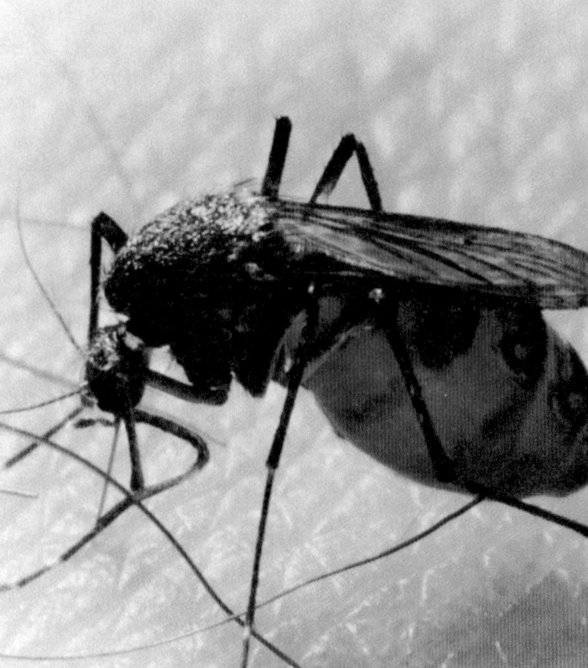

Mosquitos transmit the malaria protozoan.

▶ Causative Agent

Plasmodium species are protozoa in the sporozoan group. The genus *Plasmodium* contains four species: *P. malariae, P. vivax, P. falciparum,* and *P. ovale.* Humans are the primary vertebrate hosts for most of the species. The four species show variations in the pattern and severity of disease.

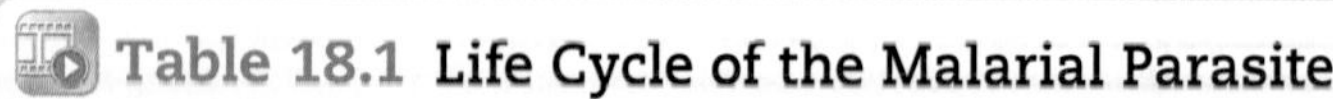

Table 18.1 Life Cycle of the Malarial Parasite

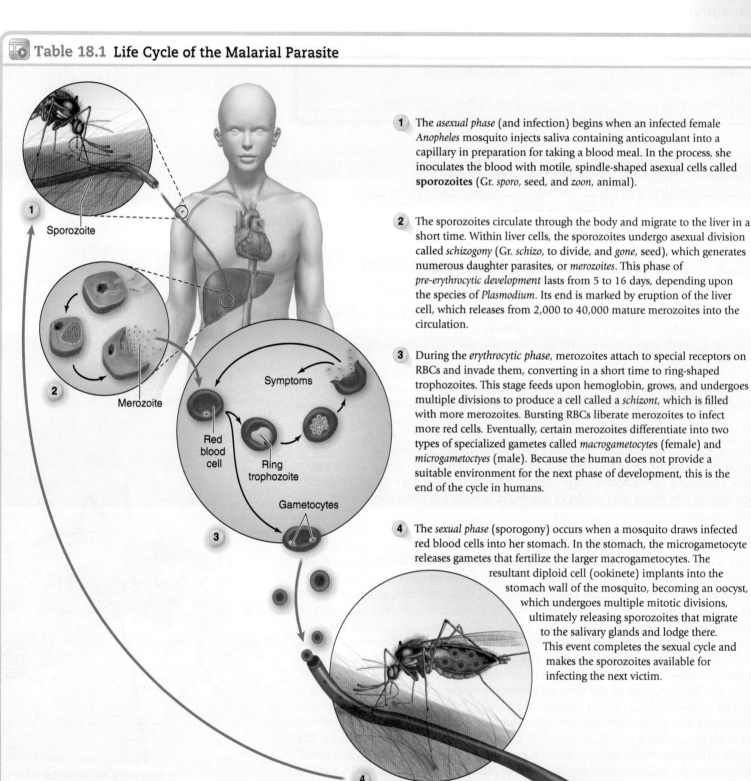

1 The *asexual phase* (and infection) begins when an infected female *Anopheles* mosquito injects saliva containing anticoagulant into a capillary in preparation for taking a blood meal. In the process, she inoculates the blood with motile, spindle-shaped asexual cells called **sporozoites** (Gr. *sporo,* seed, and *zoon,* animal).

2 The sporozoites circulate through the body and migrate to the liver in a short time. Within liver cells, the sporozoites undergo asexual division called *schizogony* (Gr. *schizo,* to divide, and *gone,* seed), which generates numerous daughter parasites, or *merozoites.* This phase of *pre-erythrocytic development* lasts from 5 to 16 days, depending upon the species of *Plasmodium.* Its end is marked by eruption of the liver cell, which releases from 2,000 to 40,000 mature merozoites into the circulation.

3 During the *erythrocytic phase,* merozoites attach to special receptors on RBCs and invade them, converting in a short time to ring-shaped trophozoites. This stage feeds upon hemoglobin, grows, and undergoes multiple divisions to produce a cell called a *schizont,* which is filled with more merozoites. Bursting RBCs liberate merozoites to infect more red cells. Eventually, certain merozoites differentiate into two types of specialized gametes called *macrogametocytes* (female) and *microgametoctyes* (male). Because the human does not provide a suitable environment for the next phase of development, this is the end of the cycle in humans.

4 The *sexual phase* (sporogony) occurs when a mosquito draws infected red blood cells into her stomach. In the stomach, the microgametocyte releases gametes that fertilize the larger macrogametocytes. The resultant diploid cell (ookinete) implants into the stomach wall of the mosquito, becoming an oocyst, which undergoes multiple mitotic divisions, ultimately releasing sporozoites that migrate to the salivary glands and lodge there. This event completes the sexual cycle and makes the sporozoites available for infecting the next victim.

Development of the malarial parasite is divided into two distinct phases: the asexual phase, carried out in the human, and the sexual phase, carried out in the mosquito. **Table 18.1** lists the steps of the malarial life cycle.

Figure 18.3 illustrates the ring trophozoite stage in a malarial infection.

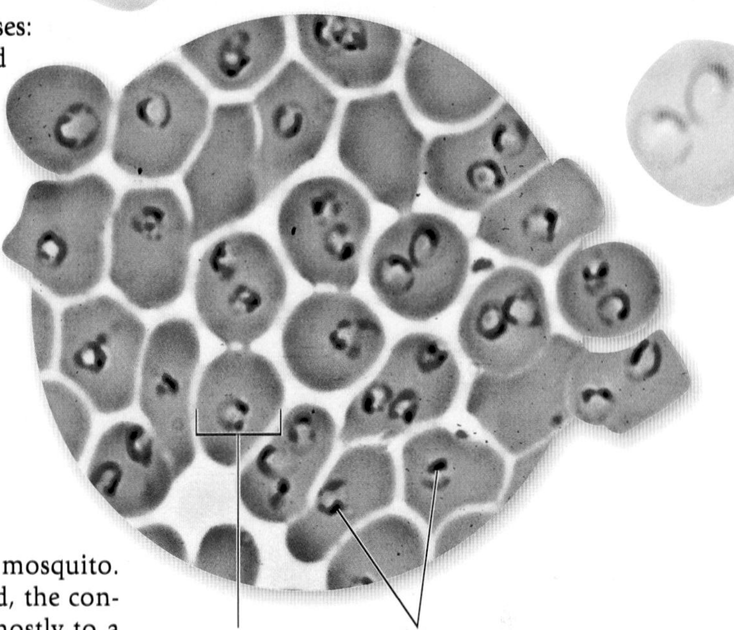

Figure 18.3 The ring trophozoite stage in a *Plasmodium falciparum* infection. A smear of peripheral blood shows ring forms in red blood cells. Some RBCs have multiple trophozoites.

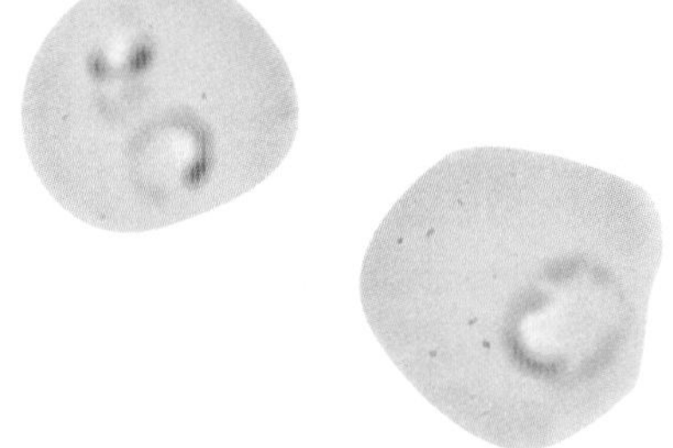

Pathogenesis and Virulence Factors

The invasion of the merozoites into RBCs leads to the release of fever-inducing chemicals into the bloodstream. Chills and fevers often occur in a cyclic pattern. *Plasmodium* also metabolizes glucose at a very high rate, leading to hypoglycemia in the human host. The damage to RBCs results in anemia. The accumulation of malarial products in the liver and the immune stimulation in the spleen can lead to enlargement of these organs.

Transmission and Epidemiology

All forms of malaria are spread primarily by the female *Anopheles* mosquito. Although malaria was once distributed throughout most of the world, the control of mosquitoes in temperate areas has successfully restricted it mostly to a belt extending around the equator (**figure 18.4**). Despite this achievement, approximately 300 million to 500 million new cases are still reported each year, about 90% of them in Africa. The most frequent victims are children and young adults, of whom at least 2 million die annually. A particular form of the malarial protozoan causes damage to the placenta in pregnant women, leading to excess mortality among fetuses and newborns. The total case rate in the United States is about 1,000 to 2,000 new cases a year, most of which occur in immigrants or travelers to endemic areas.

Culture and Diagnosis

Malaria can be diagnosed definitively by the discovery of a typical stage of *Plasmodium* in stained blood smears (see figure 18.3). Newer serological procedures have made diagnosis more accurate while requiring less skill to perform. Other indications are knowledge of the patient's residence or travel in endemic areas and symptoms such as recurring chills, fever, and sweating.

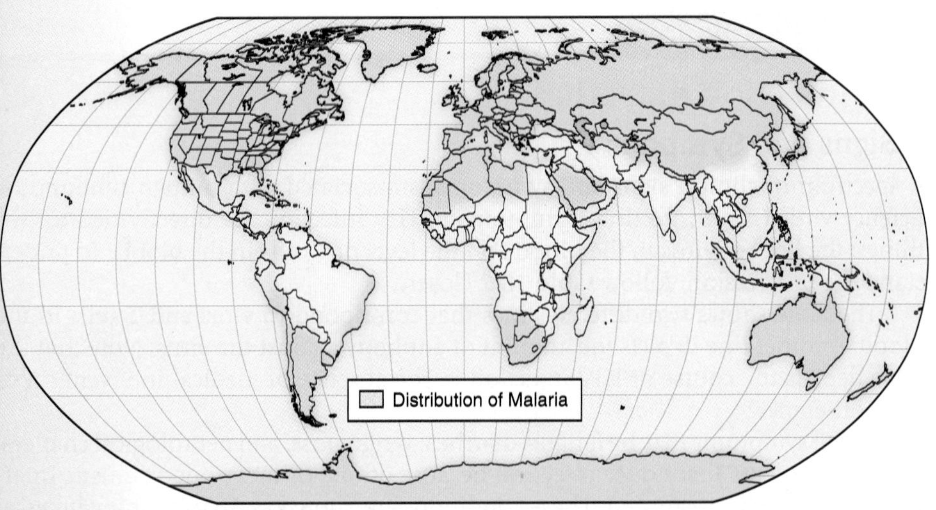

Figure 18.4 The malaria belt. Yellow zones outline the major regions that harbor malaria. The malaria belt corresponds to a band around the equator.

Disease Table 18.1 Malaria

Causative Organism(s)	*Plasmodium falciparum, P. vivax, P. ovale, P. malariae*
Most Common Modes of Transmission	Biological vector (mosquito), vertical
Virulence Factors	Multiple life stages; multiple antigenic types; ability to scavenge glucose, cytoadherence
Culture/ Diagnosis	Blood smear; serological methods
Prevention	Mosquito control; use of bed nets; no vaccine yet available; prophylactic antiprotozoal agents
Treatment	Chloroquine, mefloquine, artemisinin, pyrimethamine plus sulfadoxine (Fansidar), quinine, or proguanil

Prevention

World health officials have tried for decades to eradicate malaria. The most recent attempt is by the United Nations–backed Global Malaria Action Plan, which hopes to cut malaria by 75% between 2000 and 2015, and to reduce the number of malaria deaths to zero. Their final goal is to eradicate malaria altogether.

Malaria prevention is attempted through long-term mosquito abatement and human chemoprophylaxis. Abatement includes elimination of standing water that could serve as a breeding site and spraying of insecticides to reduce populations of adult mosquitoes, especially in and near human dwellings. Scientists have also tried introducing sterile male mosquitoes into endemic areas in an attempt to decrease mosquito populations. Humans can reduce their risk of infection considerably by using netting, screens, and repellants; by remaining indoors at night; and by taking weekly doses of prophylactic drugs. (Western travelers to endemic areas are usually prescribed antimalarials for the duration of their trips.) People with a recent history of malaria are not allowed to give blood. The WHO and other international organizations focus on efforts to distribute bed nets and to teach people how to dip the nets into an insecticide **(figure 18.5)**. The use of bed nets has been estimated to reduce childhood mortality from malaria by 20%. Here is an area where we can report some success: Bed-net use has tripled in 16 of 20 sub-Saharan African countries since 2000.

Figure 18.5
An African family sits under a treated mosquito net from the UNICEF mosquito nets program.

The best protection would come from a malaria vaccine, and scientists have struggled for decades to develop one. A successful malaria vaccine must be capable of striking a diverse and rapidly changing target. Scientists estimate that the parasite has 5,300 different antigens. Another potentially powerful strategy is the use of interfering RNAs in the mosquitoes to render them resistant to *Plasmodium* infection.

Treatment

Quinine has long been a mainstay of malaria treatment. Chloroquine, the least toxic type, is used in nonresistant forms of the disease. In areas of the world where resistant strains of *P. falciparum* and *P. vivax* predominate, a course of mefloquine or pyrimethamine plus sulfadoxine (Fansidar) may be indicated, but more commonly artemisinin, another plant compound, has been most effective. Predictably, artemisinin resistance has now been found in Cambodia. The World Health Organization now recommends only administering artemisinin in combination with other antimalarials, in order to prevent resistance development.

NCLEX® PREP

2. Of the four types of malaria, which of the following causes the most severe expression of the disease?
   a. *P. vivax*
   b. *P. ovale*
   c. *P. falciparum*
   d. *P. malariae*

HIGHLIGHT DISEASE

HIV Infection and AIDS

HIV budding out of an infected immune cell.

Signs and Symptoms

A spectrum of clinical signs and symptoms is associated with human immunodeficiency virus (HIV) infection. Symptoms in HIV infection are directly tied to two things: the level of virus in the blood and the level of T cells in the blood. To understand the progression, follow **table 18.2** closely.

The table shows two different lines that correspond to virus and T cells in the blood. Another line depicts the amount of antibody against the virus. Note that the table depicts the course of HIV infection in the absence of medical intervention or chemotherapy.

Initial symptoms may be fatigue, diarrhea, weight loss, and neurological changes, but most patients first notice infection because of one or more opportunistic infections or neoplasms (cancers). These conditions are known as AIDS-defining illnesses (ADIs) and are detailed in **table 18.3.** Other disease-related symptoms appear to

Table 18.2 Dynamics of Virus Antigen, Antibody, and T Cells in Circulation

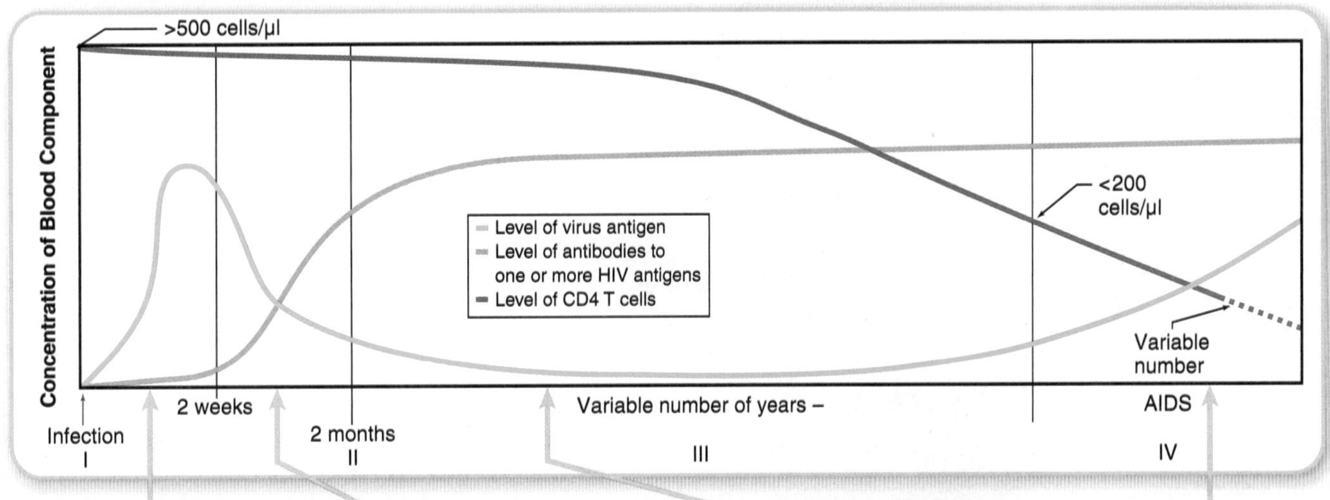

Initial infection is often attended by vague, mononucleosis-like symptoms that soon disappear. This phase corresponds to the initial high levels of virus (the green line above). Antibodies are not yet abundant.

In the second phase, virus numbers in blood drop dramatically and antibody begins to appear. CD4 T cells begin to decrease in number.

A long period of mostly asymptomatic infection ensues. During this time, which can last from 2 to 15 years, lymphadenopathy may be the prominent symptom. During the mid- to late-asymptomatic period, the number of T cells in the blood is steadily decreasing. Once the T-cell level reaches a (low) threshold, the symptoms of AIDS ensue.

Once T cells drop below 200 cells/µl, AIDS results. Note that even though antibody levels remain high, virus levels in the blood begin to rise.

Table 18.3 AIDS-Defining Illnesses

Skin and/or Mucous Membranes (includes eyes)	Nervous System	Cardiovascular and Lymphatic System or Multiple Organ Systems	Respiratory Tract	Gastrointestinal Tract	Genitourinary and/or Reproductive Tract
Cytomegalovirus retinitis (with loss of vision) Herpes simplex chronic ulcers (>1 month duration) Kaposi's sarcoma	Cryptococcosis, extrapulmonary HIV encephalopathy Lymphoma; primarily in brain Progressive multifocal leukoencephalopathy Toxoplasmosis of the brain	Coccidioidomycosis, disseminated or extrapulmonary Cytomegalovirus (other than liver, spleen, nodes) Histoplasmosis Burkitt's lymphoma Immunoblastic lymphoma *Mycobacterium kansasii*, disseminated or extrapulmonary *Mycobacterium tuberculosis*, disseminated or extrapulmonary *Salmonella* septicemia, recurrent Wasting syndrome	Candidiasis of trachea, bronchi, or lungs Herpes simplex bronchitis or pneumonitis *Mycobacterium avium* complex Tuberculosis (*Mycobacterium tuberculosis*) *Pneumocystis jiroveci* pneumonia Pneumonia, recurrent	Candidiasis of esophagus, GI tract Herpes simplex chronic ulcers (>1 month duration) or esophagitis Isosporiasis, intestinal Cryptosporidiosis, chronic intestinal (>1 month duration)	Invasive cervical carcinoma (HPV) Herpes simplex chronic ulcers (>1 month duration)

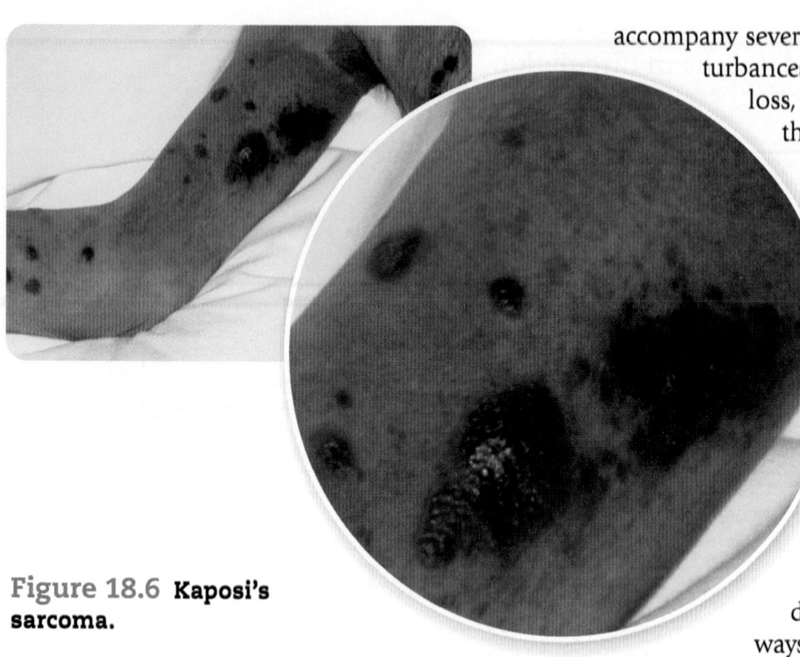

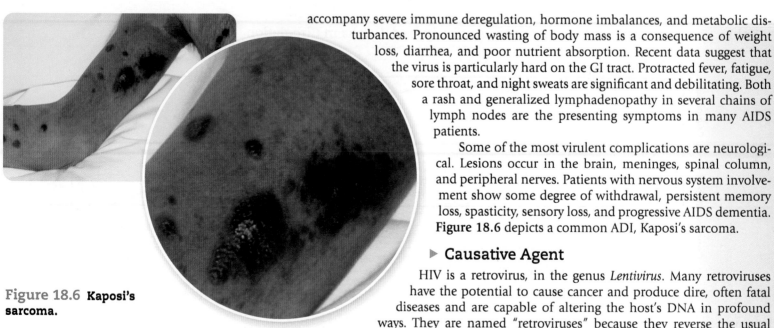

Figure 18.6 **Kaposi's sarcoma.**

accompany severe immune deregulation, hormone imbalances, and metabolic disturbances. Pronounced wasting of body mass is a consequence of weight loss, diarrhea, and poor nutrient absorption. Recent data suggest that the virus is particularly hard on the GI tract. Protracted fever, fatigue, sore throat, and night sweats are significant and debilitating. Both a rash and generalized lymphadenopathy in several chains of lymph nodes are the presenting symptoms in many AIDS patients.

Some of the most virulent complications are neurological. Lesions occur in the brain, meninges, spinal column, and peripheral nerves. Patients with nervous system involvement show some degree of withdrawal, persistent memory loss, spasticity, sensory loss, and progressive AIDS dementia. **Figure 18.6** depicts a common ADI, Kaposi's sarcoma.

▸ Causative Agent

HIV is a retrovirus, in the genus *Lentivirus*. Many retroviruses have the potential to cause cancer and produce dire, often fatal diseases and are capable of altering the host's DNA in profound ways. They are named "retroviruses" because they reverse the usual order of transcription. They contain an unusual enzyme called **reverse transcriptase (RT)** that catalyzes the replication of double-stranded DNA from single-stranded RNA. The association of retroviruses with their hosts can be so intimate that viral genes are permanently integrated into the host genome. Not only can this retroviral DNA be incorporated into the host genome as a provirus that can be passed on to progeny cells, but some retroviruses also transform cells (make them malignant) and regulate certain host genes.

HIV and other retroviruses display structural features typical of enveloped RNA viruses **(figure 18.7*a*)**. The outermost component is a lipid envelope with transmembrane glycoprotein spikes that mediate viral adsorption to the host cell. HIV can only infect host cells that present the required receptors, which is a combination receptor consisting of the CD4 marker plus a coreceptor called CCR-5. The virus uses these receptors to gain entrance to several types of leukocytes and tissue cells **(figure 18.7*b*)**.

NCLEX® PREP

3. The following are ADIs (AIDS-defining illnesses), *except*
   a. cytomegalovirus (CMV) infections.
   b. tuberculosis (TB) caused by *Mycobacterium tuberculosis*.
   c. Kaposi's sarcoma (KS).
   d. brucellosis.

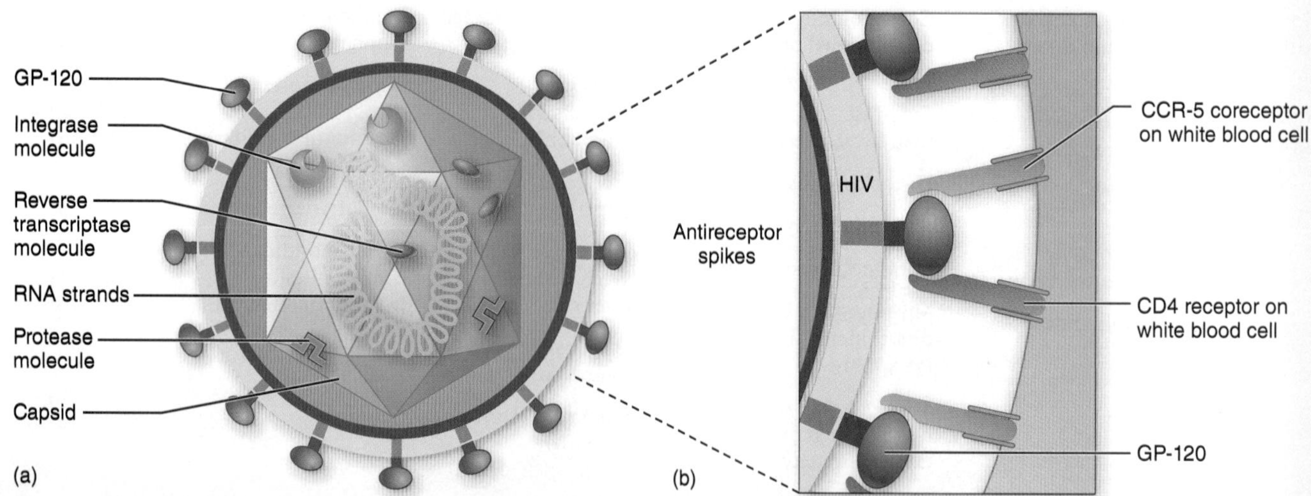

Figure 18.7 **The general structure of HIV.** **(a)** The virus consists of glycoprotein (GP) spikes in the envelope, two identical RNA strands, and several molecules of reverse transcriptase, protease, and integrase encased in a protein capsid. **(b)** The snug attachment of HIV glycoprotein molecules to their specific receptors on a human cell membrane. These receptors are CD4 and a coreceptor called CCR-5 (fusin) that permit docking with the host cell and fusion with the cell membrane.

Table 18.4 The Multiplication Cycle of HIV

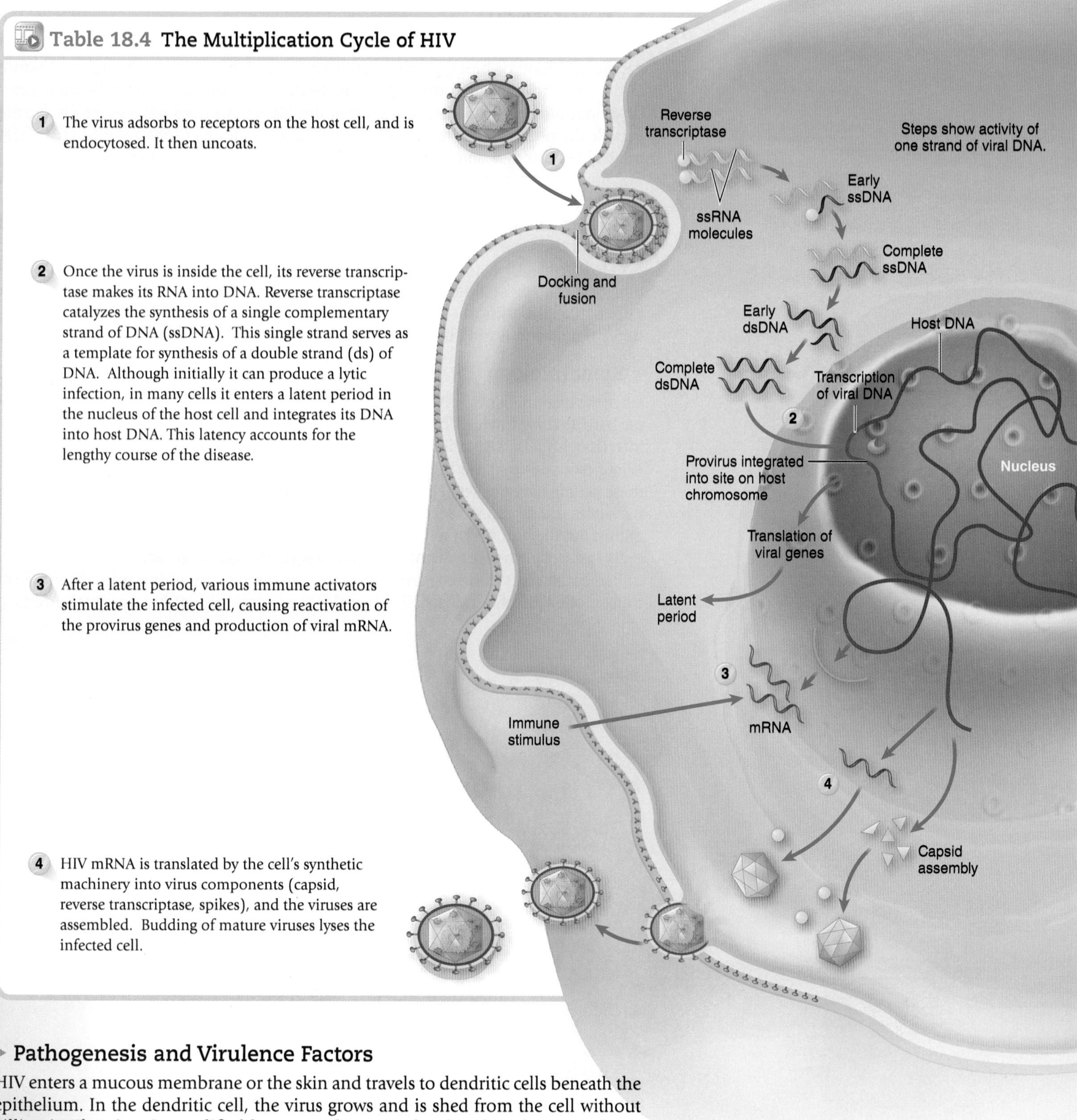
1 The virus adsorbs to receptors on the host cell, and is endocytosed. It then uncoats.
2 Once the virus is inside the cell, its reverse transcriptase makes its RNA into DNA. Reverse transcriptase catalyzes the synthesis of a single complementary strand of DNA (ssDNA). This single strand serves as a template for synthesis of a double strand (ds) of DNA. Although initially it can produce a lytic infection, in many cells it enters a latent period in the nucleus of the host cell and integrates its DNA into host DNA. This latency accounts for the lengthy course of the disease.
3 After a latent period, various immune activators stimulate the infected cell, causing reactivation of the provirus genes and production of viral mRNA.
4 HIV mRNA is translated by the cell's synthetic machinery into virus components (capsid, reverse transcriptase, spikes), and the viruses are assembled. Budding of mature viruses lyses the infected cell.
Reverse transcriptase
Steps show activity of one strand of viral DNA.
1
Early ssDNA
ssRNA molecules
Complete ssDNA
Docking and fusion
Early dsDNA
Host DNA
Complete dsDNA
Transcription of viral DNA
2
Provirus integrated into site on host chromosome
Nucleus
Translation of viral genes
Latent period
3
Immune stimulus
mRNA
4
Capsid assembly

▸ Pathogenesis and Virulence Factors

HIV enters a mucous membrane or the skin and travels to dendritic cells beneath the epithelium. In the dendritic cell, the virus grows and is shed from the cell without killing it. The virus is amplified by macrophages in the skin, lymph organs, bone marrow, and blood. One of the great ironies of HIV is that it infects and destroys many of the very cells needed to combat it, including the helper (T4 or CD4) class of lymphocytes, monocytes, macrophages, and even B lymphocytes. The virus is adapted to docking onto its host cell's surface receptors. It then induces viral fusion with the cell membrane and creates syncytia.

Table 18.4 illustrates the life cycle of the virus.

Public health officials attribute the rapid spread of HIV in Africa in part to the sexual practices of long-haul truckers along major highways on the continent.

Transmission

HIV transmission occurs mainly through two forms of contact: sexual intercourse and transfer of blood or blood products **(figure 18.8).** Babies can also be infected before or during birth, as well as through breast feeding. The mode of transmission is similar to that of hepatitis B virus, except that the AIDS virus does not survive for as long outside the host and it is far more sensitive to heat and disinfectants. And HIV is not transmitted through saliva, as hepatitis B can be. Health care workers should be aware that fluids they may come in contact with during childbirth or invasive procedures can also transmit the virus. These are amniotic fluid, synovial fluid, and spinal fluid.

Semen and vaginal secretions also harbor free virus and infected white blood cells, and thus they are significant factors in sexual transmission. The virus can be isolated from urine, tears, sweat, and saliva in the laboratory—but in such small numbers that these fluids are not considered sources of infection. Because breast milk contains significant numbers of leukocytes, neonates who have escaped infection prior to and during birth can still become infected through nursing.

Epidemiology

Since the beginning of the AIDS epidemic in the early 1980s, more than 25 million people have died worldwide. The best global estimate of the number of individuals currently infected with HIV is 33 million, with approximately 1 million in the United States. The WHO estimates that 2.6 million new infections occurred in 2009. A large number of these people have not yet begun to show symptoms. Due to efforts of many global AIDS initiatives, many more people in the developing world are receiving lifesaving treatments. But the number of new infections is still growing faster than access to drugs: For every two people receiving treatment, five new people are diagnosed.

In most parts of the world, heterosexual intercourse is the primary mode of transmission. In the industrialized world, the overall rate of heterosexual infection

HIV
HIV Transmission
Membrane or skin portal of entry
Direct blood exposure through needles
Blood exposure during sexual intercourse or other intimate contact
Semen, vaginal fluid exposure during sexual intercourse
Infected macrophage
Lacerations, sometimes microscopic
Dendritic cells underlying skin shelter and amplify virus.
HIV

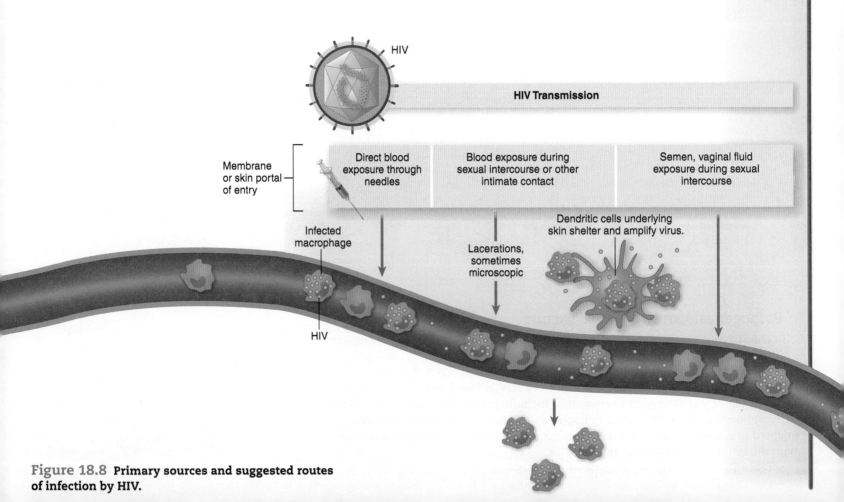

Figure 18.8 Primary sources and suggested routes of infection by HIV.

has increased dramatically in the past several years, especially in adolescent and young adult women. In the United States, about 31% of HIV infections arise from unprotected sexual intercourse with an infected partner of the opposite sex.

We should note that not everyone who becomes infected or is antibody-positive develops AIDS. About 1% of people who are antibody-positive remain free of disease, indicating that functioning immunity to the virus can develop. Any person who remains healthy despite HIV infection is termed a *nonprogressor*. These people are the object of intense scientific study. Some have been found to lack the cytokine receptors that HIV requires. Others are infected by a weakened virus mutant.

Treatment of HIV-infected mothers with an anti-HIV drug has dramatically decreased the rate of maternal-to-infant transmission of HIV during pregnancy. Current treatment regimens result in a transmission rate of approximately 11%, with some studies of multidrug regimens claiming rates as low as 5%. Evidence suggests that giving mothers protease inhibitors can reduce the transmission rate to around 1%. (Untreated mothers pass the virus to their babies at the rate of 33%.)

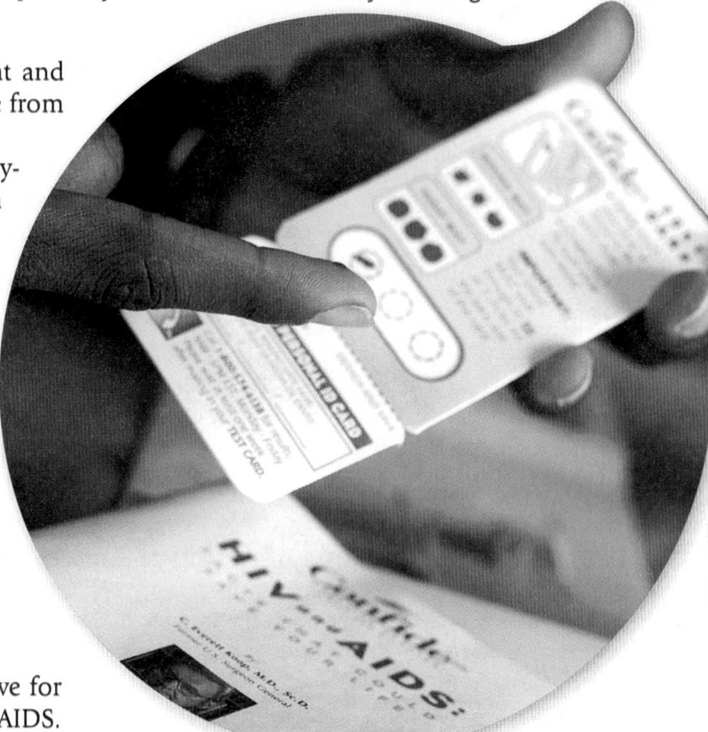

Figure 18.9 With at-home HIV tests, you apply your blood to a card and then send it to a testing center.

Culture and Diagnosis

A person is diagnosed as having HIV infection if he or she has tested positive for the human immunodeficiency virus. This diagnosis is not the same as having AIDS.

Most viral testing is based on detection of antibodies specific to the virus in serum or other fluids, which allows for the rapid, inexpensive screening of large numbers of samples. Testing usually proceeds at two levels. The initial screening tests include the older ELISA and newer latex agglutination and rapid antibody tests. **Figure 18.9** depicts the only at-home kit currently approved by the Food and Drug Administration.

Although these tests are largely accurate, around 1% of results are false positives, and they always require follow-up with a more specific test called *Western blot* analysis (see p. 421). This test detects several different anti-HIV antibodies and can usually rule out false-positive results.

Another inaccuracy can be false-negative results that occur when testing is performed before the onset of detectable antibody production. To rule out this possibility, persons who test negative, but feel they may have been exposed, should be tested a second time 3 to 6 months later.

Blood and blood products are sometimes tested for HIV antigens (rather than for HIV antibodies) to close the window of time between infection and detectable levels of antibodies during which contamination could be missed by antibody tests.

In the United States, people are diagnosed with AIDS if they meet the following criteria: (1) they are positive for the virus, *and* (2) they fulfill one of these additional criteria:

- They have a CD4 (helper T cell) count of fewer than 200 cells per microliter of blood.
- Their CD4 cells account for fewer than 14% of all lymphocytes.
- They experience one or more of a CDC-provided list of AIDS-defining illnesses (ADIs).

Prevention

Avoidance of sexual contact with infected persons is a cornerstone of HIV prevention. Abstaining from sex is an obvious prevention method, although those who are sexually active can also take steps to decrease their risk. A sexually active person should consider every partner to be infected unless proven otherwise. Barrier protection (condoms) should be used when having sex with anyone whose HIV status is not known with certainty to be negative. Although avoiding intravenous drugs is an important preventive measure, many drug addicts do not, or cannot, choose this option. In such cases, risk can be decreased by not sharing syringes or needles. Brand new research has shown that treating uninfected, or newly-infected, people with antiretrovirals can prevent the progression to AIDS. This is likely to be an area of active research.

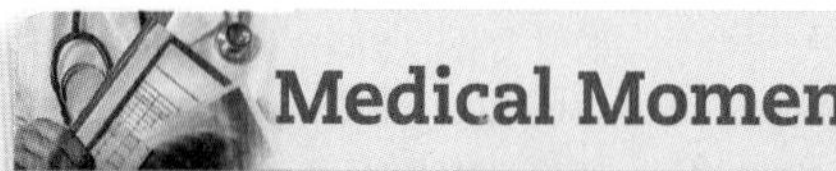

Medical Moment

Kaposi's Sarcoma

Prior to the 1980s, Kaposi's sarcoma was a cancer rarely seen in the United States. Kaposi's sarcoma primarily affected middle-aged men of Jewish or Mediterranean descent. The disease was also endemic to parts of Africa. When AIDS exploded on the scene in the 1980s, large numbers of Kaposi's sarcoma lesions began to be identified among the first AIDS patients in the United States among the male homosexual population.

Kaposi's sarcoma is not a true sarcoma, but rather arises from lymphatic tissue in which channels form and blood cells aggregate, giving Kaposi's sarcoma lesions their deep color. Lesions may be dark purple, dark red, black, or brown and are typically raised (papular). Kaposi's sarcoma may also affect other body systems, such as the gastrointestinal and respiratory tracts.

Early AIDS researchers believed that Kaposi's sarcoma could be the cause of AIDS. Of course, this theory was negated when the HIV virus was identified. Kaposi's sarcoma is now known to be caused by a herpesvirus (the eighth human herpesvirus, or HHV-8).

Kaposi's sarcoma continues to be an opportunistic infection in AIDS patients and is one of the ADIs (AIDS-defining illnesses). It is sometimes the first presenting symptom of AIDS.

From the very first years of the AIDS epidemic, the potential for creating a vaccine has been regarded as slim, because the virus presents many seemingly insurmountable problems. Among them, HIV becomes latent in cells; its cell surface antigens mutate rapidly; and although it does elicit immune responses, it is apparently not completely controlled by them. In view of the great need for a vaccine, however, none of those facts has stopped the medical community from moving ahead.

▶ Treatment

It must be clearly stated: There is no cure for HIV. None of the therapies do more than prolong life or diminish symptoms. As of mid-2011, one person in the history of the epidemic had been declared cured of HIV, after he received a stem cell transplant. Further research is needed, however, and even if this is repeatable it is not a practical approach for the millions who are infected.

Table 18.5 Mechanisms of Action of Anti-HIV Drugs

The first effective drugs developed were the synthetic nucleoside analogs (reverse transcriptase inhibitors) azidothymidine (AZT), didanosine (ddI), lamivudine (Epivir) (3TC), and stavudine (d4T). They interrupt the HIV multiplication cycle by mimicking the structure of actual nucleosides and being added to viral DNA by reverse transcriptase. Because these drugs lack all of the correct binding sites for further DNA synthesis, viral replication and the viral cycle are terminated. Other reverse transcriptase inhibitors that are not nucleosides are nevirapine and efavirenz (Sustiva), both of which bind to the viral enzyme and restructure it.

Also seen here is one of the latest additions to the arsenal, enfuvirtide (Fuzeon), a drug classified as a fusion inhibitor. It prevents the virus from fusing with the membrane of target cells, thereby stopping infection altogether.

Another important class of drugs is the protease inhibitors, which block the action of the HIV enzyme (protease) involved in the final assembly and maturation of the virus. Examples of these drugs include indinavir (Crixivan), ritonavir (Norvir), and amprenavir (Agenerase).

A class of drugs called integrase inhibitors provides a means to stop virus multiplication.

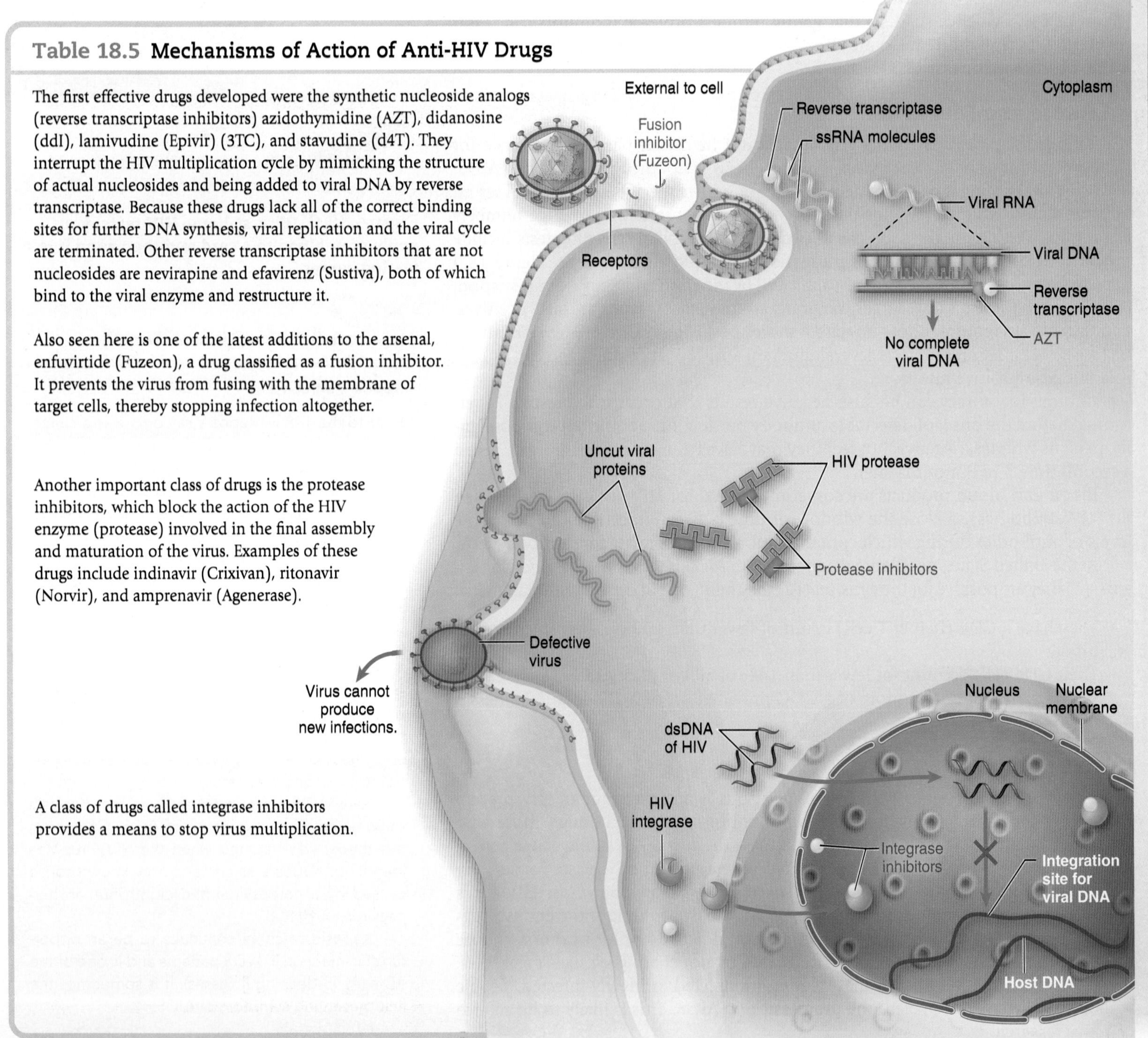

Clear-cut guidelines exist for treating people who test HIV-positive. These guidelines are updated regularly. The most recent update involves beginning treatment much earlier. Until now, recommendations called for beginning aggressive antiviral chemotherapy after AIDS manifested itself. The newer recommendations call for treatment to begin soon after HIV diagnosis. In addition to antiviral chemotherapy, HIV-positive persons should receive a wide array of drugs to prevent or treat a variety of opportunistic infections and other ADIs such as wasting disease. These treatment regimens vary according to each patient's profile and needs.

In **table 18.5** the variety of drugs available to treat HIV is depicted.

A regimen that has proved to be extremely effective in controlling AIDS and inevitable drug resistance is **HAART,** short for *highly active antiretroviral therapy*. By combining two reverse transcriptase inhibitors and one protease inhibitor in a "cocktail," the virus is interrupted in two different phases of its cycle. This therapy has been successful in reducing viral load to undetectable levels and facilitating the improvement of immune function. It has also reduced the incidence of viral drug resistance, because the virus would have to undergo three separate mutations simultaneously, at nearly impossible odds. Patients who are HIV-positive but asymptomatic can remain healthy with this therapy as well. The primary drawbacks are high cost, toxic side effects, patient noncompliance, and an inability to completely eradicate the virus.

Although we opened this section by stating "There is no cure for HIV," there have been some promising advances.

Disease Table 18.2 HIV Infection and AIDS

Causative Organism(s)	Human immunodeficiency virus 1 or 2
Most Common Modes of Transmission	Direct contact (sexual), parenteral (blood-borne), vertical (perinatal and via breast milk)
Virulence Factors	Attachment, syncytia formation, reverse transcriptase, high mutation rate
Culture/ Diagnosis	Initial screening for antibody followed by Western blot confirmation of antibody
Prevention	Avoidance of contact with infected sex partner, contaminated blood, breast milk
Treatment	HAART (reverse transcriptase inhibitors plus protease inhibitors), Fuzeon, nonnucleoside RT inhibitors

Endocarditis

Endocarditis is an inflammation of the endocardium, or inner lining of the heart. Most of the time, endocarditis refers to an infection of the valves of the heart, often the mitral or aortic valve **(figure 18.10).** Two variations of infectious endocarditis have been described: acute and subacute. Each has distinct groups of possible causative agents.

The surgical innovation of prosthetic valves presents a new hazard for development of endocarditis. Patients with prosthetic valves can acquire acute endocarditis if bacteria are introduced during the surgical procedure; alternatively, the prosthetic valves can serve as infection sites for the subacute form of endocarditis long after the surgical procedure.

Because the symptoms and the diagnostic procedures are similar for both forms of endocarditis, they are discussed first; then the specific aspects of acute and subacute endocarditis are addressed.

▶ Signs and Symptoms

The signs and symptoms are similar for both types of endocarditis, except that in the subacute condition they develop more slowly and are less pronounced than with the acute disease. Symptoms include fever, fatigue, joint pain, edema (swelling of feet, legs, and abdomen), weakness, anemia, abnormal heartbeat, and sometimes symptoms similar to myocardial infarction (heart attack). Abdominal or side pain is sometimes reported. The patient may look very ill and may have petechiae (small red-to-purple discolorations) over the upper half of the body and under the fingernails (splinter hemorrhages). Red, painless skin spots on the palms and soles (Janeway lesions) and small painful nodes on the pads of fingers and toes (Osler's nodes) may also be apparent on examination. In subacute cases, an enlarged spleen may have developed over time; cases of extremely long duration (years) can lead to clubbed fingers and toes due to lack of oxygen in the blood.

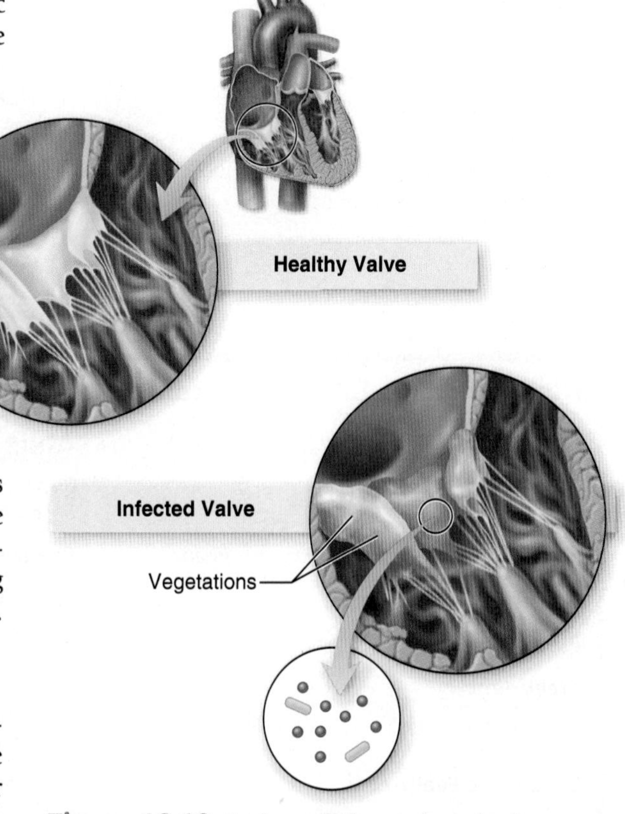

Figure 18.10 Endocarditis. Infected valves don't work properly.

Acute Endocarditis

Acute endocarditis is most often the result of an overwhelming bloodstream challenge with bacteria. Certain of these bacteria seem to have the ability to colonize normal heart valves. Accumulations of bacteria on the valves (vegetations) hamper their function and can lead directly to cardiac malfunction and death. Alternatively, pieces of the bacterial vegetation can break off and create emboli (blockages) in vital

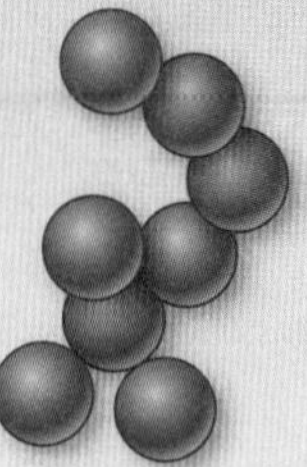

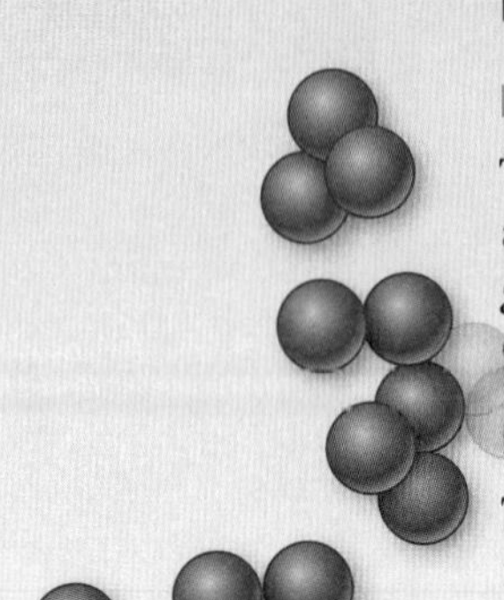

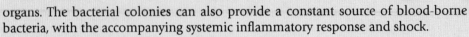

organs. The bacterial colonies can also provide a constant source of blood-borne bacteria, with the accompanying systemic inflammatory response and shock.

▸ Causative Agents

The acute form of endocarditis is most often caused by *Staphylococcus aureus.* Other agents that cause it are *Streptococcus pyogenes, Streptococcus pneumoniae,* and *Neisseria gonorrhoeae,* as well as a host of other bacteria. Each of these bacteria is described elsewhere in this book.

▸ Transmission and Epidemiology

The most common route of transmission for acute endocarditis is parenteral—that is, via direct entry into the body. Intravenous or subcutaneous drug users have been a growing risk group for the condition. Traumatic injuries and surgical procedures can also introduce the large number of bacteria required for the acute form of endocarditis.

Subacute Endocarditis

Subacute forms of this condition are almost always preceded by some form of damage to the heart valves or by congenital malformation. Irregularities in the valves encourage the attachment of bacteria, which then form biofilms and impede normal function, as well as provide an ongoing source of bacteria to the bloodstream. People who have suffered rheumatic fever and the accompanying damage to heart valves are particularly susceptible to this condition (see chapter 19 for a complete discussion of rheumatic fever).

▸ Causative Agents

Most commonly, subacute endocarditis is caused by bacteria of low pathogenicity, often originating in the oral cavity. Alpha-hemolytic streptococci, such as *Streptococcus sanguis, S. oralis,* and *S. mutans,* are most often responsible, although normal biota from the skin and other bacteria can also colonize abnormal valves and lead to this condition.

▸ Transmission and Epidemiology

Minor disruptions in the skin or mucous membranes, such as those induced by vigorous toothbrushing, dental procedures, or relatively minor cuts and lacerations, can introduce bacteria into the bloodstream and lead to valve colonization. The bacteria are not, therefore, transmitted from other people or from the environment.

▸ Prevention

The practice of prophylactic antibiotic therapy in advance of surgical and dental procedures on patients with underlying valve irregularities has decreased the incidence of this infection.

Disease Table 18.3 Endocarditis

Disease	Acute Endocarditis	Subacute Endocarditis
Causative Organism(s)	*Staphylococcus aureus, Streptococcus pyogenes, S. pneumoniae, Neisseria gonorrhoeae,* others	Alpha-hemolytic streptococci, others
Most Common Modes of Transmission	Parenteral	Endogenous transfer of normal biota to bloodstream
Culture/Diagnosis	Blood culture	Blood culture
Prevention	Aseptic surgery, injections	Prophylactic antibiotics before invasive procedures
Treatment	Nafcillin or oxacillin +/− gentamicin or tobramycin OR vancomycin + gentamicin; surgery may be necessary	Surgery may be necessary
Distinctive Features	Acute onset, high fatality rate	Slower onset

Septicemia

Septicemia occurs when organisms are actively multiplying in the blood. Many different bacteria (and a few fungi) can cause this condition. Patients suffering from these infections are sometimes described as "septic."

Disease Table 18.4 Septicemia	
Causative Organism(s)	Bacteria or fungi
Most Common Modes of Transmission	Parenteral, endogenous transfer
Virulence Factors	Cell wall or membrane components
Culture/ Diagnosis	Blood culture
Prevention	–
Treatment	Broad-spectrum antibiotic until identification and susceptibilities tested

▶ Signs and Symptoms

Fever is a prominent feature of septicemia. The patient appears very ill and may have an altered mental state, shaking chills, and gastrointestinal symptoms. Often an increased breathing rate is exhibited, accompanied by respiratory alkalosis (increased tissue pH due to breathing disorder). Low blood pressure is a hallmark of this condition and is caused by the inflammatory response to infectious agents in the bloodstream, which leads to a loss of fluid from the vasculature. This condition is the most dangerous feature of the disease, often culminating in death.

▶ Causative Agents

The vast majority of septicemias are caused by bacteria, and they are approximately evenly divided between gram-positives and gram-negatives. Perhaps 10% are caused by fungal infections. Polymicrobial bloodstream infections increasingly are being identified in which more than one microorganism is causing the infection.

▶ Pathogenesis and Virulence Factors

Gram-negative bacteria multiplying in the blood release large amounts of endotoxin into the bloodstream, stimulating a massive inflammatory response mediated by a host of cytokines. This response invariably leads to a drastic drop in blood pressure, a condition called **endotoxic shock.** Gram-positive bacteria can instigate a similar cascade of events when fragments of their cell walls are released into the blood.

▶ Transmission and Epidemiology

In many cases, septicemias can be traced to parenteral introduction of the microorganisms via intravenous lines or surgical procedures. Other infections may arise from serious urinary tract infections or from renal, prostatic, pancreatic, or gallbladder abscesses. Patients with underlying spleen malfunction may be predisposed to multiplication of microbes in the bloodstream. Meningitis infections or pneumonia occasionally can lead to sepsis. Approximately half a million cases occur each year in the United States, resulting in more than 100,000 deaths.

▶ Culture and Diagnosis

Because the infection is in the bloodstream, a blood culture is the obvious route to diagnosis. A full regimen of media should be inoculated to ensure isolation of the causative microorganism. Antibiotic susceptibilities should be assessed. Empiric therapy should be started immediately before culture and susceptibility results are available.

▶ Prevention and Treatment

Empiric therapy, which is begun immediately after blood cultures are taken, often begins with a broad-spectrum antibiotic. Once the organism is identified and its antibiotic susceptibility is known, treatment can be adjusted accordingly.

Prairie dogs in the southwest United States sometimes harbor *Yersinia pestis.*

Plague

Although pandemics of plague have probably occurred since antiquity, the first one that was reliably chronicled killed an estimated 100 million people in the 6th century AD. The last great pandemic occurred in the late 1800s and was transmitted around the world, primarily by rat-infested ships.

▶ Signs and Symptoms

Three possible manifestations of infection occur with the bacterium causing plague. **Pneumonic plague** is a respiratory disease, described in chapter 19.

Disease Table 18.5 Plague

Causative Organism(s)	*Yersinia pestis*
Most Common Modes of Transmission	Vector, biological; also droplet contact (pneumonic) and direct contact with body fluids
Virulence Factors	Capsule, Yop system, plasminogen activator
Culture/ Diagnosis	Culture or Gram stain of blood or bubo aspirate
Prevention	Flea and/or animal control; vaccine available for high-risk individuals
Treatment	Streptomycin or gentamicin

In **bubonic plague,** the bacterium, which is injected by the bite of a flea, enters the lymph and is filtered by a local lymph node. Infection causes inflammation and necrosis of the node, resulting in a swollen lesion called a **bubo,** usually in the groin or axilla **(figure 18.11).** The incubation period lasts 2 to 8 days, ending abruptly with the onset of fever, chills, headache, nausea, weakness, and tenderness of the bubo. Mortality rates, even with treatment, are greater than 15%.

These cases often progress to massive bacterial growth in the blood termed **septicemic plague.** The presence of the bacteria in the blood results in disseminated intravascular coagulation, subcutaneous hemorrhage, and **purpura** that may degenerate into necrosis and gangrene. Mortality rates, once the disease has progressed to this point, are 30% to 50% with treatment and 100% without treatment. Because of the visible darkening of the skin, the plague has often been called the "black death."

Causative Agent

The cause of this dreadful disease is a tiny gram-negative rod, *Yersinia pestis,* a member of the family *Enterobacteriaceae.* Other species members are *Y. enterocolitica* and *Y. pseudotuberculosis.* Those species cause gastrointestinal tract diseases in humans. *Y. pestis* displays unusual bipolar staining that makes it look like a safety pin **(figure 18.12).**

Pathogenesis and Virulence Factors

The number of bacteria required to initiate a plague infection is small—perhaps only 3 to 50 cells.

Transmission and Epidemiology

The principal agents in the transmission of the plague bacterium are fleas. After a flea ingests a blood meal from an infected animal, the bacteria multiply in its gut. In fleas that effectively transmit the bacterium, the esophagus becomes blocked due to coagulation factors produced by the pathogen. Being unable to feed properly, the ravenous flea jumps from animal to animal in a futile attempt to get nourishment. During this process, regurgitated infectious material is inoculated into the bite wound.

The plague bacterium exists naturally in many animal hosts, and its distribution is extensive. Although the incidence of disease has been reduced in the developed world, it has actually been increasing in Africa and other parts

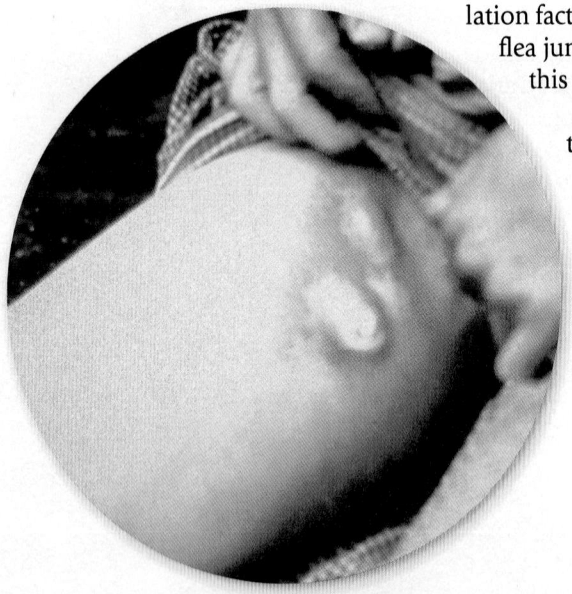

Figure 18.11 A classic inguinal bubo of bubonic plague. This hard nodule is very painful and can rupture onto the surface.

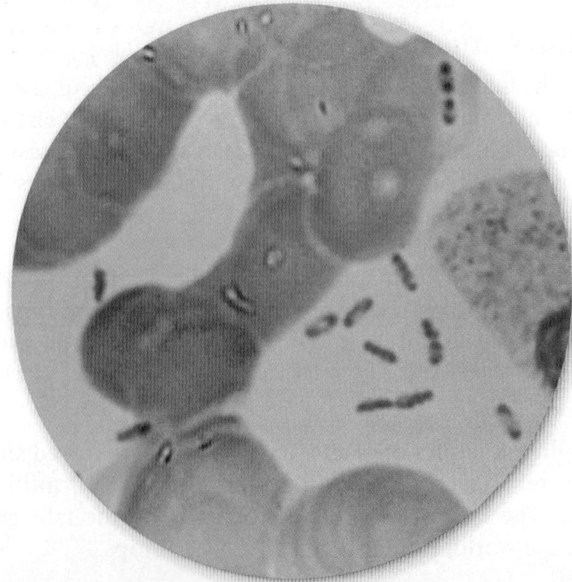

Figure 18.12 *Yersinia pestis.* Note the more darkly stained poles of the bacterium, lending it a "safety pin" appearance.

of the world. Plague still exists endemically in large areas of Africa, South America, the Mideast, Asia, and the former Soviet Union, and it sometimes erupts into epidemics. In the United States, sporadic cases (usually less than 10 per year) occur as a result of contact with wild and domestic animals. This disease is considered endemic in U.S. western and southwestern states. Persons most at risk for developing plague are veterinarians and people living and working near woodlands and forests. Dogs and cats can be infected with the plague, often from contact with infected wild animals such as prairie dogs. Human cases have been traced to a chain of events involving a flea from a prairie dog moving to a domestic cat, and then a flea from the cat moving to a human.

▸ Culture and Diagnosis

Because death can occur as quickly as 2 to 4 days after the appearance of symptoms, prompt diagnosis and treatment of plague are imperative. The patient's history, including recent travel to endemic regions, can help establish a diagnosis. Culture of the organism is the definitive method of diagnosis, although a Gram stain of aspirate from buboes often reveals the presence of the safety-pin-shaped bacteria.

Tularemia

▸ Signs and Symptoms

After an incubation period ranging from a few days to 3 weeks, acute symptoms of headache, backache, fever, chills, malaise, and weakness appear. Further clinical manifestations are tied to the portal of entry. They include ulcerative skin lesions, swollen lymph glands, conjunctival inflammation, sore throat, intestinal disruption, and pulmonary involvement. The death rate in the most serious forms of disease is 30%, but proper treatment with gentamicin or streptomycin reduces mortality to almost zero.

Disease Table 18.6 Tularemia

Causative Organism(s)	*Francisella tularensis*
Most Common Modes of Transmission	Vector, biological; also direct contact with body fluids from infected animal; airborne
Virulence Factors	Intracellular growth
Culture/ Diagnosis	Culture dangerous to lab workers and not reliable; serology most often used
Prevention	Live attenuated vaccine for high-risk individuals
Treatment	Gentamicin or streptomycin

▸ Causative Agent

The causative agent of tularemia is a facultative intracellular gram-negative bacterium called *Francisella tularensis.* It has several characteristics in common with *Yersinia pestis,* and the two species were previously often included in a single genus called *Pasteurella.* It is a zoonotic disease of assorted mammals endemic to the Northern Hemisphere. Because it has been associated with outbreaks of disease in wild rabbits, it is sometimes called rabbit fever. It is currently listed as a pathogen of concern on the lists of bioterrorism agents.

▸ Transmission and Epidemiology

Although rabbits and rodents (muskrats and ground squirrels) are the chief reservoirs, other wild animals (skunks, beavers, foxes, opossums) and some domestic animals are implicated as well. The chief route of transmission in the past had been through the activity of skinning rabbits, but with the decline of rabbit hunting, transmission via tick bites is more common. Ticks are the most frequent arthropod vector, followed by biting flies, mites, and mosquitoes.

With an estimated infective dose of between 10 and 50 organisms, *F. tularensis* is often considered one of the most infectious of all bacteria. Cases of tularemia have appeared in people who have accidentally run over rabbits while lawn mowing, presumably from inhaling aerosolized bacteria. In 2009, two different people in Alaska acquired tularemia after wresting infected rabbits from their dogs' mouths.

▸ Prevention and Treatment

Because the intracellular persistence of *F. tularensis* can lead to relapses, antimicrobial therapy must not be discontinued prematurely. Protection is available in the form of a live attenuated vaccine. Laboratory workers and other occupationally exposed personnel must wear gloves, masks, and eyewear.

Hunting and cleaning rabbits is a common cause of tularemia.

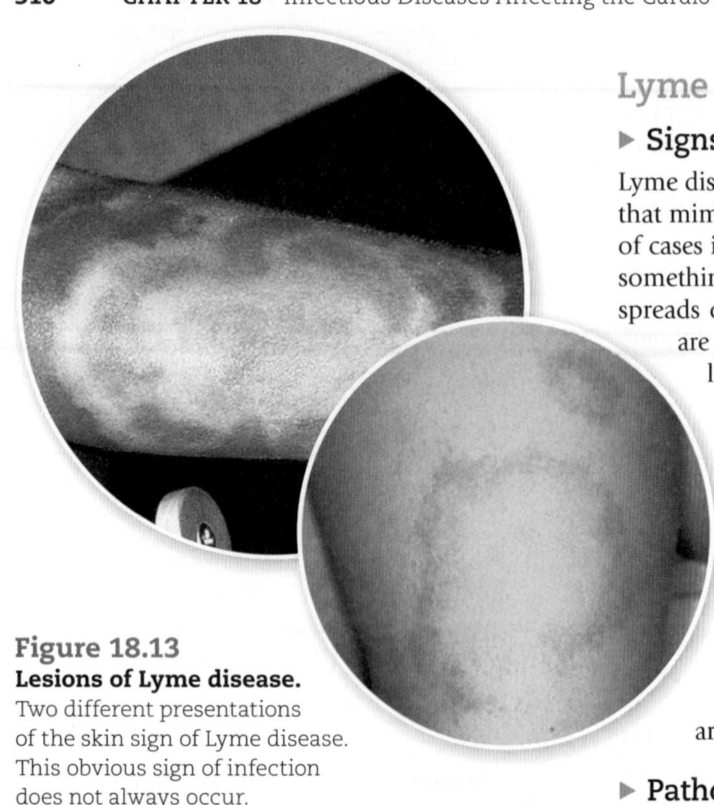

Figure 18.13
Lesions of Lyme disease.
Two different presentations of the skin sign of Lyme disease. This obvious sign of infection does not always occur.

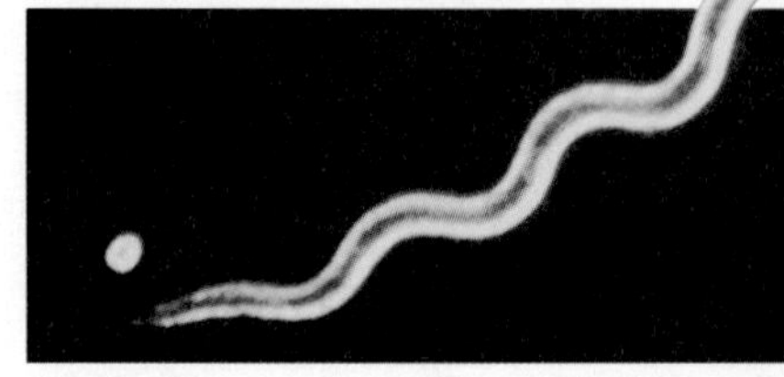

Figure 18.14 ***Borrelia* has 3 to 10 loose, irregular coils.**

Lyme Disease

▶ Signs and Symptoms

Lyme disease is slow-acting, but it often evolves into a slowly progressive syndrome that mimics neuromuscular and rheumatoid conditions. An early symptom in 70% of cases is a rash at the site of a tick bite. The lesion, called *erythema migrans,* looks something like a bull's-eye, with a raised erythematous (reddish) ring that gradually spreads outward and a pale central region **(figure 18.13).** Other early symptoms are fever, headache, stiff neck, and dizziness. If not treated or if treated too late, the disease can advance to the second stage, during which cardiac and neurological symptoms, such as facial palsy, can develop. After several weeks or months, the third stage may occur. This involves a crippling arthritis; some people acquire chronic neurological complications that are severely disabling.

▶ Causative Agent

Borrelia burgdorferi are large spirochetes, ranging from 0.2 to 0.5 micrometer in width and from 10 to 20 micrometers in length, and they contain 3 to 10 irregularly spaced and loose coils **(figure 18.14).** The nutritional requirements of *Borrelia* are so complex that the bacterium can be grown in artificial media only with difficulty.

▶ Pathogenesis and Virulence Factors

The bacterium is a master of immune evasion. It changes its surface antigens while it is in the tick and again after it has been transmitted to a mammalian host. It provokes a strong humoral and cellular immune response, but this response is mainly ineffective, perhaps because of the bacterium's ability to switch its antigens. Indeed, it is possible that the immune response contributes to the pathology of the infection.

▶ Transmission and Epidemiology

B. burgdorferi is transmitted primarily by hard ticks of the genus *Ixodes.* In the northeastern part of the United States, *Ixodes scapularis* (the black-legged deer tick, **figure 18.15**) passes through a complex 2-year cycle that involves two principal hosts. In California, the transmission cycle involves *Ixodes pacificus,* another black-legged tick, and the dusky-footed woodrat as reservoir.

The greatest concentrations of Lyme disease are found in areas having high deer populations **(figure 18.16).**

▶ Culture and Diagnosis

Diagnosis of Lyme disease can be difficult because of the range of symptoms it presents. Most suggestive are the ring-shaped lesions, isolation of spirochetes from the patient, and serological testing with an ELISA method that tracks a rising antibody titer. Tests for spirochete DNA in specimens is especially helpful for late-stage diagnosis.

▶ Prevention and Treatment

A vaccine for Lyme disease was available for a brief period of time, but it was withdrawn from the market in early 2002. Other vaccines are in development. Anyone involved in outdoor activities should wear protective clothing, boots, leggings, and insect repellent. Individuals exposed to heavy infestation should routinely inspect their bodies for ticks and remove ticks gently without crushing, preferably with forceps or fingers protected with gloves, because it is possible to become infected by tick feces or body fluids.

Early, prolonged (3 to 4 weeks) treatment with doxycycline and amoxicillin is effective, and other antibiotics such as ceftriaxone and penicillin are used in late Lyme disease therapy.

Disease Table 18.7 Lyme Disease

Causative Organism(s)	*Borrelia burgdorferi*
Most Common Modes of Transmission	Vector, biological
Virulence Factors	Antigenic shifting, adhesins
Culture/ Diagnosis	ELISA for Ab, PCR
Prevention	Tick avoidance
Treatment	Doxycycline and/or amoxicillin (3–4 weeks), also cephalosporins and penicillin

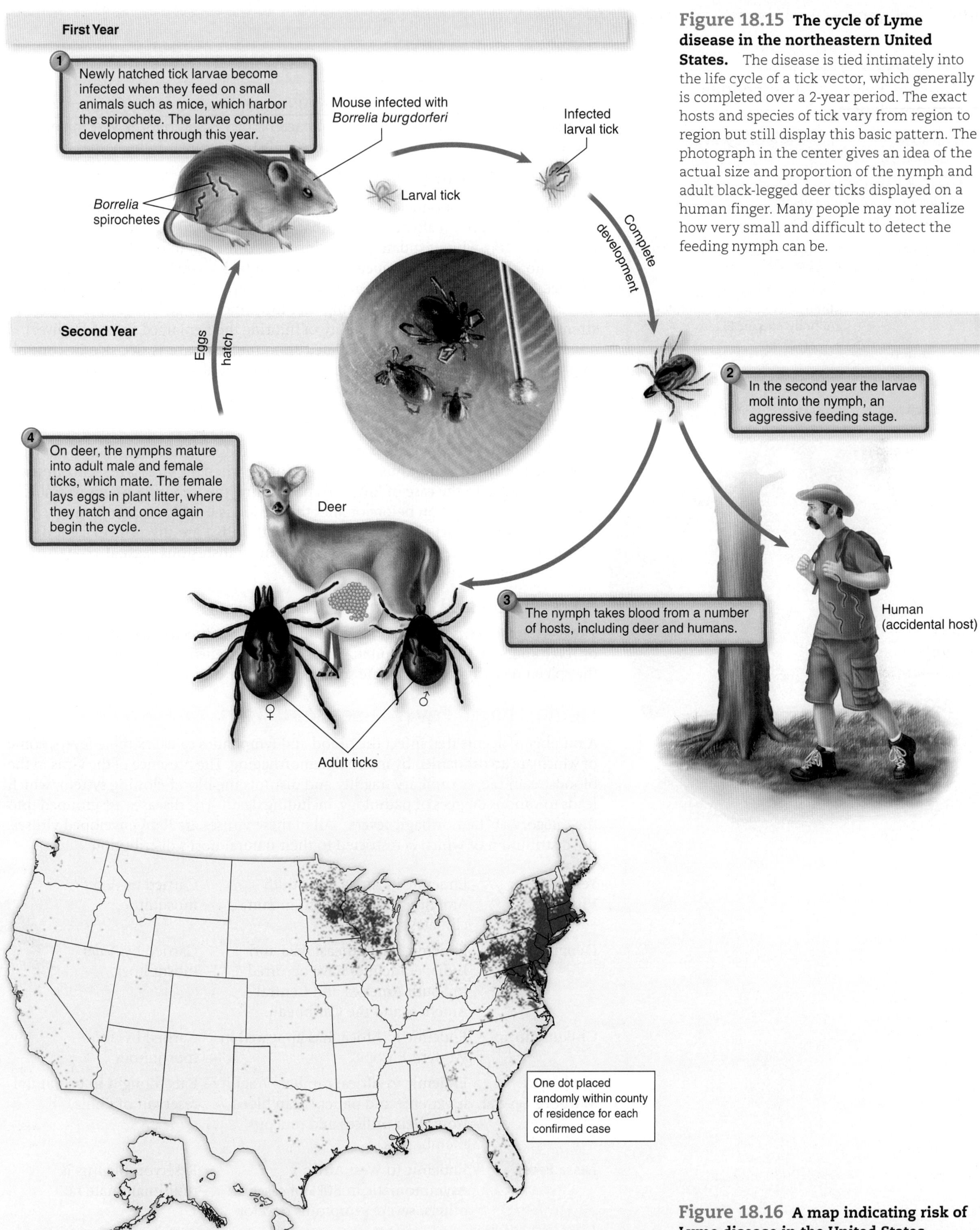
First Year
1
Newly hatched tick larvae become infected when they feed on small animals such as mice, which harbor the spirochete. The larvae continue development through this year.
Mouse infected with *Borrelia burgdorferi*
Infected larval tick
Borrelia spirochetes
Larval tick
Complete development
Second Year
Eggs hatch
2
In the second year the larvae molt into the nymph, an aggressive feeding stage.
4
On deer, the nymphs mature into adult male and female ticks, which mate. The female lays eggs in plant litter, where they hatch and once again begin the cycle.
Deer
3
The nymph takes blood from a number of hosts, including deer and humans.
Human (accidental host)
♀
♂
Adult ticks
One dot placed randomly within county of residence for each confirmed case

Figure 18.15 The cycle of Lyme disease in the northeastern United States. The disease is tied intimately into the life cycle of a tick vector, which generally is completed over a 2-year period. The exact hosts and species of tick vary from region to region but still display this basic pattern. The photograph in the center gives an idea of the actual size and proportion of the nymph and adult black-legged deer ticks displayed on a human finger. Many people may not realize how very small and difficult to detect the feeding nymph can be.

Figure 18.16 A map indicating risk of Lyme disease in the United States.

Disease Table 18.8 Infectious Mononucleosis

Causative Organism(s)	Epstein-Barr virus (EBV)
Most Common Modes of Transmission	Direct, indirect contact; parenteral
Virulence Factors	Latency, ability to incorporate into host DNA
Culture/ Diagnosis	Differential blood count, Monospot test for heterophile antibody, specific ELISA
Prevention	–
Treatment	Supportive
Distinctive Features	Most common in teens

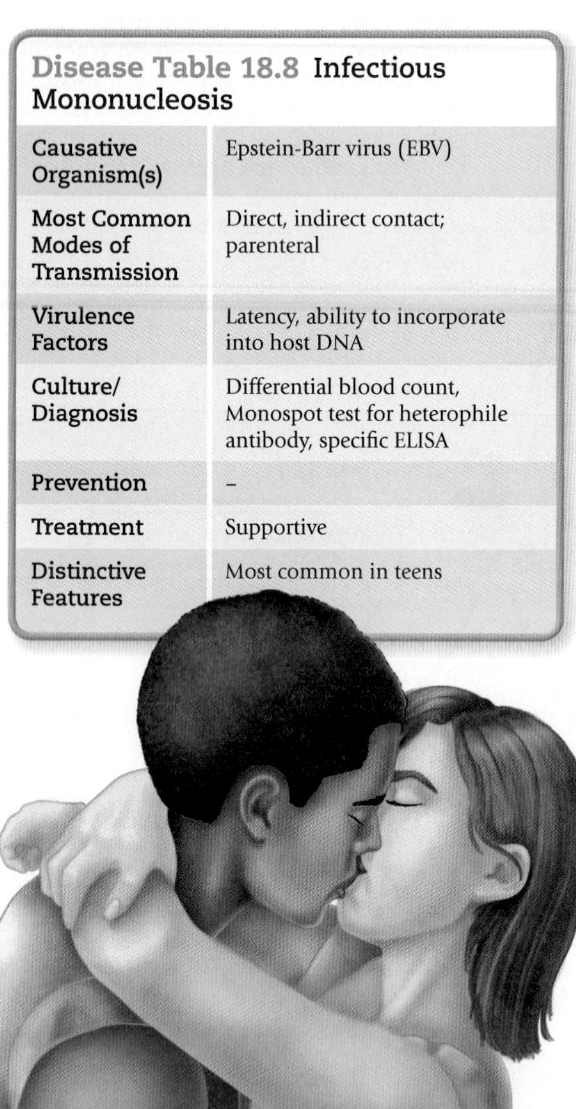

Infectious Mononucleosis

This lymphatic system disease, which is often simply called "mono" or the "kissing disease," can be caused by a number of bacteria or viruses, but the vast majority of cases are caused by the **Epstein-Barr virus (EBV)**, a member of the herpes family.

Signs and Symptoms

The symptoms of mononucleosis are sore throat, high fever, and cervical lymphadenopathy, which develop after a long incubation period (30 to 50 days). Many patients also have a gray-white exudate in the throat, a skin rash, and enlarged spleen and liver. A notable sign of mononucleosis is sudden leukocytosis, consisting initially of infected B cells and later T cells. Fatigue is a hallmark of the disease. Patients remain fatigued for a period of weeks. During that time, they are advised not to engage in strenuous activity due to the possibility of injuring their enlarged spleen (or liver).

Eventually, the strong, cell-mediated immune response is decisive in controlling the infection and preventing complications. But after recovery, people usually remain chronically infected with EBV.

Transmission and Epidemiology

More than 90% of the world's population is infected with EBV. In general, the virus causes no noticeable symptoms, but the time of life when the virus is first encountered seems to matter. In the case of EBV, infection during the teen years seems to result in disease, whereas infection before or after this period is usually asymptomatic.

Direct oral contact and contamination with saliva are the principal modes of transmission, although transfer through blood transfusions, sexual contact, and organ transplants is possible.

Prevention and Treatment

The usual treatments for infectious mononucleosis are directed at symptomatic relief of fever and sore throat. Hospitalization is rarely needed. Occasionally, rupture of the spleen necessitates immediate surgery to remove it.

Hemorrhagic Fever Diseases

A number of agents that infect the blood and lymphatics cause extreme fevers, some of which are accompanied by internal hemorrhaging. The presence of the virus in the bloodstream causes capillary fragility and disrupts the blood-clotting system, which leads to various degrees of pathology, including death. The diseases are grouped into the category of "hemorrhagic fevers." All of these viruses are RNA enveloped viruses, the distribution of which is restricted to their natural host's distribution.

Yellow Fever Virus:	Endemic in Africa and South America; more frequent in rainy climates.	Carried by *Aedes* mosquitoes.
Dengue Fever:	Endemic in southeast Asia and India; epidemics have occurred in South America and Central America, and the Caribbean.	Carried by *Aedes* mosquitoes.
Chikungunya:	Endemic in Africa; has appeared in Western Europe.	Carried by *Aedes* mosquitoes.
Ebola and Marburg Fevers:	Endemic to Africa; capillary fragility is extreme and patients can bleed from their orifices and mucous membranes.	Bats thought to be natural reservoir of Ebola.
Lassa Fever:	Endemic to West Africa. Asymptomatic in 80% of cases. In others, severe symptoms develop.	Reservoir of virus is multimammate rat.

Disease Table 18.9 Hemorrhagic Fevers

Disease	Yellow Fever	Dengue Fever	Chikungunya	Ebola and/or Marburg	Lassa Fever
Causative Organism(s)	Yellow fever virus	Dengue fever virus	Chikungunya virus	Ebola virus, Marburg virus	Lassa fever virus
Most Common Modes of Transmission	Biological vector	Biological vector	Biological vector	Direct contact, body fluids	Droplet contact (aerosolized rodent excretions), direct contact with infected fluids
Virulence Factors	Disruption of clotting factors	Disruption of clotting factors	Disruption of clotting factors	Disruption of clotting factors	Disruption of clotting factors
Culture/ Diagnosis	ELISA, PCR	Rise in IgM titers	PCR	PCR, viral culture (conducted at CDC)	ELISA
Prevention	Live attenuated vaccine available	Live attenuated vaccine being tested	–	–	Avoiding rats, safe food storage
Treatment	Supportive	Supportive	Supportive	Supportive	Ribavirin
Distinctive Features	Accompanied by jaundice	"Breakbone fever"—so named due to severe pain	Arthritic symptoms	Massive hemorrhage; rash sometimes present	Chest pain, deafness as long-term sequelae

Nonhemorrhagic Fever Diseases

In this section, we examine some infectious diseases that result in a syndrome characterized by high fever but without the capillary fragility that leads to hemorrhagic symptoms. All of the diseases in this section are caused by bacteria.

Brucellosis

This disease goes by several different names (besides brucellosis): Malta fever, undulant fever, and Bang's disease. It is on the CDC list of possible bioterror agents, though it is not designated as being "of highest concern."

▶ Signs and Symptoms

The *Brucella* bacteria responsible for this disease live in phagocytic cells. These cells carry the bacteria into the bloodstream, creating focal lesions in the liver, spleen, bone marrow, and kidney. The cardinal manifestation of human brucellosis is a fluctuating pattern of fever, which is the origin of the name *undulant fever*.

▶ Causative Agent

The bacterial genus *Brucella* contains tiny, aerobic gram-negative coccobacilli. Several species can cause this disease in humans: *B. melitensis*, *B. abortus*, and *B. suis*. Even though a principal manifestation of the disease in animals is an infection of the placenta and fetus, human placentas do not become infected.

▶ Pathogenesis and Virulence Factors

Brucella enters through damaged skin or via mucous membranes of the digestive tract, conjunctiva, and respiratory tract. From there it is taken up by phagocytic cells. Because it is able to avoid destruction in the phagocytes, the bacterium is transported easily through the bloodstream and to various organs, such as the liver, kidney, breast tissue, or joints. Scientists suspect that the up-and-down nature of the fever is related to unusual properties of the bacterial lipopolysaccharide.

4. Brucellosis causes a fever that is described as
   a. prolonged.
   b. recurrent.
   c. undulating.
   d. intermittent.

Q Fever

The name of this disease arose from the frustration created by not being able to identify its cause. The Q stands for "query." Its cause, a bacterium called *Coxiella burnetii*, was finally identified in the mid-1900s. The clinical manifestations of acute Q fever are abrupt onset of fever, chills, head and muscle ache, and, occasionally, a rash. The disease is sometimes complicated by pneumonitis (30% of cases), hepatitis, and endocarditis. About a quarter of the cases are chronic rather than acute and result in vascular damage and endocarditis-like symptoms.

C. burnetii is a very small pleomorphic (variously shaped) gram-negative bacterium, and for a time it was considered a rickettsia, in the same genus as the bacterium that causes Rocky Mountain Spotted Fever (below). It is an intracellular parasite, but it is much more resistant to environmental pressures because it produces an unusual type of endospore-like structure. *C. burnetii* is apparently harbored by a wide assortment of vertebrates and arthropods, especially ticks, which play an essential role in transmission between wild and domestic animals. Ticks do not transmit the disease to humans, however. Humans acquire infection largely by means of environmental contamination and airborne spread. Birth products, such as placentas, of infected domestic animals contain large numbers of bacteria. Other sources of infectious material include urine, feces, milk, and airborne particles from infected animals. The primary portals of entry are the lungs, skin, conjunctiva, and gastrointestinal tract.

People at highest risk are farm workers, meat cutters, veterinarians, laboratory technicians, and consumers of raw milk products.

Mild or subclinical cases resolve spontaneously, and more severe cases respond to doxycycline therapy. A vaccine is available in many parts of the world, but not in the United States.

Cat-Scratch Disease

This disease is one of a group of diseases caused by different species of the small gram-negative rod *Bartonella*. *Bartonella* species are considered to be emerging pathogens. They are fastidious but not obligate intracellular parasites, so they will grow on blood agar. In addition to cat-scratch disease, a new species of *Bartonella* that causes high fever and life-threatening anemia was identified in 2007.

Bartonella henselae is the agent of cat-scratch disease (CSD), an infection connected with being clawed or bitten by a cat. The pathogen is present in over 40% of cats, especially kittens. There are approximately 25,000 cases per year in the United States, 80% of them in children 2 to 14 years old. The symptoms start after 1 to 2 weeks, with a cluster of small papules at the site of inoculation. Most infections remain localized and resolve in a few weeks, but drugs such as azithromycin, erythromycin, and rifampin can be effective therapies. The disease can be prevented by thorough antiseptic cleansing of a cat bite or scratch.

Rocky Mountain Spotted Fever (RMSF)

This disease is named for the region in which it was first detected in the United States—the Rocky Mountains of Montana and Idaho. In spite of its name, the disease occurs infrequently in the western United States. The majority of cases are concentrated in the Southeast and Eastern Seaboard regions. It also occurs in Canada and Central and South America. Infections occur most frequently in the spring and summer, when the tick vector is most active. The yearly rate of RMSF is 20 to 40 cases per 10,000 population, with fluctuations coinciding with weather and tick infestations.

RMSF is caused by a bacterium called *Rickettsia rickettsii* transmitted by hard ticks such as the wood tick, the American dog tick, and the Lone Star tick. The dog tick is probably most responsible for transmission to humans because it is the major vector in the southeastern United States.

NCLEX® PREP

5. Early lesions in Rocky Mountain Spotted fever may resemble the rash of
   - **a.** measles.
   - **b.** chickenpox.
   - **c.** rubeola.
   - **d.** Lyme disease.

After 2 to 4 days of incubation, the first symptoms are sustained fever, chills, headache, and muscular pain. A distinctive spotted rash usually comes on within 2 to 4 days after the prodrome **(figure 18.17)**. Early lesions are slightly mottled like measles, but later ones can change shape to look like other types of rashes. In the most severe untreated cases, the enlarged lesions merge and can become necrotic, predisposing to gangrene of the toes or fingertips.

Although the spots are the most obvious symptom of the disease, the most serious manifestations are cardiovascular disruption, including hypotension, thrombosis, and hemorrhage. Conditions of restlessness, delirium, convulsions, tremor, and coma are signs of the often overwhelming effects on the central nervous system. Fatalities occur in an average of 20% of untreated cases and 5% to 10% of treated cases.

Isolating rickettsias from the patient's blood or tissues is desirable, but it is expensive and requires specially qualified lab personnel and lab facilities. Specimens taken from the rash lesions are suitable for PCR assay, which is very specific and sensitive and can circumvent the need for culture.

The drug of choice for suspected and known cases is doxycycline administered for 1 week. Other preventive measures parallel those for Lyme disease: wearing protective clothing, using insect sprays, and fastidiously removing ticks.

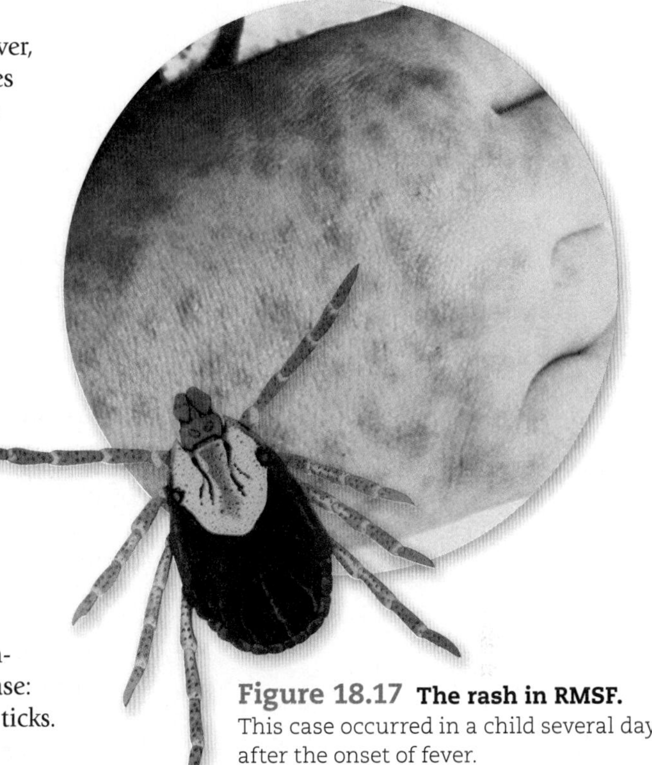

Figure 18.17 The rash in RMSF. This case occurred in a child several days after the onset of fever.

Disease Table 18.10 Nonhemorrhagic Fever Diseases

Disease	Brucellosis	Q fever	Cat-Scratch Disease	Rocky Mountain Spotted Fever
Causative Organism(s)	*Brucella* species	*Coxiella burnetii*	*Bartonella henselae*	*Rickettsia rickettsii*
Most Common Modes of Transmission	Direct contact, airborne, parenteral (needlesticks)	Airborne, direct contact, foodborne	Parenteral (cat scratch or bite)	Biological vector (tick)
Virulence Factors	Intracellular growth; avoidance of destruction by phagocytes	Endospore-like structure	Endotoxin	Induces apoptosis in cells lining blood vessels
Culture/ Diagnosis	Gram stain of biopsy material	Serological tests for antibody	Biopsy of lymph nodes plus Gram staining; ELISA (performed by CDC)	Fluorescent antibody, PCR
Prevention	Animal control, pasteurization of milk	Vaccine for high-risk population	Clean wound sites	Avoid ticks
Treatment	Doxycycline plus gentamicin or streptomycin	Doxycycline	Azithromycin	Doxycycline
Distinctive Features	Undulating fever, muscle aches	Airborne route of transmission, variable disease presentation	History of cat bite or scratch; fever not always present	Most common in eastern and southeastern United States

Anthrax

Anthrax causes disease in the lungs and in the skin, and is addressed elsewhere in this book. We discuss anthrax in this chapter because it multiplies in large numbers in the blood and because septicemic anthrax is a possible outcome of all forms of anthrax.

For centuries, anthrax has been known as a zoonotic disease of herbivorous livestock (sheep, cattle, and goats). It has an important place in the history of medical microbiology because Robert Koch used anthrax as a model for developing his postulates in 1877—and, later, Louis Pasteur used the disease to prove the usefulness of vaccination.

Signs and Symptoms

As just noted, anthrax infection can exhibit its primary symptoms in various locations of the body: on the skin (cutaneous anthrax), in the lungs (pulmonary anthrax), in the gastrointestinal tract (acquired through ingestion of contaminated foods), and in the central nervous system (anthrax meningitis). The cutaneous and pulmonary forms of the disease are the most common. In all of these forms, the anthrax bacterium gains access to the bloodstream, and death, if it occurs, is usually a result of an overwhelming septicemia. Pulmonary anthrax—and the accompanying pulmonary edema and hemorrhagic lung symptoms—can sometimes be the primary cause of death, although it is difficult to separate the effects of septicemia from the effects of pulmonary infection.

In addition to symptoms specific to the site of infection, septicemic anthrax results in headache, fever, and malaise. Bleeding in the intestine and from mucous membranes and orifices may occur in late stages of septicemia.

Causative Agent

Bacillus anthracis is a gram-positive endospore-forming rod that is among the largest of all bacterial pathogens. It is composed of block-shaped, angular rods 3 to 5 micrometers long and 1 to 1.2 micrometers wide. Central spores develop under all growth conditions except in the living body of the host **(figure 18.18)**. Because the primary habitat of many *Bacillus* species, including *B. anthracis,* is the soil, spores are continuously dispersed by means of dust into water and onto the bodies of plants and animals.

Pathogenesis and Virulence Factors

The main virulence factors of *B. anthracis* are its polypeptide capsule and what is referred to as a "tripartite" toxin—a protein complex composed of three separate exotoxins. The end result of exotoxin action is massive inflammation and initiation of shock.

Additional virulence factors for *B. anthracis* include hemolysins and other enzymes that damage host membranes.

Transmission and Epidemiology

The anthrax bacterium is a facultative parasite that undergoes its cycle of vegetative growth and sporulation in the soil. Animals become infected while grazing on grass contaminated with spores. When the pathogen is returned to the soil in animal excrement or carcasses, it can sporulate and become a long-term reservoir of infection for the animal population. The majority of natural anthrax cases are reported in livestock from Africa, Asia, and the Middle East. Most recent (natural) cases in the United States have occurred in textile workers handling imported animal hair or hide or products made from them. Because of effective control procedures, the number of cases in the United States is extremely low (fewer than 10 per year).

The anthrax attacks of 2001 aimed at two senators and several media outlets focused a great deal of attention on the threat of bioterrorism. During that attack, 22 people acquired anthrax and 5 people died.

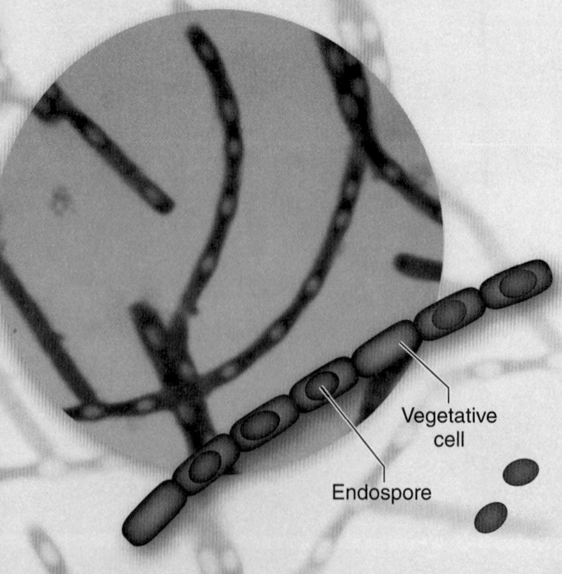

Figure 18.18 *Bacillus anthracis*. Note the centrally placed endospores and streptobacillus arrangement (600×).

Disease Table 18.11 Anthrax

Causative Organism(s)	*Bacillus anthracis*
Most Common Modes of Transmission	Vehicle (air, soil), indirect contact (animal hides), vehicle (food)
Virulence Factors	Triple exotoxin, capsule
Culture/Diagnosis	Culture, direct fluorescent antibody tests
Prevention	Vaccine for high-risk population, postexposure antibiotic prophylaxis
Treatment	Doxycycline, ciprofloxacin, penicillin

Culture and Diagnosis

Diagnosis requires a high index of suspicion. This means that anthrax must be present as a possibility in the clinician's mind or it is likely not to be diagnosed, because it is such a rare disease in the developed world and because, in all of its manifestations, it can mimic other infections that are not so rare. First-level (presumptive) diagnosis begins with culturing the bacterium on blood agar and performing a Gram stain. Ultimately, samples should be handled by the Centers for Disease Control and Prevention, which will perform confirmatory tests, usually involving direct fluorescent antibody testing and phage typing tests.

Prevention and Treatment

Humans should be vaccinated with the purified toxoid if they have occupational contact with livestock or products such as hides and bone or if they are members of the military. Effective vaccination requires six inoculations given over 1.5 years, with yearly boosters. The cumbersome nature of the vaccination has spurred research and development of more manageable vaccines. Persons who are suspected of being exposed to the bacterium are given prophylactic antibiotics, which seem to be effective at preventing disease even after exposure.

The recommended treatment for anthrax is penicillin, doxycycline, or ciprofloxacin.

ASSESS YOUR PROGRESS

4. List the possible causative agents, modes of transmission, virulence factors, diagnostic techniques, and prevention/treatment for the highlighted conditions, malaria and HIV.
5. Discuss the epidemiology of malaria.
6. Discuss the epidemiology of HIV infection in the developing world.
7. Discuss the important features of infectious cardiovascular diseases that have more than one possible cause. These are the two forms of endocarditis, septicemia, hemorrhagic fever diseases, and nonhemorrhagic fever diseases.
8. Discuss factors that distinguish hemorrhagic and nonhemorrhagic fever diseases.
9. Discuss what series of events may lead to septicemia and how it should be prevented and treated.
10. Discuss the important features of infectious cardiovascular diseases that have only one possible cause. These are plague, tularemia, Lyme disease, infectious mononucleosis, and anthrax.
11. Describe what makes anthrax a good agent for bioterrorism, and list the important presenting signs to look for in patients.

CASE FILE WRAP-UP

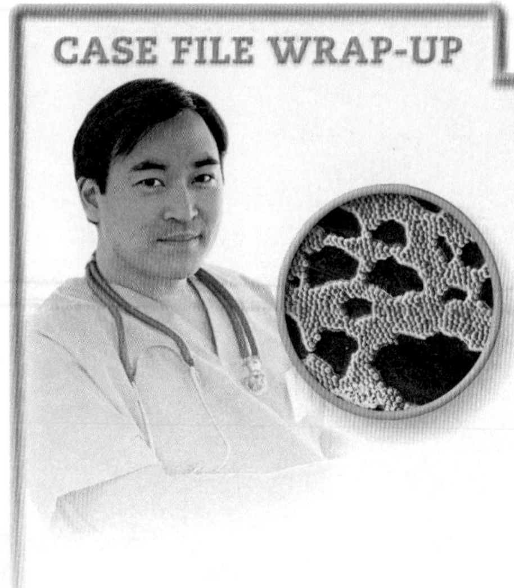

The patient was suffering from septicemia and, likely, the early stages of septic shock. Her symptoms (fever, lethargy, low blood pressure, and very ill appearance) were consistent with the diagnosis. The patient's immune system was compromised due to the fact that she was receiving chemotherapy for treatment of cancer, and the presence of the central line also increased her risk for sepsis.

Blood cultures, as well as culturing the tip of the central line, yielded the bacteria responsible for the patient's sepsis. In this case, the treating physician predicted that the patient's infection was caused by one of the bacteria that normally inhabit the skin and are common causes of catheter-associated sepsis. *Staphylococcus aureus* is the most common culprit. Treatment was commenced with an antibiotic known to be effective against *S. aureus,* and blood culture results confirmed the diagnosis 48 hours later. The patient eventually recovered.

▶ Summing Up

Taxonomic Organization Summing up Microorganisms Causing Disease in the Cardiovascular and Lymphatic Systems

Microorganism	Pronunciation	Location of Disease Table
Gram-positive endospore-forming bacteria		
Bacillus anthracis	buh-sill′-us an-thray′-sus	Anthrax, p. 517
Gram-positive bacteria		
Staphylococcus aureus	staf″-uh-lo-kok′-us are′-ee-us	Acute endocarditis, p. 506
Streptococcus pyogenes	strep″-tuh-kok′-us pie′-ah″-gen-eez	Acute endocarditis, p. 506
Streptococcus pneumoniae	strep″-tuh-kok′-us nu-mo′-nee-ay	Acute endocarditis, p. 506
Gram-negative bacteria		
Yersinia pestis	yur-sin′-ee-uh pes′-tiss	Plague, p. 508
Francisella tularensis	fran-si′-sell″-uh tew′-luh-ren″-sis	Tularemia, p. 509
Borrelia burgdorferi	bor-rill′-ee-ah berg-dorf′-fur-eye	Lyme disease, p. 510
Brucella abortus, B. suis	bru-sell′-uh uh-bort′-us	Brucellosis p. 515
Coxiella burnetii	cox-ee-ell′-uh bur-net′-tee-eye	Q fever, p. 515
Bartonella henselae	bar-ton-nell′-uh hen′-sell-ay	Cat-scratch disease, p. 515
Neisseria gonorrhoeae	nye-seer″-ee-uh′ gon′-uh-ree″-uh	Acute endocarditis, p. 506
Rickettsia rickettsii	ri-ket′-see-uh ri-ket′-see-eye	Rocky Mountain spotted fever, p. 515
DNA viruses		
Epstein-Barr virus	ep′-steen bar″ vie′-russ	Infectious mononucleosis, p. 512
RNA viruses		
Yellow fever virus	yel′-loh fee′-ver vie′-russ	Yellow fever, p. 513
Dengue fever virus	den′-gay fee′-ver vie′-russ	Dengue fever, p. 513
Ebola and Marburg viruses	ee-bowl′-uh and mar′-berg vie′-russ-suz′	Ebola and Marburg hemorrhagic fevers, p. 513
Lassa fever virus	lass′-sah fee′-ver vie′-russ	Lassa fever, p. 513
Chikungunya virus	chick-un-goon′ yah vie′-russ	Hemorrhagic fevers, p. 513
Retroviruses		
Human immunodeficiency virus 1 and 2	hew′-mun im′-muh-noh-dee-fish″-shun-see vie′-russ	HIV infection and AIDS, p. 505
Protozoa		
Plasmodium falciparum, P. vivax, P. ovale, P. malariae	plas-moh′-dee-um fals″-sih-par′-um, plas-moh′-dee-um vee′-vax, plas-moh′-dee-um oh-val′-ee, plas-moh′-dee-um ma-lair′-ee-ay	Malaria, p. 497

Inside the Clinic

The Epstein-Bar–Chronic Fatigue Connection: Fact or Fiction?

The Epstein-Barr virus (EBV), the most common cause of infectious mononucleosis, has been blamed for being a causative agent in many illnesses, such as cancer (Burkett's lymphoma, nasopharyngeal cancers), autoimmune disease, and multiple sclerosis.

In the late 1980s and 1990s, EBV was also thought to be the causative agent of chronic fatigue syndrome (CFS). Chronic fatigue syndrome is a condition characterized by severe fatigue, which does not improve with rest. The condition primarily affects women aged 30 to 50 years. CFS is diagnosed when all other possible conditions have been ruled out. The cause of CFS is not known; however, several causes have been proposed, such as stress, environment, genetics, autoimmune problems, and a viral cause.

Symptoms of CFS may mimic symptoms of numerous other conditions, including infections. Fatigue that is unrelenting and severe is the main symptom. Other symptoms include low-grade fever, lymphadenopathy (swollen lymph nodes), headaches, muscle aches, joint pain, and sore throat. Do these symptoms sound familiar? That's because they are common symptoms in many conditions, infectious and not.

Patients with CFS often report being ill with some type of infection prior to being diagnosed with CFS. While most people who fall ill with an infection experience fatigue while they are acutely ill, the fatigue ends when they recover from the infection. In CFS, however, fatigue may linger for months following a seemingly mild illness. One theory that has engaged researchers is that CSF is caused by EBV, which remains present in the body for life. Several studies in the mid-1980s demonstrated that EBV sufferers have increased levels of antibodies to EBV.

However, these studies were not borne out. Healthy people also often have elevated levels of EBV antibodies. Researchers were unable to link antibody levels with disease severity in CFS, and the idea that EBV and CFS were interlinked has gradually fallen by the wayside.

However, many researchers still believe that there is a link between the two conditions. Current research is focusing on "latent" EBV that may be able to activate an endogenous retrovirus, which may result in a cytokine increase in susceptible individuals. A current study is focusing on whether people with CFS (mostly women) may have a sort of genetic predisposition for activation of this endogenous retrovirus.

Infectious Diseases Affecting
The Cardiovascular and Lymphatic Systems

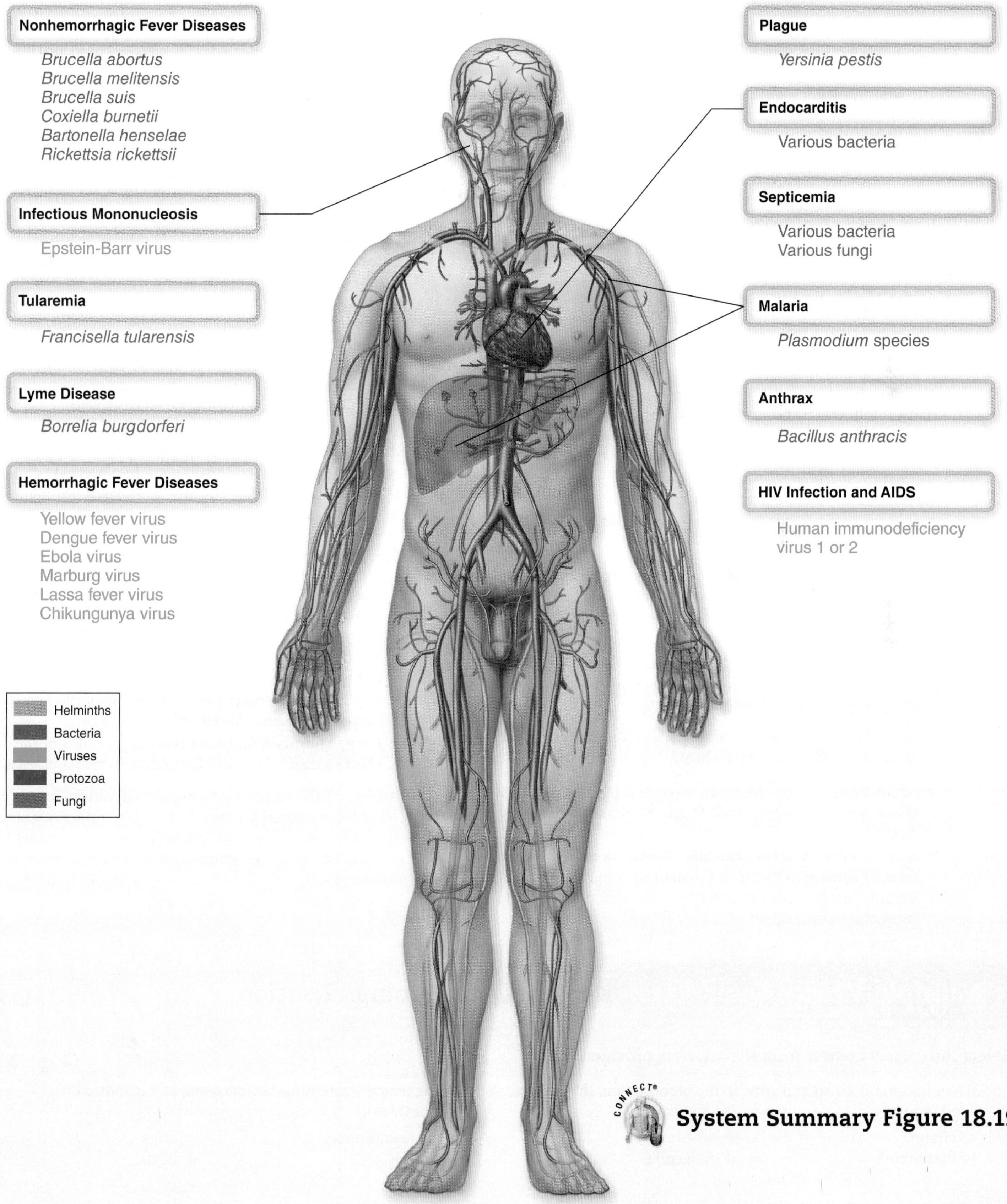

Nonhemorrhagic Fever Diseases

Brucella abortus
Brucella melitensis
Brucella suis
Coxiella burnetii
Bartonella henselae
Rickettsia rickettsii

Infectious Mononucleosis

Epstein-Barr virus

Tularemia

Francisella tularensis

Lyme Disease

Borrelia burgdorferi

Hemorrhagic Fever Diseases

Yellow fever virus
Dengue fever virus
Ebola virus
Marburg virus
Lassa fever virus
Chikungunya virus

Plague

Yersinia pestis

Endocarditis

Various bacteria

Septicemia

Various bacteria
Various fungi

Malaria

Plasmodium species

Anthrax

Bacillus anthracis

HIV Infection and AIDS

Human immunodeficiency virus 1 or 2

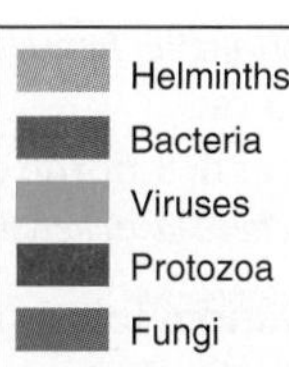

System Summary Figure 18.19

Chapter Summary

18.1 The Cardiovascular and Lymphatic Systems and Their Defenses

- The cardiovascular system is composed of the blood vessels and the heart.
- The lymphatic system is a one-way passage, returning fluid from the tissues to the cardiovascular system.
- The systems are highly protected from microbial infection, as they are not an open body system and they contain many components of the host's immune system.

18.2 Normal Biota of the Cardiovascular and Lymphatic Systems

- At the present time, we believe that the cardiovascular and lymphatic systems contain no normal biota.

18.3 Cardiovascular and Lymphatic System Diseases Caused by Microorganisms

- **Malaria:** Symptoms are malaise, fatigue, vague aches, and nausea, followed by bouts of chills, fever, and sweating. Causative organisms are *Plasmodium* species: *P. malariae, P. vivax, P. falciparum,* and *P. ovale.* Carried by *Anopheles* mosquito.
- **HIV Infection and AIDS:** Symptoms directly tied to the level of virus in the blood versus the level of T cells in the blood.
  - HIV is a retrovirus. Contains *reverse transcriptase,* which catalyzes the replication of double-stranded DNA from single-stranded RNA.
  - Destruction of T4 lymphocytes paves the way for invasion by opportunistic agents and malignant cells.
  - Transmission occurs mainly through sexual intercourse and transfer of blood or blood products.
- **Endocarditis:** Inflammation of the endocardium, usually due to infection of the valves of the heart.
  - **Acute Endocarditis:** Most often caused by *Staphylococcus aureus,* group A streptococci, *Streptococcus pneumoniae,* and *Neisseria gonorrhoeae.*
  - **Subacute Forms of Endocarditis:** Usually preceded by some form of damage to the heart valves or by congenital malformation. Alpha-hemolytic streptococci and normal biota most often responsible.
- **Septicemias/Sepsis:** Organisms actively multiplying in the blood. Most caused by bacteria, to a lesser extent by fungi.
- **Plague:** *Pneumonic plague* is a respiratory disease; *bubonic plague* causes inflammation and necrosis of the lymph nodes; *septicemic plague* is the result of multiplication of bacteria in the blood. *Yersinia pestis* is the causative organism. Fleas are principal agents in transmission of the bacterium.
- **Tularemia:** Causative agent is *Francisella tularensis,* a facultative intracellular gram-negative bacterium. Disease is often called rabbit fever.
- **Lyme Disease:** Caused by *Borrelia burgdorferi.* Syndrome mimics neuromuscular and rheumatoid conditions. *B. burgdorferi* is a spirochete transmitted primarily by *Ixodes* ticks.
- **Infectious Mononucleosis:** Vast majority of cases are caused by the herpesvirus *Epstein-Barr virus (EBV).*
- **Hemorrhagic Fever Diseases:** Extreme fevers often accompanied by internal hemorrhaging. Hemorrhagic fever diseases described here (Yellow fever, Dengue fever, Ebola and Marburg diseases, and Lassa fever) are caused by RNA enveloped viruses.
- **Nonhemorrhagic Fever Diseases:** Characterized by high fever without the capillary fragility that leads to hemorrhagic symptoms.
  - **Brucellosis:** Also called Malta fever, undulant fever, Bang's disease. Multiple species cause this disease in humans—among them *B. melitensis, B. abortus,* and *B. suis.*
  - **Q Fever:** Caused by *Coxiella burnetii,* a small pleomorphic gram-negative bacterium and intracellular parasite. *C. burnetii* is harbored by a wide assortment of vertebrates and arthropods, especially ticks.
  - **Cat-Scratch Disease:** Infection by *Bartonella henselae* connected with being clawed or bitten by a cat.
  - **Rocky Mountain Spotted Fever:** Another tick-borne disease; causes a distinctive rash. Caused by *Rickettsia rickettsii.*
- **Anthrax:** Exhibits primary symptoms in various locations: skin (cutaneous anthrax), lungs (pulmonary anthrax), gastrointestinal tract, central nervous system (anthrax meningitis). Caused by *Bacillus anthracis,* gram-positive endospore-forming rod found in soil.

Multiple-Choice Questions Knowledge and Comprehension

Select the correct answer from the answers provided.

1. When bacteria flourish and grow in the bloodstream, this is referred to as
   a. viremia.
   b. bacteremia.
   c. septicemia.
   d. fungemia.

2. The plague bacterium, *Yersinia pestis,* is transmitted mainly by
   a. mosquitoes.
   b. fleas.
   c. dogs.
   d. birds.

3. Rabbit fever is caused by
   a. *Yersinia pestis.*
   b. *Francisella tularensis.*
   c. *Borrelia burgdorferi.*
   d. *Chlamydia bunnyensis.*
4. Cat-scratch disease is effectively treated with
   a. rifampin.
   b. penicillin.
   c. amoxicillin.
   d. acyclovir.
5. Normal biota found in the oral cavity are most likely to cause
   a. acute endocarditis.
   b. subacute endocarditis.
   c. malaria
   d. tularemia.
6. A distinctive bull's-eye rash results from a tick bite transmitting
   a. Lyme disease.
   b. tularemia.
   c. Q fever.
   d. Rocky Mountain spotted fever.
7. Wool-sorter's disease is caused by
   a. *Brucella abortus.*
   b. *Bacillus anthracis.*
   c. *Coxiella burnetii.*
   d. rabies virus.
8. Which of the following is *not* a hemorrhagic fever?
   a. Lassa fever
   b. Marburg fever
   c. Ebola fever
   d. tularemia

Critical Thinking Application and Analysis

***Critical thinking* is the ability to reason and solve problems using facts and concepts. These questions can be approached from a number of angles and, in most cases, they do not have a single correct answer.**

1. In the Middle Ages, during a massive plague pandemic, one of the control measures officials instituted was the quarantine of infected people. Why was this not successful?
2. Why do you think that malarial infection is more often fatal in children than in adults in areas where it is endemic?
3. Discuss the differences between the epidemiology of AIDS in the United States and in the developing world.
4. Use the terms *prevalence* and *incidence* (see chapter 11) to explain how better treatment options have led to a higher prevalence of AIDS in the world.
5. What characteristics make tularemia a potential bioweapon?

Visual Connections Synthesis

This question connects previous images to a new concept.

1. a. **From chapter 12, figure 12.10*a*.** Imagine that the WBCs shown in this illustration are unable to control the microorganisms in the blood. Could the change that has occurred in the vessel wall help the organism spread to other locations? If so, how?

   b. If the organisms are able to survive phagocytosis, how could that impact the progress of this disease? Explain your answer.

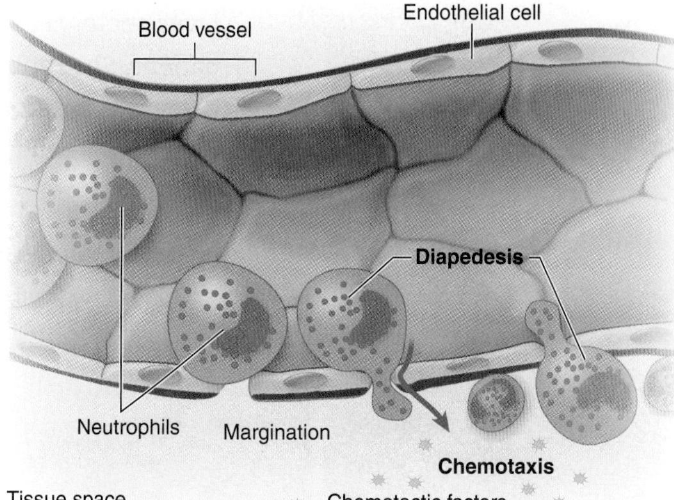

CASE FILE

Could It Be TB?

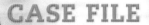

While engaged in my first practicum as a radiology technician, I performed a chest X ray on a 32-year-old recent immigrant from Mexico who had applied for work at the hospital where I was assigned. All new employees of the hospital were required to have a Mantoux test to rule out tuberculosis (TB). My patient's Mantoux skin test was positive, so he was asked to have a chest X ray done. He was concerned about his positive skin test but stated that he couldn't possibly have tuberculosis because he didn't feel sick.

When the X ray was completed, I noticed something strange. I called my preceptor, who was supervising my practicum, to help me interpret the X ray. Although I was able to identify many abnormalities on chest films, what I was seeing was something that I had never seen before in a patient so young. The X ray showed numerous areas of scarring in the patient's left lower lobe, which seemed unusual to me given my patient's young age. My preceptor viewed the X ray and immediately commented that we would have to phone the patient's physician immediately. Unable to identify what I was seeing, I asked my preceptor what she thought was wrong with the patient. She replied, "Your patient recently immigrated from Mexico, has had a positive Mantoux test, and has evidence of scarring on his chest X ray. The patient has tuberculosis."

- What other test will likely be ordered to confirm the diagnosis of tuberculosis in this patient?
- How does a chest X ray help to differentiate between primary and secondary tuberculosis?

Case File Wrap-Up appears on page 549.

CHAPTER 19

Infectious Diseases Affecting the Respiratory System

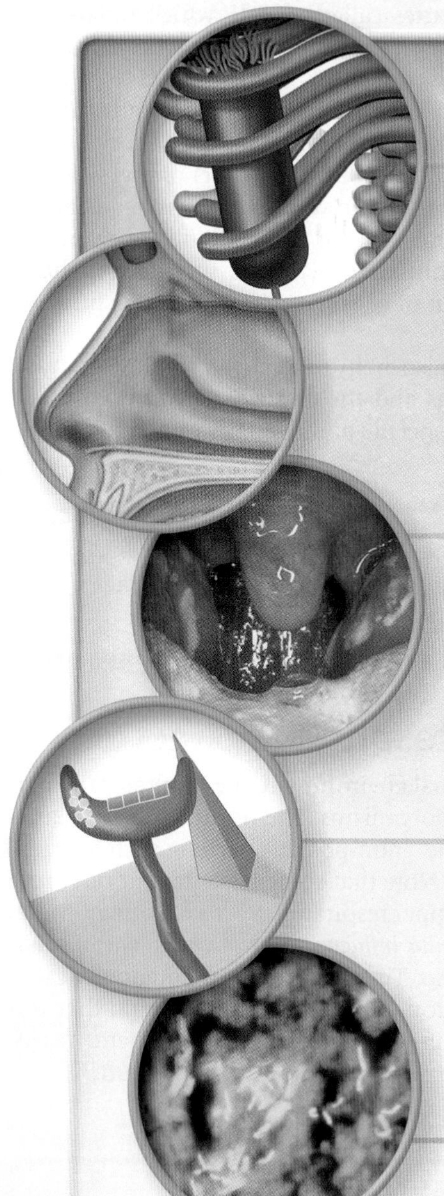

IN THIS CHAPTER...

19.1 The Respiratory Tract and Its Defenses

1. Draw or describe the anatomical features of the respiratory tract.
2. List the natural defenses present in the respiratory tract.

19.2 Normal Biota of the Respiratory Tract

3. List the types of normal biota presently known to occupy the respiratory tract.

19.3 Upper Respiratory Tract Diseases Caused by Microorganisms

4. List the possible causative agents, modes of transmission, virulence factors, diagnostic techniques, and prevention/treatment for the highlighted condition, pharyngitis.
5. Discuss important features of the other infectious diseases of the upper respiratory tract. These are rhinitis, sinusitis, acute otitis media, and diphtheria.
6. Identify two bacteria that can cause dangerous pharyngitis cases.

19.4 Diseases Caused by Microorganisms Affecting Both the Upper and Lower Respiratory Tract

7. List the possible causative agents, modes of transmission, virulence factors, diagnostic techniques, and prevention/treatment for the highlighted disease, influenza.
8. Compare and contrast antigenic drift and antigenic shift in influenza viruses.
9. Discuss important features of the other infectious diseases of the upper and lower respiratory tracts. These are pertussis and RSV disease.

19.5 Lower Respiratory Tract Diseases Caused by Microorganisms

10. List the possible causative agents, modes of transmission, virulence factors, diagnostic techniques, and prevention/treatment for the highlighted condition, tuberculosis.
11. Discuss the problems associated with MDR-TB and XDR-TB.
12. Discuss important features of the other lower respiratory tract diseases, community-acquired and healthcare-associated pneumonia.

19.1 The Respiratory Tract and Its Defenses

The respiratory tract is the most common place for infectious agents to gain access to the body. We breathe 24 hours a day, and anything in the air we breathe passes at least temporarily into this organ system.

The structure of the system is illustrated in **figure 19.1*a*.** Most clinicians divide the system into two parts, the *upper* and *lower respiratory tracts.* The upper respiratory tract includes the mouth, the nose, nasal cavity and sinuses above it, the throat or pharynx, and the epiglottis and larynx. The lower respiratory tract begins with the trachea, which feeds into the bronchi and bronchioles in the lungs. Attached to the bronchioles are small balloonlike structures called alveoli, which inflate and deflate with inhalation and exhalation. These are the sites of oxygen exchange in the lungs.

Several anatomical features of the respiratory system protect it from infection. As described in chapter 12, nasal hair serves to trap particles. Cilia **(figure 19.1*b*)** on the epithelium of the trachea and bronchi (the ciliary escalator) propel particles upward and out of the respiratory tract. Mucus on the surface of the mucous membranes lining the respiratory tract is a natural trap for invading microorganisms. Once the microorganisms are trapped, involuntary responses such as coughing, sneezing, and swallowing can move them out of sensitive areas. These are first-line defenses.

The second and third lines of defense also help protect the respiratory tract. Macrophages inhabit the alveoli of the lungs and the clusters of lymphoid tissue (tonsils) in the throat. Secretory IgA against specific pathogens can be found in the mucus secretions as well.

Medical Moment

What Is Thrush?

Oral candidiasis ("thrush") is an infection that affects the mouth and tongue. It is characterized by patches of whitish lesions on the tongue or in the oral cavity. Underneath this whitish material, the tissues affected are reddened and may bleed easily. It is caused by a fungus called *Candida albicans* that naturally inhabits the human mouth and is normally kept under control by your immune system, and also by the normal biota of your oral cavity.

Antibiotic therapy sometimes results in overgrowth of *Candida*, due to the fact that antibiotics kill some of the natural biota of the mouth that normally act to keep *Candida* in check. People with weakened immune systems are more susceptible to yeast infection, as are diabetics with uncontrolled or poorly controlled blood glucose levels. This is due to the fact that high sugar levels in the saliva act as a food source for *Candida*, allowing it to flourish.

Women who are prescribed antibiotics may also develop a vaginal yeast infection when antibiotics disrupt the normal biota of the vagina, resulting in overgrowth of *C. albicans*. Symptoms include vulvar irritation and a whitish vaginal discharge.

ASSESS YOUR PROGRESS

1. Draw or describe the anatomical features of the respiratory tract.
2. List the natural defenses present in the respiratory tract.

19.2 Normal Biota of the Respiratory Tract

Because of its constant contact with the external environment, the respiratory system harbors a large number of commensal microorganisms. The normal biota is generally limited to the upper respiratory tract, and gram-positive bacteria such as streptococci and staphylococci are very common. Note that some bacteria that can cause serious disease are frequently present in the upper respiratory tract as "normal" biota; these include *Streptococcus pyogenes, Haemophilus influenzae, Streptococcus pneumoniae, Neisseria meningitidis,* and *Staphylococcus aureus.* These bacteria can potentially cause disease if their host becomes immunocompromised for some reason, and they can cause disease in other hosts when they are innocently transferred to them. Yeasts, especially *Candida albicans,* also colonize the mucosal surfaces of the mouth.

Respiratory Tract Defenses and Normal Biota

	Defenses	Normal Biota
Upper Respiratory Tract	Nasal hair, ciliary escalator, mucus, involuntary responses such as coughing and sneezing, secretory IgA	*Moraxella,* nonhemolytic and alpha-hemolytic streptococci, *Corynebacterium* and other diphtheroids, *Candida albicans* Note: *Streptococcus pyogenes, Streptococcus pneumoniae, Haemophilus influenzae, Neisseria meningitidis,* and *Staphylococcus aureus* often present as "normal" biota.
Lower Respiratory Tract	Mucus, alveolar macrophages, secretory IgA	None

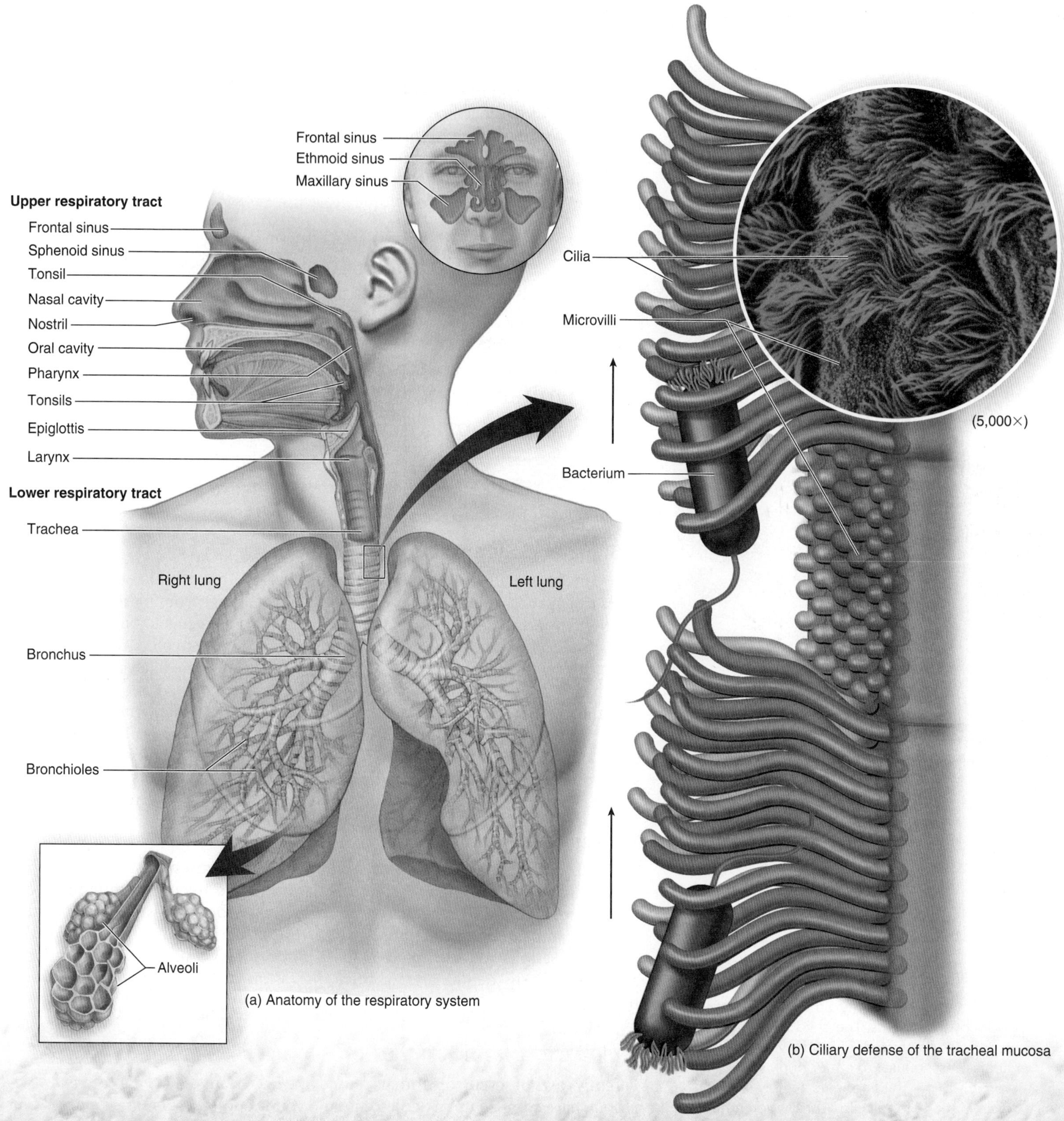

Figure 19.1 The respiratory tract. (a) Important structures in the upper and lower respiratory tract. The four pairs of sinuses are pictured in the inset. (b) Ciliary defense of the respiratory tract.

In the respiratory system, as in some other organ systems, the normal biota performs the important function of microbial antagonism (see chapter 11). This reduces the chances of pathogens establishing themselves in the same area by competing with them for resources and space. As is the case with the other body sites harboring normal biota, the microbes reported here are those we have been able to culture in the laboratory. More microbes will come to light as scientists catalog the genetic sequences in the Human Microbiome Project.

ASSESS YOUR PROGRESS

3. List the types of normal biota presently known to occupy the respiratory tract.

19.3 Upper Respiratory Tract Diseases Caused by Microorganisms

HIGHLIGHT DISEASE

Pharyngitis

▶ Signs and Symptoms

The name says it all—this is an inflammation of the throat, which the host experiences as pain and swelling. The severity of pain can range from moderate to severe, depending on the causative agent. Viral sore throats are generally mild and sometimes lead to hoarseness. Sore throats caused by group A streptococci are generally more painful than those caused by viruses, and they are more likely to be accompanied by fever, headache, and nausea.

Clinical signs of a sore throat are reddened mucosa, swollen tonsils, and sometimes white packets of inflammatory products visible on the walls of the throat, especially in streptococcal disease (**figure 19.2**). The mucous membranes may be swollen, affecting speech and swallowing. Often pharyngitis results in foul-smelling breath. The incubation period for most sore throats is generally 2 to 5 days.

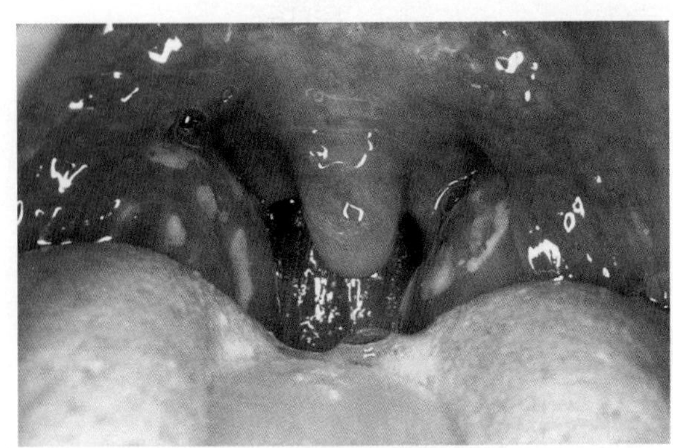

Figure 19.2 The appearance of the throat in pharyngitis and tonsillitis. The pharynx and tonsils become bright red and suppurative. Whitish pus nodules may also appear on the tonsils.

▶ Causative Agents

A sore throat is most commonly caused by the same viruses causing the common cold. It can also accompany other diseases, such as infectious mononucleosis (described in chapter 18). Pharyngitis may simply be the result of mechanical irritation from prolonged shouting or from drainage of an infected sinus cavity. The most serious cause of pharyngitis is *Streptococcus pyogenes.* We will address this infection in depth, after a brief digression about an emerging cause of pharyngitis.

NCLEX® PREP

1. A 2-year-old is brought to the emergency room by his parents. The child's parents report a 2-day history of high fever, hoarseness, refusal to eat or drink, and vomiting. The child appears acutely ill. Upon examination of the child's throat, you note swollen tonsils and a whitish exudate. The child is most likely suffering from pharyngitis caused by which common bacteria?
   a. *Fusobacterium necrophorum*
   b. *Streptococcus pneumoniae*
   c. *Streptococcus pyogenes*
   d. *Corynebacterium diphtheriae*

Fusobacterium necrophorum

Recently cases of severe sore throats caused by a bacterium called *Fusobacterium necrophorum* have cropped up in adolescents and young adults around the country. Some studies suggest it is as common as *S. pyogenes* in this age group. It can cause serious infections of the bloodstream and other organs, a condition called Lemierre's syndrome. Doctors speculate that this disease was previously rarely seen since most sore throats were empirically treated with broad-spectrum antibiotics, a treatment that generally kills *F. necrophorum*. Now that physicians are being much more judicious with antibiotic treatment, and generally not treating at all if strep tests are negative, this bacterium has a doorway to cause disease. This bacterium is sensitive to penicillin and related drugs, which are the first-line drugs for *S. pyogenes* as well. It does make the use of second-line drugs for strep throats less desirable as some of them, such as azithromycin, have no effect on this bacterium. There are currently no rapid diagnostic tests for *F. necrophorum.*

NCLEX® PREP

2. This condition typically occurs in children ages 5 to 15 and may result in damage to the heart valves. It is associated with untreated pharyngitis and may cause joint pain.
   a. diphtheria
   b. pertussis
   c. influenza
   d. rheumatic fever

Streptococcus pyogenes

S. pyogenes is a gram-positive coccus that grows in chains. It does not form spores, is nonmotile, and forms capsules and slime layers. *S. pyogenes* is a facultative anaerobe that ferments a variety of sugars. It does not form catalase, but it does have a peroxidase system for inactivating hydrogen peroxide, which allows its survival in the presence of oxygen.

▸ Pathogenesis

Untreated streptococcal throat infections occasionally can result in serious complications, either right away or days to weeks after the throat symptoms subside. These complications include scarlet fever, rheumatic fever, and glomerulonephritis. More rarely, invasive and deadly conditions such as necrotizing fasciitis can result from infection by *S. pyogenes.* These invasive conditions are described in chapter 16.

Scarlet Fever Scarlet fever is the result of infection with an *S. pyogenes* strain that is itself infected with a bacteriophage. This lysogenic virus confers on the streptococcus the ability to produce erythrogenic toxin, described in the section on virulence. Scarlet fever is characterized by a sandpaper-like rash, most often on the neck, chest, elbows, and inner surfaces of the thighs. High fever accompanies the rash. It most often affects school-age children, and was a source of great suffering in the United States in the early part of the 20th century. In epidemic form, the disease can have a fatality rate of up to 95%. Most cases seen today are mild. They are easily recognizable and amenable to antibiotic therapy. Because of the fear elicited by the name "scarlet fever," the disease is often called scarlatina in North America.

Rheumatic Fever Rheumatic fever is thought to be due to an immunologic cross-reaction between the streptococcal *M protein* and heart muscle. It tends to occur approximately 3 weeks after pharyngitis has subsided. It can result in permanent damage to heart valves. Other symptoms include arthritis in multiple joints and the appearance of nodules over bony surfaces just under the skin. Rheumatic fever is completely preventable if the original streptococcal infection is treated with antibiotics. Nevertheless, it is still a serious problem today in many parts of the world.

Glomerulonephritis Glomerulonephritis is thought to be the result of streptococcal proteins participating in the formation of antigen-antibody complexes, which then are deposited in the basement membrane of the glomeruli of the kidney. It is characterized by **nephritis** (appearing as swelling in the hands and feet and low urine output), blood in the urine, increased blood pressure, and occasionally heart failure. It can result in permanent kidney damage. The incidence of post-streptococcal glomerulonephritis has been declining in the United States, but it is still common in Africa, the Caribbean, and South America.

Toxic shock syndrome and necrotizing fasciitis are other, less frequent, consequences of streptococcal infections, and are discussed in chapter 16.

▸ Virulence Factors

The virulence of *S. pyogenes* is partly due to the substantial array of surface antigens, toxins, and enzymes it can generate.

Streptococci display numerous surface antigens (**figure 19.3**). Specialized polysaccharides on the surface of the cell wall help to

Figure 19.3 Cutaway view of group A streptococcus.

protect the bacterium from being dissolved by the lysozyme of the host. Lipoteichoic acid (LTA) contributes to the adherence of *S. pyogenes* to epithelial cells in the pharynx. A spiky surface projection called M protein contributes to virulence by resisting phagocytosis and possibly by contributing to adherence. A capsule made of hyaluronic acid (HA) is formed by most *S. pyogenes* strains. It probably contributes to the bacterium's adhesiveness. Because this HA is chemically indistinguishable from HA found in human tissues, it does not provoke an immune response from the host.

Extracellular Toxins Group A streptococci owe some of their virulence to the effects of hemolysins called **streptolysins.** The two types are streptolysin O (SLO) and streptolysin S (SLS). Both types cause beta-hemolysis of sheep blood agar (see "Culture and Diagnosis"). Both hemolysins rapidly injure many cells and tissues, including leukocytes and liver and heart muscle (in other forms of streptococcal disease).

A key toxin in the development of scarlet fever is **erythrogenic** (eh-rith'-roh-jen'-ik) **toxin.** This toxin is responsible for the bright red rash typical of this disease, and it also induces fever by acting upon the temperature regulatory center in the brain. Only lysogenic strains of *S. pyogenes* that contain genes from a temperate bacteriophage can synthesize this toxin. (For a review of the concept of lysogeny, see chapter 5.)

Some of the streptococcal toxins (erythrogenic toxin and streptolysin O) contribute to increased tissue injury by acting as *superantigens.* These toxins elicit excessively strong reactions from monocytes and T lymphocytes. When activated, these cells proliferate and produce *tumor necrosis factor* (*TNF*), which leads to a cascade of immune responses resulting in vascular injury. This is the likely mechanism for the severe pathology of toxic shock syndrome and necrotizing fasciitis.

▶ Transmission and Epidemiology

Physicians estimate that 30% of sore throats may be caused by *S. pyogenes,* adding up to several million cases each year. Most transmission of *S. pyogenes* is via respiratory droplets or direct contact with mucus secretions. This bacterium is carried as "normal" biota by 15% of the population, but transmission from this reservoir is less likely than from a person who is experiencing active disease from the infection because of the higher number of bacteria present in the disease condition. It is less common but possible to transmit this infection via fomites. Humans are the only significant reservoir of *S. pyogenes.*

More than 80 serotypes of *S. pyogenes* exist, and thus people can experience multiple infections throughout their lives because immunity is serotype-specific. Even so, only a minority of encounters with the bacterium result in disease. An immunocompromised host is more likely to suffer from strep pharyngitis as well as serious sequelae of the throat infection.

Although most sore throats caused by *S. pyogenes* can resolve on their own, they should be treated with antibiotics because serious sequelae are a possibility.

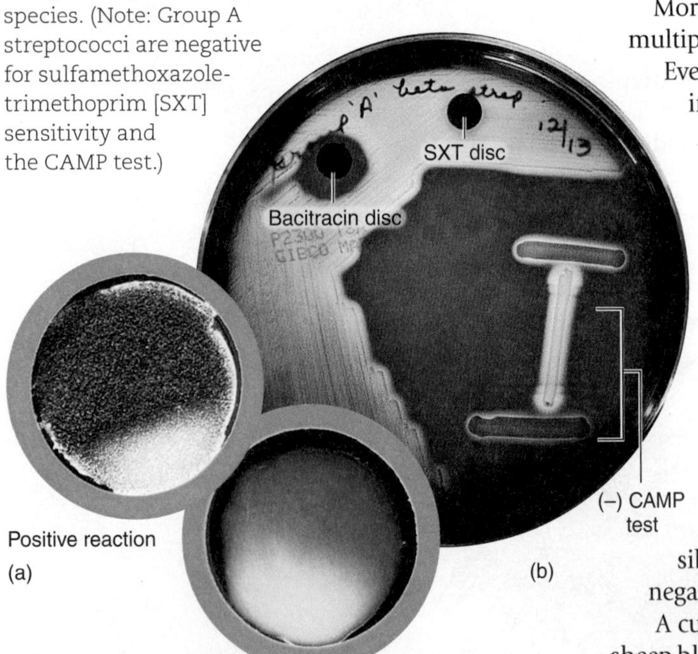

Figure 19.4 Streptococcal tests. **(a)** A rapid, direct test kit for diagnosis of group A infections. With this method, a patient's throat swab is introduced into a system composed of latex beads and monoclonal antibodies. *(Left)* In a positive reaction, the C-carbohydrate on group A streptococci produces visible clumps. *(Right)* A smooth, milky reaction is negative. **(b)** Bacitracin disc test. With very few exceptions, only *Streptococcus pyogenes* is sensitive to a minute concentration (0.02 μg) of bacitracin. Any zone of inhibition around the B disc is interpreted as a presumptive indication of this species. (Note: Group A streptococci are negative for sulfamethoxazole-trimethoprim [SXT] sensitivity and the CAMP test.)

▶ Culture and Diagnosis

The failure to recognize group A streptococcal infections can have devastating effects. Rapid cultivation and diagnostic techniques to ensure proper treatment and prevention measures are essential. Several different rapid diagnostic test kits are used in clinics and doctors' offices to detect group A streptococci from pharyngeal swab samples. These tests are based on antibodies that react with the outer carbohydrates of group A streptococci (**figure 19.4*a***). Because the rapid tests have a significant possibility of returning a false-negative result, guidelines call for confirming the negative finding with a culture, which can be read the following day.

A culture is generally taken at the same time as the rapid swab and is plated on sheep blood agar. *S. pyogenes* displays a beta-hemolytic pattern due to its streptolysins (and hemolysins) (**figure 19.4*b***). If the pharyngitis is caused by a virus, the blood

Disease Table 19.1 Pharyngitis

Causative Organism(s)	*Fusobacterium necrophorum*	*Streptococcus pyogenes*	Viruses
Most Common Modes of Transmission	Opportunistic	Droplet or direct contact	All forms of contact
Virulence Factors	Endotoxin, leukotoxin	LTA, M protein, hyaluronic acid capsule, SLS and SLO, superantigens	–
Culture/Diagnosis	Growth on anaerobic agar	Beta-hemolytic on blood agar, sensitive to bacitracin, rapid antigen tests	Goal is to rule out *S. pyogenes*, further diagnosis usually not performed
Prevention	Hygiene practices	Hygiene practices	Hygiene practices
Treatment	Penicillin, cefuroxime	Penicillin, cephalexin in penicillin-allergic	Symptom relief only
Distinctive Features	Common in adolescents and young adults, infections spread to cardiovascular system or deeper tissues	Generally more severe than viral pharyngitis	Hoarseness frequently accompanies viral pharyngitis

agar dish will show a variety of colony types, representing the normal bacterial biota. Active infection with *S. pyogenes* will yield a plate with a majority of beta-hemolytic colonies. Group A streptococci are by far the most common beta-hemolytic isolates in human diseases, but lately an increased number of infections by group B streptococci (also beta-hemolytic), as well as the existence of beta-hemolytic enterococci, have made it important to use differentiation tests. A positive bacitracin disc test (figure 19.4*b*) provides additional evidence for group A.

▶ Prevention

No vaccine exists for group A streptococci, although many researchers are working on the problem. A vaccine against this bacterium would also be a vaccine against rheumatic fever, and thus it is in great demand. In the meantime, infection can be prevented by good hand washing, especially after coughing and sneezing and before preparing foods or eating.

▶ Treatment

The antibiotic of choice for *S. pyogenes* is penicillin; many group A streptococci have become resistant to erythromycin, a macrolide antibiotic. In patients with penicillin allergies, a first-generation cephalosporin, such as cephalexin, is prescribed.

Rhinitis, or the Common Cold

Everyone is familiar with the symptoms of rhinitis: sneezing, scratchy throat, and runny nose, which usually begin 2 or 3 days after infection. An uncomplicated cold generally is not accompanied by fever, although children can experience low fevers (less than 102°F). The incubation period is usually 2 to 5 days. People with asthma and other underlying respiratory conditions, such as chronic obstructive pulmonary disease (COPD), often suffer severe symptoms triggered by the common cold.

The common cold is caused by one of over 200 different kinds of viruses. The most common type of virus leading to rhinitis is the group called rhinoviruses, of which there are 99 serotypes. Coronaviruses and adenoviruses are also major causes. Also, the respiratory syncytial virus (RSV) causes colds in most people, but in some, especially children, they can lead to more serious respiratory tract symptoms (discussed later in the chapter).

Disease Table 19.2 Rhinitis

Causative Organism(s)	Approximately 200 viruses
Most Common Modes of Transmission	Indirect contact, droplet contact
Virulence Factors	Attachment proteins; most symptoms induced by host response
Culture/Diagnosis	Not necessary
Prevention	Hygiene practices
Treatment	For symptoms only

Disease Table 19.3 Sinusitis

Causative Organism(s)	Various bacteria, often mixed infection	Various fungi
Most Common Modes of Transmission	Endogenous (opportunism)	Introduction by trauma *or* opportunistic overgrowth
Virulence Factors	–	–
Culture/Diagnosis	Culture not usually performed; diagnosis based on clinical presentation, occasionally X rays or other imaging technique used	Same
Prevention	–	–
Treatment	Broad-spectrum antibiotics	Physical removal of fungus; in severe cases antifungals used
Distinctive Features	Much more common than fungal	Suspect in immunocompromised patients

Sinusitis

Commonly called a *sinus infection,* this inflammatory condition of any of the four pairs of sinuses in the skull (see figure 19.1*c*) can actually be caused by allergy (most common), infections, or simply by structural problems such as narrow passageways or a deviated nasal septum. The infectious agents that may be responsible for the condition commonly include a variety of viruses or bacteria and, less commonly, fungi.

Figure 19.5 An infected middle ear.

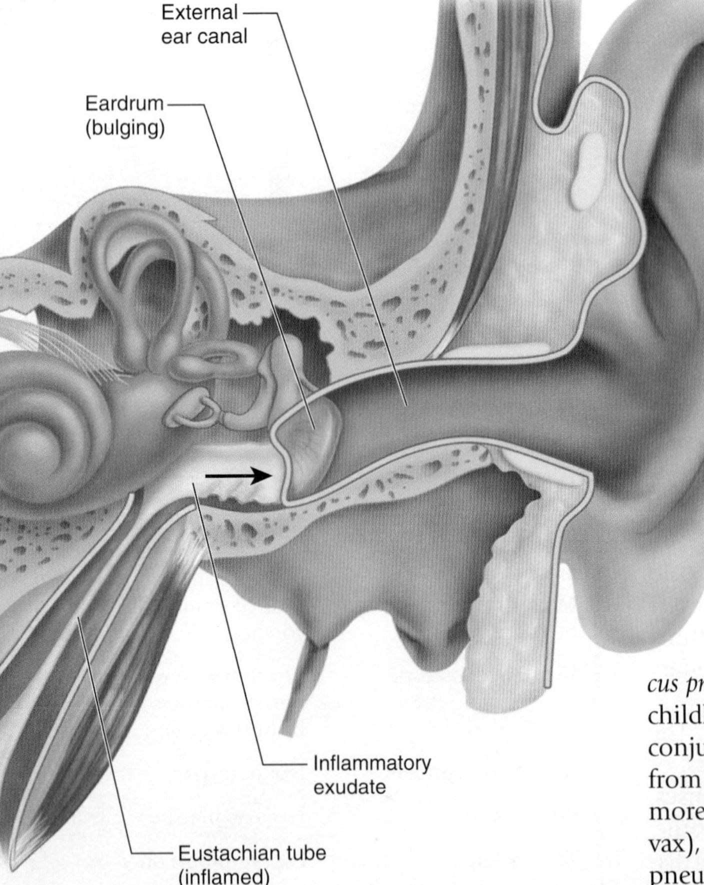

Acute Otitis Media (Ear Infection)

Viral infections of the upper respiratory tract lead to inflammation of the eustachian tubes and the buildup of fluid in the middle ear, which can lead to bacterial multiplication in those fluids. Although the middle ear normally has no biota, bacteria can migrate along the eustachian tube from the upper respiratory tract **(figure 19.5).** When bacteria encounter mucus and fluid buildup in the middle ear, they multiply rapidly. Their presence increases the inflammatory response, leading to pus production and continued fluid secretion. This fluid is referred to as *effusion.*

Another condition, known as chronic otitis media, occurs when fluid remains in the middle ear for indefinite periods of time. Until recently, physicians considered it to be the result of a noninfectious immune reaction because they could not culture bacteria from the site and because antibiotics were not effective. New data suggest that this form of otitis media is caused by a mixed biofilm of bacteria that is attached to the membrane of the inner ear. Biofilm bacteria generally are less susceptible to antibiotics (as discussed in chapter 3), and their presence in biofilm form would explain the inability to culture them from ear fluids. Scientists now believe that the majority of acute and chronic otitis media cases are mixed infections with viruses and bacteria acting together.

The single most common bacterium seen in acute otitis media is *Streptococcus pneumoniae.* A vaccine against *S. pneumoniae* has been a part of the recommended childhood vaccination schedule since 2000. The vaccine (Prevnar) is a seven-valent conjugated vaccine (see chapter 13). It contains polysaccharide capsular material from seven different strains of the bacterium complexed with a chemical that makes it more antigenic. It is distinct from another vaccine for the same bacterium (Pneumovax), which is primarily targeted to the older population to prevent pneumococcal pneumonia.

Disease Table 19.4 Otitis Media

Causative Organism(s)*	*Streptococcus pneumoniae*	Other bacteria
Most Common Modes of Transmission	Endogenous (may follow upper respiratory tract infection by *S. pneumoniae* or other microorganisms)	Endogenous
Virulence Factors	Capsule, hemolysin	–
Culture/Diagnosis	Usually relies on clinical symptoms and failure to resolve within 72 hours	Same
Prevention	Pneumococcal conjugate vaccine (heptavalent)	None
Treatment	Wait for resolution; if needed, amoxicillin (are high rates of resistance) or amoxicillin + clavulanate or cefuroxime	Wait for resolution; if needed, a broad-spectrum antibiotic (azithromycin) might be used in absence of etiologic diagnosis
Distinctive Features	–	Suspect if vaccinated against *S. pneumoniae*

*Keep in mind that many bacterial cases of otitis media are complicated with viral coinfections.

The current treatment recommendation for uncomplicated acute otitis media with a fever below 104°F is "watchful waiting" for 72 hours to allow the body to clear the infection, avoiding the use of antibiotics. When antibiotics are used, antibiotic resistance must be considered. Children who experience frequent recurrences of ear infections sometimes have small tubes placed through the tympanic membranes into their middle ears to provide a means of keeping fluid out of the site when inflammation occurs.

Diphtheria

For hundreds of years, diphtheria was a significant cause of morbidity and mortality, but in the last 50 years, both the number of cases and the fatality rate have steadily declined throughout the world. In the United States in recent years, only one or two cases have been reported each year.

The disease is caused by *Corynebacterium diphtheriae,* a non-spore-forming, gram-positive club-shaped bacterium. The most striking symptom of this disease is a characteristic membrane, usually referred to as a pseudomembrane, that forms on the tonsils or pharynx **(figure 19.6)**.

Figure 19.6 Diagnosing diphtheria. The clinical appearance in diphtheria infection includes gross inflammation of the pharynx and tonsils marked by grayish patches (a pseudomembrane) and swelling over the entire area.

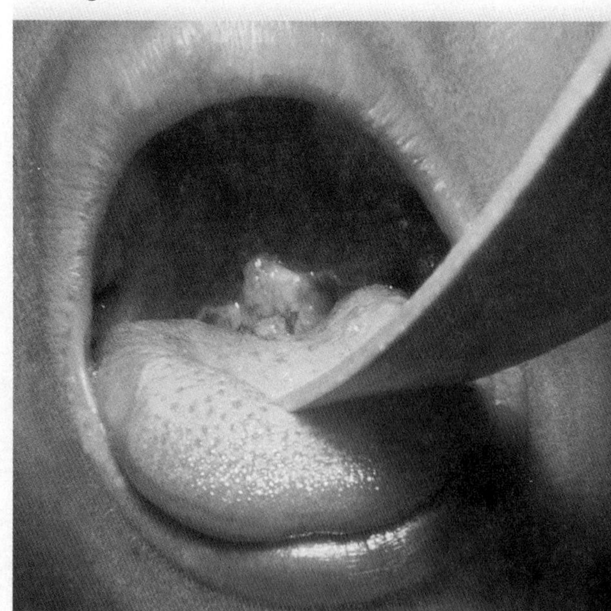

Disease Table 19.5 Diphtheria

Causative Organism(s)	*Corynebacterium diphtheriae*
Most Common Modes of Transmission	Droplet contact, direct contact or indirect contact with contaminated fomites
Virulence Factors	Exotoxin: diphtheria toxin
Culture/Diagnosis	Tellurite medium—gray/black colonies, club-shaped morphology on Gram stain; treatment begun before definitive identification
Prevention	Diphtheria toxoid vaccine (part of DTaP)
Treatment	Antitoxin plus penicillin or erythromycin

NCLEX® PREP

3. One of the hallmarks of this disease is the presence of a pseudomembrane, which may grow to block the airway and is typically gray in color:
   a. diphtheria
   b. sinusitis
   c. pneumonia
   d. pertussis

The major virulence factor is an exotoxin encoded by a bacteriophage of *C. diphtheriae.* Strains of the bacterium that are not lysogenized by this phage do not cause serious disease. The release of diphtheria toxin in the blood leads to complications in distant organs, especially myocarditis and neuritis. Neuritis affects motor nerves and may result in temporary paralysis of limbs, the soft palate, and even the diaphragm, a condition that can predispose a patient to other lower respiratory tract infections.

ASSESS YOUR PROGRESS

4. List the possible causative agents, modes of transmission, virulence factors, diagnostic techniques, and prevention/treatment for the highlighted condition, pharyngitis.
5. Discuss important features of the other infectious diseases of the upper respiratory tract. These are rhinitis, sinusitis, acute otitis media, and diphtheria.
6. Identify two bacteria that can cause dangerous pharyngitis cases.

19.4 Diseases Caused by Microorganisms Affecting Both the Upper and Lower Respiratory Tract

A number of infectious agents affect both the upper and lower respiratory tract regions. We address the more well-known diseases in this section; specifically, they are influenza, whooping cough, and respiratory syncytial virus (RSV).

HIGHLIGHT DISEASE

Influenza

The "flu" is a very important disease to study for several reasons. First of all, everyone is familiar with the cyclical increase of influenza infections occurring during the winter months in the United States. Second, many conditions are erroneously termed the "flu," while in fact only diseases caused by influenza viruses are actually the flu. Third, the way that influenza viruses behave provides an excellent illustration of the way other viruses can, and do, change to cause more serious diseases than they did previously.

Influenzas that occur every year are called "seasonal" flus. Often these are the only flus that circulate each year. Occasionally another flu strain appears, one that is new and may cause worldwide pandemics. In some years, such as in 2009, both of these flus were issues. They may have different symptoms, affect different age groups, and have separate vaccine protocols.

▶ Signs and Symptoms

Influenza begins in the upper respiratory tract but in serious cases may also affect the lower respiratory tract. There is a 1- to 4-day incubation period, after which symptoms begin very quickly. These include headache, chills, dry cough, body aches, fever, stuffy nose, and sore throat. Even the sum of all these symptoms can't describe how a person actually feels: lousy. The flu is known to "knock you off your feet." Extreme fatigue can last for a few days or even a few weeks. An infection with influenza can leave patients vulnerable to secondary infections, often bacterial. Influenza infection alone occasionally leads to a pneumonia that can cause rapid death, even in young healthy adults.

Patients with emphysema or cardiopulmonary disease, along with very young, elderly, or pregnant patients, are more susceptible to serious complications.

The latest pandemic virus, H1N1, or the swine flu of 2009, had similar symptoms but with a couple of differences. Not all patients had a fever (very unusual for influenza), and many patients had gastrointestinal distress.

Causative Agent

All influenza is caused by one of three influenza viruses: A, B, or C. They belong to the family *Orthomyxoviridae*. They are spherical particles with an average diameter of 80 to 120 nanometers. Each virion is covered with a lipoprotein envelope that is studded with glycoprotein spikes acquired during viral maturation **(figure 19.7)**. Also note that the envelope contains proteins that form a channel for ions into the virus. The two glycoproteins that make up the spikes of the envelope and contribute to virulence are called hemagglutinin (H) and neuraminidase (N). The name hemagglutinin is derived from this glycoprotein's agglutinating action on red blood cells, which is the basis for viral assays used to identify the viruses. Hemagglutinin contributes to infectivity by binding to host cell receptors of the respiratory mucosa, a process that facilitates viral penetration. Neuraminidase breaks down the protective mucous coating of the respiratory tract, assists in viral budding and release, keeps viruses from sticking together, and participates in host cell fusion.

The ssRNA genome of the influenza virus is known for its extreme variability. It is subject to constant genetic changes that alter the structure of its envelope glycoproteins. Research has shown that genetic changes are very frequent in the area of the glycoproteins recognized by the host immune response but very rare in the areas of the glycoproteins used for attachment to the host cell **(figure 19.8)**. In this way, the virus can continue to attach to host cells while managing to decrease the effectiveness of the host response to its presence. This constant mutation of the glycoproteins is called **antigenic drift**—the antigens gradually change their

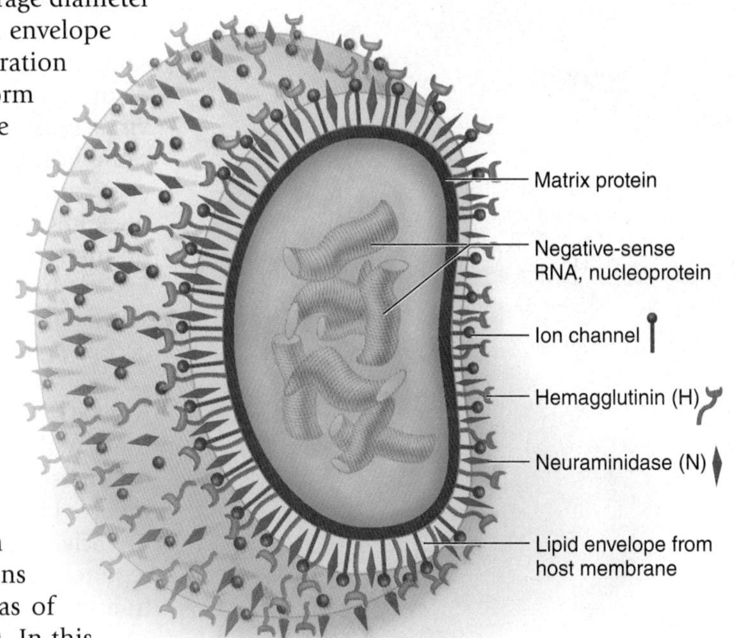

Figure 19.7 Schematic drawing of influenza virus.

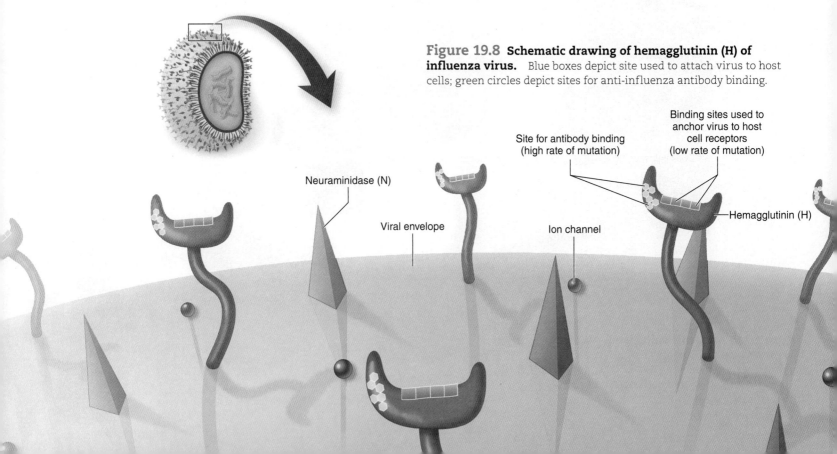

Figure 19.8 Schematic drawing of hemagglutinin (H) of influenza virus. Blue boxes depict site used to attach virus to host cells; green circles depict sites for anti-influenza antibody binding.

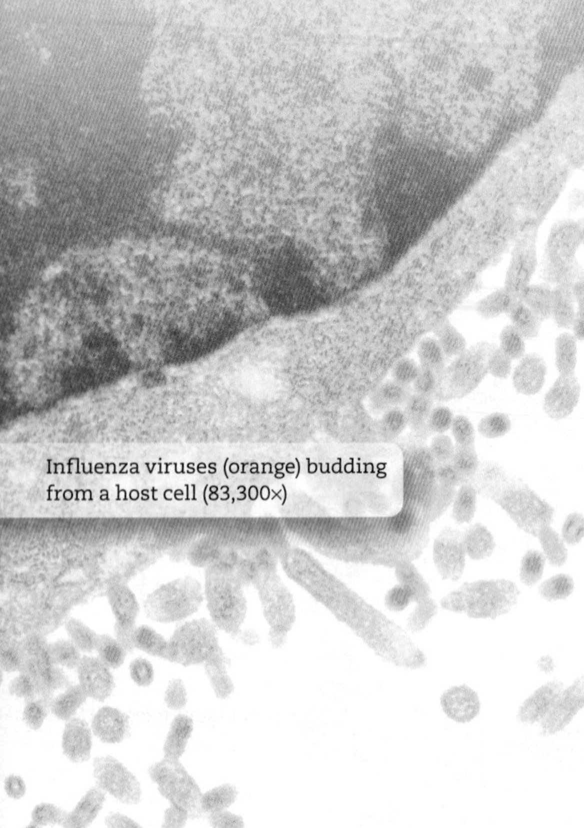
Influenza viruses (orange) budding from a host cell (83,300×)

amino acid composition, resulting in decreased ability of host memory cells to recognize them.

An even more serious phenomenon is known as **antigenic shift.** The genome of the virus consists of just 10 genes, encoded on 8 separate RNA strands. Antigenic shift is the swapping out of one of those genes or strands with a gene or strand from a different influenza virus. Some explanation is in order. First, we know that certain influenza viruses infect both humans and swine. Other influenza viruses infect birds (or ducks) and swine. All of these viruses have 10 genes coding for the same important influenza proteins (including H and N)—but the actual sequence of the genes is different in the different types of viruses. Second, when the two viruses just described infect a single swine host, with both virus types infecting the same host cell, the viral packaging step can accidentally produce a human influenza virus that contains seven human influenza virus RNA strands plus a single duck influenza virus RNA strand **(figure 19.9).** When that virus infects a human, no immunologic recognition of the protein that came from the duck virus occurs. Experts have traced the flu pandemics of 1918, 1957, 1968, 1977, and 2009 to strains of a virus that came from pigs (swine flu). Influenza A viruses are named according to the different types of H and N spikes they display on their surfaces. For instance, in 2004 the most common circulating subtypes of influenza A viruses were H1N1 and H3N2. Influenza B viruses are not divided into subtypes because they are thought to undergo only antigenic drift and not antigenic shift. Influenza C viruses are thought to cause only minor respiratory disease and are probably not involved in epidemics.

Scientists have also recently found that antigenic drift and shift are not even required to make an influenza virus deadly. It appears that a minor genetic alteration in another influenza virus gene, one that seems to produce an enzyme used

H RNA
N RNA
Duck influenza virus
Human influenza virus
H
N
Human influenza virus with duck H spike

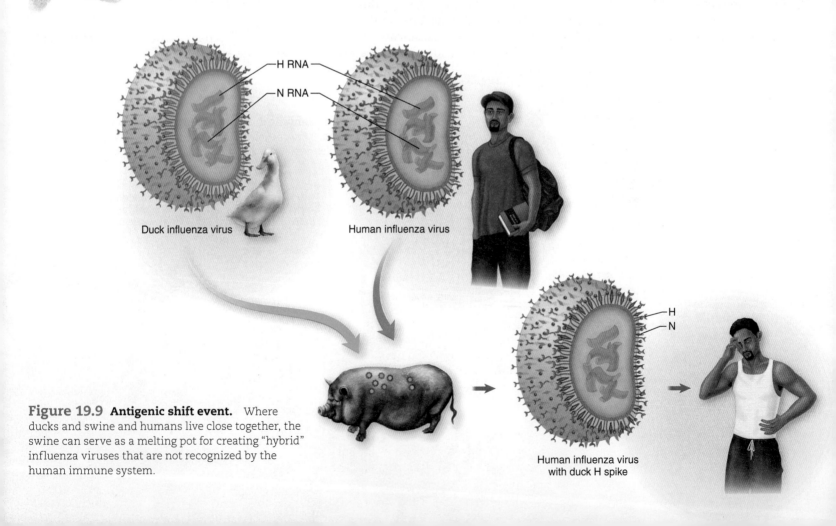

Figure 19.9 Antigenic shift event. Where ducks and swine and humans live close together, the swine can serve as a melting pot for creating "hybrid" influenza viruses that are not recognized by the human immune system.

to manufacture new viruses in the host cell, can make the difference between a somewhat pathogenic influenza virus and a lethal one. It is still not clear exactly how many of these minor changes can lead to pandemic levels of infection and a catastrophe for the public health.

Pathogenesis and Virulence Factors

The influenza virus binds primarily to ciliated cells of the respiratory mucosa. Infection causes the rapid shedding of these cells along with a load of viruses. Stripping the respiratory epithelium to the basal layer eliminates protective ciliary clearance. Combine that with what is often called a "cytokine storm" caused by the viral stimulus and the lungs experience severe inflammation and irritation. The illness is further aggravated by fever, headache, and the other symptoms just described. The viruses tend to remain in the respiratory tract rather than spread to the bloodstream. As the normal ciliated epithelium is restored in a week or two, the symptoms subside.

As just noted, the glycoproteins and their structure are important virulence determinants. First of all, they mediate the adhesion of the virus to host cells. Second, they change gradually and sometimes suddenly, evading immune recognition. One feature of the 2009 H1N1 virus is that it bound to cells lower in the respiratory tract, and at a much higher rate, leading to massive damage, and often death, in the worst-affected patients.

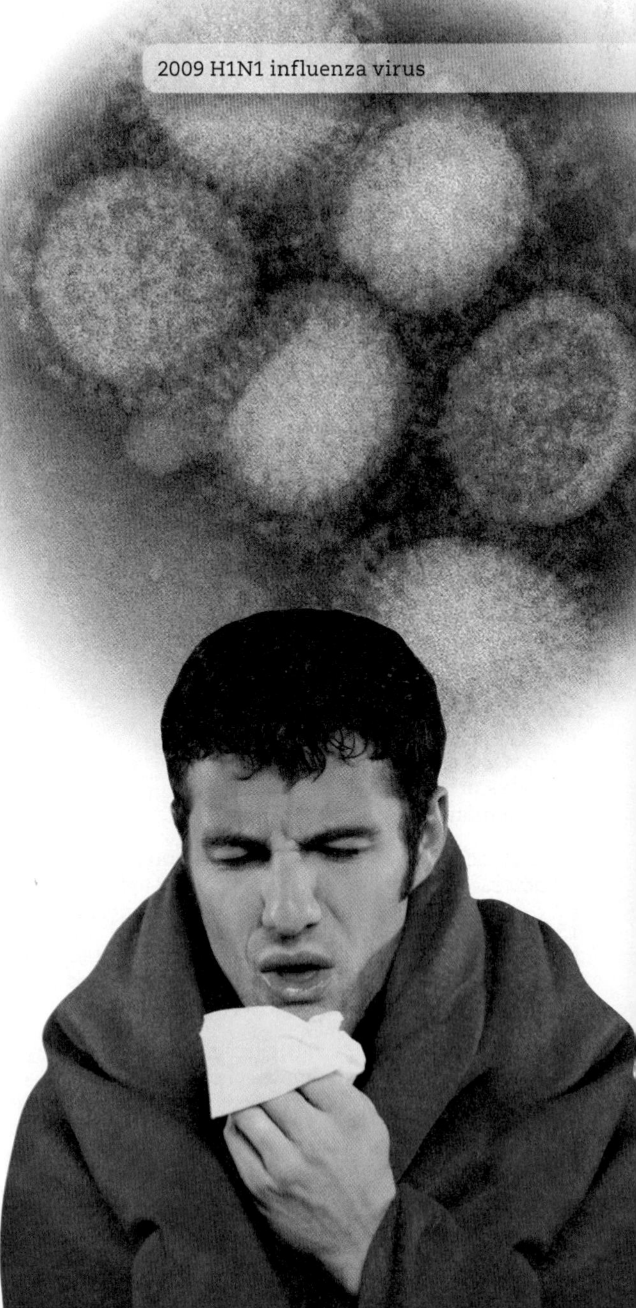
2009 H1N1 influenza virus

Transmission and Epidemiology

Inhalation of virus-laden aerosols and droplets constitutes the major route of influenza infection, although fomites can play a secondary role. Transmission is greatly facilitated by crowding and poor ventilation in classrooms, barracks, nursing homes, dormitories, and military installations in the late fall and winter. The drier air of winter facilitates the spread of the virus, as the moist particles expelled by sneezes and coughs become dry very quickly, helping the virus remain airborne for longer periods of time. In addition, the dry cold air makes respiratory tract mucous membranes more brittle, with microscopic cracks that facilitate invasion by viruses. Influenza is highly contagious and affects people of all ages. Annually, there are approximately 36,000 U.S. deaths from seasonal influenza and its complications, mainly among the very young and the very old.

The 2009 H1N1 virus took a particularly heavy toll on young people. Previously healthy children and teenagers formed a small but important risk group, with quite a few becoming ill within hours and dying within days.

Culture and Diagnosis

Very often, physicians will diagnose influenza based on symptoms alone. But there is a wide variety of culture-based and nonculture-based methods to diagnose the infection. Rapid influenza tests (such as PCR, ELISA-type assays, or immunofluorescence) provide results within 24 hours; viral culture provides results in 3 to 10 days. Cultures are not typically performed at the point of care; they must be sent to diagnostic laboratories, and they require up to 10 days for results. Despite these disadvantages, culture can be useful to identify which subtype of influenza is causing infections, which is important for public health authorities to know. In 2009, officials did not often test for H1N1 but tested for influenza A or B virus, assuming if it was A then it was H1N1, since the circulating seasonal virus was influenza B. When specimens were tested, 100% of the influenza A isolates were in fact the H1N1.

Prevention

Preventing influenza infections and epidemics is one of the top priorities for public health officials. The standard vaccine for seasonal flu contains inactivated dead

Disease Table 19.6 Influenza

Causative Organism(s)	Influenza A, B, and C viruses
Most Common Modes of Transmission	Droplet contact, direct contact, indirect contact
Virulence Factors	Glycoprotein spikes, overall ability to change genetically
Culture/ Diagnosis	Viral culture (3–10 days) or rapid antigen-based or PCR tests
Prevention	Killed injected vaccine or inhaled live attenuated vaccine—taken annually
Treatment	Amantadine, rimantadine, zanamivir, or oseltamivir

HIGHLIGHT DISEASE

viruses that had been grown in embryonated eggs. It has an overall effectiveness of 70% to 90%. The vaccine consists of three different influenza viruses (usually two influenza A and one influenza B) that have been judged to most resemble the virus variants likely to cause infections in the coming flu season. Because of the changing nature of the antigens on the viral surface, annual vaccination is considered the best way to avoid infection. Anyone over the age of 6 months can take the vaccine, and it is recommended for anyone in a high-risk group or for people who have a high degree of contact with the public.

A vaccine called FluMist is a nasal mist vaccine consisting of the three strains of influenza virus in live attenuated form. It is designed to stimulate secretory immunity in the upper respiratory tract. Its safety and efficacy have so far been demonstrated only for persons between the ages of 5 and 49. It is not advised for immunocompromised individuals, and it is significantly more expensive than the injected vaccine.

During the 2009 H1N1 pandemic, new vaccine containing the pandemic strain was quickly prepared. Officials noted that if the strain had been noticed just a few weeks earlier it could have been included in the normal, seasonal vaccine. As it was, the existence of two vaccines added to the complexity of preventing the flu that year.

One of the most promising new vaccine prospects is a vaccine that would protect against *all* flu viruses and not need to be given every year. This vaccine, in testing stages, would target the ion-channel proteins that are present on the envelope of influenza viruses. Apparently these proteins are the same on all flu viruses, and they do not mutate readily. This discovery has the possibility of revolutionizing influenza prevention.

▸ Treatment

Influenza is one of the first viral diseases for which effective antiviral drugs became available. The drugs must be taken early in the infection, preferably by the second day. This requirement is an inherent difficulty because most people do not realize until later that they may have the flu. Amantadine and rimantadine can be used to treat and prevent some influenza type A infections, but they do not work against influenza type B viruses.

Zanamivir (Relenza) is an inhaled drug that works against influenza A and B. Oseltamivir (Tamiflu) is available in capsules or as a powdered mix to be made into a drink. It can also be used for prevention of influenza A and B. Over the period of 2007–2009, different influenza viruses began to show resistance to one or more of these drugs, which called into question the practice of using the drugs preventively in epidemics. As we know with all antimicrobials, the more we use them, the more quickly we lose them (the more quickly they lose their effectiveness).

Whooping Cough (Pertussis)

This disease has two distinct symptom phases called the catarrhal and paroxysmal stages, which are followed by a long recovery (or convalescent) phase, during which a patient is particularly susceptible to other respiratory infections. After an incubation period of from 3 to 21 days, the **catarrhal** stage begins when bacteria present in the respiratory tract cause what appear to be cold symptoms, most notably a runny nose. This stage lasts 1 to 2 weeks. The disease worsens in the second **(paroxysmal)** stage, which is characterized by severe and uncontrollable coughing (a *paroxysm* can be thought of as a convulsive attack). The common name for the disease comes from the whooping sound a patient makes as he or she tries to grab a breath between uncontrollable bouts of coughing.

As in any disease, the **convalescent phase** is the time when numbers of bacteria are decreasing and no longer cause ongoing symptoms.

Pertussis outbreaks continue to occur in the United States and elsewhere. Even though it is estimated that approximately 85% of U.S. children are vaccinated against

Disease Table 19.7 Pertussis (Whooping Cough)

Causative Organism(s)	*Bordetella pertussis*
Most Common Modes of Transmission	Droplet contact
Virulence Factors	Fimbrial hemagglutinin (adhesion), pertussis toxin and tracheal cytotoxin, endotoxin
Culture/ Diagnosis	Grown on B-G, charcoal, or potato-glycerol agar; diagnosis can be made on symptoms
Prevention	Acellular vaccine (DTaP), erythromycin or trimethoprim-sulfamethoxazole for contacts
Treatment	Mainly supportive; erythromycin to decrease communicability

pertussis, it continues to be spread, perhaps by adults whose own immunity has dwindled. These adults may experience mild, unrecognized disease and unwittingly pass it to others. It has also been found that fully vaccinated children can experience the disease, possibly due to antigenic changes in the bacterium.

Respiratory Syncytial Virus Infection

As its name indicates, respiratory syncytial virus (RSV) infects the respiratory tract and produces giant multinucleated cells (syncytia). Outbreaks of droplet-spread RSV disease occur regularly throughout the world, with peak incidence in the winter and early spring. Children 6 months of age or younger, as well as premature babies, are especially susceptible to serious disease caused by this virus. RSV is the most prevalent cause of respiratory infection in the newborn age group, and nearly all children have experienced it by age 2. An estimated 100,000 children are hospitalized with RSV infection each year in the United States. Infection in older children and adults usually manifests as a cold.

The virus is highly contagious and is transmitted through droplet contact but also through fomite contamination. Diagnosis of RSV infection is more critical in babies than in older children or adults. The afflicted child is conspicuously ill, with signs typical of pneumonia and bronchitis.

There is no RSV vaccine available yet, but an effective passive antibody preparation is used as prevention in high-risk children and babies born prematurely.

Disease Table 19.8 RSV Disease

Causative Organism(s)	Respiratory syncytial virus (RSV)
Most Common Modes of Transmission	Droplet and indirect contact
Virulence Factors	Syncytia formation
Culture/Diagnosis	Direct antigen testing
Prevention	Passive antibody (humanized monoclonal) in high-risk children
Treatment	Ribavirin in severe cases

ASSESS YOUR PROGRESS

7. List the possible causative agents, modes of transmission, virulence factors, diagnostic techniques, and prevention/treatment for the highlighted disease, influenza.
8. Compare and contrast antigenic drift and antigenic shift in influenza viruses.
9. Discuss important features of the other infectious diseases of the upper and lower respiratory tracts. These are pertussis and RSV disease.

19.5 Lower Respiratory Tract Diseases Caused by Microorganisms

In this section, we consider microbial diseases that affect the lower respiratory tract primarily—namely, the bronchi, bronchioles, and lungs, with minimal involvement of the upper respiratory tract. Our discussion focuses on tuberculosis and pneumonia.

HIGHLIGHT DISEASE

Tuberculosis

Mummies from the Stone Age, ancient Egypt, and Peru provide unmistakable evidence that tuberculosis (TB) is an ancient human disease. In fact, historically it has been such a prevalent cause of death that it was called "Captain of the Men of Death" and "White Plague." After the discovery of streptomycin in 1943, the rates of tuberculosis in the developed world declined rapidly. But since the mid-1980s, it has reemerged as a serious threat. Worldwide, 2 billion people are currently infected. Two billion—that is one-third of the world's population! The cause of tuberculosis

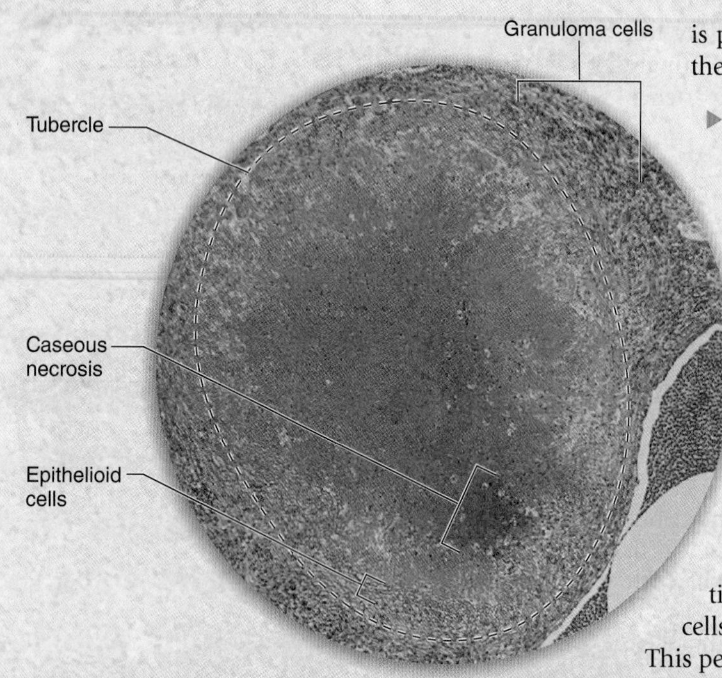

Figure 19.10 Tubercle formation. Photomicrograph of a tubercle (16×). The massive granuloma infiltrate has obliterated the alveoli and set up a dense collar of fibroblasts, lymphocytes (granuloma cells), and epithelioid cells. The core of this tubercle is a caseous (cheesy) material containing the bacilli.

is primarily the bacterial species *Mycobacterium tuberculosis,* informally called the tubercle bacillus.

Signs and Symptoms

A clear-cut distinction can be made between infection with the TB bacterium and the disease it causes. In general, humans are rather easily infected with the bacterium but are resistant to the disease. Estimates project that only about 5% of infected people actually develop a clinical case of tuberculosis. Untreated tuberculosis progresses slowly, and people with the disease may have a normal life span, with periods of health alternating with episodes of morbidity. The majority (85%) of TB cases are contained in the lungs, even though disseminated TB bacteria can give rise to tuberculosis in any organ of the body. Clinical tuberculosis is divided into primary tuberculosis, secondary (reactivation or reinfection) tuberculosis, and disseminated or extrapulmonary tuberculosis.

Primary Tuberculosis The minimum infectious dose for lung infection is around 10 bacterial cells. Alveolar macrophages phagocytose these cells, but they are not killed and continue to multiply inside the macrophages. This period of hidden infection is asymptomatic or is accompanied by mild fever. Some bacteria escape from the lungs into the blood and lymphatics. After 3 to 4 weeks, the immune system mounts a complex, cell-mediated assault against the bacteria. The large influx of mononuclear cells into the lungs plays a part in the formation of specific infection sites called **tubercles.** Tubercles are granulomas that consist of a central core containing TB bacteria in enlarged macrophages and an outer wall made of fibroblasts, lymphocytes, and macrophages **(figure 19.10).** Although this response further checks spread of infection and helps prevent the disease, it also carries a potential for damage. Frequently, as neutrophils come on the scene and release their enzymes, the centers of tubercles break down into necrotic **caseous** (kay′-see-us) **lesions** that gradually heal by *calcification*—normal lung tissue is replaced by calcium deposits. The response of T cells to *M. tuberculosis* proteins also causes a cell-mediated immune response evident in the skin test called the **tuberculin reaction,** a valuable diagnostic and epidemiological tool.

Secondary (Reactivation) Tuberculosis Although the majority of adequately treated TB patients recover more or less completely from the primary episode of infection, live bacteria can remain dormant and become reactivated weeks, months, or years later, especially in people with weakened immunity. In chronic tuberculosis, tubercles filled with masses of bacteria expand, cause cavities in the lungs, and drain into the bronchial tubes and upper respiratory tract. The patient gradually experiences more severe symptoms, including violent coughing, greenish or bloody sputum, low-grade fever, anorexia, weight loss, extreme fatigue, night sweats, and chest pain. It is the gradual wasting of the body that accounts for an older name for tuberculosis—*consumption.* Untreated secondary disease has nearly a 60% mortality rate.

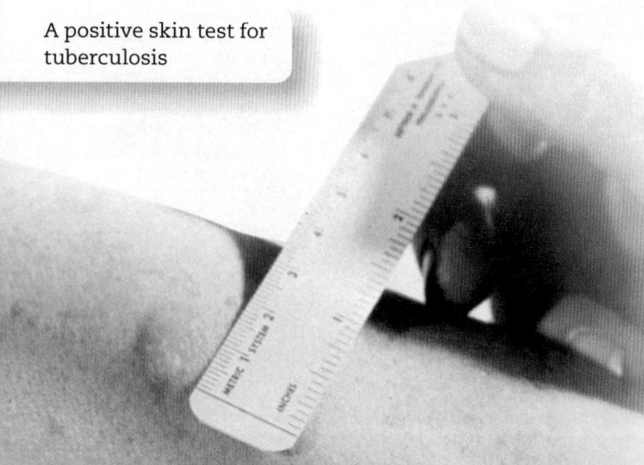

A positive skin test for tuberculosis

Extrapulmonary Tuberculosis TB infection outside of the lungs is more common in immunosuppressed patients and young children. Organs most commonly involved in **extrapulmonary TB** are the regional lymph nodes, kidneys, long bones, genital tract, brain, and meninges. Because of the debilitation of the patient and the high load of TB bacteria, these complications are usually grave. Renal tuberculosis results in necrosis and scarring of the kidney and the pelvis, ureters, and bladder. This damage is accompanied by painful urination, fever, and the presence of blood and the TB bacterium in urine. Genital tuberculosis in males damages the prostate gland, epididymis, seminal vesicle, and testes; and in females, the fallopian tubes, ovaries, and uterus. Tuberculosis of the bones and joints is a common complication.

The spine is a frequent site of infection, although the hip, knee, wrist, and elbow can also be involved. Neurological damage stemming from compression on nerves can cause extensive paralysis and sensory loss.

Tubercular meningitis is the result of an active brain lesion seeding bacteria into the meninges. Over a period of several weeks, the infection of the cranial compartments can create mental deterioration, permanent retardation, blindness, and deafness. Untreated tubercular meningitis is invariably fatal, and even treated cases can have a 30% to 50% mortality rate.

Causative Agents

M. tuberculosis is the cause of tuberculosis in most patients. It is an acid-fast rod, long and thin. It is a strict aerobe, and technically speaking, there is still debate about whether it is a gram-positive or a gram-negative organism. It is rarely called gram anything, however, because its acid-fast nature is much more relevant in a clinical setting. It grows very slowly. With a generation time of 15 to 20 hours, a period of up to 6 weeks is required for colonies to appear in culture. (Note: The prefix *Myco-* might make you think of fungi, but this is a bacterium. The prefix in the name came from the mistaken impression that colonies growing on agar resembled fungal colonies. And be sure to differentiate this bacterium from *Mycoplasma*—they are unrelated.)

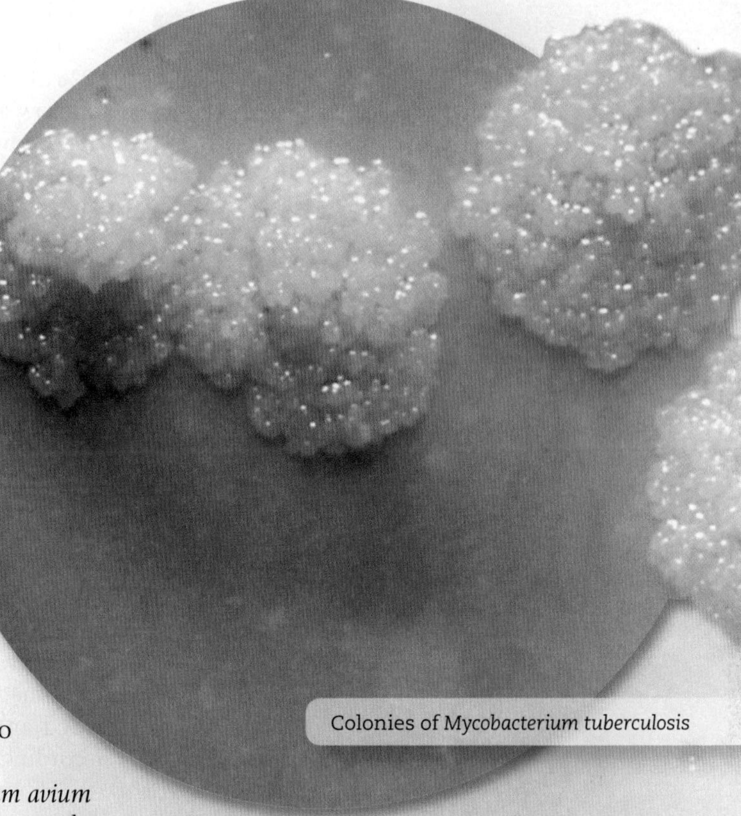
Colonies of *Mycobacterium tuberculosis*

Robert Koch identified that *M. tuberculosis* often forms serpentine cords while growing, and he called the unknown substance causing this style of growth *cord factor.* Cord factor appears to be associated with virulent strains, and it is a lipid component of the mycobacterial cell wall. All mycobacterial species have walls that have a very high content of complex lipids, including mycolic acid and waxes. This chemical characteristic makes them relatively impermeable to stains and difficult to decolorize (acid-fast) once they are stained. The lipid wall of the bacterium also influences its virulence and makes it resistant to drying and disinfectants.

In recent decades, tuberculosis-like conditions caused by *Mycobacterium avium* and related mycobacterial species (sometimes referred to as the *M. avium* complex, or MAC) have been found in AIDS patients and other immunocompromised people. In this section, we consider only *M. tuberculosis,* although *M. avium* is discussed briefly near the conclusion.

Before routine pasteurization of milk, humans acquired bovine TB, caused by a species called *Mycobacterium bovis,* from the milk they drank. It is very rare today, but in 2004, six people in a nightclub acquired bovine TB from a fellow reveler. One person died from her infection.

Pathogenesis and Virulence Factors

The course of the infection—and all of its possible variations—was previously described under "Signs and Symptoms." Important characteristics of the bacterium that contribute to its virulence are its waxy surface (contributing both to its survival in the environment and its survival within macrophages) and its ability to stimulate a strong cell-mediated immune response that contributes to the pathology of the disease.

Transmission and Epidemiology

The agent of tuberculosis is transmitted almost exclusively by fine droplets of respiratory mucus suspended in the air. The TB bacterium is highly resistant and can survive for 8 months in fine aerosol particles. Although larger particles become trapped in mucus and are expelled, tinier ones can be inhaled into the bronchioles and alveoli. This effect is especially pronounced among people sharing small closed rooms with limited access to sunlight and fresh air.

Slum in Mumbai, India

The epidemiological patterns of *M. tuberculosis* infection vary with the living conditions in a community or an area of the world. Factors that significantly affect people's susceptibility to tuberculosis are inadequate nutrition, debilitation of the immune system, poor access to medical care, lung damage, and their own genetics. Put simply, TB is an infection of poverty. People in developing countries are often infected as infants and harbor the microbe for many years until the disease is reactivated in young adulthood. Nearly 2 million people died from TB in 2008, the equivalent of 4,500 a day.

Case rates have begun to drop in the United States, from a high in 2004. About 60% of cases in the United States are among foreign-born persons. This is important to know as a health care provider so you can be alert for TB in certain populations. The top five countries of origin of people in the United States with TB in 2009 were Mexico, Philippines, Vietnam, India, and China.

Culture and Diagnosis

You are probably familiar with several methods of detecting tuberculosis in humans. Clinical diagnosis of tuberculosis relies on four techniques: (1) tuberculin testing, (2) chest X rays, (3) direct identification of acid-fast bacilli (AFB) in sputum or other specimens, and (4) cultural isolation and antimicrobial susceptibility testing.

Tuberculin Sensitivity and Testing Because infection with the TB bacillus can lead to delayed hypersensitivity to tuberculoproteins, testing for hypersensitivity has been an important way to screen populations for tuberculosis infection and disease. Although there are newer methods available, the most widely used test is still the tuberculin skin test, called the **Mantoux test.** It involves local injection of purified protein derivative (PPD), a standardized solution taken from culture fluids of *M. tuberculosis.* The injection is done intradermally into the forearm to produce an immediate small bleb. After 48 and 72 hours, the site is observed for a red wheal called an **induration,** which is measured and interpreted as positive or negative according to size **(figure 19.11).**

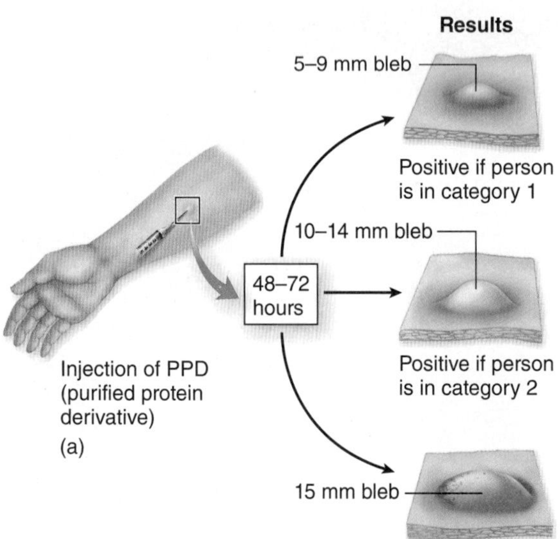

Figure 19.11 Skin testing for tuberculosis. **(a, b)** The Mantoux test. Tuberculin is injected into the dermis. A small bleb from the injected fluid develops but will be absorbed in a short time. After 48 to 72 hours, the skin reaction is rated by the degree (or size) of the raised area. The surrounding red area is *not* counted in the measurement.

Tuberculin testing is currently limited to selected groups known to have higher risk for tuberculosis infection. It is no longer used as a routine screening method among populations of children or adults who are not within the target groups. The reasoning behind this change is to allow more focused screening and to reduce expensive and unnecessary follow-up tests and treatments. Guidelines for test groups and methods of interpreting tests are listed in the following summary.

Category 1. Induration (skin reaction) that is equal to or greater than *5 millimeters* is classified as positive in persons:

- who have had contact with actively infected TB patients;
- who are HIV-positive or have risk factors for HIV infection; and
- with past history of tuberculosis as determined through chest X rays.

Category 2. Induration that is equal to or greater than *10 millimeters* is classified as positive in persons who are not in category 1 but who fit the following high-risk groups:

- HIV-negative intravenous drug users;
- persons with medical conditions that put them at risk for progressing from latent TB infection to active TB;
- persons who live or work in high-risk residences such as nursing homes, jails, or homeless shelters;
- new immigrants from countries with high rates of TB;
- low-income populations lacking access to adequate medical care;

- high-risk adults from ethnic minority populations as determined by local public health departments; and
- children who have contact with members of high-risk adult populations.

Category 3. Induration that is equal to or greater than *15 millimeters* is classified as positive in persons who do not meet criteria in categories 1 or 2.

A positive reaction in a person from one of the risk groups is fairly reliable evidence of recent infection or reactivation of a prior latent infection. Because the test is not 100% specific, false positive reactions will occasionally occur in patients who have recently been vaccinated with the BCG vaccine. Because BCG vaccination can also stimulate delayed hypersensitivity, clinicians must weigh a patient's vaccine history, especially among individuals who have immigrated from countries where the vaccine is routinely given. Another cause of a false positive reaction is the presence of an infection with a closely related species of *Mycobacterium.*

A negative skin test usually indicates that ongoing TB infection is not present. In some cases, it may be a false negative, meaning that the person is infected but is not yet reactive. One cause of a false negative test may be that it is administered too early in the infection, requiring retesting at a later time. Subgroups with severely compromised immune systems, such as those with AIDS, advanced age, and chronic disease, may be unable to mount a reaction even though they are infected. Skin testing may not be a reliable diagnostic indicator in these populations.

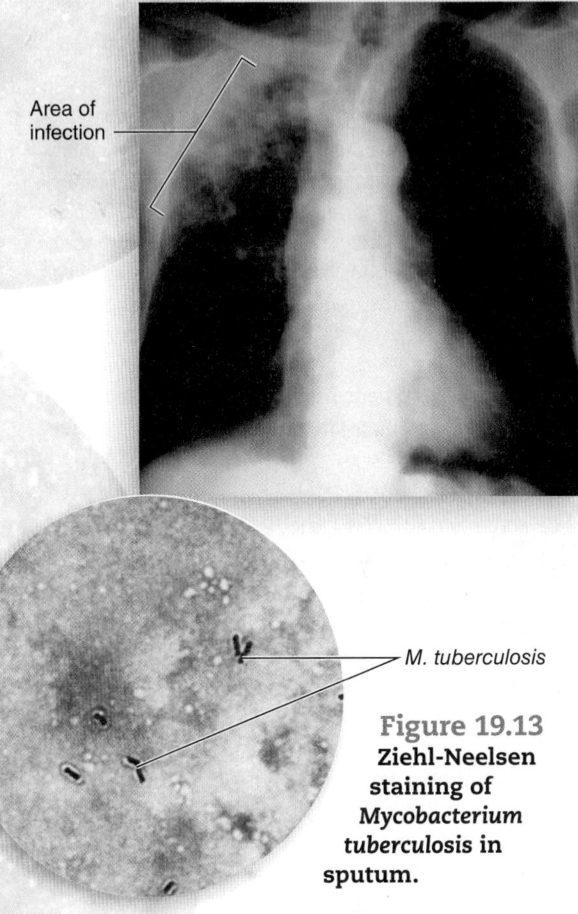

Figure 19.12 Primary tuberculosis.

Figure 19.13 Ziehl-Neelsen staining of *Mycobacterium tuberculosis* in sputum.

X Rays Chest X rays can help verify TB when other tests have given indeterminate results, and they are generally used after a positive test for further verification. X-ray films reveal abnormal radiopaque patches, the appearance and location of which can be very indicative. Primary tubercular infection presents the appearance of fine areas of infiltration **(figure 19.12)** and enlarged lymph nodes in the lower and central areas of the lungs. Secondary tuberculosis films show more extensive infiltration in the upper lungs and bronchi and marked tubercles. Scars from older infections often show up on X rays and can furnish a basis for comparison when trying to identify newly active disease.

Acid-Fast Staining The diagnosis of tuberculosis in people with positive skin tests or X rays can be backed up by acid-fast staining of sputum or other specimens. Several variations on the acid-fast stain are currently in use. The Ziehl-Neelsen stain produces bright red acid-fast bacilli (AFB) against a blue background **(figure 19.13).** Fluorescence staining shows luminescent yellow-green bacteria against a dark background **(figure 19.14).**

Diagnosis that differentiates between *M. tuberculosis* and other mycobacteria must be accomplished as rapidly as possible so that appropriate treatment and isolation precautions can be instituted. The newer fast-identification techniques such as fluorescent staining, high-performance liquid chromatography (HPLC) analysis of mycolic acids, and PCR diagnosis can and should be used to identify isolates as *Mycobacterium.* Even though newer cultivation schemes exist that shorten the incubation period from 6 weeks to several days, this delay is unacceptable for beginning treatment or isolation precautions. But a culture still must be performed because growing colonies are required to determine antibiotic sensitivities.

Because the specimens are often contaminated with rapid-growing bacteria that will interfere with the isolation of *M. tuberculosis,* they are pretreated with chemicals to remove contaminants and are plated onto selective medium (such as Lowenstein-Jensen medium).

Figure 19.14 A fluorescent acid-fast stain of *Mycobacterium tuberculosis* from sputum. Smears are evaluated in terms of the number of AFB (acid-fast bacteria) seen per field. This quantity is then applied to a scale ranging from 0 to 4+, 0 being no AFB observed and 4+ being more than 9 AFB per field.

Medical Moment

Protecting Health Care Workers from Respiratory Pathogens

Isolation rooms—Patients suspected or known to have TB or other pathogenic respiratory infections are placed in isolation rooms. Negative pressure isolation rooms work by maintaining a flow of air into the room, preventing pathogens from spreading outside the room. These rooms feature an anteroom which acts as a barrier between the actual isolation room and the hallway. Health care workers use this area to don protective equipment before entering the patient's room. Negative pressure isolation rooms have their own air supply. The air within the room is changed several times an hour. Exhaust air is forced through a HEPA filter (high-efficiency particulate air filter).

Specialized masks—Special masks are used to protect health care workers from respiratory illnesses spread through airborne or droplet infection. TB masks or N-95 masks have the following characteristics: they filter particles that are 1 micron in size or smaller, have a 95% or higher filtering efficiency, and can be sealed tightly to the face with less than a 10% leak. These masks differ from regular surgical masks due to their ability to filter smaller particles. They must be specially fitted to individual health care workers.

HIGHLIGHT DISEASE

▶ Prevention

Preventing TB in the United States is accomplished by limiting exposure to infectious airborne particles. Extensive precautions, such as isolation in negative-pressure rooms, are used in health care settings when a person with active TB is identified. Vaccine is generally not used in the United States, although an attenuated vaccine, called BCG, is used in many countries. BCG stands for Bacille Calmette-Guerin, named for two French scientists who created the vaccine in the early 1900s. It is a live strain of a bovine tuberculosis bacterium that has been made avirulent by long passage through artificial media. In 2007, scientists made the observation that the BCG vaccine currently used is fairly ineffective and that original BCG strains from a much earlier time induce stronger immunity in patients. There is talk of reviving the older BCG strains and perhaps using this new-old BCG vaccine more widely, in the face of treatment failures and the huge infection rates. Remember that persons vaccinated with BCG may respond positively to a tuberculin skin test.

In the past, prevention in the context of tuberculosis referred to preventing a person with latent TB from experiencing reactivation. This strategy is more accurately referred to as treatment of latent infection and is considered in the next section.

▶ Treatment

Treatment of latent TB infection is effective in preventing full-blown disease in persons who have positive tuberculin skin tests and who are at risk for reactivated TB. Treatment with isoniazid for 9 months or with a combination of rifampin plus an additional antibiotic called pyrazinamide for 2 months is recommended.

Treatment of active TB infection when the microorganism has been found to have no antibiotic resistance consists of 9 months of treatment with isoniazid plus rifampin, with pyrazinamide also taken for the first 2 months. If there is evidence of extrapulmonary tubercular disease, the treatment should be extended to 12 months.

When the bacterium is resistant to one or more of the preceding agents, at least three additional antibiotics must be added to the treatment regimen and the duration of treatment should be extended.

One of the biggest problems with TB therapy is noncompliance on the part of the patient. It is very difficult, even under the best of circumstances, to keep to a regimen of multiple antibiotics daily for months. And most TB patients are not living under the best of circumstances. But failure to adhere to the antibiotic regimen

Disease Table 19.9 Tuberculosis

Causative Organism(s)	*Mycobacterium tuberculosis*	*Mycobacterium avium* complex
Most Common Modes of Transmission	Vehicle (airborne)	Vehicle (airborne)
Virulence Factors	Lipids in wall, ability to stimulate strong cell-mediated immunity (CMI)	–
Culture/Diagnosis	Rapid methods plus culture; initial tests are skin testing	Positive blood culture and chest X ray
Prevention	Avoiding airborne *M. tuberculosis,* BCG vaccine in other countries	Rifabutin or azithromycin given to AIDS patients at risk
Treatment	Isoniazid, rifampin, and pyrazinamide + ethambutol or streptomycin for varying lengths of time (always lengthy); if resistant, additional drugs added to regimen	Azithromycin or clarithromycin plus one additional antibiotic
Distinctive Features	Responsible for nearly all TB except for some HIV-positive patients	Suspect this in HIV-positive patients

leads to antibiotic resistance in the slow-growing microorganism, and in fact many *M. tuberculosis* isolates are now found to be **MDR-TB,** or multidrug-resistant TB. For this reason, it has been recommended that all patients with TB be treated by directly observed therapy (DOT), in which ingestion of medications is observed by a responsible person (see Note). The threat to public health is so great when patients do not adhere to treatment regimens that the United States and other countries have occasionally incarcerated people—and isolated them—when they don't follow their treatment schedules. In 2006, a new strain of *M. tuberculosis* was identified in Africa. It is particularly lethal for HIV-infected people and has been named **XDR-TB** (extensively drug-resistant TB). XDR-TB is defined as resistance to isoniazid and rifampin plus resistance to any fluoroquinolone and at least one of three injectable second-line anti-TB drugs. Since 2006, XDR-TB has spread around the world, and the CDC estimates that 500,000 new cases are seen every year. In the United States, a handful of cases of XDR-TB occur each year.

Mycobacterium avium Complex (MAC)

Before the introduction of effective HIV treatments, described in chapter 18, disseminated tuberculosis infection with MAC was one of the biggest killers of AIDS patients. It mainly affects patients with CD4 counts below 50 cells per milliliter of blood. Antibiotics to prevent this condition should be given to all patients with AIDS.

A Note About Directly Observed Therapy

Although it is highly labor intensive, directly observed therapy (DOT) seems to be the most effective means of curbing infections and preventing further development of antibiotic resistance. The WHO estimates that 8 million deaths have been prevented by DOT over the last 15 years. Patients are referred for DOT if a physician suspects they will have trouble adhering to the very rigorous and lengthy antibiotic schedule. At that point, a public health worker is assigned to visit them at their home and/or workplace to watch them take their medicines. One innovative program to alleviate the labor-intensiveness of such an approach has been developed at the Massachusetts Institute of Technology. Patients receive a container of filter paper that dispenses a filter paper at timed intervals. They dip the paper in their urine and if the antibiotic is present in their urine, the filter paper reveals a code which the patient texts to a central database. If they miss fewer than five pills a month they receive free minutes for their cell phones.

Pneumonia

Pneumonia is a classic example of an *anatomical diagnosis.* It is defined as an inflammatory condition of the lung in which fluid fills the alveoli. The set of symptoms that we call pneumonia can be caused by a wide variety of different microorganisms. In a sense, the microorganisms need only to have appropriate characteristics to allow them to circumvent the host's defenses and to penetrate and survive in the lower respiratory tract. In particular, the microorganisms must avoid being phagocytosed by alveolar macrophages, or at least avoid being killed once inside the macrophage. Bacteria and a wide variety of viruses can cause pneumonias. Viral pneumonias are usually, but not always, milder than those caused by bacteria. At the same time, some bacterial pneumonias are very serious and others are not. In addition, fungi such as *Histoplasma* can also cause pneumonia. Overall, U.S. residents experience 2 to 3 million cases of pneumonia and more than 45,000 deaths due to this condition every year. It is much more common in the winter.

Physicians distinguish between community-acquired pneumonias and healthcare-associated pneumonias, because different bacteria are more likely to be causing the two types. Community-acquired pneumonias are those experienced by persons in the general population. Healthcare-associated pneumonias are those acquired by patients in hospitals and other health care residential facilities.

▶ Causative Agents of Community-Acquired Pneumonia

Streptococcus pneumoniae accounts for about two-thirds of community-acquired bacterial pneumonia cases. It causes more lethal pneumonia cases than any other microorganism. *Legionella* is a less common but serious cause of the disease. *Haemophilus influenzae* had been a major cause of community-acquired pneumonia, but the introduction of the Hib vaccine in 1988 has reduced its incidence. A number of bacteria cause a milder form of pneumonia that is often referred to as "walking pneumonia." Two of these are *Mycoplasma pneumoniae* and *Chlamydophila pneumoniae* (formerly known as *Chlamydia*

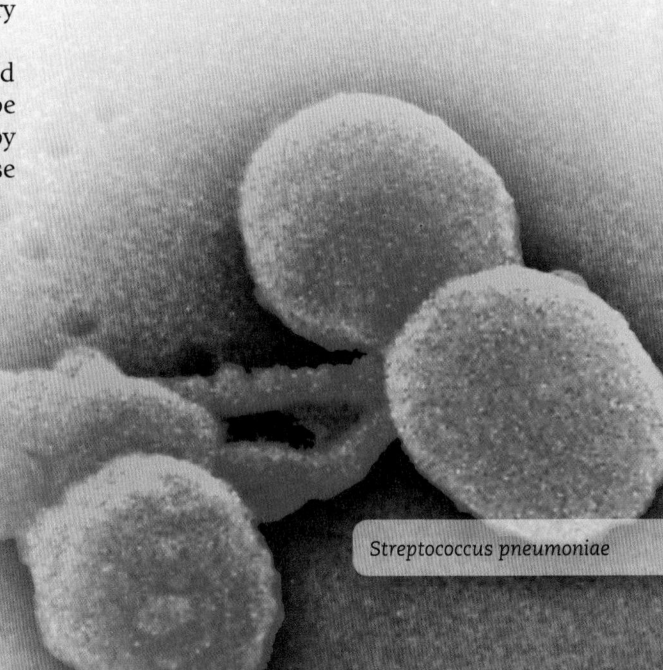

Streptococcus pneumoniae

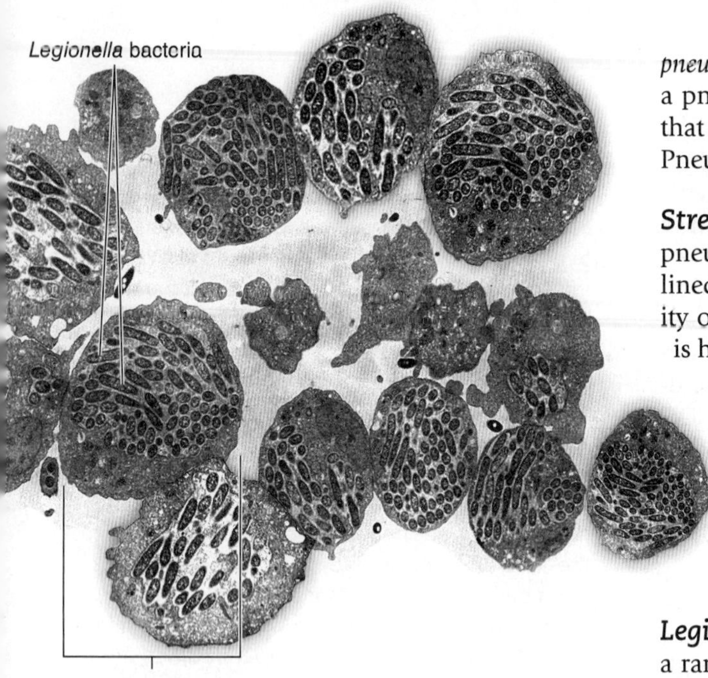

Figure 19.15 ***Legionella* living intracellularly in the amoeba *Hartmannella*.** Amoebas inhabiting natural waters appear to be the reservoir for this pathogen and a means for it to survive in rather hostile environments. The pathogenesis of *Legionella* in humans is likewise dependent on its uptake by and survival in phagocytes.

Figure 19.16 Sign in wooded area in Kentucky. The sign is covered in bird droppings. Up to 90% of the population in the Ohio Valley show evidence of past infection with *Histoplasma*.

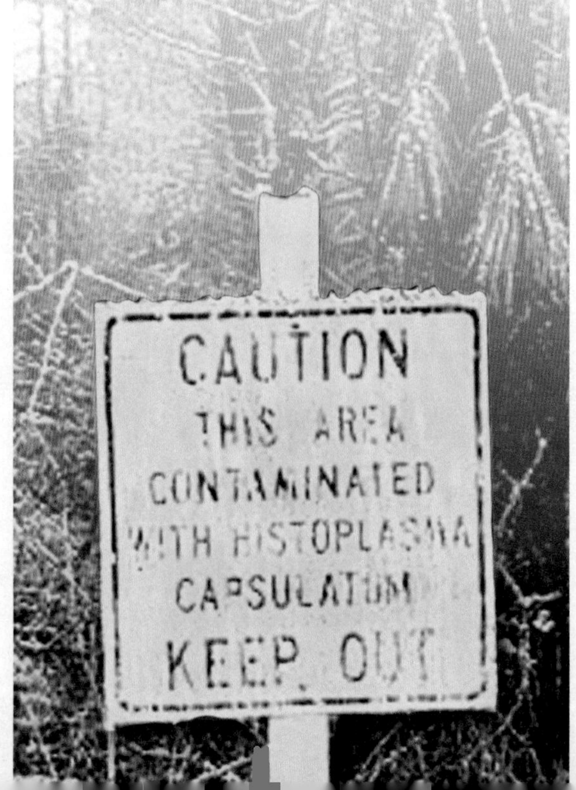

pneumoniae). *Histoplasma capsulatum* is a fungus that infects many people but causes a pneumonia-like disease in relatively few. One virus causes a type of pneumonia that can be very serious: hantavirus, which emerged in 1993 in the United States. Pneumonia may be a secondary effect of influenza disease.

Streptococcus pneumoniae This bacterium, which is often simply called the pneumococcus, is a small gram-positive flattened coccus that often appears in pairs, lined up end to end. It is alpha-hemolytic on blood agar. Factors that favor the ability of the pneumococcus to cause disease are old age, the season (rate of infection is highest in the winter), underlying viral respiratory disease, diabetes, and chronic abuse of alcohol or narcotics. Healthy people commonly inhale this and other microorganisms into the respiratory tract without serious consequences because of the host defenses present there.

Because the pneumococcus is such a frequent cause of pneumonia in older adults, this population is encouraged to seek immunization with the older pneumococcal polysaccharide vaccine, which stimulates immunity to the capsular polysaccharides of 23 different strains of the bacterium.

Legionella pneumophila *Legionella* is a weakly gram-negative bacterium that has a range of shapes, from coccus to filaments. Several species or subtypes have been characterized, but *L. pneumophila* ("lung-loving") is the one most frequently isolated from infections.

Legionella's ability to survive and persist in natural habitats has been something of a mystery, yet it appears to be widely distributed in aqueous habitats as diverse as tap water, cooling towers, spas, ponds, and other fresh waters. It is resistant to chlorine. The bacteria can live in close association with free-living amoebas **(figure 19.15)**. It is released during aerosol formation and can be carried for long distances. Cases have been traced to supermarket vegetable sprayers, hotel fountains, and even the fallout from the Mount St. Helens volcano eruption in 1980.

Atypical pneumonias Pneumonias caused by *Mycoplasma* (as well as those caused by *Chlamydophila* and some other microorganisms) are often called atypical pneumonia—atypical in the sense that the symptoms do not resemble those of pneumococcal or other severe pneumonias. *Mycoplasma* pneumonia is transmitted by aerosol droplets among people confined in close living quarters, especially families, students, and the military. Lack of acute illness in most patients has given rise to the name "walking pneumonia."

Hantavirus In 1993, hantavirus suddenly burst into the American consciousness. A cluster of unusual cases of severe lung edema among healthy young adults arose in the Four Corners area of New Mexico. Most of the patients died within a few days. They were later found to have been infected with hantavirus, an agent that had previously only been known to cause severe kidney disease and hemorrhagic fevers in other parts of the world. The new condition was named hantavirus pulmonary syndrome (HPS). Since 1993, the disease has occurred sporadically, but it has a mortality rate of at least 33%. It is considered an emerging disease.

Very soon after the initial cases in 1993, it became clear that the virus was associated with the presence of mice in close proximity to the victims. Investigators eventually determined that the virus, an enveloped virus of the *Bunyaviridae* family, is transmitted via airborne dust contaminated with the urine, feces, or saliva of infected rodents. Deer mice and other rodents can carry the virus with few apparent symptoms. Small outbreaks of the disease are usually correlated with increases in the local rodent population.

Histoplasma capsulatum The organism is endemically distributed on all continents except Australia. Its highest rates of incidence occur in the eastern and central

Disease Table 19.10 Pneumonia

Causative Organism(s)	*Streptococcus pneumoniae*	*Legionella* species	*Mycoplasma pneumoniae*	Hantavirus	*Histoplasma capsulatum*	*Pneumocystis jiroveci*
Most Common Modes of Transmission	Droplet contact or endogenous transfer	Vehicle (water droplets)	Droplet contact	Vehicle—airborne virus emitted from rodents	Vehicle—inhalation of contaminated soil	Droplet contact
Virulence Factors	Capsule	–	Adhesins	Ability to induce inflammatory response	Survival in phagocytes	–
Culture/ Diagnosis	Gram stain often diagnostic, alpha-hemolytic on blood agar	Requires selective charcoal yeast extract agar; serology unreliable	Rule out other etiologic agents	Serology (IgM), PCR identification of antigen in tissue	Usually serological (rising Ab titers)	Immuno-fluorescence
Prevention	Pneumococcal polysaccharide vaccine (23-valent)	–	No vaccine, no permanent immunity	Avoid mouse habitats and droppings	Avoid contaminated soil/ bat, bird droppings	Antibiotics given to AIDS patients to prevent this
Treatment	Cefotaxime, ceftriaxone; much resistance	Fluoroquinolone, azithromycin, clarithromycin	Recommended not to treat in most cases, doxycycline or macrolides may be used if necessary	Supportive	Amphotericin B and/or itraconazole	Trimethoprim-sulfamethoxazole
Distinctive Features	Patient usually severely ill	Mild pneumonias in healthy people; can be severe in elderly or immuno-compromised	Usually mild; "walking pneumonia"	Rapid onset; high mortality rate	Many infections asymptomatic	Vast majority occur in AIDS patients

regions of the United States, especially in the Ohio Valley. This fungus appears to grow most abundantly in moist soils high in nitrogen content, especially those supplemented by bird and bat droppings (**figure 19.16**).

A useful tool for determining the distribution of *H. capsulatum* is to inject a fungal extract into the skin and monitor for allergic reactions (much like the TB skin test). Application of this test has verified the extremely widespread distribution of the fungus. In high-prevalence areas such as southern Ohio, Illinois, Missouri, Kentucky, Tennessee, Michigan, Georgia, and Arkansas, 80% to 90% of the population show signs of prior infection.

Pneumocystis (carinii) jiroveci Although *Pneumocystis jiroveci* (formerly called *P. carinii*) was discovered in 1909, it remained relatively obscure until it was suddenly propelled into clinical prominence as the agent of *Pneumocystis* pneumonia (called PCP because of the old name of the fungus). PCP is one of the most frequent opportunistic infections in AIDS patients, most of whom will develop one or more episodes during their lifetimes.

A Note About Emerging Pneumonias

In 2003, a virus from a family previously known to cause only coldlike symptoms burst onto the world stage as it started to cause pneumonias and death in Hong Kong. The SARS epidemic ended nearly as quickly as it started, and since 2004 new cases of SARS have not been detected anywhere on the planet. Similarly, in 2007, a rare serotype of an adenovirus, which had previously only been known to cause mild respiratory disease, caused two U.S. outbreaks of severe pneumonia.

Disease Table 19.11 Healthcare-associated Pneumonia

Causative Organism(s)	Gram-negative and gram-positive bacteria from upper respiratory tract or stomach
Most Common Modes of Transmission	Endogenous (aspiration)
Virulence Factors	–
Culture/Diagnosis	Culture of lung fluids
Prevention	Elevating patient's head, preoperative education, care of respiratory equipment
Treatment	Broad-spectrum antibiotics

Traditional antifungal drugs are ineffective against *Pneumocystis* pneumonia because the chemical makeup of the organism's cell wall differs from that of most fungi.

Healthcare-associated Pneumonia

About 1% of hospitalized or institutionalized people experience the complication of pneumonia. It is the second most common healthcare-associated infection, behind urinary tract infections. The mortality rate is quite high, between 30% and 50%. Although *Streptococcus pneumoniae* is frequently responsible, in addition it is very common to find a gram-negative bacterium called *Klebsiella pneumoniae* as well as anaerobic bacteria or even coliform bacteria in healthcare-associated pneumonia. Further complicating matters, many healthcare-associated pneumonias appear to be polymicrobial in origin—meaning that there are multiple microorganisms multiplying in the alveolar spaces.

In healthcare-associated infections, bacteria gain access to the lower respiratory tract through abnormal breathing and aspiration of the normal upper respiratory tract biota (and occasionally the stomach) into the lungs. Stroke victims have high rates of healthcare-associated pneumonia. Mechanical ventilation is another route of entry for microbes. Once there, the organisms take advantage of the usually lowered immune response in a hospitalized patient and cause pneumonia symptoms.

Culture of sputum or of tracheal swabs is not very useful in diagnosing healthcare-associated pneumonia, because the condition is usually caused by normal biota. Obtaining cultures of fluids obtained through endotracheal tubes or from bronchoalveolar lavage provide better information but are fairly intrusive. It is also important to remember that if the patient has already received antibiotics, culture results will be affected.

Because most healthcare-associated pneumonias are caused by microorganisms aspirated from the upper respiratory tract, measures that discourage the transfer of microbes into the lungs are very useful for preventing the condition. Elevating patients' heads to a 45-degree angle helps reduce aspiration of secretions. Good preoperative education of patients about the importance of deep breathing and frequent coughing can reduce postoperative infection rates. Proper care of mechanical ventilation and respiratory therapy equipment is essential as well.

Studies have shown that delaying antibiotic treatment of suspected healthcare-associated pneumonia leads to a greater likelihood of death. Even in this era of conservative antibiotic use, empiric therapy should be started as soon as healthcare-associated pneumonia is suspected, using multiple antibiotics that cover both gram-negative and gram-positive organisms.

ASSESS YOUR PROGRESS

10. List the possible causative agents, modes of transmission, virulence factors, diagnostic techniques, and prevention/treatment for the highlighted condition, tuberculosis.

11. Discuss the problems associated with MDR-TB and XDR-TB.

12. Discuss important features of the other lower respiratory tract diseases, community-acquired and healthcare-associated pneumonia.

CASE FILE WRAP-UP

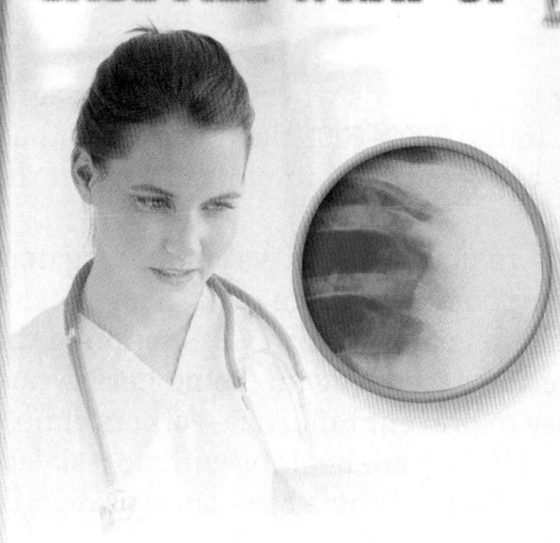

The patient is admitted to the hospital and placed on respiratory isolation precautions. An acid-fast sputum sample is obtained, and Ziehl-Neelsen staining confirms the diagnosis of tuberculosis. The patient is started immediately on isoniazid plus three other drugs, and the cultures show that there is no resistance to the drugs. The patient is told that he will need to continue taking isoniazid for at least 9 months.

Compliance with the prescribed therapy is stressed to the patient as being of utmost importance, and he is made to understand that not taking the drugs as prescribed for the duration of therapy could lead to drug resistance, putting himself and others at risk. Public health is notified when the patient is discharged from the hospital and agrees to follow up with the patient to ensure that the patient is complying with treatment.

▶ Summing Up

Taxonomic Organization Microorganisms Causing Disease in the Respiratory Tract

Microorganism	Pronunciation	Location of Disease Table
Gram-positive bacteria		
Streptococcus pneumoniae	strep'-tuh-kok"-us nu- moh' nee-ay	Otitis media, p. 533 Pneumonia, p. 547
S. pyogenes	strep'-tuh-kok"-us pie-ah'-gen-eez	Pharyngitis, p. 531
Corynebacterium diphtheriae	cor-eye'-nee-back-teer"-e-em dip-theer'-e-ay	Diphtheria, p. 533
Gram-negative bacteria		
Fusobacterium necrophorum	fuze'-oh"-back-teer"ee-em neck"-row-for'-em	Pharyngitis, p. 531
Bordetella pertussis	bor'-duh-tell'-uh per-tuss'-is	Whooping cough, p. 538
*Mycobacterium tuberculosis,** *M. avium* complex	my"-co-back-teer'-ee-em tuh-ber'-cue-loh-sis	Tuberculosis, p. 544
Legionella spp.	lee"-juhn-el'-uh	Pneumonia, p. 547
Other bacteria		
Mycoplasma pneumoniae	my"-co-plazz'-muh nu-moh'-nee-ay	Pneumonia, p. 547
RNA viruses		
Respiratory syncytial virus	ress"-pur-uh-tor'-ee sin-sish'-ull vie'-russ	RSV disease, p. 539
Influenza virus A, B, and C	in"-floo-en'-zuh vie'-russ	Influenza, p. 538
Hantavirus	haun"-tuh vie'-russ	Pneumonia, p. 547
Fungi		
Pneumocystis jiroveci	new-moh-siss'-tiss yee"-row-vet'-zee	Pneumonia, p. 547
Histoplasma capsulatum	hiss"-toe-plazz'-muh cap"-sue-lah'-tum	Pneumonia, p. 547

*There is some debate about the gram status of the genus *Mycobacterium;* it is generally not considered gram-positive or gram-negative.

Inside the Clinic

Mandatory Flu Shots for Health Care Workers: The Debate

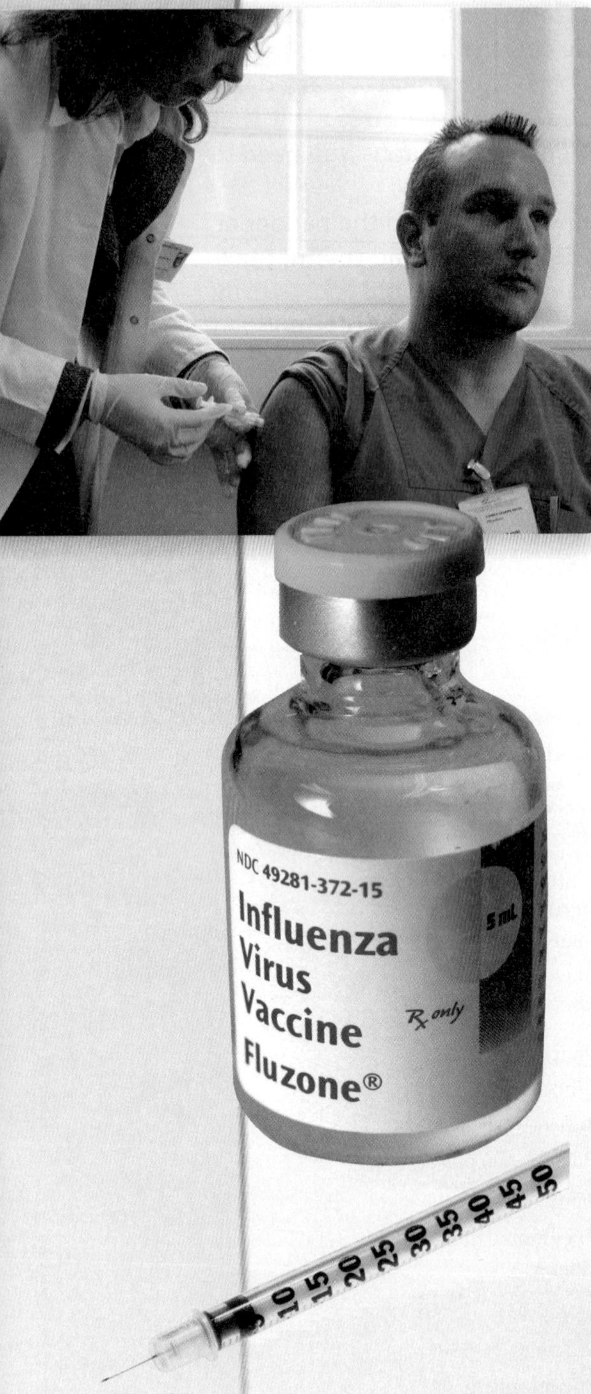

Health care workers have notoriously poor track records when it comes to yearly immunization against seasonal influenza. In the 2007–2008 flu season, less than half (approximately 46%) of all health care workers were immunized against the seasonal flu, according to the CDC.

Why are so many health care workers reluctant to get vaccinated against influenza? There are many reasons cited for poor compliance rates. Some health care workers have experienced adverse reactions to influenza vaccination in the past, making them more reluctant to have the vaccine again. Some health care workers don't believe in the vaccine's ability to prevent influenza—others simply don't believe that they need to be vaccinated if they are healthy, with no risk factors for serious disease, should they contract the flu. Others cite concerns regarding certain components of vaccines, such as thimerosal.

In 2009, during the height of fears regarding the novel H1N1 pandemic, which swept across the world within a few short months, the controversy surrounding the vaccine's rush to market and the exceptional media hype surrounding the pandemic, some health care organizations took a new approach to their yearly campaign to vaccinate their employees. The New York Health Department took the unprecedented step of mandating influenza vaccinations for health care workers, which caused a backlash of controversy as other states and organizations followed their lead. Health care workers balked at the concept of forced vaccination, with several organizations (for example, the Washington State Nurses Association) suing health care organizations over making forced vaccination a condition of employment.

There are two sides to every story, and mandatory vaccination is no exception. Those who support mandatory vaccination believe that health care workers have an obligation to protect their patients from a potentially deadly disease. They cite the fact that other vaccinations are mandatory: Health care workers must often provide proof of immunization against measles, diphtheria, rubella and other diseases that were once major health concerns before beginning employment. In short, proponents of mandatory vaccination believe that an individual's rights must be superseded by the rights of those they are charged with caring for—namely, their patients. Opponents of mandatory vaccination raise the point that individuals have the right to self-determination, and that forcing employees to submit to forced vaccinations violates human rights. Both sides raise valid points, and the controversy that raged in 2009 was one that could never be solved to everyone's satisfaction.

Several health care organizations found a compromise in this ongoing debate. In some hospitals, employees who have received the seasonal influenza wear color-coded badges that show that they have been vaccinated, while employees who do not receive the vaccine must wear masks at all times when engaged in patient care. Employees may be exempted from receiving the vaccine for valid medical reasons, such as a documented allergy to eggs (the vaccine is composed of inactivated viruses that are grown in the embryos of eggs); however, these employees are still required to wear a mask while working.

Sources: http://www.time.com/time/magazine/article/0,9171,1929232,00.html
http://www.cdc.gov/mmwr/preview/mmwrhtml/mm5912a1.htm

Infectious Diseases Affecting
The Respiratory System

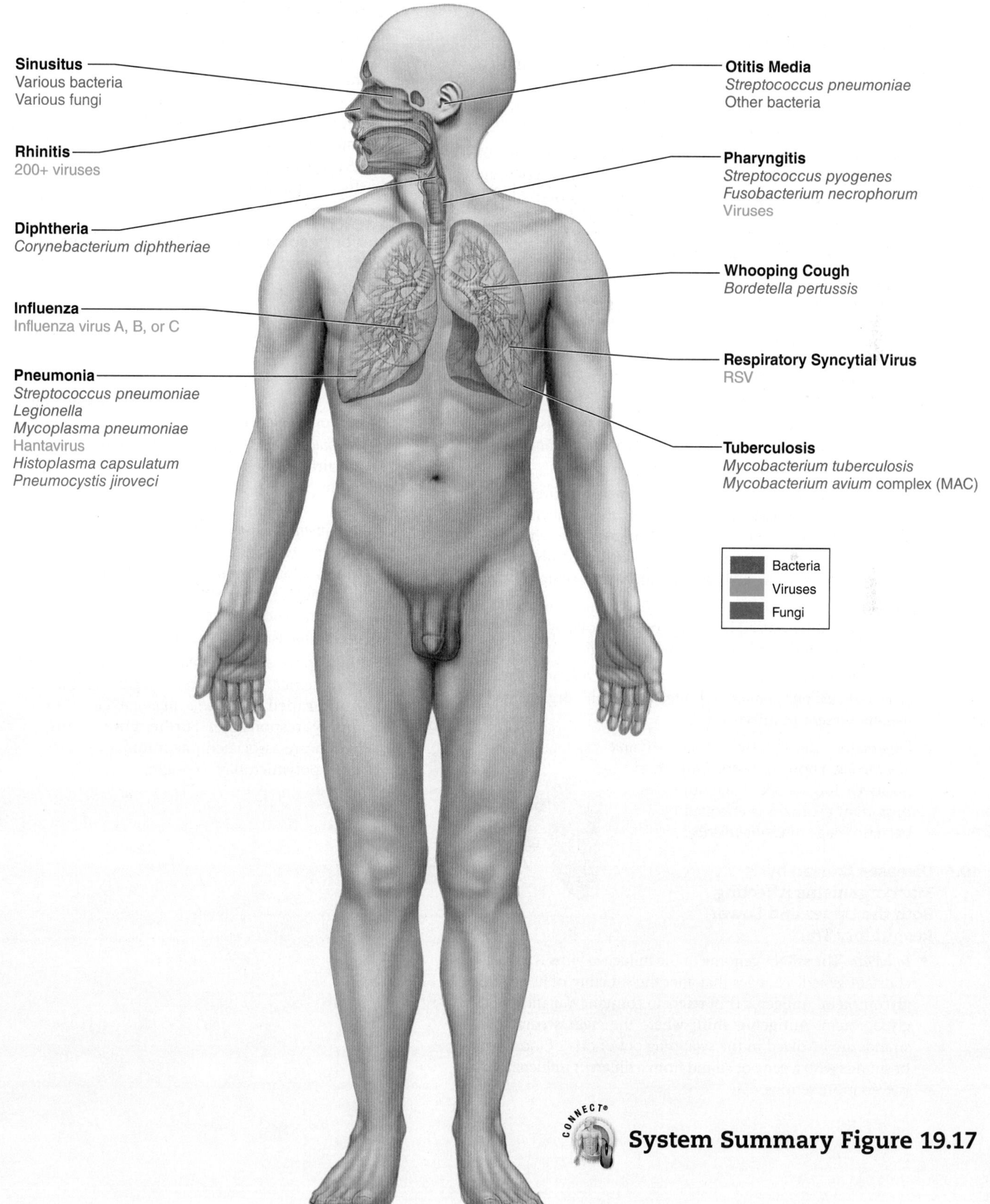

System Summary Figure 19.17

Chapter Summary

19.1 The Respiratory Tract and Its Defenses

- The upper respiratory tract includes the mouth, the nose, nasal cavity and sinuses above it, the throat or pharynx, and epiglottis and larynx.
- The lower respiratory tract consists of the trachea, the bronchi, bronchioles, and alveoli in the lungs.
- The ciliary escalator, mucus on the surface of the mucous membranes, and involuntary responses such as coughing, sneezing, and swallowing are structural defenses. Alveolar macrophages, and secretory IgA are also helpful.

19.2 Normal Biota of the Respiratory Tract

- Normal biota include *Streptococcus pyogenes, Haemophilus influenzae, Streptococcus pneumoniae, Neisseria meningitidis,* and *Staphylococcus aureus, Moraxella* and *Corynebacterium* species, and *Candida albicans.*

19.3 Upper Respiratory Tract Diseases Caused by Microorganisms

- *Pharyngitis:* Viruses are common cause of pharyngitis. However, two potentially serious causes of pharyngitis are *Streptococcus pyogenes* and *Fusobacterium necrophorum.*
- *Rhinitis,* or *the Common Cold:* Caused by one of over 200 different kinds of viruses, most commonly the rhinoviruses, followed by the coronaviruses. Respiratory syncytial virus (RSV) causes colds in many people, but in some, especially children, they can lead to more serious respiratory tract symptoms.
- *Sinusitis:* Inflammatory condition of the sinuses in the skull, most commonly caused by allergy or infections by a variety of viruses or bacteria and, less commonly, fungi.
- *Acute Otitis Media (Ear Infection):* Most common cause is *Streptococcus pneumoniae,* though multiple organisms are usually present in infections.
- *Diphtheria:* Caused by *Corynebacterium diphtheriae,* a non-spore-forming, gram-positive club-shaped bacterium. An important exotoxin is encoded by a bacteriophage of *C. diphtheriae.*

19.4 Diseases Caused by Microorganisms Affecting Both the Upper and Lower Respiratory Tract

- *Influenza:* The ssRNA genome of the influenza virus is subject to constant genetic changes that alter the structure of its envelope glycoprotein. Antigenic drift refers to constant mutation of this glycoprotein. **Antigenic shift,** where the eight separate RNA strands are involved in the swapping out of one of those genes or strands with a gene or strand from a different influenza virus, is even more serious.

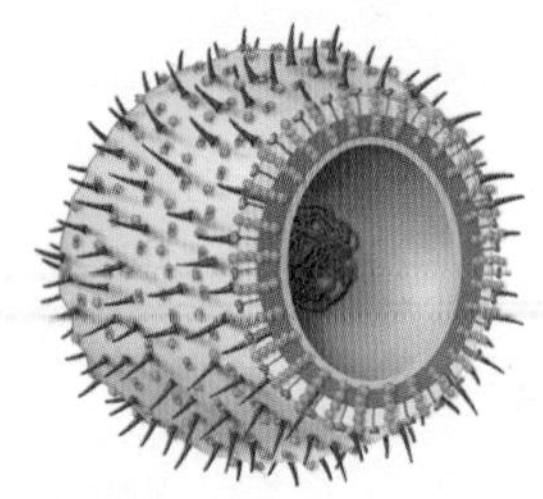

- *Whooping Cough:* Causative agent, *Bordetella pertussis,* releases multiple exotoxins—*pertussis toxin* and *tracheal cytotoxin*—that damage ciliated respiratory epithelial cells and cripple other components of the host defenses.
- RSV infects the respiratory tract and produces giant multinucleated cells (syncytia). RSV is most prevalent cause of respiratory infection in the newborn age group.

19.5 Lower Respiratory Tract Diseases Caused by Microorganisms

- *Tuberculosis:* Cause is primarily the bacterial species *Mycobacterium tuberculosis.* Vaccine generally not used in the United States, although an attenuated vaccine, BCG, is used in many countries.
- *Pneumonia:* Inflammatory condition of the lung in which fluid fills the alveoli. Caused by a wide variety of different microorganisms.
- *Streptococcus pneumoniae:* The main agent for community-acquired bacterial pneumonia cases. *Legionella* is less common but serious cause of the disease. Other bacteria: *Mycoplasma pneumoniae* and *Chlamydophila pneumoniae. Histoplasma capsulatum* is a fungus that can cause a pneumonia-like disease. A hantavirus causes a pneumonia-like condition named hantavirus pulmonary syndrome (HPS). Physicians may treat pneumonia empirically, meaning they do not determine the etiologic agent.
- *Healthcare-associated pneumonia: Streptococcus pneumoniae* and gram-negative bacterium called *Klebsiella pneumoniae* commonly responsible. Furthermore, many healthcare-associated pneumonias appear to be polymicrobial in origin.

Multiple-Choice Questions Knowledge and Comprehension

Select the correct answer from the answers provided.

1. The two most common groups of virus associated with the common cold are
   a. rhinoviruses.
   b. coronaviruses.
   c. influenza viruses.
   d. both a and b.
   e. both a and c.
2. Which is not a characteristic of *Streptococcus pyogenes*?
   a. group A streptococcus
   b. alpha-hemolytic
   c. sensitive to bacitracin
   d. gram-positive
3. Which of the following techniques are used to diagnose tuberculosis?
   a. tuberculin testing
   b. chest X rays
   c. cultural isolation and antimicrobial testing
   d. all of the above
4. The DTaP vaccine provides protection against the following diseases, *except*
   a. diphtheria.
   b. pertussis.
   c. pneumonia.
   d. tetanus.
5. Which of the following infections often has a polymicrobial cause?
   a. otitis media
   b. healthcare-associated pneumonia
   c. sinusitis
   d. all of the above
6. The vast majority of pneumonias caused by this organism occur in AIDS patients.
   a. hantavirus
   b. *Histoplasma capsulatum*
   c. *Pneumocystis jiroveci*
   d. *Mycoplasma pneumoniae*
7. The beta-hemolysis of blood agar observed with *Streptococcus pyogenes* is due to the presence of
   a. streptolysin.
   b. M protein.
   c. hyaluronic acid.
   d. catalase.
8. An estimated __________ of the world population is infected with *Mycobacterium tuberculosis*.
   a. one-half
   b. one-quarter
   c. one-third
   d. three-quarters

Critical Thinking Application and Analysis

Critical thinking **is the ability to reason and solve problems using facts and concepts. These questions can be approached from a number of angles and, in most cases, they do not have a single correct answer.**

1. What aspects of the bacterium *S. pneumoniae* do you think make it such a frequent pathogen?
2. a. Name the organisms responsible for the flu.
   b. Describe the genome of this virus.
3. What are some of the likely explanations if you are not responding to antibiotic treatment for sinusitis?
4. Why is noncompliance during TB therapy such a big concern?
5. Why do we need to take the flu vaccine every year? Why does it not confer long-term immunity to the flu like other vaccines?

Visual Connections Synthesis

This question connects previous images to a new concept.

1. **From chapter 2, figure 2.18.** Although there are many different organisms present in the respiratory tract, an acid-fast stain of sputum like the one shown here along with patient symptoms can establish a presumptive diagnosis of tuberculosis. Explain why.

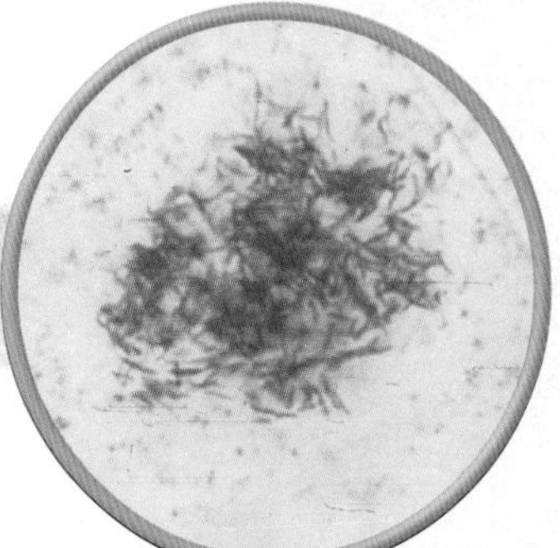

Acid-fast stain
Red cells are acid-fast.
Blue cells are non-acid-fast.

www.mcgrawhillconnect.com

Enhance your study of this chapter with study tools and practice tests. Also ask your instructor about the resources available through ConnectPlus, including the media-rich eBook, interactive learning tools, and animations.

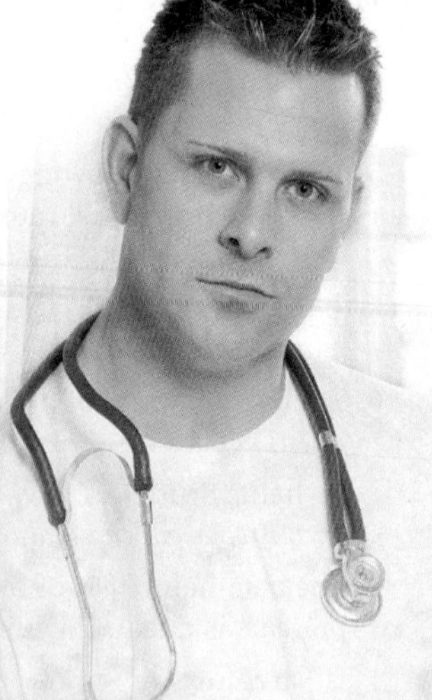

A Vacation "Souvenir"

While working as an ultrasound technician, I performed an abdominal ultrasound on a teenaged girl who had been admitted to the hospital with nausea and vomiting. In an effort to distract my nervous patient, and also to elicit more information, I asked the patient to tell me about the symptoms that had led to her hospitalization.

The patient related to me that she had recently traveled with her church youth group to Costa Rica in order to take part in an international fellowship conference. The patient had returned home to the United States 3 weeks ago. Although she initially felt well, within a week of returning home she began to experience mild fever, fatigue, and loss of appetite. She stated she "wanted to sleep all the time." She felt nauseated and would sometimes vomit when she ate. Her parents were not overly alarmed and initially thought that the symptoms would pass until the patient's skin and sclera began to turn yellow. At that point, her parents brought her to the emergency room, and she was subsequently admitted for treatment of dehydration and further testing.

- What condition is the patient likely suffering from?
- How might she have contracted it?
- What is the treatment?

Case File Wrap-Up appears on page 588.

CHAPTER 

Infectious Diseases Affecting the Gastrointestinal Tract

IN THIS CHAPTER...

20.1 The Gastrointestinal Tract and Its Defenses

1. Draw or describe the anatomical features of the gastrointestinal tract.
2. List the natural defenses present in the gastrointestinal tract.

20.2 Normal Biota of the Gastrointestinal Tract

3. List the types of normal biota presently known to occupy the gastrointestinal tract.
4. Describe how our view has changed of normal biota present in the stomach.

20.3 Gastrointestinal Tract Diseases Caused by Microorganisms (Nonhelminthic)

5. List the possible causative agents, modes of transmission, virulence factors, diagnostic techniques, and prevention/treatment for the highlighted condition, acute diarrhea.
6. Discuss important features of the conditions food poisoning and chronic diarrhea.
7. Discuss important features of the two categories of oral conditions: dental caries and periodontal diseases.
8. Identify the most important features of mumps, gastritis, and gastric ulcers.
9. Differentiate among the main types of hepatitis, and discuss the causative agents, mode of transmission, diagnostic techniques, prevention, and treatment of each.

20.4 Gastrointestinal Tract Diseases Caused by Helminths

10. Describe some distinguishing characteristics and commonalities seen in helminthic infections.
11. List four helminths that cause primarily intestinal symptoms, and identify which life cycle they follow and one unique fact about each one.

20.1 The Gastrointestinal Tract and Its Defenses

The gastrointestinal (GI) tract can be thought of as a long tube, extending from mouth to anus. It is a very sophisticated delivery system for nutrients, composed of eight main sections and augmented by four accessory organs. The eight sections are the mouth, pharynx, esophagus, stomach, small intestine, large intestine, rectum, and anus. Along the way, the salivary glands, liver, gallbladder, and pancreas add digestive fluids and enzymes to assist in digesting and processing the food we take in **(figure 20.1)**. The GI tract is often called the *digestive tract* or the *enteric tract*.

The GI tract has a very heavy load of microorganisms, and it encounters millions of new ones every day. Because of this, defenses against infection are extremely important. All intestinal surfaces are coated with a layer of mucus, which confers mechanical protection. Secretory IgA can also be found on most intestinal surfaces. The muscular walls of the GI tract keep food (and microorganisms) moving through the system through the action of peristalsis. Various fluids in the GI tract have antimicrobial properties. Saliva contains the antimicrobial proteins lysozyme and lactoferrin. The stomach fluid is antimicrobial by virtue of its extremely high acidity. Bile is also antimicrobial.

The entire system is outfitted with cells of the immune system, collectively called gut-associated lymphoid tissue (GALT). The tonsils and adenoids in the oral cavity and pharynx, small areas of lymphoid tissue in the esophagus, Peyer's patches in the small intestine, and the appendix are all packets of lymphoid tissue consisting of T and B cells as well as cells of nonspecific immunity. One of their jobs is to produce IgA, but they perform a variety of other immune functions.

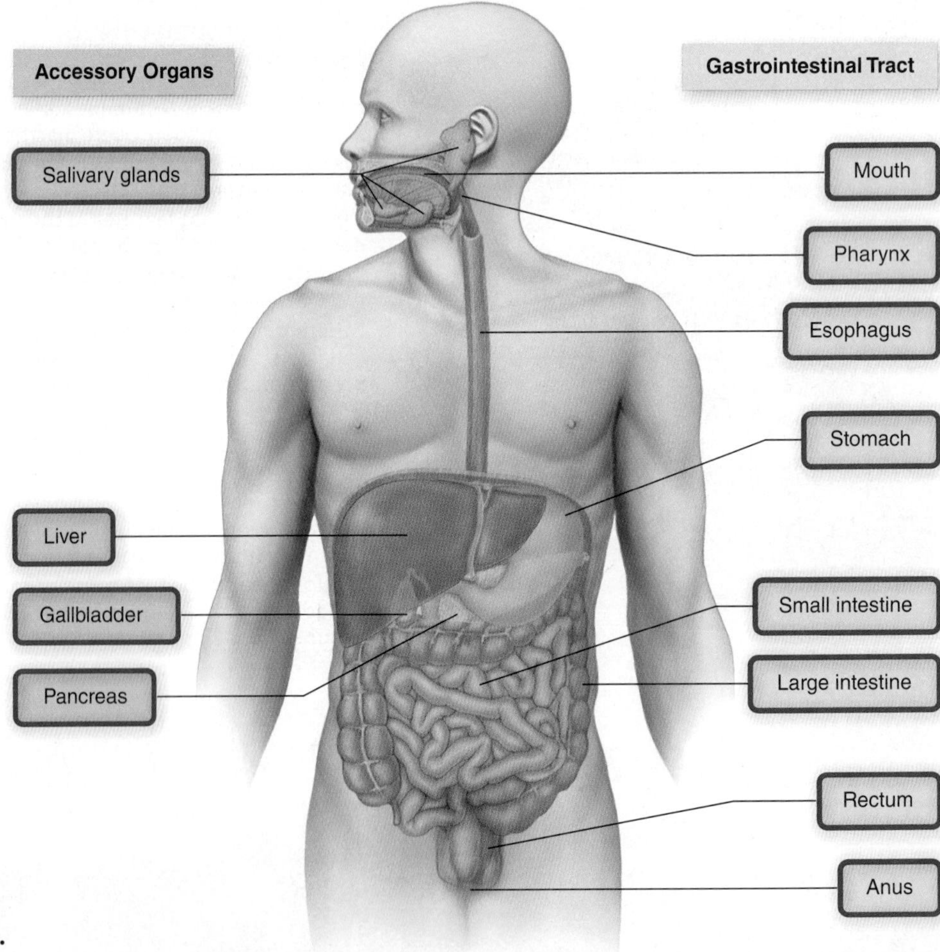

Figure 20.1 Major organs of the digestive system.

A huge population of commensal organisms lives in this system, especially in the large intestine. They avoid immune destruction through various mechanisms, including cloaking themselves with host sugars they find on the intestinal walls.

ASSESS YOUR PROGRESS

1. Draw or describe the anatomical features of the gastrointestinal tract.
2. List the natural defenses present in the gastrointestinal tract.

NCLEX® PREP

1. Gut-associated lymphoid tissue (GALT) includes
   a. Peyer's patches in the small intestine.
   b. the appendix.
   c. tonsils.
   d. adenoids.
   e. all of the above.
   f. none of the above.

20.2 Normal Biota of the Gastrointestinal Tract

As just mentioned, the GI tract is home to a large variety of normal biota. The oral cavity alone is populated by more than 550 known species of microorganisms, including *Streptococcus, Neisseria, Veillonella, Staphylococcus, Fusobacterium, Lactobacillus, Corynebacterium, Actinomyces,* and *Treponema* species. Fungi such as *Candida albicans* are also numerous. A few protozoa (*Trichomonas tenax, Entamoeba gingivalis*) also call the mouth "home." Bacteria live on the teeth as well as the soft structures in the mouth. Numerous species of normal biota bacteria live on the teeth in a synergistic community called dental plaque, which is a type of biofilm (see chapter 3). Bacteria are held in the biofilm by specific recognition molecules. Alpha-hemolytic streptococci are generally the first colonizers of the tooth surface after it has been cleaned. The streptococci attach specifically to proteins in the **pellicle,** a mucinous glycoprotein covering on the tooth. Then other species attach specifically to proteins or sugars on the surface of the streptococci, and so on.

The pharynx contains a variety of microorganisms, which were described in chapter 19. Although the stomach was previously thought to be sterile due to its very low pH, researchers in 2008 found the molecular signatures of 128 different species of microorganisms in the stomach. Though many of these are likely to be "just passing through," it would not be surprising to find a few permanent residents. The large intestine has always been known to be a haven for billions of microorganisms (10^{11} per gram of contents), including the bacteria *Bacteroides, Fusobacterium, Bifidobacterium, Clostridium, Streptococcus, Peptostreptococcus, Lactobacillus, Escherichia,* and *Enterobacter;* the fungus *Candida;* and several protozoa as well. Researchers have also found archaea species there.

The normal biota in the gut provide a protective function, but they also perform other jobs as well. Some of them help with digestion. Some provide nutrients that we can't produce ourselves. *E. coli,* for instance, synthesizes vitamin K. Its mere presence in the large intestine seems to be important for the proper formation of epithelial cell structure. And the normal biota in the gut plays an important role in "teaching" our immune system to react to microbial antigens. Scientists believe that the mix of microbiota in the healthy gut can influence a host's chances for obesity or autoimmune diseases.

The accessory organs (salivary glands, gallbladder, liver, and pancreas) are free of microorganisms, just as all internal organs are.

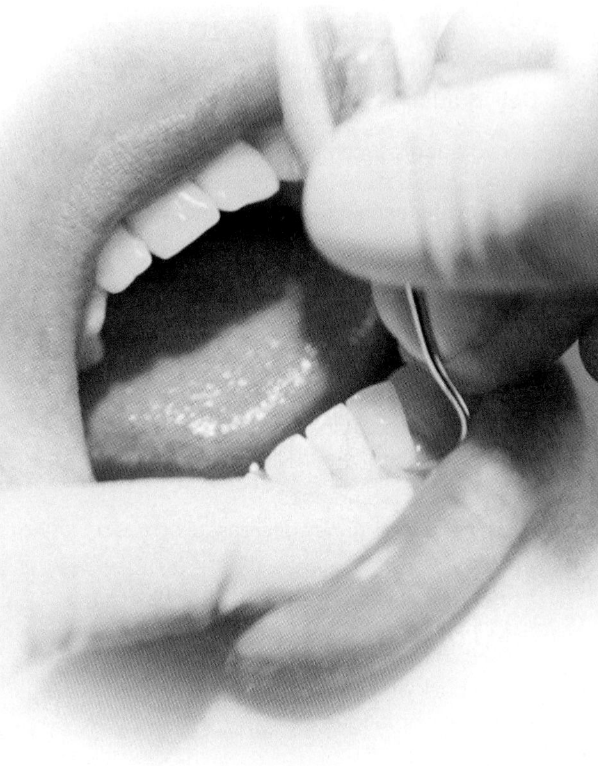

ASSESS YOUR PROGRESS

3. List the types of normal biota presently known to occupy the gastrointestinal tract.
4. Describe how our view has changed of normal biota present in the stomach.

NCLEX® PREP

2. The first colonizers of the tooth surface after it has been cleaned are
   a. *Entamoeba gingivalis* organisms.
   b. alpha-hemolytic streptococci.
   c. *Actinomyces* organisms.
   d. *Candida albicans* organisms.

Chickens and their eggs can be colonized by *Salmonella*.

Medical Moment

Dehydration

Dehydration is a common symptom experienced by individuals suffering from conditions affecting the gastrointestinal tract. Recognizing and treating dehydration is a common task of health care workers.

Dehydration can be thought of as an imbalance of fluids resulting from excessive fluid loss (as in vomiting and diarrhea) or inadequate fluid intake (due to nausea or loss of appetite).

Symptoms of dehydration may be subtle or very obvious and may include the following:

- dry mucus membranes;
- concentrated urine, decreased or absent urine output;
- lack of tears (in infants and children);
- sunken eyes;
- sunken fontanelles (the "soft spot" on the top and back of the infant's skull);
- lethargy or fatigue;
- weakness;
- tachycardia (rapid heart rate) and tachypnea (rapid breathing);
- hypotension (low blood pressure);
- poor skin turgor (skin that does not spring back into position when gently pinched);
- altered blood glucose;
- capillary refill (assessment of nail beds);
- thirst;
- headache; and
- seizures.

Health care workers classify dehydration as mild, moderate, or severe—based on the estimated amount of weight lost. This is often expressed in percentages. Capillary refill, skin turgor, and breathing are considered to be the most accurate signs in estimating degree of dehydration.

20.3 Gastrointestinal Tract Diseases Caused by Microorganisms (Nonhelminthic)

In this section, we first address microbes that cause diarrhea of various types. Then we discuss oral diseases (dental caries and periodontitis), stomach conditions (gastritis and gastric ulcers), and the spectrum of hepatitis infections.

HIGHLIGHT DISEASE

Acute Diarrhea

Diarrhea—usually defined as three or more loose stools in a 24-hour period—needs little explanation. In recent years, on average, citizens of the United States experienced 1.2 to 1.9 cases of diarrhea per person per year, and among children that number is twice as high. In tropical countries, children may experience more than 10 episodes of diarrhea a year. In fact, more than 3 million children a year, mostly in developing countries, die from a diarrheal disease. In developing countries, the high mortality rate is not the only issue. Children who survive dozens of bouts with diarrhea during their developmental years are likely to have permanent physical and cognitive effects. Diarrheal illnesses are often accompanied by fever, abdominal pain and/or cramping, nausea, vomiting, and dehydration.

In the United States, up to a third of all acute diarrhea is transmitted by contaminated food. In recent years, consumers have become much more aware of the possibility of *E. coli*–contaminated hamburgers or *Salmonella*-contaminated ice cream. New food safety measures are being implemented all the time, but it is still necessary for the consumer to be aware and to practice good food handling.

Although most diarrhea episodes are self-limiting and therefore do not require treatment, others (such as *E. coli* O157:H7) can have devastating effects. In most diarrheal illnesses, antimicrobial treatment is contraindicated (inadvisable), but some, such as shigellosis, call for quick treatment with antibiotics. For public health reasons, it is important to know which agents are causing diarrhea in the community, but in most cases identification of the agent is not performed.

In this section, we describe acute diarrhea having infectious agents as the cause. In the sections following this one, we discuss acute diarrhea and vomiting caused by toxins, commonly known as food poisoning, and chronic diarrhea and its causes.

Salmonella

A decade ago, one of every three chickens destined for human consumption was contaminated with *Salmonella*, but the rate is now about 10%. Other poultry, such as ducks and turkeys, is also affected. Eggs are infected as well because the bacteria may actually enter the egg while the shell is being formed in the chicken. In 2007, peanut butter was found to be the source of a *Salmonella* outbreak in the United States. *Salmonella* is a very large genus of bacteria, but only one species is of interest to us: *S. enterica* is divided into many variants, based on variation in the major surface antigens.

Some species of bacteria are further subdivided into variants or subtypes. Many gram-negative enteric bacteria are named and designated according to the following antigens: H, the flagellar antigen; K, the capsular antigen; and O, the cell wall antigen. Not all enteric bacteria carry the H and K antigens, but all have O, the polysaccharide portion of the lipopolysaccharide implicated in endotoxic shock (see chapter 18). Most species of gram-negative enterics exhibit a variety of subspecies, variants, or serotypes caused by slight variations in the chemical structure of the HKO antigens. Some bacteria in this chapter (e.g., *E. coli* O157:H7) are named according to their surface antigens; however, we use Latin variant names for *Salmonella*.

Salmonellae are motile; they ferment glucose with acid and sometimes gas; and most of them produce hydrogen sulfide (H_2S) but not urease. They grow

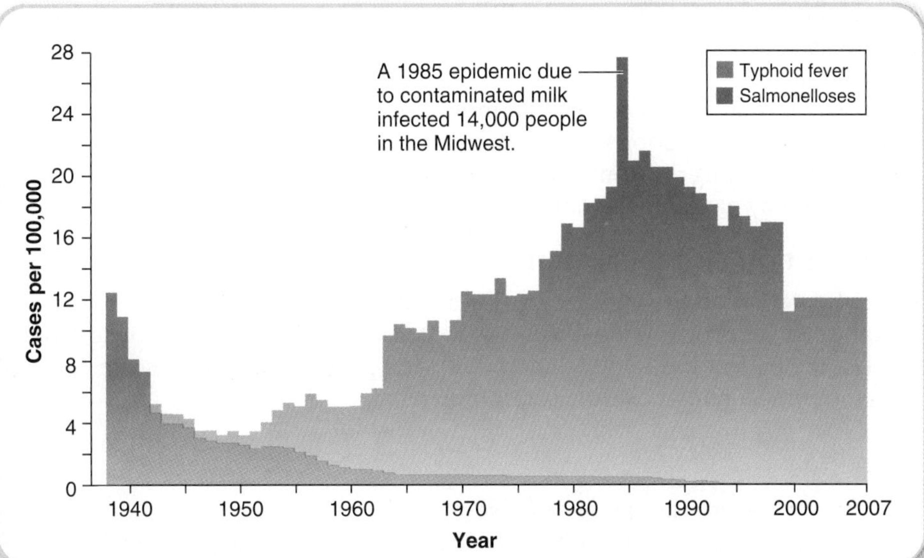

Figure 20.2 Data on the prevalence of typhoid fever and other salmonelloses from 1940 to 2007. Nontyphoidal salmonelloses did occur before 1940, but the statistics are not available.

readily on most laboratory media and can survive outside the host in inhospitable environments such as fresh water and freezing temperatures. These pathogens are resistant to chemicals such as bile and dyes, which are the basis for isolation on selective media.

▸ Signs and Symptoms

The genus *Salmonella* causes a variety of illnesses in the GI tract and beyond. Until fairly recently, its most severe manifestation was typhoid fever, which is discussed shortly. Since the mid-1900s, a milder disease usually called salmonellosis has been much more common **(figure 20.2)**. Sometimes the condition is also called enteric fever or gastroenteritis. Whereas typhoid fever is caused by the *typhi* variant, gastroenteritises are generally caused by the variants known as *paratyphi, hirschfeldii,* and *typhimurium.* Another variant, which is sometimes called *Arizona hinshawii* (even though it is still a *Salmonella*), is a pathogen found in the intestines of reptiles. Most of these strains come from animals, unlike the *typhi* strain, which infects humans exclusively. *Salmonella* bacteria are normal intestinal biota in cattle, poultry, rodents, and reptiles.

Salmonellosis can be relatively severe, with an elevated body temperature and septicemia as more prominent features than GI tract disturbance. But it can also be fairly mild, with gastroenteritis—vomiting, diarrhea, and mucosal irritation—as its major feature. Blood can appear in the stool. In otherwise healthy adults, symptoms spontaneously subside after 2 to 5 days; death is infrequent except in debilitated persons.

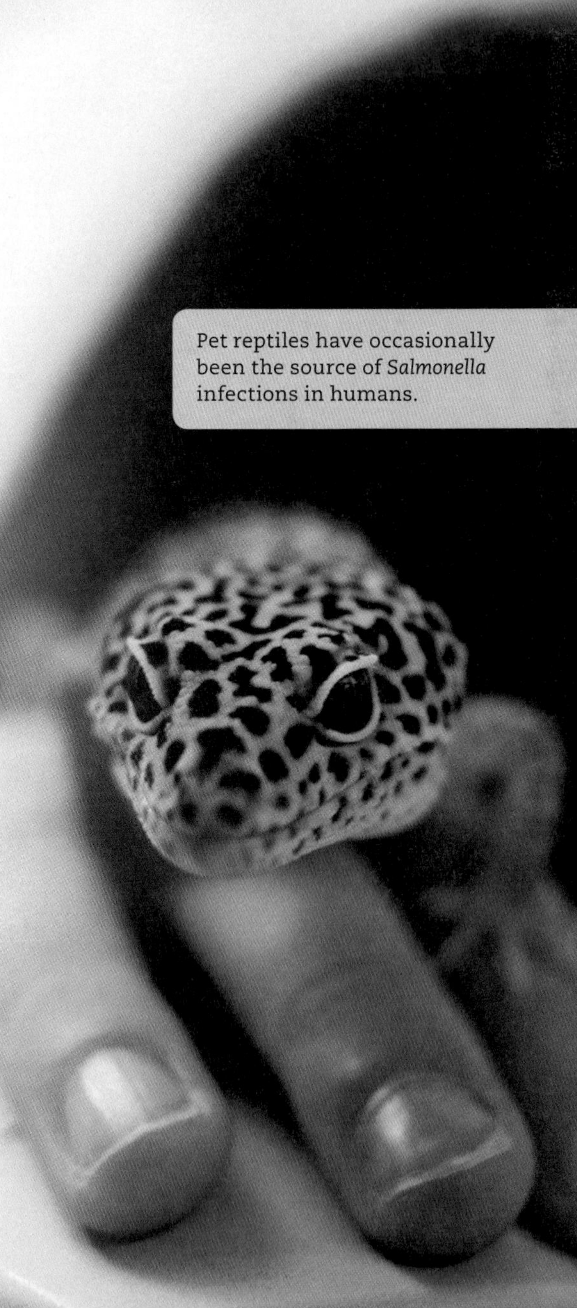

Pet reptiles have occasionally been the source of *Salmonella* infections in humans.

▸ Pathogenesis and Virulence Factors

The ability of *Salmonella* to cause disease seems to be highly dependent on its ability to adhere effectively to the gut mucosa. It is also believed that endotoxin is an important virulence factor for *Salmonella*.

▸ Transmission and Epidemiology

An important factor to consider in all diarrheal pathogens is how many organisms must be ingested to cause disease (their ID_{50}). It varies widely. These values are listed in a special row in **Disease Table 20.1.** *Salmonella* has a high ID_{50}, meaning a lot of organisms have to be ingested in order for disease to result.

Animal products such as meat and milk can be readily contaminated with *Salmonella* during slaughter, collection, and processing. A 2001 U.S. outbreak was traced to green grapes.

Most cases are traceable to a common food source such as milk or eggs. Some cases may be due to poor sanitation. In one outbreak, about 60 people became infected after visiting the Komodo dragon exhibit at the Denver zoo. They picked up the infection by handling the rails and fence of the dragon's cage.

▶ Prevention and Treatment

The only prevention for salmonellosis is avoiding contact with the bacterium. Uncomplicated cases of salmonellosis are treated with fluid and electrolyte replacement; if the patient has underlying immunocompromise or if the disease is severe, trimethoprim-sulfamethoxazole is recommended.

Shigella

The *Shigella* bacteria are gram-negative rods, nonmotile and non-spore-forming. They do not produce urease or hydrogen sulfide, traits that help in their identification. They are primarily human parasites, though they can infect apes. All produce a similar disease that can vary in intensity. These bacteria resemble some types of pathogenic *E. coli* very closely.

▶ Signs and Symptoms

The symptoms of shigellosis include frequent, watery stools, as well as fever, and often intense abdominal pain. Nausea and vomiting are common. Stools often contain obvious blood and even more often are found to have occult (not visible to the naked eye) blood. Diarrhea containing blood is also called **dysentery**. Mucus from the GI tract will also be present in the stools.

▶ Pathogenesis and Virulence Factors

Shigellosis is different from many GI tract infections in that *Shigella* invades the villus cells of the large intestine rather than the small intestine. In addition, it is not as invasive as *Salmonella* and does not perforate the intestine or invade the blood. It enters the intestinal mucosa by means of special cells in Peyer's patches. Once in the mucosa, *Shigella* instigates an inflammatory response that causes extensive tissue destruction. The release of endotoxin causes fever. **Enterotoxin**, an exotoxin that affects the enteric (or GI) tract, damages the mucosa and villi. Local areas of erosion give rise to bleeding and heavy secretion of mucus **(figure 20.3)**. *Shigella dysenteriae* (and perhaps some of the other species) produces a heat-labile exotoxin called **shiga toxin**, which seems to be responsible for the more serious damage to the intestine as well as any systemic effects, including injury to nerve cells.

▶ Transmission and Epidemiology

In addition to the usual oral route, shigellosis is also acquired through direct person-to-person contact, largely because of the small infectious dose required (from 10 to 200 bacteria). The disease is mostly associated with lax sanitation, malnutrition, and crowding; and it is spread epidemically in day care centers, prisons, mental institutions, nursing homes, and military camps. *Shigella* can establish a chronic carrier condition in some people that lasts several months.

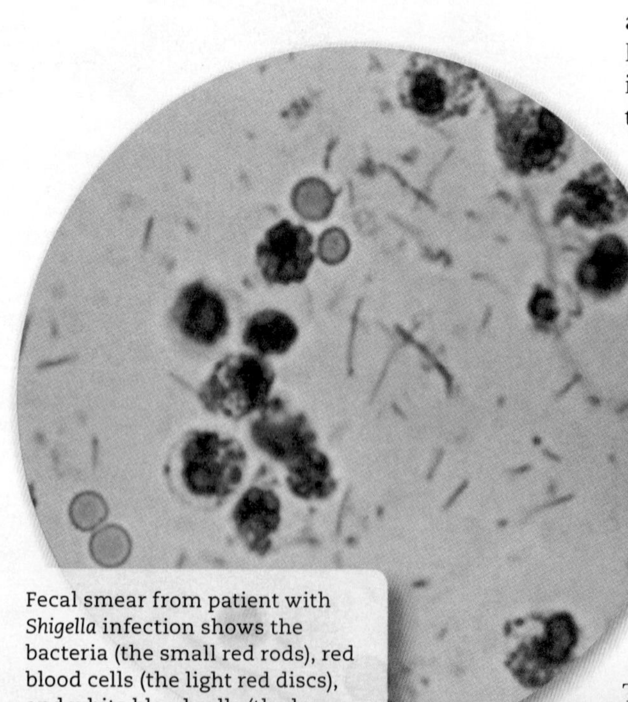

Fecal smear from patient with *Shigella* infection shows the bacteria (the small red rods), red blood cells (the light red discs), and white blood cells (the larger cells with intracellular granules).

▶ Prevention and Treatment

The only prevention of this and most other diarrheal diseases is good hygiene and avoiding contact with infected persons. Although some experts say that bloody diarrhea in this country should not be treated with antibiotics (which is generally

HIGHLIGHT DISEASE

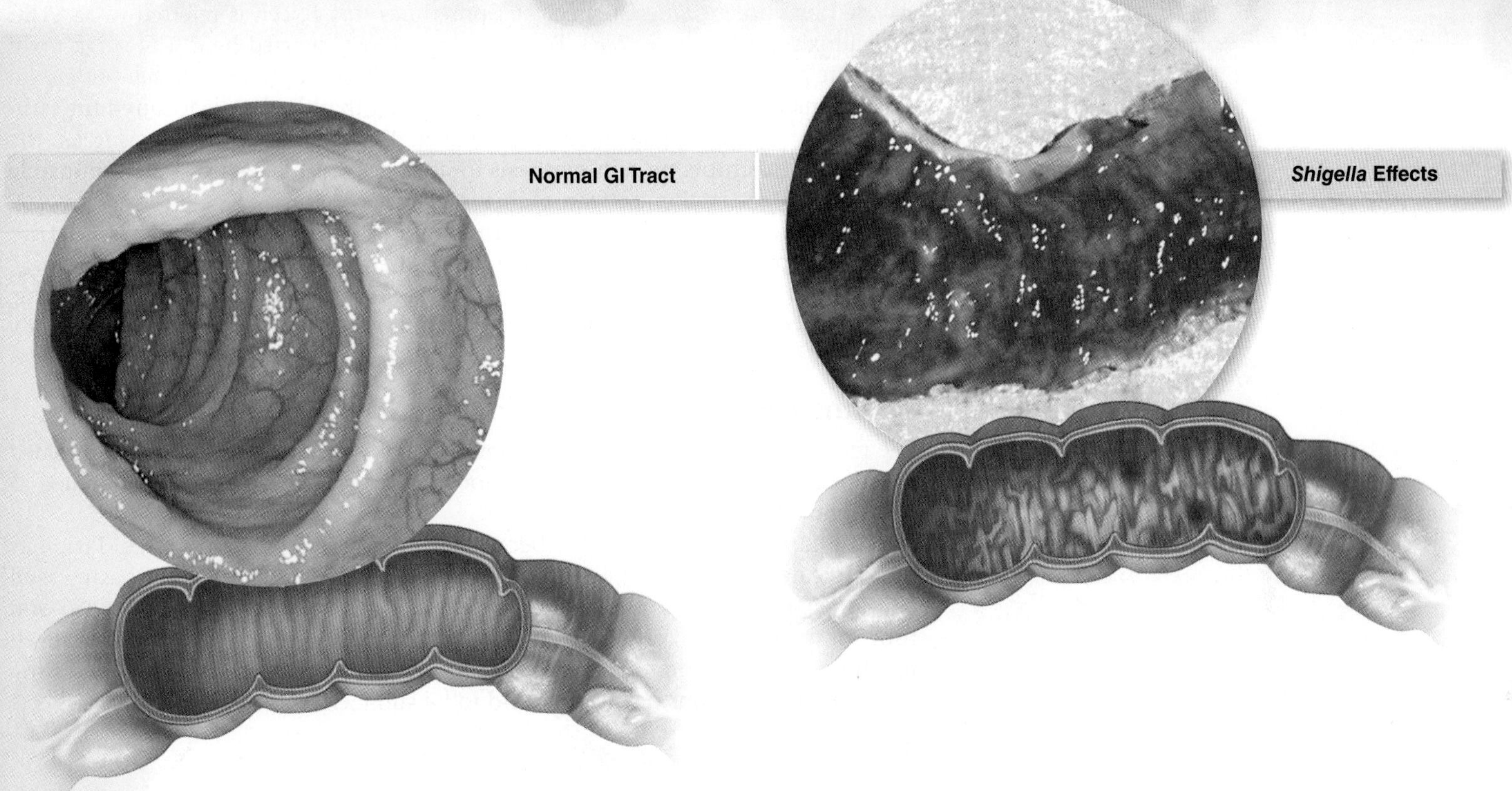

Figure 20.3 The appearance of the large intestinal mucosa in *Shigella* dysentery. Note the patches of blood and mucus, the erosion of the lining, and the absence of perforation.

accepted for *E. coli* O157:H7 infections), most physicians recommend prompt treatment of shigellosis with trimethoprim-sulfamethoxazole (TMP-SMZ).

E. coli O157:H7 (EHEC)

Dozens of different strains of *E. coli* exist, most of which cause no disease at all. A handful of them cause various degrees of intestinal symptoms, as described in this and the following section. Some of them cause urinary tract infections (see chapter 21). *E. coli* O157:H7 and its close relatives are the most virulent of them all. The group of *E. coli* of which this strain is the most famous representative is generally referred to as **enterohemorrhagic *E. coli*,** or **EHEC.**

▶ Signs and Symptoms

E. coli O157:H7 is the agent of a spectrum of conditions, ranging from mild gastroenteritis with fever to bloody diarrhea. About 10% of patients develop **hemolytic uremic syndrome (HUS),** a severe hemolytic anemia that can cause kidney damage and failure. Neurological symptoms such as blindness, seizure, and stroke (and long-term debilitation) are also possible. These serious manifestations are most likely to occur in children younger than 5 and in elderly people.

In 2011, a new HUS-causing *E. coli* strain caused a large and deadly outbreak in Germany. It was named *E. coli* O104:H4. This reminds us that bacteria are continually evolving and new ones will constantly appear.

▶ Pathogenesis and Virulence Factors

E. coli O157:H7 (and *E. coli* O104:H4, as it turns out) owes much of its virulence to shiga toxins (so named because they are identical to the shiga exotoxin secreted by virulent *Shigella* species). Sometimes this *E. coli* is referred to as STEC (shiga-toxin-producing *E. coli*). For simplicity, EHEC is used here. The shiga toxin genes are present on prophage genes donated by bacteriophage in *E. coli* but are on the chromosome of *Shigella dysenteriae,* suggesting that the *E. coli* acquired the virulence factor through phage-mediated transfer. As described earlier for *Shigella,* the shiga toxin interrupts protein synthesis in its target cells. It seems to be responsible especially for the systemic effects of this infection.

Another important virulence determinant for EHEC is the ability to efface (rub out or destroy) enterocytes, which are gut epithelial cells.

The net effect is a lesion in the gut (effacement), usually in the large intestine. The microvilli are lost from the gut epithelium, and the lesions produce bloody diarrhea.

Transmission and Epidemiology

The most common mode of transmission for EHEC is the ingestion of contaminated and undercooked beef, although other foods and beverages can be contaminated as well **(figure 20.4).**

Any farm product may also become contaminated by cattle feces. Products that are eaten raw, such as lettuce, vegetables, and apples used in unpasteurized cider, are particularly problematic. The disease can also be spread via the fecal-oral route of transmission, especially among young children in group situations. Even touching surfaces contaminated with cattle feces can cause disease, since ingesting as few as 10 organisms has been found to be sufficient to initiate this disease.

Culture and Diagnosis

Infection with this type of *E. coli* should be confirmed with stool culture or with ELISA or PCR.

Prevention and Treatment

The best prevention for this disease is never to eat raw or even rare hamburger and to wash raw vegetables well. The shiga toxin is heat-labile and the *E. coli* is killed by heat as well.

No vaccine exists for *E. coli* O157:H7. A great deal of research is directed at vaccinating livestock to break the chain of transmission to humans.

Antibiotics are contraindicated for this infection. Even with severe disease manifestations, antibiotics have been found to be of no help, and they may increase the pathology. Supportive therapy, including plasma transfusions to dilute toxin in the blood, is the only option.

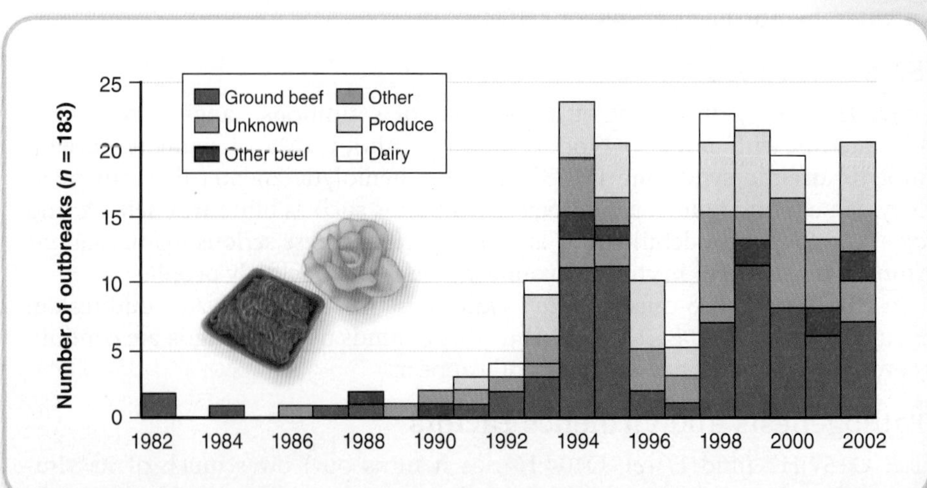

Figure 20.4 The emergence of *E. coli* O157:H7. Note how ground beef is much more often a source than other (muscle) meats.

Other E. coli

At least four other categories of *E. coli* can cause diarrheal diseases. Scientists call these **enterotoxigenic** *E. coli*, **enteroinvasive** *E. coli*, **enteropathogenic** *E. coli*, and **enteroaggregative** *E. coli*. In clinical practice, most physicians are interested in differentiating shiga-toxin-producing *E. coli* (EHEC) from all the others. In Disease Table 20.1, the non-shiga-toxin-producing *E. coli* are grouped together in one column.

Campylobacter

Although you may never have heard of *Campylobacter*, it is considered to be the most common bacterial cause of diarrhea in the United States. It probably causes more diarrhea than *Salmonella* and *Shigella* combined, with 2 million cases of diarrhea credited to it per year.

The symptoms of campylobacteriosis are frequent watery stools, fever, vomiting, headaches, and severe abdominal pain. The symptoms may last longer than most acute diarrheal episodes, sometimes extending beyond 2 weeks. They may subside and then recur over a period of weeks.

Campylobacter jejuni is the most common cause, although there are other *Campylobacter* species. Campylobacters are slender, curved, or spiral gram-negative bacteria propelled by polar flagella at one or both poles, often appearing in S-shaped or gull-winged pairs. These bacteria tend to be microaerophilic inhabitants of the intestinal tract, genitourinary tract, and oral cavity of humans and animals. A close relative, *Helicobacter pylori*, is the causative agent of most stomach ulcers (described later). Transmission of this pathogen takes place via the ingestion of contaminated beverages and food, especially water, milk, meat, and chicken.

Once ingested, *C. jejuni* cells reach the mucosa at the last segment of the small intestine (ileum) near its junction with the colon; they adhere, burrow through the mucus, and multiply. Symptoms commence after an incubation period of 1 to 7 days. The mechanisms of pathology appear to involve a heat-labile enterotoxin that stimulates a secretory diarrhea like that of cholera. In a small number of cases, infection with this bacterium can lead to a serious neuromuscular paralysis called Guillain-Barré syndrome.

Handwashing is a very effective way to reduce transmission of fecal bacteria.

Guillain-Barré syndrome (GBS) (pronounced gee″-luhn-buh-ray′) is the leading cause of acute paralysis in the United States since the eradication of polio there. The good news is that many patients recover completely from this paralysis. The condition is still mysterious in many ways, but it seems to be an autoimmune reaction that can be brought on by infection with viruses and bacteria, by vaccination in rare cases, and even by surgery. The single most common precipitating event for the onset of GBS is *Campylobacter* infection. Twenty to forty percent of GBS cases are preceded by infection with *Campylobacter*. The reasons for this are not clear. (Note that even though 20% to 40% of GBS cases are preceded by *Campylobacter* infection, only about 1 in 1,000 cases of *Campylobacter* infection results in GBS.)

Resolution of infection occurs in most instances with simple, nonspecific rehydration and electrolyte balance therapy. In more severely affected patients, it may be necessary to administer erythromycin. Antibiotic resistance is increasing in these bacteria. Because vaccines are yet to be developed, prevention depends on rigid sanitary control of water and milk supplies and care in food preparation.

Yersinia Species

Yersinia is a genus of gram-negative bacteria that includes the infamous plague bacterium, *Yersinia pestis* (discussed in chapter 18). There are two species that cause GI tract disease: *Y. enterocolitica* and *Y. pseudotuberculosis*. The infections are most notable for the high degree of abdominal pain they cause. This symptom is accompanied by fever. Often the symptoms are mistaken for appendicitis.

HIGHLIGHT DISEASE

Clostridium difficile

Clostridium difficile is a gram-positive endospore-forming rod found as normal biota in the intestine. It was once considered relatively harmless but now is known to cause a condition called pseudomembranous colitis. It is also sometimes called antibiotic-associated colitis. In most cases, this infection seems to be precipitated by therapy with broad-spectrum antibiotics such as ampicillin, clindamycin, or cephalosporins. It is a major cause of diarrhea in hospitals, although community-acquired infections have been on the rise in the last few years. Also, new studies suggest that the use of gastric acid inhibitors for the treatment of heartburn can predispose people to this infection. Although *C. difficile* is relatively noninvasive, it is able to superinfect the large intestine when drugs have disrupted the normal biota. It produces two enterotoxins, toxins A and B, that cause areas of necrosis in the wall of the intestine. The predominant symptom is diarrhea commencing late in antibiotic therapy or even after therapy has stopped. More severe cases exhibit abdominal cramps, fever, and leukocytosis. The colon is inflamed and gradually sloughs off loose, membranelike patches called pseudomembranes consisting of fibrin and cells **(figure 20.5)**. If the condition is not stopped, perforation of the cecum and death can result.

Mild, uncomplicated cases respond to the withdrawal of antibiotics and replacement therapy for lost fluids and electrolytes. More severe infections are treated with vancomycin or a new drug approved in 2011 called fidaxomicin (Dificid) for several weeks until the intestinal biota returns to normal. Some new techniques on the horizon are vaccination with *C. difficile* toxoid and restoration of normal biota by ingestion of a mixed culture of lactobacilli and yeasts.

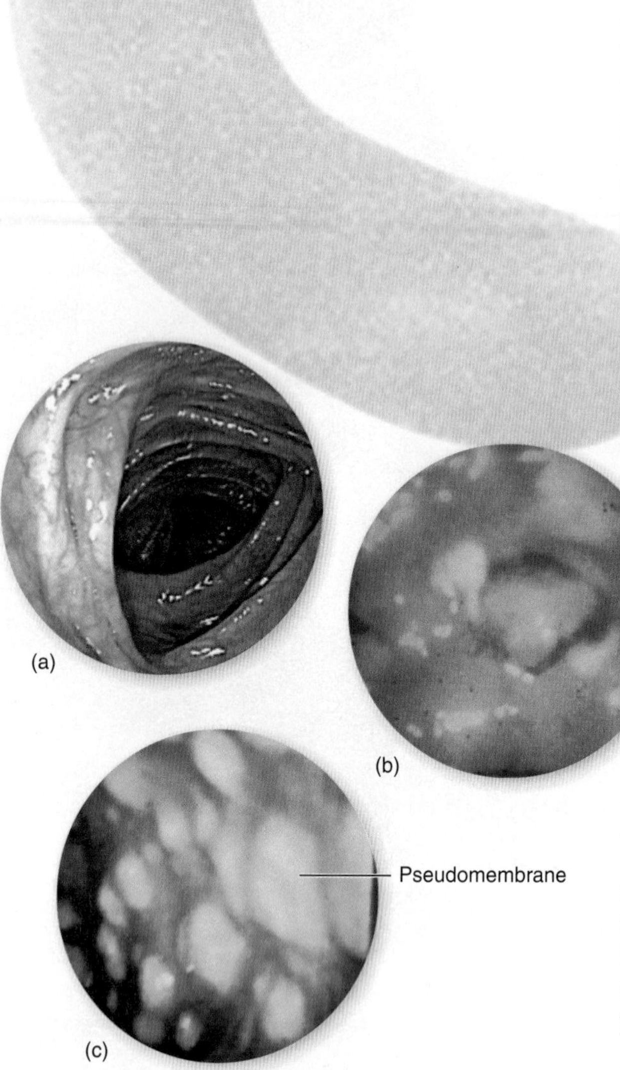

Figure 20.5 Antibiotic-associated colitis. **(a)** Normal colon. **(b)** A mild form of colitis with diffuse, inflammatory patches. **(c)** Heavy yellow plaques, or pseudomembranes, typical of more severe cases. Photographs were made by a sigmoidoscope, an instrument capable of photographing the interior of the colon.

Vibrio cholerae

Cholera has been a devastating disease for centuries. It is not an exaggeration to say that the disease has shaped a good deal of human history in Asia and Latin America, where it has been endemic. These days we have come to expect outbreaks of cholera to occur after natural disasters, war, or large refugee movements, especially in underdeveloped parts of the world.

Vibrios are rods with a single polar flagellum. They belong to the family *Vibrionaceae*. A freshly isolated specimen of *Vibrio cholerae* will contain quick, darting cells that slightly resemble a comma. *Vibrio* shares many characteristics with members of the *Enterobacteriaceae* family. Vibrios are fermentative and grow on ordinary or selective media containing bile at 37°C. They possess unique O and H antigens and membrane receptor antigens that provide some basis for classifying members of the family. There are two major types, called classic and *El Tor*.

▶ Signs and Symptoms

After an incubation period of a few hours to a few days, symptoms begin abruptly with vomiting, followed by copious watery feces called secretory diarrhea. The intestinal contents are lost very quickly, leaving only secreted fluids. This voided fluid contains flecks of mucus—hence, the description "rice-water stool." Fluid losses of nearly 1 liter per hour have been reported in severe cases, and an untreated patient can lose up to 50% of body weight during the course of this disease. The diarrhea causes loss of blood volume, acidosis from bicarbonate loss, and potassium depletion, which manifest in muscle cramps, severe thirst, flaccid skin, sunken eyes, and in young children, coma and convulsions. Secondary circulatory consequences can include hypotension, tachycardia, cyanosis, and collapse from shock within 18 to 24 hours. If cholera is left untreated, death can occur in less than 48 hours, and the mortality rate approaches 55%.

▸ Pathogenesis and Virulence Factors

V. cholerae has a relatively high infectious dose (10^8 cells). At the junction of the duodenum and jejunum, the vibrios penetrate the mucus barrier using their flagella, adhere to the microvilli of the epithelial cells, and multiply there. The bacteria never enter the host cells or invade the mucosa. The virulence of *V. cholerae* is due entirely to an enterotoxin called cholera toxin (CT), which disrupts the normal physiology of intestinal cells. Under the influence of this system, the cells shed large amounts of electrolytes into the intestine, an event accompanied by profuse water loss.

▸ Transmission and Epidemiology

The pattern of cholera transmission and the onset of epidemics are greatly influenced by the season of the year and the climate. Cold, acidic, dry environments inhibit the migration and survival of *Vibrio*, whereas warm, monsoon, alkaline, and saline conditions favor them. The bacteria survive in water sources for long periods of time. Recent outbreaks in several parts of the world have been traced to giant cargo ships that pick up ballast water in one port and empty it in another elsewhere in the world. Cholera ranks among the top seven causes of morbidity and mortality, affecting several million people in endemic regions of Asia and Africa.

In nonendemic areas such as the United States, the microbe is spread by water and food contaminated by asymptomatic carriers, but it is relatively uncommon.

▸ Culture and Diagnosis

During epidemics of this disease, clinical evidence is usually sufficient to diagnose cholera. But confirmation of the disease is often required for epidemiological studies and detection of sporadic cases. *V. cholerae* can be readily isolated and identified in the laboratory from stool samples. Direct dark-field microscopic observation reveals characteristic curved cells with brisk, darting motility as confirmatory evidence. Fluorescent staining of feces with group-specific antisera can be diagnostic as well. Difficult cases can be traced by detecting a rising antitoxin titer in the serum.

▸ Prevention and Treatment

Effective prevention is contingent on proper sewage treatment and water purification. Vaccines are available for travelers and people living in endemic regions. One vaccine contains killed *V. cholerae* but protects for only 6 months or less. An oral vaccine containing live, attenuated bacteria was developed to be a more effective alternative, but evidence suggests it also confers only short-term immunity. It is not routinely used in the United States.

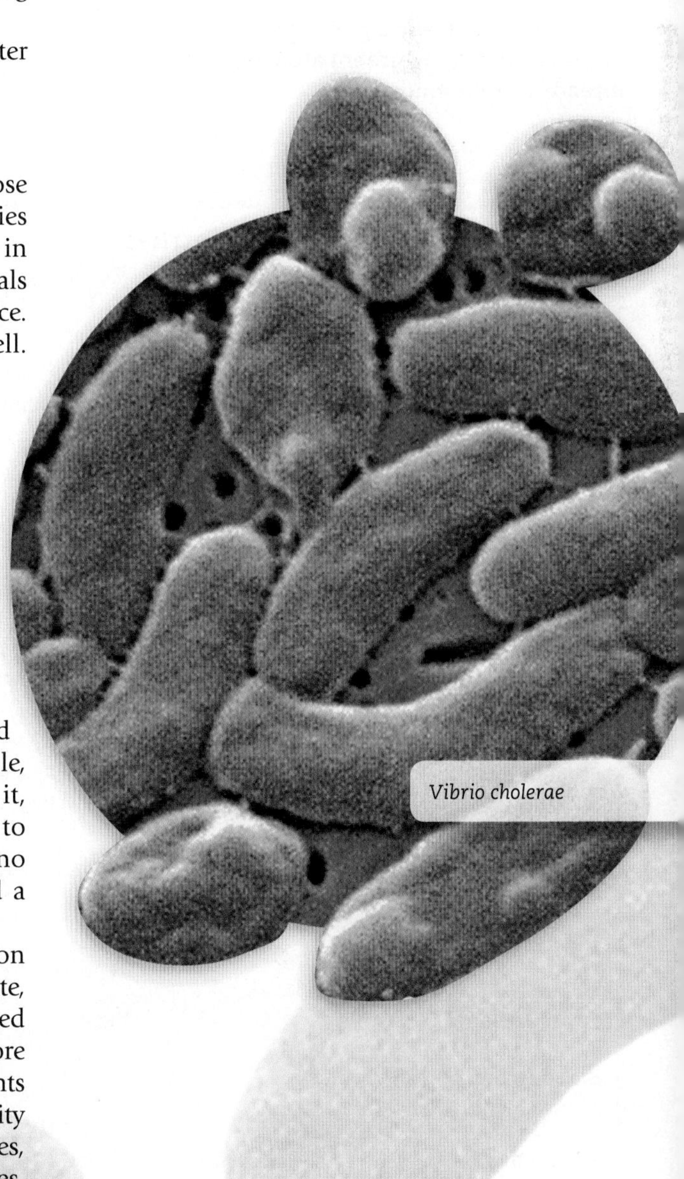
Vibrio cholerae

The key to cholera therapy is prompt replacement of water and electrolytes, because their loss accounts for the severe morbidity and mortality. This therapy can be accomplished by various rehydration techniques that replace the lost fluid and electrolytes. One of these, oral rehydration therapy (ORT), is incredibly simple, and astonishingly effective. Until the 1970s, the treatment, if one could access it, was rehydration through an IV drip. This treatment usually required traveling to the nearest clinic, often miles or days away. Most affected children received no treatment at all, and 3 million of them died every year. Then scientists tested a simple sugar-salt solution that patients could drink.

The relatively simple solution, developed by the World Health Organization (WHO), consists of a mixture of the electrolytes sodium chloride, sodium bicarbonate, potassium chloride, and glucose or sucrose dissolved in water. When administered early in amounts ranging from 100 to 400 milliliters per hour, the solution can restore patients in 4 hours, often bringing them literally back from the brink of death. Infants and small children, who once would have died, now survive so often that the mortality rate for treated cases of cholera is near zero. This therapy has several advantages, especially for countries with few resources. It does not require medical facilities, high-technology equipment, or complex medication protocols. It also eliminates the need for clean needles, which is a pressing issue in many parts of the world.

Oral antibiotics such as tetracycline and drugs such as trimethoprim-sulfamethoxazole can terminate the diarrhea in 48 hours. They also diminish the period of vibrio excretion.

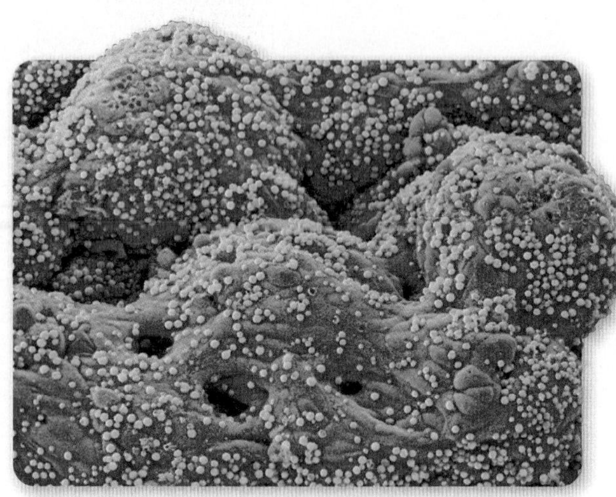

Figure 20.6 Scanning electron micrograph of *Cryptosporidium* (green) attached to the intestinal epithelium.

Cryptosporidium

Cryptosporidium is an intestinal protozoan of the apicomplexan type (see chapter 4) that infects a variety of mammals, birds, and reptiles. For many years, cryptosporidiosis was considered an intestinal ailment exclusive to calves, pigs, chickens, and other poultry, but it is clearly a zoonosis as well. The organism's life cycle includes a hardy intestinal oocyst as well as a tissue phase. Humans accidentally ingest the oocysts with water or food that has been contaminated by feces from infected animals. The oocyst "excysts" once it reaches the intestines and releases sporozoites that attach to the epithelium of the small intestine **(figure 20.6).** The organism penetrates the intestinal cells and lives intracellularly in them. It undergoes asexual and sexual reproduction in these cells, produces more oocysts, which are released into the gut lumen, excreted from the host, and after a short time become infective again. The oocysts are highly infectious and extremely resistant to treatment with chlorine and other disinfectants.

Disease Table 20.1 Acute Diarrhea

	Bacterial Causes				
Causative Organism(s)	*Salmonella*	*Shigella*	Shiga-toxin-producing *E. coli* O157:H7 (EHEC)	Other *E. coli* (non-shiga-toxin producing)	*Campylobacter*
Most Common Modes of Transmission	Vehicle (food, beverage), fecal-oral	Fecal-oral, direct contact	Vehicle (food, beverage), fecal-oral	Vehicle, fecal-oral	Vehicle (food, water), fecal-oral
Virulence Factors	Adhesins, endotoxin	Endotoxin, enterotoxin, shiga toxins in some strains	Shiga toxins; proteins for attachment, secretion, effacement	Various: proteins for attachment, secretion, effacement; heat-labile and/or heat-stable exotoxins; invasiveness	Adhesins, exotoxin, induction of autoimmunity
Culture/ Diagnosis	Stool culture, not usually necessary	Stool culture; antigen testing for shiga toxin	Stool culture, antigen testing for shiga toxin	Stool culture not usually necessary in absence of blood, fever	Stool culture not usually necessary; dark-field microscopy
Prevention	Food hygiene and personal hygiene	Food hygiene and personal hygiene	Avoid live *E. coli* (cook meat and clean vegetables)	Food and personal hygiene	Food and personal hygiene
Treatment	Rehydration; no antibiotic for uncomplicated disease	TMP-SMZ, rehydration	Antibiotics contraindicated, supportive measures	Rehydration, antimotility agent	Rehydration, erythromycin in severe cases (antibiotic resistance rising)
Fever Present?	Usually	Often	Often	Sometimes	Usually
Blood in Stool?	Sometimes	Often	Usually	Sometimes	No
Distinctive Features	Often associated with chickens, reptiles	Very low ID_{50}	Hemolytic uremic syndrome	EIEC, ETEC, EPEC	Guillain-Barré syndrome

The prominent symptoms mimic other types of gastroenteritis, with headache, sweating, vomiting, severe abdominal cramps, and diarrhea. AIDS patients may experience chronic persistent cryptosporidial diarrhea that can be used as a criterion to help diagnose AIDS. The agent can be detected in fecal samples or in biopsies (**figure 20.7**) using ELISA or acid-fast staining. Stool cultures should be performed to rule out other (bacterial) causes of infection.

Half of the outbreaks of diarrhea associated with swimming pools are caused by *Cryptosporidium*. Because chlorination is not entirely successful in eradicating the cysts, most treatment plants use filtration to remove them, but even this method can fail.

Treatment is not usually required for otherwise healthy patients. Antidiarrheal agents (antimotility drugs) may be used. Although no curative antimicrobial agent exists for *Cryptosporidium*, physicians will often try paromomycin, an aminoglycoside that can be effective against protozoa.

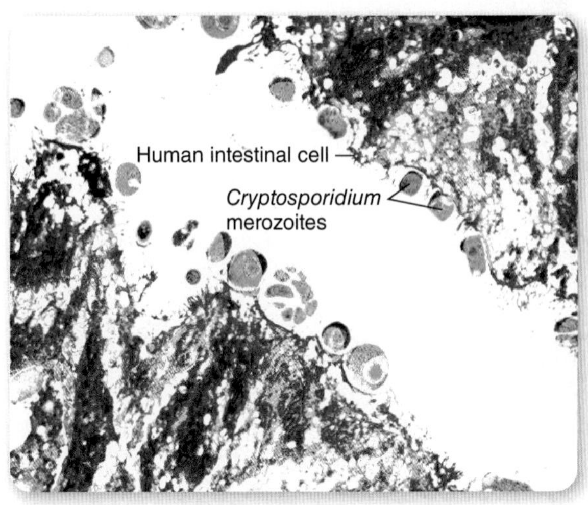

Figure 20.7 **A micrograph of a *Cryptosporidium* merozoite that has penetrated the intestinal mucosa.**

Rotavirus

Rotavirus is a member of the *Reovirus* group, which consists of an unusual double-stranded RNA genome with both an inner and an outer capsid. Globally, rotavirus is the primary viral cause of morbidity and mortality resulting from diarrhea, accounting for nearly 50% of all cases. It is estimated that there are 1 million cases of

			Nonbacterial Causes		
Yersinia	*Clostridium difficile*	*Vibrio cholerae*	*Cryptosporidium*	Rotavirus	Other viruses
Vehicle (food, water), fecal-oral, indirect contact	Endogenous (normal biota)	Vehicle (water and some foods), fecal-oral	Vehicle (water, food), fecal-oral	Fecal-oral, vehicle, fomite	Fecal-oral, vehicle
Intracellular growth	Enterotoxins A and B	Cholera toxin (CT)	Intracellular growth	–	–
Cold-enrichment stool culture	Stool culture, PCR, ELISA demonstration of toxins in stool	Clinical diagnosis, microscopic techniques, serological detection of antitoxin	Acid-fast staining, ruling out bacteria	Usually not performed	Usually not performed
Food and personal hygiene	–	Water hygiene	Water treatment, proper food handling	Oral live virus vaccine	Hygiene
None in most cases; doxycycline, gentamicin, or TMP-SMZ for bacteremia	Withdrawal of antibiotic; in severe cases metronidazole or new drug fidaxomicin (Dificid)	Rehydration; in severe cases tetracycline, TMP-SMZ	None; paromomycin used sometimes	Rehydration	Rehydration
Usually	Sometimes	No	Often	Often	Sometimes
Occasionally	Not usually; mucus prominent	No	Not usually	No	No
Severe abdominal pain	Antibiotic-associated diarrhea	Rice-water stools	Resistant to chlorine disinfection	Severe in babies	–

NCLEX® PREP

3. What fraction of the total number of acute diarrhea cases in the United States is transmitted by contaminated foods?
   a. 1/5
   b. 1/2
   c. 1/3
   d. 1/4

HIGHLIGHT DISEASE

rotavirus infection in the United States every year, leading to 70,000 hospitalizations. Peak occurrences of this infection are seasonal—in the U.S. Southwest, the peak is often in the late fall, and in the Northeast, the peak comes in the spring. The virus gets its name from its physical appearance, which is said to resemble a spoked wheel.

The virus is transmitted by the fecal-oral route, including through contaminated food, water, and fomites. For this reason, disease is most prevalent in areas of the world with poor sanitation. In the United States, rotavirus infection is relatively common, but its course is generally mild.

The effects of infection vary with the age, nutritional state, general health, and living conditions of the patient. Babies from 6 to 24 months of age lacking maternal antibodies have the greatest risk for fatal disease. These children present symptoms of watery diarrhea, fever, vomiting, dehydration, and shock. The intestinal mucosa can be damaged in a way that chronically compromises nutrition, and long-term or repeated infections can retard growth. Newborns seem to be protected by maternal antibodies. Adults can also acquire this infection, but it is generally mild and self-limiting.

Children are treated with oral replacement fluid and electrolytes. A new oral live virus vaccine has been available since 2006.

Other Viruses

A bewildering array of viruses can cause gastroenteritis, including adenoviruses, noroviruses (sometimes known as Norwalk viruses), and astroviruses. They are extremely common in the United States and around the world. They are usually "diagnosed" when no other agent (such as those just described) is identified.

Transmission is fecal-oral or via contamination of food and water. Viruses generally cause a profuse, watery diarrhea of 3 to 5 days' duration. Vomiting may accompany the disease, especially in the early phases. Mild fever is often seen.

Treatment of these infections always focuses on rehydration.

Food Poisoning (Acute Diarrhea with Vomiting)

If a patient presents with severe nausea and frequent vomiting accompanied by diarrhea, and reports that companions with whom he or she shared a recent meal (within the last 1 to 6 hours) are suffering the same fate, food poisoning should be suspected. **Food poisoning** refers to symptoms in the gut that are caused by a preformed toxin of some sort. In many cases, the toxin comes from *Staphylococcus aureus.* In others, the source of the toxin is *Bacillus cereus* or *Clostridium perfringens.* The toxin occasionally comes from nonmicrobial sources such as fish, shellfish, or mushrooms. In any case, if the symptoms are violent and the incubation period is very short, this condition, which is an *intoxication* (the effects of a toxin) rather than an *infection,* should be considered.

Staphylococcus aureus Exotoxin

This illness is associated with eating foods such as custards, sauces, cream pastries, processed meats, chicken salad, or ham that have been contaminated by handling and then left unrefrigerated for a few hours. Because of the high salt tolerance of *S. aureus,* even foods containing salt as a preservative are not exempt. The toxins produced by the multiplying bacteria do not noticeably alter the food's taste or smell. The exotoxin (which is an enterotoxin) is heat-stable; inactivation requires 100°C for at least 30 minutes. Thus, heating the food after toxin production may not prevent disease. The ingested toxin acts upon the gastrointestinal epithelium and stimulates nerves, with acute symptoms of cramping, nausea, vomiting, and diarrhea. Recovery is also rapid, usually within 24 hours. The disease is not transmissible person to person. Often, a single source will contaminate several people, leading to a mini-outbreak.

This condition is almost always self-limiting, and antibiotics are definitely not warranted.

Bacillus cereus Exotoxin

Bacillus cereus is a sporulating gram-positive bacterium that is naturally present in soil. As a result, it is a common resident on vegetables and other products in close contact with soil. It produces two exotoxins, one of which causes a diarrheal-type disease, the other of which causes an **emetic** (ee-met'-ik) or vomiting disease. The type of disease that takes place is influenced by the type of food that is contaminated by the bacterium. The emetic form is most frequently linked to fried rice, especially when it has been cooked and kept warm for long periods of time. These conditions are apparently ideal for the expression of the low-molecular-weight, heat-stable exotoxin having an emetic effect. The diarrheal form of the disease is usually associated with cooked meats or vegetables that are held at a warm temperature for long periods of time. These conditions apparently favor the production of the high-molecular-weight, heat-labile exotoxin. The symptom in these cases is a watery, profuse diarrhea that lasts only for about 24 hours.

In both cases, the only prevention is the proper handling of food.

Clostridium perfringens Exotoxin

Another sporulating gram-positive bacterium that causes intestinal symptoms is *Clostridium perfringens*. Endospores from *C. perfringens* can contaminate many kinds of foods. Those most frequently implicated in disease are animal flesh (meat, fish) and vegetables such as beans that have not been cooked thoroughly enough to destroy endospores. When these foods are cooled, spores germinate, and the germinated cells multiply, especially if the food is left unrefrigerated. If the food is eaten without adequate reheating, live *C. perfringens* cells enter the small intestine and release exotoxin. The toxin, acting upon epithelial cells, initiates acute abdominal pain, diarrhea, and nausea in 8 to 16 hours. Recovery is rapid, and deaths are extremely rare.

Disease Table 20.2 Food Poisoning (Acute Diarrhea with Vomiting)

Causative Organism(s)	*Staphylococcus aureus*	*Bacillus cereus*	*Clostridium perfringens*
Most Common Modes of Transmission	Vehicle (food)	Vehicle (food)	Vehicle (food)
Virulence Factors	Heat-stable exotoxin	Heat-stable toxin, heat-labile toxin	Heat-labile toxin
Culture/Diagnosis	Usually based on epidemiological evidence	Microscopic analysis of food or stool	Detection of toxin in stool
Prevention	Proper food handling	Proper food handling	Proper food handling
Treatment	Supportive	Supportive	Supportive
Fever Present?	Not usually	Not usually	Not usually
Blood in Stool?	No	No	No
Distinctive Features	Suspect in foods with high salt or sugar content	Two forms: emetic and diarrheal	Acute abdominal pain

C. perfringens also causes an enterocolitis infection similar to that caused by *C. difficile*. This infectious type of diarrhea is acquired from contaminated food, or it may be transmissible by inanimate objects.

Chronic Diarrhea

Chronic diarrhea is defined as lasting longer than 14 days. It can have infectious causes or can reflect noninfectious conditions. Most of us are familiar with diseases that present a constellation of bowel syndromes, such as irritable bowel syndrome and ulcerative colitis, neither of which is directly caused by a microorganism as far as we know. Increasing evidence suggests that a chronically disrupted intestinal biota (from long-term use of antibiotics, for example) can predispose people to these conditions.

People suffering from AIDS almost universally suffer from chronic diarrhea. Most of the patients who are not taking antiretroviral drugs have diarrhea caused by a variety of opportunistic microorganisms, including *Cryptosporidium*, *Mycobacterium avium*, and so forth. A patient's HIV status should be considered if he or she presents with chronic diarrhea.

Here we examine a few of the microbes that can be responsible for chronic diarrhea in otherwise healthy people.

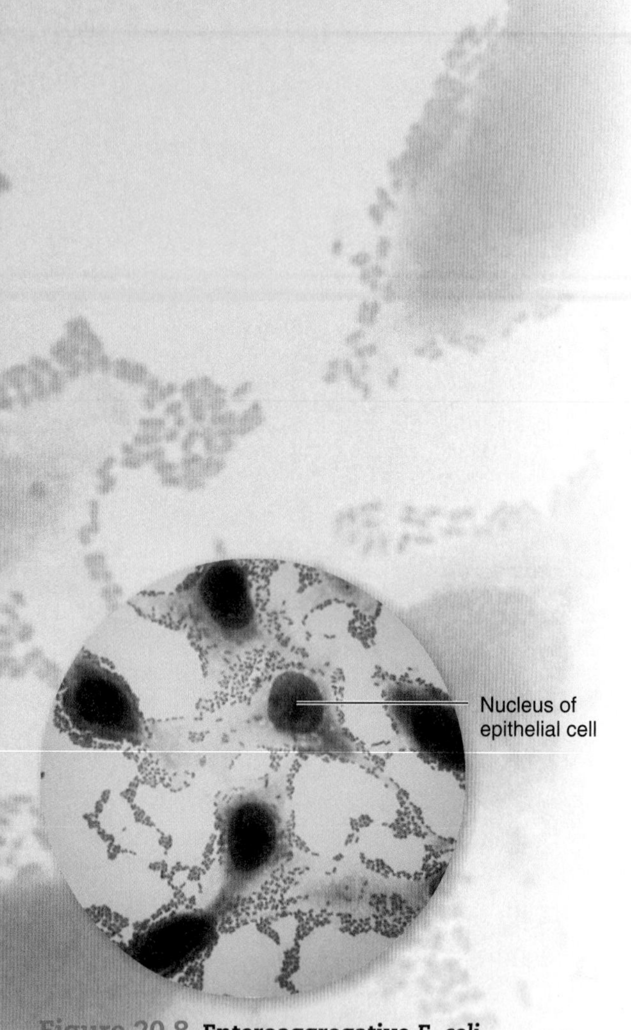

Figure 20.8 Enteroaggregative E. coli adhering to epithelial cells.

Enteroaggregative *E. coli* (EAEC)

In the section on acute diarrhea, you read about the various categories of *E. coli* that can cause disease in the gut. One type, the enteroaggregative *E. coli* (EAEC), is particularly associated with chronic disease, especially in children. This bacterium was first recognized in 1987. It secretes neither the heat-stable nor heat-labile exotoxins previously described for enterotoxigenic *E. coli* (ETEC). It is distinguished by its ability to adhere to human cells in aggregates rather than as single cells **(figure 20.8)**. Its presence appears to stimulate secretion of large amounts of mucus in the gut, which may be part of its role in causing chronic diarrhea.

Cyclospora

Cyclospora cayetanensis is an emerging protozoan pathogen. Since the first occurrence in 1979, hundreds of outbreaks have been reported in the United States and Canada. Its mode of transmission is fecal-oral, and most cases have been associated with consumption of fresh produce and water presumably contaminated with feces. This disease occurs worldwide, and although primarily of human origin, it is not spread directly from person to person. Outbreaks have been traced to imported raspberries, salad made with fresh greens, and drinking water. A major outbreak of this organism occurred on a cruise ship in April of 2009, where 135 of 1,318 passengers, and 25 crew members, became ill with *Cyclospora*.

The disease begins when oocysts enter the small intestine and release invasive sporozoites that invade the mucosa. After an incubation period of about 1 week, symptoms of watery diarrhea, stomach cramps, bloating, fever, and muscle aches appear. Patients with prolonged diarrheal illness experience anorexia and weight loss.

Most cases of infection have been effectively controlled with trimethoprim-sulfamethoxazole lasting 1 week. Traditional antiprotozoan drugs are not effective. Some cases of disease may be prevented by cooking or freezing food to kill the oocysts.

Giardia

Giardia lamblia is a pathogenic flagellated protozoan first observed by Antonie van Leeuwenhoek in his own feces. For 200 years, it was considered a harmless or weak intestinal pathogen; and only since the 1950s has its importance as a cause of diarrhea been recognized. In fact, it is the most common flagellate isolated in clinical specimens. Observed straight on, the trophozoite has a unique symmetrical heart shape with organelles positioned in such a way that it resembles a face **(figure 20.9)**.

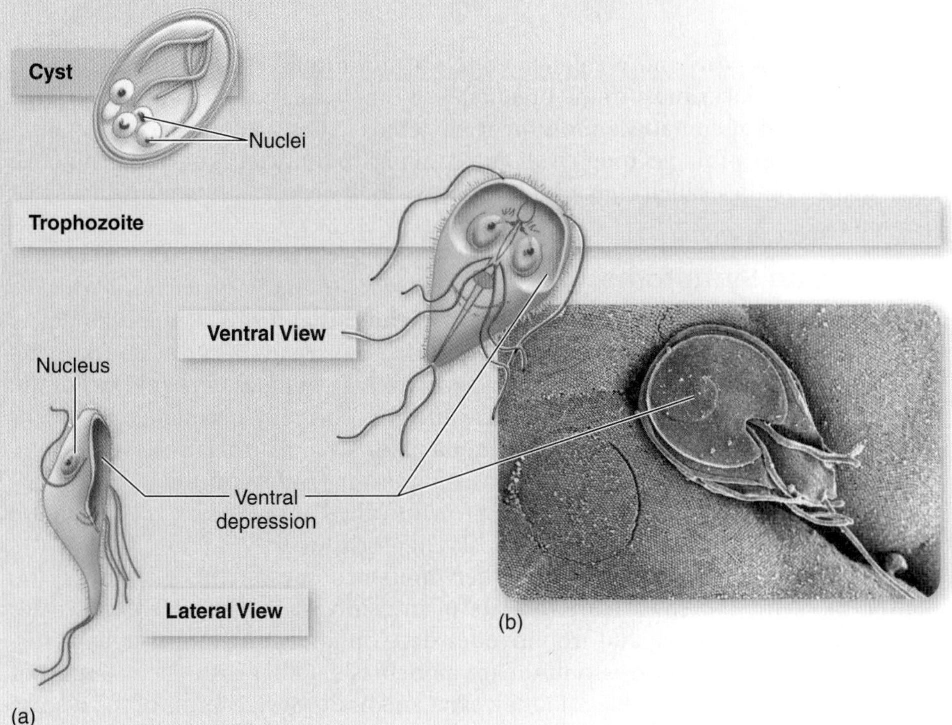

Figure 20.9 ***Giardia lamblia*** **trophozoite.** **(a)** Schematic drawing. **(b)** Scanning electron micrograph of intestinal surface, revealing (on the left) the lesion left behind by adhesive disc of a *Giardia* that has detached. The trophozoite on the right is lying on its "back" and is revealing its adhesive disc.

Four pairs of flagella emerge from the ventral surface, which is concave and acts like a suction cup for attachment to a substrate. *Giardia* cysts are small, compact, and contain four nuclei.

Typical symptoms include diarrhea of long duration, abdominal pain, and flatulence. Stools have a greasy, foul-smelling quality to them. Fever is usually not present.

▸ Transmission and Epidemiology of Giardiasis

Giardiasis has a complex epidemiological pattern. The protozoan has been isolated from the intestines of beavers, cattle, coyotes, cats, and human carriers, but the precise reservoir is unclear at this time. Although both trophozoites and cysts escape in the stool, the cysts play a greater role in transmission. Unlike other pathogenic flagellates, *Giardia* cysts can survive for 2 months in the environment. Cysts are usually ingested with water and food or swallowed after close contact with infected people or contaminated objects. Infection can occur with a dose of only 10 to 100 cysts.

▸ Prevention and Treatment

There is a vaccine against *Giardia* that can be given to animals, including dogs. No human vaccine is available. Avoiding drinking from freshwater sources is the major preventive measure that can be taken.

Treatment is with tinidazole or metronidazole.

Entamoeba

Amoebas are widely distributed in aqueous habitats and are frequent parasites of animals, but only a small number of them have the necessary virulence to invade tissues and cause serious pathology. One of the most significant pathogenic amoebas is *Entamoeba histolytica* (en″-tah-mee′-bah his″-toh-lit′-ih-kuh). The relatively simple life cycle of this parasite alternates between a large trophozoite that is motile by means of pseudopods and a smaller, compact, nonmotile cyst **(figure 20.10*a–c*)**. The trophozoite lacks most of the organelles of other eukaryotes, and it has a large single nucleus that contains a prominent nucleolus called a *karyosome*. The mature cyst is encased in a thin yet tough wall and contains four nuclei as well as distinctive cigar-shaped bodies called *chromatoidal bodies*, which are actually dense clusters of ribosomes.

Signs and Symptoms

Clinical amoebiasis exists in intestinal and extraintestinal forms. The initial targets of intestinal amoebiasis are the cecum, appendix, colon, and rectum. The amoeba secretes enzymes that dissolve tissues, and it actively penetrates deeper layers of the mucosa, leaving erosive ulcerations **(figure 20.10*d*)**. This phase is marked by dysentery (bloody, mucus-filled stools), abdominal pain, fever, diarrhea, and weight loss. The most life-threatening manifestations of intestinal infection are hemorrhage, perforation, appendicitis, and tumorlike growths called amoebomas. Lesions in the mucosa of the colon have a characteristic flasklike shape.

Extraintestinal infection occurs when amoebas invade the viscera of the peritoneal cavity. The most common site of invasion is the liver. Here, abscesses containing necrotic tissue and trophozoites develop and cause amoebic hepatitis. Another rarer complication is pulmonary amoebiasis. Other infrequent targets of infection are the spleen, adrenals, kidney, skin, and brain. Severe forms of the disease result in about a 10% fatality rate.

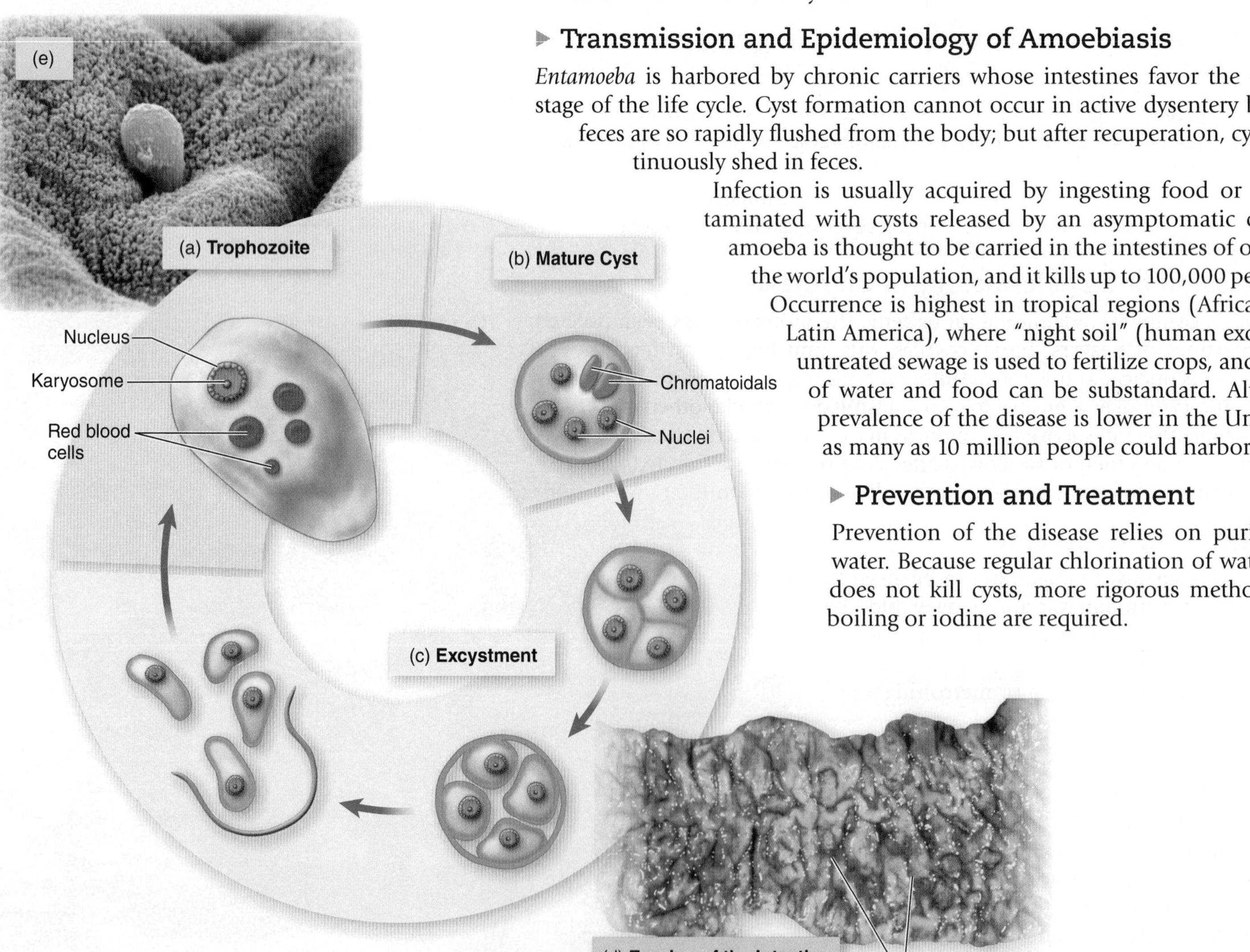

Figure 20.10 ***Entamoeba histolytica.*** **(a)** A trophozoite containing a single nucleus, a karyosome, and red blood cells. **(b)** A mature cyst with four nuclei and two blocky chromatoidals. **(c)** Stages in excystment. Divisions in the cyst create four separate cells, or metacysts, that differentiate into trophozoites and are released. **(d)** Intestinal amoebiasis and dysentery of the cecum. Red patches are sites of amoebic damage to the intestinal mucosa. **(e)** Trophozoite of *Entamoeba histolytica*. Note the fringe of very fine pseudopods it uses to invade and feed on tissue.

Transmission and Epidemiology of Amoebiasis

Entamoeba is harbored by chronic carriers whose intestines favor the encystment stage of the life cycle. Cyst formation cannot occur in active dysentery because the feces are so rapidly flushed from the body; but after recuperation, cysts are continuously shed in feces.

Infection is usually acquired by ingesting food or drink contaminated with cysts released by an asymptomatic carrier. The amoeba is thought to be carried in the intestines of one-tenth of the world's population, and it kills up to 100,000 people a year. Occurrence is highest in tropical regions (Africa, Asia, and Latin America), where "night soil" (human excrement) or untreated sewage is used to fertilize crops, and sanitation of water and food can be substandard. Although the prevalence of the disease is lower in the United States, as many as 10 million people could harbor the agent.

Prevention and Treatment

Prevention of the disease relies on purification of water. Because regular chlorination of water supplies does not kill cysts, more rigorous methods such as boiling or iodine are required.

Disease Table 20.3 Chronic Diarrhea

Causative Organism(s)	Enteroaggregative *E. coli* (EAEC)	*Cyclospora cayetanensis*	*Giardia lamblia*	*Entamoeba histolytica*
Most Common Modes of Transmission	Vehicle (food, water), fecal-oral	Fecal-oral, vehicle	Vehicle, fecal-oral, direct and indirect contact	Vehicle, fecal-oral
Virulence Factors	?	Invasiveness	Attachment to intestines alters mucosa	Lytic enzymes, induction of apoptosis, invasiveness
Culture/Diagnosis	Difficult to distinguish from other *E. coli*	Stool examination, PCR	Stool examination, ELISA	Stool examination, ELISA, serology
Prevention	?	Washing, cooking food, personal hygiene	Water hygiene, personal hygiene	Water hygiene, personal hygiene
Treatment	None, or ciprofloxacin	TMP-SMZ	Tinidazole, metronidazole	Metronidazole or tinidazole, followed by iodoquinol or paromomycin
Fever Present?	No	Usually	Not usually	Yes
Blood in Stool?	Sometimes, mucus also	No	No, mucus present (greasy and malodorous)	Yes
Distinctive Features	Chronic in the malnourished	–	Frequently occurs in backpackers, campers	–

Effective treatment usually involves the use of drugs such as iodoquinol, which acts in the feces, and metronidazole (Flagyl) or chloroquine, which work in the tissues. Dehydroemetine is used to control symptoms, but it will not cure the disease. Other drugs are given to relieve diarrhea and cramps, while lost fluid and electrolytes are replaced by oral or intravenous therapy. Infection with *E. histolytica* provokes antibody formation against several antigens, but permanent immunity is unlikely and reinfection can occur.

Tooth and Gum Infections

It is difficult to pinpoint exactly when the "normal biota biofilm" described for the oral environment becomes a "pathogenic biofilm." If left undisturbed, the biofilm structure eventually contains anaerobic bacteria that can damage the soft tissues and bones (referred to as the periodontium) surrounding the teeth. Also, the introduction of carbohydrates to the oral cavity can result in breakdown of hard tooth structure (the dentition) due to the production of acid by certain oral streptococci in the biofilm. These two separate circumstances are discussed here.

Dental Caries (Tooth Decay)

Dental caries is the most common infectious disease of human beings. The process involves the dissolution of solid tooth surface due to the metabolic action of bacteria. (**Figure 20.11** depicts the structure of a tooth.) The symptoms are often not noticeable but range from minor disruption in the outer (enamel) surface of the tooth to complete destruction of the enamel and then destruction

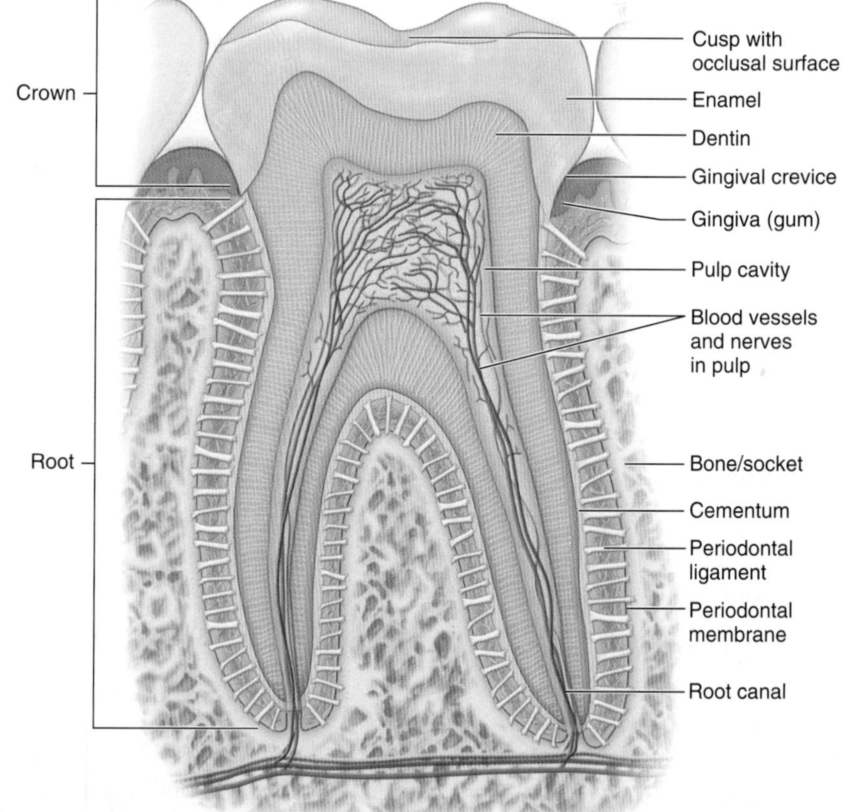

Figure 20.11 The anatomy of a tooth.

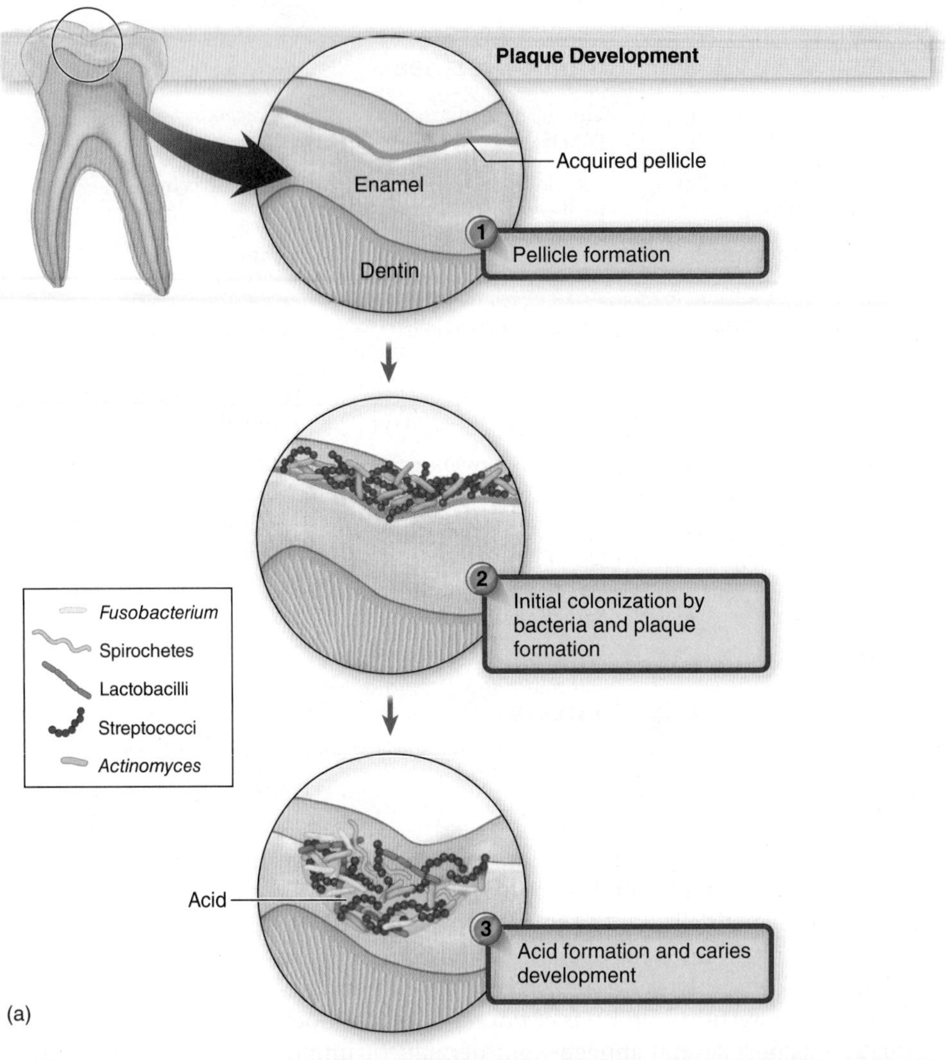

Figure 20.12 Stages in plaque development and cariogenesis. **(a)** A microscopic view of pellicle and plaque formation, acidification, and destruction of tooth enamel. **(b)** Progress and degrees of cariogenesis.

Disease Table 20.4 Dental Caries

Causative Organism(s)	*Streptococcus mutans*, *Scardovia wiggsiae*, others
Most Common Modes of Transmission	Direct contact
Virulence Factors	Adhesion, acid production
Culture/Diagnosis	–
Prevention	Oral hygiene, fluoride supplementation
Treatment	Removal of diseased tooth material

of deeper layers **(figure 20.12)**. Deeper lesions can result in infection to the soft tissue inside the tooth, called the pulp, which contains blood vessels and nerves. These deeper infections lead to pain, referred to as a "toothache."

▸ Causative Agent

An oral alpha-hemolytic streptococcus, *Streptococcus mutans*, seems to be the main cause of dental caries, although a mixed species consortium, consisting of other *Streptococcus* species and some lactobacilli, is probably the best route to caries. A specific condition called early childhood caries may also be caused by a newly identified species, *Scardovia wiggsiae*. Note that in the absence of dietary carbohydrates bacteria do not cause decay.

▶ Pathogenesis and Virulence Factors

In the presence of sucrose and, to a lesser extent, other carbohydrates, *S. mutans* and other streptococci produce sticky polymers of glucose called fructans and glucans. These adhesives help bind them to the smooth enamel surfaces and contribute to the sticky bulk of the plaque biofilm **(figure 20.13).** If mature plaque is not removed from sites that readily trap food, it can result in a carious lesion. This is due to the action of the streptococci and other bacteria that produce acid as they ferment the carbohydrates. If the acid is immediately flushed from the plaque and diluted in the mouth, it has little effect. However, in the denser regions of plaque, the acid can accumulate in direct contact with the enamel surface and lower the pH to below 5, which is acidic enough to begin to dissolve (decalcify) the calcium phosphate of the enamel in that spot. This initial lesion can remain localized in the enamel and can be repaired with various inert materials (fillings). Once the deterioration has reached the level of the dentin, tooth destruction speeds up and the tooth can be rapidly destroyed.

Figure 20.13 The microscopic and macroscopic appearance of plaque. Disclosing tablets containing vegetable dye stain heavy plaque accumulations at the junction of the tooth and gingiva and other parts of the tooth. The blown-up image is a scanning electron micrograph of the plaque biofilm with long filamentous forms and "corn cobs" that are mixed bacterial aggregates.

▶ Transmission and Epidemiology

The bacteria that cause dental caries are transmitted to babies and children by their close contacts, especially the mother or closest caregiver. There is evidence for transfer of oral bacteria between children in day care centers, as well.

▶ Culture and Diagnosis

Dental professionals diagnose caries based on the tooth condition. Culture of the lesion is not routinely performed.

▶ Prevention and Treatment

The best way to prevent dental caries is through dietary restriction of sucrose and other refined carbohydrates. Regular brushing and flossing to remove plaque are also important. Most municipal communities in the United States add trace amounts of fluoride to their drinking water, because fluoride, when incorporated into the tooth structure, can increase tooth (as well as bone) hardness. Fluoride can also encourage the remineralization of teeth that have begun the demineralization process. These and other proposed actions of fluoride could make teeth less susceptible to decay. Fluoride is also added to toothpastes and mouth rinses and can be applied in gel form. Many European countries do not fluoridate their water due to concerns over additives in drinking water.

Treatment of a carious lesion involves removal of the affected part of the tooth (or the whole tooth in the case of advanced caries), followed by restoration of the tooth structure with an artificial material.

Periodontal Diseases

Periodontal disease is so common that 97% to 100% of the population has some manifestation of it by age 45. Most kinds are due to bacterial colonization and varying degrees of inflammation that occur in response to gingival damage.

Periodontitis

The initial stage of periodontal disease is **gingivitis,** the signs of which are swelling, loss of normal contour, patches of redness, and increased bleeding of the gums (gingiva). Spaces or pockets of varying depth also develop between the tooth and the gingiva. If this condition persists, a more serious disease called periodontitis results. The deeper involvement increases the size of the pockets and can cause bone

Disease Table 20.5 Periodontitis

Disease	Periodontitis
Causative Organism(s)	Polymicrobial community including some or all of *Tannerella forsythia, Aggregatibacter actinomycetemcomitans, Porphyromonas gingivalis,* others
Most Common Modes of Transmission	–
Virulence Factors	Induction of inflammation, enzymatic destruction of tissues
Culture/ Diagnosis	–
Prevention	Oral hygiene
Treatment	Removal of plaque and calculus, gum reconstruction, tetracycline, possibly anti-inflammatory treatments

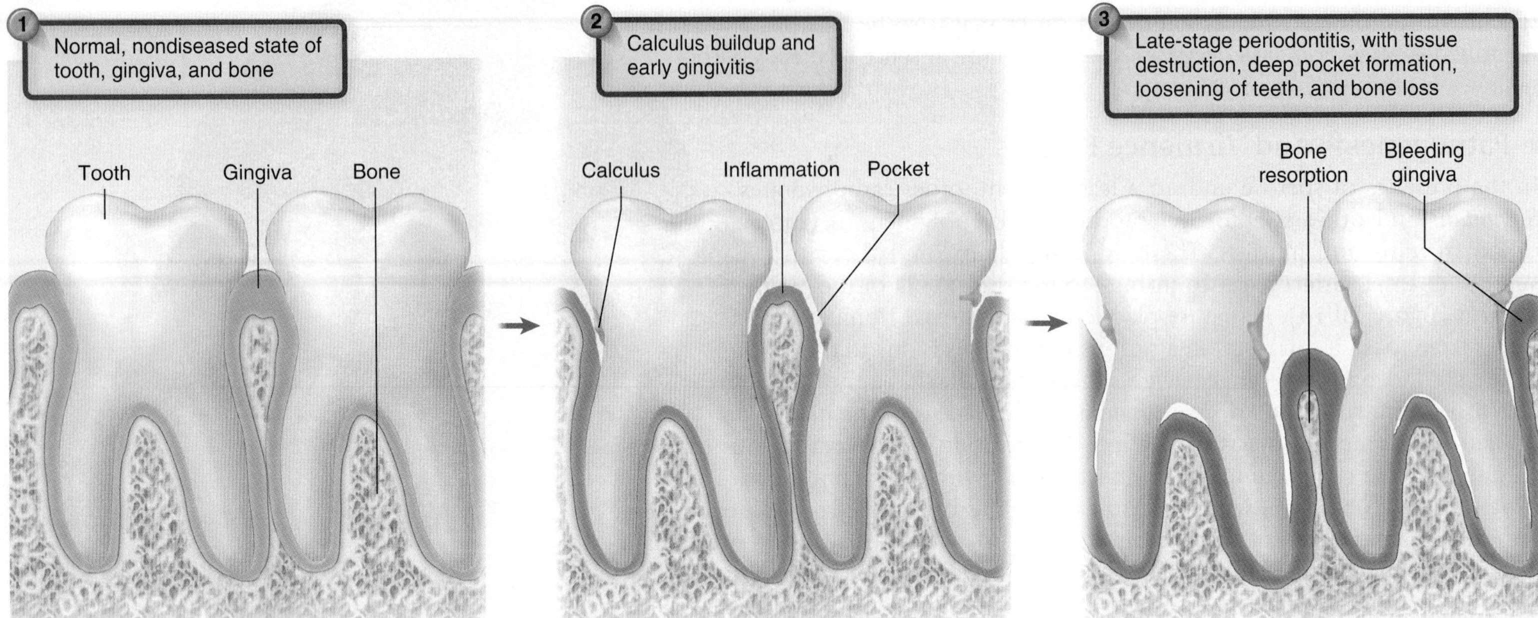

Figure 20.14 Stages in soft-tissue infection, gingivitis, and periodontitis.

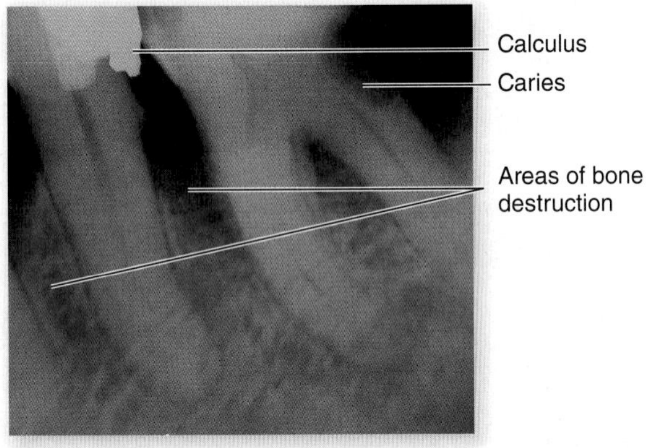

Figure 20.15 The nature of calculus. Radiograph of the lower premolar and molar, showing calculus on the top and a caries lesion on the right. Bony defects caused by periodontitis affect both teeth.

Disease Table 20.6 Mumps

Causative Organism(s)	Mumps virus (genus *Paramyxovirus*)
Most Common Modes of Transmission	Droplet contact
Virulence Factors	Spike-induced syncytium formation
Culture/Diagnosis	Clinical, fluorescent Ag tests, ELISA for Ab
Prevention	MMR live attenuated vaccine
Treatment	Supportive

resorption severe enough to loosen the tooth in its socket. If the condition is allowed to progress, the tooth can be lost **(figure 20.14).**

Causative Agent

Dental scientists stop short of stating that particular bacteria cause periodontal disease, because not all of the criteria for establishing causation have been satisfied. In fact, dental diseases (in particular, periodontal disease) provide an excellent model of disease mediated by communities of microorganisms rather than single organisms. When the polymicrobial biofilms consist of the right combination of bacteria, such as the anaerobes *Tannerella forsythia* (formerly *Bacteroides forsythus*), *Aggregatibacter actinomycetemcomitans, Porphyromonas gingivalis,* and perhaps *Fusobacterium* and spirochete species, the periodontal destruction process begins. The most common predisposing condition occurs when the plaque becomes mineralized (calcified) with calcium and phosphate crystals. This process produces a hard, porous substance called **calculus** above and below the gingival margin (edge) that can induce varying degrees of periodontal damage **(figure 20.15).** The presence of calculus leads to a series of inflammatory events that probably allow the bacteria to cause disease.

Most periodontal disease is treated by removal of calculus and plaque and maintenance of good oral hygiene. Often, surgery to reduce the depth of periodontal pockets is required. Antibiotic therapy, either systemic or applied in periodontal packings, may also be utilized.

Mumps

The word *mumps* is Old English for lump or bump. The symptoms of this viral disease are so distinctive that Hippocrates clearly characterized it in the 5th century BC as a self-limited, mildly epidemic illness associated with painful swelling at the angle of the jaw **(figure 20.16).**

Signs and Symptoms

After an average incubation period of 2 to 3 weeks, symptoms of fever, nasal discharge, muscle pain, and malaise develop. These may be followed by inflammation of the salivary glands (especially the parotids), producing the classic gopherlike swelling of the cheeks on one or both sides. Swelling of the gland is called parotitis, and it can cause considerable discomfort. Viral multiplication in salivary glands is followed by invasion of other organs, especially the testes, ovaries, thyroid gland, pancreas, meninges, heart, and kidney. Despite the invasion of multiple organs, the prognosis of most infections is complete, uncomplicated recovery with permanent immunity.

Complications in Mumps In 20% to 30% of young adult males, mumps infection localizes in the epididymis and testis, usually on one side only. The resultant syndrome of orchitis and epididymitis may be rather painful, but no permanent damage usually occurs.

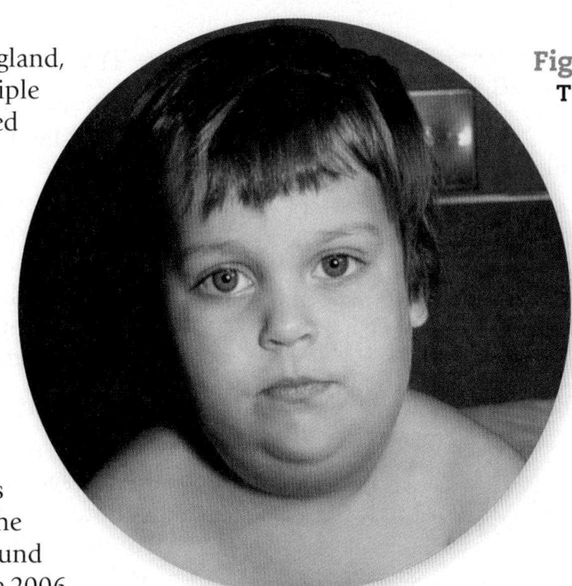

Figure 20.16 **The external appearance of swollen parotid glands in mumps (parotitis).**

▶ Transmission and Epidemiology of Mumps Virus

Humans are the exclusive natural hosts for the mumps virus. It is communicated primarily through salivary and respiratory secretions. Most cases occur in children under the age of 15, and as many as 40% are subclinical. Because lasting immunity follows any form of mumps infection, no long-term carrier reservoir exists in the population. The incidence of mumps had been reduced in the United States to around 300 cases per year. The incidence has become more unpredictable since 2006, though. In that year there were about 2,600 cases. The next 3 years saw cases in the low hundreds again, but then in 2010 there were more than 1,500 cases.

▶ Prevention and Treatment

The general pathology of mumps is mild enough that symptomatic treatment to relieve fever, dehydration, and pain is usually adequate. Vaccine recommendations call for a dose of MMR at 12 to 15 months and a second dose at 4 to 6 years. Health care workers and college students who haven't already had both doses are advised to do so.

NCLEX® PREP

4. Which of the following statements about mumps are true?
   a. The most common mode of transmission is airborne.
   b. The MMR vaccine is a live attenuated vaccine.
   c. Treatment for mumps is supportive.
   d. Mumps often results in sterility in males.
   e. both b and c

Gastritis and Gastric Ulcers

The curved cells of *Helicobacter* were first detected by J. Robin Warren in 1979 in stomach biopsies from ulcer patients. He and a partner, Barry J. Marshall, isolated the microbe in culture and even served as guinea pigs by swallowing a large inoculum to prove that it would cause gastric ulcers.

▶ Signs and Symptoms

Gastritis is experienced as sharp or burning pain emanating from the abdomen. Gastric ulcers are actual lesions in the mucosa of the stomach (gastric ulcers) or in the uppermost portion of the small intestine (duodenal ulcers). This condition is also called *peptic ulcers.* Severe ulcers can be accompanied by bloody stools, vomiting, or both. The symptoms are often worse at night, after eating, or under conditions of psychological stress.

The second most common cancer in the world is stomach cancer (although it has been declining in the United States), and ample evidence suggests that long-term infection with *H. pylori* is a major contributing factor.

▶ Causative Agent

Helicobacter pylori is a curved gram-negative rod, closely related to *Campylobacter,* which we studied earlier in this chapter.

▶ Pathogenesis and Virulence Factors

Once the bacterium passes into the gastrointestinal tract, it bores through the outermost mucus layer that lines the stomach epithelial tissue. Then it attaches to specific binding sites on the cells and entrenches itself.

Before the bacterium was discovered, spicy foods, high-sugar diets (which increase acid levels in the stomach), and psychological stress were considered to be the cause of gastritis and ulcers. Now it appears that these factors merely aggravate the underlying infection.

Disease Table 20.7 Gastritis and Gastric Ulcers

Causative Organism(s)	*Helicobacter pylori*
Most Common Modes of Transmission	?
Virulence Factors	Adhesins, urease
Culture/Diagnosis	Endoscopy, urea breath test, stool antigen test
Prevention	None
Treatment	Antibiotics plus acid suppressors (clarithromycin or metronidazole plus omeprazole or bismuth subsalicylate)

Transmission and Epidemiology

The mode of transmission of this bacterium remains a mystery. Studies have revealed that the pathogen is present in a large proportion of the human population. It occurs in the stomachs of 25% of healthy middle-age adults and in more than 60% of adults over 60 years of age. *H. pylori* is probably transmitted from person to person by the oral-oral or fecal-oral route. It seems to be acquired early in life and carried asymptomatically until its activities begin to damage the digestive mucosa. Because other animals are also susceptible to *H. pylori*, and even develop chronic gastritis, it has been proposed that the disease is a zoonosis transmitted from an animal reservoir. The bacterium has also been found in water sources.

Prevention and Treatment

The only preventive approaches available currently are those that diminish some of the aggravating factors just mentioned. Many over-the-counter remedies offer symptom relief; most of them act to neutralize stomach acid. The best treatment is a course of antibiotics augmented by acid suppressors. The antibiotics most prescribed are clarithromycin or metronidazole.

Hepatitis

When certain viruses infect the liver, they cause **hepatitis,** an inflammatory disease marked by necrosis of hepatocytes and a mononuclear response that swells and disrupts the liver architecture. This pathologic change interferes with the liver's excretion of bile pigments such as bilirubin into the intestine. When bilirubin, a greenish-yellow pigment, accumulates in the blood and tissues, it causes **jaundice,** a yellow tinge in the skin and eyes. The condition can be caused by a variety of different viruses, including cytomegalovirus and Epstein-Barr virus. The others are all called "hepatitis viruses" but only because they all can cause this inflammatory condition in the liver. They are quite different from one another. While there are some recently discovered hepatitis viruses, they are not yet well characterized so we will cover the five that are well understood, named Hepatitis A–E.

Note that noninfectious conditions can also cause inflammation and disease in the liver, including some autoimmune conditions, drugs, and alcohol overuse.

Hepatitis A and E Viruses

Hepatitis A virus (HAV) and **hepatitis E virus (HEV)** are both single-stranded nonenveloped RNA viruses. These two viruses are considered together since they are both transmitted through the fecal-oral route, and both cause relatively minor, self-limited hepatitis. The exception to this is when HEV infects pregnant women, in whom it causes a 15% to 25% fatality rate.

Signs and Symptoms

Most infections by these viruses are either subclinical or accompanied by vague, flulike symptoms. In more overt cases, the presenting symptoms may include jaundice and swollen liver. The viruses are not oncogenic (cancer causing), and in most everyone besides pregnant women, complete uncomplicated recovery results.

Transmission and Epidemiology

In general, the disease is associated with deficient personal hygiene and lack of public health measures. In countries with inadequate sewage control, most outbreaks are associated with fecally contaminated water and food. Most infections result from close institutional contact, unhygienic food handling, eating shellfish, sexual transmission, or travel to other countries.

Hepatitis A occasionally can be spread by blood or blood products, but this is the exception rather than the rule. In developing countries, children are the most common victims, because exposure to the virus tends to occur early in life, whereas in North America and Europe, more cases appear in adults. Because the virus is not carried chronically, the principal reservoirs are asymptomatic, short-term carriers (often children) or people with clinical disease.

Prevention and Treatment

Prevention of hepatitis A is based primarily on immunization. An inactivated viral vaccine (Havrix) has been in use since the mid-1990s. Short-term protection can be conferred by passive immune globulin. This treatment is useful for people who have come in contact with HAV-infected individuals, or who have eaten at a restaurant that was the source of a recent outbreak. It has also recently been discovered that administering Havrix after exposure can prevent symptoms. A combined hepatitis A/ hepatitis B vaccine, called Twinrix, is recommended for people who may be at risk for both diseases, such as people with chronic liver dysfunction, intravenous drug users, and anyone engaging in anal-oral intercourse. Travelers to areas with high rates of both diseases should obtain vaccine coverage as well. Hepatitis E has no vaccine.

No specific medicine is available for hepatitis A or E once the symptoms begin. Drinking lots of fluids and avoiding liver irritants such as aspirin or alcohol will speed recovery.

Hepatitis B Virus (and Hepatitis D virus)

Hepatitis B virus (HBV) is an enveloped DNA virus in the family *Hepadnaviridae.* Intact viruses are often called Dane particles. The genome is partly double-stranded and partly single-stranded.

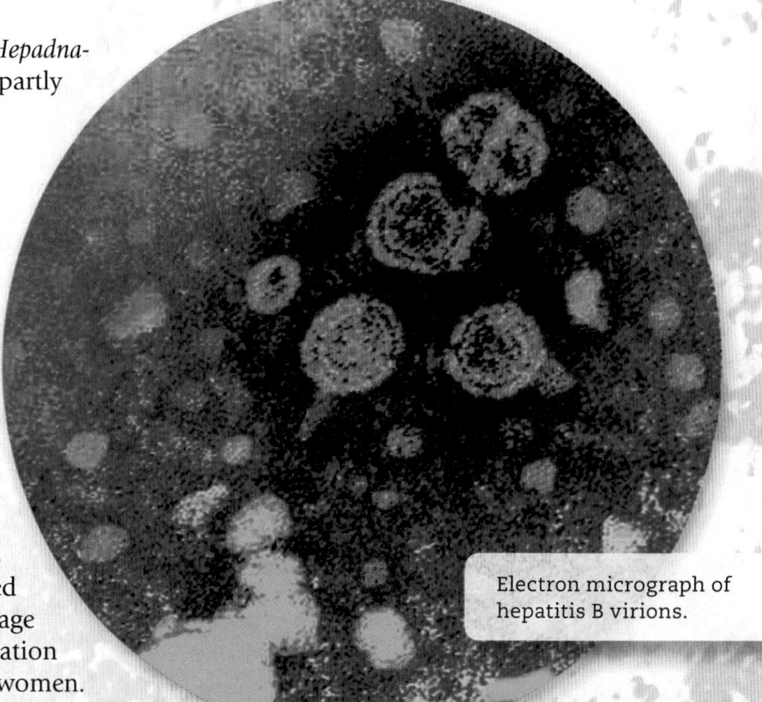

Electron micrograph of hepatitis B virions.

Signs and Symptoms

In addition to the direct damage to liver cells just outlined, the spectrum of hepatitis disease may include fever, chills, malaise, anorexia, abdominal discomfort, diarrhea, and nausea. Rashes may appear and arthritis may occur. Hepatitis B infection can be very serious, even life-threatening. A small number of patients develop glomerulonephritis and arterial inflammation. Complete liver regeneration and restored function occur in most patients; however, a small number of patients develop chronic liver disease in the form of necrosis or cirrhosis (permanent liver scarring and loss of tissue). In some cases, chronic HBV infection can lead to liver cancer.

Patients who become infected as children have significantly higher risks of long-term infection and disease. In fact, 90% of neonates infected at birth develop chronic infection, as do 30% of children infected between the ages of 1 and 5, but only 6% of persons infected after the age of 5. This finding is one of the major justifications for the routine vaccination of children. Also, infection becomes chronic more often in men than in women. The mortality rate is 15% to 25% for people with chronic infection. HBV is known to be a cause of liver cancer.

Some patients infected with hepatitis B are coinfected with a particle called the delta agent, sometimes also called a **hepatitis D** virus. This agent seems to be a defective RNA virus that cannot produce infection unless a cell is also infected with HBV. Hepatitis D virus invades host cells by using the same host cell as HBV does. When HBV infection is accompanied by the delta agent, the disease becomes more severe and is more likely to progress to permanent liver damage.

Pathogenesis and Virulence Factors

The hepatitis B virus enters the body through a break in the skin or mucous membrane or by injection into the bloodstream. Eventually, it reaches the liver cells (hepatocytes) where it multiplies and releases viruses into the blood during an incubation period of 4 to 24 weeks (7 weeks average). Surprisingly, the majority of those infected exhibit few overt symptoms and eventually develop an immunity to HBV, but some people experience the symptoms described earlier.

Transmission and Epidemiology

An important factor in the transmission pattern of hepatitis B virus is that it multiplies exclusively in the liver, which continuously seeds the blood with viruses. Electron microscopic studies have revealed up to 10^7 virions per milliliter of infected

blood. Even a minute amount of blood (a *millionth* of a milliliter) can transmit infection. The abundance of circulating virions is so high and the minimal dose so low that such simple practices as sharing a toothbrush or a razor can transmit the infection. HBV has also been detected in semen and vaginal secretions, and it can be transmitted by these fluids. Spread of the virus by means of close contact in families or institutions is also well documented. Vertical transmission is possible, and it predisposes the child to development of the carrier state and increased risk of liver cancer. It is sometimes known as *serum hepatitis.*

This virus is one of the major infectious concerns for health care workers. Needlesticks can easily transmit the virus, and therefore most workers are required to have the full series of HBV vaccinations. Unlike the more notorious HIV, HBV remains infective for days in dried blood, for months when stored in serum at room temperature, and for decades if frozen. Although it is not inactivated after 4 hours of exposure to 60°C, boiling for the same period can destroy it. Disinfectants containing chlorine, iodine, and glutaraldehyde show potent anti-hepatitis B activity.

▸ Culture and Diagnosis

Serological tests can detect either virus antigen or antibodies. Radioimmunoassay and ELISA testing permit detection of the important surface antigen (S antigen) of HBV very early in infection. Antibody tests are most valuable in patients who are negative for the antigen.

▸ Prevention and Treatment

The primary prevention for HBV infection is vaccination. The most widely used vaccines are recombinant, containing the pure surface antigen cloned in yeast cells. Vaccination is a must for medical and dental workers and students, patients receiving multiple transfusions, immunodeficient persons, and cancer patients. The vaccine is also now strongly recommended for all newborns as part of a routine immunization schedule. As just mentioned, a combined vaccine for HAV/HBV may be appropriate for certain people.

Passive immunization with hepatitis B immune globulin (HBIG) gives significant immediate protection to people who have been exposed to the virus through needle puncture, broken blood containers, or skin and mucosal contact with blood. Another group for whom passive immunization is highly recommended is neonates born to infected mothers.

Mild cases of hepatitis B are managed by symptomatic treatment and supportive care. Chronic infection can be controlled with recombinant human interferon, adefovir dipivoxil, lamivudine (another nucleotide analog best known for its use in HIV patients), or a newly approved drug called entecavir (Baraclude). All of these can help to stop virus multiplication and prevent liver damage in many but not all patients. None of the drugs are considered curative.

Hepatitis C Virus

Hepatitis C is sometimes referred to as the "silent epidemic" because more than 4 million Americans are infected with the virus, but it takes many years to cause noticeable symptoms. In the United States, its incidence fell between 1992 and 2003, but no further decreases have been seen since then. Liver failure from hepatitis C is one of the most common reasons for liver transplants in this country. Hepatitis C is an RNA virus in the *Flaviviridae* family. It used to be known as "non-A non-B" virus. It is usually diagnosed with a blood test for antibodies to the virus.

▸ Signs and Symptoms

People have widely varying experiences with this infection. It shares many characteristics of hepatitis B disease, but it is much more likely to become chronic. Of those infected, 75% to 85% will remain infected indefinitely. (In contrast, only about 6% of persons who acquire hepatitis B after the age of 5 will

Disease Table 20.8 Hepatitis

Causative Organism(s)	Hepatitis A or E virus	Hepatitis B virus	Hepatitis C virus
Most Common Modes of Transmission	Fecal-oral, vehicle	Parenteral (blood contact), direct contact (especially sexual), vertical	Parenteral (blood contact), vertical
Virulence Factors	–	Latency	Core protein suppresses immune function
Culture/Diagnosis	IgM serology	Serology (ELISA, radioimmunoassay)	Serology
Prevention	Hepatitis A vaccine or combined HAV/HBV vaccine	HBV recombinant vaccine	–
Treatment	Hep A: hepatitis A vaccine or immune globulin; hep E: immune globulin	Interferon, nucleoside analogs	(Pegylated) interferon, with or without ribavirin
Incubation Period	2–7 weeks	1–6 months	2–8 weeks

be chronically infected.) With HCV infection, it is possible to have severe symptoms without permanent liver damage, but it is more common to have chronic liver disease even if there are no overt symptoms. Cancer may also result from chronic hepatitis C virus (HCV) infection. Worldwide, HBV infection is the most common cause of liver cancer, but in the United States it is more likely to be caused by HCV.

▶ Transmission and Epidemiology

This virus is acquired in similar ways to HBV. It is more commonly transmitted through blood contact (both "sanctioned," such as in blood transfusions, and "unsanctioned," such as needle sharing by injecting drug users) than through transfer of other body fluids. Vertical transmission is also possible.

Before a test was available to test blood products for this virus, it seems to have been frequently transmitted through blood transfusions. Hemophiliacs who were treated with clotting factor prior to 1985 were infected with HCV at a high rate. Once blood began to be tested for HIV (in 1985) and screened for so-called "non-A non-B" hepatitis, the risk of contracting HCV from blood was greatly reduced.

▶ Prevention and Treatment

There is currently no vaccine for hepatitis C. The current treatment regimen is ribavirin plus a form of interferon called pegylated interferon. The treatments are not curative, but they may prevent or lessen damage to the liver. In 2011 two new protease inhibitor drugs were approved for treating Hepatitis C.

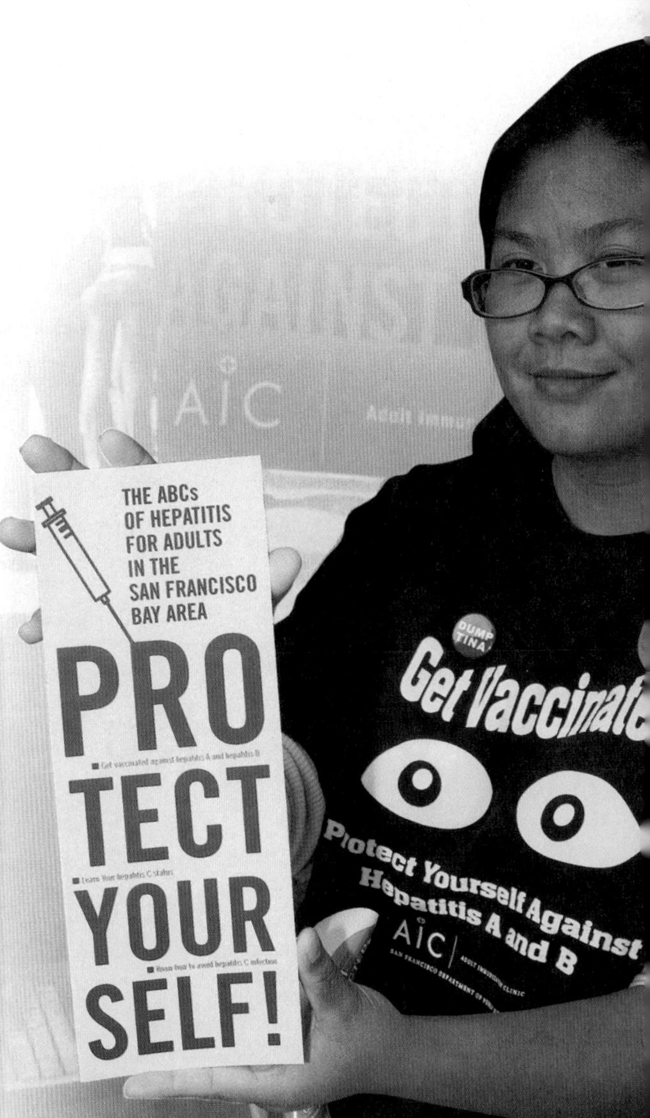

ASSESS YOUR PROGRESS

5. List the possible causative agents, modes of transmission, virulence factors, diagnostic techniques, and prevention/treatment for the highlighted condition, acute diarrhea.
6. Discuss important features of the conditions food poisoning and chronic diarrhea.
7. Discuss important features of the two categories of oral conditions: dental caries and periodontal diseases.
8. Identify the most important features of mumps, gastritis, and gastric ulcers.
9. Differentiate among the main types of hepatitis, and discuss the causative agents, mode of transmission, diagnostic techniques, prevention, and treatment of each.

Trained sushi chefs are skilled at detecting helminth infection in the raw fish they prepare.

20.4 Gastrointestinal Tract Diseases Caused by Helminths

Helminths that parasitize humans are amazingly diverse, ranging from barely visible roundworms (0.3 mm) to huge tapeworms (25 m long). In the introduction to these organisms in chapter 4, we grouped them into three categories: nematodes (roundworms), trematodes (flukes), and cestodes (tapeworms), and we discussed basic characteristics of each group. You may wish to review those sections before continuing. In this section, we examine the intestinal diseases caused by helminths. Although they can cause symptoms that might be mistaken for some of the diseases discussed elsewhere in this chapter, helminthic diseases are usually accompanied by an additional set of symptoms that arise from the host response to helminths. Worm infection usually provokes an increase in granular leukocytes called eosinophils, which have a specialized capacity to destroy worms. This increase, termed **eosinophilia,** is a hallmark of helminthic infection and is detectable in blood counts. If the following symptoms occur coupled with eosinophilia, helminthic infection should be suspected.

Helminthic infections may be acquired through the fecal-oral route or through penetration of the skin, but most of these organisms spend part of their lives in the intestinal tract. **Figure 20.17** depicts the four different types of life cycles of the helminths. While the worms are in the intestines, they can produce a gamut of intestinal symptoms. Some of them also produce symptoms outside of the intestines.

Clinical Considerations

There is a very wide variety of helminthic diseases that afflict humans (and animals, for that matter). We don't have space in this book to describe them all, but we will present two classic types of infections in some detail and provide you disease tables for several more.

Figure 20.17 Four basic helminth life and transmission cycles.

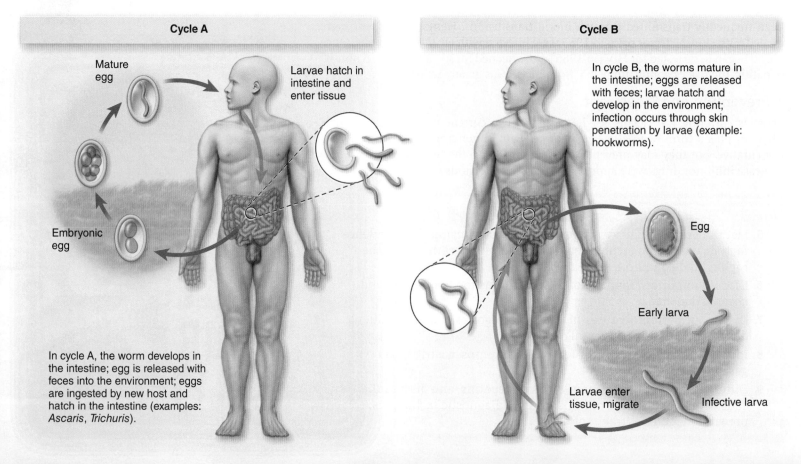

Cycle A

Mature egg

Larvae hatch in intestine and enter tissue

Embryonic egg

In cycle A, the worm develops in the intestine; egg is released with feces into the environment; eggs are ingested by new host and hatch in the intestine (examples: *Ascaris*, *Trichuris*).

Cycle B

In cycle B, the worms mature in the intestine; eggs are released with feces; larvae hatch and develop in the environment; infection occurs through skin penetration by larvae (example: hookworms).

Egg

Early larva

Larvae enter tissue, migrate

Infective larva

We talk about diagnosis, pathogenesis and prevention, and treatment of the helminths as a group in the next subsections. We'll then highlight one of the most common forms of helminthic disease, and finish with summaries of the others.

Pathogenesis and Virulence Factors in General

In most cases, helminths that infect humans do not have sophisticated virulence factors. They do have numerous adaptations that allow them to survive in their hosts. They have specialized mouthparts for attaching to tissues and for feeding, enzymes with which they liquefy and penetrate tissues, and a cuticle or other covering to protect them from host defenses. In addition, their organ systems are usually reduced to the essentials: getting food and processing it, moving, and reproducing. The damage they cause in the host is very often the result of the host's response to the presence of the invader.

Many helminths have more than one host during their lifetimes. If this is the case, the host in which the adult worm is found is called the **definitive host** (usually a vertebrate). Sometimes the actual definitive host is not the host usually used by the parasite but an accidental bystander. Humans often become the accidental definitive hosts for helminths whose normal definitive host is a cow, pig, or fish. Larval stages of helminths are found in intermediate hosts. Humans can serve as intermediate hosts, too. Helminths may require no intermediate host at all or may need one or more intermediate hosts for their entire life cycle.

Diagnosis in General

Diagnosis of almost all helminthic infections follows a similar series of steps. A differential blood count showing eosinophilia and serological tests indicating sensitivity to helminthic antigens all provide indirect evidence of worm infection. A history of travel to the tropics or immigration from those regions is also helpful, even if it occurred years ago, because some flukes and nematodes persist for decades. The

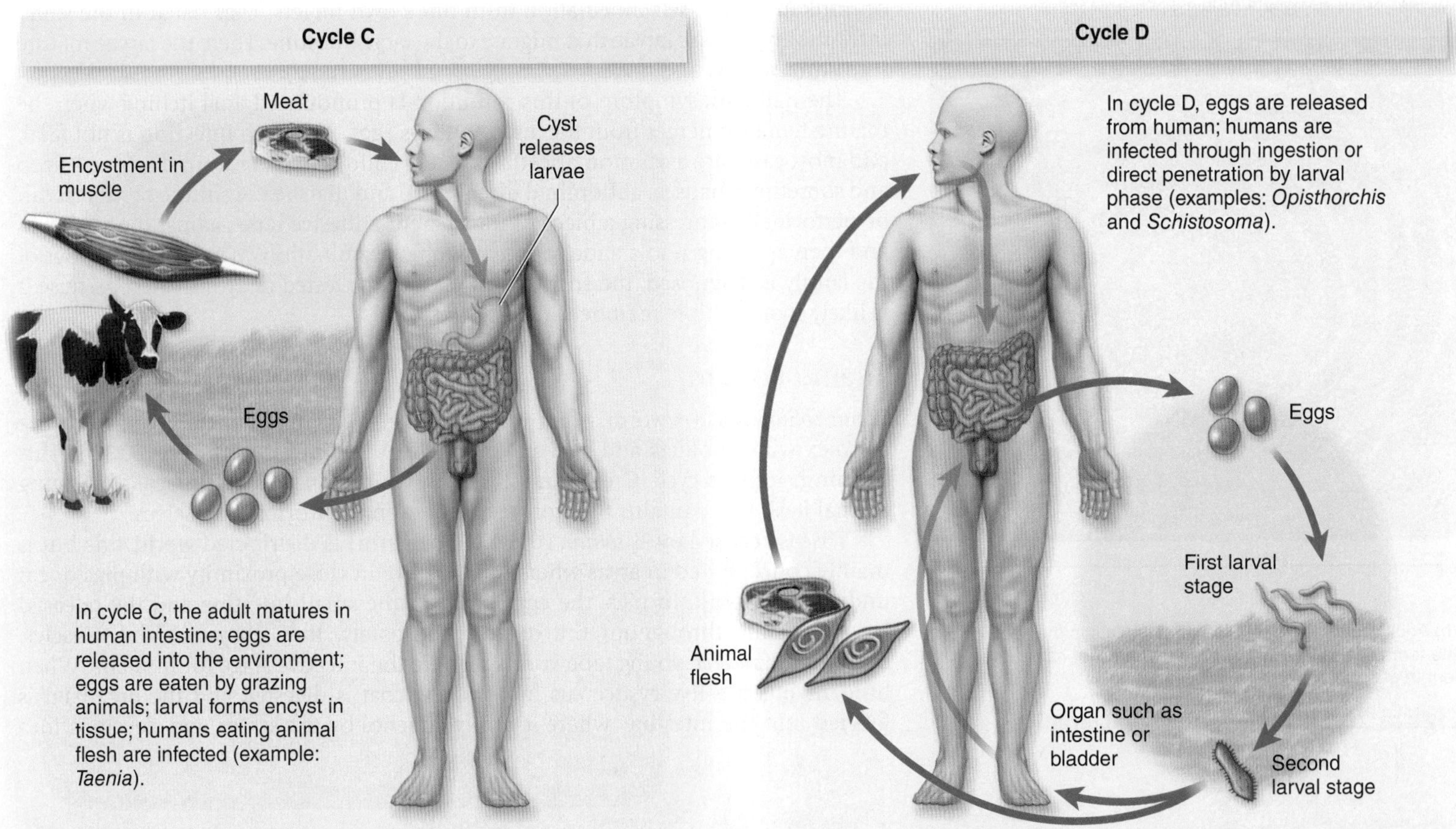
Cycle C
Meat
Encystment in muscle
Cyst releases larvae
Eggs
In cycle C, the adult matures in human intestine; eggs are released into the environment; eggs are eaten by grazing animals; larval forms encyst in tissue; humans eating animal flesh are infected (example: *Taenia*).
Cycle D
In cycle D, eggs are released from human; humans are infected through ingestion or direct penetration by larval phase (examples: *Opisthorchis* and *Schistosoma*).
Eggs
First larval stage
Animal flesh
Organ such as intestine or bladder
Second larval stage

NCLEX® PREP

5. Blood in the stool may occur in which of the following?
   a. *Salmonella* infection
   b. rotavirus infection
   c. *Clostridium difficile* infection
   d. *Shigella* infection
   e. b, c, and d
   f. a, c, and d

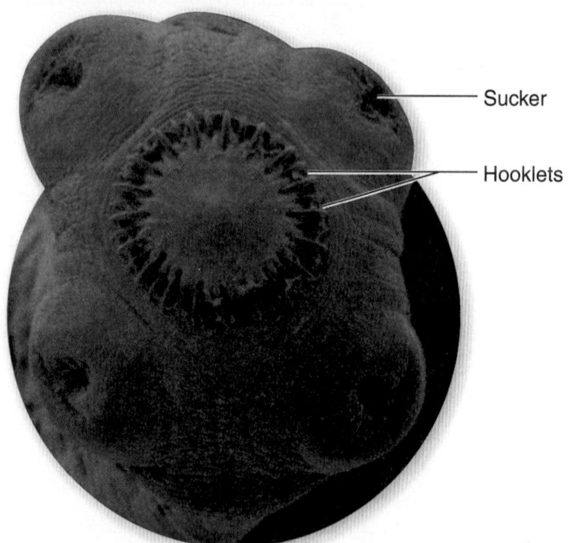

(a) Tapeworm scolex showing sucker and hooklets.

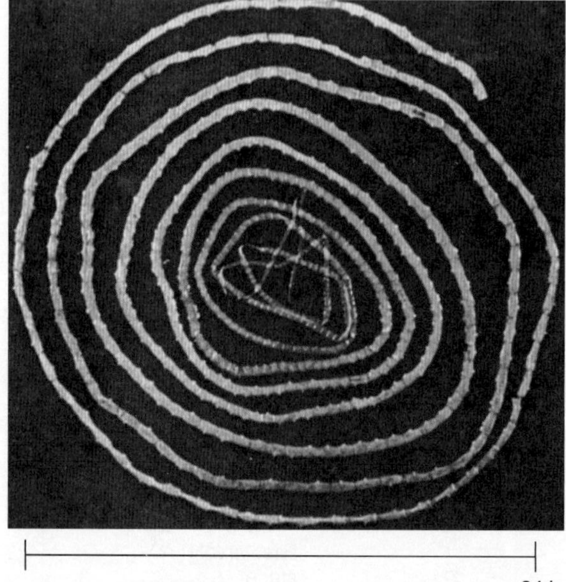

(b) Adult *Taenia saginata*. The arrow points to the scolex; the remainder of the tape, called the strobila, has a total length of 5 meters.

Figure 20.18 Tapeworm characteristics.

most definitive evidence, however, is the discovery of eggs, larvae, or adult worms in stools or other tissues. The worms are sufficiently distinct in morphology that positive identification can be based on any stage, including eggs. That said, not all of these diseases result in eggs or larval stages that can easily be found in stool.

Prevention and Treatment in General

None of these diseases has vaccines to prevent them. Preventive measures are aimed at minimizing human contact with the parasite or interrupting its life cycle.

Although several useful antihelminthic medications exist, the cellular physiology of the eukaryotic parasites resembles that of humans, and drugs toxic to them can also be toxic to us. Some antihelminthic drugs suppress a metabolic process that is more important to the worm than to the human. Others inhibit the worm's movement and prevent it from maintaining its position in a certain organ. Note that some helminths have developed resistance to the drugs used to treat them. In some cases, surgery may be necessary to remove worms or larvae.

HIGHLIGHT DISEASE

Disease: Intestinal Distress as the Primary Symptom

Both tapeworms and roundworms can infect the intestinal tract in such a way as to cause primary symptoms there. We will highlight one nematode and one tapeworm, and include the rest of the probable agents in our summary table.

Enterobius vermicularis

This nematode is often called the pinworm, or seatworm. It is the most common worm disease of children in temperate zones. The transmission of this roundworm is of the cycle A type. Freshly deposited eggs have a sticky coating that causes them to lodge beneath the fingernails and to adhere to fomites. Upon drying, the eggs become airborne and settle in house dust. Eggs are ingested from contaminated food or drink and from self-inoculation from one's own fingers. Eggs hatch in the small intestine and release larvae that migrate to the large intestine. There the larvae mature into adult worms and mate.

The hallmark symptom of this condition is pronounced anal itching when the mature female emerges from the anus and lays eggs. Although infection is not fatal, and most cases are asymptomatic, the afflicted child can suffer from disrupted sleep and sometimes nausea, abdominal discomfort, and diarrhea. A simple rapid test can be performed by pressing a piece of transparent adhesive tape against the anal skin and then applying it to a slide for microscopic examination. When one member of the family is diagnosed, the entire family should be tested and/or treated because it is likely that multiple members are infected.

Taenia solium

Taenia solium is a tapeworm. Adult worms are usually around 5 meters long and have a scolex with hooklets and suckers to attach to the intestine **(figure 20.18)**. This helminth follows cycle C in figure 20.17, in which humans are infected by eating animal flesh that contains the worm eggs, or even the worms themselves.

Disease caused by *T. solium* (the pig tapeworm) is distributed worldwide but is mainly concentrated in areas where humans live in close proximity with pigs or eat undercooked pork. In pigs, the eggs hatch in the small intestine and the released larvae migrate throughout the organs. Ultimately, they encyst in the muscles, becoming *cysticerci*, young tapeworms that are the infective stage for humans. When humans ingest a live cysticercus in pork, the coat is digested and the organism is flushed into the intestine, where it firmly attaches by the scolex and develops into an adult tapeworm. Infection with *T. solium* can take another form when humans ingest the tapeworm eggs rather than cysticerci. Although humans are not the usual intermediate hosts, the eggs can still hatch in the intestine, releasing tapeworm larvae that migrate to all tissues. They form bladderlike sacs throughout the body that can cause serious damage.

For such a large organism, it is remarkable how few symptoms a tapeworm causes. Occasionally, a patient discovers proglottids in his or her stool, and some patients complain of vague abdominal pain and nausea.

Other tapeworms of the genus *Taenia* infect humans. One of them is the beef tapeworm, *Taenia saginata*. It usually causes similar general symptoms of helminthic infection. But humans are not known to acquire *T. saginata* infection by ingesting the eggs.

Other Helminths Responsible for Intestinal Distress

Trichuris trichiura, the whipworm, has a cycle A lifestyle. Trichuriasis has its highest incidence in areas of the tropics and subtropics that have poor sanitation. Symptoms of this infection may include localized hemorrhage of the bowel caused by worms burrowing and piercing intestinal mucosa. This can also provide a portal of entry for secondary bacterial infection. Heavier infections can cause dysentery, loss of muscle tone, and rectal prolapse, which can prove fatal in children.

The tapeworm *Diphyllobothrium latum* has an intermediate host in fish. It follows cycle C just as *Taenia solium* does. It is common in the Great Lakes, Alaska, and Canada. Humans are its definitive host. It develops in the intestine and can cause long-term symptoms. It can be transmitted in raw food such as sushi and sashimi made from salmon.

Hymenolepis species are small tapeworms and are the most common human tapeworm infections in the world. They follow cycle C. There are two species: *Hymenolepis nana*, known as the dwarf tapeworm because it is only 15 to 40 mm in length, and *H. diminuta*, the rat tapeworm, which is usually 20 to 60 cm in length as an adult.

Disease Table 20.9 Intestinal Distress

Causative Organism(s)	*Enterobius vermicularis* (pinworm)	*Taenia solium* (pork tapeworm)	*Trichuris trichiura* (whipworm)	*Diphyllobothrium latum* (fish tapeworm)	*Hymenolepis nana* and *H. diminuta*
Most Common Modes of Transmission	Cycle A: vehicle (food, water), fomites, self-inoculation	Cycle C: vehicle (pork), fecal-oral	Cycle A: vehicle (soil), fecal-oral	Cycle C: vehicle (seafood)	Cycle C: vehicle (ingesting insects), fecal-oral
Virulence Factors	–	–	Burrowing and invasiveness	Vitamin B_{12} usage	–
Culture/Diagnosis	Adhesive tape + microscopy	Blood count, serology, egg or worm detection	Blood count, serology, egg or worm detection	Blood count, serology, egg or worm detection	Blood count, serology, egg or worm detection
Prevention	Hygiene	Cook meat, avoid pig feces	Hygiene, sanitation	Cook meat	Hygienic environment
Treatment	Mebendazole, piperazine	Praziquantel	Mebendazole	Praziquantel	Praziquantel
Distinctive Features	Common in United States	Tapeworm; intermediate host is pigs	Humans sole host	Large tapeworm; anemia	Most common tapeworm infection

Disease Table 20.10 Intestinal Distress Plus Migratory Symptoms

Causative Organism(s)	*Ascaris lumbricoides* (intestinal roundworm)	*Necator americanus and Ancylostoma duodenale* (hookworms)	*Strongyloides stercoralis* (threadworm)
Most Common Modes of Transmission	Cycle A: vehicle (soil/fecal-oral), fomites, self-inoculation	Cycle B: vehicle (soil), fomite	Cycle B: vehicle (soil), fomite
Virulence Factors	Induction of hypersensitivity, adult worm migration, abdominal obstruction	Induction of hypersensitivity, adult worm migration, abdominal obstruction	Induction of hypersensitivity, adult worm migration, abdominal obstruction
Culture/Diagnosis	Blood count, serology, egg or worm detection	Blood count, serology, egg or worm detection	Blood count, serology, egg or worm detection
Prevention	Hygiene	Sanitation	Sanitation
Treatment	Albendazole	Albendazole	Ivermectin or thiabendazole
Distinctive Features	1 billion persons infected	Penetrates skin, serious intestinal symptoms	Penetrates skin, severe for immunocompromised

Disease Table 20.11 Muscle and Neurological Symptoms

Causative Organism(s)	*Trichinella* species
Most Common Modes of Transmission	Vehicle (food)
Virulence Factors	–
Culture/Diagnosis	Serology combined with clinical picture; muscle biopsy
Prevention	Cook meat
Treatment	Mebendazole, steroids
Distinctive Features	Brain and heart involvement can be fatal

Disease: Intestinal Distress Accompanied by Migratory Symptoms

A diverse group of helminths enter the body as larvae or eggs, mature to the worm stage in the intestine, and then migrate into the circulatory and lymphatic systems, after which they travel to the heart and lungs, migrate up the respiratory tree to the throat, and are swallowed. This journey returns the mature worms to the intestinal tract where they then take up residence. All of these conditions, in addition to causing symptoms in the digestive tract, may induce inflammatory reactions along their migratory routes, resulting in eosinophilia and, during their lung stage, pneumonia. Three different examples of this type of infection appear in **Disease Table 20.10**.

Trichinosis: Muscle and Neurological Symptoms

Trichinosis is an infection transmitted by eating pork (and sometimes other wildlife) with the cysts of *Trichinella* species embedded in the meat **(figure 20.19).** The life cycle of this nematode is spent entirely within the body of a mammalian host such as a pig, bear, cat, dog, or rat. The disease cannot be transmitted from one human to another except in the event of cannibalism.

Figure 20.19 ***Trichinella*** **cysts embedded in pork muscle.**

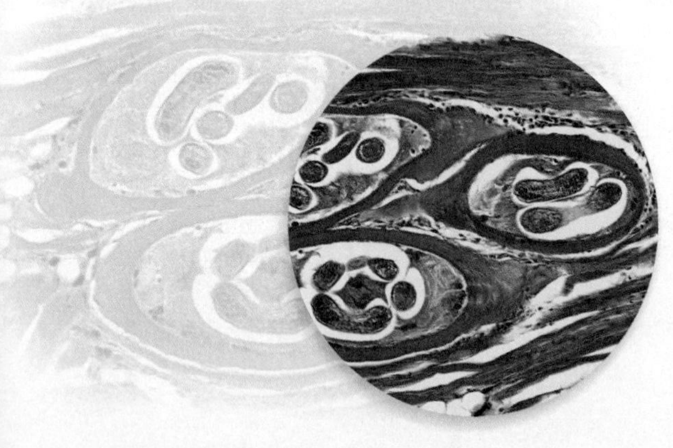

Schistosomiasis: Liver Disease

When liver swelling or malfunction is accompanied by eosinophilia, **schistosomiasis** should be suspected. Schistosomiasis has afflicted humans for thousands of years. The disease described here is caused by the blood flukes *Schistosoma mansoni* or *S. japonicum*, species that are morphologically and geographically distinct but share similar life cycles, transmission methods, and general disease manifestations. It is one of the few infectious agents that can invade intact skin.

Another species called *Schistosoma haematobium* causes disease in the bladder.

▸ Signs and Symptoms

The most severe consequences associated with chronic infection are hepatomegaly, liver disease, and splenomegaly. Occasionally, eggs from the worms are carried into the central nervous system and heart, and create a severe granulomatous response. Adult flukes can live for many years and, by eluding the immune defenses, cause a chronic affliction.

▶ Causative Agent

Schistosomes are trematodes, or flukes (see chapter 4), but they are more cylindrical than flat (figure 20.19). They are often called blood flukes. Humans are the definitive hosts for the blood fluke, and snails are the intermediate host.

▶ Pathogenesis and Virulence Factors

This parasite is clever indeed. Once inside the host, it coats its outer surface with proteins from the host's bloodstream, basically "cloaking" itself from the host defense system. This coat reduces its surface antigenicity and allows it to remain in the host indefinitely.

▶ Transmission and Epidemiology

The life cycle of the schistosome is of the "D" type, and is very complex (**figure 20.20**). The cycle begins when infected humans release eggs into irrigated fields or ponds, either by deliberate fertilization with excreta or by defecating or urinating directly into the water.

The disease is endemic to 74 countries located in Africa, South America, the Middle East, and the Far East. Schistosomiasis (including the urinary tract form) is the second most prominent parasitic disease after malaria, probably affecting 200 million people at any one time worldwide.

Disease Table 20.12 Liver Disease

Causative Organism(s)	*Schistosoma mansoni, S. japonicum*
Most Common Modes of Transmission	Cycle D: vehicle (contaminated water)
Virulence Factors	Antigenic "cloaking"
Culture/ Diagnosis	Identification of eggs in feces, scarring of intestines detected by endoscopy
Prevention	Avoiding contaminated vehicles
Treatment	Praziquantel
Distinctive Features	Penetrates skin, lodges in blood vessels of intestine, damages liver

ASSESS YOUR PROGRESS

10. Describe some distinguishing characteristics and commonalities seen in helminthic infections.

11. List four helminths that cause primarily intestinal symptoms, and identify which life cycle they follow and one unique fact about each one.

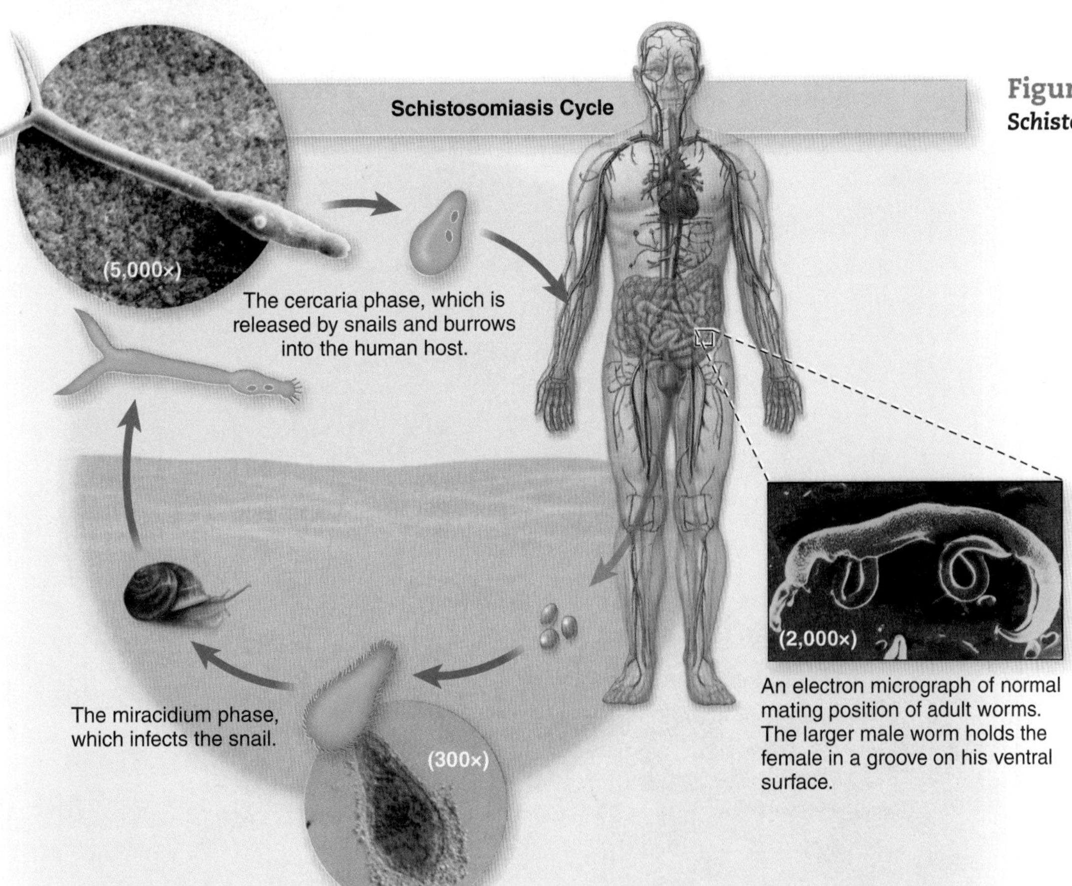
Schistosomiasis Cycle
(5,000×)
The cercaria phase, which is released by snails and burrows into the human host.
(2,000×)
An electron micrograph of normal mating position of adult worms. The larger male worm holds the female in a groove on his ventral surface.
The miracidium phase, which infects the snail.
(300×)

Figure 20.20 Stages in the life cycle of *Schistosoma*.

CASE FILE WRAP-UP

The patient described at the beginning of the chapter was found to have an abnormality of the liver on ultrasound, referred to as a "starry sky" appearance caused by pathologic changes of the organ. The ultrasound findings, coupled with elevated liver enzymes, the patient's symptoms (particularly jaundice), and serology results led to a diagnosis of hepatitis A. The patient likely contracted the disease while traveling in South America and consuming contaminated food or water.

There is no specific treatment for hepatitis A. Most patients recover fully within 3 to 6 months. Symptomatic treatment may involve hydration, antiemetics for nausea and vomiting, and rest. Avoidance of fatty foods and alcohol is important to avoid further irritation of the liver.

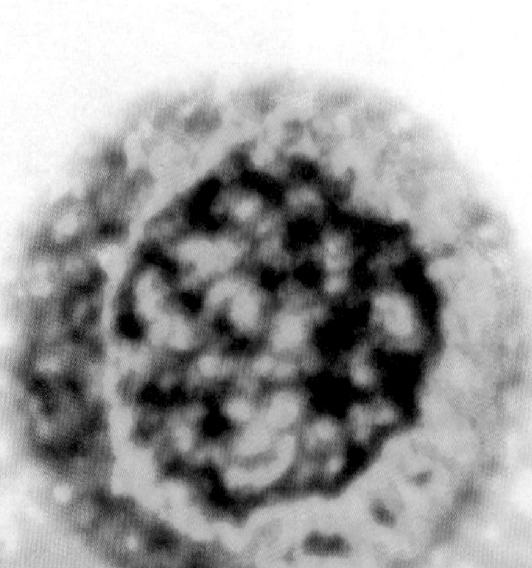

Summing Up

Taxonomic Organization Microorganisms Causing Disease in the GI Tract

Microorganism	Pronunciation	Location of Disease Table
Gram-positive endospore-forming bacteria		
Clostridium difficile	klos-trid″-ee-um dif″-i-sil	Acute diarrhea, p. 566
Clostridium perfringens	klos-trid″-ee-um purr-frinj′-unz	Acute diarrhea and/or vomiting, p. 569
Bacillus cereus	buh-sill′-us seer′-ee-uhs	Acute diarrhea and/or vomiting, p. 569
Gram-positive bacteria		
Streptococcus mutans	strep″-tuh-kok′-us mew′-tans	Dental caries, p. 574
Streptococcus sobrinus	strep″-tuh-kok′-us so-brin′-us	Dental caries, p. 574
Staphylococcus aureus	staf″-uh-lo-kok′-us are′-ee-us	Acute diarrhea and/or vomiting, p. 569
Scardovia wiggsiae	skar-doh″-vee-uh′ wig′-zee-ay	Dental caries, p. 574
Gram-negative bacteria		
Campylobacter jejuni	cam″-plo-bac′-ter juh-june′-ee	Acute diarrhea, p. 566
Helicobacter pylori	heel″-i-coe-back′-tur pie-lor′-ee	Gastritis/gastric ulcers, p. 578
Escherichia coli O157:H7	esh′-shur-eesh″ ee -uh-col′-eye	Acute diarrhea plus hemolytic syndrome, p. 566
Other *E. coli*		Acute diarrhea, p. 566 Chronic diarrhea, p. 573
Salmonella	sal′-muh-nel″-luh	Acute diarrhea, p. 566
Shigella	shi-gel′-luh	Acute diarrhea, p. 566
Vibrio cholerae	vib′-ree-oh col′-er-ee	Acute diarrhea, p. 566
Yersinia enterocolitica and *Y. pseudotuberculosis*	yur-sin′-ee-ah en-ter-oh-coe-lit′-i-cuh, yur-sin′-ee-ah soo′-doh-tuh-bur′-cue-loh″ sis	Acute diarrhea, p. 566
Tannerella forsythia, Aggregatibacter actinomycetemcomitans, Porphyromonas gingivalis, Treponema vincentii, Prevotella intermedia, Fusobacterium	tan-er-rel′-ah for-sye′-thee-ah, ag-gruh-ga″-ti-bac′-tur ack-tin′-oh-my-see″-tem-cah′-mi-tans, por-fuhr′-oh-moan″-as jin-ji-vall′-is, trep′-oh-nee-ma vin-cen′-tee-eye, prev′-oh-tell-ah in-ter-meed′-ee-ah, few′-zo-bac-teer′-ee′-um	Periodontal disease, p. 575
DNA viruses		
Hepatitis B virus	hep-uh-tie′-tis B vie′-russ	Hepatitis, p. 581
RNA viruses		
Hepatitis A virus	hep-uh-tie′-tis A vie′-russ	Hepatitis, p. 581
Hepatitis C virus	hep-uh-tie′-tis C vie′-russ	Hepatitis, p. 581
Hepatitis E virus	hep-uh-tie′-tis E vie′-russ	Hepatitis, p. 581
Mumps virus	mumps vie′-russ	Mumps, p. 576
Rotavirus	ro′-ta-vie′-russ	Acute diarrhea, p. 566
Protozoa		
Entamoeba histolytica	en″-tah-mee′-ba his″-toh-lit′-ih-kuh	Chronic diarrhea, p. 573
Cryptosporidium	crip′-toe-spor-id″-ee-um	Acute diarrhea, p. 566
Cyclospora	Sie″-clo-spor′-ah	Chronic diarrhea, p. 573
Giardia lamblia	jee-ar′-dee-ah lam′-blee-ah	Chronic diarrhea, p. 573
Helminths—nematodes		
Ascaris lumbricoides	a-scare′-is lum′-bri-coi″-dees	Intestinal distress plus migratory symptoms, p. 586
Enterobius vermicularis	en′-ter-oh″-bee-us ver-mick″-u-lar′-is	Intestinal distress, p. 585
Trichuris trichiura	tri-cur′-is trick-ee-ur′-ah	Intestinal distress, p. 585
Necator americanus and *Ancylostoma duodenale*	neh-cay′-ter a-mer′-i-can″-us, an′-sy-lo-sto″-mah dew-ah′-den-al″-ee	Intestinal distress plus migratory symptoms, p. 586
Strongyloides stercoralis	stron-jil-oid′-ees ster-cor-al′-is	Intestinal distress plus migratory symptoms, p. 586
Trichinella spp.	trick-i-nell′-ah	Muscle and neurological symptoms, p. 586
Helminths—cestodes		
Hymenolepis	hie′-men-oh″-lep-is	Intestinal distress, p. 585
Taenia solium	te′-ne-ah so′-lee-um	Intestinal distress, p. 585
Diphyllobothrium latum	dif′-oh-lo-both″-ree-um lah′-tum	Intestinal distress, p. 585
Helminths—trematodes		
Schistosoma mansoni and *S. japonicum*	shis′-toh-so-my″-a-sis man-sohn″-ee, ja-pawn′-i-cum	Helminthic liver disease, p. 587

Inside the Clinic

Understanding Jaundice

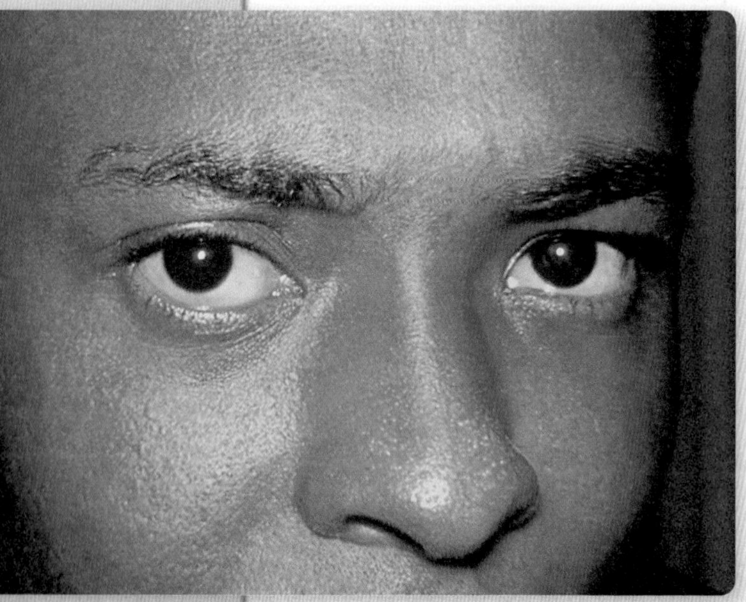

The first thing to understand about jaundice is that it is a symptom, not a disease. Jaundice is caused by elevated levels of bilirubin in the blood. Bilirubin is a chemical that remains in the blood following the breakdown and destruction of red blood cells. Iron is removed from hemoglobin prior to red blood cell destruction, and bilirubin is the chemical that remains. Bilirubin is a waste product that is normally removed from the blood by the liver.

Jaundice occurs under the following circumstances:

1. there is too much bilirubin for the liver to dispose of (i.e., hemolytic anemia, in which red blood cells are destroyed at too rapid a rate for the liver to keep up);
2. there is a problem in the liver that prevents the liver from being able to remove bilirubin; or
3. there is a blockage of the bile ducts that prevents bile and bilirubin from leaving the liver and traveling to the intestines (i.e., gallstones).

Jaundice can turn the sclerae (white portions of the eye) and the skin yellow. Stool may be clay-colored due to the lack of bilirubin that gives stool its brown color. Urine may become dark or even brown in color due to bilirubin being excreted in the urine. By far the worst symptom of jaundice is pruritus (itching) which can be very severe and has even caused some tormented patients to commit suicide.

Jaundice is associated with many conditions such as hepatitis, gallbladder and bile duct disorders, liver diseases (cirrhosis, drug-induced hepatitis), pancreatic cancer, pregnancy (caused by bile pooling in the liver), and newborn jaundice.

Treatment of jaundice is aimed at discovering and treating its underlying cause. For example, jaundice caused by gallstones may require removal of the gallbladder, while jaundice in newborns may be treated with phototherapy or with exchange transfusion.

Drugs that have been associated with the development of jaundice include antidepressants, antihypertensives, hormonal contraceptives, antibiotics, antifungals, antidiabetic medications, nonsteroidal anti-inflammatory drugs (NSAIDs), acetaminophen, and herbal remedies. Essentially, any drug may cause jaundice in susceptible individuals. It is important for patients with jaundice to disclose all medications they are taking, including herbs and over-the-counter (OTC) drugs.

Alcoholic hepatitis is a frequent cause of jaundice. The condition develops in individuals after a period of increased alcohol consumption. The condition may occur in patients with chronic alcoholic liver disease or alcoholic cirrhosis and can be fatal.

Jaundice is never normal. Any individual experiencing jaundice should be investigated to determine the underlying cause.

Infectious Diseases Affecting
The Gastrointestinal Tract

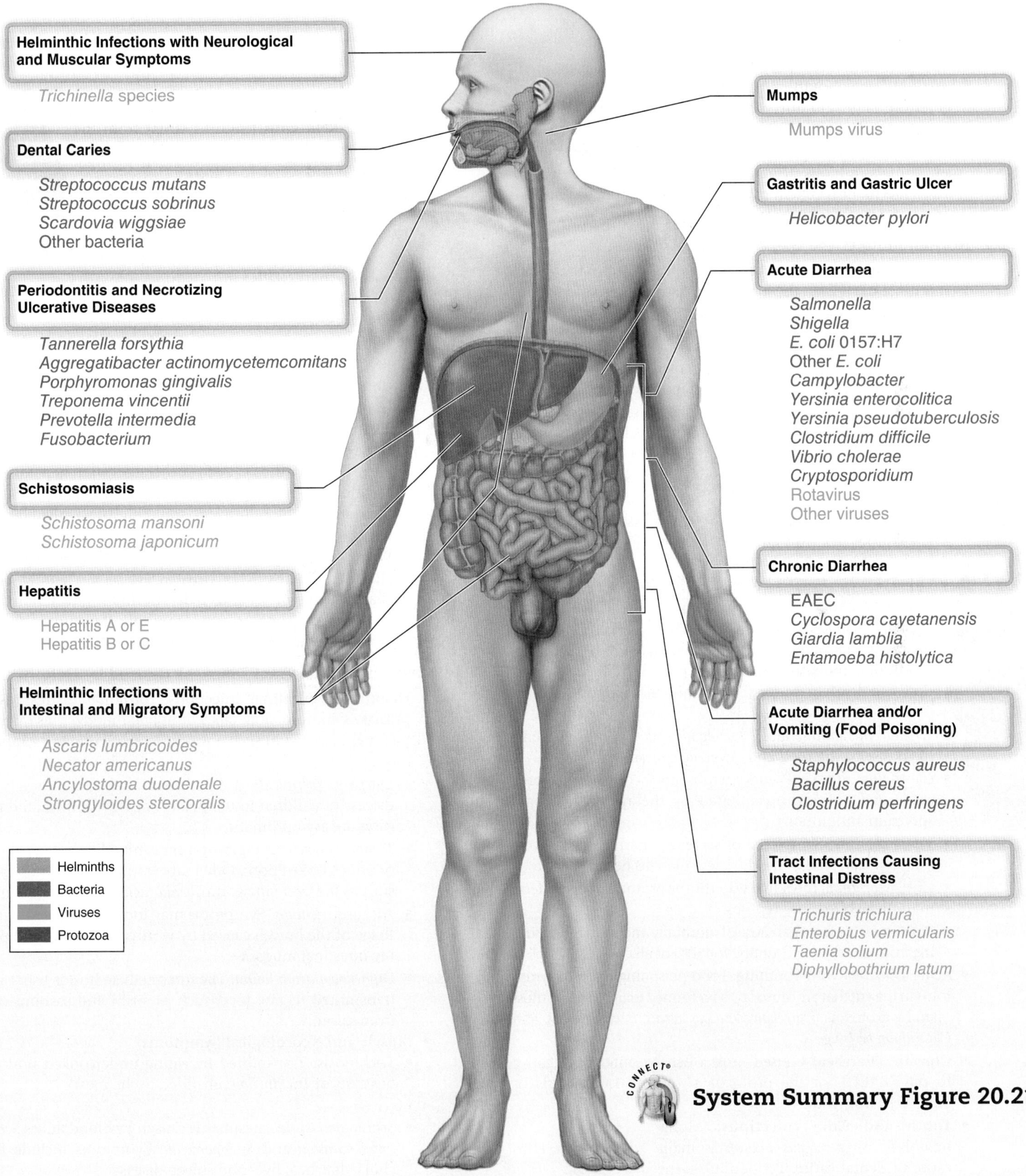

Helminthic Infections with Neurological and Muscular Symptoms

Trichinella species

Dental Caries

Streptococcus mutans
Streptococcus sobrinus
Scardovia wiggsiae
Other bacteria

Periodontitis and Necrotizing Ulcerative Diseases

Tannerella forsythia
Aggregatibacter actinomycetemcomitans
Porphyromonas gingivalis
Treponema vincentii
Prevotella intermedia
Fusobacterium

Schistosomiasis

Schistosoma mansoni
Schistosoma japonicum

Hepatitis

Hepatitis A or E
Hepatitis B or C

Helminthic Infections with Intestinal and Migratory Symptoms

Ascaris lumbricoides
Necator americanus
Ancylostoma duodenale
Strongyloides stercoralis

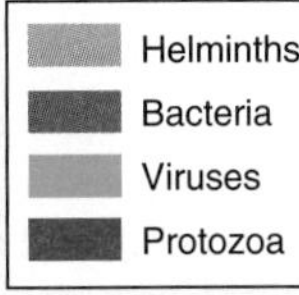

Mumps

Mumps virus

Gastritis and Gastric Ulcer

Helicobacter pylori

Acute Diarrhea

Salmonella
Shigella
E. coli 0157:H7
Other *E. coli*
Campylobacter
Yersinia enterocolitica
Yersinia pseudotuberculosis
Clostridium difficile
Vibrio cholerae
Cryptosporidium
Rotavirus
Other viruses

Chronic Diarrhea

EAEC
Cyclospora cayetanensis
Giardia lamblia
Entamoeba histolytica

Acute Diarrhea and/or Vomiting (Food Poisoning)

Staphylococcus aureus
Bacillus cereus
Clostridium perfringens

Tract Infections Causing Intestinal Distress

Trichuris trichiura
Enterobius vermicularis
Taenia solium
Diphyllobothrium latum

CONNECT® **System Summary Figure 20.21**

Chapter Summary

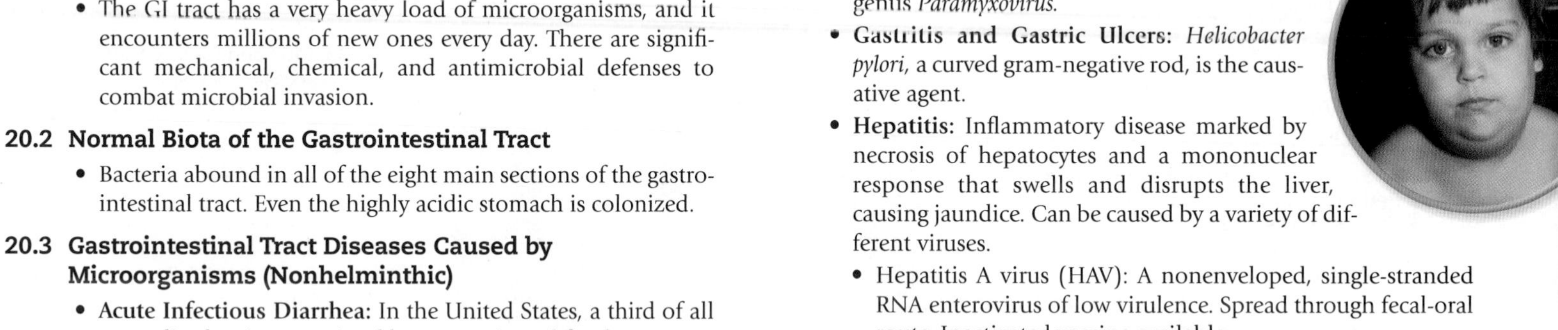

20.1 The Gastrointestinal Tract and Its Defenses

- The gastrointestinal (GI) tract is composed of eight main sections—the mouth, pharynx, esophagus, stomach, small intestine, large intestine, rectum, and anus, and four accessory organs—the salivary glands, liver, gallbladder, and pancreas.
- The GI tract has a very heavy load of microorganisms, and it encounters millions of new ones every day. There are significant mechanical, chemical, and antimicrobial defenses to combat microbial invasion.

20.2 Normal Biota of the Gastrointestinal Tract

- Bacteria abound in all of the eight main sections of the gastrointestinal tract. Even the highly acidic stomach is colonized.

20.3 Gastrointestinal Tract Diseases Caused by Microorganisms (Nonhelminthic)

- **Acute Infectious Diarrhea:** In the United States, a third of all acute diarrhea is transmitted by contaminated food.
  - *Salmonella:* The *Salmonella* species that causes gastrointestinal disease is divided into many serotypes, based on major surface antigens.
  - *Shigella* species: Frequent, watery, bloody stools, fever, and often intense abdominal pain. The bacterium *Shigella dysenteriae* produces a heat-labile exotoxin called shiga toxin.
  - *E. coli* O157:H7: This group of *E. coli* is referred to as enterohemorrhagic *E. coli,* or **EHEC.**
  - Other *E. coli:* Enterotoxigenic *E. coli* (traveler's diarrhea), enteroinvasive *E. coli,* enteropathogenic *E. coli,* and enteroaggregative *E. coli* also cause diarrhea.
  - *Campylobacter:* Frequent, watery stools, fever, vomiting, headaches, and severe abdominal pain. Infrequently, infection can lead to serious neuromuscular paralysis called *Guillain-Barré syndrome.*
  - *Yersinia enterocolitica* and *Y. pseudotuberculosis:* Both are agents of GI disease via food and beverage contamination.
  - *Clostridium difficile*: Pseudomembranous colitis (antibiotic-associated colitis), precipitated by therapy with broad-spectrum antibiotics.
  - *Vibrio cholerae:* Symptoms of secretory diarrhea and severe fluid loss can lead to death in less than 48 hours.
  - *Cryptosporidium:* Intestinal waterborne protozoan that infects mammals, birds, and reptiles.
  - Rotavirus: Primary viral cause of morbidity and mortality resulting from diarrhea, accounting for 50% of all cases.
- **Acute Diarrhea with Vomiting:** Food poisoning refers to symptoms in the gut that are caused by a preformed toxin. Caused most often by exotoxins from *Staphylococcus aureus, Bacillus cereus,* and *Clostridium perfringens.*
- **Chronic Diarrhea:** Caused most often by enteroaggregative *E. coli* (EAEC), or the protozoa *Cyclospora cayetanensis* or *Entamoeba histolytica.*
- **Tooth and Gum Infections:** Alpha-hemolytic *Streptococcus mutans* is main cause of dental caries. Periodontitis: The anaerobic bacteria *Tannerella forsythia, Aggregatibacter actinomycetemcomitans, Porphyromonas, Fusobacterium,* and spirochete species are causative agents.
- **Mumps:** Caused by an enveloped, single-stranded RNA virus (mumps virus) from the genus *Paramyxovirus.*
- **Gastritis and Gastric Ulcers:** *Helicobacter pylori,* a curved gram-negative rod, is the causative agent.
- **Hepatitis:** Inflammatory disease marked by necrosis of hepatocytes and a mononuclear response that swells and disrupts the liver, causing jaundice. Can be caused by a variety of different viruses.
  - Hepatitis A virus (HAV): A nonenveloped, single-stranded RNA enterovirus of low virulence. Spread through fecal-oral route. Inactivated vaccine available.
  - Hepatitis B virus (HBV): Enveloped DNA virus in the family *Hepadnaviridae.* Can be very serious, even life-threatening; some patients develop chronic liver disease in the form of necrosis or cirrhosis. Also associated with hepatocellular carcinoma. Some patients infected with hepatitis B are co-infected with the delta agent, sometimes also called hepatitis D virus. HBV transmitted by blood and other bodily fluids. Virus is major infectious concern for health care workers.
  - Hepatitis C virus: RNA virus in *Flaviviridae* family. Shares characteristics of hepatitis B disease, but is much more likely to become chronic. More commonly transmitted through blood contact than through other body fluids.

20.4 Gastrointestinal Tract Diseases Caused by Helminths

- **Helminthic Intestinal Infections: Intestinal distress as the primary symptom:** Both tapeworms and roundworms can infect the intestinal tract in such a way as to cause primary symptoms there.
  - *Enterobius vermicularis:* "Pinworm"; most common worm disease of children in temperate zones. Not fatal, and most cases are asymptomatic.
  - *Taenia solium:* This tapeworm transmitted to humans by raw or undercooked pork. Other tapeworms of the genus *Taenia,* such as the beef tapeworm *Taenia saginata,* infect humans.
  - *Trichuris trichiura:* Symptoms may include localized hemorrhage of the bowel, caused by worms burrowing and piercing intestinal mucosa.
  - *Diphyllobothrium latum:* The intermediate host is fish; can be transmitted in raw food such as sushi and sashimi made from salmon.
- **Muscle and Neurological Symptoms**
  - Trichinosis: Transmitted by eating undercooked pork that has cysts of *Trichinella* embedded in the meat.
- **Liver Disease**
  - *Schistosomiasis* in intestines is caused by blood flukes *Schistosoma mansoni* and *S. japonicum.* Symptoms include fever, chills, diarrhea, liver and spleen disease.

Multiple-Choice Questions Knowledge and Comprehension

Select the correct answer from the answers provided.

1. Food moves down the GI tract through the action of
   a. cilia.
   b. peristalsis.
   c. gravity.
   d. microorganisms.
2. Gastric ulcers are caused by
   a. *Treponema vincentii.*
   b. *Prevotella intermedia.*
   c. *Helicobacter pylori.*
   d. all of the above.
3. Which of these microorganisms is considered the most common cause of diarrhea in the United States?
   a. *E. coli*
   b. *Salmonella*
   c. *Campylobacter*
   d. *Shigella*
4. Which of these microorganisms is associated with Guillain-Barré syndrome?
   a. *E. coli*
   b. *Salmonella*
   c. *Campylobacter*
   d. *Shigella*
5. This hepatitis virus is an enveloped DNA virus.
   a. hepatitis A virus
   b. hepatitis B virus
   c. hepatitis C virus
   d. hepatitis E virus

Critical Thinking Application and Analysis

Critical thinking **is the ability to reason and solve problems using facts and concepts. These questions can be approached from a number of angles and, in most cases, they do not have a single correct answer.**

1. Chicken eggs are often used as incubators for virus culture and vaccine production because they are a sterile source of living cells. Is this always true? Can the sterility of the shelled egg be breached?
2. Why is it thought that the Shiga toxin found in *E. coli* originated in *Shigella,* and not vice versa?
3. Why is heating food contaminated with *Staphylococcus aureus* no guarantee that the associated food poisoning will be prevented?
4. What are some of the ways we can prevent or slow down the spread of helminthic diseases?
5. Which members of the population are most at risk for hepatitis C? Why?

Visual Connections Synthesis

This question connects previous images to a new concept.

1. **From chapter 11, figure 11.3*b*.** Imagine for a minute that the organism in this illustration is *E. coli* O157:H7. What would be one reason not to treat a patient having this infection with powerful antibiotics?

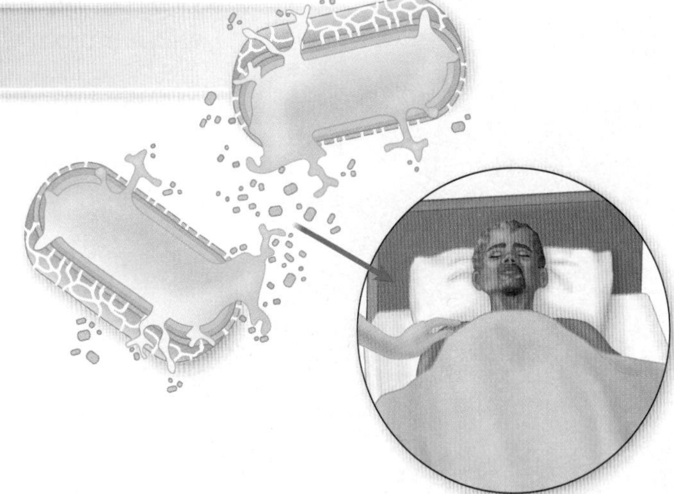

Outer membrane component causes fever, malaise, aches, and shock.

www.mcgrawhillconnect.com
Enhance your study of this chapter with study tools and practice tests. Also ask your instructor about the resources available through ConnectPlus, including the media-rich eBook, interactive learning tools, and animations.

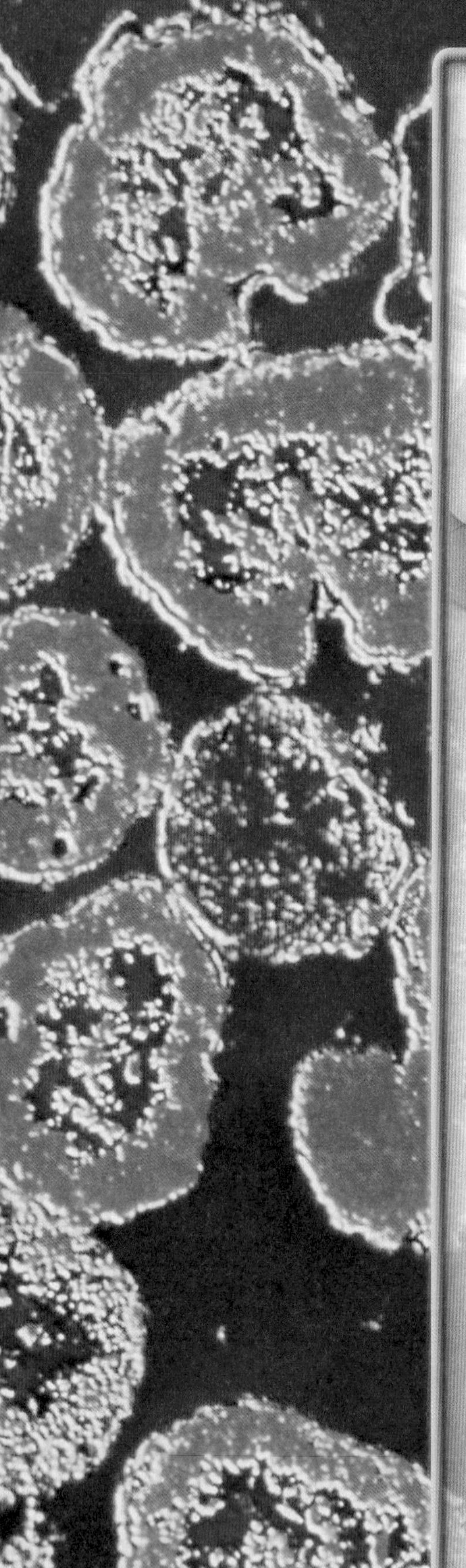

CASE FILE

It's All In the Walk

One of the most disturbing and gut-wrenching cases I was ever involved in concerned a 10-year-old girl who was brought to the emergency room by her mother, who was afraid her daughter had appendicitis. What her daughter turned out to have was far more troubling.

The patient had developed a high fever (39.4°C [103°F]) and was complaining of severe lower abdominal pain. Upon questioning, the patient also admitted to painful urination. As I led her into an examining room, I noticed that she walked taking very small steps. She did not lift her feet off the floor and seemed reluctant or unable to straighten up fully. Her odd gait raised a red flag in my mind.

After performing a quick abdominal examination and obtaining vital signs, I found the physician on call and told her about the patient's symptoms. I also described how the patient moved with an odd shuffling gait. Although I could not recall what I had learned about the symptom, I knew that it was a diagnostic feature. The physician asked me how old the patient was and asked if I had had the opportunity to ask the patient whether she was sexually active. I had not done so due to the patient's age. To my surprise, the physician asked me to prepare for an internal (vaginal) exam in another room while she examined the patient and spoke to her mother.

- What condition did the physician suspect?
- Is the condition reportable? If so, to whom would you report it?

Case File Wrap-Up appears on page 619.

CHAPTER 21

Infectious Diseases Affecting the Genitourinary System

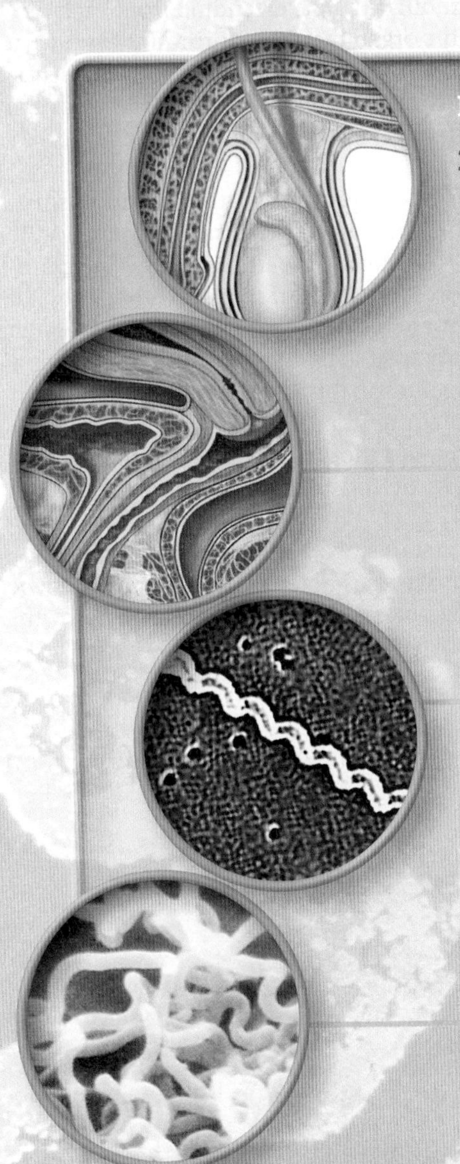

IN THIS CHAPTER...

21.1 The Genitourinary Tract and Its Defenses

1. Draw or describe the anatomical features of the genitourinary tracts of both genders.
2. List the natural defenses present in the genitourinary tracts.

21.2 Normal Biota of the Genitourinary Tract

3. List the types of normal biota presently known to occupy the genitourinary tracts of both genders.

21.3 Urinary Tract Diseases Caused by Microorganisms

4. List the possible causative agents, modes of transmission, virulence factors, diagnostic techniques, and prevention/treatment for the highlighted condition, urinary tract infection.
5. Discuss important features of leptospirosis.

21.4 Reproductive Tract Diseases Caused by Microorganisms

6. List the possible causative agents, modes of transmission, virulence factors, and prevention/treatment for gonorrhea and *Chlamydia* infection.
7. Distinguish between vaginitis and vaginosis.
8. Discuss prostatitis.
9. Name three diseases that result in genital ulcers, and discuss their important features.
10. Differentiate between the two diseases causing warts in the reproductive tract.
11. Provide some detail about the first "cancer vaccine" and how it works.
12. Identify the most important risk group for group B *Streptococcus* infection and why.

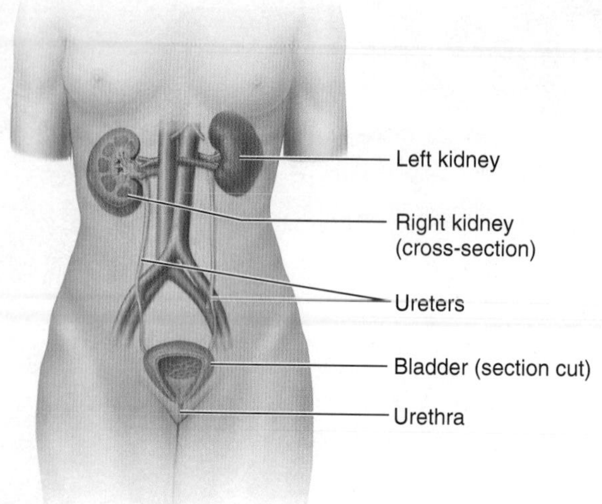

Figure 21.1 **The urinary system.**

21.1 The Genitourinary Tract and Its Defenses

As suggested by the name, the structures considered in this chapter are really two distinct organ systems. The *urinary tract* has the job of removing substances from the blood, regulating certain body processes, and forming urine and transporting it out of the body. The *genital system* has reproduction as its major function. It is also called the *reproductive system*.

The urinary tract includes the kidneys, ureters, bladder, and the urethra **(figure 21.1)**. The kidneys remove metabolic wastes from the blood, acting as a sophisticated filtration system. Ureters are tubular organs extending from each kidney to the bladder. The bladder is a collapsible organ that stores urine and empties it into the urethra, which is the conduit of urine to the exterior of the body. In males, the urethra is also the terminal organ of the reproductive tract, but in females the urethra is separate from the vagina, which is the outermost organ of the reproductive tract.

The most obvious defensive mechanism in the urinary tract is the flushing action of the urine flowing out of the system. The flow of urine also encourages the **desquamation** (shedding) of the epithelial cells lining the urinary tract. For example, each time a person urinates, he or she loses hundreds of thousands of epithelial cells! Any microorganisms attached to them are also shed, of course. Probably the most common microbial threat to the urinary tract is the group of microorganisms that comprise the normal biota in the gastrointestinal tract, because the two organ systems are in close proximity. But the cells of the epithelial lining of the urinary tract have different chemicals on their surfaces than do those lining the GI tract. For that reason, most bacteria that are adapted to adhere to the chemical structures in the GI tract cannot gain a foothold in the urinary tract.

Urine, in addition to being acidic, also contains two antibacterial proteins, lysozyme and lactoferrin. You may recall that lysozyme is an enzyme that breaks down peptidoglycan. Lactoferrin is an iron-binding protein that inhibits bacterial growth.

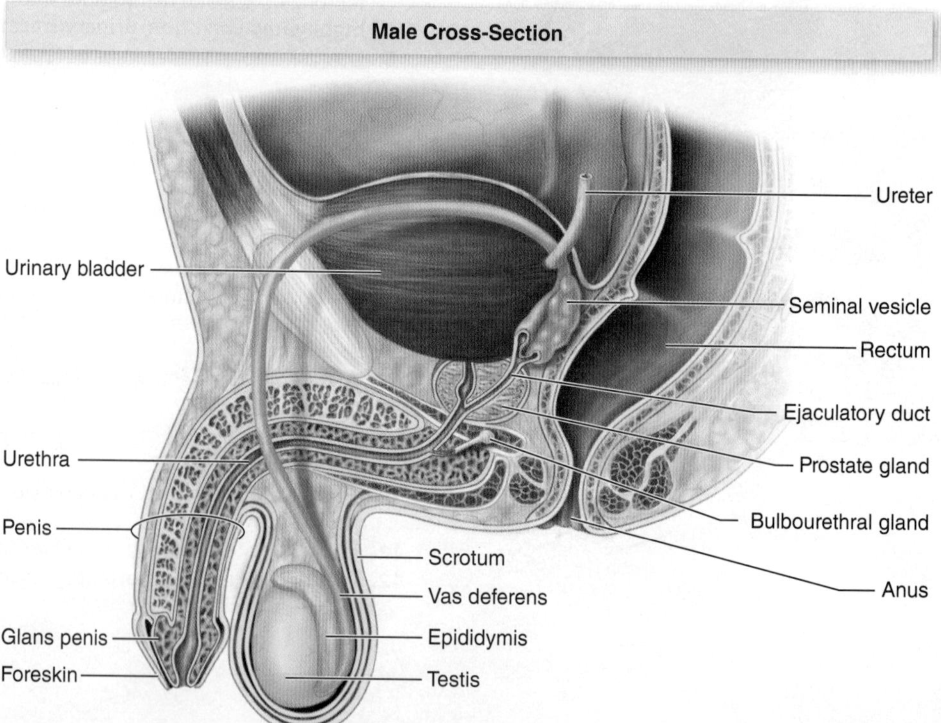

Figure 21.2 **The male reproductive system.**

Finally, secretory IgA specific for previously encountered microorganisms can be found in the urine.

The male reproductive system produces, maintains, and transports sperm cells and is the source of male sex hormones. It consists of the *testes,* which produce sperm cells and hormones, and the *epididymides,* which are coiled tubes leading out of the testes. Each epididymis terminates in a *vas deferens,* which combines with the seminal vesicle and terminates in the ejaculatory duct **(figure 21.2).** The contents of the ejaculatory duct empty into the urethra during ejaculation. The *prostate gland* is a walnut-shaped structure at the base of the urethra. It also contributes to the released fluid (semen). The external organs are the scrotum, containing the testes, and the *penis,* a cylindrical organ that houses the urethra. As for its innate defenses, the male reproductive system also benefits from the flushing action of the urine, which helps move microorganisms out of the system.

The female reproductive system consists of the *uterus,* the *fallopian tubes* (also called uterine tubes), *ovaries,* and *vagina* **(figure 21.3).** One very important tissue of the female reproductive tract is the *cervix,* which is the lower one-third of the uterus and the part that connects to the vagina. The cervix serves as the opening to the uterus. The cervix is a common site of infection in the female reproductive tract.

The natural defenses of the female reproductive tract vary over the lifetime of the woman. The vagina is lined with mucous membranes and, thus, has the protective covering of secreted mucus. During childhood and after menopause, this mucus is the major nonspecific defense of this system. Secretory IgA antibodies specific for any previously encountered infections would be present on these surfaces. During a woman's reproductive years, a major portion of the defense is provided by changes in the pH of the vagina brought about by the release of estrogen. This hormone stimulates the vaginal mucosa to secrete glycogen, which certain bacteria can ferment into acid, lowering the pH of the vagina to about 4.5. Before puberty, a girl produces little estrogen and little glycogen and has a vaginal pH of about 7. The change in

NCLEX® PREP

1. The ________is/are a common site of infection in the female reproductive tract.
   a. vagina
   b. fallopian tubes
   c. cervix
   d. ovaries

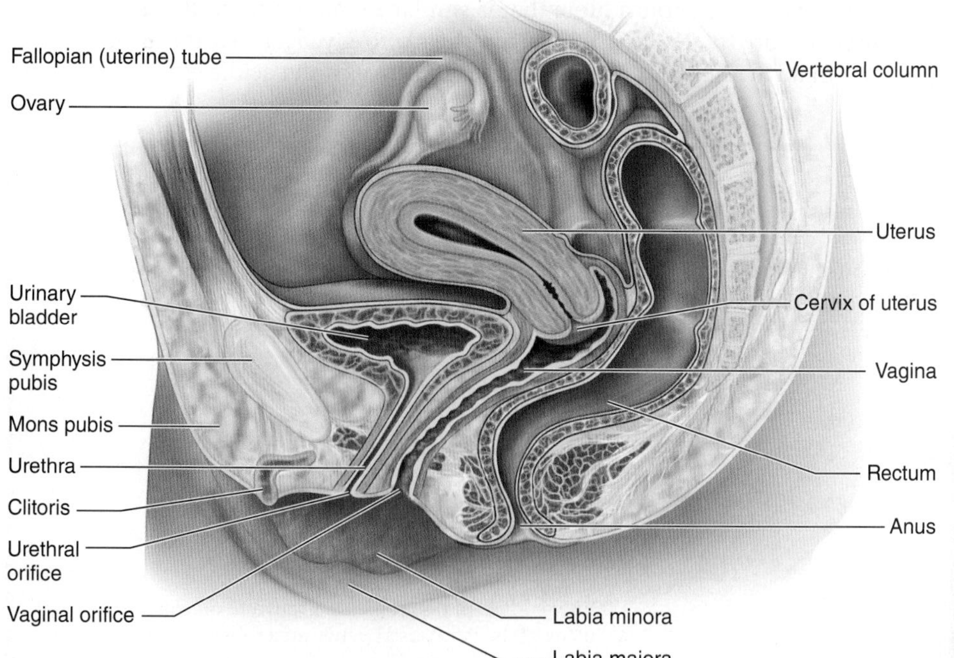

Figure 21.3 The female reproductive system.

The genitourinary tract includes the reproductive organs.

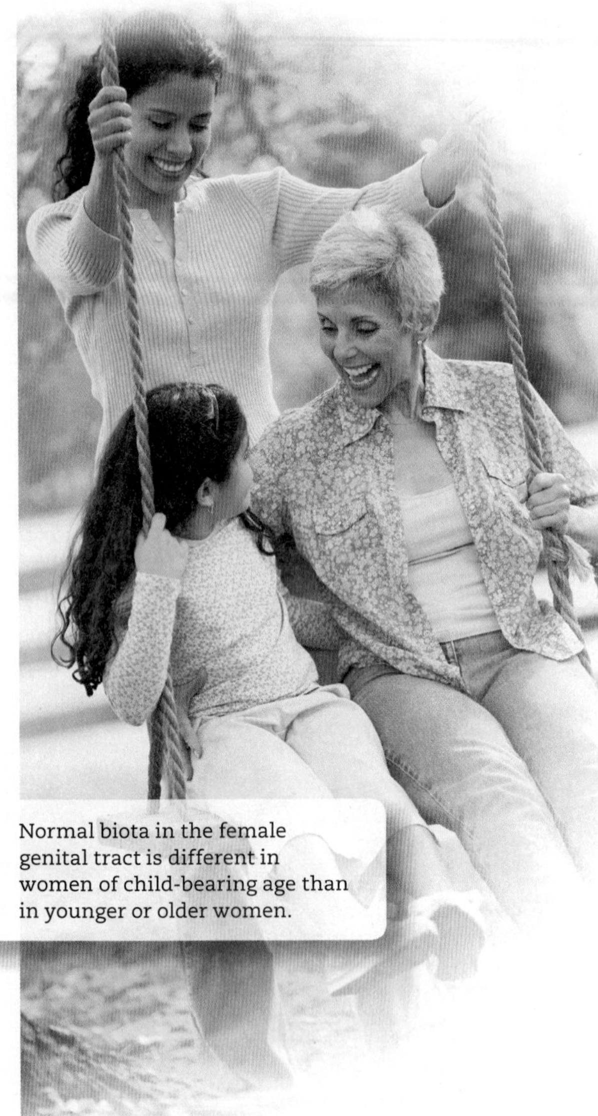

Normal biota in the female genital tract is different in women of child-bearing age than in younger or older women.

pH beginning in adolescence results in a vastly different normal biota in the vagina, described later. The biota of women in their childbearing years is thought to prevent the establishment and invasion of microbes that might have the potential to harm a developing fetus.

ASSESS YOUR PROGRESS

1. Draw or describe the anatomical features of the genitourinary tracts of both genders.
2. List the natural defenses present in the genitourinary tracts.

21.2 Normal Biota of the Genitourinary Tract

In both genders, the outer region of the urethra harbors some normal biota. The kidney, ureters, bladder, and upper urethra are presumably kept sterile by urine flow and regular bladder emptying (urinating). The principal known residents of the urethra are the nonhemolytic streptococci, staphylococci, corynebacteria, and some lactobacilli. Because the urethra in women is so short (about 3.5 cm long) and is in such close proximity to the anus, it can act as a pipeline for bacteria from the GI tract to the bladder, resulting in urinary tract infections. The outer surface of the penis is colonized by *Pseudomonas* and *Staphylococcus* species—aerobic bacteria. In an uncircumcised penis, the area under the foreskin is colonized by anaerobic gram-negatives.

Normal Biota of the Male Genital Tract

Because the terminal "tube" of the male genital tract is the urethra, the normal biota of the male genital tract (i.e., in the urethra) is comprised of the same residents just described.

Normal Biota of the Female Genital Tract

In the female genital tract, only the vagina harbors a normal population of microbes. Starting at the cervix and for all organs above it, there is no normal biota. As just mentioned, before puberty and after menopause, the pH of the vagina is close to neutral and the vagina harbors a biota that is similar to that found in the urethra. After the onset of puberty, estrogen production leads to glycogen release in the vagina, resulting in an acidic pH. *Lactobacillus* species thrive in the acidic environment and

Genitourinary Tract Defenses and Normal Biota

	Defenses	Normal Biota
Urinary Tract (both genders)	Flushing action of urine; specific attachment sites not recognized by most nonnormal biota; shedding of urinary tract epithelial cells, secretory IgA, lysozyme, and lactoferrin in urine	Nonhemolytic *Streptococcus, Staphylococcus, Corynebacterium, Lactobacillus*
Female Genital Tract (childhood and postmenopause)	Mucus secretions, secretory IgA	Same as for urinary tract
Female Genital Tract (childbearing years)	Acidic pH, mucus secretions, secretory IgA	Predominantly *Lactobacillus* but also *Candida*
Male Genital Tract	Same as for urinary tract	Urethra: Same as for urinary tract Outer surface of penis: *Pseudomonas* and *Staphylococcus* Sulcus of uncircumcised penis: anaerobic gram-negatives

contribute to it, converting sugars to acid. Their predominance in the vagina, combined with the acidic environment, discourages the growth of many microorganisms. The estrogen-glycogen effect continues, with minor disruptions, throughout the childbearing years until menopause, when the biota gradually returns to a mixed population similar to that of prepuberty. Note that the fungus *Candida albicans* is also present at low levels in the healthy female reproductive tract. When the normal vaginal microbiota is altered, and *Candida albicans* is not kept in check, an overgrowth of the fungus may occur, resulting in a symptomatic yeast infection.

ASSESS YOUR PROGRESS

3. List the types of normal biota presently known to occupy the genitourinary tracts of both genders.

21.3 Urinary Tract Diseases Caused by Microorganisms

We consider two types of diseases in this section. **Urinary tract infections (UTIs)** result from invasion of the urinary system by bacteria or other microorganisms. **Leptospirosis,** by contrast, is a spirochete-caused disease transmitted by contact of broken skin or mucous membranes with contaminated animal urine.

HIGHLIGHT DISEASE

Urinary Tract Infections (UTIs)

Even though the flushing action of urine helps to keep infections to a minimum in the urinary tract, urine itself is a good growth medium for many microorganisms. When urine flow is reduced, or bacteria are accidentally introduced into the bladder, an infection of that organ (known as *cystitis*) can occur. Occasionally, the infection can also affect the kidneys, in which case it is called *pyelonephritis*. If an infection is limited to the urethra, it is called *urethritis*.

▸ Signs and Symptoms

Cystitis is a disease of sudden onset. Symptoms include pain, frequent urges to urinate even when the bladder is empty, and burning pain accompanying urination (called *dysuria*). The urine can be cloudy due to the presence of bacteria and white blood cells. It may have an orange tinge from the presence of red blood cells (*hematuria*). Low-grade fever and nausea are frequently present. If back pain is present, and fever is high, it is an indication that the kidneys may also be involved (pyelonephritis). Pyelonephritis is a serious infection that can result in permanent damage to the kidneys if improperly or inadequately treated. If only the bladder is involved, the condition is sometimes called acute uncomplicated UTI.

▸ Causative Agents

In 95% of cystitis and pyelonephritis cases, the cause is bacteria that are normal biota in the gastrointestinal tract. *Escherichia coli* is by far the most common of these, accounting for approximately 80% of urinary tract infections. *Staphylococcus saprophyticus* and *Proteus mirabilis* are also common culprits. These last two are only referenced in **Disease Table 21.1** following the discussion of *E. coli.*

The *E. coli* species that cause UTIs are ones that exist as normal biota in the gastrointestinal tract. They are not the ones that cause diarrhea and other digestive tract diseases.

NCLEX® PREP

2. __________ that accompanies a UTI is an indication that the __________ may also be involved, a condition known as ________.
   a. Fever; bladder; urethritis
   b. Nausea; kidneys; cystitis
   c. Blood in the urine; bladder; pyelonephritis
   d. Back pain; kidneys; pyelonephritis

HIGHLIGHT DISEASE

Disease Table 21.1 Urinary Tract Infections (Cystitis, Pyelonephritis)

Causative Organism(s)	*Escherichia coli*	*Staphylococcus saprophyticus*	*Proteus mirabilis*
Most Common Modes of Transmission	Endogenous transfer from GI tract (opportunism)	Opportunism	Opportunism
Virulence Factors	Adhesins, motility	–	Urease enzyme, leads to kidney stone formation
Culture/Diagnosis	Often "bacterial infection" diagnosed on basis of increased white cells in urinalysis; if culture performed, bacteria may or may not be identified to species level	Often "bacterial infection" diagnosed on basis of increased white cells in urinalysis; if culture performed, bacteria may or may not be identified to species level	Often "bacterial infection" diagnosed on basis of increased white cells in urinalysis; if culture performed, bacteria may or may not be identified to species level
Prevention	Hygiene practices	Hygiene practices	Hygiene practices
Treatment	Cephalosporins: check for resistance	Ampicillin, amoxicillin, trimethoprimsulfamethoxazole	Ampicillin or cephalosporins
Distinctive Features	–	–	Kidney stones and severe pain may ensue

NCLEX® PREP

3. A vaccine is in development for these bacteria, which are responsible for causing most urinary tract infections (UTIs):
   a. *Proteus mirabilis*
   b. *Staphylococcus saprophyticus*
   c. *Leptospira interrogans*
   d. *Escherichia coli*

▸ Transmission and Epidemiology

Community-acquired UTIs are nearly always "transmitted" *not* from one person to another but from one organ system to another, namely from the GI tract to the urinary system. They are much more common in women than in men because of the nearness of the female urethral opening to the anus (see figure 21.3). Many women experience what have been referred to as "recurrent urinary tract infections," although it is now known that some *E. coli* can invade the deeper tissue of the urinary tract and therefore avoid being destroyed by antibiotics. They can emerge later to cause symptoms again. It is not clear how many "recurrent" infections are actually infections that reactivate in this way.

Note that urinary tract infections are also the most common of nosocomial infections. Patients of both sexes who have urinary catheters are susceptible to infections with a variety of microorganisms, not just the three mentioned here.

▸ Treatment

Ampicillin, amoxicillin, cephalosporins, or sulfa drugs such as trimethoprimsulfamethoxazole are most often used for UTIs of various etiologies. Often another nonantibiotic drug called phenazopyridine (Pyridium) is administered simultaneously. This drug relieves the very uncomfortable symptoms of burning and urgency. However, some physicians are reluctant to administer this medication for fear that it may mask worsening symptoms; when Pyridium is used, it should be used only for a maximum of 2 days. Pyridium is an azo dye and causes the urine to turn a dark orange to red color. It may also color contact lenses. A large percentage of *E. coli* strains is resistant to penicillin derivatives, so these should be avoided. Also, a new strain of *E. coli* (ST131) has arisen, which is highly virulent, and more troubling, resistant to multiple antibiotics. Medical professionals are ringing alarm bells about this strain, saying that if it acquires resistance to one more class of antibiotics it will become virtually untreatable.

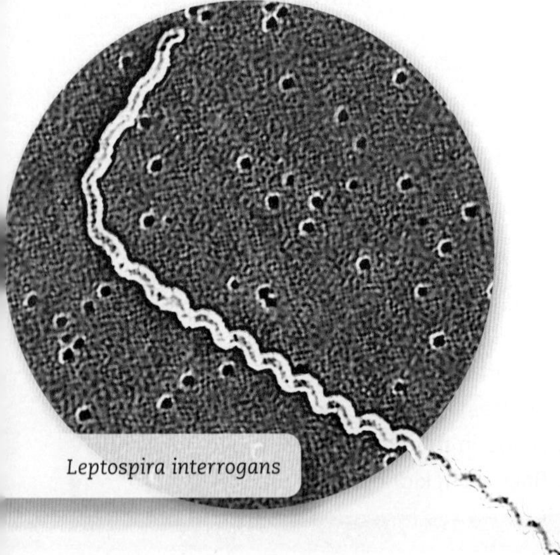

Leptospira interrogans

Leptospirosis

This infection is a zoonosis associated with wild animals and domesticated animals. It can affect the kidneys, liver, brain, and eyes. It is considered in this section because it can have its major effects on the kidneys and because its presence in animal urinary tracts causes it to be shed into the environment through animal urine.

▶ Signs and Symptoms

Leptospirosis has two phases. During the early, or leptospiremic, phase, the pathogen appears in the blood and cerebrospinal fluid. Symptoms are sudden high fever, chills, headache, muscle aches, conjunctivitis, and vomiting. During the second phase (called the immune phase), the blood infection is cleared by natural defenses. This period is marked by milder fever; headache due to leptospiral meningitis; and *Weil's syndrome,* a cluster of symptoms characterized by kidney invasion, hepatic disease, jaundice, anemia, and neurological disturbances. Long-term disability and even death can result from damage to the kidneys and liver, but they occur primarily with the most virulent strains and in elderly persons.

▶ Causative Agent

Leptospires are typical spirochete bacteria marked by tight, regular, individual coils with a bend or hook at one or both ends. *Leptospira interrogans* (lep″-toh-spy′-rah in-terr′-oh-ganz) is the species that causes leptospirosis in humans and animals. There are nearly 200 different serotypes of this species distributed among various animal groups, which accounts for extreme variations in the disease manifestations in humans.

▶ Transmission and Epidemiology

Infection occurs almost entirely through contact of skin abrasions or mucous membranes with animal urine or some environmental source containing urine. In 1998, dozens of athletes competing in the swimming phase of a triathlon in Illinois contracted leptospirosis from the water.

▶ Treatment

Early treatment with amoxicillin or doxycycline rapidly reduces symptoms and shortens the course of disease, but delayed therapy is less effective. Other spirochete diseases, such as syphilis (described later), exhibit this same pattern of being susceptible to antibiotics early in the infection but less so later on.

Disease Table 21.2 Leptospirosis

Causative Organism(s)	*Leptospira interrogans*
Most Common Modes of Transmission	Vehicle—contaminated soil or water
Virulence Factors	Adhesins? Invasion proteins?
Culture/Diagnosis	Slide agglutination test of patient's blood for antibodies
Prevention	Avoiding contaminated vehicles
Treatment	Doxycycline, amoxicillin

ASSESS YOUR PROGRESS

4. List the possible causative agents, modes of transmission, virulence factors, diagnostic techniques, and prevention/treatment for the highlighted condition, urinary tract infection.
5. Discuss important features of leptospirosis.

21.4 Reproductive Tract Diseases Caused by Microorganisms

Not all reproductive tract diseases are sexually transmitted, though many are. Vaginitis/vaginosis may or may not be; prostatitis probably is not.

It was very difficult to choose a "highlight" disease for this chapter, though we were sure we wanted it to be a sexually transmitted disease (now often called sexually transmitted infections, due to the fact that so many of them are silent, while still being serious). Sexually transmitted infections (STIs) now are more common in the United States than in any other industrialized country. The discharge diseases are responsible for unprecedented numbers of infertility cases. Herpes and human papillomavirus (HPV) infections are incurable, and therefore simply increase in their prevalence over time. Americans have become more familiar with the dangers of HPV infection since the introduction of the HPV vaccine, so, in a split decision, we have decided to highlight the dangers of curable—but usually undetected—discharge diseases.

A Note About STI Statistics

It is difficult to compare the incidence of different STIs to one another, for several reasons. The first is that many, many infections are "silent," and therefore infected people don't access the health care system, and don't get counted. Of course, we know that many silent infections are actually causing damage that won't be noticed for years—and when it is, the original causative organism is almost never sought out. The second reason is that only some STIs are officially reportable to health authorities. *Chlamydia* infection and gonorrhea are reported, for example, but herpes and HPV infections are not. In each section, we will try to present accurate estimates of the prevalence and/or incidence of the diseases as we know them.

HIGHLIGHT DISEASE

Discharge Diseases with Major Manifestation in the Genitourinary Tract

Discharge diseases are those in which the infectious agent causes an increase in fluid discharge in the male and female reproductive tracts. Examples are trichomoniasis, gonorrhea, and *Chlamydia* infection. The causative agents are transferred to new hosts when the fluids in which they live contact the mucosal surfaces of the receiving partner.

Gonorrhea

Gonorrhea has been known as a sexually transmitted disease since ancient times. It was named by the Greek physician Claudius Galen, who thought that it was caused by an excess flow of semen.

▶ Signs and Symptoms

In the male, infection of the urethra elicits urethritis, painful urination, and a yellowish discharge, although a relatively large number of cases are asymptomatic. In most cases, infection is limited to the distal urogenital tract, but it can occasionally spread from the urethra to the prostate gland and epididymis (refer to figure 21.2). Scar tissue formed in the spermatic ducts during healing of an invasive infection can render a man infertile.

In the female, it is likely that both the urinary and genital tracts will be infected during sexual intercourse. A mucopurulent (containing mucus and pus) or bloody vaginal discharge occurs in about half of the cases, along with painful urination if the urethra is affected. Major complications occur when the infection ascends from the vagina and cervix to higher reproductive structures such as the uterus and fallopian tubes **(figure 21.4)**. One disease resulting from this progression is **salpingitis** (sal″-pin-jy′-tis). This inflammation of the fallopian tubes may be isolated, or it may

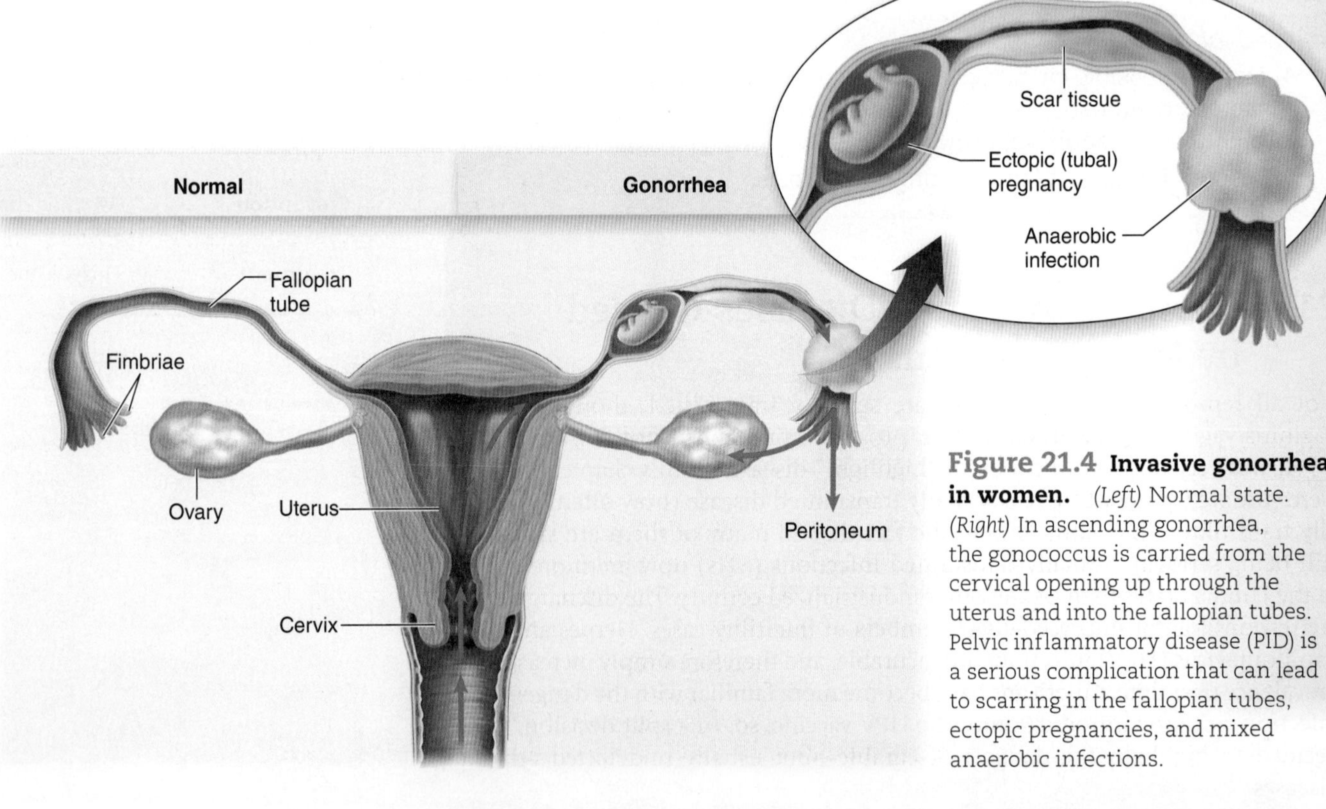

Figure 21.4 Invasive gonorrhea in women. *(Left)* Normal state. *(Right)* In ascending gonorrhea, the gonococcus is carried from the cervical opening up through the uterus and into the fallopian tubes. Pelvic inflammatory disease (PID) is a serious complication that can lead to scarring in the fallopian tubes, ectopic pregnancies, and mixed anaerobic infections.

also include inflammation of other parts of the upper reproductive tract, termed pelvic inflammatory disease (PID). It is not unusual for the microbe that initiates PID to become involved in mixed infections with anaerobic bacteria. The buildup of scar tissue from PID can block the fallopian tubes, causing sterility or ectopic pregnancies.

Serious consequences of gonorrhea can occur outside of the reproductive tract. In a small number of cases, the gonococcus enters the bloodstream and is disseminated to the joints and skin. Involvement of the wrist and ankle can lead to chronic arthritis and a painful, sporadic, papular rash on the limbs. Rare complications of gonococcal bacteremia are meningitis and endocarditis.

Children born to gonococcus carriers are also in danger of being infected as they pass through the birth canal. Because of the potential harm to the fetus, physicians usually screen pregnant mothers for its presence. Gonococcal eye infections are very serious and often result in keratitis, ophthalmia neonatorum, and even blindness **(figure 21.5)**. A universal precaution to prevent such complications is the use of antibiotic eyedrops or ointments (usually erythromycin) for newborn babies. The pathogen may also infect the pharynx and respiratory tract of neonates. Finding gonorrhea in children other than neonates is strong evidence of sexual abuse by infected adults, and it calls for child welfare consultation along with thorough bacteriologic analysis.

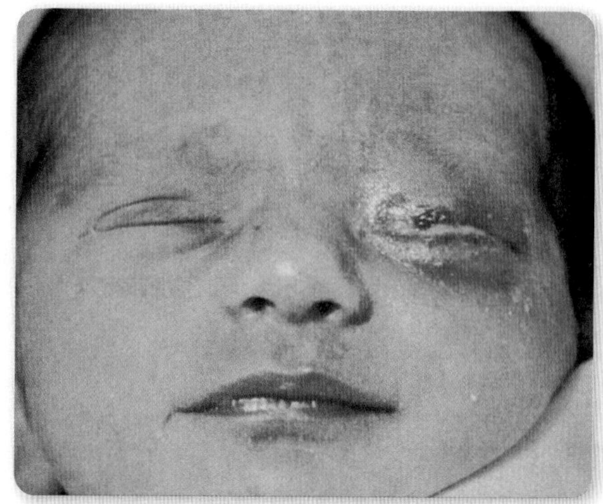

Figure 21.5 Gonococcal ophthalmia neonatorum in a week-old infant. The infection is marked by intense inflammation and edema; if allowed to progress, it causes damage that can lead to blindness. Fortunately, this infection is completely preventable and treatable.

Causative Agent

N. gonorrhoeae is a pyogenic gram-negative diplococcus. It appears as pairs of kidney bean–shaped bacteria, with their flat sides touching **(figure 21.6)**.

Pathogenesis and Virulence Factors

Successful attachment is key to the organism's ability to cause disease. Gonococci use specific chemical groups on the tips of fimbriae to anchor themselves to mucosal epithelial cells. Once the bacterium attaches, it invades the cells and multiplies on the basement membrane.

The fimbriae may also play a role in slowing down effective immunity. The fimbrial proteins are controlled by genes that can be turned on or off, depending on the bacterium's situation. This phenotypic change is called phase variation. In addition, the genes can rearrange themselves to put together fimbriae of different configurations. This antigenic variation confuses the body's immune system. Antibodies that previously recognized fimbrial proteins may not recognize them once they are rearranged.

The gonococcus also possesses an enzyme called IgA protease, which can cleave IgA molecules stationed on mucosal surfaces. In addition, pieces of its outer membrane are shed during growth. These "blebs," containing endotoxin, probably play a role in pathogenesis because they can stimulate portions of the nonspecific defense response, resulting in localized damage.

Transmission and Epidemiology

Except for neonatal infections, the gonococcus is spread through some form of sexual contact.

Gonorrhea is a strictly human infection that occurs worldwide and ranks among the most common sexually transmitted diseases. Although about 350,000 cases are reported in the United States each year, it is estimated that the actual incidence is much higher—in the millions if one counts asymptomatic infections.

It is important to consider the reservoir of asymptomatic males and females when discussing the transmission of the infection. Because approximately 10% of infected males and 50% of infected females experience no symptoms, it is often spread unknowingly.

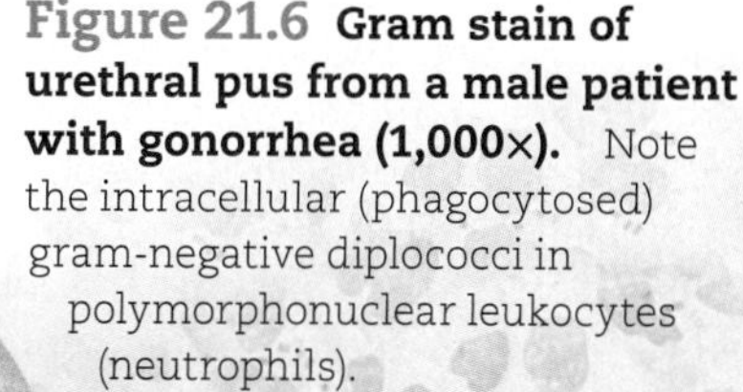

Figure 21.6 Gram stain of urethral pus from a male patient with gonorrhea (1,000×). Note the intracellular (phagocytosed) gram-negative diplococci in polymorphonuclear leukocytes (neutrophils).

Culture and Diagnosis

In males, it is easy to diagnose this disease; a Gram stain of urethral discharge is diagnostic. The normal biota of the male urethra is so sparse that it is easy to see

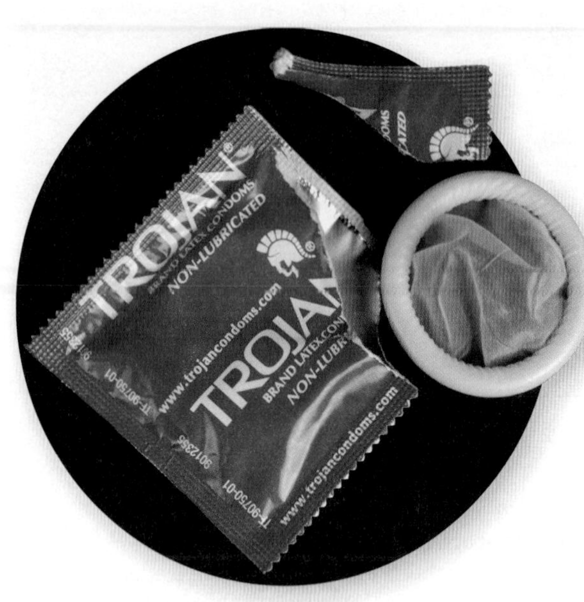

the diplococcus inside of neutrophils (figure 21.6). In females, other methods, such as ELISA or PCR tests, are called for. Alternatively, the bacterium can be cultured on Thayer-Martin agar, a rich chocolate agar base with added antibiotics that inhibit competing bacteria.

N. gonorrhoeae grows best in an atmosphere containing increased CO_2. Because *Neisseria* is so fragile, it is best to inoculate it onto media directly from the patient rather than using a transport tube. Gonococci produce catalase, enzymes for fermenting various carbohydrates, and the enzyme cytochrome oxidase, which can be used for identification as well. Gonorrhea is a reportable disease.

▶ Prevention

No vaccine is yet available for gonorrhea. Using condoms is an effective way to avoid transmission of this and other discharge diseases.

▶ Treatment

The CDC runs a program called the Gonococcal Isolate Surveillance Project (GISP) to monitor the occurrence of antibiotic resistance in *N. gonorrhoeae.* Penicillin was traditionally the drug of choice, but a large percentage of isolates now are able to produce penicillinase. Others are resistant to tetracycline and quinolones (like ciprofloxacin). In 2011 a strain of *N. gonorrhoeae* that is resistant to all existing antibiotics was identified in Japan. This development highlights the need for practitioners to be aware of local resistance patterns before prescribing antibiotics for gonorrhea. The GISP provides this local data. Every month in 28 local STD clinics around the country, *N. gonorrhoeae* isolates from the first 25 males diagnosed with the infection are sent to regional testing labs, their antibiotic sensitivities are determined, and the data are provided to the GISP program at the CDC.

A Note About Pelvic Inflammatory Disease (PID) and Infertility

The National Center for Health Statistics estimates that more than 6 million women in the United States have impaired fertility. There are many different reasons for infertility, but the leading cause is pelvic inflammatory disease, or PID. PID is caused by infection of the upper reproductive structures in women—namely, the uterus, fallopian tubes, and ovaries. These organs have no normal biota, and when bacteria from the vagina are transported higher in the tract, they start a chain of inflammatory events that may or may not be noticeable to the patient. The inflammation can be acute, resulting in pain, abnormal vaginal discharge, fever, and nausea, or it can be chronic, with less noticeable symptoms. In acute cases, women usually seek care; in some ways, these can be considered the lucky ones. If the inflammation is curbed at an early stage by using antibiotics to kill the bacteria, chances are better that the long-term sequelae of PID can be avoided. *Chlamydia* infection is the leading cause of PID, followed closely by *N. gonorrhoeae* infection. But other bacteria, perhaps also including normal biota of the reproductive tract, can also cause PID if they are traumatically introduced into the uterus.

Chlamydia

Genital chlamydial infection is the most common reportable infectious disease in the United States. Annually, more than 1 million cases are reported, but the actual infection rate may be five to seven times that number. The overall prevalence among young adults in the United States is 4%. It is at least two to three times as common as gonorrhea. The vast majority of cases are asymptomatic. When we consider the serious consequences that may follow *Chlamydia* infection, those facts are very disturbing.

▶ Signs and Symptoms

In males who experience symptoms of *Chlamydia* infection, the bacterium causes an inflammation of the urethra. The symptoms mimic gonorrhea—namely, discharge and painful urination. Untreated infections may lead to epididymitis. Females who experience symptoms have cervicitis, a discharge, and often salpingitis. Pelvic inflammatory disease is a frequent sequela of female chlamydial infection. A woman is even more likely to experience PID as a result of a *Chlamydia* infection than as a result of gonorrhea. Up to 75% of *Chlamydia* infections are asymptomatic, which puts women at risk for developing PID because they don't seek treatment for initial infections. The PID itself may be acute and painful, or it may be relatively asymptomatic, allowing damage to the upper reproductive tract to continue unchecked.

Certain strains of *C. trachomatis* can invade the lymphatic tissues, resulting in another condition called lymphogranuloma venereum. This condition is accompanied by headache, fever, and muscle aches. The lymph nodes near the lesion begin to fill with granuloma cells and become enlarged and tender. These "nodes" can cause long-term lymphatic obstruction that leads to chronic, deforming edema of the genitalia or anus. The disease is endemic to South America, Africa, and Asia, but occasionally occurs in other parts of the world. Its incidence in the United States is about 500 cases per year.

Babies born to mothers with *Chlamydia* infections can develop eye infections and also pneumonia if they become infected during passage through the birth canal. Infant conjunctivitis caused by contact with maternal *Chlamydia* infection is the most prevalent form of conjunctivitis in the United States (100,000 cases per year). Antibiotic drops or ointment applied to newborns' eyes are chosen to eliminate both *Chlamydia* and *N. gonorrhoeae*.

Causative Agent

C. trachomatis is a very small gram-negative bacterium. It lives inside host cells as an obligate intracellular parasite. All *Chlamydia* species alternate between two distinct stages, illustrated in **table 21.1.**

Pathogenesis and Virulence Factors

Chlamydia's ability to grow intracellularly contributes to its virulence because it escapes certain aspects of the host's immune response. Also, the bacterium has a unique cell wall that apparently prevents the phagosome from fusing with the lysosome inside phagocytes. The presence of the bacteria inside cells causes the release of cytokines that provoke intense inflammation. This defensive response leads to most of the actual tissue damage in *Chlamydia* infection. Of course, the last step of inflammation is repair, which often results in scarring. This can have disastrous effects on a narrow-diameter structure like the fallopian tube.

Transmission and Epidemiology

The reservoir of pathogenic strains of *C. trachomatis* is the human body. The microbe shows an astoundingly broad distribution within the population. Adolescent women are more likely than older women to harbor the bacterium because it prefers to infect cells that are particularly prevalent on the adolescent cervix. It is transmitted through sexual contact and also vertically. Fifty percent of (untreated) babies born to infected mothers will acquire chlamydial conjunctivitis or pneumonia.

Culture and Diagnosis

Infection with this microorganism is usually detected initially using a rapid technique such as PCR or ELISA. Direct fluorescent antibody detection is also used. Serology is not always reliable. In addition, antibody to *Chlamydia* is very common in adults and often indicates past, not present, infection. A urine test is available, which has definite advantages for widespread screening, but it is slightly less accurate for females than males.

Prevention

Avoiding contact with infected tissues and secretions through abstinence or barrier protection (condoms) is the only means of prevention.

Treatment

Treatment for this infection relies on being aware of it, so one of the guidelines issued by the CDC is a recommendation for annual screening of young women for presence of the bacterium. It is also recommended that older women with some risk factor (new sexual partner, for instance) also be screened. If infection is found, treatment is usually with azithromycin, a macrolide antibiotic. Note that according to public health officials, many patients become reinfected soon after treatment; therefore, the recommendation is that patients be rechecked for *Chlamydia* infection 3 to 4 months after treatment. Repeated infections with *Chlamydia* increase the likelihood of PID and other serious sequelae.

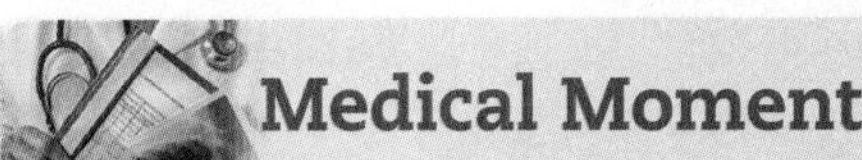

Medical Moment

Female Condoms

Condoms are a reliable way to prevent the spread of STIs. Although not 100% effective, they greatly reduce the risk of contracting a sexually transmitted disease.

Male condoms have been used for years. In an effort to provide more choice and control to women, the female condom was introduced in the 1990s. Despite numerous changes over the past two decades, the female condom has not "caught on" as agencies tasked with controlling STIs had once hoped.

Why are women (and men) not embracing the female condom? Several reasons have been put forth, including the following:

- higher cost of female condoms;
- awkwardness of insertion/application;
- possibility of leakage of sperm upon removal from the vagina;
- reduced availability of female condoms, in some areas, compared with male condoms; and
- decreased sensation for some women.

Female condoms are being provided to women in developing countries in the hopes that they will be able to protect themselves against HIV. Women in developing countries seem to be more receptive to female condoms; however, experts argue that men who are opposed to male condoms are not likely to embrace female condoms.

HIGHLIGHT DISEASE

Table 21.1 The Life Cycle of *Chlamydia*

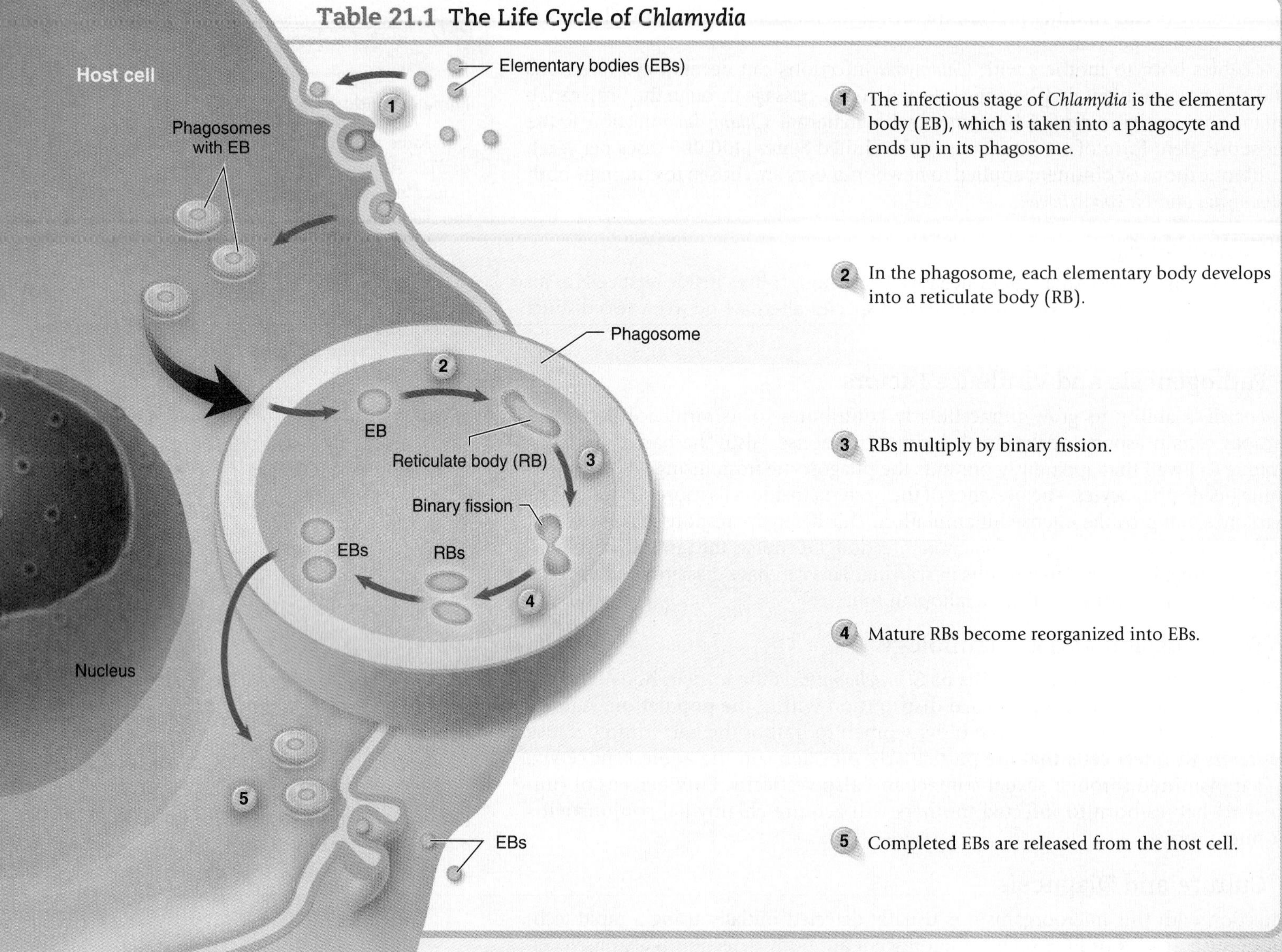

1 The infectious stage of *Chlamydia* is the elementary body (EB), which is taken into a phagocyte and ends up in its phagosome.

2 In the phagosome, each elementary body develops into a reticulate body (RB).

3 RBs multiply by binary fission.

4 Mature RBs become reorganized into EBs.

5 Completed EBs are released from the host cell.

Disease Table 21.3 Genital "Discharge" Diseases

	Gonorrhea	Chlamydia
Causative Organism(s)	*Neisseria gonorrhoeae*	*Chlamydia trachomatis*
Most Common Modes of Transmission	Direct contact (STI), also vertical	Direct contact (STI), vertical
Virulence Factors	Fimbrial adhesins, antigenic variation, IgA protease, membrane blebs/endotoxin	Intracellular growth resulting in avoiding immune system and cytokine release, unusual cell wall preventing phagolysosome fusion
Culture/Diagnosis	Gram stain in males, rapid tests (PCR, ELISA) for females, culture on Thayer-Martin agar	PCR or ELISA, can be followed by cell culture
Prevention	Avoid contact; condom use	Avoid contact; condom use
Treatment	Many strains resistant to various antibiotics; local and current guidelines must be consulted	Azithromycin, doxycycline, and follow-up to check for reinfection
Distinctive Features	Rare complications include arthritis, meningitis, endocarditis	More commonly asymptomatic than gonorrhea
Effects on Fetus	Eye infections, blindness	Eye infections, pneumonia

Vaginitis and Vaginosis

▶ Signs and Symptoms

Vaginitis, an inflammation of the vagina, is a condition characterized by some degree of vaginal itching, depending on the etiologic agent. Symptoms may also include burning, and sometimes a discharge, which may take different forms as well. Vaginosis is similar, but does not include significant inflammation.

▶ Causative Agents

The most common cause of vaginitis is *Candida albicans*. The vaginal condition caused by this fungus is known as a *yeast infection*. Most women experience this condition one or multiple times during their lives.

Candida albicans

C. albicans is a dimorphic fungus that is normal biota in from 50% to 100% of humans, living in low numbers on many mucosal surfaces such as the mouth, gastrointestinal tract, vagina, and so on. The vaginal condition it causes is also called vulvovaginal candidiasis. The yeast is easily detectable on a wet prep or a Gram stain of material obtained during a pelvic exam **(figure 21.7)**. The presence of pseudohyphae in the smear is a clear indication that the yeast is growing rapidly and causing a yeast infection.

In otherwise healthy people, the fungus is not invasive and limits itself to this surface infection. Please note, however, that *Candida* infections of the bloodstream do occur and they have high mortality rates. They do not normally stem from vaginal infections with the fungus, however, but are seen most frequently in hospitalized patients. AIDS patients are also at risk of developing systemic *Candida* infections.

▶ Transmission and Epidemiology

Vaginal infections with this organism are nearly always opportunistic. Disruptions of the normal bacterial biota or even minor damage to the mucosal epithelium in the vagina can lead to overgrowth by this fungus. Disruptions may be mechanical, such as trauma to the vagina, or they may be chemical, as when broad-spectrum antibiotics taken for some other purpose temporarily diminish the vaginal bacterial population. Diabetics and pregnant women are also predisposed to vaginal yeast overgrowths. Some women are prone to this condition during menstruation.

It is possible to transmit this yeast through sexual contact, especially if a woman is experiencing an overgrowth of it. The recipient's immune system may well subdue the yeast so that it acts as normal biota in them. But the yeast may be passed back to the original partner during further sexual contact after treatment. Women with HIV infection experience frequently recurring yeast infections. Also, a small percentage of women with no underlying immune disease experience chronic or recurrent vaginal infection with *Candida* for reasons that are not clear.

▶ Prevention and Treatment

No vaccine is available for *C. albicans*. Topical and oral azole drugs are used to treat vaginal candidiasis, and many of them are now available over the counter. If infections recur frequently or fail to resolve, it is important to see a physician for evaluation.

Gardnerella Species

The bacterium *Gardnerella* is associated with a particularly common condition in women in their childbearing years. This condition is usually called vaginosis rather than vaginitis because it doesn't appear to induce inflammation in the vagina. It is also known as BV, or bacterial vaginosis. Despite the absence of an inflammatory response, a vaginal discharge is associated with the condition, which often has a very

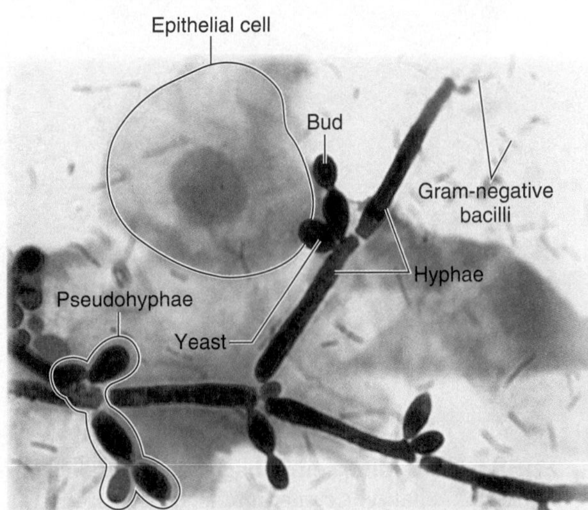

Figure 21.7 Gram stain of *Candida albicans* in a vaginal smear.

Disease Table 21.4 Vaginitis/Vaginosis

Causative Organism(s)	*Candida albicans*	Mixed infection, usually including *Gardnerella*	*Trichomonas vaginalis*
Most Common Modes of Transmission	Opportunism	Opportunism?	Direct contact (STI)
Virulence Factors	–	–	–
Culture/Diagnosis	Wet prep or Gram stain	Visual exam of vagina, or clue cells seen in Pap smear or other smear	Protozoa seen on Pap smear or Gram stain
Prevention	–	–	Barrier use during intercourse
Treatment	Topical or oral azole drugs, some over-the-counter drugs	Metronidazole or clindamycin	Metronidazole, tinidazole
Distinctive Features	White curdlike discharge	Discharge may have fishy smell	Discharge may be greenish

fishy odor. Itching is common. But it is also true that many women have this condition with no noticeable symptoms.

Vaginosis is most likely a result of a shift from a predominance of "good" bacteria (lactobacilli) in the vagina to a predominance of "bad" bacteria, and one of those is *Gardnerella vaginalis.* This genus of bacteria is aerotolerant and gram-positive, although in a Gram stain it usually appears gram-negative. (Some texts refer to it as gram-variable for this reason.) Probably a mixed infection leads to the condition, however. Anaerobic streptococci and other bacteria, particularly a genus known as *Mobiluncus,* that are normally found in low numbers in a healthy vagina can also often be found in high numbers in this condition. The often-mentioned fishy odor comes from the metabolic by-products of anaerobic metabolism by these bacteria.

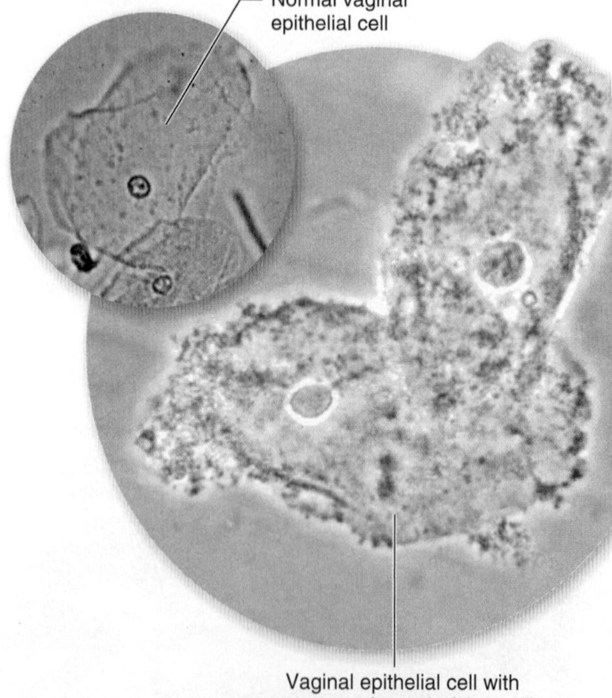

Figure 21.8 Clue cell in bacterial vaginosis. These epithelial cells came from a pelvic exam. The cells in the large circle have an abundance of bacteria attached to them.

▶ Pathogenesis and Virulence Factors

The mechanism of damage in this disease is not well understood. But some of the outcomes are. Besides the symptoms just mentioned, vaginosis can lead to complications such as pelvic inflammatory disease, infertility, and more rarely, ectopic pregnancies. Babies born to some mothers with vaginosis have low birth weights.

▶ Transmission and Epidemiology

This mixed infection is not considered to be sexually transmitted, although women who have never had sex rarely develop the condition. It is very common in sexually active women. It may be that the condition is associated with sex but not transmitted by it. This situation could occur if the act of penetration or the presence of semen (or saliva) causes changes in the vaginal epithelium, or in the vaginal biota. We do not know exactly what causes the increased numbers of *Gardnerella* and other normally rare biota. The low pH typical of the vagina is usually higher in vaginosis. It is not clear whether this causes or is caused by the change in bacterial biota.

▶ Culture and Diagnosis

The condition can be diagnosed by a variety of methods. Sometimes a simple stain of vaginal secretions is used to examine sloughed vaginal epithelial cells. In vaginosis, some cells will appear to be nearly covered with adherent bacteria. In normal times, vaginal epithelial cells are sparsely covered with bacteria. These cells are called clue cells and are a helpful diagnostic indicator **(figure 21.8).** They can also be found on Pap smears.

Prevention and Treatment

Women who find the condition uncomfortable or who are planning on becoming pregnant should be treated. Women who use intrauterine devices (IUDs) for contraception should also be treated because IUDs can provide a passageway for the bacteria to gain access to the upper reproductive tract. The usual treatment is oral or topical metronidazole or clindamycin.

NCLEX® PREP

4. Which of the following statements are true regarding bacterial vaginosis (BV)?
   a. BV likely results from a shift in a predominance of "good" bacteria in the vagina to a predominance of "bad" bacteria.
   b. *Gardnerella* may appear gram-negative in a Gram stain, although it is a gram-positive bacterium.
   c. BV often causes a fishy odor.
   d. Although itching is common, some women have no symptoms.
   e. all of the above

Trichomonas vaginalis

Trichomonads are small, pear-shaped protozoa with four anterior flagella and an undulating membrane. *Trichomonas vaginalis* seems to cause asymptomatic infections in approximately 50% of females and males. Trichomonads are considered asymptomatic infectious agents rather than normal biota because of evidence that some people experience long-term negative effects. Even though *Trichomonas* is a protozoan, it has no cyst form, and it does not survive long outside of the host.

Many cases are asymptomatic, and men seldom have symptoms. Women often have vaginitis symptoms, which can include a white to green frothy discharge. Chronic infection can make a person more susceptible to other infections, including HIV. Also, women who become infected during pregnancy are predisposed to premature labor and low-birth-weight infants. Chronic infection may also lead to infertility.

Because *Trichomonas* is common biota in so many people, it is easily transmitted through sexual contact. It has been called the most common nonviral sexually transmitted infection. It does not appear to undergo opportunistic shifts within its host (i.e., to become symptomatic under certain conditions), but rather, the protozoan causes symptoms when transmitted to a noncarrier.

Prostatitis

Prostatitis is an inflammation of the prostate gland (see figure 21.2). It can be acute or chronic. Acute prostatitis is virtually always caused by bacterial infection. The bacteria are usually normal biota from the intestinal tract or may have caused a previous urinary tract infection. Chronic prostatitis is also often caused by bacteria. Researchers have found that chronic prostatitis, often unresponsive to antibiotic treatment, can be caused by mixed biofilms of bacteria in the prostate. Some forms of chronic prostatitis have no known microbial cause, though many infectious disease specialists feel that one or more bacteria are involved, but they are simply not culturable with current techniques.

Symptoms may include pain in the groin and lower back, frequent urge to urinate, difficulty in urinating, blood in the urine, and painful ejaculation. Treatment is with broad-spectrum antibiotics.

Disease Table 21.5 Prostatitis

Causative Organism(s)	GI tract biota
Most Common Modes of Transmission	Endogenous transfer from GI tract; otherwise unknown
Virulence Factors	Various
Culture/Diagnosis	Digital rectal exam to examine prostate; culture of urine or semen
Prevention	None
Treatment	Antibiotics, muscle relaxers, alpha blockers
Distinctive Features	Pain in genital area and/or back, difficulty urinating

NCLEX® PREP

5. Prostatitis symptoms may include
   a. hematuria (blood in the urine).
   b. painful ejaculation.
   c. groin pain.
   d. GI tract disturbance.
   e. a, b, and d.
   f. a, b, and c.

Genital Ulcer Diseases

Three common infectious conditions can result in lesions (ulcers) on the genitals: syphilis, chancroid, and genital herpes. In this section, we consider each of these. One very important fact to remember about the ulcer diseases is that having one of them increases the chances of infection with HIV because of the open lesions.

Syphilis

Untreated syphilis is marked by distinct clinical stages designated as *primary, secondary,* and *tertiary syphilis*. The disease also has latent periods of varying duration during which it is quiescent. The spirochete appears in the lesions and blood during the primary and secondary stages and, thus, is transmissible at these times. During the early latency period between secondary and tertiary syphilis, it is also transmissible. Syphilis is largely nontransmissible during the "late latent" and tertiary stages.

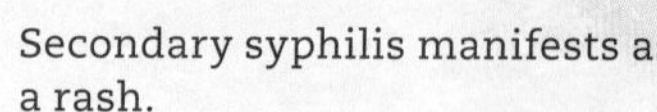

Secondary syphilis manifests as a rash.

▶ Primary Syphilis

The earliest indication of syphilis infection is the appearance of a hard **chancre** (shang′-ker) at the site of entry of the pathogen. Because these ulcers tend to be painless, they may escape notice, especially when they are on internal surfaces. The chancre heals spontaneously without scarring in 3 to 6 weeks, but the healing is deceptive because the spirochete has escaped into the circulation and is entering a period of tremendous activity.

▶ Secondary Syphilis

About 3 weeks to 6 months after the chancre heals, the secondary stage appears. By then, many systems of the body have been invaded, and the signs and symptoms are more profuse and intense. Initial symptoms are fever, headache, and sore throat, followed by lymphadenopathy and a peculiar red or brown rash that breaks out on all skin surfaces, including the palms of the hands and the soles of the feet. A person's hair often falls out. Like the chancre, the lesions contain viable spirochetes and disappear spontaneously in a few weeks. The major complications of this stage, occurring in the bones, hair follicles, joints, liver, eyes, and brain, can linger for months and years.

▶ Latency and Tertiary Syphilis

After resolution of secondary syphilis, about 30% of infections enter a highly varied latent period that can last for 20 years or longer. During latency, although antibodies to the bacterium are readily detected, the bacterium itself is not. The final stage of the disease, tertiary syphilis, is relatively rare today because of widespread use of antibiotics. But it is so damaging that it is important to recognize. By the time a patient reaches this phase, numerous pathologic complications occur in susceptible tissues and organs. Cardiovascular syphilis results from damage to the small arteries in the aortic wall. As the fibers in the wall weaken, the aorta is subject to distension and fatal rupture. The same pathologic process can damage the aortic valves, resulting in heart failure.

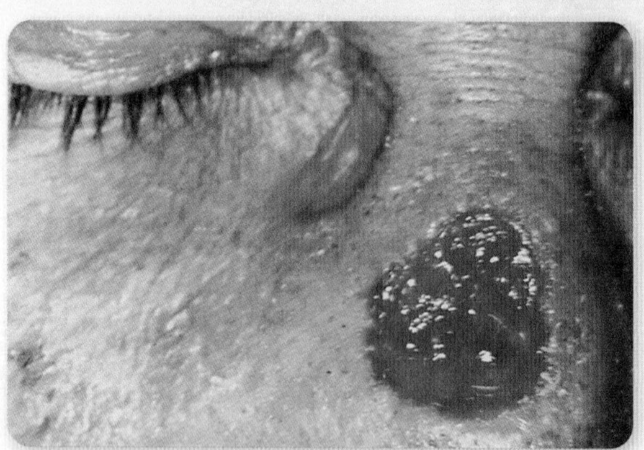

Figure 21.9 The pathology of late, or tertiary, syphilis. An ulcerating syphilis tumor, or gumma, appears on the nose of this patient. Other gummas can be internal.

In one form of tertiary syphilis, painful swollen syphilitic tumors called **gummas** (goo-mahz′) develop in tissues such as the liver, skin, bone, and cartilage **(figure 21.9)**. Gummas are usually benign and only occasionally lead to death, but they can impair function. Neurosyphilis can involve any part of the nervous system, but it shows particular affinity for the blood vessels in the brain, cranial nerves, and dorsal roots of the spinal cord. The diverse results include severe headaches, convulsions, atrophy of the optic nerve, blindness, dementia, and a sign called the Argyll-Robertson pupil—a condition caused by adhesions along the inner edge of the iris that fix the pupil's position into a small irregular circle.

Congenital Syphilis

The syphilis bacterium can pass from a pregnant woman's circulation into the placenta and can be carried throughout the fetal tissues. An infection leading to congenital syphilis can occur in any of the three trimesters, but it is most common in the second and third. The pathogen inhibits fetal growth and disrupts critical periods of development with varied consequences, ranging from mild to the extremes of spontaneous miscarriage or stillbirth. Early congenital syphilis encompasses the period from birth to 2 years of age and is usually first detected 3 to 8 weeks after birth. Infants often demonstrate such signs as profuse nasal discharge **(figure 21.10*a*)**, skin eruptions, bone deformation, and nervous system abnormalities. The late form gives rise to an unusual assortment of problems in the bones, eyes, inner ear, and joints, and causes the formation of Hutchinson's teeth **(figure 21.10*b*)**.

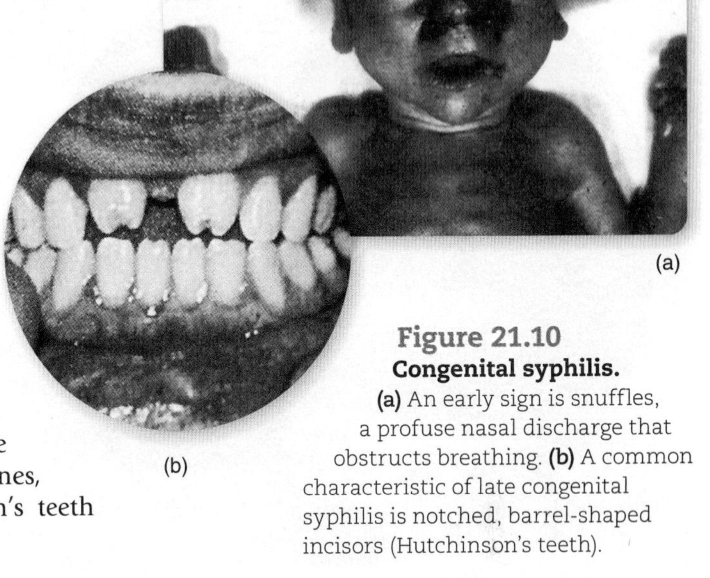

Figure 21.10 **Congenital syphilis.** **(a)** An early sign is snuffles, a profuse nasal discharge that obstructs breathing. **(b)** A common characteristic of late congenital syphilis is notched, barrel-shaped incisors (Hutchinson's teeth).

Causative Agent

Treponema pallidum, a spirochete, is a thin, regularly coiled cell with a gram-negative cell wall. It is a strict parasite with complex growth requirements that necessitate cultivating it in living host cells.

Pathogenesis and Virulence Factors

Brought into direct contact with mucous membranes or abraded skin, *T. pallidum* binds avidly by its hooked tip to the epithelium **(figure 21.11)**. At the binding site, the spirochete multiplies and penetrates the capillaries nearby. Within a short time, it moves into the circulation, and the body is literally transformed into a large receptacle for incubating the pathogen. Virtually any tissue is a potential target.

T. pallidum produces no toxins and does not appear to kill cells directly. Studies have shown that, although phagocytes seem to act against it and several types of antitreponemal antibodies are formed, immune responses are unable to contain it.

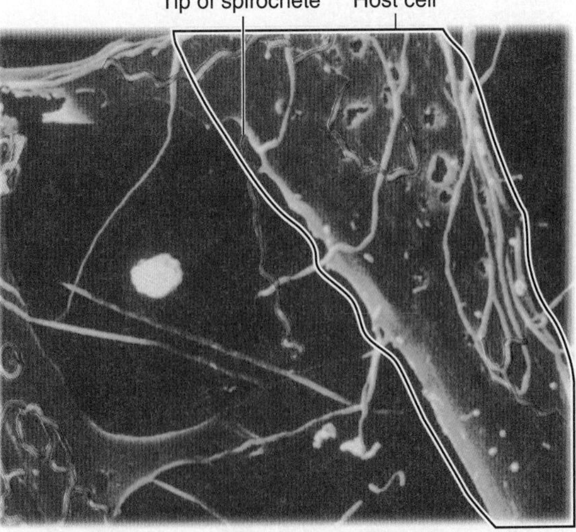

Figure 21.11 **Electron micrograph of the syphilis spirochete attached to cells.**

Transmission and Epidemiology

Humans are evidently the sole natural hosts and source of *T. pallidum*. The bacterium is extremely fastidious and sensitive and cannot survive for long outside the host, being rapidly destroyed by heat, drying, disinfectants, soap, high oxygen tension, and pH changes. It survives a few minutes to hours when protected by body secretions and about 36 hours in stored blood. The risk of infection from an infected sexual partner is 12% to 30% per encounter.

For centuries, syphilis was a common and devastating disease in the United States, so much so that major medical centers had "Departments of Syphilology." Its effect on social life was enormous. This effect diminished quickly when antibiotics were discovered. But since 2003, the rates have been increasing again in the United States. And syphilis continues to be a serious problem worldwide, especially in Africa and Asia. As mentioned previously, persons with syphilis often suffer concurrent infections with other STIs. Coinfection with the AIDS virus can be an especially deadly combination with a rapidly fatal course.

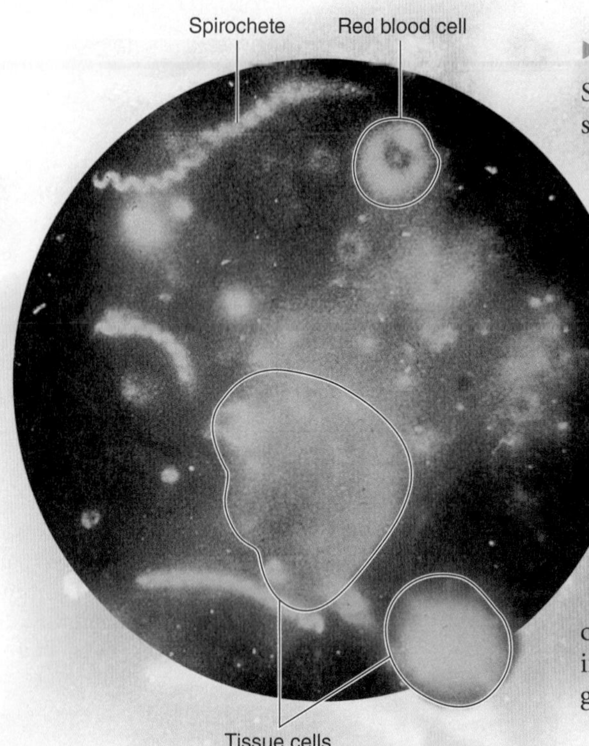

Figure 21.12 *Treponema pallidum* from a syphilitic chancre, viewed with dark-field illumination. Its tight spirals are highlighted next to human cells and tissue debris.

Treponema pallidum has a corkscrew shape that helps it burrow through the body.

Culture and Diagnosis

Syphilis can be detected in patients most rapidly by using dark-field microscopy of a suspected lesion **(figure 21.12).** A single negative test is not enough to exclude syphilis because the patient may have removed the organisms by washing, so follow-up tests are recommended.

Very commonly, blood tests are used for this diagnosis. These tests are based on detection of antibody formed in response to *T. pallidum* infection. Two kinds of antibodies are formed: those that specifically react with treponemal antigens and, perhaps surprisingly, those that are formed against nontreponemal antigens. After infection with *T. pallidum*, the body abnormally produces antibodies to a natural constituent of human cells called *cardiolipin*, and the presence of these cardiolipin antibodies is also indicative of *T. pallidum* infection. Several different tests detect these antibodies, such as rapid plasma reagin (RPR), VDRL, Kolmer, and the Wasserman test.

Prevention

The core of an effective prevention program depends on detection and treatment of the sexual contacts of syphilitic patients. Public health departments and physicians are charged with the task of questioning patients and tracing their contacts. All individuals identified as being at risk, even if they show no signs of infection, are given immediate prophylactic penicillin in a single long-acting dose.

The barrier effect of a condom provides excellent protection during the primary phase. Protective immunity apparently does arise in humans, allowing the prospect of an effective immunization program in the future, although no vaccine exists currently.

Treatment

Throughout most of history, the treatment for syphilis was a dose of mercury or even a "mercurial rub" applied to external lesions. In 1906, Paul Ehrlich discovered that a derivative of arsenic called salvarsan could be very effective. The fact that toxic compounds like mercury and arsenic were used to treat syphilis gives some indication of how dreaded the disease was and to what lengths people would go to rid themselves of it.

Once penicillin became available, it replaced all other treatments, and penicillin G retains its status as a wonder drug in the treatment of all stages and forms of syphilis.

Chancroid

This ulcerative disease usually begins as a soft papule, or bump, at the point of contact. It develops into a "soft chancre" (in contrast to the hard syphilis chancre), which is very painful in men, but may be unnoticed in women **(Disease Table 21.6).** Inguinal lymph nodes can become very swollen and tender.

Chancroid is caused by a pleomorphic gram-negative rod called *Haemophilus ducreyi*. Recent research indicates that a hemolysin (exotoxin) is important in the pathogenesis of chancroid disease. It is very common in the tropics and subtropics and is becoming more common in the United States. Chancroid is transmitted exclusively through direct contact, especially sexually. This disease is associated with lower socioeconomic status and poor hygiene; uncircumcised men seem to be more commonly infected than those who have been circumcised. People may carry this bacterium asymptomatically.

Genital Herpes

Genital herpes is much more common than most people think. It is caused by herpes simplex viruses (HSVs). Two types of HSV have been identified, HSV-1 and HSV-2.

Signs and Symptoms

Genital herpes infection has multiple presentations. After initial infection, a person may notice no symptoms. Alternatively, herpes could cause the appearance of single

Disease Table 21.6 Genital Ulcer Diseases

	Syphilis	Chancroid	Herpes
Causative Organism(s)	*Treponema pallidum*	*Haemophilus ducreyi*	Herpes simplex 1 and 2
Most Common Modes of Transmission	Direct contact and vertical	Direct contact (vertical transmission not documented)	Direct contact, vertical
Virulence Factors	Lipoproteins	Hemolysin (exotoxin)	Latency
Culture/ Diagnosis	Direct tests (immunofluorescence, dark-field microscopy), blood tests for treponemal and nontreponemal antibodies, PCR	Culture from lesion	Clinical presentation, PCR, Ab tests, growth of virus in cell culture
Prevention	Antibiotic treatment of all possible contacts, avoiding contact	Avoiding contact	Avoiding contact, antivirals can reduce recurrences
Treatment	Penicillin G	Azithromycin, ceftriaxone, ciprofloxacin	Acyclovir and derivatives
Distinctive Features	Three stages of disease plus latent period, possibly fatal	No systemic effects	Range from asymptomatic to frequent recurrences
Effects on Fetus	Congenital syphilis	None	Blindness, disseminated herpes infection
Appearance of Lesions			Vesicles

or multiple vesicles on the genitalia, perineum, thigh, and buttocks. The vesicles are small and are filled with a clear fluid (see Disease Table 21.6). They are intensely painful to the touch. The appearance of lesions the first time you get them can be accompanied by malaise, anorexia, fever, and bilateral swelling and tenderness in the groin. Occasionally central nervous system symptoms such as meningitis or encephalitis can develop. Thus, we see that initial infection can either be completely asymptomatic or be serious enough to require hospitalization.

After recovery from initial infection, a person may have recurrent episodes of lesions. They are generally less severe than the original symptoms, although the whole gamut of possible severity is seen here as well. Some people never have recurrent lesions. Others have nearly constant outbreaks with little recovery time between them. On average, the number of recurrences is four or five a year. Their frequency tends to decrease over the course of years.

In most cases, patients remain asymptomatic or experience recurrent "surface" infections indefinitely. Very rarely, complications can occur. Every year, one or two persons per million with chronic herpes infections develop encephalitis. The virus disseminates along nerve pathways to the brain (although it can also infect the spinal cord). The effects on the central nervous system begin with headache and stiff neck and can progress to mental disturbances and coma. The fatality rate in untreated encephalitis cases is 70%, although treatment with acyclovir is effective. Patients with underlying immunodeficiency are more prone to severe, disseminated herpes infection than are immunocompetent patients.

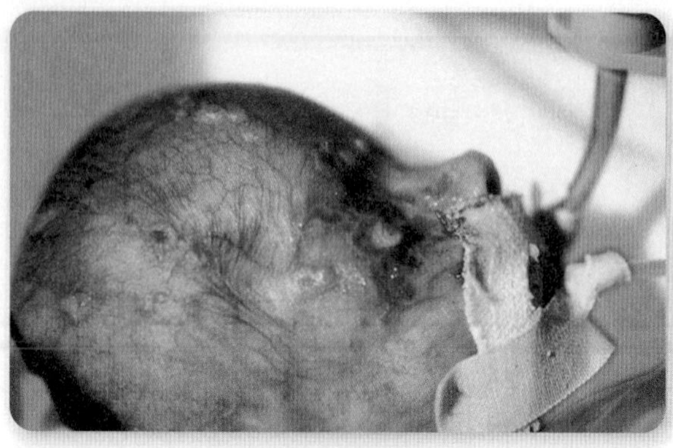

Figure 21.13 Neonatal herpes simplex. This premature infant was born with the classic "cigarette burn" pattern of HSV infection. Babies can be born with the lesions or develop them 1 to 2 weeks after birth.

Herpes of the Newborn

Although HSV infections in healthy adults are annoying and unpleasant, only rarely are they life-threatening. However, in the neonate and the fetus **(figure 21.13)**, HSV infections are very destructive and can be fatal. Most cases occur when infants are contaminated by the mother's reproductive tract immediately before or during birth, but they have also been traced to hand transmission from the mother's lesions to the baby. In infants whose disease is confined to the mouth, skin, or eyes, the mortality rate is 30%, but disease affecting the central nervous system has a 50% to 80% mortality rate.

Pregnant women with a history of recurrent infections must be monitored for any signs of viral shedding, especially in the last 4 weeks of pregnancy. If no evidence of recurrence is seen, vaginal birth is indicated, but any evidence of an outbreak at the time of delivery necessitates a cesarean section.

Causative Agent

Both HSV-1 and HSV-2 can cause genital herpes if the virus contacts the genital epithelium, although HSV-1 is thought of as a virus that infects the oral mucosa, resulting in "cold sores" or "fever blisters" **(figure 21.14)**, and HSV-2 is thought of as the genital virus. In reality, either virus can infect either region, depending on the type of contact.

Pathogenesis and Virulence Factors

Herpesviruses have a strong tendency to become latent. The molecular basis of latency is not entirely clear. During latency, some type of signal causes most of the HSV genome not to be transcribed. This allows the virus to be maintained within cells of the nervous system between episodes. Recent research has found that microRNAs are responsible for the latency of HSV-1. It is further suggested that in some peripheral cells, viral replication takes place at a constant, slow rate, resulting in constant low-level shedding of the virus without lesion production.

Reactivation of the virus can be triggered by a variety of stimuli, including stress, UV radiation (sunlight), injury, menstruation, or another microbial infection. At that point, the virus begins manufacturing large numbers of entire virions, which cause new lesions on the surface of the body served by the neuron, usually in the same site as previous lesions.

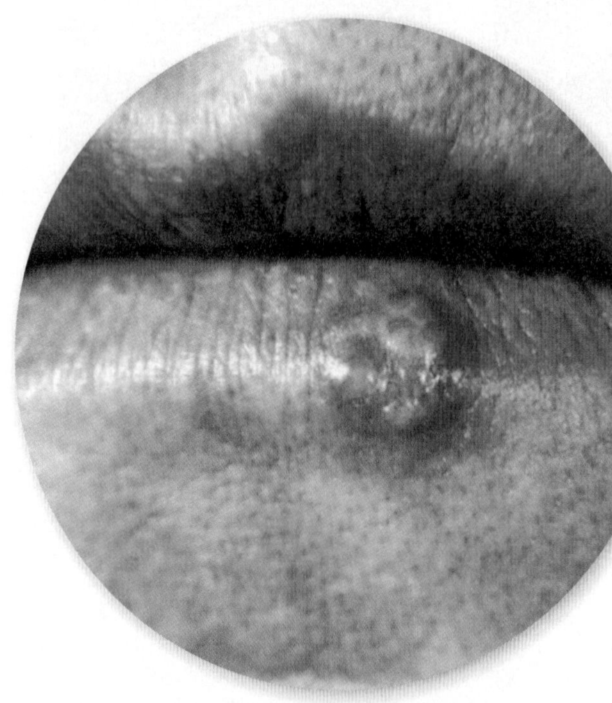

Figure 21.14 Oral herpes infection. Tender itchy papules erupt around the mouth and progress to vesicles that burst, drain, and scab over. These sores and fluid are highly infectious and should not be touched.

Transmission and Epidemiology

Herpes simplex infection occurs globally in all seasons and among all age groups. Because these viruses are relatively sensitive to the environment, transmission is primarily through direct exposure to secretions containing the virus. People with active lesions are the most significant source of infection, but studies indicate that genital herpes can be transmitted even when no lesions are present (due to the constant shedding just discussed).

Earlier in this chapter, you read that *Chlamydia* infection is the most common *reported* infectious disease in the United States. Elsewhere you might hear that gonorrhea is one of the most common reportable *STDs* in the United States. Both statements are true. It is also true that genital herpes is much more common than either of these diseases. Herpes, however, is not an officially *reportable* disease.

It is estimated that about 20% of American adults have genital herpes. That estimate would put the number of infected people in this country at more than 42 million. Two-thirds of people who are infected don't even know it, either because they have rare symptoms that they fail to recognize or because they have no symptoms at all.

Culture and Diagnosis

These two viruses are sometimes diagnosed based on the characteristic lesions alone. PCR tests are available to test for these viruses directly from lesions. Alternatively, antibody to either of the viruses can be detected from blood samples. Detecting antibody to either HSV-1 or HSV-2 in blood does not necessarily indicate whether the infection is oral or genital, or whether the infection is new or preexisting.

Herpes-infected mucosal cells display notable characteristics in a Pap smear **(figure 21.15)**. Laboratory culture and specific tests are essential for diagnosing severe or complicated herpes infections.

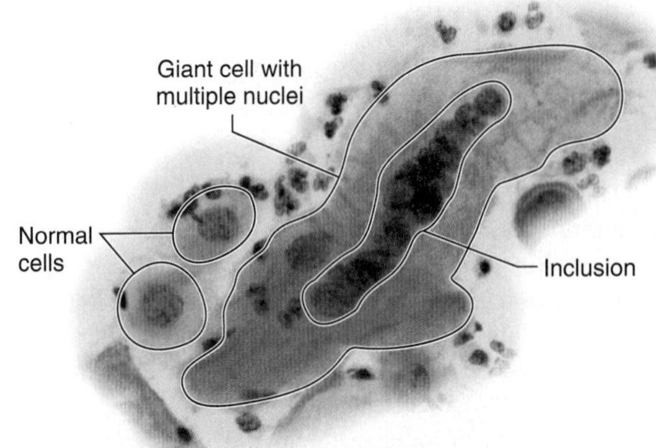

Figure 21.15 The appearance of herpesvirus infection in a Pap smear. A Pap smear of a cervical scraping shows enlarged (multinucleate) (giant) cells and intranuclear inclusions typical of herpes simplex type 2. This appearance is not specific for HSV, but most other herpesviruses do not infect the reproductive mucosa.

▶ Prevention

No vaccine is currently licensed for HSV, but more than one is being tested in clinical trials, meaning that vaccines may become available very soon. In the meantime, avoiding contact with infected body surfaces is the only way to avoid HSV. Condoms provide good protection when they actually cover the site where the lesion is, but lesions can occur outside of the area covered by a condom.

Mothers with cold sores should be careful in handling their newborns; they should never kiss their infants on the mouth.

▶ Treatment

Several agents are available for treatment. These agents often result in reduced viral shedding and a decrease in the frequency of lesion occurrence. They are not curative. Acyclovir (Zovirax) and valacyclovir (Valtrex) are very effective. Topical formulations can be applied directly to lesions, and pills are available as well. Sometimes medicines are prescribed on an ongoing basis to decrease the frequency of recurrences, and sometimes they are prescribed to be taken at the beginning of a recurrence to shorten it.

Wart Diseases

In this section, we describe two viral STIs that cause wartlike growths. The more serious disease is caused by the *human papillomavirus* (*HPV*); the other condition, called *molluscum contagiosum*, apparently has no serious effects.

Human Papillomavirus Infection

These viruses are the causative agents of genital warts. But an individual can be infected with these viruses without having any warts, while still risking serious consequences.

▶ Signs and Symptoms

Symptoms, if present, may manifest as warts—outgrowths of tissue on the genitals **(Disease Table 21.7)**. In females, these growths can occur on the vulva and in and around the vagina. In males, the warts can occur in or on the penis and the scrotum. In both sexes, the warts can appear in or on the anus and even on the skin around the groin, such as the area between the thigh and the pelvis. The warts themselves range from tiny, flat, inconspicuous bumps to extensively branching, cauliflower-like masses called **condyloma acuminata.** The warts are unsightly and can be obstructive, but they don't generally lead to more serious symptoms.

Other types of HPV can lead to more subtle symptoms. Certain types of the virus infect cells on the female cervix. This infection may be "silent," or it may lead to abnormal cell changes in the cervix. Some of these cell changes can eventually result in malignancies of the cervix. The vast majority of cervical cancers are caused by HPV infection. (It is possible that chronic infections with other microorganisms cause a very small percentage of cervical malignancies.) Approximately 4,000 women die each year in the United States from cervical cancer.

Males can also get cancer from infection with these viruses. The sites most often affected are the penis and the anus. These cases are much less common than cervical cancer. Mouth and throat cancers in both genders have also been more recently associated with HPV infection and are thought to be a consequence of oral sex.

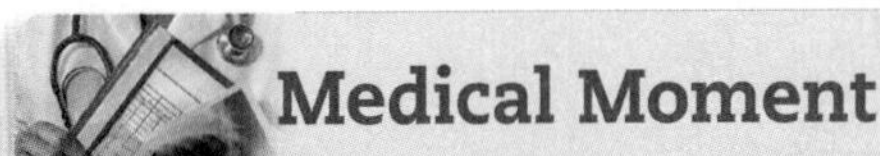

Medical Moment

Crabs

Pediculosis pubis, commonly known as crabs, is caused by infestation of the pubic hair by *Phthirus pubis*, a tiny (1 mm or less) insect that can multiply rapidly. The condition can be spread from person to person through sexual contact and can therefore be considered a sexually transmitted condition. The eyebrows, eyelashes, chest hair, scalp hair, and facial hair may also be affected, generally through oral sexual activities.

Although these tiny creatures do not pose much of a risk to human health, infestation with crabs may lead to a higher risk for other STIs. It is estimated that approximately 3 million people are infected yearly in the United States.

Symptoms include intense itching of the affected areas. Some people do not experience itching but may observe the insects while they are bathing, as the lice are visible to the naked eye.

Treatment is applied topically in the form of creams, shampoos, or lotions. Manual removal of adult insects and their eggs is recommended using a fine-toothed metal comb. Clothing and bedding should be laundered in hot water to prevent reinfestation. Abstinence is the only way to reliably prevent the condition.

A Note About HIV and Hepatitis B and C

This chapter is about diseases *whose major (presenting) symptoms occur in the genitourinary tract.* But some sexually transmitted diseases do not have their major symptoms in this system. HIV and hepatitis B and C can all be transmitted in several ways, one of them being through sexual contact. HIV is considered in chapter 18 because its major symptoms occur in the cardiovascular and lymphatic systems. Because the major disease manifestations of hepatitis B and C occur in the gastrointestinal tract, these diseases are discussed in chapter 20. Anyone diagnosed with any sexually transmitted disease should also be tested for HIV.

▸ Causative Agent

The human papillomaviruses are a group of nonenveloped DNA viruses belonging to the Papovaviridae family. There are more than 100 different types of HPV. Some types are specific for the mucous membranes; others invade the skin. Some of these viruses are the cause of plantar warts, which often occur on the soles of the feet. Other HPVs cause the common or "seed" warts and flat warts. In this chapter, we are concerned only with the HPVs that colonize the genital tract.

Among the HPVs that infect the genital tract, some are more likely to cause the appearance of warts. Others that have a preference for growing on the cervix can lead to cancerous changes. Five types in particular, HPV-16, -18, -31, -33, and -35, are closely associated with development of cervical cancer. Other types put you at higher risk for vulvar or penile cancer.

▸ Pathogenesis and Virulence Factors

Scientists are working hard to understand how viruses cause the growths we know as warts and also how some of them can cause cancer. The major virulence factor for cancer-causing HPVs is their **oncogenes,** which code for proteins that interfere with normal host cell function, resulting in uncontrolled growth.

▸ Transmission and Epidemiology

Young women have the highest rate of HPV infections; 25% to 46% of women under the age of 25 are infected with genital HPV. It is estimated that 14% of female college students become infected with this incurable condition each year. Overall, about 15% of people between 15 and 49 are HPV-positive. It is difficult to know whether genital herpes or HPV is more common, but it is probably safe to assume that any unprotected sex carries a good chance of encountering either HSV or HPV.

The mode of transmission is direct contact. Autoinoculation is also possible—meaning that the virus can be spread to other parts of the body by touching warts. Indirect transmission occurs but is more common for nongenital warts caused by HPV.

▸ Culture and Diagnosis

PCR-based screening tests can be used to test samples from a pelvic exam for the presence of dangerous HPV types. These tests are now recommended for women over the age of 30.

▸ Prevention

When discussing HPV prevention, we must consider two possibilities. One of these is infection with the viruses, which is prevented the same way other sexually transmitted infections are prevented—by avoiding direct, unprotected contact, but also by one of two vaccines that are now available (Gardasil and Cervarix). The vaccines prevent infection by a small number of types of HPV and are recommended in girls as young as age 9. Despite the fears of some parents, being vaccinated against the virus does not encourage girls to become sexually active, but instead causes them to realize the dangers of sex, according to a study conducted in 2009 among 553 teenage girls in Britain.

The second issue is the prevention of cervical cancer. Even though women now have access to the vaccines, cancer can still result from HPV types not included in the vaccines. The good news is that cervical cancer is slow in developing, so that even if a woman is infected with a malignant HPV type, regular screening of the cervix can detect abnormal changes early. The standardized screen for cervical cell changes is the Pap smear. Precancerous changes show up very early, and the development process can be stopped by removal of the affected tissue. Women should have their first Pap smear by age 21 or within 3 years of their first sexual activity, whichever comes first. New Pap smear technologies have been developed; and depending on which one your physician uses, it is now possible that you need to be screened only once every 2 or 3 years. But you should base your screening practices on the sound advice of a physician.

▶ Treatment

Infection with any HPV is incurable. Genital warts can be removed through a variety of methods, some of which can be used at home. But the virus causing them will most likely remain with you. It is possible for the viral infection to resolve itself, but this is very unpredictable.

Incurable Infections

In 1960, the first birth control pill was approved by the Food and Drug Administration. This changed the landscape for sexual relations. Previously, the only reliable pregnancy preventer was a condom. But with the rush of enthusiasm for birth control pills, the need for barrier protection to prevent disease transmission was underemphasized. As a result, sexually transmitted infections of all types surged. Many of the curable (bacterial) infections peaked and decreased in incidence in later decades. But two notable infections, herpes and HPV, are not curable. Thus, the prevalence of these infections in the population only increases. When your children are ready to have sexual relations, the likelihood that their partners will carry one of these viruses will be much higher than that of the previous generation. Eventually this likelihood can decrease again if the uptake of the HPV vaccines increases and an HSV vaccine becomes available.

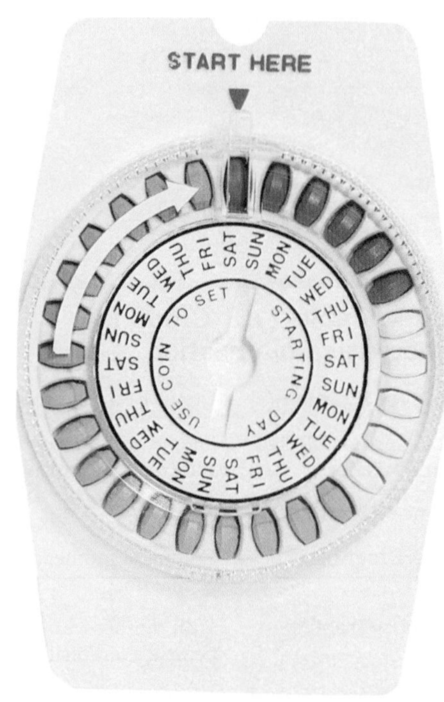

Molluscum Contagiosum

An unclassified virus in the family *Poxviridae* can cause a condition called molluscum contagiosum. This disease can take the form of skin lesions, and it can also be transmitted sexually. The wartlike growths that result from this infection can be found on the mucous membranes or the skin of the genital area (see Disease Table 21.7). Few problems are associated with these growths beyond the warts themselves. In severely immunocompromised people, the disease can be more serious.

Disease Table 21.7 Wart Diseases

	HPV	Molluscum Contagiosum
Causative Organism(s)	Human papillomaviruses	Poxvirus, sometimes called the molluscum contagiosum virus (MCV)
Most Common Modes of Transmission	Direct contact (STI)—also autoinoculation, indirect contact	Direct contact (STI), also indirect and autoinoculation
Virulence Factors	Oncogenes (in the case of malignant types of HPV)	–
Culture/Diagnosis	PCR tests for certain HPV types, clinical diagnosis	Clinical diagnosis, also histology, PCR
Prevention	Vaccine available; avoid direct contact; prevent cancer by screening cervix	Avoid direct contact
Treatment	Warts or precancerous tissue can be removed; virus not treatable	Warts can be removed; virus not treatable
Distinguishing Features	Infection may or may not result in warts; infection may result in malignancy	Wartlike growths are only known consequence of infection
Effects on Fetus	May cause laryngeal warts	–
Appearance of Lesions		

The virus causing these growths can also be transmitted through fomites such as clothing or towels and through autoinoculation. For a more detailed description of this condition, see chapter 16.

Group B *Streptococcus* "Colonization"—Neonatal Disease

Ten to forty percent of women in the United States are colonized, asymptomatically, by a beta-hemolytic *Streptococcus* in Lancefield group B. Nonpregnant women experience no ill effects from this colonization. But colonization of pregnant women with this organism is associated with preterm delivery. Additionally, about half of their infants become colonized by the bacterium during passage through the birth canal or by ascension of the bacteria through ruptured membranes; thus, this colonization is considered a reproductive tract disease.

A small percentage of infected infants experience life-threatening bloodstream infections, meningitis, or pneumonia. If they recover from these acute conditions, they may have permanent disabilities, such as developmental disabilities, hearing loss, or impaired vision. In some cases, the mothers also experience disease, such as amniotic infection or subsequent stillbirths.

In 2002, the CDC recommended that all pregnant women be screened for group B *Streptococcus* colonization at 35 to 37 weeks of pregnancy. These recommendations may be modified to recommend earlier screening now that colonization has been associated with preterm birth. Women positive for the bacterium should be treated with penicillin or ampicillin, unless the bacterium is found to be resistant to these, and unless allergy to penicillin is present, in which case erythromycin may be used.

Disease Table 21.8 Group B *Streptococcus* Colonization

Causative Organism(s)	Group B *Streptococcus*
Most Common Modes of Transmission	Endogenous in mother; vertical in newborns
Virulence Factors	–
Culture/Diagnosis	Culture of mother's genital tract
Prevention/Treatment	Treat mother with penicillin/ampicillin

ASSESS YOUR PROGRESS

6. List the possible causative agents, modes of transmission, virulence factors, and prevention/treatment for gonorrhea and *Chlamydia* infection.
7. Distinguish between vaginitis and vaginosis.
8. Discuss prostatitis.
9. Name three diseases that result in genital ulcers, and discuss their important features.
10. Differentiate between the two diseases causing warts in the reproductive tract.
11. Provide some detail about the first "cancer vaccine" and how it works.
12. Identify the most important risk group for group B *Streptococcus* infection and why.

CASE FILE WRAP-UP

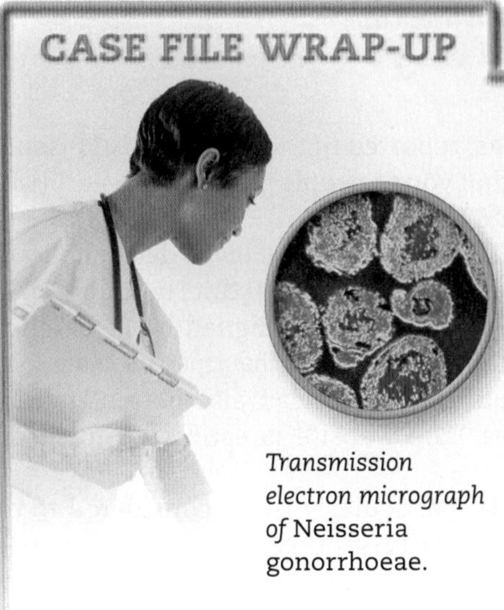

Transmission electron micrograph of Neisseria gonorrhoeae.

The young patient featured in the opening case study was given a pelvic exam after consent was obtained from the patient's mother. The patient was found to have a purulent and foul-smelling vaginal discharge, in addition to fever and lower abdominal pain. Cultures of the vaginal discharge and the cervix were obtained. Blood work and an ultrasound were also ordered. The blood work revealed an elevated white blood cell count and erythrocyte sedimentation rate (ESR), while the ultrasound revealed an abscess near the left ovary. The patient was admitted with a diagnosis of pelvic inflammatory disease (PID) for IV antibiotics and possible surgical drainage of the abscess. Cultures eventually yielded the specific causative agent, *Neisseria gonorrhoeae*. The "PID shuffle" is a term used to describe the typical gait of a patient with PID, in which the feet are advanced in a shuffling manner to avoid jarring the pelvic organs, which results in severe pain.

The patient was only 10 years of age, which should raise suspicion of child abuse. Not only should the case be reported to the appropriate state health authority, but it should also be reported to social services or the police in order to determine whether the patient was a victim of abuse.

Inside the Clinic

Testing at Home for STIs: Trading Privacy for Accuracy?

New research from Johns Hopkins, reported in the February 2011 issue of *Sexually Transmitted Diseases*, has shown that young people prefer to do everything online—including testing themselves for STIs.

A program that was begun in Baltimore in 2004 was designed to provide kits for testing for STIs from an online site, www.IWantTheKit.org. The website, which is now available in several states, was designed by researchers at Johns Hopkins and provides confidential testing for *Trichomonas vaginalis, Neisseria gonorrhoeae,* and *Chlamydia trachomatis*. Site users can also obtain treatment advice and options if they test positive. The website is estimated to receive 100,000 monthly "hits."

Data show that young people, particularly those considered to be high risk (urban, poor, harder to reach minority groups), prefer to obtain kits online, although kits were also made available in public health clinics and pharmacies for the purposes of the study. In fact, 9 out of 10 users preferred to order their kit online. Although the kits were initially available only to females, kits for males are now also available. Alaska; Washington, D.C.; Maryland; Denver, Colorado; Philadelphia, Pennsylvania; West Virginia; and parts of Illinois are the areas currently served by the site, but the program could easily be made available in all 50 states.

The supplied kits come with instructions for use, a unique identifier number, and a prepaid envelope to return the swabs collected (vaginal, rectal, or penile swabs) to a lab at Johns Hopkins. The kits are packaged and mailed discreetly and also include questionnaires designed to collect crucial demographic information. Within 2 weeks, individuals can call a phone number, provide their secure identification code, and receive the results of their test. As of February 2011, more than 600 individuals have tested positive for a protozoan or bacterial infection. Those who test positive are referred to a nearby public health clinic. All but 5 individuals sought treatment after receiving their results.

The encouraging results of this study show that young people prefer online anonymity to visiting a clinic and speaking to a professional face-to-face. They appreciate the privacy, confidentiality, and practicality of obtaining test kits online and receiving their results over the phone.

Charlotte Gaydos, an STI and public health expert from Johns Hopkins, who was involved with the preceding study, attempted to survey the quality of testing services provided by for-profit companies offering online STI test kits. She discovered that the reliability of these companies was less than stellar. She received results from only four out of six companies she sent samples to. Worse yet, half of the companies returned false negative results, despite the fact that she purposely infected the samples with *Chlamydia*. Thus far, the FDA has not given approval to any of these companies. These results were the reason Gaydos and colleagues at Johns Hopkins set out to create www.IWantTheKit.org, which has proven to be very successful.

Ideally, counseling and testing through an individual's health care provider should be the standard, but young people may be reluctant to go to their doctor to ask to be tested. Online testing from a reputable source, such as the program started at Johns Hopkins, offers a safe, effective alternative, particularly for a younger generation that is used to doing everything online.

▶ Summing Up

Taxonomic Organization Microorganisms Causing Disease in the Genitourinary Tract

Microorganism	Pronunciation	Location of Disease Table
Gram-positive bacteria		
Staphylococcus saprophyticus	staf″-uh-lo-kok′-us sap′-pro-fit″-uh-cus	Urinary tract infection, p. 600
Gardnerella (note: stains gram-negative)	gard′-ner-el″-uh	Vaginitis or vaginosis, p. 608
Group B *Streptococcus*	groop bee′ strep′-tuh-kok″-us	Group B *Streptococcus* neonatal disease, p. 618
Gram-negative bacteria		
Escherichia coli	esh′shur-eesh″-ee-uh col′-eye	Urinary tract infection, p. 600
Leptospira interrogans (spirochete)	lep′-toh-spy′-ruh in-ter′-ruh-ganz	Leptospirosis, p. 601
Proteus mirabilis	pro′-tee-us meer-ab′-ah-lus	Urinary tract infection and kidney stones, p. 600
Neisseria gonorrhoeae	nye-seer″-ee-uh′ gon′-uh-ree″-uh	Gonorrhea, p. 606
Chlamydia trachomatis	kluh-mi″-dee-uh′ truh-koh′-muh-tis	Chlamydia, p. 606
Treponema pallidum (spirochete)	trep′-oh-nee″-ma pal′-uh-dum	Syphilis, p. 613
Haemophilus ducreyi	huh-mah′-fuh-luss doo-cray′-ee-eye	Chancroid, p. 613
DNA viruses		
Herpes simplex virus 1 and 2	hur′-peez sim′-plex vie′-russ	Genital herpes, p. 613
Human papillomavirus	hew′-mun pap′-uh-loh″-muh-vie′-russ	Genital warts and cervical carcinoma, p. 617
Poxvirus	pox′-vie′-russ	Molluscum contagiosum, p. 617
Fungi		
Candida albicans	can′-duh-duh al″-buh-cans′	Vaginitis or vaginosis, p. 608
Protozoa		
Trichomonas vaginalis	trick″-uh-mon′-us vaj′-ih-nal″-us	Trichomoniasis or vaginitis, p. 608

Infectious Diseases Affecting
The Genitourinary System

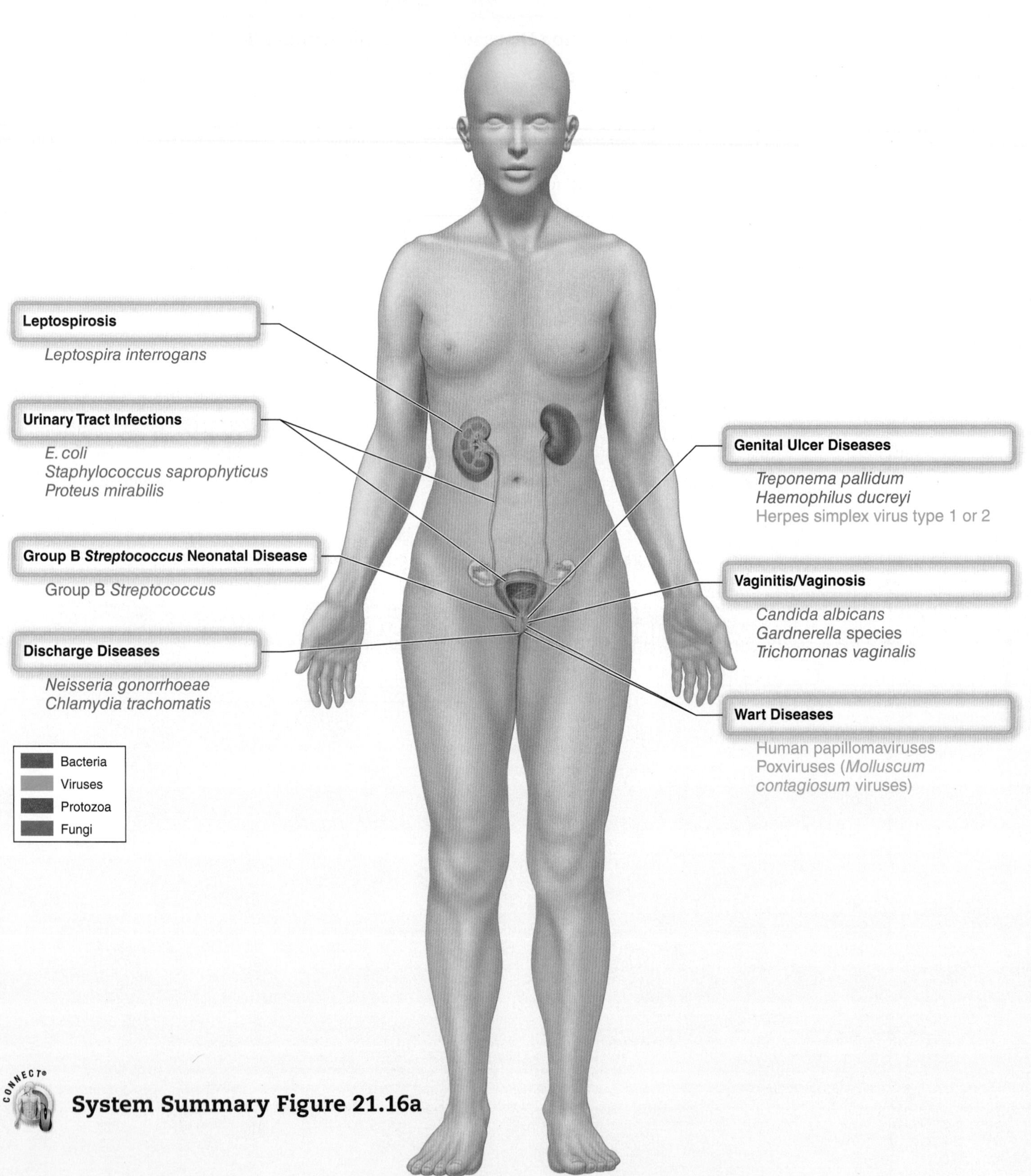

System Summary Figure 21.16a

Infectious Diseases Affecting
The Genitourinary System

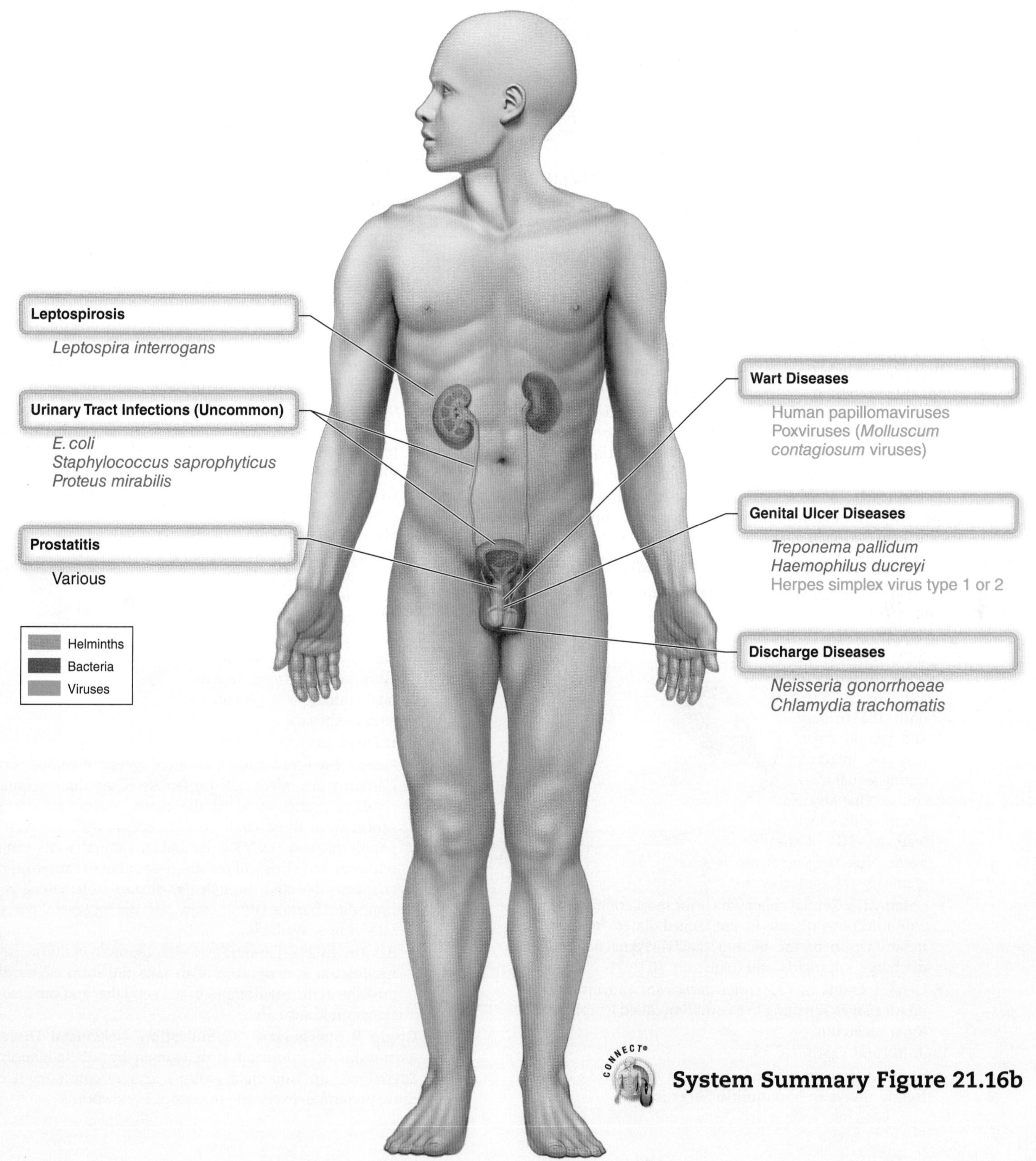

System Summary Figure 21.16b

Chapter Summary

21.1 The Genitourinary Tract and Its Defenses

- The urinary system allows excretion of fluid and wastes from the body. It has mechanical, chemical defense mechanisms.
- The reproductive tract is composed of structures and substances that allow for sexual intercourse and the creation of a new fetus; protected by normal mucosal defenses and specialized features (such as low pH.)

21.2 Normal Biota of the Genitourinary Tract

- Normal biota in the male reproductive and urinary systems are in the distal part of the urethra and resemble skin biota. Same is generally true for the female urinary system. Normal biota in the female reproductive tract changes over the course of her lifetime.

21.3 Urinary Tract Diseases Caused by Microorganisms

- **Urinary Tract Infections (UTIs):** Can occur in the bladder (*cystitis*), the kidneys (*pyelonephritis*), and the urethra (*urethritis*). Most common causes are *Escherichia coli, Staphylococcus saprophyticus,* and *Proteus mirabilis.* Community-acquired UTIs are most often transmitted from the GI tract to the urinary system. UTIs are the most common nosocomial infection.
- **Leptospirosis:** Zoonosis associated with wild animals that affects the kidneys, liver, brain, and eyes. Causative agent is spirochete *Leptospira interrogans*.

21.4 Reproductive Tract Diseases Caused by Microorganisms

- **Discharge Diseases with Major Manifestation in the Genitourinary Tract**
  - Gonorrhea can elicit urethritis in males, but many cases are asymptomatic. In females, both the urinary and genital tracts may be infected during sexual intercourse. One sequela is salpingitis, which can lead to PID. Causative agent, *Neisseria gonorrhoeae,* is a gram-negative diplococcus.
  - **Chlamydia:** Genital chlamydia is the most common reportable infectious disease in the United States. In males: an inflammation of the urethra (NGU). Females: cervicitis, discharge, salpingitis, and frequently PID.
  - Certain strains of *Chlamydia trachomatis* can invade lymphatic tissues, resulting in a condition called lymphogranuloma venereum.
- **Vaginitis and Vaginosis**
  - Vaginitis is most commonly caused by *Candida albicans*. Nearly always an opportunistic infection.
  - *Gardnerella* is associated with vaginosis; has a discharge but no inflammation. Could lead to complications such as pelvic inflammatory disease (PID).
  - *Trichomonas vaginalis* causes mostly asymptomatic infections in females and males. *Trichomonas,* a flagellated protozoan, is easily transmitted through sexual contact.
- **Prostatitis:** Inflammation of the prostate; can be acute or chronic. Not all cases established to have microbial cause, but most do.
- **Genital Ulcer Diseases**
  - **Syphilis**: Caused by spirochete *Treponema pallidum.* Three distinct clinical stages: *primary, secondary,* and *tertiary syphilis,* with a latent period between secondary and tertiary. Spirochete appears in lesions, blood during primary and secondary stages; is transmissible at these times, also during early latency period. Largely nontransmissible during "late latent" and tertiary stages. The syphilis bacterium can lead to congenital syphilis, inhibiting fetal growth and disrupting critical periods of development. This can lead to spontaneous miscarriage or stillbirth.
  - **Chancroid:** Caused by *Haemophilus ducreyi,* a pleomorphic gram-negative rod. Transmitted exclusively through direct—mainly sexual—contact.
  - **Genital Herpes**: Caused by two types of herpes simplex viruses (HSVs): HSV-1 and HSV-2. May be no symptoms, or may be fluid-filled, painful vesicles on genitalia, perineum, thigh, and buttocks. In severe cases, meningitis or encephalitis can develop. Patients remain asymptomatic or experience recurrent "surface" infections indefinitely. Infections in neonate and fetus can be fatal.
- **Wart Diseases**
  - *Human papillomaviruses:* Causative agents of genital warts. Certain types infect cells on female cervix that eventually result in malignancies of the cervix. Males can also get cancer from these viral types. Infection with any human papillomavirus (HPV) is incurable. Genital warts can be removed, but virus will remain. Treatment of cancerous cell changes—detected through Pap smears in females—is an important part of HPV therapy. Vaccine for several types of HPV is now available.
  - A virus in the family *Poxviridae* causes condition called molluscum contagiosum. Can take the form of wartlike growths in the membranes of the genitalia, and can also be transmitted sexually.
- **Group B *Streptococcus* "Colonization"—Neonatal Disease:** Asymptomatic colonization of women by a beta-hemolytic *Streptococcus* in Lancefield group B is very common. It can cause preterm delivery and infections in newborns.

Multiple-Choice Questions Knowledge and Comprehension

Select the correct answer from the answers provided.

1. Cystitis is an infection of the
   a. bladder.
   b. urethra.
   c. kidney.
   d. vagina.
2. Leptospirosis is transmitted to humans by
   a. person to person.
   b. fomites.
   c. mosquitoes.
   d. contaminated soil or water.
3. Syphilis is caused by
   a *Treponema pallidum.*
   b. *Neisseria gonorrhoeae.*
   c. *Trichomonas vaginalis.*
   d. *Haemophilus ducreyi.*
4. Bacterial vaginosis is commonly associated with the following organism:
   a. *Candida albicans*
   b. *Gardnerella*
   c. *Trichomonas*
   d. all of the above
   e. none of the above
5. This dimorphic fungus is a common cause of vaginitis.
   a. *Candida albicans*
   b. *Gardnerella*
   c. *Trichomonas*
   d. all of the above
6. Genital herpes transmission can be reduced or prevented by all of the following, *except*
   a. a condom.
   b. abstinence.
   c. the contraceptive pill.
   d. a female condom.
7. This protozoan can be treated with the drug metronidazole (Flagyl).
   a. *Neisseria gonorrhoeae*
   b. *Chlamydia trachomatis*
   c. *Treponema pallidum*
   d. *Trichomonas vaginalis*
8. Which group has the highest rate of HPV infection?
   a. female college students
   b. male college students
   c. college professors of either gender
   d. baby-boomers

Critical Thinking Application and Analysis

Critical thinking **is the ability to reason and solve problems using facts and concepts. These questions can be approached from a number of angles and, in most cases, they do not have a single correct answer.**

1. Infection with *Gardnerella* does not induce inflammation in the vagina. Can you speculate on characteristics of the infection or the organism which could result in no inflammation?.
2. What advantages does the life cycle of *Chlamydia* confer on the pathogen?
3. What are some of the stimuli that can trigger reactivation of a latent herpesvirus infection? Speculate on why.
4. Why do you suppose a urine screening test for *Chlamydia* is more accurate for males than for females?
5. It has been stated that the actual number of people in the United States who have genital herpes may be a lot higher than official statistics depict. What are some possible reasons for this discrepancy?

Visual Connections Synthesis

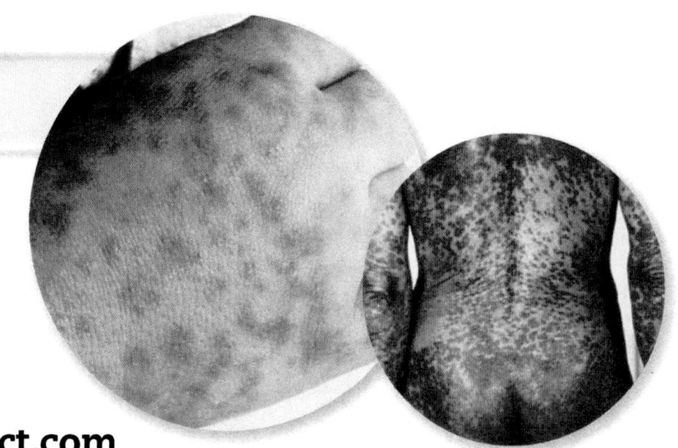

This question connects previous images to a new concept.

1. **From chapters 18 and 21, figure 18.17 and the photo on page 610.** Compare these two rashes. What kind of information would help you determine the diagnosis in both cases?

APPENDIX

Exponents

Dealing with concepts such as microbial growth often requires working with numbers in the billions, trillions, and even greater. A mathematical shorthand for expressing such numbers is with exponents. The exponent of a number indicates how many times (designated by a superscript) that number is multiplied by itself. These exponents are also commonly called *logarithms,* or logs. The following chart, based on multiples of 10, summarizes this system.

Exponential Notation for Base 10

Number	Quantity	Exponential Notation*	Number Arrived at By:	One Followed By:
1	One	10^0	Numbers raised to zero power are equal to one	No zeros
10	Ten	10^1**	10×1	One zero
100	Hundred	10^2	10×10	Two zeros
1,000	Thousand	10^3	$10 \times 10 \times 10$	Three zeros
10,000	Ten thousand	10^4	$10 \times 10 \times 10 \times 10$	Four zeros
100,000	Hundred thousand	10^5	$10 \times 10 \times 10 \times 10 \times 10$	Five zeros
1,000,000	Million	10^6	10 times itself 6 times	Six zeros
1,000,000,000	Billion	10^9	10 times itself 9 times	Nine zeros
1,000,000,000,000	Trillion	10^{12}	10 times itself 12 times	Twelve zeros
1,000,000,000,000,000	Quadrillion	10^{15}	10 times itself 15 times	Fifteen zeros
1,000,000,000,000,000,000	Quintillion	10^{18}	10 times itself 18 times	Eighteen zeros

Other large numbers are sextillion (10^{21}), septillion (10^{24}), and octillion (10^{27}).

*The proper way to say the numbers in this column is 10 raised to the *n*th power, where *n* is the exponent. The numbers in this column can also be represented as 1×10^n, but for brevity, the $1 \times$ can be omitted.

**The exponent 1 is usually omitted.

Converting Numbers to Exponent Form

As the chart shows, using exponents to express numbers can be very economical. When simple multiples of 10 are used, the exponent is always equal to the number of zeros that follow the 1, but this rule will not work with numbers that are more varied. Other large whole numbers can be converted to exponent form by the following operation: First, move the decimal (which we assume to be at the end of the number) to the left until it sits just behind the first number in the series (example: 3568. = 3.568). Then count the number of spaces (digits) the decimal has moved;

that number will be the exponent. (The decimal has moved from 8. to 3., or 3 spaces.) In final notation, the converted number is multiplied by 10 with its appropriate exponent: 3568 is now 3.568×10^3.

Rounding Off Numbers

The notation in the previous example has not actually been shortened, but it can be reduced further by rounding off the decimal fraction to the nearest thousandth (three digits), hundredth (two digits), or tenth (one digit). To round off a number, drop its last digit and either increase the one next to it or leave it as it is. If the number dropped is 5, 6, 7, 8, or 9, the subsequent digit is increased by one (rounded up); if it is 0, 1, 2, 3, or 4, the subsequent digit remains as is. Using the example of 3.528, removing the 8 rounds off the 2 to a 3 and produces 3.53 (two digits). If further rounding is desired, the same rule of thumb applies, and the number becomes 3.5 (one digit). Other examples of exponential conversions follow.

Number	Is the Same As	Rounded Off, Placed in Exponent Form
16,825.	$1.6825 \times 10 \times 10 \times 10 \times 10$	1.7×10^4
957,654.	$9.57654 \times 10 \times 10 \times 10 \times 10 \times 10$	9.58×10^5
2,855,000.	$2.855000 \times 10 \times 10 \times 10 \times 10 \times 10 \times 10$	2.86×10^6

Negative Exponents

The numbers we have been using so far are greater than 1 and are represented by positive exponents. But the correct notation for numbers less than 1 involves negative exponents (10 raised to a negative power, or 10^{-n}). A negative exponent says that the number has been divided by a certain power of 10 (10, 100, 1,000). This usage is handy when working with concepts such as pH that are based on very small numbers otherwise needing to be represented by large decimal fractions—for example, 0.003528. Converting this and other such numbers to exponential notation is basically similar to converting positive numbers, except that you work from left to right and the exponent is negative. Using the example of 0.003528, first convert the number to a whole integer followed by a decimal fraction and keep track of the number of spaces the decimal point moves (example: 0.003528 = 3.528). The decimal has moved three spaces from its original position, so the finished product is 3.528×10^{-3}. Other examples follow.

Number	Is the Same As	Rounded Off, Expressed with Exponents
0.0005923	$\frac{5.923}{10 \times 10 \times 10 \times 10}$	5.92×10^{-4}
0.00007295	$\frac{7.295}{10 \times 10 \times 10 \times 10 \times 10}$	7.3×10^{-5}

APPENDIX B

Answers to NCLEX® Prep and Multiple-Choice Questions

Chapter 1

NCLEX® Prep
1. a
2. c

Multiple-Choice
1. d
2. d
3. a
4. c
5. c
6. d
7. c
8. a

Chapter 2

NCLEX® Prep
1. b
2. d
3. c
4. c
5. d

Multiple-Choice
1. c
2. b
3. b
4. c
5. c
6. a
7. b
8. d

Chapter 3

NCLEX® Prep
1. c
2. a
3. b

Multiple-Choice
1. d
2. d
3. c
4. b
5. b
6. d
7. c
8. c

Chapter 4

NCLEX®Prep
1. d
2. b
3. a
4. c
5. a

Multiple-Choice
1. b
2. d
3. b
4. d
5. d
6. b
7. c
8. a

Chapter 5

NCLEX® Prep
1. d
2. a
3. d

Multiple-Choice
1. c
2. d
3. d
4. a
5. a
6. b
7. d
8. a

Chapter 6

NCLEX® Prep
1. d
2. e
3. b
4. c
5. d

Multiple-Choice
1. a
2. c
3. b
4. a
5. a
6. b
7. c
8. b

Chapter 7

NCLEX® Prep
1. b
2. c
3. b
4. c

Multiple-Choice
1. a
2. d
3. b
4. b
5. d
6. b
7. c
8. c

Chapter 8

NCLEX® Prep
1. b
2. c
3. c
4. d

Multiple-Choice
1. b
2. b
3. b
4. c
5. a
6. b
7. a
8. c

Chapter 9

NCLEX® Prep
1. c
2. d
3. a
4. b

Multiple-Choice
1. c
2. a
3. c
4. b
5. d
6. b
7. d
8. b

Chapter 10

NCLEX® Prep
1. a or b
2. d
3. c
4. a

Multiple-Choice
1. b
2. c
3. b
4. d
5. d
6. b
7. c
8. b

Chapter 11

NCLEX® Prep
1. c
2. b
3. d
4. c

Multiple-Choice
1. a
2. b
3. d
4. d
5. b
6. c
7. a
8. a

Chapter 12

NCLEX® Prep
1. a
2. b
3. c
4. e
5. c

Multiple-Choice
1. b
2. d
3. b
4. c
5. d
6. a
7. d
8. c

Chapter 13

NCLEX® Prep
1. a
2. c
3. d
4. b

Multiple-Choice
1. a
2. c
3. c
4. c
5. a
6. e
7. c
8. d

Chapter 14

NCLEX® Prep
1. e
2. b
3. c
4. d

Multiple-Choice
1. a
2. d
3. a
4. b
5. b
6. b
7. d
8. d

Chapter 15

NCLEX® Prep
1. d
2. e
3. e

Multiple-Choice
1. b
2. a
3. c
4. c
5. b
6. c
7. b
8. c

Chapter 16

NCLEX® Prep
1. c
2. a
3. b
4. e

Multiple-Choice
1. b
2. a
3. d
4. e
5. d
6. d
7. b
8. c

Chapter 17

NCLEX® Prep
1. a
2. e
3. d
4. d
5. d

Multiple-Choice
1. d
2. a
3. c
4. d
5. b
6. b
7. a
8. d

Chapter 18

NCLEX® Prep
1. b
2. c
3. d
4. c
5. a

Multiple-Choice
1. c
2. b
3. b
4. a
5. b
6. a
7. b
8. d

Chapter 19

NCLEX® Prep
1. c
2. d
3. a

Multiple-Choice
1. d
2. b
3. d
4. c
5. d
6. c
7. a
8. c

Chapter 20

NCLEX® Prep
1. e
2. b
3. c
4. e
5. f

Multiple-Choice
1. b
2. c
3. c
4. c
5. b

Chapter 21

NCLEX® Prep
1. c
2. d
3. d
4. e
5. f

Multiple-Choice
1. a
2. d
3. a
4. b
5. a
6. c
7. d
8. a

Chapter 22

NCLEX® Prep
1. c
2. d
3. a

Multiple-Choice
1. b
2. c
3. b
4. d
5. d
6. b
7. a
8. d

Displaying Disease Statistics

Infectious disease specialists use a number of different methods to visually represent the numbers of disease cases or deaths.

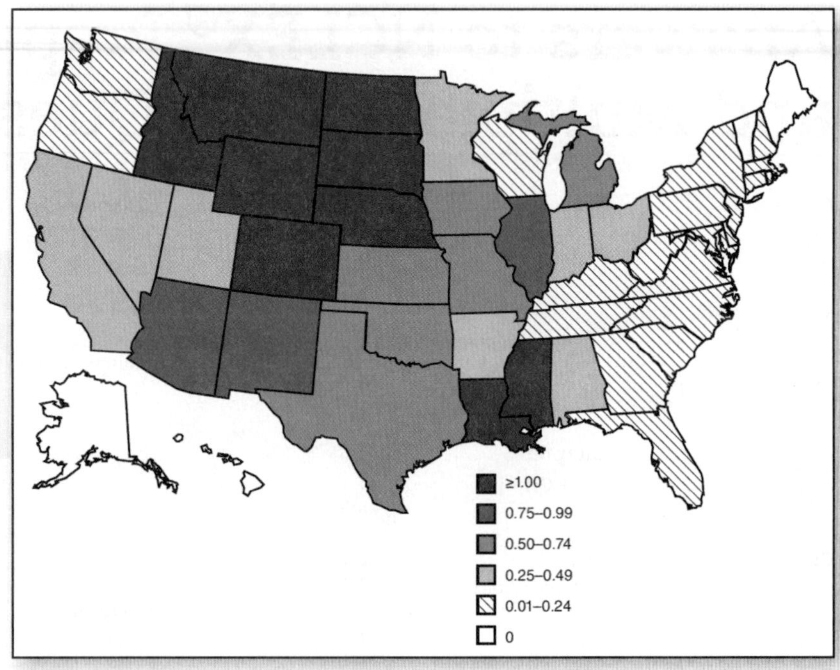

Average annual incidence* per 100,000 population of West Nile virus neuroinvasive disease (n = 11,822), by state of residence—United States, 1999–2008.

*Calculated using U.S. Census Bureau population estimates for July 1, 2004.

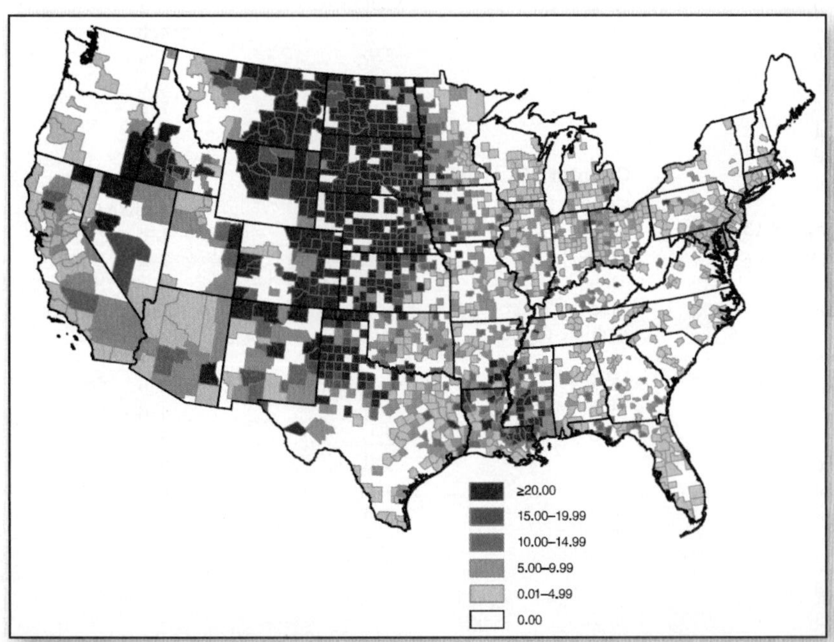

Average annual incidence* per 100,000 population of West Nile virus neuroinvasive disease (n = 11,822), by county of residence—United States, 1999–2008.

*Calculated using U.S. Census Bureau population estimates for July 1, 2004.

Some methods emphasize the geographical distribution of disease.

Other methods may represent trends over time.

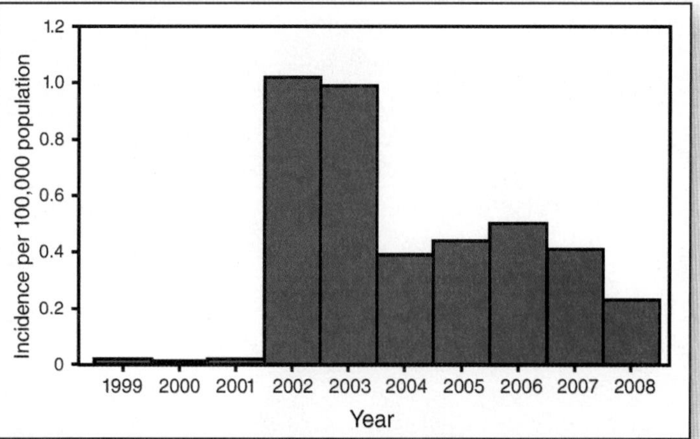

Annual incidence* of West Nile virus neuroinvasive disease (n = 11,822), by year—United States, 1999–2008.

*Calculated using U.S. Census Bureau population estimates for July 1 of each year of the reporting period.

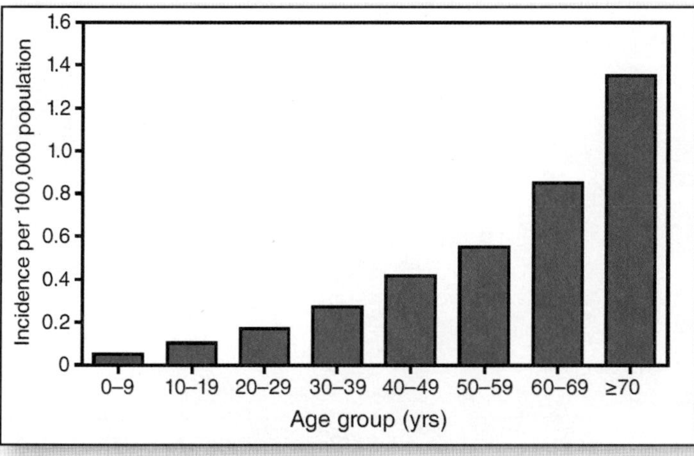

West Nile virus neuroinvasive disease case-fatality ratios*, by age group—United States, 1999–2008.

*Calculated using U.S. Census Bureau population estimates for July 1 of each year of the reporting period.

Or, the image may depict information by age.

Visit www.cdc.gov/mmwr for more in-depth discussions and visual representations of disease statistics.

Glossary

A

A-B toxin A class of bacterial exotoxin consisting of two components: a binding (B) component and an active (A) or enzymatic component.

abiogenesis The belief in spontaneous generation as a source of life.

abiotic Nonliving factors such as soil, water, temperature, and light that are studied when looking at an ecosystem.

ABO blood group system Developed by Karl Landsteiner in 1904; the identification of different blood groups based on differing isoantigen markers characteristic of each blood type.

abscess An inflamed, fibrous lesion enclosing a core of pus.

abyssal zone The deepest region of the ocean; a sunless, high-pressure, cold, anaerobic habitat.

acellular vaccine A vaccine preparation that contains specific antigens such as the capsule or toxin from a pathogen and not the whole microbe. Acellular (without a cell).

acid-fast A term referring to the property of mycobacteria to retain carbol fuchsin even in the presence of acid alcohol. The staining procedure is used to diagnose tuberculosis.

acid-fast stain A solution containing carbol-fuchsin which, when bound to lipids in the envelopes of *Mycobacterium* species, cannot be removed with an acid wash.

acidic A solution with a pH value below 7 on the pH scale.

acidic fermentation An anaerobic degradation of pyruvic acid that results in organic acid production.

acquired immunodeficiency syndrome See *AIDS.*

actin Protein component of long filaments of protein arranged under the cell membrane of bacteria; contribute to cell shape and division.

actin cytoskeleton A scaffoldlike structure made of protein that lies under the cytoplasmic membrane of some bacteria.

actinomycetes A group of filamentous, funguslike bacteria.

active immunity Immunity acquired through direct stimulation of the immune system by antigen.

active site The specific region on an apoenzyme that binds substrate. The site for reaction catalysis.

active transport Nutrient transport method that requires carrier proteins in the membranes of the living cells and the expenditure of energy.

acute Characterized by rapid onset and short duration.

acyclovir A synthetic purine analog that blocks DNA synthesis in certain viruses, particularly the herpes simplex viruses.

adenine (A) One of the nitrogen bases found in DNA and RNA, with a purine form.

adenosine deaminase (ADA) deficiency An immunodeficiency disorder and one type of SCIDS that is caused by an inborn error in the metabolism of adenine. The accumulation of adenine destroys both B and T lymphocytes.

adenosine triphosphate (ATP) A nucleotide that is the primary source of energy to cells.

adhesion The process by which microbes gain a more stable foothold at the portal of entry; often involves a specific interaction between the molecules on the microbial surface and the receptors on the host cell.

adjuvant In immunology, a chemical vehicle that enhances antigenicity, presumably by prolonging antigen retention at the injection site.

adsorption A process of adhering one molecule onto the surface of another molecule.

aerobe A microorganism that lives and grows in the presence of free gaseous oxygen (O_2).

aerobic respiration Respiration in which the final electron acceptor in the electron transport chain is oxygen (O_2).

aerosols Suspensions of fine dust or moisture particles in the air that contain live pathogens.

aerotolerant The state of not utilizing oxygen but not being harmed by it.

aflatoxin From ***Aspergillus flavus*** toxin, a mycotoxin that typically poisons moldy animal feed and can cause liver cancer in humans and other animals.

agammaglobulinemia Also called hypogammaglobulinemia. The absence of or severely reduced levels of antibodies in serum.

agar A polysaccharide found in seaweed and commonly used to prepare solid culture media.

agglutination The aggregation by antibodies of suspended cells or similar-size particles (agglutinogens) into clumps that settle.

agranulocyte One form of leukocyte (white blood cell) having globular, nonlobed nuclei and lacking prominent cytoplasmic granules.

AIDS Acquired immunodeficiency syndrome. The complex of signs and symptoms characteristic of the late phase of human immunodeficiency virus (HIV) infection.

alcoholic fermentation An anaerobic degradation of pyruvic acid that results in alcohol production.

algae Photosynthetic, plantlike organisms that generally lack the complex structure of plants; they may be single-celled or multicellular and inhabit diverse habitats such as marine and freshwater environments, glaciers, and hot springs.

allele A gene that occupies the same location as other alternative (allelic) genes on paired chromosomes.

allergen A substance that provokes an allergic response.

allergy The altered, usually exaggerated, immune response to an allergen. Also called hypersensitivity.

alloantigen An antigen that is present in some but not all members of the same species.

allograft Relatively compatible tissue exchange between nonidentical members of the same species. Also called homograft.

allosteric Pertaining to the altered activity of an enzyme due to the binding of a molecule to a region other than the enzyme's active site.

alternative splicing The ability of eukaryotic organisms to create variant mRNAs from a single genetic sequence by cutting it in different places.

amantadine Antiviral agent used to treat influenza; prevents fusion and uncoating of virus.

Ames test A method for detecting mutagenic and potentially carcinogenic agents based upon the genetic alteration of nutritionally defective bacteria.

amination The addition of an amine ($—NH_2$) group to a molecule.

amino acids The building blocks of protein. Amino acids exist in 20 naturally occurring forms that impart different characteristics to the various proteins they compose.

aminoglycoside A complex group of drugs derived from soil actinomycetes that impairs ribosome function and has antibiotic potential. Example: streptomycin.

ammonification Phase of the nitrogen cycle in which ammonia is released from decomposing organic material.

amphibolism Pertaining to the metabolic pathways that serve multiple functions in the breakdown, synthesis, and conversion of metabolites.

amphipathic Relating to a compound that has contrasting characteristics, such as hydrophilic-hydrophobic or acid-base.

amphitrichous Having a single flagellum or a tuft of flagella at opposite poles of a microbial cell.

amplicon DNA strand that has been primed for replication during polymerase chain reaction.

anabolism The energy-consuming process of incorporating nutrients into protoplasm through biosynthesis.

anaerobe A microorganism that grows best, or exclusively, in the absence of oxygen.

anaerobic digesters Closed chambers used in a microbial process that converts organic sludge from waste treatment plants into useful fuels such as methane and hydrogen gases. Also called bioreactors.

anaerobic respiration Respiration in which the final electron acceptor in the electron transport chain is an inorganic molecule containing sulfate, nitrate, nitrite, carbonate, and so on.

analog In chemistry, a compound that closely resembles another in structure.

anamnestic response In immunology, an augmented response or memory related to a prior stimulation of the immune system by antigen. It boosts the levels of immune substances.

anaphylaxis The unusual or exaggerated allergic reaction to antigen that leads to severe respiratory and cardiac complications.

anion A negatively charged ion.

anoxygenic Non-oxygen-producing.

annotating In the context of genome sequencing, it is the process of assigning biological function to genetic sequence.

antagonism Relationship in which microorganisms compete for survival in a common environment by taking actions that inhibit or destroy another organism.

antibiotic A chemical substance from one microorganism that can inhibit or kill another microbe even in minute amounts.

antibody A large protein molecule evoked in response to an antigen that interacts specifically with that antigen.

antibody-mediated immunity Specific protection from disease provided by the products of B cells.

anticodon The trinucleotide sequence of transfer RNA that is complementary to the trinucleotide sequence of messenger RNA (the codon).

antigen Any cell, particle, or chemical that induces a specific immune response by B cells or T cells and can stimulate resistance to an infection or a toxin. See ***immunogen.***

antigen binding site Specific region at the ends of the antibody molecule that recognize specific antigens. These sites have numerous shapes to fit a wide variety of antigens.

antigenic drift Minor antigenic changes in the influenza A virus due to mutations in the spikes' genes.

antigenic shift Major changes in the influenza A virus due to recombination of viral strains from two different host species.

antigenicity The property of a substance to stimulate a specific immune response such as antibody formation.

antigen-presenting cell (APC) A macrophage or dendritic cell that ingests and degrades an antigen and subsequently places the antigenic determinant molecules on its surface for recognition by CD4 T lymphocytes.

antigen-presenting cells Cells of the immune system that digest foreign cells and particles and place pieces of them on their own surfaces in such a way that other cells of the immune system recognize them.

antihistamine A drug that counters the action of histamine and is useful in allergy treatment.

antimetabolite A substance such as a drug that competes with, substitutes for, or interferes with a normal metabolite.

antimicrobial A special class of compounds capable of destroying or inhibiting microorganisms.

antimicrobial peptides Short protein molecules found in epithelial cells; have the ability to kill bacteria.

antisense DNA A DNA oligonucleotide that binds to a specific piece of RNA, thereby inhibiting translation; used in gene therapy.

antisense RNA An RNA oligonucleotide that binds to a specific piece of RNA, thereby inhibiting translation; used in gene therapy.

antisepsis Chemical treatments to kill or inhibit the growth of all vegetative microorganisms on body surfaces.

antiseptic A growth-inhibiting agent used on tissues to prevent infection.

antiserum Antibody-rich serum derived from the blood of animals (deliberately immunized against infectious or toxic antigen) or from people who have recovered from specific infections.

antitoxin Globulin fraction of serum that neutralizes a specific toxin. Also refers to the specific antitoxin antibody itself.

apicomplexans A group of protozoans that lack locomotion in the mature state.

apoenzyme The protein part of an enzyme, as opposed to the nonprotein or inorganic cofactors.

apoptosis The genetically programmed death of cells that is both a natural process of development and the body's means of destroying abnormal or infected cells.

appendages Accessory structures that sprout from the surface of bacteria. They can be divided into two major groups: those that provide motility and those that enable adhesion.

applied microbiology The study of the practical uses of microorganisms.

aquifer A subterranean water-bearing stratum of permeable rock, sand, or gravel.

archaea Prokaryotic single-celled organisms of primitive origin that have unusual anatomy, physiology, and genetics and live in harsh habitats; when capitalized **(Archaea)**, the term refers to one of the three domains of living organisms as proposed by Woese.

arthroconidia Reproductive body of *Coccidioides immitis*, also ***arthrospore***.

Arthus reaction An immune complex phenomenon that develops after repeat injection. This localized inflammation results from aggregates of antigen and antibody that bind, complement, and attract neutrophils.

artificial immunity Immunity that is induced as a medical intervention, either by exposing an individual to an antigen or administering immune substances to him or her.

ascospore A spore formed within a saclike cell (ascus) of Ascomycota following nuclear fusion and meiosis.

ascus Special fungal sac in which haploid spores are created.

asepsis A condition free of viable pathogenic microorganisms.

aseptic technique Methods of handling microbial cultures, patient specimens, and other sources of microbes in a way that prevents infection of the handler and others who may be exposed.

assay medium Microbiological medium used to test the effects of specific treatments to bacteria, such as antibiotic or disinfectant treatment.

assembly (viral) The step in viral multiplication in which capsids and genetic material are packaged into virions.

astromicrobiology A branch of microbiology that studies the potential for and the possible role of microorganisms in space and on other planets.

asymptomatic An infection that produces no noticeable symptoms even though the microbe is active in the host tissue.

asymptomatic carrier A person with an inapparent infection who shows no symptoms of being infected yet is able to pass the disease agent on to others.

atmosphere That part of the biosphere that includes the gaseous envelope up to 14 miles above the earth's surface. It contains gases such as carbon dioxide, nitrogen, and oxygen.

atom The smallest particle of an element to retain all the properties of that element.

atomic number (AN) A measurement that reflects the number of protons in an atom of a particular element.

atomic weight The average of the mass numbers of all the isotopic forms for a particular element.

atopy Allergic reaction classified as type I, with a strong familial relationship; caused by allergens such as pollen, insect venom, food, and dander; involves IgE antibody; includes symptoms of hay fever, asthma, and skin rash.

ATP synthase A unique enzyme located in the mitochondrial cristae and chloroplast grana that harnesses the flux of hydrogen ions to the synthesis of ATP.

attenuate To reduce the virulence of a pathogenic bacterium or virus by passing it through a non-native host or by long-term subculture.

AUG (start codon) The codon that signals the point at which translation of a messenger RNA molecule is to begin.

autoantibody An "anti-self" antibody having an affinity for tissue antigens of the subject in which it is formed.

autoclave A sterilization chamber that allows the use of steam under pressure to sterilize materials. The most common temperature/pressure combination for an autoclave is 121 °C and 15 psi.

autograft Tissue or organ surgically transplanted to another site on the same subject.

autoimmune disease The pathologic condition arising from the production of antibodies against autoantigens. Example: rheumatoid arthritis. Also called autoimmunity.

autoimmune regulator (AIRE) A protein that regulates the transcription of self antigens in the thymus; defects in AIRE can lead to inappropriate responses to self antigens.

autotroph A microorganism that requires only inorganic nutrients and whose sole source of carbon is carbon dioxide.

axenic A sterile state such as a pure culture. An axenic animal is born and raised in a germ-free environment. See ***gnotobiotic.***

axial filament A type of flagellum (called an endoflagellum) that lies in the periplasmic space of spirochetes and is responsible for locomotion. Also called periplasmic flagellum.

azole Five-membered heterocyclic compounds typical of histidine, which are used in antifungal therapy.

B

B lymphocyte (B cell) A white blood cell that gives rise to plasma cells and antibodies.

bacillus Bacterial cell shape that is cylindrical (longer than it is wide).

bacitracin Antibiotic that targets the bacterial cell wall; component of over-the-counter topical antimicrobial ointments.

back-mutation A mutation that counteracts an earlier mutation, resulting in the restoration of the original DNA sequence.

bacteremia The presence of viable bacteria in circulating blood.

bacteremic Bacteria present in the bloodstream.

Bacteria When capitalized can refer to one of the three domains of living organisms proposed by Woese, containing all nonarchaea prokaryotes.

bacteria (plural of bacterium) Category of prokaryotes with peptidoglycan in their cell walls and circular chromosome(s). This group of small cells is widely distributed in the earth's habitats.

bacterial chromosome A circular body in bacteria that contains the primary genetic material. Also called nucleoid.

bactericide An agent that kills bacteria.

bacteriocin Proteins produced by certain bacteria that are lethal against closely related bacteria and are narrow spectrum compared with antibiotics; these proteins are coded and transferred in plasmids.

bacteriophage A virus that specifically infects bacteria.

bacteristatic Any process or agent that inhibits bacterial growth.

bacterium A tiny unicellular prokaryotic organism that usually reproduces by binary fission and usually has a peptidoglycan cell wall, has various shapes, and can be found in virtually any environment.

barophile A microorganism that thrives under high (usually hydrostatic) pressure.

basement membrane A thin layer (1–6 μm) of protein and polysaccharide found at the base of epithelial tissues.

basic A solution with a pH value above 7 on the pH scale.

basidiospore A sexual spore that arises from a basidium. Found in basidiomycota fungi.

basidium A reproductive cell created when the swollen terminal cell of a hypha develops filaments (sterigmata) that form spores.

basophil A motile polymorphonuclear leukocyte that binds IgE. The basophilic cytoplasmic granules contain mediators of anaphylaxis and atopy.

beta oxidation The degradation of long-chain fatty acids. Two-carbon fragments are formed as a result of enzymatic attack directed against the second or beta carbon of the hydrocarbon chain. Aided by coenzyme A, the fragments enter the Krebs cycle and are processed for ATP synthesis.

beta-lactamase An enzyme secreted by certain bacteria that cleaves the beta-lactam ring of penicillin and cephalosporin and thus provides for resistance against the antibiotic. See ***penicillinase.***

binary fission The formation of two new cells of approximately equal size as the result of parent cell division.

binomial system Scientific method of assigning names to organisms that employs two names to identify every organism—genus name plus species name.

biochemistry The study of organic compounds produced by (or components of) living things. The four main categories of biochemicals are carbohydrates, lipids, proteins, and nucleic acids.

biodegradation The breaking down of materials through the action of microbes or insects.

bioenergetics The study of the production and use of energy by cells.

bioethics The study of biological issues and how they relate to human conduct and moral judgment.

biofilm A complex association that arises from a mixture of microorganisms growing together on the surface of a habitat.

biogenesis Belief that living things can only arise from others of the same kind.

biogeochemical cycle A process by which matter is converted from organic to inorganic form and returned to various nonliving reservoirs on earth (air, rocks, and water) where it becomes available for reuse by living things. Elements such as carbon, nitrogen, and phosphorus are constantly cycled in this manner.

biological vector An animal that not only transports an infectious agent but plays a role in the life cycle of the pathogen, serving as a site in which it can multiply or complete its life cycle. It is usually an alternate host to the pathogen.

biomes Particular climate regions in a terrestrial realm.

bioremediation Decomposition of harmful chemicals by microbes or consortia of microbes.

biosensor A device used to detect microbes or trace amounts of compounds through PCR, genome techniques, or electrochemical signaling.

biosphere Habitable regions comprising the aquatic (hydrospheric), soil-rock (lithospheric), and air (atmospheric) environments.

biota Beneficial or harmless resident bacteria commonly found on and/or in the human body.

biotechnology The intentional use by humans of living organisms or their products to accomplish a goal related to health or the environment.

biotic Living factors such as parasites, food substrates, or other living or once-living organisms that are studied when looking at an ecosystem.

blast cell An immature precursor cell of B and T lymphocytes. Also called a lymphoblast.

blocking antibody The IgG class of immunoglobulins that competes with IgE antibody for allergens, thus blocking the degranulation of basophils and mast cells.

blood cells Cellular components of the blood consisting of red blood cells, primarily responsible for the transport of oxygen and carbon dioxide, and white blood cells, primarily responsible for host defense and immune reactions.

blood-brain barrier Decreased permeability of the walls of blood vessels in the brain, restricting access to that compartment.

botulinum ***Clostridium botulinum*** toxin. Ingestion of this potent exotoxin leads to flaccid paralysis.

bradykinin An active polypeptide that is a potent vasodilator released from IgE-coated mast cells during anaphylaxis.

broad spectrum Denotes drugs that have an effect on a wide variety of microorganisms.

Brownian movement The passive, erratic, nondirectional motion exhibited by microscopic particles. The jostling comes from being randomly bumped by submicroscopic particles, usually water molecules, in which the visible particles are suspended.

brucellosis A zoonosis transmitted to humans from infected animals or animal products; causes a fluctuating pattern of severe fever in humans as well as muscle pain, weakness, headache, weight loss, and profuse sweating. Also called undulant fever.

bubo The swelling of one or more lymph nodes due to inflammation.

bubonic plague The form of plague in which bacterial growth is primarily restricted to the lymph and is characterized by the appearance of a swollen lymph node referred to as a bubo.

budding See ***exocytosis.***

bulbar poliomyelitis Complication of polio infection in which the brain stem, medulla, or cranial nerves are affected. Leads to loss of respiratory control and paralysis of the trunk and limbs.

bullous Consisting of fluid-filled blisters.

C

calculus Dental deposit formed when plaque becomes mineralized with calcium and phosphate crystals. Also called tartar.

Calvin cycle A series of reactions in the second phase of photosynthesis that generates glucose.

cancer Any malignant neoplasm that invades surrounding tissue and can metastasize to other locations. A carcinoma is derived from epithelial tissue, and a sarcoma arises from proliferating mesodermal cells of connective tissue.

capsid The protein covering of a virus's nucleic acid core. Capsids exhibit symmetry due to the regular arrangement of subunits called capsomers. See ***icosahedron.***

capsomer A subunit of the virus capsid shaped as a triangle or disc.

capsular staining Any staining method that highlights the outermost polysaccharide and/or protein structure on a bacterial, fungal, or protozoal cell.

capsule In bacteria, the loose, gel-like covering or slime made chiefly of polysaccharides. This layer is protective and can be associated with virulence.

carbohydrate A compound containing primarily carbon, hydrogen, and oxygen in a 1:2:1 ratio.

carbohydrate fermentation medium A growth medium that contains sugars that are converted to acids through fermentation. Usually contains a pH indicator to detect acid protection.

carbon cycle That pathway taken by carbon from its abiotic source to its use by producers to form organic compounds (biotic), followed by the breakdown of biotic compounds and their release to a nonliving reservoir in the environment (mostly carbon dioxide in the atmosphere).

carbon fixation Reactions in photosynthesis that incorporate inorganic carbon dioxide into organic compounds such as sugars. This occurs during the Calvin cycle and uses energy generated by the light reactions. This process is the source of all production on earth.

carbuncle A deep staphylococcal abscess joining several neighboring hair follicles.

carotenoid Yellow, orange, or red photosynthetic pigments.

carrier A person who harbors infections and inconspicuously spreads them to others. Also, a chemical agent that can accept an atom, chemical radical, or subatomic particle from one compound and pass it on to another.

caseous lesion Necrotic area of lung tubercle superficially resembling cheese. Typical of tuberculosis.

catabolism The chemical breakdown of complex compounds into simpler units to be used in cell metabolism.

catalyst A substance that alters the rate of a reaction without being consumed or permanently changed by it. In cells, enzymes are catalysts.

catalytic site The niche in an enzyme where the substrate is converted to the product (also active site).

catarrhal A term referring to the secretion of mucus or fluids; term for the first stage of pertussis.

cation A positively charged ion.

cell An individual membrane-bound living entity; the smallest unit capable of an independent existence.

cell wall In bacteria, a rigid structure made of peptidoglycan that lies just outside the cytoplasmic membrane; eukaryotes also have a cell wall but may be composed of a variety of materials.

cell-mediated immunity The type of immune responses brought about by T cells, such as cytotoxic and helper effects.

cellulitis The spread of bacteria within necrotic tissue.

cellulose A long, fibrous polymer composed of β-glucose; one of the most common substances on earth.

cephalosporins A group of broad-spectrum antibiotics isolated from the fungus ***Cephalosporium***.

cercaria The free-swimming larva of the schistosome trematode that emerges from the snail host and can penetrate human skin, causing schistosomiasis.

cestode The common name for tapeworms that parasitize humans and domestic animals.

chancre The primary sore of syphilis that forms at the site of penetration by ***Treponema pallidum***. It begins as a hard, dull red, painless papule that erodes from the center.

chancroid A lesion that resembles a chancre but is soft and is caused by ***Haemophilus ducreyi***.

chemical bond A link formed between molecules when two or more atoms share, donate, or accept electrons.

chemical mediators Small molecules that are released during inflammation and specific immune reactions that allow communication between the cells of the immune system and facilitate surveillance, recognition, and attack.

chemiosmosis The generation of a concentration gradient of hydrogen ions (called the proton motive force) by the pumping of hydrogen ions to the outer side of the membrane during electron transport.

chemoautotroph An organism that relies upon inorganic chemicals for its energy and carbon dioxide for its carbon. Also called a chemolithotroph.

chemoheterotroph Microorganisms that derive their nutritional needs from organic compounds.

chemokine Chemical mediators (cytokines) that stimulate the movement and migration of white blood cells.

chemostat A growth chamber with an outflow that is equal to the continuous inflow of nutrient media. This steady-state growth device is used to study such events as cell division, mutation rates, and enzyme regulation.

chemotactic factors Chemical mediators that stimulate the movement of white blood cells. See ***chemokines***.

chemotaxis The tendency of organisms to move in response to a chemical gradient (toward an attractant or to avoid adverse stimuli).

chemotherapy The use of chemical substances or drugs to treat or prevent disease.

chemotroph Organism that oxidizes compounds to feed on nutrients.

chitin A polysaccharide similar to cellulose in chemical structure. This polymer makes up the horny substance of the exoskeletons of arthropods and certain fungi.

chloramphenicol Antibiotic that inhibits protein synthesis by binding to the 50S subunit of the ribosome.

chlorophyll A group of mostly green pigments that are used by photosynthetic eukaryotic organisms and cyanobacteria to trap light energy to use in making chemical bonds.

chloroplast An organelle containing chlorophyll that is found in photosynthetic eukaryotes.

cholesterol Best-known member of a group of lipids called steroids. Cholesterol is commonly found in cell membranes and animal hormones.

chromatin The genetic material of the nucleus. Chromatin is made up of nucleic acid and stains readily with certain dyes.

chromosome The tightly coiled bodies in cells that are the primary sites of genes.

chronic Any process or disease that persists over a long duration.

cilium (plural: *cilia*) Eukaryotic structure similar to a flagellum that propels a protozoan through the environment.

class In the levels of classification, the division of organisms that follows phylum.

classical pathway Pathway of complement activation initiated by a specific antigen-antibody interaction.

clonal selection theory A conceptual explanation for the development of lymphocyte specificity and variety during immune maturation.

clone A colony of cells (or group of organisms) derived from a single cell (or single organism) by asexual reproduction. All units share identical characteristics. Also used as a verb to refer to the process of producing a genetically identical population of cells or genes.

cloning host An organism such as a bacterium or a yeast that receives and replicates a foreign piece of DNA inserted during a genetic engineering experiment.

coagulase A plasma-clotting enzyme secreted by ***Staphylococcus aureus***. It contributes to virulence and is involved in forming a fibrin wall that surrounds staphylococcal lesions.

coccobacillus An elongated coccus; a short, thick, oval-shaped bacterial rod.

coccus A spherical-shaped bacterial cell.

codon A specific sequence of three nucleotides in mRNA (or the sense strand of DNA) that constitutes the genetic code for a particular amino acid.

coenzyme A complex organic molecule, several of which are derived from vitamins (e.g., nicotinamide, riboflavin). A coenzyme operates in conjunction with an enzyme. Coenzymes serve as transient carriers of specific atoms or functional groups during metabolic reactions.

coevolution A biological process whereby a change in the genetic composition in one organism leads to a change in the genetics of another organism.

cofactor An enzyme accessory. It can be organic, such as coenzymes, or inorganic, such as Fe^{2+}, Mn^{2+}, or Zn^{2+} ions.

cold sterilization The use of nonheating methods such as radiation or filtration to sterilize materials.

coliform A collective term that includes normal enteric bacteria that are gram-negative and lactose-fermenting.

colony A macroscopic cluster of cells appearing on a solid medium, each arising from the multiplication of a single cell.

colostrum The clear yellow early product of breast milk that is very high in secretory antibodies. Provides passive intestinal protection.

commensalism An unequal relationship in which one species derives benefit without harming the other.

common source epidemic An outbreak of disease in which all affected individuals were exposed to a single source of the pathogen, even if they were exposed at different times.

communicable infection Capable of being transmitted from one individual to another.

community The interacting mixture of populations in a given habitat.

competitive inhibition Control process that relies on the ability of metabolic analogs to control microbial growth by successfully competing with a necessary enzyme to halt the growth of bacterial cells.

complement In immunology, serum protein components that act in a definite sequence when set in motion either by an antigen-antibody complex or by factors of the alternative (properdin) pathway.

complementary DNA (cDNA) DNA created by using reverse transcriptase to synthesize DNA from RNA templates.

compounds Molecules that are a combination of two or more different elements.

concentration The expression of the amount of a solute dissolved in a certain amount of solvent. It may be defined by weight, volume, or percentage.

condyloma acuminata Extensive, branched masses of genital warts caused by infection with human papillomavirus.

congenital Transmission of an infection from mother to fetus.

congenital rubella Transmission of the rubella virus to a fetus in utero. Injury to the fetus is generally much more serious than it is to the mother.

congenital syphilis A syphilis infection of the fetus or newborn acquired from maternal infection in utero.

conidia Asexual fungal spores shed as free units from the tips of fertile hyphae.

conidiospore A type of asexual spore in fungi; not enclosed in a sac.

conjugation In bacteria, the contact between donor and recipient cells associated with the transfer of genetic material such as plasmids. Can involve special (sex) pili. Also a form of sexual recombination in ciliated protozoans.

conjunctiva The thin fluid-secreting tissue that covers the eye and lines the eyelid.

consortium A group of microbes that includes more than one species.

constitutive enzyme An enzyme present in bacterial cells in constant amounts, regardless of the presence of substrate. Enzymes of the central catabolic pathways are typical examples.

consumer An organism that feeds on producers or other consumers. It gets all nutrients and energy from other organisms (also called heterotroph). May exist at several levels, such as primary (feeds on producers) and secondary (feeds on primary consumers).

contagious Communicable; transmissible by direct contact with infected people and their fresh secretions or excretions.

contaminant An impurity; any undesirable material or organism.

contaminated culture A medium that once held a pure (single or mixed) culture but now contains unwanted microorganisms.

convalescence Recovery; the period between the end of a disease and the complete restoration of health in a patient.

corepressor A molecule that combines with inactive repressor to form active repressor, which attaches to the operator gene site and inhibits the activity of structural genes subordinate to the operator.

covalent A type of chemical bond that involves the sharing of electrons between two atoms.

covalent bond A chemical bond formed by the sharing of electrons between two atoms.

Creutzfeldt-Jakob disease (CJD) A spongiform encephalopathy caused by infection with a prion. The disease is marked by dementia, impaired senses, and uncontrollable muscle contractions.

crista The infolded inner membrane of a mitochondrion that is the site of the respiratory chain and oxidative phosphorylation.

cryptosporidiosis A gastrointestinal disease caused by ***Cryptosporidium parvum***, a protozoan.

culture The visible accumulation of microorganisms in or on a nutrient medium. Also, the propagation of microorganisms with various media.

curd The coagulated milk protein used in cheese making.

cutaneous Second level of skin, including the stratum corneum and occasionally the upper dermis.

cyanosis Blue discoloration of the skin or mucous membranes indicative of decreased oxygen concentration in blood.

cyst The resistant, dormant but infectious form of protozoans. Can be important in spread of infectious agents such as ***Entamoeba histolytica*** and ***Giardia lamblia***.

cystine An amino acid, $HOOC—CH(NH_2)—CH_2—S—S—CH_2—CH(NH_2)COOH$. An oxidation product of two cysteine molecules in which the OSH (sulfhydryl) groups form a disulfide union. Also called dicysteine.

cytochrome A group of heme protein compounds whose chief role is in electron and/or hydrogen transport occurring in the last phase of aerobic respiration.

cytokine Regulatory chemical released by cells of the immune system that serves as signal between different cells.

cytopathic effect The degenerative changes in cells associated with virus infection. Examples: the formation of multinucleate giant cells (Negri bodies), the prominent cytoplasmic inclusions of nerve cells infected by rabies virus.

cytoplasm Dense fluid encased by the cell membrane; the site of many of the cell's biochemical and synthetic activities.

cytoplasmic membrane Lipid bilayer that encloses the cytoplasm of bacterial cells.

cytosine (C) One of the nitrogen bases found in DNA and RNA, with a pyrimidine form.

cytotoxicity The ability to kill cells; in immunology, certain T cells are called cytotoxic T cells because they kill other cells.

D

daptomycin A lipopetide antibiotic that disrupts the cytoplasmic membrane.

deamination The removal of an amino group from an amino acid.

death phase End of the cell growth due to lack of nutrition, depletion of environment, and accumulation of wastes. Population of cells begins to die.

debridement Trimming away devitalized tissue and foreign matter from a wound.

decomposer A consumer that feeds on organic matter from the bodies of dead organisms. These microorganisms feed from all levels of the food pyramid and are responsible for recycling elements (also called saprobes).

decomposition The breakdown of dead matter and wastes into simple compounds that can be directed back into the natural cycle of living things.

decontamination The removal or neutralization of an infectious, poisonous, or injurious agent from a site.

deduction Problem-solving process in which an individual constructs a hypothesis, tests its validity by outlining particular events that are predicted by the hypothesis, and then performs experiments to test for those events.

deductive approach Method of investigation that uses **deduction.** See ***deduction***.

definitive host The organism in which a parasite develops into its adult or sexually mature stage. Also called the final host.

degerm To physically remove surface oils, debris, and soil from skin to reduce the microbial load.

degranulation The release of cytoplasmic granules, as when cytokines are secreted from mast cell granules.

dehydration synthesis During the formation of a carbohydrate bond, the step in which one carbon molecule gives up its OH group and the other loses the H from its OH group, thereby producing a water molecule. This process is common to all polymerization reactions.

denaturation The loss of normal characteristics resulting from some molecular alteration. Usually in reference to the action of heat or chemicals on proteins whose function depends upon an unaltered tertiary structure.

dendritic cell A large, antigen-processing cell characterized by long, branchlike extensions of the cell membrane.

denitrification The end of the nitrogen cycle when nitrogen compounds are returned to the reservoir in the air.

dental caries A mixed infection of the tooth surface that gradually destroys the enamel and may lead to destruction of the deeper tissue.

deoxyribonucleic acid (DNA) The nucleic acid often referred to as the "double helix." DNA carries the master plan for an organism's heredity.

deoxyribose A 5-carbon sugar that is an important component of DNA.

dermatophytes A group of fungi that cause infections of the skin and other integument components. They survive by metabolizing keratin.

dermolytic Capable of damaging the skin.

desensitization See ***hyposensitization.***

desiccation To dry thoroughly. To preserve by drying.

desquamate To shed the cuticle in scales; to peel off the outer layer of a surface.

diabetes mellitus A disease involving compromise in insulin function. In one form, the pancreatic cells that produce insulin are destroyed by autoantibodies, and in another, the pancreas does not produce sufficient insulin.

diapedesis The migration of intact blood cells between endothelial cells of a blood vessel such as a venule.

dichotomous keys Flow charts that offer two choices or pathways at each level.

differential medium A single substrate that discriminates between groups of microorganisms on the basis of differences in their appearance due to different chemical reactions.

differential stain A technique that utilizes two dyes to distinguish between different microbial groups or cell parts by color reaction.

diffusion The dispersal of molecules, ions, or microscopic particles propelled down a concentration gradient by spontaneous random motion to achieve a uniform distribution.

DiGeorge syndrome A birth defect usually caused by a missing or incomplete thymus gland that results in abnormally low or absent T cells and other developmental abnormalities.

dimorphic In mycology, the tendency of some pathogens to alter their growth form from mold to yeast in response to rising temperature.

diplococci Spherical or oval-shaped bacteria, typically found in pairs.

direct or total cell count 1. Counting total numbers of individual cells being viewed with magnification. 2. Counting isolated colonies of organisms growing on a plate of media as a way to determine population size.

disaccharide A sugar containing two monosaccharides. Example: sucrose (fructose + glucose).

disease Any deviation from health, as when the effects of microbial infection damage or disrupt tissues and organs.

disinfection The destruction of pathogenic nonsporulating microbes or their toxins, usually on inanimate surfaces.

division In the levels of classification, an alternate term for phylum.

DNA See *deoxyribonucleic acid.*

DNA polymerase Enzyme responsible for the replication of DNA. Several versions of the enzyme exist, each completing a unique portion of the replication process.

DNA profiling A pattern of restriction enzyme fragments that is unique for an individual organism.

DNA sequencing Determining the exact order of nucleotides in a fragment of DNA. Most commonly done using the Sanger dideoxy sequencing method.

DNA vaccine A newer vaccine preparation based on inserting DNA from pathogens into host cells to encourage them to express the foreign protein and stimulate immunity.

domain In the levels of classification, the broadest general category to which an organism is assigned. Members of a domain share only one or a few general characteristics.

doubling time Time required for a complete fission cycle—from parent cell to two new daughter cells. Also called generation time.

droplet nuclei The dried residue of fine droplets produced by mucus and saliva sprayed while sneezing and coughing. Droplet nuclei are less than 5 μm in diameter (large enough to bear a single bacterium and small enough to remain airborne for a long time) and can be carried by air currents. Droplet nuclei are drawn deep into the air passages.

drug resistance An adaptive response in which microorganisms begin to tolerate an amount of drug that would ordinarily be inhibitory.

dysentery Diarrheal illness in which stools contain blood and/or mucus.

dyspnea Difficulty in breathing.

E

echinocandins Antifungal drugs that inhibit the manufacture of fungal cell walls.

ecosystem A collection of organisms together with its surrounding physical and chemical factors.

ectoplasm The outer, more viscous region of the cytoplasm of a phagocytic cell such as an amoeba. It contains microtubules, but not granules or organelles.

eczema An acute or chronic allergy of the skin associated with itching and burning sensations. Typically, red, edematous, vesicular lesions erupt, leaving the skin scaly and sometimes hyperpigmented.

edema The accumulation of excess fluid in cells, tissues, or serous cavities. Also called swelling.

electrolyte Any compound that ionizes in solution and conducts current in an electrical field.

electron A negatively charged subatomic particle that is distributed around the nucleus in an atom.

electrophoresis The separation of molecules by size and charge through exposure to an electrical current.

electrostatic Relating to the attraction of opposite charges and the repulsion of like charges. Electrical charge remains stationary as opposed to electrical flow or current.

element A substance comprising only one kind of atom that cannot be degraded into two or more substances without losing its chemical characteristics.

ELISA Abbreviation for enzyme-linked immunosorbent assay, a very sensitive serological test used to detect antibodies in diseases such as AIDS.

emerging disease Newly identified diseases that are becoming more prominent.

emetic Inducing to vomit.

encephalitis An inflammation of the brain, usually caused by infection.

endemic disease A native disease that prevails continuously in a geographic region.

endergonic reaction A chemical reaction that occurs with the absorption and storage of surrounding energy. Antonym: exergonic.

endocytosis The process whereby solid and liquid materials are taken into the cell through membrane invagination and engulfment into a vesicle.

endoenzyme An intracellular enzyme, as opposed to enzymes that are secreted.

endogenous Originating or produced within an organism or one of its parts.

endoplasmic reticulum (ER) An intracellular network of flattened sacs or tubules with or without ribosomes on their surfaces.

endospore A small, dormant, resistant derivative of a bacterial cell that germinates under favorable growth conditions into a vegetative cell. The bacterial genera *Bacillus* and *Clostridium* are typical sporeformers.

endosymbiosis Relationship in which a microorganism resides within a host cell and provides a benefit to the host cell.

endotoxic shock A massive drop in blood pressure caused by the release of endotoxin from gram-negative bacteria multiplying in the bloodstream.

endotoxin A bacterial toxin that is not ordinarily released (as is exotoxin). Endotoxin is composed of a phospholipid-polysaccharide complex that is an integral part of gram-negative bacterial cell walls. Endotoxins can cause severe shock and fever.

energy of activation The minimum energy input necessary for reactants to form products in a chemical reaction.

energy pyramid An ecological model that shows the energy flow among the organisms in a community. It is structured like the food pyramid but shows how energy is reduced from one trophic level to another.

enriched medium A nutrient medium supplemented with blood, serum, or some growth factor to promote the multiplication of fastidious microorganisms.

enteric Pertaining to the intestine.

enteroaggregative The term used to describe certain types of intestinal bacteria that tend to stick to each other in large clumps.

enterohemorrhagic *E. coli* (EHEC) A group of *E. coli* species that induce bleeding in the intestines and also in other organs; *E. coli* O157:H7 belongs to this group.

enteroinvasive Predisposed to invade the intestinal tissues.

enteropathogenic Pathogenic to the alimentary canal.

enterotoxigenic Having the capacity to produce toxins that act on the intestinal tract.

enterotoxin A bacterial toxin that specifically targets intestinal mucous membrane cells. Enterotoxigenic strains of *Escherichia coli* and *Staphylococcus aureus* are typical sources.

enumeration medium Microbiological medium that does not encourage growth and allows for the counting of microbes in food, water, or environmental samples.

enveloped virus A virus whose nucleocapsid is enclosed by a membrane derived in part from the host cell. It usually contains exposed glycoprotein spikes specific for the virus.

enzyme A protein biocatalyst that facilitates metabolic reactions.

enzyme induction One of the controls on enzyme synthesis. This occurs when enzymes appear only when suitable substrates are present.

enzyme repression The inhibition of enzyme synthesis by the end product of a catabolic pathway.

eosinophil A leukocyte whose cytoplasmic granules readily stain with red eosin dye.

eosinophilia An increase in eosinophil concentration in the bloodstream, often in response to helminth infection.

epidemic A sudden and simultaneous outbreak or increase in the number of cases of disease in a community.

epidemiology The study of the factors affecting the prevalence and spread of disease within a community.

epitope The precise molecular group of an antigen that defines its specificity and triggers the immune response.

Epstein-Barr virus (EBV) Herpes virus linked to infectious mononucleosis, Burkitt's lymphoma, and nasopharyngeal carcinoma.

erysipelas An acute, sharply defined inflammatory disease specifically caused by hemolytic ***Streptococcus***. The eruption is limited to the skin but can be complicated by serious systemic symptoms.

erythroblastosis fetalis Hemolytic anemia of the newborn. The anemia comes from hemolysis of Rh-positive fetal erythrocytes by anti-Rh maternal antibodies. Erythroblasts are immature red blood cells prematurely released from the bone marrow.

erythrocytes (red blood cells) Blood cells involved in the transport of oxygen and carbon dioxide.

erythrogenic toxin An exotoxin produced by lysogenized group A strains of β-hemolytic streptococci that is responsible for the severe fever and rash of scarlet fever in the nonimmune individual. Also called a pyrogenic toxin.

eschar A dark, sloughing scab that is the lesion of anthrax and certain rickettsioses.

essential nutrient Any ingredient such as a certain amino acid, fatty acid, vitamin, or mineral that cannot be formed by an organism and must be supplied in the diet. A growth factor.

ester bond A covalent bond formed by reacting carboxylic acid with an OH group:

$$(R-\overset{\overset{\displaystyle O}{||}}{C}-O-R9)$$

Olive and corn oils, lard, and butter fat are examples of triacylglycerols—esters formed between glycerol and three fatty acids.

ethylene oxide A potent, highly water-soluble gas invaluable for gaseous sterilization of heat-sensitive objects such as plastics, surgical and diagnostic appliances, and spices.

etiologic agent The microbial cause of disease; the pathogen.

eubacteria Term used for nonarchaea prokaryotes, means "true bacteria."

Eukarya One of the three domains (sometimes called superkingdoms) of living organisms, as proposed by Woese; contains all eukaryotic organisms.

eukaryotic cell A cell that differs from a prokaryotic cell chiefly by having a nuclear membrane (a well-defined nucleus), membrane-bounded subcellular organelles, and mitotic cell division.

eutrophication The process whereby dissolved nutrients resulting from natural seasonal enrichment or industrial pollution of water cause overgrowth of algae and cyanobacteria to the detriment of fish and other large aquatic inhabitants.

evolution Scientific principle that states that living things change gradually through hundreds of millions of years, and these changes are expressed in structural and functional adaptations in each organism. Evolution presumes that those traits that favor survival are preserved and passed on to following generations, and those traits that do not favor survival are lost.

exanthem An eruption or rash of the skin.

exergonic A chemical reaction associated with the release of energy to the surroundings. Antonym: endergonic.

exfoliative toxin A poisonous substance that causes superficial cells of an epithelium to detach and be shed. Example: staphylococcal exfoliatin. Also called an epidermolytic toxin.

exocytosis The process that releases enveloped viruses from the membrane of the host's cytoplasm.

exoenzyme An extracellular enzyme chiefly for hydrolysis of nutrient macromolecules that are otherwise impervious to the cell membrane. It functions in saprobic decomposition of organic debris and can be a factor in invasiveness of pathogens.

exogenous Originating outside the body.

exon A stretch of eukaryotic DNA coding for a corresponding portion of mRNA that is translated into peptides. Intervening stretches of DNA that are not expressed are called introns. During transcription, exons are separated from introns and are spliced together into a continuous mRNA transcript.

exotoxin A toxin (usually protein) that is secreted and acts upon a specific cellular target. Examples: botulin, tetanospasmin, diphtheria toxin, and erythrogenic toxin.

exponential Pertaining to the use of exponents, numbers that are typically written as a superscript to indicate how many times a factor is to be multiplied. Exponents are used in scientific notation to render large, cumbersome numbers into small workable quantities.

exponential growth phase The period of maximum growth rate in a growth curve. Cell population increases logarithmically.

extrapulmonary tuberculosis A condition in which tuberculosis bacilli have spread to organs other than the lungs.

extremophiles Organisms capable of living in harsh environments, such as extreme heat or cold.

F

facilitated diffusion The passive movement of a substance across a plasma membrane from an area of higher concentration to an area of lower concentration utilizing specialized carrier proteins.

facultative Pertaining to the capacity of microbes to adapt or adjust to variations; not obligate. Example: The presence of oxygen is not obligatory for a facultative anaerobe to grow. See ***obligate.***

family In the levels of classification, a midlevel division of organisms that groups more closely related organisms than previous levels. An order is divided into families.

fastidious Requiring special nutritional or environmental conditions for growth. Said of bacteria.

fecal coliforms Any species of gram- negative lactose-positive bacteria (primarily *Escherichia coli*) that live primarily in the intestinal tract and not the environment. Finding evidence of these bacteria in a water or food sample is substantial evidence of fecal contamination and potential for infection (see ***coliform***).

feedback inhibition Temporary end to enzyme action caused by an end-product molecule binding to the regulatory site and preventing the enzyme's active site from binding to its substrate.

fermentation The extraction of energy through anaerobic degradation of substrates into simpler, reduced metabolites. In large industrial processes, fermentation can mean any use of microbial metabolism to manufacture organic chemicals or other products.

fermentor A large tank used in industrial microbiology to grow mass quantities of microbes that can synthesize desired products. These devices are equipped with means to stir, monitor, and harvest products such as drugs, enzymes, and proteins in very large quantities.

ferritin An intracellular protein that binds and stores iron.

fertility (F′) factor Donor plasmid that allows synthesis of a pilus in bacterial conjugation. Presence of the factor is indicated by F^+, and lack of the factor is indicated by $F^{\boxtimes}$.

filament A helical structure composed of proteins that is part of bacterial flagella.

fimbria A short, numerous-surface appendage on some bacteria that provides adhesion but not locomotion.

Firmicutes Taxonomic category of bacteria that have gram-positive cell envelopes.

flagellar staining A staining method that highlights the flagellum of a bacterium.

flagellum A structure that is used to propel the organism through a fluid environment.

fluid mosaic model A conceptualization of the molecular architecture of cellular membranes as a bilipid layer containing proteins. Membrane proteins are embedded to some degree in this bilayer, where they float freely about.

fluorescence The property possessed by certain minerals and dyes to emit visible light when excited by ultraviolet radiation. A fluorescent dye combined with specific antibody provides a sensitive test for the presence of antigen.

fluoroquinolones Synthetic antimicrobial drugs chemically related to quinine. They are broad spectrum and easily adsorbed from the intestine.

focal infection Occurs when an infectious agent breaks loose from a localized infection and is carried by the circulation to other tissues.

folliculitis An inflammatory reaction involving the formation of papules or pustules in clusters of hair follicles.

fomite Virtually any inanimate object an infected individual has contact with that can serve as a vehicle for the spread of disease.

food chain A simple straight-line feeding sequence among organisms in a community.

food fermentations Addition to and growth of known cultures of microorganisms in foods to produce desirable flavors, smells, or textures. Includes cheeses, breads, alcoholic beverages, and pickles.

food poisoning Symptoms in the intestines (which may include vomiting) induced by preformed exotoxin from bacteria.

food web A complex network that traces all feeding interactions among organisms in a community (see ***food chain***). This is considered to be a more accurate picture of food relationships in a community than a food chain.

formalin A 37% aqueous solution of formaldehyde gas; a potent chemical fixative and microbicide.

fosfomycin trimethamine Antibiotic that inhibits an enzyme necessary for cell wall synthesis.

frameshift mutation An insertion or deletion mutation that changes the codon reading frame from the point of the mutation to the final codon. Almost always leads to a nonfunctional protein.

free energy Energy in a chemical system that can be used to do work.

fructose One of the carbohydrates commonly referred to as sugars. Fructose is commonly fruit sugars.

functional group In chemistry, a particular molecular combination that reacts in predictable ways and confers particular properties on a compound. Examples: —COOH, —OH, —CHO.

fungemia The condition of fungi multiplying in the bloodstream.

fungi Macroscopic and microscopic heterotrophic eukaryotic organisms that can be uni- or multicellular.

fungus Heterotrophic unicellular or multicellular eukaryotic organism that may take the form of a larger macroscopic organism, as in the case of mushrooms, or a smaller microscopic organism, as in the case of yeasts and molds.

furuncle A boil; a localized pyogenic infection arising from a hair follicle.

fuzeon Anti-HIV drug that inhibits viral attachment to host cells.

G

Gaia Theory The concept that biotic and abiotic factors sustain suitable conditions for one another simply by their interactions. Named after the mythical Greek goddess of earth.

gamma globulin The fraction of plasma proteins high in immunoglobulins (antibodies). Preparations from pooled human plasma containing normal antibodies make useful passive immunizing agents against pertussis, polio, measles, and several other diseases.

gas gangrene Disease caused by a clostridial infection of soft tissue or wound. The name refers to the gas produced by the bacteria growing in the tissue. Unless treated early, it is fatal. Also called myonecrosis.

gastritis Pain and/or nausea, usually experienced after eating; result of inflammation of the lining of the stomach.

gel electrophoresis A laboratory technique for separating DNA fragments according to length by employing electricity to force the DNA through a gel-like matrix typically made of agarose. Smaller DNA fragments move more quickly through the gel, thereby moving farther than larger fragments during the same period of time.

gene A site on a chromosome that provides information for a certain cell function. A specific segment of DNA that contains the necessary code to make a protein or RNA molecule.

gene probe Short strands of single-stranded nucleic acid that hybridize specifically with complementary stretches of nucleotides on test samples and thereby serve as a tagging and identification device.

gene therapy The introduction of normal functional genes into people with genetic diseases such as sickle cell anemia and cystic fibrosis. This is usually accomplished by a virus vector.

generation time Time required for a complete fission cycle—from parent cell to two new daughter cells. Also called doubling time.

genetic engineering A field involving deliberate alterations (recombinations) of the genomes of microbes, plants, and animals through special technological processes.

genetics The science of heredity.

genital warts A prevalent STD linked to some forms of cancer of the reproductive organs. Caused by infection with human papillomavirus.

genome The complete set of chromosomes and genes in an organism.

genomics The systematic study of an organism's genes and their functions.

genotype The genetic makeup of an organism. The genotype is ultimately responsible for an organism's phenotype, or expressed characteristics.

genus In the levels of classification, the second most specific level. A family is divided into several genera.

geomicrobiology A branch of microbiology that studies the role of microorganisms in the earth's crust.

germ free See ***axenic.***

germ theory of disease A theory first originating in the 1800s that proposed that microorganisms can be the cause of diseases. The concept is actually so well established in the present time that it is considered a fact.

germicide An agent lethal to nonendospore-forming pathogens.

giardiasis Infection by the *Giardia* flagellate. Most common mode of transmission is contaminated food and water. Symptoms include diarrhea, abdominal pain, and flatulence.

gingivitis Inflammation of the gum tissue in contact with the roots of the teeth.

gluconeogenesis The formation of glucose (or glycogen) from noncarbohydrate sources such as protein or fat. Also called glyconeogenesis.

glucose One of the carbohydrates commonly referred to as sugars. Glucose is characterized by its 6-carbon structure.

glycerol A 3-carbon alcohol, with three OH groups that serve as binding sites.

glycocalyx A filamentous network of carbohydrate-rich molecules that coats cells.

glycogen A glucose polymer stored by cells.

glycolysis The energy-yielding breakdown (fermentation) of glucose to pyruvic or lactic acid. It is often called anaerobic glycolysis because no molecular oxygen is consumed in the degradation.

glycosidic bond A bond that joins monosaccharides to form disaccharides and polymers.

gnotobiotic Referring to experiments performed on germ-free animals.

Golgi apparatus An organelle of eukaryotes that participates in packaging and secretion of molecules.

gonococcus Common name for ***Neisseria gonorrhoeae,*** the agent of gonorrhea.

Gracilicutes Taxonomic category of bacteria that have gram-negative envelopes.

graft Live tissue taken from a donor and transplanted into a recipient to replace damaged or missing tissues such as skin, bone, blood vessels.

graft versus host disease (GVHD) A condition associated with a bone marrow transplant in which T cells in the transplanted tissue mount an immune response against the recipient's (host) normal tissues.

Gram stain A differential stain for bacteria useful in identification and taxonomy. Gram-positive organisms appear purple from crystal violet mordant retention, whereas gram-negative organisms appear red after loss of crystal violet and absorbance of the safranin counterstain.

gram-negative A category of bacterial cells that describes bacteria with an outer membrane, a cytoplasmic membrane, and a thin cell wall.

gram-positive A category of bacterial cells that describes bacteria with a thick cell wall and no outer membrane.

grana Discrete stacks of chlorophyll-containing thylakoids within chloroplasts.

granulocyte A mature leukocyte that contains noticeable granules in a Wright stain. Examples: neutrophils, eosinophils, and basophils.

granuloma A solid mass or nodule of inflammatory tissue containing modified macrophages and lymphocytes. Usually a chronic pathologic process of diseases such as tuberculosis or syphilis.

granzymes Enzymes secreted by cytotoxic T cells that damage proteins of target cells.

Graves' disease A malfunction of the thyroid gland in which autoantibodies directed at thyroid cells stimulate an overproduction of thyroid hormone (hyperthyroidism).

greenhouse effect The capacity to retain solar energy by a blanket of atmospheric gases that redirects heat waves back toward the earth.

group translocation A form of active transport in which the substance being transported is altered during transfer across a plasma membrane.

growth curve A graphical representation of the change in population size over time. This graph has four periods known as lag phase, exponential or log phase, stationary phase, and death phase.

growth factor An organic compound such as a vitamin or amino acid that must be provided in the diet to facilitate growth. An essential nutrient.

guanine (G) One of the nitrogen bases found in DNA and RNA in the purine form.

Guillain-Barré syndrome A neurological complication of infection or vaccination.

gumma A nodular, infectious granuloma characteristic of tertiary syphilis.

gut-associated lymphoid tissue (GALT) A collection of lymphoid tissue in the gastrointestinal tract that includes the appendix, the lacteals, and Peyer's patches.

gyrase The enzyme responsible for supercoiling DNA into tight bundles; a type of topoisomerase.

H

HAART Highly active antiretroviral therapy; three-antiviral treatment for HIV infection.

habitat The environment to which an organism is adapted.

halogens A group of related chemicals with antimicrobial applications. The halogens most often used in disinfectants and antiseptics are chlorine and iodine.

halophile A microbe whose growth is either stimulated by salt or requires a high concentration of salt for growth.

Hansen's disease A chronic, progressive disease of the skin and nerves caused by infection by a *Mycobacterium* that is a slow-growing, strict parasite. Hansen's disease is the preferred name for leprosy.

hapten An incomplete or partial antigen. Although it constitutes the determinative group and can bind antigen, hapten cannot stimulate a full immune response without being carried by a larger protein molecule.

Hashimoto's thyroiditis An autoimmune disease of the thyroid gland that damages the thyroid follicle cells and results in decreased production of thyroid hormone (hypothyroidism).

hay fever A form of atopic allergy marked by seasonal acute inflammation of the conjunctiva and mucous membranes of the respiratory passages. Symptoms are irritative itching and rhinitis.

helical Having a spiral or coiled shape. Said of certain virus capsids and bacteria.

helminth A term that designates all parasitic worms.

helper T cell A class of thymus-stimulated lymphocytes that facilitate various immune activities such as assisting B cells and macrophages. Also called a T helper cell.

hemagglutinin A molecule that causes red blood cells to clump or agglutinate. Often found on the surfaces of viruses.

hematopoiesis The process by which the various types of blood cells are formed, such as in the bone marrow.

hemoglobin A protein in red blood cells that carries iron.

hemolysin Any biological agent that is capable of destroying red blood cells and causing the release of hemoglobin. Many bacterial pathogens produce exotoxins that act as hemolysins.

hemolytic disease Incompatible Rh factor between mother and fetus causes maternal antibodies to attack the fetus and trigger complement-mediated lysis in the fetus.

hemolytic uremic syndrome (HUS) Severe hemolytic anemia leading to kidney damage or failure; can accompany *E. coli* O157:H7 intestinal infection.

hemolyze When red blood cells burst and release hemoglobin pigment.

hepatitis Inflammation and necrosis of the liver, often the result of viral infection.

hepatitis A virus (HAV) Enterovirus spread by contaminated food responsible for short-term (infectious) hepatitis.

hepatitis B virus (HBV) DNA virus that is the causative agent of serum hepatitis.

hepatocellular carcinoma A liver cancer associated with infection with hepatitis B virus.

herd immunity The status of collective acquired immunity in a population that reduces the likelihood that nonimmune individuals will contract and spread infection. One aim of vaccination is to induce herd immunity.

heredity Genetic inheritance.

hermaphroditic Containing the sex organs for both male and female in one individual.

herpes zoster A recurrent infection caused by latent chickenpox virus. Its manifestation on the skin tends to correspond to dermatomes and to occur in patches that "girdle" the trunk. Also called shingles.

heterotroph An organism that relies upon organic compounds for its carbon and energy needs.

hexose A 6-carbon sugar such as glucose and fructose.

hierarchies Levels of power. Arrangement in order of rank.

histamine A cytokine released when mast cells and basophils release their granules. An important mediator of allergy, its effects include smooth muscle contraction, increased vascular permeability, and increased mucus secretion.

histiocyte Another term for macrophage.

histone Proteins associated with eukaryotic DNA. These simple proteins serve as winding spools to compact and condense the chromosomes.

HLA An abbreviation for human leukocyte antigens. This closely linked cluster of genes programs for cell surface glycoproteins that control immune interactions between cells and is involved in rejection of allografts. Also called the major histocompatibility complex (MHC).

holoenzyme An enzyme complete with its apoenzyme and cofactors.

hops The ripe, dried fruits of the hop vine (***Humulus lupulus***) that are added to beer wort for flavoring.

horizontal gene transfer Transmission of genetic material from one cell to another through nonreproductive mechanisms; i.e., from one organism to another living in the same habitat.

host Organism in which smaller organisms or viruses live, feed, and reproduce.

host range The limitation imposed by the characteristics of the host cell on the type of virus that can successfully invade it.

human diploid cell vaccine (HDCV) A vaccine made using cell culture that is currently the vaccine of choice for preventing infection by rabies virus.

human immunodeficiency virus (HIV) A retrovirus that causes acquired immunodeficiency syndrome (AIDS).

Human Microbiome Project A project of the National Institutes of Health to identify microbial inhabitants of the human body and their role in health and disease; uses metagenomic techniques instead of culturing.

human papillomavirus (HPV) A group of DNA viruses whose members are responsible for common, plantar, and genital warts.

humoral immunity Protective molecules (mostly B lymphocytes) carried in the fluids of the body.

hybridization A process that matches complementary strands of nucleic acid (DNA-DNA, RNA-DNA, RNA-RNA). Used for locating specific sites or types of nucleic acids.

hybridoma An artificial cell line that produces monoclonal antibodies. It is formed by fusing (hybridizing) a normal antibody-producing cell with a cancer cell, and it can produce pure antibody indefinitely.

hydration The addition of water as in the coating of ions with water molecules as ions enter into aqueous solution.

hydrogen bond A weak chemical bond formed by the attraction of forces between molecules or atoms—in this case, hydrogen and either oxygen or nitrogen. In this type of bond, electrons are not shared, lost, or gained.

hydrologic cycle The continual circulation of water between hydrosphere, atmosphere, and lithosphere.

hydrolysis A process in which water is used to break bonds in molecules. Usually occurs in conjunction with an enzyme.

hydrophilic The property of attracting water. Molecules that attract water to their surface are called hydrophilic.

hydrophobic The property of repelling water. Molecules that repel water are called hydrophobic.

hydrosphere That part of the biosphere that encompasses water-containing environments such as oceans, lakes, or rivers.

hypertonic Having a greater osmotic pressure than a reference solution.

hyphae The tubular threads that make up filamentous fungi (molds). This web of branched and intertwining fibers is called a mycelium.

hypogammaglobulinemia An inborn disease in which the gamma globulin (antibody) fraction of serum is greatly reduced. The condition is associated with a high susceptibility to pyogenic infections.

hyposensitization A therapeutic exposure to known allergens designed to build tolerance and eventually prevent allergic reaction.

hypothesis A tentative explanation of what has been observed or measured.

hypotonic Having a lower osmotic pressure than a reference solution.

I

icosahedron A regular geometric figure having 20 surfaces that meet to form 12 corners. Some virions have capsids that resemble icosahedral crystals.

immune complex reaction Type III hypersensitivity of the immune system. It is characterized by the reaction of soluble antigen with antibody, and the deposition of the resulting complexes in basement membranes of epithelial tissue.

immunity An acquired resistance to an infectious agent due to prior contact with that agent.

immunoassays Extremely sensitive tests that permit rapid and accurate measurement of trace antigen or antibody.

immunocompetence The ability of the body to recognize and react with multiple foreign substances.

immunodeficiency Immune function is incompletely developed, suppressed, or destroyed.
immunodeficiency disease A form of immunopathology in which white blood cells are unable to mount a complete, effective immune response, which results in recurrent infections. Examples would be AIDS and agammaglobulinemia.
immunogen Any substance that induces a state of sensitivity or resistance after processing by the immune system of the body.
immunoglobulin (Ig) The chemical class of proteins to which antibodies belong.
immunology The study of the system of body defenses that protect against infection.
immunopathology The study of disease states associated with overreactivity or underreactivity of the immune response.
immunotherapy Preventing or treating infectious diseases by administering substances that produce artificial immunity. May be active or passive.
in utero Literally means "in the uterus"; pertains to events or developments occurring before birth.
in vitro Literally means "in glass," signifying a process or reaction occurring in an artificial environment, as in a test tube or culture medium.
in vivo Literally means "in a living being," signifying a process or reaction occurring in a living thing.
incidence In epidemiology, the number of new cases of a disease occurring during a period.
incineration Destruction of microbes by subjecting them to extremes of dry heat. Microbes are reduced to ashes and gas by this process.
inclusion A relatively inert body in the cytoplasm such as storage granules, glycogen, fat, or some other aggregated metabolic product.
inclusion body One of a variety of different storage compartments in bacterial cells.
incubate To isolate a sample culture in a temperature-controlled environment to encourage growth.
incubation period The period from the initial contact with an infectious agent to the appearance of the first symptoms.
index case The first case of a disease identified in an outbreak or epidemic.
indicator bacteria In water analysis, any easily cultured bacteria that may be found in the intestine and can be used as an index of fecal contamination. The category includes coliforms and enterococci. Discovery of these bacteria in a sample means that pathogens may also be present.
induced mutation Any alteration in DNA that occurs as a consequence of exposure to chemical or physical mutagens.
inducible enzyme An enzyme that increases in amount in direct proportion to the amount of substrate present.
inducible operon An operon that under normal circumstances is not transcribed. The presence of a specific inducer molecule can cause transcription of the operon to begin.
induction The process whereby a bacteriophage in the prophage state is activated and begins replication and enters the lytic cycle.
induration Area of hardened, reddened tissue associated with the tuberculin test.
infection The entry, establishment, and multiplication of pathogenic organisms within a host.
infectious disease The state of damage or toxicity in the body caused by an infectious agent.
inflammation A natural, nonspecific response to tissue injury that protects the host from further damage. It stimulates immune reactivity and blocks the spread of an infectious agent.
inoculation The implantation of microorganisms into or upon culture media.
inorganic chemicals Molecules that lack the basic framework of the elements of carbon and hydrogen.
integument The outer surfaces of the body: skin, hair, nails, sweat glands, and oil glands.
interferon (IFN) Natural human chemical that inhibits viral replication; used therapeutically to combat viral infections and cancer.
interferon gamma A protein produced by a virally infected cell that induces production of antiviral substances in neighboring cells. This defense prevents the production and maturation of viruses and thus terminates the viral infection.
interleukins A class of chemicals released from host cells that have potent effects on immunity.
intermediate filament Proteinaceous fibers in eukaryotic cells that help provide support to the cells and their organelles.
intoxication Poisoning that results from the introduction of a toxin into body tissues through ingestion or injection.
intron The segments on split genes of eukaryotes that do not code for polypeptide. They can have regulatory functions. See ***exon.***
iodophor A combination of iodine and an organic carrier that is a moderate-level disinfectant and antiseptic.
ion An unattached, charged particle.
ionic bond A chemical bond in which electrons are transferred and not shared between atoms.
ionization The aqueous dissociation of an electrolyte into ions.
ionizing radiation Radiant energy consisting of short-wave electromagnetic rays (X ray) or high-speed electrons that cause dislodgment of electrons on target molecules and create ions.
irradiation The application of radiant energy for diagnosis, therapy, disinfection, or sterilization.
irritability Capacity of cells to respond to chemical, mechanical, or light stimuli. This property helps cells adapt to the environment and obtain nutrients.
isograft Transplanted tissue from one monozygotic twin to the other; transplants between highly inbred animals that are genetically identical.
isolation The separation of microbial cells by serial dilution or mechanical dispersion on solid media to create discrete colonies.
isoniazid Older drug that targets the bacterial cell wall; used against *M. tuberculosis.*
isotonic Two solutions having the same osmotic pressure such that, when separated by a semipermeable membrane, there is no net movement of solvent in either direction.
isotope A version of an element that is virtually identical in all chemical properties to another version except that their atoms have slightly different atomic masses.

J

jaundice The yellowish pigmentation of skin, mucous membranes, sclera, deeper tissues, and excretions due to abnormal deposition of bile pigments. Jaundice is associated with liver infection, as with hepatitis B virus and leptospirosis.
JC virus (JCV) Causes a form of encephalitis (progressive multifocal leukoencephalopathy), especially in AIDS patients.

K

Kaposi sarcoma A malignant or benign neoplasm that appears as multiple hemorrhagic sites on the skin, lymph nodes, and viscera, and apparently involves the metastasis of abnormal blood vessel cells. It is a clinical feature of AIDS.
keratin Protein produced by outermost skin cells provides protection from trauma and moisture loss.
killed or inactivated vaccine A whole cell or intact virus preparation in which the microbes are dead or preserved and cannot multiply but are still capable of conferring immunity.
killer T cells A T lymphocyte programmed to directly affix cells and kill them. See ***cytotoxicity.***
kingdom In the levels of classification, the second division from more general to more specific. Each domain is divided into kingdoms.
Koch's postulates A procedure to establish the specific cause of disease. In all cases of infection: (1) The agent must be found; (2) inoculations of a pure culture must reproduce the same disease in animals; (3) the agent must again be present in the experimental animal; and (4) a pure culture must again be obtained.
Koplik's spots Tiny red blisters with central white specks on the mucosal lining of the cheeks. Symptomatic of measles.
Krebs cycle or tricarboxylic acid cycle (TCA) The second pathway of the three pathways that complete the process of primary catabolism. Also called the citric acid cycle.

L

L form A stage in the lives of some bacteria in which they have no peptidoglycan.
labile In chemistry, molecules, or compounds that are chemically unstable in the presence of environmental changes.
lactoferrin A protein in mucosal secretions, tears and milk that contains iron molecules and has antimicrobial activity.
lactose One of the carbohydrates commonly referred to as sugars. Lactose is commonly found in milk.
lactose (*lac*) operon Control system that manages the regulation of lactose metabolism. It is composed of three DNA segments, including a regulator, a control locus, and a structural locus.
lag phase The early phase of population growth during which no signs of growth occur.
lager The maturation process of beer, which is allowed to take place in large vats at a reduced temperature.
lagging strand The newly forming 5′ DNA strand that is discontinuously replicated in segments (Okazaki fragments).

lantibiotics Short peptides produced by bacteria that inhibit the growth of other bacteria.

latency The state of being inactive. Example: a latent virus or latent infection.

leading strand The newly forming 3′ DNA strand that is replicated in a continuous fashion without segments.

leaven To lighten food material by entrapping gas generated within it. Example: the rising of bread from the CO_2 produced by yeast or baking powder.

Legionnaire's disease Infection by ***Legionella*** bacterium. Weakly gram-negative rods are able to survive in aquatic habitats. Some forms may be fatal.

legumes Plants that produce seeds in pods. Examples include soybeans and peas.

lepromas Skin nodules seen on the face of persons suffering from lepromatous leprosy. The skin folds and thickenings are caused by the overgrowth of ***Mycobacterium leprae.***

lepromatous leprosy Severe, disfiguring leprosy characterized by widespread dissemination of the leprosy bacillus in deeper lesions.

leprosy See ***Hansen's disease.***

lesion A wound, injury, or some other pathologic change in tissues.

leukocidin A heat-labile substance formed by some pyogenic cocci that impairs and sometimes lyses leukocytes.

leukocytes White blood cells. The primary infection-fighting blood cells.

leukocytosis An abnormally large number of leukocytes in the blood, which can be indicative of acute infection.

leukopenia A lower-than-normal leukocyte count in the blood that can be indicative of blood infection or disease.

leukotriene An unsaturated fatty acid derivative of arachidonic acid. Leukotriene functions in chemotactic activity, smooth muscle contractility, mucus secretion, and capillary permeability.

ligase An enzyme required to seal the sticky ends of DNA pieces after splicing.

light-dependent reactions The series of reactions in photosynthesis that are driven by the light energy (photons) absorbed by chlorophyll. They involve splitting of water into hydrogens and oxygen, transport of electrons by NADP, and ATP synthesis.

light-independent reactions The series of reactions in photosynthesis that can proceed with or without light. It is a cyclic system that uses ATP from the light reactions to incorporate or fix carbon dioxide into organic compounds, leading to the production of glucose and other carbohydrates (also called the Calvin cycle).

lipase A fat-splitting enzyme. Example: Triacylglycerol lipase separates the fatty acid chains from the glycerol backbone of triglycerides.

lipid A term used to describe a variety of substances that are not soluble in polar solvents, such as water, but will dissolve in nonpolar solvents such as benzene and chloroform. Lipids include triglycerides, phospholipids, steroids, and waxes.

lipopolysaccharide A molecular complex of lipid and carbohydrate found in the bacterial cell wall. The lipopolysaccharide (LPS) of gram-negative bacteria is an endotoxin with generalized pathologic effects such as fever.

lipoteichoic acid Anionic polymers containing glycerol that are anchored in the cytoplasmic membranes of gram-positive bacteria.

liquid media Growth-supporting substance in fluid form.

lithoautotroph Bacteria that rely on inorganic minerals to supply their nutritional needs. Sometimes referred to as chemoautotrophs.

lithosphere That part of the biosphere that encompasses the earth's crust, including rocks and minerals.

lithotroph An autotrophic microbe that derives energy from reduced inorganic compounds such as N_2S.

lobar pneumonia Infection involving whole segments (lobes) of the lungs, which may lead to consolidation and plugging of the alveoli and extreme difficulty in breathing.

localized infection Occurs when a microbe enters a specific tissue, infects it, and remains confined there.

locus A site on a chromosome occupied by a gene. Plural: loci.

log phase Maximum rate of cell division during which growth is geometric in its rate of increase. Also called exponential growth phase.

lophotrichous Describing bacteria having a tuft of flagella at one or both poles.

lumen The cavity within a tubular organ.

lymphadenitis Inflammation of one or more lymph nodes. Also called lymphadenopathy.

lymphatic system A system of vessels and organs that serve as sites for development of immune cells and immune reactions. It includes the spleen, thymus, lymph nodes, and GALT.

lymphocyte The second most common form of white blood cells.

lyophilization A method for preserving microorganisms (and other substances) by freezing and then drying them directly from the frozen state.

lyse To burst.

lysin A complement-fixing antibody that destroys specific targeted cells. Examples: hemolysin and bacteriolysin.

lysis The physical rupture or deterioration of a cell.

lysogenic conversion A bacterium acquires a new genetic trait due to the presence of genetic material from an infecting phage.

lysogeny The indefinite persistence of bacteriophage DNA in a host without bringing about the production of virions.

lysosome A cytoplasmic organelle containing lysozyme and other hydrolytic enzymes.

lysozyme An enzyme found in sweat, tears, and saliva that breaks down bacterial peptidoglycan.

M

macromolecules Large, molecular compounds assembled from smaller subunits, most notably biochemicals.

macronutrient A chemical substance required in large quantities (phosphate, for example).

macrophage A white blood cell derived from a monocyte that leaves the circulation and enters tissues. These cells are important in nonspecific phagocytosis and in regulating, stimulating, and cleaning up after immune responses.

macroscopic Visible to the naked eye.

major histocompatibility complex A set of genes in mammals that produces molecules on surfaces of cells that differentiate among different individuals in the species.

malt The grain, usually barley, that is sprouted to obtain digestive enzymes and dried for making beer.

maltose One of the carbohydrates referred to as sugars. A fermentable sugar formed from starch.

Mantoux test An intradermal screening test for tuberculin hypersensitivity. A red, firm patch of skin at the injection site greater than 10 mm in diameter after 48 hours is a positive result that indicates current or prior exposure to the TB bacillus.

mapping Determining the location of loci and other qualities of genomic DNA.

marine microbiology A branch of microbiology that studies the role of microorganisms in the oceans.

marker Any trait or factor of a cell, virus, or molecule that makes it distinct and recognizable. Example: a genetic marker.

mash In making beer, the malt grain is steeped in warm water, ground up, and fortified with carbohydrates to form mash.

mass number (MN) Measurement that reflects the number of protons and neutrons in an atom of a particular element.

mast cell A nonmotile connective tissue cell implanted along capillaries, especially in the lungs, skin, gastrointestinal tract, and genitourinary tract. Like a basophil, its granules store mediators of allergy.

matrix The dense ground substance between the cristae of a mitochondrion that serves as a site for metabolic reactions.

matter All tangible materials that occupy space and have mass.

maximum temperature The highest temperature at which an organism will grow.

MDRTB Multidrug-resistant tuberculosis.

mechanical vector An animal that transports an infectious agent but is not infected by it, such as houseflies whose feet become contaminated with feces.

medium (plural, *media*) A nutrient used to grow organisms outside of their natural habitats.

meiosis The type of cell division necessary for producing gametes in diploid organisms. Two nuclear divisions in rapid succession produce four gametocytes, each containing a haploid number of chromosomes.

membrane In a single cell, a thin double-layered sheet composed of lipids such as phospholipids and sterols and proteins.

memory (immunologic memory) The capacity of the immune system to recognize and act against an antigen upon second and subsequent encounters.

memory cell The long-lived progeny of a sensitized lymphocyte that remains in circulation and is genetically programmed to react rapidly with its antigen.

Mendosicutes Taxonomic category of bacteria that have unusual cell walls; archaea.

meninges The tough tri-layer membrane covering the brain and spinal cord. Consists of the dura mater, arachnoid mater, and pia mater.

meningitis An inflammation of the membranes (meninges) that surround and protect the brain. It is often caused by bacteria such as ***Neisseria meningitidis*** (the meningococcus) and ***Haemophilus influenzae***.

merozoite The motile, infective stage of an apicomplexan parasite that comes from a liver or red blood cell undergoing multiple fission.

mesophile Microorganisms that grow at intermediate temperatures.

messenger RNA (mRNA) A single-stranded transcript that is a copy of the DNA template that corresponds to a gene.

metabolic analog Enzyme that mimics the natural substrate of an enzyme and vies for its active site.

metabolism A general term for the totality of chemical and physical processes occurring in a cell.

metabolites Small organic molecules that are intermediates in the stepwise biosynthesis or breakdown of macromolecules.

metabolomics The study of the complete complement of small chemicals present in a cell at any given time.

metachromatic Exhibiting a color other than that of the dye used to stain it.

metachromatic granules A type of inclusion in storage compartments of some bacteria that stain a contrasting color when treated with colored dyes.

metagenomics The study of all the genomes in a particular ecological niche, as opposed to individual genomes from single species.

methanogens Methane producers.

MHC Major histocompatibility complex. See ***HLA***.

MIC Abbreviation for minimum inhibitory concentration. The lowest concentration of antibiotic needed to inhibit bacterial growth in a test system.

microaerophile An aerobic bacterium that requires oxygen at a concentration less than that in the atmosphere.

microbe See ***microorganism***.

microbial antagonism Relationship in which microorganisms compete for survival in a common environment by taking actions that inhibit or destroy another organism.

microbial ecology The study of microbes in their natural habitats.

microbicides Chemicals that kill microorganisms.

microbiology A specialized area of biology that deals with living things ordinarily too small to be seen without magnification, including bacteria, archaea, fungi, protozoa, and viruses.

microbistatic The quality of inhibiting the growth of microbes.

microfilaments Cellular cytoskeletal element formed by thin protein strands that attach to cell membrane and form a network through the cytoplasm. Responsible for movement of cytoplasm.

micronutrient A chemical substance required in small quantities (trace metals, for example).

microorganism A living thing ordinarily too small to be seen without magnification; an organism of microscopic size.

microscopic Invisible to the naked eye.

microscopy Science that studies structure, magnification, lenses, and techniques related to use of a microscope.

microtubules Long hollow tubes in eukaryotic cells; maintain the shape of the cell and transport substances from one part of cell to another; involved in separating chromosomes in mitosis.

miliary tuberculosis Rapidly fatal tuberculosis due to dissemination of mycobacteria in the blood and formation of tiny granules in various organs and tissues. The term ***miliary*** means resembling a millet seed.

mineralization The process by which decomposers (bacteria and fungi) convert organic debris into inorganic and elemental form. It is part of the recycling process.

minimum inhibitory concentration (MIC) The smallest concentration of drug needed to visibly control microbial growth.

minimum temperature The lowest temperature at which an organism will grow.

miracidium The ciliated first-stage larva of a trematode. This form is infective for a corresponding intermediate host snail.

missense mutation A mutation in which a change in the DNA sequence results in a different amino acid being incorporated into a protein, with varying results.

mitochondrion A double-membrane organelle of eukaryotes that is the main site for aerobic respiration.

mitosis Somatic cell division that preserves the somatic chromosome number.

mixed acid fermentation An anaerobic degradation of pyruvic acid that results in more than one organic acid being produced (e.g., acetic acid, lactic acid, succinic acid).

mixed culture A container growing two or more different, known species of microbes.

mixed infection Occurs when several different pathogens interact simultaneously to produce an infection. Also called a synergistic infection.

molecule A distinct chemical substance that results from the combination of two or more atoms.

molluscum contagiosum Poxvirus-caused disease that manifests itself by the appearance of small lesions on the face, trunk, and limbs. Can be associated with sexual transmission.

monoclonal antibodies (MAbs) Antibodies that have a single specificity for a single antigen and are produced in the laboratory from a single clone of B cells.

monocyte A large mononuclear leukocyte normally found in the lymph nodes, spleen, bone marrow, and loose connective tissue. This type of cell makes up 3% to 7% of circulating leukocytes.

monomer A simple molecule that can be linked by chemical bonds to form larger molecules.

mononuclear phagocyte system A collection of monocytes and macrophages scattered throughout the extracellular spaces that function to engulf and degrade foreign molecules.

monosaccharide A simple sugar such as glucose that is a basic building block for more complex carbohydrates.

monotrichous Describing a microorganism that bears a single flagellum.

morbidity A diseased condition.

morbidity rate The number of persons afflicted with an illness under question or with illness in general, expressed as a numerator, with the denominator being some unit of population (as in $x/100{,}000$).

mordant A chemical that fixes a dye in or on cells by forming an insoluble compound and thereby promoting retention of that dye. Example: Gram's iodine in the Gram stain.

morphology The study of organismic structure.

mortality rate The number of persons who have died as the result of a particular cause or due to all causes, expressed as a numerator, with the denominator being some unit of population (as in $x/100{,}000$).

most probable number (MPN) Test used to detect the concentration of contaminants in water and other fluids.

motility Self-propulsion.

mumps Viral disease characterized by inflammation of the parotid glands.

must Juices expressed from crushed fruits that are used in fermentation for wine.

mutagen Any agent that induces genetic mutation. Examples: certain chemical substances, ultraviolet light, radioactivity.

mutant strain A subspecies of microorganism that has undergone a mutation, causing expression of a trait that differs from other members of that species.

mutation A permanent inheritable alteration in the DNA sequence or content of a cell.

mutualism Organisms living in an obligatory but mutually beneficial relationship.

mycelium The filamentous mass that makes up a mold. Composed of hyphae.

mycoplasma A genus of bacteria; contain no peptidoglycan/cell wall, but the cytoplasmic membrane is stabilized by sterols.

mycorrhizae Various species of fungi adapted in an intimate, mutualistic relationship to plant roots.

mycosis Any disease caused by a fungus.

myonecrosis Death of muscle tissue.

N

NAD/NADH Abbreviations for the oxidized/reduced forms of nicotinamide adenine dinucleotide, an electron carrier. Also known as the vitamin niacin.

nanobacteria (also *nanobes*) Bacteria that are up to 100 times smaller than average bacteria.

nanobes Cell-like particles found in sediments and other geologic deposits that some scientists speculate are the smallest bacteria. Short for nanobacteria.

narrow spectrum Denotes drugs that are selective and limited in their effects. For example, they inhibit either gram-negative or gram-positive bacteria, but not both.

natural immunity Any immunity that arises naturally in an organism via previous experience with the antigen.

natural selection A process in which the environment places pressure on organisms to adapt and survive changing conditions. Only the survivors will be around to continue the life cycle and contribute their genes to future generations. This is considered a major factor in evolution of species.

necrosis A pathologic process in which cells and tissues die and disintegrate.

negative stain A staining technique that renders the background opaque or colored and leaves the object unstained so that it is outlined as a colorless area.

nematode A common name for helminths called roundworms.

nephritis Inflammation of the kidney.

neurotropic Having an affinity for the nervous system. Most likely to affect the spinal cord.

neutralization The process of combining an acid and a base until they reach a balanced proportion, with a pH value close to 7.

neutron An electrically neutral particle in the nuclei of all atoms except hydrogen.

neutrophil A mature granulocyte present in peripheral circulation, exhibiting a multilobular nucleus and numerous cytoplasmic granules that retain a neutral stain. The neutrophil is an active phagocytic cell in bacterial infection.

niche In ecology, an organism's biological role in or contribution to its community.

nitrification Phase of the nitrogen cycle in which ammonium is oxidized.

nitrogen base A ringed compound of which pyrimidines and purines are types.

nitrogen cycle The pathway followed by the element nitrogen as it circulates from inorganic sources in the nonliving environment to living things and back to the nonliving environment. The longtime reservoir is nitrogen gas in the atmosphere.

nitrogen fixation A process occurring in certain bacteria in which atmospheric N_2 gas is converted to a form (NH_4) usable by plants.

nitrogenous base A nitrogen-containing molecule found in DNA and RNA that provides the basis for the genetic code. Adenine, guanine, and cytosine are found in both DNA and RNA, while thymine is found exclusively in DNA and uracil is found exclusively in RNA.

nomenclature A set system for scientifically naming organisms, enzymes, anatomical structures, and so on.

noncommunicable An infectious disease that does not arrive through transmission of an infectious agent from host to host.

noncompetitive inhibition Form of enzyme inhibition that involves binding of a regulatory molecule to a site other than the active site.

nonionizing radiation Method of microbial control, best exemplified by ultraviolet light, that causes the formation of abnormal bonds within the DNA of microbes, increasing the rate of mutation. The primary limitation of nonionizing radiation is its inability to penetrate beyond the surface of an object.

nonpolar A term used to describe an electrically neutral molecule formed by covalent bonds between atoms that have the same or similar electronegativity.

nonself Molecules recognized by the immune system as containing foreign markers, indicating a need for immune response.

nonsense codon A triplet of mRNA bases that does not specify an amino acid but signals the end of a polypeptide chain.

nonsense mutation A mutation that changes an amino-acid-producing codon into a stop codon, leading to premature termination of a protein.

normal biota The native microbial forms that an individual harbors.

nosocomial infection An infection not present upon admission to a hospital but incurred while being treated there.

nucleocapsid In viruses, the close physical combination of the nucleic acid with its protective covering.

nucleoid The basophilic nuclear region or nuclear body that contains the bacterial chromosome.

nucleolus A granular mass containing RNA that is contained within the nucleus of a eukaryotic cell.

nucleosome Structure in the packaging of DNA. Formed by the DNA strands wrapping around the histone protein to form nucleus bodies arranged like beads on a chain.

nucleotide The basic structural unit of DNA and RNA; each nucleotide consists of a phosphate, a sugar (ribose in RNA, deoxyribose in DNA), and a nitrogenous base such as adenine, guanine, cytosine, thymine (DNA only), or uracil (RNA only).

numerical aperture In microscopy, the amount of light passing from the object and into the object in order to maximize optical clarity and resolution.

nutrient Any chemical substance that must be provided to a cell for normal metabolism and growth. Macronutrients are required in large amounts, and micronutrients in small amounts.

nutrition The acquisition of chemical substances by a cell or organism for use as an energy source or as building blocks of cellular structures.

O

obligate Without alternative; restricted to a particular characteristic. Example: An obligate parasite survives and grows only in a host; an obligate aerobe must have oxygen to grow; an obligate anaerobe is destroyed by oxygen.

Okazaki fragment In replication of DNA, a segment formed on the lagging strand in which biosynthesis is conducted in a discontinuous manner dictated by the 5′→ 3′ DNA polymerase orientation.

oligodynamic action A chemical having antimicrobial activity in minuscule amounts. Example: Certain heavy metals are effective in a few parts per billion.

oligonucleotides Short pieces of DNA or RNA that are easier to handle than long segments.

oligotrophic Nutrient-deficient ecosystem.

oncogene A naturally occurring type of gene that when activated can transform a normal cell into a cancer cell.

oncovirus Mammalian virus capable of causing malignant tumors.

oocyst The encysted form of a fertilized macrogamete or zygote; typical in the life cycles of apicomplexan parasites.

operator In an operon sequence, the DNA segment where transcription of structural genes is initiated.

operon A genetic operational unit that regulates metabolism by controlling mRNA production. In sequence, the unit consists of a regulatory gene, inducer or repressor control sites, and structural genes.

opportunistic In infection, ordinarily nonpathogenic or weakly pathogenic microbes that cause disease primarily in an immunologically compromised host.

opsonization The process of stimulating phagocytosis by affixing molecules (opsonins such as antibodies and complement) to the surfaces of foreign cells or particles.

optimum temperature The temperature at which a species shows the most rapid growth rate.

orbitals The pathways of electrons as they rotate around the nucleus of an atom.

order In the levels of classification, the division of organisms that follows class. Increasing similarity may be noticed among organisms assigned to the same order.

organelle A small component of eukaryotic cells that is bounded by a membrane and specialized in function.

organic chemicals Molecules that contain the basic framework of the elements carbon and hydrogen.

osmophile A microorganism that thrives in a medium having high osmotic pressure.

osmosis The diffusion of water across a selectively permeable membrane in the direction of lower water concentration.

osteomyelitis A focal infection of the internal structures of long bones, leading to pain and inflammation. Often caused by ***Staphylococcus aureus.***

outer membrane An additional membrane possessed by gram-negative bacteria; a lipid bilayer containing specialized proteins and polysaccharides. It lies outside of the cell wall.

oxidation In chemical reactions, the loss of electrons by one reactant.

oxidation-reduction Redox reactions in which paired sets of molecules participate in electron transfers.

oxidative phosphorylation The synthesis of ATP using energy given off during the electron transport phase of respiration.

oxidizing agent An atom or a compound that can receive electrons from another in a chemical reaction.

oxygenic Any reaction that gives off oxygen; usually in reference to the result of photosynthesis in eukaryotes and cyanobacteria.

P

palindrome A word, verse, number, or sentence that reads the same forward or backward. Palindromes of nitrogen bases in DNA have genetic significance as transposable elements, as regulatory protein targets, and in DNA splicing.

palisades The characteristic arrangement of ***Corynebacterium*** cells resembling a row of fence posts and created by snapping.

PAMPs Pathogen-associated molecular patterns. Chemical signatures present on many different microorganisms, but not on host, which are recognized by host as foreign.

pandemic A disease afflicting an increased proportion of the population over a wide geographic area (often worldwide).

papilloma Benign, squamous epithelial growth commonly referred to as a wart.

parasite An organism that lives on or within another organism (the host) from which it obtains nutrients and enjoys protection. The parasite produces some degree of harm in the host.

parasitism A relationship between two organisms in which the host is harmed in some way while the colonizer benefits.

parenteral Administering a substance into a body compartment other than through the gastrointestinal tract, such as via intravenous, subcutaneous, intramuscular, or intramedullary injection.

paroxysmal Events characterized by sharp spasms or convulsions; sudden onset of a symptom such as fever and chills.

passive carrier Persons who mechanically transfer a pathogen without ever being infected by it. For example, a health care worker who doesn't wash his/her hands adequately between patients.

passive immunity Specific resistance that is acquired indirectly by donation of preformed immune substances (antibodies) produced in the body of another individual.

passive transport Nutrient transport method that follows basic physical laws and does not require direct energy input from the cell.

pasteurization Heat treatment of perishable fluids such as milk, fruit juices, or wine to destroy heat-sensitive vegetative cells, followed by rapid chilling to inhibit growth of survivors and germination of spores. It prevents infection and spoilage.

pathogen Any agent (usually a virus, bacterium, fungus, protozoan, or helminth) that causes disease.

pathogen-associated molecular patterns molecules on the surfaces of many types of microbes that are not present on host cells that mark the microbes as foreign; PAMPs.

pathogenicity The capacity of microbes to cause disease.

pathogenicity islands Areas of the genome containing multiple genes, which contribute to a new trait for the organism that increases its ability to cause disease.

pathognomic Distinctive and particular to a single disease; suggestive of a diagnosis.

pathologic Capable of inducing physical damage on the host.

pathology The structural and physiological effects of disease on the body.

pattern recognition receptors Molecules on the surface of host defense cells that recognize pathogen-associated molecular patterns on microbes; PRRs.

pellicle A membranous cover; a thin skin, film, or scum on a liquid surface; a thin film of salivary glycoproteins that forms over newly cleaned tooth enamel when exposed to saliva.

pelvic inflammatory disease (PID) An infection of the uterus and fallopian tubes that has ascended from the lower reproductive tract. Caused by gonococci and chlamydias.

penetration (viral) The step in viral multiplication in which virus enters the host cell.

penicillinase An enzyme that hydrolyzes penicillin; found in penicillin-resistant strains of bacteria.

penicillins A large group of naturally occurring and synthetic antibiotics produced by *Penicillium* mold and active against the cell wall of bacteria.

pentose A monosaccharide with five carbon atoms per molecule. Examples: arabinose, ribose, xylose.

peptide Molecule composed of short chains of amino acids, such as a dipeptide (two amino acids), a tripeptide (three), and a tetrapeptide (four).

peptide bond The covalent union between two amino acids that forms between the amine group of one and the carboxyl group of the other. The basic bond of proteins.

peptidoglycan A network of polysaccharide chains cross-linked by short peptides that forms the rigid part of bacterial cell walls. Gram-negative bacteria have a smaller amount of this rigid structure than do gram-positive bacteria.

perforin Proteins released by cytotoxic T cells that produce pores in target cells.

perinatal In childbirth, occurring before, during, or after delivery.

period of invasion The period during a clinical infection when the infectious agent multiplies at high levels, exhibits its greatest toxicity, and becomes well established in the target tissues.

periodontal Involving the structures that surround the tooth.

periplasmic space The region between the cell wall and cell membrane of the cell envelopes of gram-negative bacteria.

peritrichous In bacterial morphology, having flagella distributed over the entire cell.

petechiae Minute hemorrhagic spots in the skin that range from pinpoint- to pinhead-size.

Peyer's patches Oblong lymphoid aggregates of the gut located chiefly in the wall of the terminal and small intestine. Along with the tonsils and appendix, Peyer's patches make up the gut-associated lymphoid tissue that responds to local invasion by infectious agents.

pH The symbol for the negative logarithm of the H ion concentration; p (power) or $[H^+]_{10}$. A system for rating acidity and alkalinity.

phage A bacteriophage; a virus that specifically parasitizes bacteria.

phagocyte A class of white blood cells capable of engulfing other cells and particles.

phagocytosis A type of endocytosis in which the cell membrane actively engulfs large particles or cells into vesicles.

phagolysosome A body formed in a phagocyte, consisting of a union between a vesicle containing the ingested particle (the phagosome) and a vacuole of hydrolytic enzymes (the lysosome).

phase variation The process of bacteria turning on or off a group of genes that changes its phenotype in a heritable manner.

phenotype The observable characteristics of an organism produced by the interaction between its genetic potential (genotype) and the environment.

phosphate An acidic salt containing phosphorus and oxygen that is an essential inorganic component of DNA, RNA, and ATP.

phospholipid A class of lipids that compose a major structural component of cell membranes.

phosphorylation Process in which inorganic phosphate is added to a compound.

photoactivation (light repair) A mechanism for repairing DNA with ultraviolet-light-induced mutations using an enzyme (photolyase) that is activated by visible light.

photoautotroph An organism that utilizes light for its energy and carbon dioxide chiefly for its carbon needs.

photolysis The splitting of water into hydrogen and oxygen during photosynthesis.

photon A subatomic particle released by electromagnetic sources such as radiant energy (sunlight). Photons are the ultimate source of energy for photosynthesis.

photophosphorylation The process of electron transport during photosynthesis that results in the synthesis of ATP from ADP.

photosynthesis A process occurring in plants, algae, and some bacteria that traps the sun's energy and converts it to ATP in the cell. This energy is used to fix CO_2 into organic compounds.

phototrophs Microbes that use photosynthesis to feed.

phycobilin Red or blue-green pigments that absorb light during photosynthesis.

phylum In the levels of classification, the third level of classification from general to more specific. Each kingdom is divided into numerous phyla. Sometimes referred to as a division.

physiology The study of the function of an organism.

phytoplankton The collection of photosynthetic microorganisms (mainly algae and cyanobacteria) that float in the upper layers of aquatic habitats where sun penetrates. These microbes are the basis of aquatic food pyramids and, together with zooplankton, make up the plankton.

pili Small, stiff filamentous appendages in gram-negative bacteria that function in DNA exchange during bacterial conjugation.

pilus A hollow appendage used to bring two bacterial cells together to transfer DNA.

pinocytosis The engulfment, or endocytosis, of liquids by extensions of the cell membrane.

plague Zoonotic disease caused by infection with ***Yersinia pestis.*** The pathogen is spread by flea vectors and harbored by various rodents.

plankton Minute animals (zooplankton) or plants (phytoplankton) that float and drift in the limnetic zone of bodies of water.

plantar warts Deep, painful warts on the soles of the feet as a result of infection by human papillomavirus.

plaque In virus propagation methods, the clear zone of lysed cells in tissue culture or chick embryo membrane that corresponds to the area containing viruses. In dental application, the filamentous mass of microbes that adheres tenaciously to the tooth and predisposes to caries, calculus, or inflammation.

plasma The carrier fluid element of blood.

plasma cell A progeny of an activated B cell that actively produces and secretes antibodies.

plasmids Extra chromosomal genetic units characterized by several features. A plasmid is a double-stranded DNA that is smaller than and replicates independently of the cell chromosome; it bears genes that are not essential for cell growth; it can bear genes that code for adaptive traits; and it is transmissible to other bacteria.

platelet-activating factor A substance released from basophils that causes release of allergic mediators and the aggregation of platelets.

platelets Formed elements in the blood that develop when megakaryocytes disintegrate. Platelets are involved in hemostasis and blood clotting.

pleomorphism Normal variability of cell shapes in a single species.

pluripotential Stem cells having the developmental plasticity to give rise to more than one type. Example: undifferentiated blood cells in the bone marrow.

pneumococcus Common name for ***Streptococcus pneumoniae,*** the major cause of bacterial pneumonia.

pneumonia An inflammation of the lung leading to accumulation of fluid and respiratory compromise.

pneumonic plague The acute, frequently fatal form of pneumonia caused by ***Yersinia pestis***.

point mutation A change that involves the loss, substitution, or addition of one or a few nucleotides.

point source epidemic An outbreak of disease in which all affected individuals were exposed to a single source of the pathogen at a single point in time.

polar Term to describe a molecule with an asymmetrical distribution of charges. Such a molecule has a negative pole and a positive pole.

poliomyelitis An acute enteroviral infection of the spinal cord that can cause neuromuscular paralysis.

polyclonal In reference to a collection of antibodies with mixed specificities that arose from more than one clone of B cells.

polyclonal antibodies A mixture of antibodies that were stimulated by a complex antigen with more than one antigenic determinant.

polymer A macromolecule made up of a chain of repeating units. Examples: starch, protein, DNA.

polymerase An enzyme that produces polymers through catalyzing bond formation between building blocks (polymerization).

polymerase chain reaction (PCR) A technique that amplifies segments of DNA for testing. Using denaturation, primers, and heat-resistant DNA polymerase, the number can be increased several-million-fold.

polymicrobial Involving multiple distinct microorganisms.

polymorphonuclear leukocytes (PMNLs) White blood cells with variously shaped nuclei. Although this term commonly denotes all granulocytes, it is used especially for the neutrophils.

polymyxin A mixture of antibiotic polypeptides from ***Bacillus polymyxa*** that are particularly effective against gram-negative bacteria.

polypeptide A relatively large chain of amino acids linked by peptide bonds.

polyribosomal complex An assembly line for mass production of proteins composed of a chain of ribosomes involved in mRNA transcription.

polysaccharide A carbohydrate that can be hydrolyzed into a number of monosaccharides. Examples: cellulose, starch, glycogen.

population A group of organisms of the same species living simultaneously in the same habitat. A group of different populations living together constitutes the community level.

porin Transmembrane proteins of the outer membrane of gram-negative cells that permit transport of small molecules into the periplasmic space but bar the penetration of larger molecules.

portal of entry Route of entry for an infectious agent; typically a cutaneous or membranous route.

portal of exit Route through which a pathogen departs from the host organism.

positive stain A method for coloring microbial specimens that involves a chemical that sticks to the specimen to give it color.

potable Describing water that is relatively clear, odor-free, and safe to drink.

PPNG Penicillinase-producing ***Neisseria gonorrhoeae.***

prebiotics Nutrients used to stimulate the growth of favorable biota in the intestine.

prevalence The total number of cases of a disease in a certain area and time period.

primary infection An initial infection in a previously healthy individual that is later complicated by an additional (secondary) infection.

primary response The first response of the immune system when exposed to an antigen.

primary structure Initial protein organization described by type, number, and order of amino acids in the chain. The primary structure varies extensively from protein to protein.

primers Synthetic oligonucleotides of known sequence that serve as landmarks to indicate where DNA amplification will begin.

prion A concocted word to denote "proteinaceous infectious agent"; a cytopathic protein associated with the slow-virus spongiform encephalopathies of humans and animals.

probes Small fragments of single-stranded DNA (RNA) that are known to be complementary to the specific sequence of DNA being studied.

probiotics Preparations of live microbes used as a preventive or therapeutic measure to displace or compete with potential pathogens.

prodromal stage A short period of mild symptoms occurring at the end of the period of incubation. It indicates the onset of disease.

producer An organism that synthesizes complex organic compounds from simple inorganic molecules. Examples would be photosynthetic microbes and plants. These organisms are solely responsible for originating food pyramids and are the basis for life on earth (also called autotroph).

product(s) In a chemical reaction, the substance(s) that is(are) left after a reaction is completed.

proglottid The egg-generating segment of a tapeworm that contains both male and female organs.

progressive multifocal leukoencephalopathy (PML) An uncommon, fatal complication of infection with JC virus (polyoma virus).

prokaryotic cells Small cells, lacking special structures such as a nucleus and organelles. All prokaryotes are microorganisms.

promastigote A morphological variation of the trypanosome parasite responsible for leishmaniasis.

promoter Part of an operon sequence. The DNA segment that is recognized by RNA polymerase as the starting site for transcription.

promoter region The site composed of a short signaling DNA sequence that RNA polymerase recognizes and binds to commence transcription.

propagated epidemic An outbreak of disease in which the causative agent is passed from affected persons to new persons over the course of time.

prophage A lysogenized bacteriophage; a phage that is latently incorporated into the host chromosome instead of undergoing viral replication and lysis.

prophylactic Any device, method, or substance used to prevent disease.

prostaglandin A hormonelike substance that regulates many body functions. Prostaglandin comes from a family of organic acids containing 5-carbon rings that are essential to the human diet.

protease Enzymes that act on proteins, breaking them down into component parts.

protease inhibitors Drugs that act to prevent the assembly of functioning viral particles.

protein Predominant organic molecule in cells, formed by long chains of amino acids.

proteomics The study of an organism's complement of proteins (its ***proteome***) and functions mediated by the proteins.

proton An elementary particle that carries a positive charge. It is identical to the nucleus of the hydrogen atom.

protoplast A bacterial cell whose cell wall is completely lacking and that is vulnerable to osmotic lysis.

protozoa A group of single-celled, eukaryotic organisms.

provirus The genome of a virus when it is integrated into a host cell's DNA.

PRRs Pattern recognition receptors. Molecules on the surface of host cells that recognize pathogen-associated molecular patterns (PAMPs) on microbial cells.

pseudohypha A chain of easily separated, spherical to sausage-shaped yeast cells partitioned by constrictions rather than by septa.

pseudomembrane A tenacious, noncellular mucous exudate containing cellular debris that tightly blankets the mucosal surface in infections such as diphtheria and pseudomembranous enterocolitis.

pseudopodium A temporary extension of the protoplasm of an amoeboid cell. It serves both in amoeboid motion and for food gathering (phagocytosis).

pseudopods Protozoan appendage responsible for motility. Also called "false feet."

psychrophile A microorganism that thrives at low temperature (0°C–20°C), with a temperature optimum of 0°C–15°C.
pulmonary Occurring in the lungs. Examples include pulmonary anthrax and pulmonary nocardiosis.
pure culture A container growing a single species of microbe whose identity is known.
purine A nitrogen base that is an important encoding component of DNA and RNA. The two most common purines are adenine and guanine.
purpura Purple-colored spots or blotches on the skin.
pus The viscous, opaque, usually yellowish matter formed by an inflammatory infection. It consists of serum exudate, tissue debris, leukocytes, and microorganisms.
pyogenic Pertains to pus formers, especially the pyogenic cocci: pneumococci, streptococci, staphylococci, and neisseriae.
pyrimidine Nitrogen bases that help form the genetic code on DNA and RNA. Uracil, thymine, and cytosine are the most important pyrimidines.
pyrimidine dimer The union of two adjacent pyrimidines on the same DNA strand, brought about by exposure to ultraviolet light. It is a form of mutation.
pyrogen A substance that causes a rise in body temperature. It can come from pyrogenic microorganisms or from polymorphonuclear leukocytes (endogenous pyrogens).

Q

quaternary structure Most complex protein structure characterized by the formation of large, multiunit proteins by more than one of the polypeptides. This structure is typical of antibodies and some enzymes that act in cell synthesis.
quats A word that pertains to a family of surfactants called quaternary ammonium compounds. These detergents are only weakly microbicidal and are used as sanitizers and preservatives.
quinine A substance derived from cinchona trees that was used as an antimalarial treatment; has been replaced by synthetic derivatives.
quinolone A class of synthetic antimicrobic drugs with broad-spectrum effects.
quorum sensing The ability of bacteria to regulate their gene expression in response to sensing bacterial density.

R

rabies The only rhabdovirus that infects humans. Zoonotic disease characterized by fatal meningoencephalitis.
radiation Electromagnetic waves or rays, such as those of light given off from an energy source.
radioactive isotopes Unstable isotopes whose nuclei emit particles of radiation. This emission is called radioactivity or radioactive decay. Three naturally occurring emissions are alpha, beta, and gamma radiation.
rales Sounds in the lung, ranging from clicking to rattling; indicate respiratory illness.
reactants Molecules entering or starting a chemical reaction.
real image An image formed at the focal plane of a convex lens. In the compound light microscope, it is the image created by the objective lens.
receptor Cell surface molecules involved in recognition, binding, and intracellular signaling.
recombinant An organism that contains genes that originated in another organism, whether through deliberate laboratory manipulation or natural processes.
recombinant DNA technology A technology, also known as genetic engineering, that deliberately modifies the genetic structure of an organism to create novel products, microbes, animals, plants, and viruses.
recombination A type of genetic transfer in which DNA from one organism is donated to another.
recycling A process that converts unusable organic matter from dead organisms back into their essential inorganic elements and returns them to their nonliving reservoirs to make them available again for living organisms. This is a common term that means the same as mineralization and decomposition.
redox Denoting an oxidation-reduction reaction.
reducing agent An atom or a compound that can donate electrons in a chemical reaction.
reducing medium A growth medium that absorbs oxygen and allows anaerobic bacteria to grow.
reduction In chemistry, the gain of electrons.
redundancy The property of the genetic code that allows an amino acid to be specified by several different codons.
refraction In optics, the bending of light as it passes from one medium to another with a different index of refraction.
regulated enzymes Enzymes whose extent of transcription or translation is influenced by changes in the environment.
regulator DNA segment that codes for a protein capable of repressing an operon.
regulatory B cells (B_{reg} cells) A type of activated B cell that controls the immune response.
regulatory site The location on an enzyme where a certain substance can bind and block the enzyme's activity.
rennin The enzyme casein coagulase, which is used to produce curd in the processing of milk and cheese.
replication In DNA synthesis, the semiconservative mechanisms that ensure precise duplication of the parent DNA strands.
replication fork The Y-shaped point on a replicating DNA molecule where the DNA polymerase is synthesizing new strands of DNA.
reportable disease Those diseases that must be reported to health authorities by law.
repressible operon An operon that under normal circumstances is transcribed. The buildup of the operon's amino acid product causes transcription of the operon to stop.
repressor The protein product of a repressor gene that combines with the operator and arrests the transcription and translation of structural genes.
reservoir In disease communication, the natural host or habitat of a pathogen.
resident biota The deeper, more stable microbiota that inhabit the skin and exposed mucous membranes, as opposed to the superficial, variable, transient population.
resistance (R) factor Plasmids, typically shared among bacteria by conjugation, that provide resistance to the effects of antibiotics.
resolving power The capacity of a microscope lens system to accurately distinguish between two separate entities that lie close to each other. Also called resolution.
respiratory chain A series of enzymes that transfer electrons from one to another, resulting in the formation of ATP. It is also known as the electron transport chain. The chain is located in the cell membrane of bacteria and in the inner mitochondrial membrane of eukaryotes.
respiratory syncytial virus (RSV) An RNA virus that infects the respiratory tract. RSV is the most prevalent cause of respiratory infection in newborns.
restriction endonuclease An enzyme present naturally in cells that cleaves specific locations on DNA. It is an important means of inactivating viral genomes, and it is also used to splice genes in genetic engineering.
reticuloendothelial system Also known as the mononuclear phagocyte system, it pertains to a network of fibers and phagocytic cells (macrophages) that permeates the tissues of all organs. Examples: Kupffer cells in liver sinusoids, alveolar phagocytes in the lung, microglia in nervous tissue.
retrovirus A group of RNA viruses (including HIV) that have the mechanisms for converting their genome into a double strand of DNA that can be inserted on a host's chromosome.
reverse transcriptase (RT) The enzyme possessed by retroviruses that carries out the reversion of RNA to DNA—a form of reverse transcription.
Reye's syndrome A sudden, usually fatal neurological condition that occurs in children after a viral infection. Autopsy shows cerebral edema and marked fatty change in the liver and renal tubules.
Rh factor An isoantigen that can trigger hemolytic disease in newborns due to incompatibility between maternal and infant blood factors.
rhizobia Bacteria that live in plant roots and supply supplemental nitrogen that boosts plant growth.
rhizosphere The zone of soil, complete with microbial inhabitants, in the immediate vicinity of plant roots.
ribonucleic acid (RNA) The nucleic acid responsible for carrying out the hereditary program transmitted by an organism's DNA.
ribose A 5-carbon monosaccharide found in RNA.
ribosomal RNA (rRNA) A single-stranded transcript that is a copy of part of the DNA template.
ribosome A bilobed macromolecular complex of ribonucleoprotein that coordinates the codons of mRNA with tRNA anticodons and, in so doing, constitutes the peptide assembly site.
ribozyme A part of an RNA-containing enzyme in eukaryotes that removes intervening sequences of RNA called introns and splices together the true coding sequences (exons) to form a mature messenger RNA.

rickettsias Medically important family of bacteria, commonly carried by ticks, lice, and fleas. Significant cause of important emerging diseases.

ringworm A superficial mycosis caused by various dermatophytic fungi. This common name is actually a misnomer.

RNA editing The alteration of RNA molecules before translation, found only in eukaryotes.

RNA polymerase Enzyme process that translates the code of DNA to RNA.

rolling circle An intermediate stage in viral replication of circular DNA into linear DNA.

root nodules Small growths on the roots of legume plants that arise from a symbiotic association between the plant tissues and bacteria (Rhizobia). This association allows fixation of nitrogen gas from the air into a usable nitrogen source for the plant.

rosette formation A technique for distinguishing surface receptors on T cells by reacting them with sensitized indicator sheep red blood cells. The cluster of red cells around the central white blood cell resembles a little rose blossom and is indicative of the type of receptor.

rough endoplasmic reticulum (RER) Microscopic series of tunnels that originates in the outer membrane of the nuclear envelope and is used in transport and storage. Large numbers of ribosomes, partly attached to the membrane, give the rough appearance.

rubeola (red measles) Acute disease caused by infection with Morbillivirus.

S

saccharide Scientific term for sugar. Refers to a simple carbohydrate with a sweet taste.

salpingitis Inflammation of the fallopian tubes.

sanitize To clean inanimate objects using soap and degerming agents so that they are safe and free of high levels of microorganisms.

saprobe A microbe that decomposes organic remains from dead organisms. Also known as a saprophyte or saprotroph.

sarcina A cubical packet of 8, 16, or more cells; the cellular arrangement of the genus ***Sarcina*** in the family Micrococcaceae.

satellitism A commensal interaction between two microbes in which one can grow in the vicinity of the other due to nutrients or protective factors released by that microbe.

saturation The complete occupation of the active site of a carrier protein or enzyme by the substrate.

schistosomiasis Infection by blood fluke, often as a result of contact with contaminated water in rivers and streams. Symptoms appear in liver, spleen, or urinary system depending on species of ***Schistosoma.*** Infection may be chronic.

schizogony A process of multiple fission whereby first the nucleus divides several times, and subsequently the cytoplasm is subdivided for each new nucleus during cell division.

scientific method Principles and procedures for the systematic pursuit of knowledge, involving the recognition and formulation of a problem, the collection of data through observation and experimentation, and the formulation and testing of a hypothesis.

scolex The anterior end of a tapeworm characterized by hooks and/or suckers for attachment to the host.

sebaceous glands The sebum- (oily, fatty) secreting glands of the skin.

sebum Low pH, oil-based secretion of the sebaceous glands.

secondary infection An infection that compounds a pre-existing one.

secondary response The rapid rise in antibody titer following a repeat exposure to an antigen that has been recognized from a previous exposure. This response is brought about by memory cells produced as a result of the primary exposure.

secondary structure Protein structure that occurs when the functional groups on the outer surface of the molecule interact by forming hydrogen bonds. These bonds cause the amino acid chain to either twist, forming a helix, or to pleat into an accordion pattern called a β-pleated sheet.

secretory antibody The immunoglobulin (IgA) that is found in secretions of mucous membranes and serves as a local immediate protection against infection.

selective media Nutrient media designed to favor the growth of certain microbes and to inhibit undesirable competitors.

selectively toxic Property of an antimicrobial agent to be highly toxic against its target microbe while being far less toxic to other cells, particularly those of the host organism.

self Natural markers of the body that are recognized by the immune system.

self-limited Applies to an infection that runs its course without disease or residual effects.

semiconservative replication In DNA replication, the synthesis of paired daughter strands, each retaining a parent strand template.

semisolid media Nutrient media with a firmness midway between that of a broth (a liquid medium) and an ordinary solid medium; motility media.

semisynthetic Drugs that, after being naturally produced by bacteria, fungi, or other living sources, are chemically modified in the laboratory.

sensitizing dose The initial effective exposure to an antigen or an allergen that stimulates an immune response. Often applies to allergies.

sepsis The state of putrefaction; the presence of pathogenic organisms or their toxins in tissue or blood.

septic shock Blood infection resulting in a pathological state of low blood pressure accompanied by a reduced amount of blood circulating to vital organs. Endotoxins of all gram-negative bacteria can cause shock, but most clinical cases are due to gram-negative enteric rods.

septicemia Systemic infection associated with microorganisms multiplying in circulating blood.

septicemic plague A form of infection with ***Yersinia pestis*** occurring mainly in the bloodstream and leading to high mortality rates.

septum A partition or cellular cross wall, as in certain fungal hyphae.

sequela A morbid complication that follows a disease.

sequencing Determining the actual order and types of bases in a segment of DNA.

serology The branch of immunology that deals with ***in vitro*** diagnostic testing of serum.

seropositive Showing the presence of specific antibody in a serological test. Indicates ongoing infection.

serotonin A vasoconstrictor that inhibits gastric secretion and stimulates smooth muscle.

serotyping The subdivision of a species or subspecies into an immunologic type, based upon antigenic characteristics.

serum The clear fluid expressed from clotted blood that contains dissolved nutrients, antibodies, and hormones but not cells or clotting factors.

serum sickness A type of immune complex disease in which immune complexes enter circulation, are carried throughout the body, and are deposited in the blood vessels of the kidney, heart, skin, and joints. The condition may become chronic.

severe acute respiratory syndrome (SARS) A severe respiratory disease caused by infection with a newly described coronavirus.

severe combined immunodeficiencies A collection of syndromes occurring in newborns caused by a genetic defect that knocks out both B- and T-cell types of immunity. There are several versions of this disease, termed SCIDS for short.

sex pilus A conjugative pilus.

sexually transmitted disease (STD) Infections resulting from pathogens that enter the body via sexual intercourse or intimate, direct contact.

shiga toxin Heat-labile exotoxin released by some *Shigella* species and by *E. coli* O157:H7; responsible for worst symptoms of these infections.

shingles Lesions produced by reactivated human herpesvirus 3 (chickenpox) infection; also known as herpes zoster.

siderophores Low-molecular-weight molecules produced by many microorganisms that can bind iron very tightly.

sign Any abnormality uncovered upon physical diagnosis that indicates the presence of disease. A sign is an objective assessment of disease, as opposed to a symptom, which is the subjective assessment perceived by the patient.

silent mutation A mutation that, because of the degeneracy of the genetic code, results in a nucleotide change in both the DNA and mRNA but not the resultant amino acid and thus, not the protein.

simple stain Type of positive staining technique that uses a single dye to add color to cells so that they are easier to see. This technique tends to color all cells the same color.

slime layer A diffuse, unorganized layer of polysaccharides and/or proteins on the outside of some bacteria.

smooth endoplasmic reticulum (SER) A microscopic series of tunnels lacking ribosomes that functions in the nutrient processing function of a cell.

solute A substance that is uniformly dispersed in a dissolving medium or solvent.

solution A mixture of one or more substances (solutes) that cannot be separated by filtration or ordinary settling.

solvent A dissolving medium.

somatic (O or cell wall antigen) One of the three major antigens commonly used to differentiate gram-negative enteric bacteria.

source The person or item from which an infection is directly acquired. See ***reservoir.***

Southern blot A technique that separates fragments of DNA using electrophoresis and identifies them by hybridization.

species In the levels of classification, the most specific level of organization.

specificity In immunity, the concept that some parts of the immune system only react with antigens that originally activated them.

spheroplast A gram-negative cell whose peptidoglycan, when digested by lysozyme, remains intact but is osmotically vulnerable.

spike A receptor on the surface of certain enveloped viruses that facilitates specific attachment to the host cell.

spirillum A type of bacterial cell with a rigid spiral shape and external flagella.

spirochete A coiled, spiral-shaped bacterium that has endoflagella and flexes as it moves.

spontaneous generation Early belief that living things arose from vital forces present in nonliving, or decomposing, matter.

spontaneous mutation A mutation in DNA caused by random mistakes in replication and not known to be influenced by any mutagenic agent. These mutations give rise to an organism's natural, or background, rate of mutation.

sporadic Description of a disease that exhibits new cases at irregular intervals in unpredictable geographic locales.

sporangiospore A form of asexual spore in fungi; enclosed in a sac.

sporangium A fungal cell in which asexual spores are formed by multiple cell cleavage.

spore A differentiated, specialized cell form that can be used for dissemination, for survival in times of adverse conditions, and/or for reproduction. Spores are usually unicellular and may develop into gametes or vegetative organisms.

sporicide A chemical agent capable of destroying bacterial endospores.

sporozoite One of many minute elongated bodies generated by multiple division of the oocyst. It is the infectious form of the malarial parasite that is harbored in the salivary gland of the mosquito and inoculated into the victim during feeding.

sporulation The process of spore formation.

start codon The nucleotide triplet AUG that codes for the first amino acid in protein sequences.

starter culture The sizable inoculation of pure bacterial, mold, or yeast sample for bulk processing, as in the preparation of fermented foods, beverages, and pharmaceuticals.

stasis A state of rest or inactivity; applied to nongrowing microbial cultures. Also called microbistasis.

stationary growth phase Survival mode in which cells either stop growing or grow very slowly.

stem cells Pluripotent, undifferentiated cells.

sterile Completely free of all life forms, including spores and viruses.

sterilization Any process that completely removes or destroys all viable microorganisms, including viruses, from an object or habitat. Material so treated is sterile.

STORCH Acronym for common infections of the fetus and neonate. Storch stands for syphilis, toxoplasmosis, other diseases (hepatitis B, AIDS, and chlamydiosis), rubella, cytomegalovirus, and herpes simplex virus.

strain In microbiology, a set of descendants cloned from a common ancestor that retain the original characteristics. Any deviation from the original is a different strain.

streptolysin A hemolysin produced by streptococci.

strict or obligate anaerobe An organism that does not use oxygen gas in metabolism and cannot survive in oxygen's presence.

stroma The matrix of the chloroplast that is the site of the dark reactions.

structural gene A gene that codes for the amino acid sequence (peptide structure) of a protein.

subacute Indicates an intermediate status between acute and chronic disease.

subacute sclerosing panencephalitis (SSPE) A complication of measles infection in which progressive neurological degeneration of the cerebral cortex invariably leads to coma and death.

subcellular vaccine A vaccine preparation that contains specific antigens, such as the capsule or toxin from a pathogen, and not the whole microbe.

subclinical A period of inapparent manifestations that occurs before symptoms and signs of disease appear.

subculture To make a second-generation culture from a well-established colony of organisms.

subcutaneous The deepest level of the skin structure.

substrate The specific molecule upon which an enzyme acts.

subunit vaccine A vaccine preparation that contains only antigenic fragments such as surface receptors from the microbe. Usually in reference to virus vaccines.

sucrose One of the carbohydrates commonly referred to as sugars. Common table or cane sugar.

sulfonamide Antimicrobial drugs that interfere with the essential metabolic process of bacteria and some fungi.

superantigens Bacterial toxins that are potent stimuli for T cells and can be a factor in diseases such as toxic shock.

superficial mycosis A fungal infection located in hair, nails, and the epidermis of the skin.

superinfection An infection occurring during antimicrobial therapy that is caused by an overgrowth of drug-resistant microorganisms.

superoxide A toxic derivative of oxygen; (O_2^-).

surfactant A surface-active agent that forms a water-soluble interface. Examples: detergents, wetting agents, dispersing agents, and surface tension depressants.

sylvatic Denotes the natural presence of disease among wild animal populations. Examples: sylvatic (sylvan) plague, rabies.

symbiosis An intimate association between individuals from two species; used as a synonym for mutualism.

symptom The subjective evidence of infection and disease as perceived by the patient.

syncytium A multinucleated protoplasmic mass formed by consolidation of individual cells.

syndrome The collection of signs and symptoms that, taken together, paint a portrait of the disease.

synergism The coordinated or correlated action by two or more drugs or microbes that results in a heightened response or greater activity.

syngamy Conjugation of the gametes in fertilization.

synthesis (viral) The step in viral multiplication in which viral genetic material and proteins are made through replication and transcription/translation.

synthetic biology The use of known genes to produce new applications.

syntrophy The productive use of waste products from the metabolism of one organism by a second organism.

syphilis A sexually transmitted bacterial disease caused by the spirochete ***Treponema pallidum***.

systemic Occurring throughout the body; said of infections that invade many compartments and organs via the circulation.

T

T lymphocyte (T cell) A white blood cell that is processed in the thymus gland and is involved in cell-mediated immunity.

Taq polymerase DNA polymerase from the thermophilic bacterium ***Thermus aquaticus*** that enables high-temperature replication of DNA required for the polymerase chain reaction.

tartar See ***calculus.***

taxa Taxonomic categories.

taxonomy The formal system for organizing, classifying, and naming living things.

teichoic acid Anionic polymers containing glycerol that appear in the walls of gram-positive bacteria.

temperate phage A bacteriophage that enters into a less virulent state by becoming incorporated into the host genome as a prophage instead of in the vegetative or lytic form that eventually destroys the cell.

template The strand in a double-stranded DNA molecule that is used as a model to synthesize a complementary strand of DNA or RNA during replication or transcription.

Tenericutes Taxonomic category of bacteria that lack cell walls.

teratogenic Causing abnormal fetal development.

tertiary structure Protein structure that results from additional bonds forming between functional groups in a secondary structure, creating a three-dimensional mass.

tetanospasmin The neurotoxin of ***Clostridium tetani***, the agent of tetanus. Its chief action is directed upon the inhibitory synapses of the anterior horn motor neurons.

tetracyclines A group of broad-spectrum antibiotics with a complex 4-ring structure.

tetrads Groups of four.

theory A collection of statements, propositions, or concepts that explains or accounts for a natural event.

theory of evolution The evidence cited to explain how evolution occurs.

therapeutic index The ratio of the toxic dose to the effective therapeutic dose that is used to assess the safety and reliability of the drug.

thermal death point The lowest temperature that achieves sterilization in a given quantity of broth culture upon a 10-minute exposure. Examples: 55°C for *Escherichia coli,* 60°C for *Mycobacterium tuberculosis,* and 120°C for spores.

thermal death time The least time required to kill all cells of a culture at a specified temperature.

thermocline A temperature buffer zone in a large body of water that separates the warmer water (the epilimnion) from the colder water (the hypolimnion).

thermoduric Resistant to the harmful effects of high temperature.

thermophile A microorganism that thrives at a temperature of 50°C or higher.

thrush *Candida albicans* infection of the oral cavity.

thylakoid Vesicles of a chloroplast formed by elaborate folding of the inner membrane to form "discs." Solar energy trapped in the thylakoids is used in photosynthesis.

thymine (T) One of the nitrogen bases found in DNA but not in RNA. Thymine is in a pyrimidine form.

thymus Butterfly-shaped organ near the tip of the sternum that is the site of T-cell maturation.

tincture A medicinal substance dissolved in an alcoholic solvent.

tinea Ringworm; a fungal infection of the hair, skin, or nails.

tinea versicolor A condition of the skin appearing as mottled and discolored skin pigmentation as a result of infection by the yeast *Malassezia furfur.*

titer In immunochemistry, a measure of antibody level in a patient, determined by agglutination methods.

toll-like receptors (TLRs) A category of pattern recognition receptors that binds to pathogen-associated molecular patterns on microbes.

tonsils A ring of lymphoid tissue in the pharynx that acts as a repository for lymphocytes.

topoisomerases Enzymes that can add or remove DNA twists and thus regulate the degree of supercoiling.

toxemia Condition in which a toxin (microbial or otherwise) is spread throughout the bloodstream.

toxigenicity The tendency for a pathogen to produce toxins. It is an important factor in bacterial virulence.

toxin A specific chemical product of microbes, plants, and some animals that is poisonous to other organisms.

toxinosis Disease whose adverse effects are primarily due to the production and release of toxins.

toxoid A toxin that has been rendered nontoxic but is still capable of eliciting the formation of protective antitoxin antibodies; used in vaccines.

trace elements Micronutrients (zinc, nickel, and manganese) that occur in small amounts and are involved in enzyme function and maintenance of protein structure.

transamination The transfer of an amino group from an amino acid to a carbohydrate fragment.

transcript A newly transcribed RNA molecule.

transcription mRNA synthesis; the process by which a strand of RNA is produced against a DNA template.

transduction The transfer of genetic material from one bacterium to another by means of a bacteriophage vector.

transferrin A protein in the plasma fraction of blood that transports iron.

transfer RNA (tRNA) A transcript of DNA that specializes in converting RNA language into protein language.

transformation In microbial genetics, the transfer of genetic material contained in "naked" DNA fragments from a donor cell to a competent recipient cell.

transfusion Infusion of whole blood, red blood cells, or platelets directly into a patient's circulation.

translation Protein synthesis; the process of decoding the messenger RNA code into a polypeptide.

transposon A DNA segment with an insertion sequence at each end, enabling it to migrate to another plasmid, to the bacterial chromosome, or to a bacteriophage.

transport medium Microbiological medium that is used to transport specimens.

traveler's diarrhea A type of gastroenteritis typically caused by infection with enterotoxigenic strains of *E. coli* that are ingested through contaminated food and water.

trematode A category of helminth; also known as flatworm or fluke.

trichinosis Infection by the *Trichinella spiralis* parasite, usually caused by eating the meat of an infected animal. Early symptoms include fever, diarrhea, nausea, and abdominal pain that progress to intense muscle and joint pain and shortness of breath. In the final stages, heart and brain function are at risk, and death is possible.

trichomoniasis Sexually transmitted disease caused by infection by the trichomonads, a group of protozoa. Symptoms include urinary pain and frequency and foul-smelling vaginal discharge in females, or recurring urethritis, with a thin milky discharge, in males.

triglyceride A type of lipid composed of a glycerol molecule bound to three fatty acids.

triplet See *codon.*

trophozoite A vegetative protozoan (feeding form) as opposed to a resting (cyst) form.

true pathogen A microbe capable of causing infection and disease in healthy persons with normal immune defenses.

trypomastigote The infective morphological stage transmitted by the tsetse fly or the reduviid bug in African trypanosomiasis and Chagas disease.

tubercle In tuberculosis, the granulomatous well-defined lung lesion that can serve as a focus for latent infection.

tuberculin A glycerinated broth culture of *Mycobacterium tuberculosis* that is evaporated and filtered. Formerly used to treat tuberculosis, tuberculin is now used chiefly for diagnostic tests.

tuberculin reaction A diagnostic test in which PPD, or purified protein derivative (of *M. tuberculosis*), is injected superficially under the skin and the area of reaction measured; also called the Mantoux test.

tuberculoid leprosy A superficial form of leprosy characterized by asymmetrical, shallow skin lesions containing few bacterial cells.

tubulin Protein component of long filaments of protein arranged under the cell membrane of bacteria; contribute to cell shape and division.

turbid Cloudy appearance of nutrient solution in a test tube due to growth of microbe population.

tyndallization Fractional (discontinuous, intermittent) sterilization designed to destroy spores indirectly. A preparation is exposed to flowing steam for an hour, and then the mineral is allowed to incubate to permit spore germination. The resultant vegetative cells are destroyed by repeated steaming and incubation.

typhoid fever Form of salmonellosis. It is highly contagious. Primary symptoms include fever, diarrhea, and abdominal pain. Typhoid fever can be fatal if untreated.

U

ubiquitous Present everywhere at the same time.

ultraviolet (UV) radiation Radiation with an effective wavelength from 240 nm to 260 nm. UV radiation induces mutations readily but has very poor penetrating power.

uncoating The process of removal of the viral coat and release of the viral genome by its newly invaded host cell.

undulant fever See *brucellosis.*

universal donor In blood grouping and transfusion, a group O individual whose erythrocytes bear neither agglutinogen A nor B.

universal precautions (UPs) Centers for Disease Control and Prevention guidelines for health care workers regarding the prevention of disease transmission when handling patients and body substances.

uracil (U) One of the nitrogen bases in RNA but not in DNA. Uracil is in a pyrimidine form.

urinary tract infection (UTI) Invasion and infection of the urethra and bladder by bacterial residents, most often *E. coli.*

V

vaccination Exposing a person to the antigenic components of a microbe without its pathogenic effects for the purpose of inducing a future protective response.

vaccine Originally used in reference to inoculation with the cowpox or vaccinia virus to protect against smallpox. In general, the term now pertains to injection of whole microbes (killed or attenuated), toxoids, or parts of microbes as a prevention or cure for disease.

vacuoles In the cell, membrane-bounded sacs containing fluids or solid particles to be digested, excreted, or stored.

valence The combining power of an atom based upon the number of electrons it can either take on or give up.

van der Waals forces Weak attractive interactions between molecules of low polarity.

vancomycin Antibiotic that targets the bacterial cell wall; used often in antibiotic-resistant infections.

variable region The antigen binding fragment of an immunoglobulin molecule, consisting of a combination of heavy and light chains whose molecular conformation is specific for the antigen.

varicella Informal name for virus responsible for chickenpox as well as shingles; also known as human herpesvirus 3 (HHV-3).

variolation A hazardous, outmoded process of deliberately introducing smallpox material scraped from a victim into the nonimmune subject in the hope of inducing resistance.

vector An animal that transmits infectious agents from one host to another, usually a biting or piercing arthropod like the tick, mosquito, or fly. Infectious agents can be conveyed mechanically by simple contact or biologically whereby the parasite develops in the vector. A genetic element such as a plasmid or a bacteriophage used to introduce genetic material into a cloning host during recombinant DNA experiments.

vegetative In describing microbial developmental stages, a metabolically active feeding and dividing form, as opposed to a dormant, seemingly inert, nondividing form. Examples: a bacterial cell versus its spore; a protozoan trophozoite versus its cyst.

vehicle An inanimate material (solid object, liquid, or air) that serves as a transmission agent for pathogens.

vesicle A blister characterized by a thin-skinned, elevated, superficial pocket filled with serum.

viable nonculturable (VNC) A description of a state in which bacteria are alive but are not metabolizing at an appreciable rate and will not grow when inoculated onto laboratory medium.

vibrio A curved, rod-shaped bacterial cell.

viremia The presence of viruses in the bloodstream.

virion An elementary virus particle in its complete morphological and thus infectious form. A virion consists of the nucleic acid core surrounded by a capsid, which can be enclosed in an envelope.

viroid An infectious agent that, unlike a virion, lacks a capsid and consists of a closed circular RNA molecule. Although known viroids are all plant pathogens, it is conceivable that animal versions exist.

virtual image In optics, an image formed by diverging light rays; in the compound light microscope, the second, magnified visual impression formed by the ocular from the real image formed by the objective.

virucide A chemical agent that inactivates viruses, especially on living tissue.

virulence In infection, the relative capacity of a pathogen to invade and harm host cells.

virulence factors A microbe's structures or capabilities that allow it to establish itself in a host and cause damage.

virus Microscopic, acellular agent composed of nucleic acid surrounded by a protein coat.

virus particle A more specific name for a virus when it is outside of its host cells.

vitamins A component of coenzymes critical to nutrition and the metabolic function of coenzyme complexes.

W

wart An epidermal tumor caused by papillomaviruses. Also called a verruca.

Western blot test A procedure for separating and identifying antigen or antibody mixtures by two-dimensional electrophoresis in polyacrylamide gel, followed by immune labeling.

wheal A welt; a marked, slightly red, usually itchy area of the skin that changes in size and shape as it extends to adjacent area. The reaction is triggered by cutaneous contact or intradermal injection of allergens in sensitive individuals.

whey The residual fluid from milk coagulation that separates from the solidified curd.

whitlow A deep inflammation of the finger or toe, especially near the tip or around the nail. Whitlow is a painful herpes simplex virus infection that can last several weeks and is most common among health care personnel who come in contact with the virus in patients.

whole blood A liquid connective tissue consisting of blood cells suspended in plasma.

Widal test An agglutination test for diagnosing typhoid.

wild type The natural, nonmutated form of a genetic trait.

wort The clear fluid derived from soaked mash that is fermented for beer.

X

XDRTB Extensively drug-resistant tuberculosis (worse than multidrug-resistant tuberculosis).

xenograft The transfer of a tissue or an organ from an animal of one species to a recipient of another species.

Z

zoonosis An infectious disease indigenous to animals that humans can acquire through direct or indirect contact with infected animals.

zooplankton The collection of nonphotosynthetic microorganisms (protozoa, tiny animals) that float in the upper regions of aquatic habitat and together with phytoplankton comprise the plankton.

zygospore A thick-walled sexual spore produced by the zygomycete fungi. It develops from the union of two hyphae, each bearing nuclei of opposite mating types.

Credits

Line Art

Chapter 1

Table 1.1: Data from latest "World Health Report"

Chapter 11

Table 9.5: From Perkins, *Principles and Methods of Sterilization in Health Science*, 2nd ed. Courtesy of Charles C. Thomas Publisher, Ltd., Springfield, Illinois

Chapter 20

Figure 20.4: From *American Scientist*, 95:6, 2007; "Safer Salads" by Fonseca and Ravishankar. Reprinted by permission.

Photo

Chapter 1

Opener (clockwise top left - first, second): CDC/Janice Haney Carr; (third): CDC/Dr. Erskine Palmer & Byron Skinner; (fourth): CDC/Dr. Stan Erlandsen; (fifth, sixth): © Science Photo Library RF/Getty Images; (seventh): NIAID, NIH/ Rocky Mountain Laboratories; (author): Courtesy of Kelly Cowan; p. 3 (cells): © T. J. Beveridge/Biological Photo Service; p. 3 (pond): © Ian Murray/Loop Images/Corbis; p. 4 (top): © MedicalRF.com/Getty Images; p. 4 (bottom): NASA; 1.1: NASA GSFC image by Robert Simmon and Reto Stöckli; 1.2: © Ian Murray/Loop Images/Corbis; p. 6: © The McGraw-Hill Companies, Inc./Don Rubbelke, photographer; 1.3: U.S. Coast Guard photo by Chief Petty Officer John Kepsimelis, Atlantic Strike Team; p. 8: © PhotoLink/Getty Images (RF); 1.5 (both): © Kathy Park Talaro/Visuals Unlimited; Table 1.2: © Steve Gschmeissner/SPL/Getty Images (RF); p. 11: © Corbis (RF); 1.6: © Bettmann/Corbis; 1.7 (taenia, herpes): Centers for Disease Control; 1.7 (vorticella): © Carolina Biological Supply/Phototake; 1.7 (e. coli): CDC/Janice Haney Carr; 1.7 (syncephalastrum): © Dr. Arthur Siegelman/Visuals Unlimited; p. 14: © Stephen Durr (RF); 1.8: © H Lansdown/Alamy (RF); 1.9: © Stockbyte/PunchStock (RF); p. 18: © Guy Crittenden/ Getty Images (RF); p. 20: © Comstock/JupiterImages (RF); p. 21, 24: © Ingram Publishing (RF); p. 25: CDC/Janice Haney Carr; p. 26: © Stephen Durr (RF); p. 28 (web): © Tony Sweet/ Digital Vision/Getty Images (RF); p. 28 (soil): © Pixtal/AGE Fotostock (RF); p. 30 (author): Courtesy of Kelly Cowan; p. 30 (cell): © Science Photo Library RF/Getty Images; p. 30 (background): © Stephen Durr (RF); p. 31: © Roll Call/Getty Images

Chapter 2

Opener: © Dr. Edward Chan/Visuals Unlimited; p. 34 (doctor): © Blend Images/Getty Images (RF); p. 35: © Peter Skinner/ Photo Researchers; 2.2a–c: © Kathy Park Talaro; p. 37: Centers for Disease Control; p. 38: © Dan Ippolito (RF); 2.3a–c: © Kathy Park Talaro; p. 40: © Image Source/Corbis (RF); p. 40–41: Centers for Disease Control; 2.4a,b, 2.5: © Kathy Park Talaro; 2.7: © Harold J. Benson; p. 44–45: © Ryan McVay/Getty Images (RF); 2.9a–c: © Kathy Park Talaro and Harold Benson; 2.11: © Peter Skinner/Photo Researchers; p. 48–49: Centers for Disease Control; 2.13a,b: Coutesy of Nikon Instruments Inc.; Table 2.6 (first): © Carolina Biological Supply, Co/Visuals Unlimited; Table 2.6 (second–fourth): © Michael Abbey/ Visuals Unlimited; Table 2.6 (fifth): © 2011 Life Technologies Corporation. Used under permission. www.lifetechnologies .com; Table 2.6 (sixth): Courtesy of Dr. Jeremy Allen/University of Salford, Biosciences Research Institute; Table 2.6: © CDC/ Dr. Erskine Palmer; Table 2.6 (eighth): © Science Photo Library RF/Getty Images; p. 52: © Digital Vision/Getty Images (RF); p. 53: CDC/DPDx - Melanie Moser; 2.17a: © Kathy Park Talaro; 2.17b: © Harold J. Benson; 2.18a,b: © Jack Bostrack/Visuals Unlimited; 2.18c: © Manfred Kage/Peter Arnold/Photolibrary; 2.19a: © A.M. Siegelman/Visuals Unlimited; 2.19b: © David Frankhauser; p. 55 (dish): © Flying Colours Ltd/Getty Images (RF); p. 56 (dish): © Dr. Edward Chan/Visuals Unlimited; p. 56 (doctor): © Blend Images/Getty Images (RF); p. 56 (bread): © imagebroker/Alamy (RF); p. 56 (tomato): © Emily Keegin/ fStop/Getty Images (RF); p. 57 (bacteria): © Kathy Park Talaro and Harold Benson; p. 57 (nurse): © Science Photo Library RF/ Getty Images; p. 59: © Kathy Park Talaro and Harold Benson

Chapter 3

Opener: © Eye of Science/Photo Researchers; p. 60 (doctor): © Purestock/Getty Images (RF); p. 61 (second): Fig 1A from S. Knutton, D.R. Lloyd, A. McNeish, "Identification of a New Fimbrial Structure in Enterotoxigenic Escherichia coli (ETEC) Serotype 0148 H28 Which Adheres to Human Intestinal Mucosa: a Potentially New Human ETEC Colonization Factor," Infection and Immunity, January 1987, Vol 55, No 1., p. 86–92. Reproduced with permission from American Society for Microbiology.; p. 61 (third): © T. J. Beveridge/ Biological Photo Service; p. 61 (fifth): © Corbis (RF); p. 61 (sixth): Courtesy of Bergey's Manual Trust; p. 62–63: © Science Photo Library RF/Getty Images; 3.2: © Max Planck Institute for Marine Microbiology, Germany; 3.3: © David M. Phillips/ Visuals Unlimited; Table 3.1a,b: CDC/Janice Haney Carr; Table 3.1c: Fig 2b from Jacob S. Teppema, "In Vivo Adherence and Colonization of Vibro Cholerae Strains that differ in Hemagglutinating Activity and Motility" Journal of Infection and Immunity, 55(9): 2093–2102, Sept. 1987. Reprinted by permission of American Society for Microbiology.; Table 3.1d: USDA/Photo by De Wood. Digital colorization by Chris Pooley; Table 3.1e: © VEM/Photo Researchers; Table 3.1f: © Science VU/Frederick Mertz/Visuals Unlimited; 3.5: © Dr. Elmer Koneman/Visuals Unlimited; 3.6b: Noreen R. Francis, Gina E. Sosinsky, Dennis Thomas and David J. DeRosier, "Isolation, Characterization and Structure of Bacterial Flagellar Motors Containing the Switch Complex," Journal of Molecular Biology, Vol 235, Issue 4, 27 January 1994, Pages 1261–1270.; 3.7a: © Science VU/Visuals Unlimited; 3.7b: © Dennis Kunkel Microscopy, Inc./Visuals Unlimited; 3.7c: © Dr. Edward Chan/Visuals Unlimited; 3.7d: © Dr. Fred Hossler/Visuals Unlimited; 3.9a: © Eye of Science/Photo Researchers; 3.9b: Fig 1A from S. Knutton, D.R. Lloyd, A. McNeish, "Identification of a New Fimbrial Structure in Enterotoxigenic Escherichia coli (ETEC) Serotype 0148 H28 Which Adheres to Human Intestinal Mucosa: a Potentially New Human ETEC Colonization Factor," Infection and Immunity, January 1987, Vol 55, No 1., p. 86–92. Reproduced with permission from American Society for Microbiology.; 3.10: © L. Caro/SPL/Photo Researchers; 3.11a: © John D. Cunningham/Visuals Unlimited; 3.11b: Fig 1 from Brett J. Pellock, Max Teplitski, Ryan P. Boinay, W. Dietz Bauer, and Graham C. Walker, "A LuxR Homolog Controls Production of Symbiotically Active Extracellular Polysaccharide II by Sinorhizobium meliloti." Journal of Bacteriology, September 15, 2002, Vol. 184, No. 18, p. 5067–5076. Reproduced with permission from American Society for Microbiology.; 3.12b: © Science VU–Charles W. Stratton/Visuals Unlimited; 3.14 (left): © S.C Holt/Biological Photo Service; 3.14 (right): © T. J. Beveridge/Biological Photo Service; 3.15: © McGraw-Hill Companies, Inc.; p. 73: © Steven P. Lynch (RF); p. 76: © Digital Vision/Getty Images (RF); 3.18: © Paul W. Johnson/ Biological Photo Service; 3.19, 3.20: © George Chapman/ Visuals Unlimited; p. 78–79: CDC/Laura Rose & Janice Haney Carr; p. 80: © Corbis (RF); p. 81 (top): Courtesy of Bergey's Manual Trust; p. 81 (bottom): © Purestock/Getty Images (RF); p. 82 (background): CDC/Janice Haney Carr; p. 82 (doctor): © Purestock/Getty Images (RF); p. 82 (bacteria): © Eye of Science/Photo Researchers; p. 83 (shot): © Blend Images/JupiterImages (RF); p. 83 (infant): Centers for Disease Control; p. 84: © T. J. Beveridge/Biological Photo Service; p. 85: © Eye of Science/Photo Researchers

Chapter 4

Opener: © Dr. Tony Brain/Photo Researchers, Inc.; p. 86 (doctor): © Image Source/Veer (RF); p. 87 (third): © Dennis Kunkel Microscopy, Inc./Visuals Unlimited; p. 87 (fourth): © David M. Phillips/Visuals Unlimited; p. 87 (fifth): © Arthur Siegelman/Visuals Unlimited; 4.1 (frog): © Adam Jones/ Getty Images (RF); 4.1 (protozoa): © Melba Photo Agency/ PunchStock (RF); 4.1 (mushroom): © Tinke Hamming/ Ingram Publishing (RF); 4.1 (algae): © Stephen Durr (RF); 4.1 (sprout): © Digital Vision (RF); p. 89: © EM Research Services, Newcastle University (RF); 4.3: © RMF/FDF/Visuals Unlimited; 4.4a: © John J. Cardamone, Jr./Biological Photo Service; 4.5: © Donald Fawcett/Visuals Unlimited; 4.6: © Don W. Fawcett/Photo Researchers; 4.7: © EM Research Services, Newcastle University (RF); p. 94–95: © Science Photo Library RF/Getty Images; 4.10: © Donald Fawcett/Visuals Unlimited; p. 96: © EM Research Services, Newcastle University (RF); 4.11, p. 97: © Albert Tousson/PhotoTake; p. 98: © Science Photo Library RF/Getty Images; p. 99: © Dennis Kunkel Microscopy, Inc./Visuals Unlimited; 4.12a,b: Courtesy of Dr. Judy A. Murphy, Murphy Consuitancy Microscopy & Digital Imaging, Stockton, CA; 4.13b: © David M. Phillips/Visuals Unlimited; p. 102 (top): © Kathy Park Talaro; p. 102–103: © William Marin, Jr./The Image Works; p. 104,105: © Stephen Durr (RF); 4.15: CDC/Dr. Stan Erlandsen; Table 4.4 (amoeboid): © Stephen Durr (RF); Table 4.4 (ciliated): © J. R. Factor/Photo Researchers; Table 4.4 (apicomplexan): © Dennis Kunkel Microscopy, Inc./Visuals Unlimited; Table 4.4 (flagelated): © David M. Phillips/Visuals Unlimited; p. 106: M W Riggs, V A Cama, H L Leary, Jr, and C R Sterling,"Bovine antibody against Cryptosporidium parvum elicits a circumsporozoite precipitate-like reaction and has immunotherapeutic effect against persistent cryptosporidiosis in SCID mice." Infection and Immunity, May 1994, p. 1927–1939, Vol. 62, No. 5. Reproduced with permission from American Society for Microbiology; 4.16 (liver fluke): © Arthur Siegelman/Visuals Unlimited; 4.16 (tape worm): © Carol Geake/Animals Animals; p. 108 (flatworm): © NHPA/M. I. Walker (RF); 4.17b: Centers for Disease Control; p. 110 (doctor): © Image Source/Veer (RF); p. 110 (giardia): © Dr. Tony Brain/Photo Researchers, Inc.; p. 110 (bottom): CDC/Dr. Stan Erlandsen; p. 111: CDC/James Gathany

Chapter 5

Opener: © L. Bassett/Visuals Unlimited; p. 114 (doctors): © Masterfile (RF); p. 115 (first): © Eye of Science/Photo Researchers; p. 115 (fourth): Centers for Disease Control; p. 115 (fifth): © Pr. J.J. Hauw/ISM/Phototake; p. 115 (sixth): CDC/Cynthia Goldsmith; p. 116: © Science VU/Wayside/Visuals Unlimited; p. 117: CDC/Cynthia Goldsmith; 5.2a: © K.G. Murti/Visuals Unlimited; 5.2b: © Phototake; 5.2c: © A.B. Dowsette/SPL/Photo Researchers; p. 119: CDC/Dr. Fred Murphy; Table 5.2 (mosaic): © Dennis Kunkel/CNRI/Phototake; Table 5.2 (flu): © K.G. Murti/Visuals Unlimited; Table 5.2 (adeno, hep B): © Dr. Linda M. Stannard, University of Cape Town/Photo Researchers; Table 5.2 (herpes): © Eye of Science/Photo Researchers; Table 5.2 (capsid): © Harold Fisher/Visuals Unlimited; p. 122: © Science Photo Library RF/Getty Images; p. 123: CDC/Dr. Fred Murphy; p. 124: CDC/Cynthia Goldsmith; p. 127: CDC/James Gathany; 5.6b: © Chris Bjornberg/Photo Researchers; 5.7a: © Patricia Barber/Custom Medical Stock; 5.7b: Courtesy of Massimo Battaglia, INeMM CNR, Rome Italy; 5.11: © Lee D. Simon/Photo Researchers; p. 132: © Corbis (RF); 5.12a,b: Centers for Disease Control; 5.12c: © Jack Bostrack/Visuals Unlimited; p. 134 (left): © M. Abbey/Photo Researchers; p. 134 (right): © Pr. J.J. Hauw/ISM/Phototake; p. 135: CDC/C. S. Goldsmith and A. Balish; p. 136: CDC/Cynthia Goldsmith; p. 136 (doctors): © Masterfile (RF); p. 136 (x-ray): © L. Bassett/Visuals Unlimited; p. 137 (top): © Logical Images, Inc. All rights reserved; p. 137 (child): © Brand X Pictures/PunchStock (RF); p. 137 (virus): © Science Photo Library RF/Getty Images

Chapter 6

Opener: © Dr. Gary Gaugler/Photo Researchers; p. 140 (doctor): © Jon Feingersh Photography/Getty Images (RF); p. 141: © Terese M. Barta, Ph.D.; p. 142: © The McGraw-Hill Companies, Inc./Barry Barker, photographer; p. 142 (inset): © Michael Aw/Photodisc/Getty Images (RF); p. 143: CDC/Peggy S. Hayes & Elizabeth H. White, M.S.; 6.1a: © Dennis Kunkel Microscopy, Inc./Visuals Unlimited; 6.1b: © Martin Oeggerli/Photo Researchers; 6.6a: © Francois Gohier/Photo Researchers; 6.6b: Courtesy of Nozomu Takeuchi; p. 151: courtesy of Submarine Ring of Fire 2004 Exploration, NOAA Vents Program; 6.7: © Terese M. Barta, Ph.D.; p. 152 (pickles): © Photodisc/Alamy (RF); Table 6.5 (first): CDC/Laura Rose & Janice Haney Carr; Table 6.5 (second): © Science Photo Library RF/Getty Images; Table 6.5 (third–fifth): CDC/Janice Haney Carr; p. 154: © Getty Images (RF); 6.8b: Courtesy of Ellen Swogger and Garth James, Center for Biofilm Engineering, Montana State University; p. 156–158 (all): CDC/Janice Haney Carr; p. 159: © Getty Images/Jonelle Weaver (RF); p. 160: © Corbis (RF); 6.13: © Kathy Park Talaro/Visuals Unlimited; p. 161: Centers for Disease Control; p. 162 (doctor): © Jon Feingersh Photography/Getty Images (RF); p. 162 (inset): © Dr. Gary Gaugler/Photo Researchers; p. 162 (e. coli): © Science Photo Library RF/Getty Images; p. 163: © Ingram Publishing (RF)

Chapter 7

Opener: © Getty Images/Brand X (RF); p. 166 (doctor): © Jose Luis Pelaez Inc/Blend Images (RF); p. 170: © Ingram Publishing (RF); p. 172: © The McGraw-Hill Companies, Inc./Jill Braaten, photographer; p. 173: © Frederick Bass/Getty Images (RF); p. 175: © Digital Vision/PunchStock (RF); p. 177: © Lars A. Niki (RF); p. 179: © imageshop - zefa visual media uk ltd/Alamy (RF); p. 183 (grapes): © Imagestate Media (John Foxx)/Imagestate (RF); p. 183 (barrels): © Ingram Publishing/SuperStock (RF); p. 184: © Ingram Publishing (RF); p. 185: © Joseph Sohm/Visions of America/Corbis (RF); p. 188 (doctor): © Jose Luis Pelaez Inc/Blend Images (RF); p. 188 (EKG): © Getty Images/Brand X (RF); p. 188 (girl): © Ingram Publishing (RF); Table 7.17: National Institute of Health/National Institute of General Medical Sciences

Chapter 8

Opener: © Don Farrall/Getty Images (RF); p. 192 (doctors): © Image Source/Getty Images (RF); p. 193: © Kathy Park Talaro; p. 194: © Adrian Neal/Getty Images (RF); 8.2: © K.G. Murti/Visuals Unlimited; p. 197: © Blend Images/Getty Images (RF); p. 202 (background): © EM Research Services, Newcastle University (RF); Table 8.4: © Center for Molecular Biology of RNA, UC–Santa Cruz; 8.9: Courtesy of Steven McKnight, PhD; p. 209: © Ingram Publishing (RF); p. 211 (cow): © Imagestate Media (John Foxx)/Imagestate (RF); p. 211 (snake): © Ingram Publishing/Fotosearch (RF); p. 212, 213: CDC/Janice Haney Carr; p. 217: CDC/James Gathany; p. 218: © The McGraw-Hill Companies, Inc./Barry Barker, photographer; p. 220: © ERproductions Ltd/Blend Images (RF); p. 222: © Chad Baker/Getty Images (RF); 8.17b: © Kathy Park Talaro; p. 223: © Rob Melnychuk/Getty Images (RF); p. 225: © Science Photo Library RF/Getty Images; p. 226: CDC/Hsi Liu, Ph.D., MBA, James Gathany; p. 228 (doctors): © Image Source/Getty Images (RF); p. 228 (EKG): © Don Farrall/Getty Images (RF); p. 228 (bottle): © Jon Feingersh Photography/Getty Images (RF); p. 229: © Ingram Publishing (RF); p. 231: © Eye of Science/Photo Researchers

Chapter 9

Opener: © Ingram Publishing (RF); p. 232 (doctor): © Purestock/Getty Images (RF); p. 233 (second): © The McGraw-Hill companies, Inc./Charles D. Winters, photographer; p. 233 (third): © Kathy Park Talaro/Visuals Unlimited; p. 234: © Corbis (RF); p. 236: © Doug Sherman/Geofile (RF); p. 237: USDA/Ken Hammond; p. 240: © Bruce Chambers, The Orange County Register/Newscom; p. 241 (man): © Fuse/Getty Images (RF); p. 241 (sardines): © Burke/Triolo Productions/Getty Images (RF); Table 9.5 (pot): © The McGraw-Hill companies, Inc./Charles D. Winters, photographer; Table 9.5 (pasteurization): © James King-Holmes/Photo Researchers; Table 9.5 (beer): © John A. Rizzo/Getty Images (RF); Table 9.5 (autoclave): © Science VU/Visuals Unlimited; p. 242–243 (background): © Corbis (RF); Table 9.6 (top): © Raymond B. Otero/Visuals Unlimited; Table 9.6 (bottom): © Steve Allen/Brand X Pictures (RF); p. 244 (background): © PhotoAlto/PunchStock (RF); p. 245: USDA/Courtesy of Dr. Brendan A. Niemira; Table 9.7 (top): © Adam Hart-Davis/Photo Researchers; Table 9.7 (bottom): © Tom Pantages; 9.6: © Fred Hossler/Visuals Unlimited; p. 248: © Ingram Publishing (RF); p. 249: © Stockbyte/PunchStock (RF); Table 9.9 (bleach): © Richard Hutchings (RF); Table 9.9 (peroxide): © The McGraw-Hill Companies, Inc./Jill Braaten, photographer; Table 9.9 (alcohol): © Richard Hutchings (RF); Table 9.9 (heavy metal): © The McGraw-Hill Companies, Inc./Stephen Frisch, photographer; p. 254 (doctor): © Purestock/Getty Images (RF); p. 254 (needles): © Ingram Publishing (RF); p. 254 (alcohol): © Richard Hutchings (RF); p. 255: © Keith Brofsky/Getty Images RF

Chapter 10

Opener: © Dr. David Phillips/Visuals Unlimited; p. 258 (doctor): © Sheer Photo, Inc/Getty Images (RF); p. 259 (top): Etest® is a registered trademark belonging to AB BIODISK, Sweden, and the product and underlying technologies are patented by AB BIODISK in all major markets; p. 260 (top): Armed Forces Institute of Pathology; Table 10.1: CDC/Janice Haney Carr; p. 261: Library of Congress; p. 262–263: CDC/Janice Carr; 10.1b: © Kathy Park Talaro; 10.2: Etest® is a registered trademark belonging to AB BIODISK, Sweden, and the product and underlying technologies are patented by AB BIODISK in all major markets; 10.3b: Courtesy of David Ellis; p. 264: © Creatas/PunchStock (RF); p. 265 (test): Courtesy of David Ellis; p. 265 (pills): © Thinkstock/JupiterImages (RF); p. 266: © MedicalRF.com/Getty Images; Table 10.4: © Jon Feingersh Photography/Getty Images (RF); p. 268–269 (bottom): © Peter Dazeley/Photographer's Choice/Getty Images (RF); p. 270: © Image Source/JupiterImages (RF); p. 272: © Forest & Kim Starr (RF); p. 274: © NHPA/M. I. Walker (RF); p. 276: © L. Caro/SPL/Photo Researchers; p. 279 (virus): CDC/Frederick Murphy; 10.6: © Kathy Park Talaro; p. 280, 283: Centers for Disease Control; p. 284 (doctor): © Sheer Photo, Inc/Getty Images (RF); p. 284 (bacteria): © Dr. David Phillips/Visuals Unlimited; p. 284 (pill): © Jon Feingersh Photography/Getty Images (RF); p. 285 (top): © JGI/Blend Images (RF); p. 285 (bottom): © Jon Feingersh Photography/Getty Images (RF); p. 286: CDC/Janice Haney Carr; p. 287: © Stockbyte/Getty Images (RF)

Chapter 11

Opener: © James Cavallini/Photo Researcher; p. 288 (doctor): © Seth Joel/Getty Images (RF); p. 289 (first), 290: NIH Roadmap for Medical Research website—*Source:* http://nihroadmap.nih.gov/; p. 289 (second): © The McGraw-Hill Companies, Inc./Christopher Kerrigan, photographer; p. 291: © Brand X Pictures/JupiterImages (RF); p. 294 (nose): © Ingram Publishing (RF); p. 294–295: NIAID, NIH/Rocky Mountain Laboratories; p. 296: © Brand X Pictures (RF); 11.4a: © Dr. Gladden Willis/Visuals Unlimited; 11.4b: © L.M. Pope and D.R. Grote/Biological Photo Service; p. 300: © Rubberball/Getty Images (RF); p. 302: © Getty Images/Photodisc (RF); Table 11.6 (writing): © Thinkstock/Getty Images (RF); Table 11.6 (top man): © Brand X Pictures/PunchStock (RF); Table 11.6 (mosquito): Centers for Disease Control; Table 11.6 (coughing): © The McGraw-Hill Companies, Inc./Christopher Kerrigan, photographer; Table 11.8 (raccoon): © imagebroker/Alamy (RF); Table 11.8 (pig): © Creatas/PunchStock (RF); Table 11.8 (cat): © Ingram Publishing/SuperStock (RF); p. 305 (mouse): © Punchstock/BananaStock (RF); p. 306 (plane): © Tony Cordoza/Alamy (RF); p. 306 (passengers): © ColorBlind Images/Getty Images (RF); p. 308: © Dynamic Graphics/JupiterImages (RF); p. 312: © Donald Nausbaum/Getty Images (RF); Table 11.11: NIAID, NIH/photo by Arthur Friedlander; p. 316 (doctor): © Seth Joel/Getty Images (RF); p. 316 (inset): © James Cavallini/Photo Researcher; p. 316 (background): CDC/Fred Murphy and Sylvia Whitfield; p. 317: © Plush Studios/Blend Images/Corbis (RF); Table 11.27: © Kathy Park Talaro

Chapter 12

Opener: © Ted Kinsman/Photo Researchers; p. 320 (doctor): © Image Source/Getty Images (RF); p. 321 (top): © Ellen R. Dirksen/Visuals Unlimited; p. 321–322: © Science Photo Library RF/Getty Images; p. 322: © Ingram Publishing (RF); p. 323: © Andersen Ross/Blend Images (RF); 12.3: © Ellen R. Dirksen/Visuals Unlimited; p. 327: © MedicalRF.com/Getty Images; p. 328: © Graham Bell/Corbis (RF); p. 329: © fStop/PunchStock (RF); 12.8a: © David M. Phillips/Visuals Unlimited; 12.9: © Dennis Kunkel/Phototake; p. 334: © Brand X Pictures/PunchStock (RF); 12.10b: Courtesy of Steve Kunkel; p. 336: © Brand X Pictures/Punchstock (RF); p. 337: © Science Photo Library RF/Getty Images; 12.12: © 1966 Rockefeller University Press. The Journal of Experimental Medicine, June 1966, Vol 123, p. 969–984.; p. 342 (doctor): © Image Source/Getty Images (RF); p. 342 (inset): © Ted Kinsman/Photo Researchers; p. 342 (child): © S. Olsson/PhotoAlto (RF); p. 343: © Comstock Images/PictureQuest (RF)

Chapter 13

Opener: CDC/Janice Haney Carr; p. 346 (doctor): © Keith Brofsky/Getty Images (RF); p. 347: © Steve Gschmeissner/Photo Researchers; p. 348: © MedicalRF.com/Getty Images; p. 350: © Comstock Images/PictureQuest (RF); p. 351: © MedicalRF.com/Getty Images; p. 358–359: © Photographer's Choice/Getty Images (RF); 13.7: © Steve Gschmeissner/Photo Researchers; 13.8b: U.S. National Library of Medicine; p. 365: © Blend Images/Getty Images (RF); p. 366: © Image Source/Getty Images (RF); Table 13.10 (girl): © Floresco Productions/Corbis RF; Table 13.10 (mother): © Ingram Publishing/Superstock (RF); Table 13.10 (boy): © The McGraw-Hill companies, Inc./Jill Braaten, photographer; Table 13.10 (patient): © Brooke Fasani Auchincloss/Corbis (RF); 13.9: James Gillray (English, 1757–1815), The Cow-Pock. Library of Congress Prints and Photographs Division Washington, D.C.;

p. 370: © Ingram Publishing/SuperStock (RF); p. 371: CDC/James Gathany; p. 372 (top): © Blend Images/JupiterImages (RF); p. 372 (doctor): © Keith Brofsky/Getty Images (RF); p. 372 (bacteria): CDC/Janice Haney Carr; p. 373: © AP Photo/Elise Amendola

Chapter 14

Opener: CDC/Dr. Paul M. Feorino; p. 376 (doctors): © Getty Images/OJO Images (RF); p. 377 (first): © Pixtal/age fotostock (RF); p. 377 (second): © STU/Custom Medical Stock; p. 377 (fourth): © Phototake; p. 377 (sixth): © SIU/Visuals Unlimited; p. 377 (seventh), 14.1 (top left): Courtesy of Baylor College of Medicine, Public Affairs; 14.1 (top right): © The McGraw-Hill Companies, Inc./Christopher Kerrigan, photographer; 14.1 (sneeze): © Pixtal/age fotostock (RF); 14.1 (tranfusion): © Roc Canals Photography/Getty Images; 14.1 (arthritis): © Dynamic Graphics/JupiterImages (RF); 14.1: © Kenneth E. Greer/Visuals Unlimited; p. 379: © Pixtal/age fotostock (RF); p. 380: © Ivan Hunter/Getty Images (RF); p. 381: © JupiterImages/Photos.com/Alamy (RF); 14.3c (headache): © Ingram Publishing (RF); 14.3c (skin): © STU/Custom Medical Stock; 14.3c (stomache ache): © Brand X Pictures (RF); 14.3c (blowing nose): © Ingram Publishing (RF); 14.3c (inhaler): © Science Photo Library (RF); 14.4 (infant): © Dr. P. Marazzi/Photo Researchers; 14.4 (arm): © Biophoto Associates/Photo Researchers; 14.5: © Dr. P. Marazzi/Photo Researchers; 14.6a: © STU/Custom Medical Stock; p. 387: © Flying Colours Ltd/Getty Images (RF); p. 389: © Image Source/Getty Images (RF); 14.9a: © Phototake; 14.9b: Courtesy of Gary P. Wiliams, M.D.; 14.10a: © Kathy Park Talaro; 14.10b: © Kenneth E. Greer/Visuals Unlimited; p. 392: © Rubberball/Getty Images (RF); p. 393: © Getty Images/OJO Images (RF); 14.13a: © ISM/Phototake; 14.13b: © SIU/Visuals Unlimited; p. 396: © Realistic Reflections/Getty Images (RF); p. 397 (top): Curtis J. Donskey, M.D., and Brittany C. Eckstein, B.S., "The Hands Give It Away." New England Journal of Medicine 2009; 360:e3. January 15, 2009. Courtesy of Curtis J. Donskey; p. 397 (bottom): Curtis J. Donskey, M.D., and Brittany C. Eckstein, B.S., "The Hands Give It Away." New England Journal of Medicine 2009; 360:e3. January 15, 2009. Courtesy of Curtis J. Donskey; 14.16a: Courtesy of Baylor College of Medicine, Public Affairs; 14.16b, p. 398: © The McGraw-Hill Companies, Inc./Christopher Kerrigan, photographer; p. 400 (background): © ERproductions Ltd/Blend Images (RF); p. 400 (doctors): © Keith Brofsky/Getty Images (RF); p. 400 (antibodies): CDC/Dr. Paul M. Feorino; p. 401: © Comstock/Alamy (RF); p. 402: © Pixtal/age fotostock (RF)

Chapter 15

Opener: © Scimat/Photo Researchers; p. 404 (doctor): © Ingram Publishing (RF); p. 405 (first): Image provided by AdvanDx, Inc.; p. 405 (fourth): © Steven Puetzer/Getty Images (RF); p. 406: © Adam Gault/Getty Images (RF); Table 15.1 (phenotypic): CDC/Arthur F. DiSalvo, M.D.; Table 15.1 (genotypic): © Steven Puetzer/Getty Images (RF); p. 407: © Don Carstens/Artville (RF); p. 408: © Ingram Publishing (RF); p. 412: © Punchstock/BananaStock (RF); p. 413: CDC/Janice Haney Carr; 15.6: Courtesy of The University of Leeds; 15.8: Image provided by AdvanDx, Inc.; 15.9 (top): © AP Photo/Kenneth Lambert; 15.9 (bottom), p. 417: Centers for Disease Control; p. 418: © Adam Gault/Getty Images (RF); Table 15.2 (agglutination): © Image Source/Getty Images (RF); Table 15.2 (precipitation): © Joel Gordon; Table 15.2 (western blot): Rigurat; Table 15.2 (fixation): © LeBeau/Custom Medical Stock Photo; Table 15.2 (fluorescence): Centers for Disease Control; Table 15.2 (tube): © Comstock/PunchStock (RF); Table 15.2 (elisa): © Hank Morgan/Science Source/Photo Researchers; Table 15.2 (in vivo): CDC/Gabrielle Benenson; 15.13: Rigurat; 15.14: © Fred Marsik/Visuals Unlimited; 15.16b: © Hank Morgan/Science Source/Photo Researchers; p. 424: Courtesy of EM Scrimgeour et el. First report of Q fever in Oman. Emerging Infectious Diseases. Jan–Feb 2000. vol. 6, no 1; 15.17 (lesion): Centers for Disease Control; 15.17 (herpes virus): © A.M. Siegelman/Visuals Unlimited; 15.17 (flu): © Science VU/CDC/Visuals Unlimited; 15.17 (rotavirus): © K.G. Murti/Visuals Unlimited; 15.17 (hep B): © Dr. Linda M. Stannard, University of Cape Town/Photo Researchers; 15.17 (western blot): Rigurat; p. 426 (doctor): © Ingram Publishing (RF); p. 426 (bacteria): © Scimat/Photo Researchers; p. 426 (background): © Adam Gault/Getty Images (RF); p. 427: © Purestock/Getty Images (RF); p. 429: © Kenneth E. Greer/Visuals Unlimited

Chapter 16

Opener: © Eye of Science/Photo Researchers; p. 430 (doctor): © Graham Bell/Corbis (RF); p. 431 (second): Centers for Disease Control; p. 431 (third): © World Health Org./Peter Arnold/Photolibrary; p. 431 (fifth): CDC/Janice Haney Carr/Jeff Hageman, M.H.S.; p. 431 (sixth): © ISM/Phototake; p. 432: © Corbis (RF); 16.1: © Dennis Kunkel Microscopy, Inc./Visuals Unlimited; p. 433: Centers for Disease Control; 16.2: © Phototake; 16.3: © James Stevenson/Photo Researchers; p. 436: CDC/Dr. Fred Murphy; Sylvia Whitfield; Table 16.1 (measles): © Phototake; Table 16.1 (rubella): Centers for Disease Control; Table 16.1 (fifth disease): © Jack Ballard/Visuals Unlimited; Table 16.1 (roseola): © Scott Camazine/Phototake; Table 16.1 (scarlet fever): © Mediscan/Corbis; 16.4: © Dr. Ken Greer/Visuals Unlimited; 16.5: © Kathy Park Talaro/Visuals Unlimited; p. 440–441: © Image Source/Getty Images (RF); 16.7a: National Institute Slide Bank/The Welcome Centre for Medical Sciences; 16.7b: © Dr. Ken Greer/Visuals Unlimited; 16.8 (all): Centers for Disease Control; 16.9a: © Logical Images, Inc. All rights reserved; p. 444: Centers for Disease Control; Table 16.5 (left): © Phil Degginger; Table 16.5 (right): © World Health Org./Peter Arnold/Photolibrary; p. 445 (both): Centers for Disease Control; Table 16.6 (warts): © Kenneth E. Greer/Visuals Unlimited; Table 16.6 (molluscum): © Dr. Jack Jerjian/Phototake; Table 16.7 (left): Centers for Disease Control; Table 16.7 (right): © Science VU-Charles W. Stratton/Visuals Unlimited; p. 447 (neck): Centers for Disease Control; p. 447 (bacteria): CDC/Dr. William A. Clark; Table 16.1 (scalp): © Everett S. Beneke/Visuals Unlimited; Table 16.1 (chin): Centers for Disease Control; Table 16.1 (body, foot): © Kenneth E. Greer/Visuals Unlimited; Table 16.1 (groin): © Dr. Harout Tanielian/Photo Researchers; Table 16.1 (nails): Reprinted from J. Walter Wilson, Fungous Diseases of Man, Plate 42 (middle right), © 1965, The Regents of the University of California; 16.10a: Elmer W. Koneman and Roberts, Practical Laboratory Mycology. © 1985, Williams and Wilkins Co., Baltimore, MD; 16.10b: © A.M. Siegelman/Visuals Unlimited; 16.10c: Elmer W. Koneman and Roberts, Practical Laboratory Mycology. © 1985, Williams and Wilkins Co., Baltimore, MD; 16.11: © Biophoto Associates/Photo Researchers; p. 451: © Comstock Images/PictureQuest (RF); 16.14: © Science VU-Bascom Palmer Institute/Visuals Unlimited; p. 452 (bottom): CDC/Janice Haney Carr/Jeff Hageman, M.H.S.; 16.15: © ISM/Phototake; p. 454 (doctor): © Graham Bell/Corbis (RF); p. 454 (virus): © Eye of Science/Photo Researchers; p. 456: © 2005 The Regents of the University of California; p. 458: © Dr. Ken Greer/Visuals Unlimited; p. 459: Centers for Disease Control

Chapter 17

Opener: © MedicalRF.com/Getty Images; p. 460 (doctor): © Purestock/Getty Images (RF); p. 461: © Pr. J.J. Hauw/ISM/Phototake; 17.4: © Dr. Ken Greer/Visuals Unlimited; 17.5: © Kathy Park Talaro/Visuals Unlimited; 17.6: © Dr. Gary Gaugler/Visuals Unlimited; 17.7 (both): © Gordon Love, M.D. VA, North CA Healthcare System, Martinez, CA; p. 468 (bottom): CDC/Maryam I. Daneshvar, Ph.D.; 17.8a: CDC/Dr. Hardin; 17.8b: CDC/Mercy Hosp Toledo OH; Brian J. Harrington; 17.9: © Science VU/CDC/Visuals Unlimited; 17.10: Centers for Disease Control; p. 473: © Corbis (RF); p. 474: Centers for Disease Control; p. 477: © Tom Pepeira, photographer/Iconotec (RF); 17.12a: © M. Abbey/Photo Researchers; 17.12b: © Pr. J.J. Hauw/ISM/Phototake; p. 478, 17.13 (bat): © PhotoLink/Getty Images (RF); 17.13 (skunk): © Stockbyte/Getty Images (RF); 17.13 (raccoon): © Corbis (RF); 17.13 (tx fox): © Ingram Publishing (RF); 17.13 (az fox): © Corbis (RF); 17.14: © John D. Cunningham/Visuals Unlimited; 17.15: Centers for Disease Control; 17.16c: CDC/Dr. Thomas F. Sellers/Emory University; p. 481 (bottom): © Image Source/Getty Images (RF); p. 484 (doctor): © Purestock/Getty Images (RF); p. 484 (cells): © MedicalRF.com/Getty Images; Table 17.6: © The McGraw-Hill Companies; p. 489 (bottom): © A.M. Siegelman/Visuals Unlimited

Chapter 18

Opener: © SciMAT/Photo Researchers; p. 490 (doctor): © Getty Images/Image Source (RF); p. 492–493: © Purestock/Getty Images (RF); p. 495: Centers for Disease Control; 18.3: Courtesy of Stephen B. Aley, PhD., University of Texas at El Paso; 18.5: © Anthony Asael/Art in All of Us/Corbis; p. 498 (HIV): CDC/Cynthia Goldsmith; 18.6: © SPL/Photo Researchers; p. 502: © Comstock Images/Alamy (RF); 18.9: © Yoav Levy/Phototake; p. 507: © Corbis (RF); 18.11: Centers for Disease Control; 18.12: JAMA; p. 509: © Ingram Publishing/SuperStock (RF); 18.13 (top): CDC/Peter Arnold/Photolibrary; 18.13 (bottom): Centers for Disease Control; 18.14: © Science VU-Charles W. Stratton/Visuals Unlimited; 18.15: © Scott Camazine/Photo Researchers; p. 514: © Comstock Images/Alamy (RF); 18.17 (hand): Centers for Disease Control; 18.17 (tick): © PhotoLink/Getty Images (RF); 18.18: © A.M. Siegelman/Visuals Unlimited; p. 517 (doctor): © Getty Images/Image Source (RF); p. 517 (bacteria): © SciMAT/Photo Researchers; p. 518: © Ingram Publishing (RF); p. 523: CDC/Peter Arnold/Photolibrary

Chapter 19

Opener: © Barts Hospital/Getty Images; p. 522 (doctor): © Tom Grill/Getty Images (RF); p. 523 (third): © Pulse Picture Library/CMP Images/PhotoTake; p. 523 (fifth): © Elmer Koneman/Visuals Unlimited; p. 524–525: © Science Photo Library RF/Getty Images; 19.1b: © Ellen R. Dirksen/Visuals Unlimited; 19.2: © Pulse Picture Library/CMP Images/PhotoTake; p. 526: © Photodisc Collection/Getty Images (RF); 19.4a (both): Courtesy of Siemens Healthcare Diagnostics © 2011 Siemens Healthcare Diagnostics Inc.; 19.4b: © Dr. David Schlaes/John D. Cunningham/Visuals Unlimited; p. 529: © ballyscanlon/Getty Images (RF); 19.6: Centers for Disease Control; p. 532: © Getty Images (RF); p. 534: © Science Photo Library RF/Getty Images; p. 535 (virus): CDC/C. S. Goldsmith and A. Balish; p. 535 (man): © RubberBall/SuperStock (RF); p. 537: © Thinkstock/JupiterImages (RF); 19.10: © John D. Cunningham/Visuals Unlimited; p. 538: CDC/Donald Kopanoff; p. 539: CDC/Dr. George Kubica; p. 540: © The McGraw-Hill Companies, Inc./Barry Barker, photographer; 19.12: © SIU Bio Med/Custom Medical Stock Photo; 19.13: © Dr. Leonid Heifets, National Jewish Medical Research Center; 19.14: © Elmer Koneman/Visuals Unlimited; p. 543: CDC/Janice Carr; 19.15: Centers for Disease Control; 19.16: © Tom Volk; p. 545: © Travel Ink/Getty Images; p. 547 (doctor): © Tom Grill/Getty Images (RF); p. 547 (x-ray): © Barts Hospital/Getty Images; p. 548 (top): © Getty Images; p. 548 (vaccine): CDC/Jim Gathany; p. 548 (shot): © Creatas/PunchStock (RF); p. 550: © Thinkstock/JupiterImages (RF); p. 551: © Jack Bostrack/Visuals Unlimited

Chapter 20

Opener: © SPL/Photo Researchers; p. 554 (doctor): © Purestock/Getty Images (RF); p. 555 (second): © Ingram Publishing (RF); p. 555 (third): © Moredun Animal Health Ltd./Photo Researchers; p. 555 (fourth): © Stanley Flegler/Visuals Unlimited; p. 556: © Kate Mitchell/Corbis (RF); p. 557: © Ingram Publishing (RF); p. 558: © Kent Knudson/PhotoLink/Getty Images (RF); p. 559: © Ryan McVay/Getty Images (RF); p. 560: Centers for Disease Control; 20.3 (left): © Gastrolab/Photo Researchers; 20.3 (right): Centers for Disease Control; p. 562: Lynn Betts, USDA, Natural Resources Conservation Center; p. 563: © BananaStock/

PunchStock (RF); 20.5a: © David Musher/Photo Researchers; 20.5b: Courtesy of Fred Pittman; p. 565: CDC/Janice Haney Carr; 20.5c: Farrar, W. Edmund, Infectious Diseases. © 1984, Williams and Wilkins, Baltimore, MD; 20.6: © Moredun Animal Health Ltd./Photo Researchers; 20.7: © Custom Medical Stock Photo; p. 568–569: © McGraw-Hill Companies, Inc./Erica Simone Leeds, photographer; 20.8: © Iruka Okeke; 20.9: CDC/Dr. Stan Erlandsen; p. 571: © The McGraw-Hill Companies, Inc./Barry Barker, photographer; 20.10d: © Science VU-Charles W. Stratton/Visuals Unlimited; 20.10e: © Eye of Science/Photo Researchers; 20.13 (plaque): © Stanley Flegler/Visuals Unlimited; 20.13 (tooth): © R. Gottsegen/Peter Arnold/Photolibrary; 20.15: © Science VU-Max A. Listgarten/Visuals Unlimited; 20.16: Centers for Disease Control; p. 577: © MedicalRF.com/Getty Images; p. 579: CDC/Dr. Erskine Palmer; p. 580: © Ingram Publishing (RF); p. 581: © The McGraw-Hill Companies, Inc./Christopher Kerrigan, photographer; p. 582: © Getty Images/Stockbyte (RF); 20.18a: © Stanley Flegler/Visuals Unlimited; 20.18b: Courtesy of Dickson Despommier; p. 585: © John A. Rizzo/Getty Images (RF); 20.19: © Ed Reschke/Photolibrary; 20.20 (cercaria): © Dr. Harvey Blankespoor; 20.20 (mating): © Science VU/Visuals Unlimited; 20.20 (miracidium): © Cabisco/Visuals Unlimited; p. 588 (doctor): © Purestock/Getty Images (RF); p. 588 (virus): © SPL/Photo Researchers; p. 590, 592: Centers for Disease Control

Chapter 21

Opener: © Moredun Animal Health Ltd/Photo Researchers; p. 594 (doctor): © Jose Luis Pelaez Inc./Getty Images (RF); p. 595 (third, fourth): Centers for Disease Control; p. 597: © Andersen Ross/Getty Images (RF); p. 598: © Ariel Skelley/Blend Images (RF); p. 599: © Photodisc/Getty Images (RF); p. 600: Centers for Disease Control; p. 602: © Corbis (RF); 21.5: James Bingham, Sexually Transmitted Diseases. © 1984 Williams and Wilkins Co., Baltimore, MD; 21.6: © George J. Wilder/Visuals Unlimited; p. 604: © The McGraw-Hill Companies, Inc./Christopher Kerrigan, photographer; 21.7: Courtesy of Danny L. Wiedbrauk; 21.8 (both): Centers for Disease Control; p. 609: © David M. Phillips/Visuals Unlimited; p. 610: © Science VU/Visuals Unlimited; 21.9: CDC/J. Pledger; 21.10a,b: © Science VU/CDC/Visuals Unlimited; 21.11: © Custom Medical Stock Photo; 21.12: © Science VU/CDC/Visuals Unlimited; p. 612: Centers for Disease Control; Table 21.6 (syphilis): © ISM/Phototake; Table 21.6 (chancroid): © Dr. M.A. Ansary/Photo Researchers; Table 21.6 (herpes): © Dr. P. Marazzi/Photo Researchers; 21.13: © Kenneth E. Greer/Visuals Unlimited; 21.14: Centers for Disease Control; 21.15: © Dr. Walker/Photo Researchers; p. 616 (woman): © The McGraw-Hill Companies, Inc./Jill Braaten, photographer; p. 616 (virus): © Science Photo Library RF/Getty Images; p. 617: © Comstock/Alamy (RF); Table 21.7 (HPV): © Kenneth E. Greer/Visuals Unlimited; Table 21.7 (molluscum): © Dr. Jack Jerjian/Phototake; p. 619 (doctor): © Jose Luis Pelaez Inc./Getty Images (RF); p. 619 (virus): © Moredun Animal Health Ltd/Photo Researchers; p. 620: © Corbis (RF); p. 624: © Dr. Walker/Photo Researchers; p. 625 (lip, hand): Centers for Disease Control; p. 625 (back): © Science VU/Visuals Unlimited

Chapter 22

Opener: © Moredun Animal Health Ltd./Photo Researchers; p. 626 (doctor): © Jose Luis Pelaez Inc./Getty Images (RF); p. 627 (second): Reprinted from EPA Method 1604 (EPA-821-R-02-024) courtesy of Dr. Kristen Brenner from the Microbial Exposure Research Branch, Microbiological and Chemical Exposure Assessment Research Division, National Exposure Research Laboratory, Office of Research and Development, U.S Environmental Protection Agency; p. 627 (third): © Ingram Publishing (RF); p. 627 (fourth): © J.T. MacMillan; p. 630: © Stockbyte (RF); p. 631: © Jim Reed/Getty Images (RF); p. 632: © The McGraw-Hill Companies, Inc./Pat Watson, photographer; 22.5a: © Dr. David Phillips/Visuals Unlimited; 22.5b: © Carleton Ray/Photo Researchers; 22.5c: © Phillip Slattery/Visuals Unlimited; p. 633 (child): © JupiterImages/Comstock Premium/Alamy (RF); 22.7a,b: Courtesy of Sanitation Districts of Los Angeles County; p. 635: © Corbis/SuperStock (RF); p. 636: © Dr. Parvinder Sethi (RF); p. 637: © Corbis (RF); 22.8 (top): © Kathy Park Talaro; 22.8 (middle, bottom): Reprinted from EPA Method 1604 (EPA-821-R-02-024) courtesy of Dr. Kristen Brenner from the Microbial Exposure Research Branch, Microbiological and Chemical Exposure Assessment Research Division, National Exposure Research Laboratory, Office of Research and Development, U.S Environmental Protection Agency; p. 639: © J. Luke/PhotoLink/Getty Images (RF); p. 640: © Ingram Publishing (RF); 22.11: © Kathy Park Talaro; 22.13: © Volker Steger/SPL/Photo Researchers; 22.14: © J.T. MacMillan; p. 646 (doctor): © Jose Luis Pelaez Inc./Getty Images (RF); p. 646 (bacteria): © Moredun Animal Health Ltd./Photo Researchers; p. 649: © Vanessa Vick/Photo Researchers; p. 651: © Kathy Park Talaro

Index

Note: In this index, page numbers followed by a t refer to tables, page numbers followed by an f refer to figures, page numbers set in **boldface** refer to boxed material, and page numbers set in *italics* refer to definitions or introductory discussions.

B

D

E

H

I

J

K

L

M

N

O

P